Managing
Brands:
A Contemporary
Perspective

Managing Brands: A Contemporary Perspective

Sylvie Laforet

The **McGraw·Hill** *Companies*

London Boston Burr Ridge, IL Dubuque, IA Madison, WI New York San Francisco
St. Louis Bangkok Bogotá Caracas Kuala Lumpur Lisbon Madrid Mexico City
Milan Montreal New Delhi Santiago Seoul Singapore Sydney Taipei Toronto

Managing Brands: A Contemporary Perspective
Sylvie Laforet
ISBN-13 978-0-07-711748-1
ISBN-10 0-07-711748-4

Published by McGraw-Hill Education
Shoppenhangers Road
Maidenhead
Berkshire
SL6 2QL
Telephone: 44 (0) 1628 502 500
Fax: 44 (0) 1628 770 224
Website: www.mcgraw-hill.co.uk

Reprinted 2011

British Library Cataloguing in Publication Data
A catalogue record for this book is available from the British Library

Library of Congress Cataloging in Publication Data
The Library of Congress data for this book has been applied for from the Library of Congress

Commissioning Editor: Rachel Gear
Head of Development: Caroline Prodger
Freelance Editor: Emma Gain
Marketing Director: Alice Duijser
Production Editor: Alison Holt

Text design by Fakenham Photosetting Ltd, Fakenham, Norfolk NR21 8NN
Cover design by Adam Renvoize
Printed and bound in the UK by CPI Antony Rowe, Chippenham, Wiltshire

ISBN-13 978-0-07-711748-1
ISBN-10 0-07-711748-4

Dedication

I would like to dedicate this book to Pierre, Marie, Pareesa and Hadi.

Brief Table of Contents

Detailed Table of Contents

Guided Tour

Each chapter opens with a detailed **table of contents**, a **chapter overview** summarizing key themes, and helpful **learning objectives** to enable the reader to structure their learning of the material.

Illustrations and photos throughout the book bring branding to life, showing how companies such as Unilever, Hyundai and Apple have developed their brands.

Branding Brief boxes contain short examples of leading brands, or interesting snippets from the press or research about a branding topic. They provide numerous examples to show the relevance of the discussions in the surrounding text to real branding decisions.

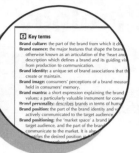

Key terms are provided at the end of each chapter, giving students an at-a-glance glossary of industry jargon and academic terms and concepts in branding.

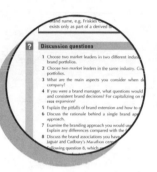

Discussion questions at the end of each chapter encourage readers to pause and reflect on the ideas in the chapter, and can be set either as revision questions or used as a revision tool. **Projects** at the end of chapters provide activities and assignments for students of branding, involving wider research or surveys.

Mini case studies and longer end of chapter cases appear at the close of each chapter, reflecting themes discussed on the previous pages and featuring brands such as Levi's, Cathay Pacific, Virgin, Starbucks, and many more European and internationally renowned brands. Each full end of chapter case is accompanied by case questions for reflection or assessment.

For lecturers: technology to enhance your teaching

*Visit **www.mcgraw-hill.co.uk/textbooks/Laforet** today*

Online Learning Centre (OLC)

An Online Learning Centre website is available for lecturers who adopt this textbook for their teaching. The website offers lecturers the following useful resources to help them deliver an effective branding or brand management module:

- case study teaching notes
- PowerPoint slides
- links to other online sources.

Custom Publishing Solutions

Let us help make our content your solution

At McGraw-Hill Education our aim is to help lecturers to find the most suitable content for their needs delivered to their students in the most appropriate way. Our **custom publishing solutions** offer the ideal combination of content delivered in the way that best suits lecturer and students.

Our custom publishing programme offers lecturers the opportunity to select just the chapters or sections of material they wish to deliver to their students from a database called Primis at www. primisonline.com

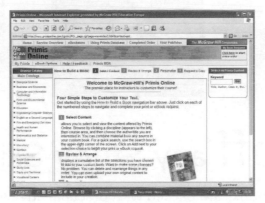

Primis contains over two million pages of content from:

- textbooks
- professional books
- case books – Harvard Articles, Insead, Ivey, Darden, Thunderbird and BusinessWeek
- Taking Sides – debate materials.

Across the following imprints:

- McGraw-Hill Education
- Open University Press
- Harvard Business School Press
- US and European material.

There is also the option to include additional material authored by lecturers in the custom product – this does not necessarily have to be in English.

We will take care of everything from start to finish in the process of developing and delivering a custom product to ensure that lecturers and students receive exactly the material needed, in the most suitable way.

With a Custom Publishing Solution, students enjoy the best selection of material deemed to be the most suitable for learning everything they need for their courses – something of real value to support their learning. Teachers are able to use exactly the material they want, in the way they want, to support their teaching on the course.

Please contact your local McGraw-Hill representative with any questions or alternatively contact Warren Eels e: warren_eels@mcgraw-hill.com.

Acknowledgements

Our thanks go to the following reviewers for their comments at various stages in the text's development:

Alan Seymour, The University of Northampton
HB Klopper, University of Johannesburg
Mike Flynn, University of Gloucestershire
Charlene Gerber Nel, University of South Africa
Benedik Samuelsen, BI Norwegian School of Management
Dr Berk Ataman, Erasmus Universiteit Rotterdam
Gareth Smith, Loughborough University
Madele Tait, Nelson Mandela Metropolitan University
Mary Brennan, Newcastle University
Julie McColl, Glasgow Caledonian University

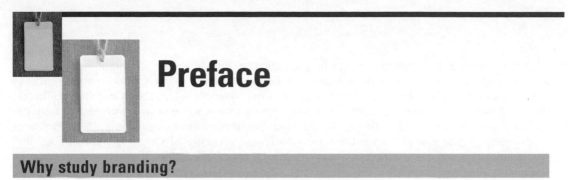

Preface

Why study branding?

It is important to study brands and branding because, first, it is part of our lives, whether we like it or not. It is also important to students to study strategic brand management to appreciate how part of the business world functions.

For a long time branding has also been seen as part of the marketing discipline, and marketing is studied by students across the board, including engineers. Traditionally, branding is part of the marketing mix, or the 4Ps: Product, Price, Promotion and Place. The *product* has two levels: core and augmented. Branding is not the core product but the augmented level of the product. The way marketing evolves from being 'production' to 'sales' functions, to 'customer orientation' and now to 'competition led' has great implications for branding, which explains how it became central to the marketing discipline.

In its early phases, around the 1960s, marketing was concerned only with production and the selling of the output of the factory or the service centre. Its function was to sell what the company produced. The next phase began as the process of producing only the products that fulfil customers' needs and wants; the emphasis of marketing was then on 'meeting customers' needs'. This phase has implications for new product development and segmentation, and these took centre stage in marketing departments. The third phase began in the 1980s, by which time the customer-orientation strategy was no longer sufficient. Competition was fierce and demand started to wane. There were no longer any unfulfilled needs. Instead there were many suppliers with products and services of increasingly higher quality and value to the customer. Accordingly, it has become vital for companies to be number one and to ensure that their brands are selected, and are in the consumer mindset. Strategic brand management can create customer preference by ensuring that the products or services sold are perceived to be superior to those of competitors, and that these products and services offer the best possible perceived value for money.

In recent years there have been shifts in academic thoughts and management practice. Some may argue that brand management is no longer part of marketing but has evolved, and become a discipline of its own. As brands become the core of many businesses, nowadays brands are considered to be the responsibility of senior management and the boardroom (Chapter 4).

Aim of the book

Our aim is to provide an interesting and detailed account and analysis of contemporary brand management as well as offering tools for brand decision-making. The book covers both theoretical and practical issues of branding, and incorporates pedagogical features. The primary market for this book is upper-level undergraduates and postgraduate students studying marketing and branding modules for the first time. The book also caters for students who wish to gain an understanding of how brands are made and managed in the marketplace, as well as those who are interested in pursuing a career as a product/brand manager.

We hope to add value to the teaching of brand management and student learning through short, interesting brand stories – branding briefs, case studies and other pedagogical features; these are combined with years of research in the field. The book focuses on the fundamentals of branding and strategic brand management and, at the same time, it discusses emerging trends and issues in branding, and the environmental factors affecting contemporary brand management. Thus the book aims to provide a comprehensive synthesis of the subject, by including, where possible, all the developments in the area of brand management.

This book has a further advantage in presenting assimilated ideas on branding by various authors and researchers; the book is also based on the author's research work, current practices and innovation in the area of branding and brand management with a good number of illustrations and exercises. It covers a number of contemporary topics, some of which are drawn from the author's own research work – 'Brand Structure and Brand Portfolio Management', 'New Pressures in Branding', 'Design and Branding for the Consumer', 'Country of Origin Branding', 'Building Brand and Corporate Reputation', 'Managing Brands across a Life Cycle'. It also discusses issues of online branding and branding in the Internet age, the use of deep metaphors in branding, brand risk management, marketing ethics and sustainability of brands, as well as providing a comprehensive and detailed analysis of retail versus manufacturer brands. Finally, it examines brand and business building in an innovative way by adopting business management principles to building brands.

Outline of the book

PART 1 Strategic Implications of Branding

Chapter 1 Introduction to contemporary brand management

This covers: the definition of brand, various paradigms of brand, its meanings, functions and importance; brand and its relationship to customer relationship management; the components of brand; the brand management process, branding decisions, deep metaphors of branding, online branding and branding in the Internet age; marketing ethics and sustainability of brands – key challenges.

Chapter 2 Brand equity and brand valuation

This covers: the conceptual foundation of brand equity; how brands are valued and why it is important to calculate brand value; situations on which companies should go for brand valuation; the financial methods of brand valuation; the behavioural approach and customer-based brand equity; modern and new methods of valuations such as the Brand Asset Valuator (BAV), the Interbrand brand valuation methodology and emerging trends of narrative reporting by the Institute of Practitioners in Advertising (IPA).

Chapter 3 Brand building and business building

This examines: the relationship between building a business and building a brand (arguing that one cannot build the brand without building a business first and brands are built on business models). It compares brand building to classic and modern business building models; applying business management principles to building brands.

Chapter 4 Brands as strategic assets – moving up the corporate agenda

This examines: the role of brands as strategic assets and discusses the view that brand management is now part of the corporate agenda. It looks at some evidence from both academic literature and practitioners' insights, suggesting that a more strategic view of brands is taking hold. Examples from various industries are included; comparisons between large and small companies are illustrated.

PART 2 Managing Brands – Creating and Sustaining Brand Equity

Chapter 5 Brand identity and positioning

This covers: the concept of brand identity system, elements of brand identity and its facets, brand image and its dimensions, image formation and brand image building, strategic brand image concept management; brand positioning and its role in the marketing mix; the process of brand positioning; brand positioning strategies; perceptual mapping; the gap between brand identity and brand image; the integrated brand communication process; Aaker's model of brand equity building and the PCDL model.

Chapter 6 Brand architecture

This explains: what brand structure is about; it describes the management of brands and product relationships, and discusses the different branding approaches used on product packs such as corporate branding, corporate endorsement, mixed brands, dual brands, standalone brands, furtive brands, super branding, sub-branding, etc. Examples from fmcg companies are included. It examines: the rationale behind each brand approach and how to choose an appropriate brand strategy; international brand structure. It discusses: new pressures in branding; where brands are going; the latest strategies, and future trends such as brand licensing.

Chapter 7 Brand extension

This covers: the definition and rationale of brand extension; the options for brand extension; the advantages and disadvantages of brand extensions; the benefits and risks of line and category extension, vertical and horizontal extension, key factors for success of both types of extensions, factors influencing the vertical extension strategy, process of brand extension; the brand linkage – brand symbiosis, brand relationship and interaction matrix, extending into a mature vs new market; extending with a corporate brand, family brand or product brand; brand dilution and distancing techniques; brand extension procedure and the effect of brand extension strategies on brand equity.

Chapter 8 Managing brands across a life cycle

This chapter shifts the focus from building brand equity to managing and sustaining brand equity over the brand life cycle. It covers an analysis of brand decline and failure, commoditization of brands, managing the brand based on the product life-cycle model, revitalization strategies, positioning and repositioning of brands over their life cycle as well as the various brand life-cycle models such as the five stages of a BLC, the Goodyear model, Mootee's BLC model and the BCM model.

Chapter 9 Building brand and corporate reputation

This examines: the principle of corporate and brand reputation building, which is a new area of branding. It includes the management and measurement of corporate and brand reputation; brand vulnerability assessment; the effects of reputation on firm performance. It introduces the notion of corporate social responsibility, and discusses recent research into consumer nationalism and corporate reputation in international markets; competitive intelligence and corporate reputation, etc., illustrating this with examples from various industries.

PART 3 The New Business Environment

Chapter 10 The new competitive environment and branding

This analyses: environmental pressures in branding, the rise of technology and the Internet, the fragmentation of media and the challenges of modern markets; the impact of these on branding strategies and brand communications; competitive branding; strategic brand alliances; cause branding and social marketing; new creative media and branding, etc. It discusses the implications for many companies around the world.

Chapter 11 Retail brands vs manufacturer brands

This discusses: the growth and changing nature of retail brands; why retailers should have their own brands; how retail brands grow in the long term. It examines the building of retail business and of a retail brand; how manufacturers compete against retail brand and defend against retail imitation; how manufacturers face low-cost competition.

Chapter 12 Packaging design and branding for the consumer

This examines: the relationship between branding and packaging design; the role of packaging to reinforce the brand message and understanding of consumers' values; what consumers want from their packaged brand – functionality or interaction? How packaging influences brand choice under involvement and time pressure; how manufacturers overcome the dichotomy between food quality and the processed appearance of their brand packaging to engender trust in the consumer. It discusses: the relevancy and recognition debate, and how environmental issues influence consumer buying behaviour; recent trends and the use of new technologies in packaging designs to meet consumers' packaging needs (new innovative packaging design examples are illustrated). It explains: how branding efforts go hand-in-hand with packaging design and sub-branding initiatives; how brand strategy is executed on the package; when and how to optimise the relationships among brands.

Chapter 13 Country of origin branding

This discusses: the concept of country-of-origin branding, consumer perceptions of products from France, Britain and Germany, and from multiple countries of origin; the nature of country umbrella brands and the role such brands play in the promotion of a country; success criteria of country associations. It also reviews recent conceptual frameworks and describes examples from newly industrialized or less developed countries (LDCs). It discusses successful umbrella branding communication programmes and examines the benefits of country-of-origin in relation to increased market share, equity and positioning for small companies and services, as well as its effects on brand origin. It looks at the influence of brand origin and country image association on the perceptions and purchase intentions of Chinese MNC brands, and discusses the overall managerial implications.

Introduction

What is strategic brand management?

A brand enables customers to remember the core information about a product, and prevents competitors from making imitations (Aaker, 1991). Successful brand building helps profitability by adding value that entices customers to buy (De Chernatony and McDonald, 1994). It is also becoming clearer that companies creating strong brands can obtain important competitive advantage over those that do not (Kohli and Thakor, 1997). Whenever a marketer creates a new name, logo or symbol for a new product, he or she has created a brand (Keller, 2003). The above observations made by past authors in various ways sum up the American Marketing Association's definition of a brand as: a 'name, term, sign, symbol or design, or a combination of these, intended to identify the goods and services of one seller or group of sellers, and to differentiate them from those of [the] competition'. Additionally, according to De Chernatony and McDonald, if successfully built, a brand will add value for customers, and is the underlying reason for purchase. This can bring profitability to the firm.

Good branding is based on a clear strategy and sound management. Strategic brand management achieves its results through vision, analytic skills and talent. Entrepreneurs build brands (e.g. the Virgin brand of entrepreneur and businessman Richard Branson; Microsoft from entrepreneur and businessman Bill Gates). How did the discipline first develop? Strategic brand management started at Procter & Gamble plc, based on a famous memo by Neil McElroy. It involved analysing all aspects of a brand and devising a strategic brand plan in order to build brand equity. Brand managers have responsibility for the sale and profitability of their brand, as well as building brand equity and value over a period of time.

The main driver of strategic brand management is the customer, because the overall need is to adapt brands to suit the requirements of that customer. Strategic brand management seeks to increase the customer's perceived value of a product, thereby increasing brand franchise and equity. Marketers see a brand as an implied promise of the level of quality consumers can come to expect from a brand, which will enable them to use it as a benchmark in their future purchase choice. In other words, a brand can bring a company customer loyalty as well as profits. Consequently, strategic brand management is also concerned with creating, nurturing and building the brand, as well as managing customer and stakeholder relationships.

Today's business environment for brand building is much more complex thanks to intense competition, the emergence of new marketing tools, technological changes in media advertising, social and cultural changes (see the section below on 'Brands and society'); fashion (in popular culture, which is faster moving than in the past; reflected in new consumption trends and the emergence of new lifestyles, people seeking new ways to connect and interact socially) also changes more quickly and we are on a faster track, all of which combines to present a challenge for brand building (see the section below on 'The new competitive environment and its impact on modern brand management'). Yet, more than ever before, consumers want the predictable performance and unique experience that strong brands promise. Creating strong brands that connect with consumers in such an environment requires thoughtfully developed, creatively designed, carefully implemented and scrupulously maintained brand platforms.

History of branding

Branding is more than fifty years old. It was the child of television and the needs that drive consumption in a mass market. Communicating with a mass market requires mass media. It is fast-moving consumer goods that have driven branding for fifty years. Branding theory came from fast-moving consumer goods (fmcg); it was not interactive or relationship based. It was all about the product and the communication around the product. The drive to differentiate a product on a shelf was a driving force behind branding methods and the rise of advertising agencies. It was all about the packaging, the product and volume.

For all that time branding focused on product and communication only. Thus, for a long time, branding and advertising were simply ways to publicize and identify one's products. The brand was a method for ranchers to identify their cattle. By burning a distinct symbol on to the cattle, the owner could ensure that the animals were his legal property. When manufacturers of products adopted the brand as a way of guaranteeing the quality of their goods, its function remained the same. Buying a package of cornflakes with a Kellogg's label meant that these otherwise generic cornflakes could be traced back to their source or the company that owned them. Moreover, if the cornflakes were of superior quality, the customer knew where he could get them again.

Communication about the product was done mainly through advertising. Advertising then meant publicizing the existence of a brand, and its sole objective was to increase consumers' awareness of the product or the company that made it. It was not until the 1930s, 1940s and 1950s, when people in the West turned towards movies and television and away from newspapers and radio, that advertisers' focus shifted from describing their brand to creating images for it. In the 1960s it was much the same: new techniques were designed to promote brand image. It was not until the 1970s that advertising theory, demographic research and brand image were combined to develop campaigns that worked on two levels. To this day, consumers know to associate Volvos with safety, Dr Pepper with individuality and Cadbury with British heritage. However, modern marketers are less concerned with creating brand images to reflect the products they sell, and more focused on the target market's psychological profile. Thus, there is a shift from the audience and the product to the audience and brand marketers.

Brands and society

Our dependence on brands is obvious and non-debatable – we live brands, from the clothes we dress in, to the drink we have, the food we eat and the car we drive. Whether we like it or not, we are a generation that consumes brands. This consumption of brands is deeply rooted in modern life. Brands are what drive a modern citizen of a Western materialistic culture.

At a basic level, we use brands to differentiate ourselves from our neighbours, our co-workers and the outside world. Brands allow us to be unique individuals in our own minds. At a higher level, our expectations from brands go beyond the use of brands to express our individuality. Nowadays, consumers expect brands to give them pleasure, to be their friend, to understand their fear and emotions as well as to help them achieve self-actualization and self-fulfilment (e.g. ownership of a BMW could be translated into: 'I have worked hard enough to be able to afford this car's brand or I have won money on the lottery so can I could afford this car's brand, which I have always dreamt of possessing'). Brands also have a wider impact on mankind. Their ROI becomes Return on Intention, where intention embodies what is good for the business and good for the ecosystem in which it operates. These brands are known as 'heroic' brands, because they make a difference. These brands actively seek ways to turn day-to-day business activities into catalysts for social and ecological improvement.

Unfortunately, not all brands share this good intention. When a brand shifts its focus from its customers and towards itself, the impact on its equity can be disastrous. Brand equity is a function of consumer trust, but when that trust is abused because of companies' greed, it starts eroding (see PlanetFeedback.com for untrustworthy brands). People do not trust brands that charge a high price, that do not do deliver on their promises, that misuse power, miss focus, mistake beliefs and misplace concerns.

Misusing power refers to brands that use their size to crowd out smaller players from the market. Companies must realize sooner or later that consumers care and that the winners are those brands that play by the book. *Missing focus* refers to the fact that brands must be seen as more than a marketing connotation or under the sole responsibility of the marketing department. There is a need for marketing to be coordinated with the production, financial and other departments in the company. Financial scams and non-conformance to ethical production norms can harm the brand by showing that it does not live up to what it promises. Similarly, brands that do not disseminate their values across the company will find that non-marketing functions can erode brand equity faster than the marketing department can build it. *Mistaken beliefs* describes a situation in which brands (or brand managers) feel that they need to do something different to break negative or slow growth, and end up making things worse. Therefore, it is important for brand managers to have the belief that they can outlast a tough period. Finally, *misplaced concerns* occur when a brand is seen as lacking a proper concern for one set of values that consumers care about, so that it is difficult for the same brand to be seen as possessing overwhelming concern for another set of values that consumers care about. For instance, it is difficult for consumers to believe that the same brand that would destroy the environment in the course of production would have genuine concerns for its customers.

According to Aaker, Fournier and Brasel (2004), sincere brands enjoy stronger relationships than exciting ones. *Sincere brands* are those that are positively related to relationship strength and satisfaction. These brands have traits of nurture, family orientation and tradition. Although exciting brands can be attractive and attention getting, they may be seen as less legitimate and therefore less able to win consumer trust. However, sincere brands are also more likely to run a higher risk of offending or losing customers when something goes wrong.

The role and importance of brands in business

Where two products resemble each other and may be of the same quality, but one of the products has no associated branding (such as a generic, store-branded product), shoppers often select the more expensive branded product on the basis of the quality promise of the brand or the reputation of the brand owner. Therefore, brands can be seen as the primary competitive differentiator for products, services and organizations that build ongoing relationships with customers and consumers, which will result in competitive advantage gain, long-term profitability and growth.

Furthermore, brands can last longer than products and do not have to go through a life cycle from introduction to growth, maturity and decline. They can live on and continue through the growth or maturity stage. If well managed, brands can be kept vital and growing, and tired brands can be revived (see Chapter 8).

A brand is therefore one of the most valuable assets of a company (see Chapter 2), so much so that many companies try to acquire them. However, companies might buy brands, but how do they use them in a brand portfolio, for instance (see Chapter 6)?

Branding has four components: brand identity, brand image, brand positioning and brand equity. *Brand identity* refers to the strategic goal of a brand; *brand image* is what currently resides in the minds of consumers; *brand positioning* is the process by which companies try to create an image or identity in the minds of their target market for their brand (see Chapter 5); *brand equity* is a set of assets and liabilities limited to a brand. Marketers can sustain the customer–brand relationship by giving value and relevance to the chosen target audience over the long term, and through quality and innovation. Additionally, marketers also use emotional marketing and metaphors to connect with their customers (see Chapter 1).

Central to good branding is creating a brand that people value enough to buy and buy again. These brand values or images can then be used to extend or to leverage to new products in the same product class or in a different product category, which can be targeted at the same customers or different ones. This is known as *brand extension*. To the firm, the benefit of brand leverage or brand extension is mainly cost reduction compared with developing and launching a completely new product. Brand extensions can also have long-term advantages in that brand equity can be built and sustained. However, these advantages are counterbalanced by a number of problems (see Chapter 7).

Increasingly, the perception of brands goes beyond the simple marketing context, since they are also seen as ambassadors of an organization. They represent what the organization stands for, and are constantly under pressure to deliver greater and greater returns to their investors, becoming responsible for employees' morale, the environment and the wider communities. With such roles to play, it is important that companies ensure that corporate and brand values are never compromised, and are consistently maintained over time and space in ways that do nothing to sully their reputation. Maintaining a strong reputation for leadership, innovation, success and fairness to customers will also have a much stronger direct effect on brand equity and sales than ethics (see Chapter 9). New evidence suggests that consumers also pay significant attention to country-related information as well as brand reputation, when evaluating and selecting brands. Country-of-origin branding (COOB) is seen as a way for producers to brand a product, by taking advantage of the positive perceived image of the country from which the product originates. The benefits of COOB can be seen to contribute to some companies' sales and market share. In particular, COOB could contribute to a small company's brand equity, and increase its international visibility and positioning (see Chapter 13).

The challenges brand managers face today are identifying the new, upcoming currents and their significance, and developing an understanding of sociological and cultural diversity (see Chapters 1 and 10), which is discussed below.

The new competitive environment and its impact on modern brand management

The emergence of new marketing tools (network digital, online tools and interactive TV, web TV and ATM marketing), technological changes in media advertising, fashion (see the section entitled 'What is strategic brand management?', above), and social and cultural changes (see 'Brands and society', above), all present a challenge for brand managers. In addition, increasing competition, the rising number of mergers and acquisitions, the differing characteristics of consumers, and the power of the media and public opinion can make it difficult to communicate with consumers (Barich and Kotler, 1991). In order to handle these dynamics, organizations must attempt to create their own individual and distinctive features to distinguish them and their brands in the very competitive environment.

Technological advancement

The Internet is a very powerful brand-building tool, which can be tailored to the needs of the brand, and the relationship between the customer and the brand. It can transmit information, impart experiential associations and leverage other brand-building programmes. All these experiences and associations can also largely be controlled (Aaker and Joachimsthaler, 2000). The Internet also significantly increases market transparency, empowering consumers to consider and compare many more options while making their purchasing decisions. The Internet primarily delivers information about non-physical product attributes. It also offers a means through which consumers can obtain information about the physical or experiential characteristics of a product. Whether consumers perceive this information to be reliable or not depends on several factors.

Online brands can often also provide more competitive offerings than offline manufacturer brands because of their low maintenance costs. Thus, the Internet and online brands may be seen as a threat to manufacturers' brands on a large scale.

Fragmentation of communication and media advertising

Fragmentation challenges mass media. Ever since consumers' media consumption habits began to fragment, the importance of mass media has declined along with the level of its consumption. Specialist magazines, the Internet, SMS, direct marketing, ambient media, and email or viral marketing are emerging as significant alternative channels for advertisers to communicate their messages. Even the established media are fragmenting, as newspapers sectionalize and add magazines, pay TV dilutes the reach of free-to-air channels and digital radio stations operate outside the AF/FM band. In addition, all mass media are available in one form or another on the Internet, and such expansion of media is having a serious effect on consumers' media consumption and media planning.

As consumers are drawn to emerging media, and away from mass media, advertisers are under increasing pressure to reach the right market and to decide how they should split their media budget between the diverse range of media, and which people are using which media. As technology introduces new and innovative things to the mainstream, and our lifestyles become busier to varying degrees, we still require information. Accordingly, sometimes we go to different places to gain our knowledge, such as the Internet.

Globalization and shorter product life cycles

The European Union contributes to consumers' mobility, thus making it more difficult for sellers to reach buyers. Additionally, working hours have become longer. Some people are constantly travelling for their jobs and spend less time in front of the television. Sellers need, therefore, to find other ways of reaching buyers effectively. Time is another important factor in people's lives; consumers will have less and less time to choose products in supermarkets and other retail outlets. The paradox is that there will be more and more choice available to them. Therefore, communication with the target market needs to be to the point and interesting to capture consumers' attention.

So, advancement of technology, fragmentation of communication and media advertising, globalization and shorter product life cycles, as well as issues of the role of brands in society as mentioned in the previous paragraph, fashion and cultural diversity (note that cultural diversity refers not just to ethnic cultures in a society or a country but also different cultures may be adopted in different groups within a society, which are separated by demographics or psychographics, such as age or lifestyle and social class, which in turn have an effect on their brand choice) will have an impact on branding.

Retailer competition

Consumer studies show that brand switching is frequent in fast-moving consumer goods (fmcg). Few brands are perceived as giving real value to the consumer, either functional or symbolic. There is also a lot more choice on offer and shopping behaviour has changed. The shopper is less involved with the product and more economical with time. They want to be able to find the brand they want there and then, and shopping decisions are often made in the store. Consumers are also easily bored. Thousands of products are launched by companies each year, sometimes merely updates, sometimes completely new products, just to maintain brand loyalty. This is the dilemma facing many national and manufacturer brands. The changing nature of competition is reflected in power being shifted to the retailer, which can produce in bulk and keep costs low, and thus dictate price; can provide more choice; and is no longer regarded as producing for the low end of the market (see Chapter 11).

Furthermore, despite companies spending large amounts on research and advertising, most packaging in fmcg is similar, and does not stand out enough from the crowd of products displayed on the supermarket shelf. Attracting consumers through innovative packaging and product innovation will overcome competition to a great extent. Understanding what consumers need, their value and purchase motivations, and using these in designing a package that meets these needs is central to branding and packaging design (see Chapter 12).

Brand building

All of the factors mentioned above will have an impact on the brand proposition and brand messages, based on the provision of clear brand differentiation. Brand marketers will have to work harder to create bonds between customers and their brands, as well as unique relationships and brand experiences. Brand building will, therefore, take on a completely different dimension and will be required to focus on the following key themes.

- *Building quality, values and relevance.* It is not the volume of information that is instrumental in the creation and enhancement of brand value, but its quality and relevance, and the choice of media that carry the key message.
- *Managing perceptual assets.* This is concerned with managing those messages or types of information that marketers want consumers to notice.
- *CEO branding.* Brand building is also concerned with top management branding or chief executive branding. Thus the CEO must be seen to be the key spokesperson for the company. This also includes corporate social responsibility and significant event officiation.
- *Building social capital.* Companies must invest in corporate sponsorship for charitable causes, and support government programmes and philanthropical initiatives. In other words, they are required to play a significant part in building social goodwill, because this ensures trust and credibility with the consumer.
- *Nation's equity.* Companies operating internationally do better if they are associated with the value attributes of their country of origin. Studies conducted by an American research company show that a nation's image plays a significant role in marketing products and services internationally.
- *Energizing and updating to accommodate changes in technology, fashion and cultural diversity.* Also adopting innovative packaging and products.
- *Brand building linked to managing rankings and surveys.* This is done with the help of media coverage that leads to consumers' greater awareness of companies. This, in turn, leads to better-ranking status in international surveys (based on Nair's discussion of branding as a public relations discipline, at Brandchannel.com).

It should also be noted that brands are built on their business models and, therefore, customers and environmental influences are unique to each brand. Therefore, we need to look at the business model of that brand. A business model describes how a business positions itself within the value chain of its industry and how it intends to sustain itself in order to generate revenue. Brand building is based on a similar principle. The brand needs to position itself in the value chain of its industry, product market or product category, and to maintain its capacity to generate revenue in the long term (see Chapter 3).

Who is branding for?

Modern-day branding goes beyond traditional product branding in also being concerned with personal branding, celebrity branding, country and city branding. Nowadays, we can brand almost anything.

In this book we will explore the key areas of branding – its strategic impact, the principles of successful brand management, and branding in the new competitive business environment.

References

Aaker, D. (1991), *Managing Brand Equity*, New York: Free Press.

Aaker, D. and Joachimstahler, E. (2000), *Brands Leadership*, New York: The Free Press.

Aaker, J., Fournier, S. and Brasel, S. A. (2004), 'When good brands do bad', *Journal of Consumer Research,* Vol. 31, No. 1, pp. 1–16.

Barich, H. and Irotler, P. (1991) 'A framework for marketing image management', *Sloan Management Review*, Vol. 32, No. 2, pp. 94–104.

De Chernatony, L. and McDonald, M. (1994), *Creating Powerful Brands*, Oxford: Butterworth-Heinemann.

Keller, K. (2003), 'Brand synthesis: the multidimensionality of brand knowledge', *Journal of Consumer Research*, Vol. 29, No. 1, pp. 595–600.

Kohli, C. and Thakor, M. (1997), 'Branding consumer goods: insights from theory and practice', *Journal of Consumer Marketing*, Vol. 14, No. 3, pp. 206–19.

PART 1

Strategic Implications of Branding

CHAPTER 01

Introduction to Contemporary Brand Management

Chapter contents

Chapter overview

This chapter provides an introduction to contemporary brand management. It examines branding from three perspectives: first, from the brand's perspectives we look at the functions of brands; next, what branding means, first, to the customer; and, then, to the manufacturer/the producer/the brand owner or the company.

The chapter begins with a discussion of the meanings, functions and importance of brands. Concepts of customer–brand relationship and branding metaphors will be explored, as part of the new brand-management philosophy. Brand components, brand types and branding decisions are described. The chapter moves swiftly on to examine today's environmental influences on branding, by exploring the issues for branding in the information technology age. Among these, online branding, marketing ethics and the sustainability of brands will be discussed.

Part 1 focuses on the strategic implications of branding. It is divided in four chapters: Chapter 1 is an introduction to contemporary brand management; Chapter 2 looks at brand equity and brand valuation, and discusses the concept of brand equity, which views brands as a financial asset to the company, and brand evaluation, i.e. how this asset is measured or valued; Chapter 3 examines the foundation of brand building, which involves building a successful business; finally, Chapter 4 explains why branding is seen as a corporate issue.

❖ LEARNING OBJECTIVES

After completing this chapter, you should be able to:

- ❖ Understand the meaning, function and importance of brands
- ❖ Explain and discuss the metaphors of branding
- ❖ Explain the role of brands from the consumer, company and societal perspectives
- ❖ Explain what brand relationships mean
- ❖ Debate the customer–brand relationship
- ❖ Understand what a brand is made up of and its components

- ❖ Study different types of brands
- ❖ Compare brands to online brands
- ❖ Study how branding decisions are made
- ❖ Discuss the advantages and disadvantages of branding
- ❖ Discuss the issues of branding in the Internet age
- ❖ Discuss sociological and cultural diversity influences on branding
- ❖ Discuss other challenges faced by brands

Introduction

In the past customers looked more into the functional value added of the brand when purchasing it. As consumers have become more sophisticated, new lifestyles and new consumption trends have emerged. There is now a shift towards hedonic and symbolic consumption. Our purchasing behaviour often underlines the construction of our identities. Self-concept and self-image have, therefore, become more influential in buying behaviour. As a result, two major trends in branding have emerged: the first is creating brand meanings using metaphors; the second is about developing customer–brand relationships. The branding of personal identity, rather than branding features of products and companies, has also become central to branding strategy.

Other factors affecting contemporary brand management and the development of modern branding are the rise of information technology and the Internet, and sociological and cultural diversity. With regard to the Internet, this provides a platform for brands to be promoted and experienced in new ways, since it is not only used for obtaining information but can also be interactive and entertaining (Mathwick and Rigdon, 2004; Wolfinbarger and Gilly, 2001). The drawbacks are, first, competitive offerings of online brands compared with non-online brands could weaken the latter on a large scale. The Internet also poses a threat to brands, when it is used by political activists or disgruntled customers to spread malicious rumours about brands. The sociological influence on branding strategy concerns ecology and the environment, which have assumed a growing importance in creating brand loyalty and shaping corporate culture, while cultural diversity now has an impact on branding techniques in identifying, capturing, developing and retaining niche markets. Part of brand management is also to recognize that some people will accept or reject brands, while others will actively seek them out, and to be able to manage the different branding environments.

This chapter examines how brands are managed in the modern world, first covering the basic functions and aspects of branding, and branding decisions. It then moves on to examine new concepts and the use of metaphors in branding. Finally, it discusses the social and environmental factors affecting modern brand management and the key challenges facing it.

Definition, meanings, functions and importance of brands

Definition and meanings of brands

A brand is a 'name, symbol, design or mark that enhances the value of a product beyond its functional purposes' (Farquhar, 1989). Let us examine this definition from Farquhar by looking at the distinction between the product and the brand (see Figure 1.1).

The product includes characteristics, such as product attributes (the classic Coke glass bottle is curvy, dark and red), features, uses (Apple computers are great for graphical applications), quality/ value (Marks & Spencer delivers quality products), and functional benefits (Tesco provides extra value). In addition to these characteristics, a brand includes user imagery (those who wear designer clothes), country of origin (Audi has German craftsmanship), organizational associations (3M is an innovative company), brand personality (Crédit Lyonnais is a banking brand expressing reliability and integrity), symbols (the bottle shape represents Absolut Vodka), brand–customer relationships (Henkel is a 'brand like a friend'), self-expressive (Nike is sporty) and emotional benefits (Maserati makes its drivers feel sporty and sophisticated).

The brand creates a more favourable view of the product, relative to others in the market. The value of the brand is determined by the amount of profit it generates. In an attempt to increase perceived value, companies have added brands to their balance sheet. Rank Hovis McDougall has been a leader in this and, in late 1988, added over $1 billion worth of brands to its balance sheet and tripled its recorded shareholders' funds overnight. Arthur Young and Company (1989) found that 25 per cent of the companies it surveyed included some amount for brand names or intellectual property in their accounts.

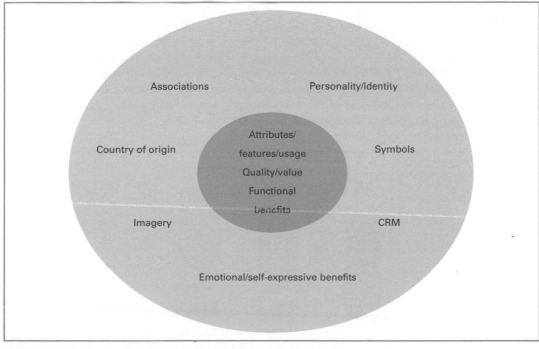

FIGURE 1.1 A brand is more than a product

In consumer durable markets, where variants of products are only on the market for a short time, the brand is essential for retaining consumer confidence and recognition. Brands are a major reason for companies making acquisitions. In 1988, the chance to acquire such brand names as Kit Kat, Quality Street, Smarties, Rolo and Yorkie was the reason Nestlé paid six times the book value of its Rowntree acquisition. This is discussed further in Chapter 2 (p. 37).

A brand is also a complex entity in the mind of the consumer. It is more than simply a trademark or a sales and marketing tool, as is explained in the section 'Importance of brands', below. Here we have to look at the meanings of a brand and what it does to people. It is a well-known fact that people form an attachment to a brand. This is known as 'brand engagement' – the process of forming an attachment between a person and a brand. Furthermore, branding creates and changes perceptions, attitudes, beliefs, behaviours, and engages many of consumers' senses (e.g. 'I love my iPod').

Consumers do not just buy a product, they also buy the image associations of the product – see Figure 1.1 above. In our world, we define ourselves by our possessions, or better – we constantly try to inherit the image of a brand for ourselves. This is why branding a product is so important. The brand image (or one of the brand's components) is the key to developing the most powerful 'pictures' in the consumer's mind.

For example, Dr Pepper, Oasis and Five Alive are all owned by the Coca-Cola Company. The differences between these products are in each of their brand positioning (another brand's components). Each of these brands targets a specific market segment and associates it with different values.

Functions of brands

Efficiency of information

Brands facilitate the information process, because they provide information regarding the manufacturer and the origin of a product or service. Additionally, the recognition effect helps consumers to repeatedly find trusted brands quickly and easily. As a result, brands increase the efficiency of information processes in early stages of the purchase-decision process (Fischer, Meffert and Perrey, 2004).

Reduction of risk

Furthermore, brands help to reduce the consumer's risk of making a wrong purchase decision. According to Solomon et al. (2003) and Meffert (2000), risks, both real and perceived, of an incorrect purchase decision can be a monetary risk (the product or service could be cheaper in another store), a functional risk (qualitative insufficiencies of the product or service), a physical risk (e.g. allergies resulting from the use of the product or service), a social risk (e.g. lacking acceptance in social groups due to the choice of incorrect brands), and a psychological risk (dissatisfaction with the purchased product or service, or potentially negative consequences for a person's self-image).

Exhibit 1: Dr Pepper, Oasis and Five Alive

Brands provide reassurance regarding the possible negative effects of the purchase. They create trust in the expected performance of the product and offer continuity, by making product or service benefits predictable (Fischer, Meffert and Perrey, 2004).

Image benefit creation

Emotional benefits exist, for instance, when the buyer or user of a brand feels something during the purchase process or use experience. For example, the way a customer feels safe in a Volvo, strong and rugged when wearing Levi's Jeans, or comfortable and 'at home' when drinking a coffee at Starbucks. The image benefit can also be directed outward to the public to allow consumers to use the brand to cultivate an image for themselves. Such a self-expressive benefit relates to the ability of a brand to provide a medium by which a person can proclaim a particular self-image. For example, it is hip to buy clothes from Diesel; a person can also project a sophisticated image by wearing Ralph Lauren fashions; or a successful and in-control image by driving a BMW. The purchase and use of a brand is a way to fulfil these emotional and self-expressive needs.

Importance of brands

From the consumer's point of view, branding is an important value-added aspect of products or services, as it often serves to denote a certain attractive quality or characteristic (Anholt, 2003). In order to create distinguishable value for consumers, differentiation is crucial, as mentioned earlier. The value must be unique, i.e. it must separate the company's offer from the competition, and it must be sustainable over time (Aaker and Joachimsthaler, 2000). Increasingly, marketing managers realize that it is difficult to compete merely on product or service differentiation. In the end, it is not the product or service the customer has a relationship with, it is the brand, 'the emotional tie the customer has with what he or she perceives to be the value, benefit, and, yes, even psychological comfort that a strong brand brings to the marketplace'. While mere products and services can be more or less easily imitated, this is incomparably more difficult, if not impossible, with brands (Aaker and Joachimsthaler, 2000).

The corresponding value for the brand-owning company might be profitable customers, valuable customer relationships, effective and efficient use of its resources, and in the end the ability to gain profits in order to survive, or even to grow in the future (Aaker and Joachimsthaler, 2000; Kapferer, 1997). Brands can be a means to increase profits, because branded products or services usually enable brand owners to charge higher prices (Aaker and Joachimsthaler, 2000; Keller, 2003; Kotler et al., 1996). Where two products resemble each other, but one of the products

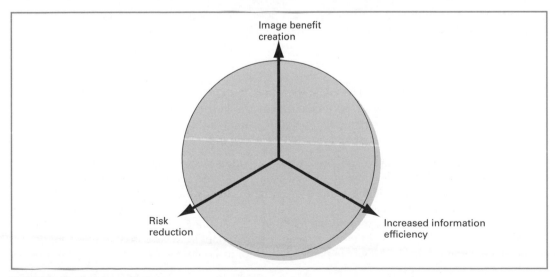

FIGURE 1.2 The functions of brands

has no associated branding (such as a generic, store-branded product), people may often select the more expensive branded product, on the basis of the quality promise of the brand or the reputation of the brand owner; assets that the no-name product does not have, although it might in fact be of the same objective quality (Kalita, Jagpal and Lehmann, 2004). Brands can be seen as the primary competitive differentiator for products, services, and organizations that build ongoing relationships with customers and consumers. A brand is therefore one of the most valuable assets of a company as mentioned before (also, referring to the concept of brand equity in Chapter 2), building a competitive advantage that will result in long-term profitability.

Branding Brief 1.1: The development of a brand name

What's in a name?

There is great value to be gained from a strong brand name. The right name clears the way for market acceptance. The development of the right brand name is crucial to the success of a product and the business (www.ashtonbg.com, 2001). If managed properly, a new brand name can become one of a company's most valuable and vital assets.

Businessmen believe that opportunity knocks only once. Thus, with a name, nothing can be left to chance. There must be a conscious effort to develop a brand that is both distinct and 'trademarkable'. Likewise, the business owner must ensure that the brand name is successful both in its product introduction and its management over time.

'What is the right name?', that is the question

A brand name is right when it effectively performs two important functions:

1 The name gives recognizability to the new product.
2 The name lends a positive, relevant meaning to the new product.

Of the two, the second function is more important because it embodies the essence of the brand name as the product's 'identity' or its 'core indicator'.

Other considerations in choosing the right name are:

1 The name must be hard to imitate, especially once it has been established.
2 A name which is a mere product descriptor, especially of what the product does, should be avoided.

A name which simply denotes what the product does reflects a poor understanding of what a brand really entails. The brand name should not merely describe the product; it should distinguish it.

Ideographs

A third consideration is important in countries where the language is ideographic and based on Chinese characters. The ideographic character of the language must be considered when developing and promoting a brand name. A study (Schmitt and Pan, 1994) suggested that the consideration must include at least four linguistic aspects:

1 *How the consumers in these countries regard a written name.* A name is like a work of art. This implies that in developing a brand name, the focus must be on creating 'distinct writings' for the name. It is the name's calligraphic strokes that count in making it both memorable and rich in imagery.
2 *Consider the characters composing the name as 'sign symbols'.* Characters are inherently meaningful, even in their smaller units. Thus, it is important to make sure that there are no negative meanings in: 1) the whole name, 2) each of its component characters, and 3) the character's smaller units.

3   *Beware of the different homonyms the pronunciations of the name's characters carry.* The spoken name may have homonyms with undesirable meanings. The right name for a brand must sound good to consumers or at least have no negative sound associations.

4   *The tonal character of the names as pronounced.* Cantonese and Mandarin are tonal. A name with the same phonetic pronunciation will have different meanings depending on how it is pronounced, for example with a falling, rising or flat tone. This suggests that the right brand name has no or minimal 'tonal confusions'.

Basic types of names, their advantages and drawbacks

An important element in the development of a brand name that should be discussed in greater detail is what type of name would best suit the entity in question.

Neologisms

A neologism, or new word, is a word that is created. Examples of neologisms are Pepsi and Xerox.

Advantages of neologisms

■   The distinctive nature of new words would mean fewer trademark difficulties. 'Extremely inventive products and companies that represent new ideas can make their names almost synonymous with the industry itself' (www.ashtonadams.com, 2001). Companies like Kleenex and Xerox practically invented their own product class.

■   Most neologisms can be understood and recognized in different languages, thus neologisms are considered to be globally friendly.

Drawbacks of neologisms

■   One problem with neologisms is that they have no meaning when they are first introduced. This means that a company must invest more in advertising the name.

■   Most of the time, a neologism does not mention the product's key benefit, thus missing the opportunity to position the product using its name.

■   Neologisms might encounter difficulties in spelling and pronunciation when first introduced. Most of the now famous neologisms were mispronounced when they were first introduced, a typical problem when introducing new words.

Current usage words

Unlike neologisms, current usage words are words that already have meaning in our language. The names 'people' and 'sprint' are current usage names. 'All send messages about the product or company to which they are affixed. All possess an element of description, but trigger something more in the minds of their market' (www.ashtonadams.com, 2001). These names are descriptive enough to inform, but can also distinctively evoke positive images in the mind of the consumer. In the world of fashion, the name Polo refers to clothing for sporty men, and also suggests sophistication and good taste.

Drawbacks

■   The problem with current usage words is that their being too descriptive will prevent them from being legally owned and registered. For example, the word 'cola' is not protectable because it describes an entire product class: beverages from the kola nut.

■   Current usage words can also pose problems in their translation to other languages. Thus, one must make certain that the messages conveyed by these words are all positive.

Hybrids

Hybrids are combinations of current usage words or recognizable syllables. Like current usage words, hybrids can send the right messages with the name. Moreover, one may actually be able to communicate better with hybrids since the combination of words can highlight several attributes of the product. The probability of legal problems is also less, since hybrids are not likely to be the same as other regular words. Like neologisms, hybrids must be pronounceable and memorable. Like current usage words, they too must convey positive messages (www.ashtonadams.com, 2001).

Acronyms

Acronyms are collection of letters that send out a targeted message. Most acronyms have technical backgrounds. Examples of such are ATM (automated teller machine), GE (General Electric) and IBM (International Business Machines). Acronyms, like neologisms, are advantageous because there are fewer legal problems in their registration. The problem, however, is that initially these acronyms mean nothing and may leave customers' minds blank. Nevertheless, companies like AT&T, which took the risk with acronyms, have made it big.

Brand relationships

We can also view the brand as a relationship. Ultimately, the brand reflects a relationship between the buyer and the product bought (and so indirectly with the supplier). It is the promise that a company makes to its current and future customers. This relationship, like all others, is based on trust, the fulfilment of promises and common values.

Over time the brand relationship changes as needs change. Buyers can become footloose, find new interests, become bored with their usual habits. Brands, on the other hand, can stagnate and wither, become focused on new customers or change in their essence. The brand relationship is also fragile. A single event, such as contamination (e.g. Perrier) or a misplaced word (e.g. Ratners) can irreparably damage this trust. Brands can suffer chronic damage over time through the constant failure to deliver on promises, unreliability, or failure to deliver on specification, which can diminish and destroy brand value (e.g. the underperformance of Virgin Trains threatens the entire perceptions of the Virgin brand).

There are cases where companies have focused purely on the brand's imagery and completely overlooked the implicit specification, and assurance aspects of a brand which rely on basic quality, and meeting the implicit service promises (e.g. Boo.com). This means that companies should also look at the way they deal with distribution channels, as part of brand management, to ensure that the brand is not compromised on its journey to the customer.

Marketers can sustain the customer–brand relationship by giving value and relevance to the relevant target audience over the long term, and through quality and innovation. However, it is worth noting that the strongest brands have been selling the same product for more than a hundred years (e.g. Coke, Kellogg's Cornflakes, Guinness, Wrigleys) through marketing, rather than product innovation. Additionally, marketers also use emotional marketing and metaphors to connect with their customers (see below).

Metaphors of branding

The dictionary definition of a metaphor is 'a symbol', 'image', 'figure of speech' or 'allegory'. Deep metaphors are basic frames or orientations we have towards the world around us. Deep metaphors are largely unconscious and universal, and shape the way we engage with the world. These constitute a silent but rich and powerful language of thought and expression. Study after study around the world has shown that deep metaphors are the most powerful predictors of what customers think, and how they react to new or existing goods and services. Metaphors are important for effective marketing because marketers need to understand and connect meaningfully with their customers at a deeper or emotional level.

Deep metaphors have three main aspects for marketers. First, they are the best, and some linguists argue the only, way to learn about the content of emotions. For example, when an advertisement, brand name, scent or some other stimulus produces a negative reaction, deep metaphors enable us to discover whether shame, guilt or some other negative feeling is producing the adverse or negative experience.

Second, deep metaphors provide the basic foundations for the brand stories people create around marketing communications. If managers are to influence the stories consumers create, or their relationship with a brand or company, they need to know what deep metaphors are operating. These insights then allow managers to leverage them in advertising, packaging, product design, and so on. For this reason, they are fundamental building blocks for developing customer relationships.

Third, because deep metaphors are shared by consumers who may be very different from each other on the surface, they become very powerful tools for developing new product concepts, communicating about them, restructuring market segmentation strategies and simplifying product design processes. They are the way of answering the important question, 'What is the common denominator around or about which consumers vary?'

Two examples of effective marketing campaigns that have used deep metaphors are:

1 Coca-Cola's 'I'd like to teach the world to sing', which invoked the deep metaphor of connection and the ability of the brand to bring diverse people together. It also engaged the deep metaphor of social balance by stressing the concept of harmony with a music metaphor.

2 The Michelin tyre ad portraying the tyre as a container; another deep metaphor of safety for one's family, especially children. The last version of the ad, which ran for many years, showed a child positioned within a tyre on a wet surface accompanied by several pairs of animals. This invoked imagery of Noah's Ark, one of the most famous containers of all time that withstood a major catastrophe.

Researchers often use applied ethnographic approaches to see how deep metaphors influence the behaviours and actions of consumers by spending time with them in their actual environment, observing them in their homes, on shopping trips, at social functions or at their workplace.

Brand components

Branding comprises four components. These are: brand identity, brand image, brand position and brand equity. *Brand identity* is a unique set of functional and mental associations the brand aspires to create or maintain. These associations represent what the brand should ideally stand for in the minds of customers, and imply a potential promise to customers. It is important to keep in mind that the brand identity refers to the strategic goal for a brand, and is aspirational from the brand owner's point of view; while *brand image* is what currently resides in the minds of consumers. *Brand positioning* is the process by which companies try to create an image or identity in the minds of their target market for their brand (see Chapter 5). It is also the 'relative competitive comparison' the companies' brand occupies in a given market, as perceived by the target market. Companies that present a cohesive, distinctive and relevant brand identity can create a preference in the marketplace, add value to their products and services, and command a price premium that leads to the creation of *brand equity*, which is an asset to the firm.

Exhibit 2: Graphic design and brand identity: Optimal Ribbon for Breast Cancer

Types of brand

There are different kinds of brands: generic, manufacturer's or national, private or supermarket, captive and online. (Also refer to Chapter 6 for brand architecture and more brand type names.) *Generic brands* are those whose names are used like a common name, e.g. Paracetamol and Hoover which, when they were first introduced onto the market, were leaders in their product category. As time goes by, their names have been used like common names. For example 'Hoover', the brand name of the vacuum cleaner, is used as a verb to describe the act of vacuuming. The two uses of the word are used interchangeably, so that 'hoover' has now become generic.

Manufacturer's brands, also known as *national brands*, are made by the manufacturer. For example, Coke is manufactured and owned by the Coca-Cola Company, as opposed to Tesco's Coke, which is owned by Tesco. *Private brands* or *supermarket brands*, also known as 'private labels', include Tesco's Coke, Asda's George, and Marks & Spencer's St Michael. Many manufacturers produce for retailers, who put their own labels on these products. *Captive brands* are national brands that are sold exclusively by a retail chain like Marks & Spencer. This form of private brand often involves a specific mode, such as a given brand being sold exclusively in a given retail store. *Online brands* (also see section below on 'Branding in the Internet age') include Yahoo!, Google, MySpace and SearchEngine. These are well-known online brands and online sites but there are many more online brands that sell almost anything, from books to shoes.

Branding decisions

The role of a brand manager is to manage a brand or brands and to make decisions regarding branding. These decisions are briefly described below.

The branding decisions a brand manager takes must consider: brand strategy, brand sponsorship, brand name, brand portfolio and brand positioning/repositioning. These are discussed throughout the book.

Brand strategy involves the brand manager deciding in the first place whether to brand a product or not. This decision can be taken only after considering the nature of the product, the type of outlets envisaged for the product, the perceived advantages of branding and the estimated costs of developing brands; then, finally, whether to add or maintain brands within the company's product portfolio. The brand manager must decide whether to create new brands or use existing brand elements (e.g. same brand name, symbol, colour and packaging for new products). This sometimes refers to brand extension or brand leverage; although, brand extension is concerned only with the use of the existing brand name on the new product (see Chapter 7).

Brand naming involves the brand manager deciding on a name for the brand (see Branding Brief 1.1). A simple brand name will be effective if the overall brand personality supports the brand promise. Brand names have to be relevant to both product category and audience. A brand name is also expected to generate favourable associations. Three types of brand names often apply. These are: descriptive brand name; suggestive brand name; free-standing brand name, e.g. Kodak.

Brand sponsorship involves the brand manager deciding whether the company should manufacture the brand itself if it is a manufacturer, or using a private label and/or going half and half, i.e. partly manufacturer brand/partly private brand. This strategy is often adopted by retailers.

Brand portfolio concerns a multi-product company, e.g. large fmcg companies like Nestlé operating in a multi-product market such as coffee, baby products, condiments, etc. The multi-product firm must manage its brand portfolio in such a way that each brand in the portfolio keeps its distinct and unique features, differentiated value, brand promise and distinct image in the consumer's mind. Sometimes, these products may also be competing with each other (see Chapter 6).

Finally, *brand positioning/repositioning* involves attaching a permanent meaning and relevance to the product in the mind of the consumer. It determines what kind of value the brand will deliver, and how. It tells the consumer what role the brand plays in his or her life. It convinces the consumer to choose the company's brand over competitors' brands. When a brand is repositioned, it is clearly trying to redefine its value to the consumer (see Chapter 5).

Branding in the Internet age

In this section we will look at the role of the brand in social media marketing, and the issues of online branding. Traditionally, marketers would try to create connections with customers at various points and through various channels such as point-of-sale, promotions, local media ads, etc. These promotions were meant to generate sales, and branding was simply a welcome side effect. In the Internet age, all these media lost their importance and, as a result, branding, i.e. the original side effect, has become key. Information technology allows companies to focus on fewer marketing points. Thus, if companies concentrate on relationships and branding, today they can market effectively.

As far as consumers are concerned, they seek more and more new ways to connect and interact in a social context. The recent popularity of online social networks bears witness to people's most primitive desire to belong as they congregate around the things they are most passionate about. The Internet has also transformed passive consumers into brand influencers and ambassadors. These are not to be underestimated. This is also when the Internet can create problems for companies. Many brands are wary of exposing themselves on social media sites, but as anyone who has been involved in social media for more than five minutes knows, they are too late. Their brands are already exposed, and the community is talking about them, whether they choose to get involved or not.

Using the Internet, virtual pressure groups or disgruntled customers spread ideas so quickly that a local problem can suddenly become a global disaster (Murray, 2003). These conflagrations typically occur when a global brand meets a destructive idea that is as sweet and simple as the brand itself. In 1999 Coca-Cola Beverages suddenly faced declining sales all across Europe when a number of Belgian consumers became sick after drinking contaminated Coke (Murray, 2004). In anti-globalization movements, global brands attract protesters as well as customers (Held, 2002; Notes from Nowhere, 2003). For example, in Europe Cadbury's was targeted in the 'obesity debate' in the anti-globalization protest against global corporations. This is now exacerbated by the activists' use of the Internet (Murray, 2003). So, rather than trying to dodge the debate, brand marketers need to create a strategy to engage online influencers and social media users who have the power to make or break their brand.

Next, we will look at the issues of online branding. In the early years of the Internet, there was considerable discussion about branding in the new environment. Apart from those companies that were created as mere online brands, the question was whether to create new brands for the new environment or to rely on established brand names. At first, it was believed that established brands were not suitable for the new online environment. Hence, new online brands have been created at considerable expense, such as, e.g., Myworld created by the German Karstadt or the Advance Bank created by Hypovereinsbank. After the dotcom bubble burst, companies realized that it is not only very expensive to build up new brands and corresponding trust in the new brands, but that existing brands were already established in the minds of many consumers (Porter, 2001). There were existing relationships that just needed to be expanded to the online environment.

Smith and Brynjolfsson (2001) state that consumers use brand names as a signal of reliability and credibility, especially in the non-contractible aspects of a product bundle, such as shipping or promised delivery times. Consumers are more willing to engage in e-commerce with known brands than with brands they do not know (Smith and Brynjolfsson, 2001). Accordingly, established brands initiated hybrid forms of marketing, the so-called 'clicks-and-mortar strategies', working both in the online and the offline environments (also referred to as 'enabled' e-brands). At the same time, brands that have been created on the Internet (so-called 'generated' e-brands) such as Amazon, Yahoo! or Google, were able to gain trust among consumers over time.

Brand management is somewhat similar for brands that have been created on the Internet and brands that have been created offline (Chiagouris and Wansley, 2000). Furthermore, the Internet is a very powerful brand-building tool, because it can be tailored to the needs of the brand, and the relationship between the customer and the brand. It can transmit information, impart experiential associations, and leverage other brand-building programmes. All these experiences and associations can also largely be controlled (Aaker and Joachimsthaler, 2000). The Internet also significantly increases market transparency, thus empowering consumers to consider and compare many more options during the purchase decision process. The Internet primarily delivers information about non-physical product attributes. It also offers means by which consumers can obtain information about sensory or experiential characteristics of a good. Whether consumers perceive this information to be reliable or not depends on a number of factors. It is not unreasonable to assume that consumers may well have similar expectations of online shopping, especially those consumers who already use the Internet for entertainment and interaction (Wolfinbarger and Gilly, 2001). Last but not least, brands may deliver values that cannot be simply displaced, such as feelings and emotions (Klaming, 2006).

Branding Brief 1.2: Online branding

Source: www.iprospect.com

The web is vital to successful marketing, including branding. Online branding strategies should include search engine marketing initiatives since it is critical that your website is easy to find by the major search engines where your audience is searching for your products or services. Unlike other online advertising and methods such as pop-ups and banners, search engine listings are presented to consumers as they are in the process of searching for products or solutions. When your site is returned in response to a query, it gives your brand added credibility that it corresponds to the needs of the consumer. As a result, achieving prominent listings within search engines for keywords that relate to your products or services is vital in creating brand loyalty among consumers. This brand loyalty results in more sales opportunities.

Branding Brief 1.3: What is cult branding?

Source: Cultbranding.com

Brands fail for one primary reason: instead of building a brand some people love, companies build brands no one hates. Most marketers live in a world where they are constantly searching for the flashy, the instant – in short, the trivial.

We must recognize that brands don't belong to marketers. Brands belong to the customer. The customer's embrace is the only vote that counts, yet it is constantly ignored by strategies that position our products and services as the 'goal' rather than the means by which to satisfy our customers' needs, wishes and fantasies.

Successful brands embrace their customers by anticipating basic and spiritual human needs. Success creates magnetic brands – cult brands.

Why cult branding works

Cult brands aren't just companies with products or services to sell. To many of their followers, they are a living, breathing surrogate family filled with like-minded individuals. They are a support group that just happens to sell products and services. Picture a cult brand in this context, and you will have a much better understanding of why these brands all have such high customer loyalty and devoted followers.

That is how cult branding works. Society only helps to accelerate the drivers behind its success.

Marketing ethics and sustainability of brands – key challenges

The challenge brand managers face today is identifying the new, upcoming currents and their significance, as well as developing an understanding of sociological and cultural diversity. The sociological aspects refer to the environment, and social responsibility through marketing and brand ethics. These are of growing importance in creating brand loyalty and corporate culture, which is discussed below. Cultural diversity allows for the deployment of branding techniques in order to identify, capture, develop and retain niche markets. This will also be examined below.

Marketing and sustainability are two conflicting philosophies because marketing is about selling more, while sustainability is about consuming less. Sustainability or corporate social responsibility is a subject that is most talked about in today's business environment. Therefore, it also affects marketing; similarly, the social and cultural changes impact on the health of the brand. The question is how marketers can pursue these two goals at the same time, and what brands can do to win over the consumer, and create a sustainable value or advantage.

The Chartered Institute of Marketing (CIM) has conducted some investigations to identify emerging issues in this area and the challenges marketers face. The first challenge refers to obstacles and barriers to change, and how marketing can be sustainable. The remainder are concerned with sustainable processes applied to marketing: what new ideas of sustainable business are available; how marketing and sustainability relate to new issues of intangible value; and whether anti-materialism can keep pace with increases in consumption. The CIM's investigation resulted in some proposals for marketing reconvergence. Marketing needs to move away from the old notion of material volume increase as being the only route to great profitability, and towards reducing sales by volume to values such as reputation, integrity, trust and relationships. It needs to focus on what matters to consumers and how companies perform in terms of those attributes. As for brands, the questions are: whether sustainable branding has greater impact and which sustainability practices drive brand equity; whether certification labels clarify or confuse customers; and how branding can build trust, avoid consumer backlash and break through the clutter; what are success factors for building green brands in the mainstream marketplace; how do we create and sustain ethical brands, and to what extent do markets have to be savvy. (At this point in time, the big question for consumers is how to make the best choice of green brands.) The solution is not to use too many messages at the same time, and communicate personal direct benefit as well as giving clear information about products by improvements to labelling. The other remaining issues will also need to be resolved soon.

The other challenge is fashion and cultural diversity. Too often brands have been accused of losing touch with their customers and culture, a lack of differentiation and relevance, as well as not getting through to their customers. A brand can lose touch with the customer and its place in popular culture, which is shifting more rapidly than in the past. Fashions change more quickly and we are on a faster track. Brands that do not keep up can quickly get lost. Lack of differentiation is a factor that diminishes brands over time. For example, each of General Motors' brands lost its clear identity, and they even began competing with each other on price. Brand managers must play a key role; they have to do more than make day-to-day decisions about the marketing, and management of the brand. They must be attuned to changes in technology, fashion and culture. They need to invest in R&D and increase advertising budgets as well as keeping the brand energized and updated. Nike has kept in touch with its customers and expanded its brand from sneakers to related categories of athletic clothing and equipment. Companies such as Sony and Campbell's Soup invest constantly in product innovation. Even the image of Betty Crocker on food packages has been updated over the decades so that she always looks contemporary. It is difficult to energize a brand if its category is dying. In this case a new brand must be created instead. Effective brand strategy should be about developing brand vision and insight to engage the target market, together with an excellent integrated marketing mix to bring this into play, as well as a commitment from everyone in the company to live the brand's value proposition.

The following is a summary of the challenges faced by branding executives from *Fortune* 500 companies, which can be placed into six categories:

1 *Creating relevance.* The pendulum has swung from consumers valuing premium products to products that are simply 'good enough'.

2 *Protecting the brand.* Misbehaving senior managers and poor product quality; many marketers worry that the corporate reputation, and thus the brand, will become tainted.

3 *Reaching target consumers.* Highly fragmented media and products, such as TiVo are causing marketers to rethink old techniques.

4 *Nurturing employees.* Companies are only as good as their frontline people. Taking care of employees is paramount to creating a leading brand.

5 *Competing and partnering at the same time.* Partnering with mass merchandisers that have their own private-label brands while competing against those same merchandisers' brands can create a challenging business environment.

6 *Implementation of programmes.* Marketers have little room for error and virtually no opportunity to make a second impression. Everything must work well out of the gate.

Conclusion

A brand is a 'name, symbol, design or mark that enhances the value of a product beyond its functional purposes'. From being a trademark stamped on goods, branding has become a part of corporate strategy, as companies try to include brands in their balance sheets or make major acquisitions in order to get them. Branding increases the product's perceived value to the customer and increases sales. It creates a more favourable view of the product relative to others on the market. The value of the brand is determined by the amount of profit it generates. Brands are also viewed as a relationship. Ultimately the brand reflects a relationship between the buyer and the product bought (and so indirectly with the supplier). Marketers can sustain the customer–brand relationship by giving value and relevance to the relevant target audience over the long term, through quality and innovation. A brand is also a complex entity in the mind of the consumer. It is more than simply a trademark and beyond its role as a sales and marketing tool. Consumers do not just buy a product, but also the image associations of the product. This is why branding a product is so important. The brand image (or one of the brand's components) is the key to developing the most powerful 'pictures' in consumers' minds. More and more marketers use emotional marketing and metaphors to connect with their customers.

Brands have three functions: facilitating information processing; helping consumers find the product they want in a short time; reducing the risk of making the wrong purchase, and creating benefits through fulfilling consumers' emotional and self-expressive needs. Branding is composed of four elements: *brand identity*, *brand image*, *brand position* and *brand equity*. There are different kinds of brands: generic, manufacturer's or national, private or supermarket, captive and online. See Chapter 6 for more brand type names. Consumers are more willing to engage in e-commerce with known brands than with brands they do not know. Hence, established brands have initiated hybrid forms of marketing – so called 'clicks-and-mortar strategies' – working both in the online and the offline environment (also referred to as enabled e-brands). At the same time brands that have been created on the Internet (so-called 'generated' e-brands), such as for instance Amazon, Yahoo! and Google, have been able to gain trust among consumers over time. A brand manager's role is to manage a brand or brands and to make decisions regarding branding. The branding decisions a brand manager must take include brand strategy, brand sponsorship, brand name, brand portfolio and brand positioning/repositioning.

Nowadays, consumers seek more and more new ways to connect socially. The Internet has transformed passive consumers into brand influencers and ambassadors, who are not to be underestimated. Using the Internet, virtual pressure groups or disgruntled customers spread ideas so quickly that a local problem can suddenly become a global one. Anti-globalization protests against global corporations can increase by the activists' use of the Internet. This means that brand management now has been taken up a level, to include dealing with the Internet and using online chat rooms to counteract bad publicity about the company or its brands, and to communicate the brand in a better light. Not only that, brand management has also been challenged more than ever before as we enter the era of social responsibility and cultural diversity. The new strategic brand management must have an understanding of sociological and cultural diversity issues, as these will become significant in creating brand loyalty and corporate culture.

🔒 Key terms

Brand: a brand is a name, term, sign, symbol, design, logo or some combination that identifies a company's product. A brand provides functional benefits plus added values that some customers value enough to buy.

Brand associations: see Chapter 7.

Brand equity: see Chapter 2.

Brand extension: see Chapter 7.

Brand identity: see Chapter 2.

Brand image: see Chapter 2.

Brand personality: see Chapter 2.

Brand positioning: see Chapter 2.

Brand relationships: the relationship between the buyer and the product bought (and so indirectly with the supplier). It is also known as the brand–customer relationship.

Branding: from being a trademark stamped on goods, branding has become a part of corporate strategy, as companies try to include it in their balance sheets or make major acquisitions in order to get it (Saunders, 1990).

Branding metaphors: the attached meanings that people give to brands.

Captive brands: national brands that are sold exclusively by a retail chain like Marks & Spencer.

Cult branding: is about creating cult brands. Cult brands are magnetic brands. They embrace their customers by anticipating basic and spiritual human needs. These brands are a living, breathing surrogate family filled with like-minded individuals. Cult brands have high customer loyalty and devoted followers.

National brand: see Chapter 11.

Own brand: see Chapter 11.

Private label: see Chapter 11.

? Discussion questions

1 How does a product differ from a brand?

2 Discuss the role of the brand from a:
   a) customer perspective
   b) company perspective
   c) society perspective.

3 Explain what brand relationships are. Support your answer with examples.

4 What are the metaphors of branding? Give examples.

5 How are online brands different from brands? How are online brands managed?

?

6 What are the managerial issues of branding in the Internet age?

7 Explain what captive branding is. In your opinion, how should captive brands be managed?

8 Discuss the functions of brands.

9 Explain the differences in branding an:

   a) industrial product

   b) consumer product

   c) agricultural product.

10 Can you describe the brand personality of:

   a) Cadbury

   b) British Airways

   c) Virgin

   d) Yorkshire Bank?

Projects

1 Conduct a questionnaire survey to find out the top ten brands among junior school children living in an urban area and those living in a rural area.

2 Find out the brand image of the following online brands among young adults:

   a) Google

   b) Yahoo!

   c) MyWebSearch

   d) MySpace.

3 Conduct a focus group among housewives to find out what they associate the following brands with:

   a) Bird's Custard

   b) Nescafé

   c) British Beef

   d) Tesco Cola.

4 How would you position a bicycle for three different segments of the market of your choice?

5 Conduct a market survey among the lower-income and upper-income groups to find out what they think about the following retailers:

   a) KwikSave

   b) Morrisons

   c) Asda.

MINI CASE 1.1: USING CUSTOMER RELATIONSHIP INTERACTION TO BUILD A GREAT BRAND

Source: Janet Holian, VistaPrint

Let's face it, every organization wants a great brand: one that exemplifies your company's best qualities, making every customer want to purchase your products and services. Some of the most successful organizations in the world have worked hard to build and maintain a brand that people remember. But what is a brand and how can you use it to effectively convey the right message to your customers?

A brand is the identity of your organization. It is a unique and identifiable symbol, association, name or trademark which serves to differentiate competing products or services. A brand isn't made up by just one element. It is both a physical and emotional trigger used to create a relationship between consumers and the product or service.

A combination of elements is used to define a brand in a way that creates visual consistency, character and style – beyond the logo.

In addition to the visual elements, there are verbal elements such as the tone and voice that tell your customers what you stand for and the type of products or services they will receive when doing business with you.

The first items that companies typically consider when building a brand are the positioning statement, tagline, logo and method of conveying those symbols and words in an easy form. While these are important components to reaching brand nirvana, they, alone, are not enough. The biggest mistake organizations make with regards to brand is thinking their brand is only conveyed visually.

Instead, organizations need to think about all of the customer communication channels and consider how interaction with customers can make or break a brand. After all, customer experience is a critical component of your brand, regardless of the products you sell or the services you offer.

Whether you are a physical retail establishment, an online business, or both, the first interaction any customer has with your company defines your brand. As a result, it is critical to ensure that you have correctly positioned your brand and that your impression delivers on the promise. Are you friendly and helpful like Jet Blue, or consistently fast and efficient like McDonald's? Are your products high-end like Nordstrom, or bargain basement like Wal-Mart? Do you offer something no one else does like Sharper Image or are you competing on price in a competitive market like Staples?

Communicating the company brand

Whatever you decide, be sure to consistently communicate company-brand values across all channels. Don't just assume your employees know what your organization stands for. Tell them and tell them often through regular training activities such as new-hire training, new-position training and quarterly-update training. Reward personnel for behaviour that exemplifies the values of your company and be sure to correct those that do not follow the appropriate course of action.

Beyond that, build your company's structure around those values in order to enable your employees to carry out the brand that has been defined for them. Consider what you want to portray to customers. Be sure to take customer wait times, customer satisfaction and customer experience into account, and train personnel to operate within the goals defined for them. Hire the right people with the right skill set for your customer base and choose the supporting technology that will enable better service.

Another important part of branding is the crafting of appropriate policies. Do you offer a satisfaction guarantee, a lenient return policy or do you deny returns after 30 days? Do you empower your agents to make amends with unhappy customers or are customers out of luck when not happy with your service?

Each and every customer should be treated appropriately to ensure positive results.

Arm your organization with tools that protect

While companies often spend millions to build their brands across every aspect of their organization, each salesperson within an organization needs to carry that brand through in order to achieve success. Corporations can and should provide all of their frontline sales personnel with the tools necessary to build the corporate brand successfully.

These tools include templates of marketing materials such as presentations, direct-mail pieces and company literature that can be customized and personalized depending on the target market. They could also include special customer promotions, new product or service announcements, even birthday- or holiday-card wishes. Presentation folders, letterheads and business cards should also be provided.

Beyond the basic tools necessary to protect the brand, consider arming your sales force with gifts for customers. Appropriate giveaways can make a strong impact on brand communication, ensuring that your customers think of you when they need to purchase.

Consistency is key; evolution is natural

Regardless of brand choice and implementation, consistency across the board is the key. You must ensure that every aspect of your organization, from marketing materials and websites to customer service personnel, maintains the values outlined in your brand. Reaching brand nirvana is not a difficult task, it is just one that needs perpetual focus and constant attention.

Once clearly defined, communicated and practised, your brand will likely evolve over time as your organization grows and expands. Perhaps you expand your product line, refine it or maybe you even want to target a new market. Do not be afraid of the growth. Simply make sure it's communicated appropriately and practised through delivering on the promise. The investment will pay you back in spades.

Janet Holian is the chief marketing officer of VistaPrint (www.vistaprint.com), an online supplier of high-quality graphic design services and customized printed products for small businesses and consumers. She has been helping small businesses grow since joining the company in 2000. A customer-focused organization, VistaPrint offers toll-free customer service and free design services to its customers.

Questions:

1 Explain what customer relationship interaction (CRI) means?

2 How can companies use CRI to build brands in a) the consumer goods market; b) the business-to-business market.

MINI CASE 1.2: MANAGING A BRAND: AN INDIAN PERSPECTIVE

Source: Kanishk Gupta and Indira Bisht at www.pitchonnet.com, the website of the Indian marketing magazine *Pitch*

A new species has emerged in the domestic marketplace – the aware customer, a creature of the information economy, who's informed and not bashful about asking questions and expressing his opinions. This aware customer is throwing a volley of challenges, and also opportunities, to the discerning brand marketers. What does this signify for marketers?

Marketers aren't oblivious to this paradigm change either, and that some of them, if not all, are increasingly gearing up to meet these challenges. For instance, while LG, the largest durables marketer in the country, says there's a distinct change in customer attitude, which is mainly veering around the realm of product involvement as an offshoot of rising expectations from them, Yum! Restaurants note that the informed customer is making the marketer take another look at what brand communication means; as a result, no longer do consumers base their opinion about brands on advertising.

'The new customer is seeking labels to associate with an increased rational component in brands and has a high involvement in the retail environment with greater expectations at points-of-purchase', is how LG's marketing vice-president Girish Bapat puts it. Jyothy Laboratories' marketing vice-president R. Ravi also takes note of it. '[The c]ustomer is now looking closely at what you call the brand truth, which is a function of the features, attributes and the advantages that the brand possesses', is how he explains the demands of the new discerning customer. 'No longer do consumers base their opinions about brands on advertising. It's about the experience – the service, packaging, WoM and this is especially accentuated in case of high-ticket items,' says Yum!

And this leads to another important challenge of marketing – the fickleness of the consumer, whose loyalty now can't be taken for granted. It's noticed by other marketers too. Jyothy's Ravi feels that the consumer is also willing to experiment more and is looking for alternatives, as he is flooded with choices. Today the consumer's focus is clear – how does this brand improve my life? You can see how marketers have taken their cues from this. For instance, Santro moved from the 'tall big car' platform to 'shining car,' he explains.

The combination of the changing customer and an evolving marketplace creates a scenario where the brand manager can no longer rely on the marketing wisdom fine-tuned in the yesteryears, which was driven largely by the 4Ps model, which has been criticized for being outmoded.

Let's take a close look at the issues and challenges facing the brand management domain.

The challenges

In these rapidly changing times, it's only natural for things to get difficult, and this creates a challenging state for the marketer to build strong brands. Our analysis of these challenges that have emerged in the last decade or so has found that marketers are gearing up to meet these challenges.

Samsung's Ravinder Zutshi says: 'With the rise in information channels and globalization of brands, maintaining consistency in brand communication and staying relevant across different geographies, demographic segments and psychographic profiles is challenging.'

This media fragmentation gets further confounded with another trend, as is being argued by Mediratta. The new-age consumer has a fleeting attention span, and coupled with this is the clutter of messages and fragmented media channels, further exacerbating the communication problem, he says.

Amidst this, the focus on innovation is seen to be a prerequisite for marketers. 'The ability to continuously innovate in terms of products, features or technology, and adopt those that meet consumer requirements, is imperative in the present situation,' argues Zutshi.

Ravi also echoes the role of innovations in engaging the new customer, especially innovation that is relevant and meets consumer needs. LG's Bapat cites two hurdles when it comes to building strong brands, and the problem, as he puts it, is mostly from non-innovating brands. 'The lowering differentiation between brands and a shorter timeline between innovation and the competition following suit, dilutes the benefits,' he complains.

Besides these challenges, there are some nagging problems that are the result of the kneejerk reaction of marketers to adapt to the market conditions, which sometimes can prove to be detrimental in the long run. As Ravi points out, 'in the mad rush to attract consumers, many brands are coming out with an array of promotional offers. But pegging the brand on this becomes problematic, as it dilutes the brand as, sooner or later, consumers would not buy your brand unless it comes with a promotion.' But Mediratta says the more serious problem is the increasing tendency amongst marketers, especially among fmcg players, to adopt the easy route of price cuts to circumvent the tedious route of innovation. 'Fmcg brands have not innovated in the past two decades. Further confounding this is frequent price cuts, whereby you create commodities, not brands,' he says.

Another development that needs to be taken into consideration is the debate on umbrella brands versus product brands. There isn't a clear-cut trend emerging anywhere. Corporate houses like Samsung and Sony are doing well with umbrella brands, whereas others have tried to focus on individual brands.

We quizzed the marketers for their views about the benefits of different branding models. While Samsung's Zutshi is all for umbrella branding, LG's Bapat takes a balanced view. 'Both of them are equally sustainable. For instance, BMW is a dominant umbrella brand,' explains Bapat, and points out that in certain categories, like durables, an umbrella brand becomes important as it provides reassurance. 'When benefits offered across product groups are similar, umbrella branding makes sense,' he says, adding that, in the case of durables and automobiles, the figure is four to five per cent and in case of fmcgs it's eight to ten per cent. But Zutshi doesn't agree and argues that an umbrella brand ensures that there is no dilution of brand equity over different brands, and no conflicting positions arise out of different positioning of products. Also, the marketer can invest in one brand while not diluting it across different product groups. Jyothy Labs' Ravi also considers both the model kinds of branding serving specific roles. 'While an umbrella brand infuses the fundamental, guiding principles and beliefs into the brand, a product brand works more strongly on the specific brand values,' he argues.

Now let's move on to retail brands, which is touted to be the next wave of change that's sweeping the domestic marketing landscape.

Retail brands

No doubt the emergence of organized retailing is a big challenge as well as a huge opportunity. Currently at a three to four per cent of the total Rs 2.5-lakh-crore domestic retail market, the future looks set to change all of that. In the developed markets, store brands compete with manufacturers' brands and retailers' strong-arm brand managers; this is one wave that's causing sleepless nights for the marketing fraternity. The aware consumer, who's constantly seeking value and is ready to give up brand loyalty if he finds a suitable replacement, further accentuates this worry.

'The intensity of the threat is not the same for every product category. For food and dairy products, the threat is high but for durables it isn't the case. If the retail brands want to cater to the mass market, they would require high investments and this is a deterrent. In the initial years, they are better off catering to niche segments,' says Jyothy's Ravi. Mediratta echoes this: 'The threat isn't so much in case of retail brands, which need technology to appeal to consumers. For low differentiated brand categories, it's surely a threat that they need to prepare for.'

Professor Nirmalaya Kumar of the London Business School, who is a leading expert on marketing, on the other hand, warns that 'it isn't a question of if the retail brands will dominate the market, but only when. Soon, retail brands are likely to garner a 40 per cent share of the market.'

Marketing thinkers around the world believe that the only way for manufacturers to salvage their brands is to build strong equity, so that the customer demands your brand. It's a case of creating brand pull rather than brand push. The situation today displays some trends like the preference of consumers for certain categories when buying a store brand, and the association of 'budget brands' with store brands.

Also, over the long run, looking at a collaborative relationship will work for both entities, but again the strength of the brand determines the openness of retailers to synergize.

The way forward

There is goods news too! The state of affairs in the marketplace, though fraught with many threats, also presents a host of opportunities. The most important challenge is for new brands to establish themselves, thanks to the opening up of new communication channels and newer ways to reach out to consumers. American coffee major Starbucks is one case of brand building without mass media communications. Back in our own market, small companies are already on the way to do that – Café Mocha, Tantra T-shirts, etc. are some of the names.

The second opportunity is to do with the nature of consumer interaction. LG's Bapat highlights how the new communication channels like the Internet and mobile phones are helping marketers to engage the consumer in an interactive dialogue. 'The benefits are tremendous. These technologies allow one-on-one communication and avoid the dangers inherent to interpreting the consumer,' he points out. YLR Moorthi, of the IIM-B's marketing faculty, also agrees: 'IT is giving greater access to the purses and minds of consumers.' Zutshi also considers that this explosion in channels of communication will be helpful to marketers who are seeking to enter markets: 'Enhanced awareness and the availability of many options to communicate with the consumer, lowers the entry barriers, especially across geographical diversities.'

Strategy that works

What, then, should be the future course? Zutshi believes that there is no general rule of thumb, but 'product quality and the way a product is marketed makes all the difference. That is why Samsung also has select IT channels for its digital products like Samsung Digital Homes/Plazas and Samsung Digital Zones.'

But Moorthi says multiple focus points won't be effective and hence recommends 'a single-minded focus, clear positioning and organizational commitments, all of which need to translate into a product that delivers', as the mantra for brand success. The role of the company is, critically, 'in constantly underscoring the values for which the brand stands. For example, when Tata Finance failed, Tata gave back every penny it owed to depositors. This was essential, as the Tata brand name stands for "trust" in the country,' argues Moorthi.

Mediratta believes that an obsessive customer focus is the need of the hour. 'We, at Yum! believe in customer mania; the passion to put a yum on the face of every customer. This kind of obsession will make the marketer pay attention to small details and do everything to engage the customer.' He also emphasizes three other marketing techniques that he believes will yield a rich dividend to marketers – first, CRM and customer loyalty programmes, along with using word-of-mouth and buzz marketing; second is product quality; and third is service quality. But all of this has to be balanced with value for money, the slogan of the aware consumer, he says. Product quality seems to be an important consideration for consumers too. 'Product quality has been the reason that there are repeat purchases of LG; customer satisfaction is high and this is translated into positive WoM and helps reduce after-sales service costs,' says Bapat.

Some, like Ravi, believe that the quality consciousness of the consumer needs to be qualified further. 'The consumer has become quality-conscious, but the aspect of price-consciousness is also present. So, most marketers are walking a tightrope between the two. There are three main approaches such as making the brand relevant to the consumer at both the functional as well as the self-expressive level; making the brand stand apart, and, third, adequately meeting product delivery needs, that can be applied to increase brand value,' he argues.

The writing on the wall seems clear: marketers need to create strong brands by exploiting new and emerging ways of communication and brand building. This also puts the onus on organizations to appreciate the role of marketing and put their money where their mouth is.

■ *Exit the customer, enter the guest: customer experience.* The world of shopping is no longer the same. With the marketing paradigm changing fast, shopping has attained a more holistic approach where it no longer means just buying a product, but the ambience of the place of offering makes a major difference. We are talking about the new mantra that lately marketers have laid their hands on to bring in more footfall by twisting their business motive from selling a product or service to one that offers a unique experience through the same process and product.

- *Many to many: delivery models.* With 15 million mom-and-pop stores dotting every corner of it, India has the world's highest density of distribution or retail outlets, contributing to over 10 per cent of the gross domestic product and valued at around Rs 2.5 lakh crore. But, the modern retail trade is still a far cry from our neighbouring markets, let alone the emerged economies.

- *Integrate or perish: integrating communications.* Integration: that's the mantra by which to manage – and even encourage – the new marketing communication world order. The bedrock of this concept was a flux in the developed markets in the 1980s, which was marked by an explosion of media and increasing globalization of brands. IMC gives a model for marketers to create order out of this chaos by strategically integrating a plethora of marketing communications created by the same company.

Questions:

1 Discuss the main challenges faced by brand managers of today.

2 Discuss the possible strategic collaboration for retail brands.

3 What are the recommendations for marketers and/or brand managers to succeed in today's competitive environment?

4 Explain what the following terms mean: 'customer experience', 'delivery models' and 'integrating communications'.

END OF CHAPTER CASE STUDY: VIRGIN

Virgin, a leading branded venture capital organization, is one of the world's most recognized and respected brands. Conceived in 1970 by Sir Richard Branson, the Virgin Group has gone on to grow very successful businesses in sectors ranging from mobile telephony, to transportation, travel, financial services, leisure, music, holidays, publishing and retailing.

Virgin has created more than 200 branded companies worldwide, employing approximately 50 000 people, in 29 countries. Revenues around the world in 2006 exceeded £10 billion.

Virgin believes in making a difference. In its customers' eyes, Virgin stands for value for money, quality, innovation, fun and a sense of competitive challenge. It delivers a quality service by empowering employees, and facilitates and monitors customer feedback to continually improve the customer's experience through innovation.

When Virgin starts a new venture, it bases it on hard research and analysis. Typically, Virgin reviews the industry and puts itself in the customer's shoes to see what could make it better.

It is also able to draw on talented people from throughout the group. New ventures are often steered by people seconded from other parts of Virgin, who bring with them the trademark management style, skills and experience. They frequently create partnerships with others to combine skills, knowledge, market presence, and so on.

Contrary to what some people may think, Virgin's constantly expanding and eclectic empire is neither random nor reckless. Each successive venture demonstrates its skill in picking the right market and the right opportunity.

Once a Virgin company is up and running, several factors contribute to making it a success. The power of the Virgin name; Richard Branson's personal reputation; its unrivalled network of friends, contacts and partners; the Virgin management style; the way talent is empowered to flourish within the group. To some traditionalists, these may not seem hard-headed enough; to them, the fact that Virgin has minimal management layers, no bureaucracy, a tiny board and no massive global HQ is an anathema.

Its companies are part of a family rather than a hierarchy. They are empowered to run their own affairs, yet other companies help one another, and solutions to problems come from all kinds of sources. In a sense it is a community, with shared ideas, values, interests and goals. The proof of its success is real and tangible.

All the markets in which Virgin operates tend to have features in common: they are typically markets where the customer has been ripped off or under-served, where there is confusion and/ or where the competition is complacent.

Questions:

1 By looking at www.virgin.com and conducting your own research, can you find out and explain what is the marketing mix used in building the Virgin brand?

2 What is the target market of Virgin?

3 What are Virgin's organizational values? How are these transferred into its brand image?

4 In your opinion, what is Virgin's brand identity, brand personality and brand image?

5 In your opinion, why is Virgin so successful?

References

Aaker, D. (1991), *Managing Brand Equity*, New York: Free Press.

Aaker, D. and Joachimsthaler, E. (2000), *Brands Leadership*, New York: The Free Press.

Aaker, D. and Keller, K. (1990), 'Consumer evaluations of brand extensions', *Journal of Marketing*, Vol. 54, No. 1, pp. 27–33.

Anholt, S. (2003), *Brand New Justice: The Upside of Global Branding* (paperback edn), Oxford: Butterworth-Heinemann.

Chiagouris, L. and Wansley B. (2000), 'Branding on the Internet', *Marketing Management*, Vol. 9, No. 2.

Constantinides, E. (2008), 'The empowered customer and the digital myopia', *Business Strategy Series*, Vol. 9, No. 5.

Fischer, M., Meffert, H. and Perrey, J. (2004), 'Markenpolitik: Ist sie für jedes Unternehmen gleichermaßen relevant?', *Die Betriebswirtschaft*, Vol. 64 No. 3, pp. 333–56.

Held, D. (2002), *Globalization and Anti-Globalization*, Cambridge, UK: Polity Press.

Implications for Australian Business (1989), Sydney, Australia: Arthur Young and Company.

Jones, J. P. (1986), *What's In a Name?*, Aldershot: Gower.

Kalita, J. K., Jagpal, S. and Lehmann, D. R. (2004), 'Do high prices signal high quality? A theoretical model and empirical results', *Journal of Product and Brand Management*, Vol. 13 No. 5, pp. 279–88.

Kapferer, J.-N. (1997), *Strategic Brand Management*, Great Britain: Kogan Page.

Keller, K. (2003), 'Brand synthesis: the multidimensionality of brand knowledge', *Journal of Consumer Research*, Vol. 29 No.1, pp. 595–600.

Klaming, G. (2006), 'The changing role of brands in the age of empowered consumers', PhD thesis (04-983-862).

Kotler, P., Armstrong, G. and Wong, V. (1996), *Principles of Marketing – European Edition*, London: Prentice Hall.

Mathwick, C. and Rigdon, E. (2004), 'Play, flow, and the online search experience', *Journal of Consumer Research*, Vol. 3, No.2, pp. 324–32.

Murray, S. (2003), 'Reputation risk: big PR to companies' aid', *Financial Times*, 30 September.

Murray, S. (2004), 'Defending a brand: what's in a name? A crisis will tell', *Financial Times*, 8 March.

ACNielsen Co. (1984), 'Extending brands', *The Nielsen Researcher*, April.

Notes from Nowhere (2003), *We Are Everywhere: The Irresistible Rise of Anti-Capitalism*, London: Verso Books.

Porter, M. (2001), 'Strategy and the Internet', *Harvard Business Review*, March, pp. 62–78.

Saunders, J. (1990), 'Brands and valuation', *International Journal of Advertising*, Vol. 8, No. 2, pp. 95–110.

Schmitt, B. H. and Pan, Y. (1994), 'Managing corporate and brand identities in the Asia-Pacific region', *California Management Review*, Vol. 36 (Summer), pp. 32–48.

Smith, M. and Brynjolfsson, E. (2001), 'Customer decision making at an Internet shopbot: brand still matters', *The Journal of Industrial Economics*, Vol. 49, No. 4.

Solomon, M., Bamossy, G. and Aaskegard, S. (2003), *Consumer Behaviour – A European Perspective*, Europe: Prentice Hall.

Wolfinbarger, M. and Gilly, M. (2001), 'Shopping online for freedom, control, and fun', *California Management Review*, Vol. 43, No. 2, pp. 34–55.

Further reading and online sites

Beverland, M. (2005) 'Brand management and the challenge of authenticity', *Journal of Product & Brand Management*, Vol. 14, No. 7.

Da Silva, R. V. and Alwi, S. F. (2008), 'Online brand attributes and online corporate brand images', *European Journal of Marketing*, Vol. 42, No. 9/10, pp. 1039–58.

De Chernatony, L., Harris, F. and Dall'Olmo R. F. (2000), 'Added value: its nature, roles and sustainability', *European Journal of Marketing*, Vol. 34, No. 1/2, pp. 39–56.

Delgado-Ballester, E. and Hernández-Espallardo, M. (2008), 'Building online brands through brand alliances in Internet', *European Journal of Marketing*, Vol. 42, No. 9/10.

'Ethics and sustainability, the canon project', Chartered Institute of Marketing at http://www.cim.co.uk/knowledgehub/marketingknowledge/ethics%20and %20sustainability/topichome.aspx

Farquhar, P. (1989), 'Managing brand equity', *Market Research*, pp. 24–33.

Horppu, M., Kuivalainen, O., Tarkiainen, A. and Ellonen, H. K. (2008), 'Online satisfaction, trust and loyalty, and the impact of the offline parent brand', *Journal of Product & Brand Management*, Vol. 17, No. 6.

Jensen, M. B. (2008), 'Online marketing communication potential: Priorities in Danish firms and advertising agencies', *European Journal of Marketing*, Vol. 42, No. 3/4.

Millison, D. and Moon, M. (2000), *Firebrands: Building Brand Loyalty in the Internet Age*, New Delhi: McGraw-Hill.

Power, J., Whelan, S. and Davies, G. (2008), 'The attractiveness and connectedness of ruthless brands: the role of trust', *European Journal of Marketing*, Vol. 42, No. 5/6.

Ward, S. and Lewandowska, A. (2008), 'Is the marketing concept always necessary? The effectiveness of customer, competitor and societal strategies in business environment types', *European Journal of Marketing*, Vol. 42, No. 1/2.

Watson, T. (2007), 'Reputation and ethical behaviour in a crisis: predicting survival', *Journal of Communication Management*, Vol. 11 No. 4.

CHAPTER

02

Brand Equity and Brand Valuation

Chapter contents

Chapter overview

This chapter examines why and how brands are valued, otherwise known as 'brand valuation'. The chapter opens with an examination of the concepts of brand equity, brand value, brand asset and brand valuation. It then covers methods of brand valuation based on accounting, behavioural and customer-oriented approaches, together with emerging trends as well as the applications of brand valuation. One of the reasons for putting a value on brands is strategic and is part of strategic brand management. Therefore, brand valuation is evaluated from the firm's perspective. The previous chapter was an introduction to contemporary brand management. The next chapter relates business models to the foundation of successful brand building.

Introduction

As we saw in Chapter 1, the brand is more than a product because it provides emotional and symbolic value over and above the mere functional value given by the product to the customer. Consumers buy brands not only for pleasure and for the brand's symbolic value, but also to reflect their lifestyle image and their own identities. Accordingly, brands have become part of the consumer's life and are so valuable to him he wants to own them and is ready to pay a higher price for them (e.g. there are many brands in the world that some people value enough to be willing to pay a premium price for; examples are fashion designer brands such as Gucci, Ralph Lauren and Luis Vuitton, or high-quality technological brands of automobiles, computers, etc.). Brands are also valuable to companies because they generate immense returns as well as customer confidence and customer loyalty. In the past brands were perceived as a valuable asset only when it was a question of buying and selling from one owner to another. Brands were valued in the cases of sale, merger or takeover. Now, however, marketers have realized the significant contribution of brands and their long-term value for generating cross-sales and increased sales, as well as making it possible to charge a premium price for their products. As a result, the concepts of brand equity and brand valuation have emerged. The concept of *brand equity* means that brands are seen as valuable assets to the company which enable it to make profits, increase market share and enhance organizational performance over a period of time. *Brand valuation* is concerned with methods of valuing brands based on three different aspects: the financial, the organizational and the customer-orientated. This chapter starts with a definition of brand equity, the rationale for putting a value on brands and how brands are valued. The financial brand valuation methods, behavioural approaches and customer-based brand equity are examined. The advantages and applications of brand valuation and emerging trends are discussed.

What is brand equity?

Technically, a brand is a trademark but behind this trademark are values that can make profits, increase market share and enhance organizational performance. That sum of value is called 'brand equity'.

Brand equity is defined as 'the set of associations and behaviour on the part of a brand's customers, channel members and parent corporation that permits the brand to earn greater volume or greater margins than it could without the brand name' (Leuthesser, 1988). This partly explains why brands have been added to companies' balance sheets, and has been given as a major reason for companies making acquisitions in the late 1980s. For instance, Rank Hovis McDougall was among the first companies in the UK to add its brands to the balance sheet in the late 1980s. In 1988 Nestlé paid six times the book value of its Rowntree acquisition to acquire brand names such as Kit Kat, Quality Street, Smarties, Rolo and Yorkie.

In acquisitions, there is a need for the acquiring company to achieve a perfect match between what has been bought (the book value of the company assets to include goodwill, i.e. a measure of the financial market's attitude to the future of the company, to include the acquired company's brands minus debts) and the price paid. Sometimes there are huge goodwill payments when major corporations are sold, e.g. when Nestlé bought Rowntree. When a brand is purchased individually, the value of this asset must also be made explicit. That is, only transactions involving external brands used to be recorded on a company's balance sheet.

A financially orientated approach to measure brand equity in hypothetical mergers is based on the balance model developed by Farquhar and Rao (1976). This model suggests a match between the acquiring firm and the acquired firm in terms of a variety of attributes. It is based on a multi-attribute approach for evaluating acquisition partners. This approach estimates the brand equity component implicitly in terms of total annual sales, average return on equity, average debt, total assets, market/book value ration and insider share ownership. It evaluates each brand to be acquired in terms of return on equity vs market/book/value, return on equity vs debt/assets, return on equity vs insider ownership (see Table 2 and Figures 2 and 3 in Rao et al. (1991)).

There are two implications of Leuthesser's definition of brand equity: one, unless a brand earns a high volume of sales with high margins the brand has no value; two, this definition only takes into account the financial value of the brand and is simply measured at the level of earnings before interest and tax (EBIT). However, the value of branding to a company goes beyond the financial value that it has been given. Firms that develop strong brands will gain significant competitive advantage over those that do not. The value of brand equity in this case is known as 'the beliefs customers have about a brand'. It helps companies to identify where they are and where they need to go. Another reason for putting value on brands is said to be for a company to proclaim its purpose and to signal the health and development of its brands to other audiences such as shareholders, journalists, the government and, above all, to the company's employees at all levels – to inspire people and help them understand the corporate ethos.

Kapferer (2004) suggested that brand equity should be examined at three levels – brand assets, brand strength and brand value – including four main elements: brand name awareness, brand loyalty, perceived quality and brand associations.

Brand equity is therefore the appropriate measure for evaluating the long-run impact of marketing decisions. Generally, the concept of brand equity and what goes in and out of it helps managers understand how and where brands add value. Brand equity is a brand asset that is built over time. To track brand equity, Kapferer suggested that managers should measure brand strength regularly and make a diagnosis of why this strength is going up or down, and try to improve the level of brand assets – for example, through advertising and other marketing communications.

How internal brands are valued

The financial brand valuation methods

The very first brand valuation was done by Interbrand in the mid-80s for the company Rank Hovis McDougall (RHM) (see above). Interbrand is a brand consultancy which, to date, has become an international brand authority. Interbrand's approach was a ranking one. The rankings reflect the important developments of the previous year and show how much these have affected the

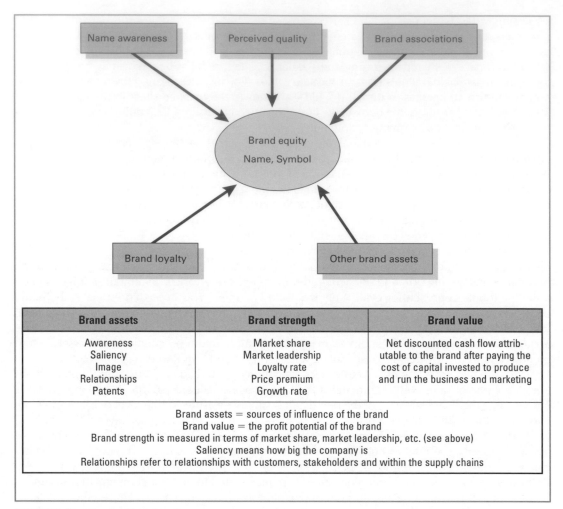

FIGURE 2.1 Three levels of brand equity

company's brand value. Since then this brand authority has published a list of most valuable companies in the world (see Table 2.1). Interbrand's methodology is covered in Branding Brief 2.1.

Brand	Market
Hovis	Bread
Stork	Margarine
Kellogg's	Cornflakes
Gillette	Razor
Schweppes	Mixers
Colgate	Toothpaste
Kodak	Film
Hoover	Vacuum cleaner

TABLE 2.1 Leading brands in the UK since 1933

Brands on the balance sheet

In 1989 the London Stock Exchange endorsed the concept of brand valuation as used by RHM by allowing the inclusion of intangible assets in the class tests for shareholder approvals during takeovers. This proved to be the impetus for a wave of major branded-goods companies to recognize the value of brands as intangible assets on their balance sheets. In the UK these included Cadbury Schweppes, Grand Metropolitan (when it acquired Pillsbury for $5 billion), Guinness, Ladbrokes (when it acquired Hilton) and United Biscuits (including the Smith's brand).

Today, many companies, including LVMH, L'Oréal, Gucci, Prada and PPR, have recognized acquired brands on their balance sheets. Some companies have used the balance-sheet recognition of their brands as an investor-relations tool by providing historic brand values and using brand value as a financial performance indicator.

A number of valuation methods are recommended, such as discounted cash flow (DCF) and market value approaches, among others discussed below. The valuations need to be performed on the business unit (or subsidiary) that generates revenues and profit. The accounting treatment of goodwill upon acquisition is an important step in improving the financial reporting of intangibles such as brands. It is still insufficient, as only acquired goodwill is recognized, and the detail of the reporting is reduced to a minor footnote in the accounts. This can lead to distortion. The McDonald's brand does not appear on the company's balance sheet, even though it is estimated to account for about 70 per cent of the firm's stock market value, yet the Burger King brand is recognized on the balance sheet. In addition, there is still a problem with the quality of brand valuations for balance sheet recognition. Although some companies use a brand-specific valuation approach, others use less sophisticated valuation techniques that often produce questionable values. The debate about bringing financial reporting more in line with the reality of long-term corporate value is likely to continue, but if there is greater consistency in brand valuation approaches and greater reporting of brand values, corporate asset values will become much more transparent (source: Brandchannel. com).

The cost-based method

This is one of the simplest forms of brand evaluation, whereby the value of the brand equals the amount of costs that go into product development, test marketing and all marketing communications, including historical cost. Historical cost is about the resources that have already been invested in the brand. The method also focuses on the amount of money that will be needed to replace a brand: the 'replacement cost'. Replacement cost is based on the estimate of what it will cost to build a brand today from scratch. It therefore seeks to measure the future benefits of ownership by quantifying the amount of money that would be required to replace the future service capability of the brand. The problem with brand valuation by replacement cost is that it requires expert opinion and guesswork, which tend to be subjective. The historical cost approach assumes that there is a direct relationship between the level of past expenditure and the prospective profits and underlying value of the brand. The problem with this method is that it tends to place an excessive value on less successful brands at which high levels of expenditure have been directed, and vice versa. It also ignores inflation. Other pitfalls include the difficulty in determining a period over which costs can be accounted for. Many established brands are old ones: for example, Coca-Cola dates back to 1807, Danone to 1919 and those listed in Table 2.1 have been around since 1933. Should cost be included right from the beginning? Similarly, investment in advertising cannot always be measured in the present time, as one part of the investment goes on building brand awareness and image to facilitate future sales; the other part can generate current extra sales. It has also been argued that it might be better to look at the projections of the brand's future income, but this again may be subjective.

The market-based approach

This method is based on the amount which the customer or the market is willing to pay for the brand. For the manufacturer or the marketer of the brand, this method looks at the future benefits of its brand, upon which the brand value would be determined. The evaluations tend to be hypothetical. Thus, a brand value can be calculated from a company's stock market capitalization or market value. This method is analogous to Simon and Sullivan's (1993) pioneer model of capital, market-orientated brand valuation. It is however only useful to those companies listed on the stock market. This method also ignores the reasons behind the brand's purchase which may be specific to the individual buyer, so that the value cannot be determined by proxy.

The method is based on the idea that the stock price of a company will perform to reflect its brand's potential. The brand value can be calculated using the following formula:

Brand value = (Stock price × Number of shares) −
(Tangible assets + All remaining intangible assets)

The income-based method

This approach takes the value of the earning stream credited to the brand V to be equal to the net income of the brand I (i.e. all outflows minus all inflows) over the capitalization rate R reflecting all business, economic and regulatory risk associated with the brand. In this

$V = I/R.$

In the same family as the income-based method, the discounted cash-flow approach is a method in which the value of the brand is measured by the present worth of the net economic benefit to be received over the life of the brand. This approach takes into account the amount of the income stream that can be generated by the brand, the assumed duration of income stream and the assumed risk associated with the realization of the forecast income. There are three ways to evaluate the brand under this method: by royalties, by premium profit and by excess earnings. The *royalty relief* way, as it is known, is based on the annual royalties a company could hope to receive if it licensed the rights to others to use its brand. These royalty fees are based on a percentage of sales and not profits. Here, careful attention should be paid to identify and compare actual royalty rates paid by franchisees of similar brands to estimate what it would cost to license the brand. This method is practised only in limited areas such as the luxury markets. It is also difficult to separate out the value of the brand, as the royalty fee includes not only the use of the brand but also the packaging supplied by the brand owner, the know-how and services (sometimes including training), which helps the licensee to maintain the brand's appropriate quality level.

The *premium profit* method involves valuing the premium profit generated by a business that uses a brand name and comparing it with a business that does not. This method takes into account the price differential between the branded products and other brands, the additional cost towards the maintenance and strengthening of the brand, as well as the risk associated with future cash flow streams.

The *excess earning* approach is based on the increase in profit or cash flow attributable to the brand. These cash flows are then projected over the life of the brand across a ten-year period through a discounted cash-flow analysis. The problem with this method is in the estimation of the incremental effects of the brand on sales or profits.

Comparables

Another approach is to arrive at a value for a brand on the basis of something comparable. However, comparability is difficult in the case of brands as by definition they should be distinct and thus very different from each other. Furthermore, the value creation of brands in the same category can be very different, even if most other aspects of the underlying business such as target groups, advertising expenditure, price promotions and distribution channel are similar or identical. Comparables can provide an interesting cross-check, however, even though they should never be relied on solely for valuing brands.

Premium price

In the premium price method, the value is calculated as the net present value of future price premiums that a branded product would command over an unbranded or generic equivalent.

However, the primary purpose of many brands is not necessarily to obtain a price premium, but rather to secure the highest level of future demand. The value generation of these brands lies in securing future volumes rather than securing a premium price. This is true for many durable and non-durable consumer goods categories.

This method is flawed since there are rarely generic equivalents to which the premium price of a branded product can be compared. Today almost everything is branded, and in some cases store brands can be as strong as producer brands charging the same or similar prices. The price difference between a brand and competing products can be an indicator of its strength, but it does not represent the sole and most important value contribution a brand makes to the underlying business (source: Brandchannel.com).

Financial brand equity research

Simon and Sullivan (1993) developed methods of separating the brand value from the other assets of a company. They showed how the firm's total brand equity can be measured by subtracting the estimated economic (not just book) value of tangible and non-brand intangible assets from its total stock market value. This approach can also be used ex-post to show the impact of major events like the Coke reformulation on the market's valuation of brand equity.

Another financial approach to measure brand equity focuses on the application of 'momentum accounting' (e.g. Ijiri's work in 1988). This approach suggests a brand's 'momentum' is the rate at which it generates sales, and that the accounting system should focus attention in a disciplined way on changes in this momentum from period to period. The aim is for all such change to be fully accounted for in terms of 1) general dissipation of momentum, in relation to tangible asset depreciation, and 2) the impact of specific marketing activities by the firm and its competitors. However, in general, there has been very little academic research on brands as financial assets. In contrast, most research has focused on the consumer behavioural aspects of brand equity, e.g. the brand's customer franchise. Most of this has been specifically about brand extensions, but there have also been attempts to define and measure customer-based brand equity as a whole.

Financial models of brand valuation have been challenged over time, following a variety of proposals by theoreticians and their limited application to either buy/sale or takeover situations. These models also concentrate too much on stock market capitalization, earning capacity and future cash flows of the brand, licence revenue, etc., many of which lead to the assumption that brand equity is equivalent to future returns and/or profits. Not all influencing factors have been taken into account when calculating future returns or profits such as the behaviour of customers and competitors. Additional influences are sales expenditure, the efficiency of the distribution system and human resources. There is also the strategic issue in mergers and acquisitions reflected in the takeover of Rowntree by Nestlé, which cost Nestlé three times more than the value of Rowntree's shares on the stock exchange and 26 times more than Rowntree's returns. This cannot be explained by financial management methods. Instead, it reflects the important influence of other factors, such as Nestlé's massive strategic interest in Rowntree. Generally, the financial orientation of brand valuation so far only offers rough and partial information about brand equity because it involves a mass of subjective estimations. This is when behavioural brand valuation comes into play. This school of thought takes into consideration customer response and behaviour-related issues for valuing brands. This is discussed in the following section.

The behavioural approach

The behavioural approach offers a market or customer orientation rather than the company one reflected in the financial approaches described above. This approach takes into account the attitudes of the consumer, and defines brand equity as 'the set of associations and the behaviour on the part of a brand's customers, channel members and parent corporation that permits the brand to earn greater volume or greater margins than it could without the brand name' (Leuthesser, 1988), and acknowledges that, 'it gives the brand a strong, sustainable and differentiated competitive advantage' (Srivastava and Shocker, 1991). The early definition of brand equity was centred round the customers. However, it was later extended to include other target audiences as well. It has been defined as 'the strength, currency and value of the brand, the description, the assessment of the appeal, of a brand to all the target audiences who interact with it' (Cooper and Simons, 1997, quoted in Pickton and Broderick, 2005) or 'the value of the brand's name, symbols, associations and reputation to all target audiences who interact with it' (Pickton and Broderick, 2005).

Aaker presented a similar argument, but he underlined the brand as a formal sign and also believed that brand equity can be negative. According to him, 'brand equity comprises a collection of advantages and disadvantages which are connected with a brand, the brand's name or symbol and which increases or decreases the value of a product or service from a company's or customer's perspective. If these characteristics should be the basis of brand equity, they must be linked with the name and/or symbol of the brand.' Aaker examined brand equity from both the customer's and the firm's perspectives. Brand equity is made up of five elements: brand awareness, brand associations, perceived quality, proprietary brand assets and brand loyalty. The first four elements are what determine the fifth: brand loyalty, which is a 'measure of the attachment that a customer has to a brand'. Pickton and Broderick's brand equity has three major components: brand description, brand strength and brand future. The perceived quality and brand association can be categorized as *brand description*. Brand awareness, brand loyalty and proprietary brand assets (in Pickton and Broderick (2005) it is known as 'brand heritage') can be categorized as *brand strength*. The brand description is about what the brand owner can do to exert and maintain a positive image to customers, while brand strength reflects how customers react to the brand. An organization carries out branding with the aim of delivering a positive brand image to its targeted audiences, and high-level brand awareness, consistent and stable brand loyalty from its customers are the expected results. Thus, brand equity lies in the interface between the organization and its customers. Aaker also pointed out five steps in building a brand:

1 Select a name and symbol to represent the company or the product.
2 Create awareness.
3 Position the brand to begin differentiating it from competing brands.
4 Create a brand image to help further differentiate the brand and make it easier to recognize and recall.
5 Create trust in the mind of customers and prospects about the brand by maintaining consistency and delivering expectations.

Brand awareness always occurs in consumers' minds at the beginning of a purchase, and is a significant impetus towards taking action. To create and enhance brand awareness among customers, a high rate of exposure is required. As Keller (2003) stated, brand awareness is created by increasing the familiarity of the brand through repeated exposure and strong association with the appropriate product category or other relevant purchase or consumption. High-level brand awareness among customers can be considered as a solid base for a good financial statement, and also for brand loyalty development. Along with repeated exposure, brand awareness can be generated and can play a prominent role in the entire branding campaign, while a brand image can be a powerful influence on the purchasing decision, through brand awareness. Keller (2003) pointed out that 'a positive brand image is created by marketing programmes that link strong, favourable and unique associations to the brand in memory'. These programmes can be operated in a variety of ways: 'by direct experience; from information communication about the brand from the firm and word-of-mouth; and, by assumptions or inferences from the brand itself or from the identification of the brand or some particular person, place or event' (Pickton and Broderick, 2005). Brand image can be reinforced by the adoption of marketing communications. However, strong, favourable and unique associations of brand image are not always equally valuable in all situations. As Keller (2003) pointed out, the evaluation of brand image may be situation or context dependent and vary according to the particular goals that consumers have in the purchase or consumption decision.

Brand awareness generated in the customer's mind, together with the brand image, evoke customers' purchasing interests and provide persuasive factors in the purchasing decision, while brand loyalty determines the opportunities for repeat business, which are vital for increasing profits and extending the customer base. Therefore, brand loyalty is an asset; without the loyalty of its customers, a brand is merely a trademark, an ownable, identifiable symbol with little value. Light and Morgan (1994) have suggested that brand loyalty identifies not only a product, a service, a corporation, but represents a promise from the corporation, while creating and increasing brand loyalty results in a corresponding increase in the value of the trust mark. These authors also indicated that to maintain long-term and stable brand loyalty, bilateral benefit should be taken into consideration. For example, a loyalty reward system can be a good method to provoke purchase repetition, thus achieving the goal of maintaining brand loyalty.

Marketers tend to focus on brand strength, which is based on market share and profit. Pitta and Katsanis (1995) suggest that brand equity increases the probability of brand choice leading to brand loyalty, and protects the brand from a degree of competition. Achieving a high degree of brand strength may be considered an important objective for managers of brands. The higher the brand strength, the higher the brand value; brand value is based on the future earnings of a brand. The long-term outcome of this should be increased profitability. Furthermore, the brand provides value to the organization by enhancing the efficiency and effectiveness of the marketing programme, prices and margins, brand extensions, trade leverage and competitive advantage. From the customer's perspective, the brand provides value to the customer by enhancing customers' interpretation and evaluation of brand meanings, giving them confidence in their purchasing decision and providing satisfaction. In a sense, brand equity can be defined as 'the totality of consumers' associations, imaginations, ideas and reflections with regard to a brand, which are initiated or evoked by branding a product and which are expressed in a certain esteem for a brand' (source: Association for Consumer Research). From the customer-orientated perspective, brand strength depends on the customer's attitude towards its image. The following section discusses the concept of customer-based brand equity.

Customer-based brand equity

Keller posits that the value of the brand and its equity is derived from the actions of the consumers. Consumers ultimately decide which brands provide more added value, i.e. equity, than others. Keller defined customer-based brand equity as: 'the differential effect that consumer brand knowledge has on their response to brand marketing activity' (Keller, 2003). Thus, from a customer-based brand equity perspective, the indirect approach to measuring brand equity attempts to assess potential sources for brand equity by measuring the consumer mindset or brand knowledge. In a sense, Keller's concept of brand equity provides a useful yardstick for interpreting marketing strategies and assessing the value of the brand.

Brand knowledge is all the thoughts, feelings, perceptions, images, experiences, and so on that become linked to the brand in the minds of consumers. Thus it can be viewed as an associative network memory model containing a network of nodes and links where the brand can be thought of as being a node in memory with a variety of different types of potential associations linked to it. A 'mental map' can be a useful way to portray some of the important dimensions of brand knowledge.

Brand knowledge is characterized by brand awareness and brand image. Brand awareness is related to the strength of the brand node or trace in memory as reflected by consumers' ability to recall or recognize the brand under different conditions. The depth of brand awareness is the likelihood that the brand can be recognized or recalled. The breadth of brand awareness relates to the variety of purchase and consumption situations in which the brand comes to mind. Brand image is the consumer's perception of a brand reflected by the brand associations held in his memory. Consumer-based brand equity occurs when the consumer has a high level of awareness and familiarity with the brand and holds a strong, favourable and unique association with it in his mind.

The indirect approach is useful in identifying what aspects of the brand knowledge may cause the distinctive response that creates brand equity in the marketplace. Because any one measure typically captures only one particular aspect of brand knowledge, multiple measures need to be employed to account for the multi-dimensional nature of brand knowledge. Brand awareness can be assessed through a variety of aided and unaided memory measures that can be applied to test brand recall and recognition; brand image can be assessed through a variety of qualitative and quantitative techniques.

While several studies have tried to estimate the contribution that brands make to shareholder value, a study by Interbrand in association with JP Morgan (see Table 2.2) concluded that on average brands account for more than one-third of shareholder value. The study also reveals that brands create significant value either as consumer or corporate brands, or as a combination of the two. Table 2.2 shows how big the economic contribution made by brands to companies can be.

The McDonald's brand accounts for more than 70 per cent of shareholder value. The Coca-Cola brand alone accounts for 51 per cent of the stock market value of the Coca-Cola Company. This is despite the fact that the company owns a large portfolio of other drinks brands such as Sprite and Fanta (source: Brandchannel.com).

The new approach: Brand Asset Valuator (BAV) for brand management

BAV is a database of consumer perception of brands; it is created and managed by Brand Asset Consulting, a division of Young & Rubicam Brands, to provide information to enable firms to improve the marketing decision-making process and to manage brands better. BAV measures the value of a brand along four dimensions: 'Differentiation', 'Relevance', 'Esteem' and 'Knowledge'. Differentiation and Relevance build up to 'Brand Strength'. Esteem and Knowledge are used to calculate 'Brand Stature' as follows:

- 'Differentiation' quantifies the brand's point of difference.
- 'Relevance' means how appropriate the brand is to you.
- 'Esteem' means how well regarded the brand is.

Company	2002 brand value ($bn)	Brand contribution to market capitalization of parent company (%)	2001 brand value ($bn)
Coca-Cola	69.6	51	69.0
Microsoft	64.1	21	65.1
IBM	51.2	39	52.8
GE	41.3	14	42.4
Intel	30.9	22	34.7
Nokia	30.0	51	35.0
Disney	29.3	68	32.6
McDonald's	26.4	71	25.3
Marlboro	24.2	20	22.1
Mercedes-Benz	21.0	47	21.7

Source: *BusinessWeek*, Interbrand/JP Morgan league table, 2002.

TABLE 2.2 The contribution of brands to shareholder value

- 'Knowledge' means an intimate understanding of the brand.
- 'Brand Strength' describes the brand's growth potential.
- 'Brand Stature' describes the brand's current power.

BAV's database is the result of the world's most extensive research project on branding. It is based on data covering 30 000 brands across 400 000 consumers in 48 countries through 240 studies (source: Wikipedia). It is not only a body of research, but also a brand concept that has been tested many times and is constantly being updated. Data gathered in BAV show that brands are created as a result of the development of the four main dimensions mentioned above, which characterize the image existing in customers' perception (see Figures 2.2 and 2.3).

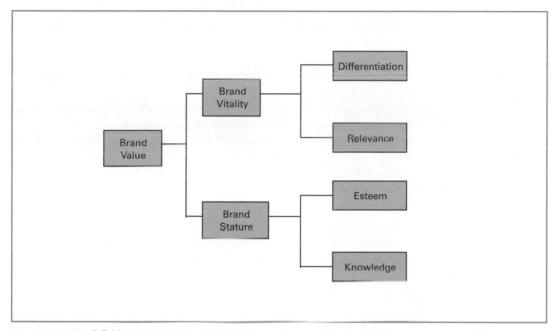

FIGURE 2.2 Young & Rubicam Brand Asset Valuator (BAV)

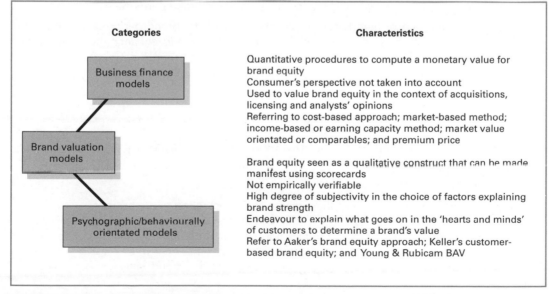

FIGURE 2.3 Summary of Brand Valuation Models

Advantages and applications of brand valuation

Brand valuation is helpful for the following:

- Making decisions on business investments. By making the brand asset comparable to other intangible and tangible company assets, resource allocation between the different asset types can follow the same economic criteria and rationale: for example, capital allocation and return requirements.

- Measuring the return on brand investments based on brand value to arrive at an ROI that can be directly compared with other investments. Brand management and marketing service providers can be measured against clearly identified performance targets related to the value of the brand asset.

- Making decisions on brand investments. By prioritizing them by brand, customer segment, geographic market, product or service, distribution channel, and so on, brand investments can be assessed for cost and impact, and judged on which will produce the highest returns.

- Making decisions on licensing the brand to subsidiary companies. Under a licence the subsidiaries will be accountable for the brand's management and use, and an asset that has to be paid for will be managed more rigorously than one that is free.

- Turning the marketing department from a cost centre into a profit centre by connecting brand investments and brand returns (royalties from the use of the brand by subsidiaries). The relationship between investments in and returns from the brand becomes transparent and manageable. Remuneration and career development of marketing staff can be linked to and measured by brand-value development.

- Allocating marketing expenditures according to the benefit each business unit derives from the brand asset.

- Organizing and optimizing the use of different brands in the business (for example, corporate, product and subsidiary brands) according to their respective economic value contribution.

- Assessing co-branding initiatives according to their economic benefits and risks to the value of the company's brand.

- Deciding the appropriate branding after a merger, according to a clear economic rationale.

- Managing brand migration more successfully as a result of a better understanding of the value of different brands, and therefore of what can be lost or gained if brand migration occurs.

- Establishing brand value scorecards based on the understanding of the drivers of brand value that provide focused and actionable measures for optimal brand performance.

- Managing a portfolio of brands across a variety of markets. Brand performance and brand investments can be assessed on an equally comparable basis to enhance the overall return from the brand portfolio.

- Communicating where appropriate the economic value creation of the brand to the capital markets in order to support share prices and obtain funding.

Branding Brief 2.1: The Interbrand brand valuation methodology

The Interbrand methodology is the most easily recognized of all methodologies. Interbrand builds its valuations up from three elements:

1 The *Financial Analysis*, to establish the ongoing profit generation of the business.
2 The *Market Analysis*, to establish the extent to which the brand contributes to those profits. Just because a brand appears on a tin does not mean that people buy this tin because of this brand.
3 The *Brand Analysis*, to establish the ongoing strength of the brand, and therefore a risk discount factor.

How does Interbrand derive the value of brands?

Interbrand's valuation approach is a derivative of the way businesses and financial assets are valued. It fits with current corporate finance theory and practice. There are three key elements.

Financial forecasting

It identifies the revenues from products or services that are generated with the brand. From these branded revenues it deducts operating costs, applicable taxes and a charge for the capital employed to derive intangible earnings. Intangible earnings are the earnings that are generated by all of the business's intangibles, including brands, patents, R&D, management expertise, etc. This is a prudent and conservative approach, as it only rewards the intangible assets after the tangible assets have received their required return. The concept of intangible earnings is, therefore, similar to value-based management concepts, such as economic profit or EVA (Economic Value Added is Stern Stuart's branded concept). On the basis of reports from financial analysts, we prepare a forecast of intangible earnings for six years.

Role of brand

Since intangible earnings include the returns for all intangibles employed in the business, Interbrand needs to identify the earnings that are specifically attributable to the brand. Through its proprietary analytical framework, called 'role of brand', it can calculate the percentage of intangible earnings that is entirely generated by the brand. In some businesses, e.g. fragrances or packaged goods, the role of brand is very high – as the brand is the predominant driver of the customer purchase decision. However, in other businesses (in particular B2B), the brand is only one purchase driver among many, and the role of the brand is therefore lower. For example, people are buying Microsoft not only because of the brand but mostly because the company has an installed base of 80 per cent of the market and it would be for most users extremely difficult to switch their existing files to a new software platform. In the case of Shell, people buy not only because of the brand but because of the location of its petrol stations. For each of the brands (and categories) we have assessed the role of brand.

The role of brand is a percentage – thus, if it is 50 per cent, we take 50 per cent of the intangible earnings as brand earnings. If it is 10 per cent, we take only 10 per cent of the earnings.

Brand strength

For deriving the net present value of the forecast brand earnings, Interbrand needs a discount rate that represents the risk profile of these earnings. There are two factors at play: first, the time value of money (i.e. $100 today is more valuable than $100 in five years because one can earn interest on the money in the meantime); second, the risk that the forecast earnings will actually materialize. The discount rate represents these factors, as it provides an asset-specific risk rate. The higher the risk of the future earnings stream, the higher will be the discount rate. To derive today's value of a future expected-earnings stream, it needs to be 'discounted' by a rate that reflects the risk of the earnings actually materializing and the time for which it is expected. For example, $100 from the Coca-Cola brand in five years requires a lower discount rate than $100 from the Fanta brand in five years, as the Coca-Cola brand is stronger and, therefore, more likely to deliver the expected earnings.

The assessment of brand strength is a structured way of assessing the specific risk of the brand. Interbrand compares the brand against a notional ideal and scores it against common factors of brand strength. The ideal brand is virtually 'risk free' and would be discounted at a rate almost as low as government bonds or similar risk-free investments. The lower the brand strength, the further it is from the risk-free investment and so, the higher the discount rate (and therefore the lower the net present value).

Branding Brief 2.2: Applications of brand valuation

Internal marketing management

Brand valuation is increasingly being used as a management tool in leading organizations. For example, brand valuation figures can be used to evaluate new product and market development opportunities, to set business objectives, allocate budgets and to help measure performance and reward staff.

Internal royalty rates

Across a large organization there may be many affiliates, subsidiaries or divisions that make use of any particular brand. As the profit potential of brands becomes more clearly understood, more companies are charging royalties across their business operations for the use of these brand assets.

Licensing and franchising

Where companies allow outside organizations to use their brand, on a licensing or franchising basis, a brand valuation can lay the foundation for appropriate charges.

Tax planning

As the management of brands as financial assets becomes more sophisticated, so tax authorities around the world have started to take an interest in how these assets are managed. The result is that more and more international organizations are planning the most cost-effective domicile for their brand portfolios and are organizing their tax affairs with their brands in mind.

Securitized borrowing

Even in the conservative world of banking, the asset value of brands has been recognized. As a result brands have been used to secure loans, especially in the US, where companies such as Disney have borrowed significant amounts of money against their brand name.

Litigation support

Brand valuations have been used to support litigation against the illegal use of a brand name (as a basis for calculating damages, for example) and also in cases of receivership, to prevent the assets of the business being undervalued.

Branding Brief 2.3: Brand valuation for non-profits

Why would a non-profit company go to the trouble of valuing its brand?

Establishing the value of a non-profit brand can open the door to co-branding, licensing and partnering opportunities. Additionally, it allows one to determine reasonable expenditure on marketing and offers a point from which to explain the power of the brand.

Interbrand's brand valuation for non-profits considers factors such as the public's level of trust that the donation will be used effectively, the public's perception of the organization's financial stability, the public's personal experience of the cause, the organization's level of contact with the donor, and the ease of transaction for the donor.

What are the factors that drive a non-profit brand's value?

UNICEF, for instance, is a strong brand. It has respect and value. One of the goals for UNICEF is to educate the public. If the public understands what it is that UNICEF does, they will support it.

There are internal barriers to overcome – e.g. the perception that branding is for the crass commercial world.

There seems to be a clear distinction between business school approaches and the way in which charities and causes have evolved over the years. They don't necessarily match in many people's mind. However, there are not only synergies, but also common elements in the way that a private-sector organization evolves and grows, and the way that a non-profit or charity would evolve or grow.

What portion of funds should be allocated to branding for non-profits?

For instance, a for-profit brand like a perfume manufacturer devotes perhaps 2 per cent of its money to mixing the concoction and 98 per cent to the branding (e.g. packaging, brand protection, promotion).

However, serious non-profit with a social mission would be more like the reverse of that – ideally 98 per cent to the cause and 2 per cent to the brand. It may be enough in one instance and not in another.

There are organic ways to harness the passion of members, volunteers and organizational staff to keep that number small for non-profits.

The best thing about having a strong brand is that it makes it easier to attract funding and donations, thereby making the fundraising process more efficient by harnessing the brand to work towards growing the support base. The more non-profits understand the value of their brand, the better control they can exercise over how and when that brand gets used and the better use they can put their donations to in furthering their cause.

Emerging trends

Apart from the financial and behavioural approaches to brand valuations, the new financial reporting looks at different ways to recognize intangible assets. International organizations for standardization have recently proposed a new international standard on brand valuation based on narrative reporting. The reason for this and the issues in accounting intangibles are discussed below.

Sixty-two per cent of the value of the world's quoted companies resides in intangibles not reported in the company's books; 20 per cent of quoted global intangible asset value resides in brands in which the position is understated; while 12 per cent of the value of the world's quoted companies resides in brand intangibles. This varies by sector: for example, luxury goods are high in brand intangibles but in utilities the level is low, although there is an increase in own brands. Generally, the trend in intangibles is for growth. The problem is how to account for intangibles and how to describe them. The exclusion of internally generated intangibles from financial reporting will limit the reduction in the large unexplained 'intangible gap'. Improved narrative reporting is required to plug the gap. This is a chance for companies to prove how much their brands are worth.

The Institute of Practitioners in Advertising (IPA) has come up with new ways of reporting brand intangibles through narrative reporting, using non-financial key performance indicators. The IPA framework for narrative reporting employs the following criteria to help companies think how they should be reporting. The best narrative reporting should be: concise; comprehensive; material; cohesive; strategic; forward looking; explicit; comparative; and comparable over time. Narrative reporting should also be credible and reliable, and these two criteria should be included in the IPA's framework.

Non-financial reporting emphasizes the following: human capital; customer service; less marketing; customer service in KPIs; customer service in terms of customer satisfaction, numbers, retention rates, service award and customer complaints.

Narrative reporting helps to explain what happens to a company's investment, what it spends resources on (although some companies are reluctant to say too much about their investment). Narrative reporting is what is seen through the eyes of the management and is also a reflection of the dynamic of the market. It is a good approach, and helps to show how brands contribute and drive the business forward. It also helps to raise customer awareness of the company's brands. One of the measures in brand strength is shown by the brand index and the customer relationships with the brands.

Conclusion

Brands are valuable assets to companies. This is because of the associations and meanings that consumers attach to them. People buy brands because of the functional and emotional benefits they get from them. Keller posits that the value of the brand and its equity are derived from the actions of consumers. Consumers ultimately decide which brands provide more added value, i.e. more equity than others. Consumer-based brand equity occurs when the consumer has a high level of awareness and familiarity with the brand, and it holds a strong, favourable and unique association in his mind. A study by Interbrand in association with JP Morgan reveals that brands create significant value either as consumer or corporate brands, or as a combination of the two. Brand equity is a concept which gives value to the brand. This value can make profits, increase market share and enhance organizational performance over time. Brand equity has been viewed from the financial, organizational and customer-orientated perspectives. Brand valuation as a method of valuing brands has gained momentum from its cost orientation to the comprehensive approach in which the brand valuator takes the cost and finance factors, the market and competition factors, and the consumer behaviour and response factors into account while valuing brands. The finance-based approach views brand equity in terms of incremental discounted future cash flows that would result from a branded product revenue compared with that of the same product without the brand name. The financial market value-based technique for estimating a firm's brand equity is centred round the stock price, which is used as a basis to estimate the value of the brand. The estimation technique extracts the value of brand equity from the value of the firm's other assets.

The income-based method takes the value of the earning stream credited to the brand V to be equalled to the net income of the brand I (i.e. all outflows minus all inflows) over the capitalization rate R reflecting all business, economic and regulatory risk associated with the brand. In the premium price method, the value is calculated as the net present value of future price premiums that a branded product would command over an unbranded or generic equivalent. Another approach is to arrive at a value for a brand on the basis of something comparable. Overall, the financial orientation of brand valuation offers only rough and partial information about brand equity because it contains a great deal of guesswork, while financial models of brand valuation have also been challenged over time, with a variety of proposals by theoreticians and their limited application to either buy/sale or takeover situations.

The behavioural approach is based on an orientation towards the market, customers and other target audiences. It views the brand as a strong, sustainable, differentiated and competitive tool, whose advantage is contained in its name, symbols, associations and reputation to all target audiences who interact with it. However, brand equity can also be negative, as it comprises a collection of advantages and disadvantages which are connected with the brand's name or symbol, and which can increase or decrease the value of a product or service from a company's or customer's perspective. Brand equity is made up of five elements: brand awareness, brand associations, perceived quality, proprietary brand assets and brand loyalty. The first four elements are what determine the fifth, brand loyalty, which is a measure of the attachment that a customer has to a brand. Brand equity also has three major components: brand description, brand strength and brand future.

Brand equity thus lies in the interface between the organization and its customers. The customer orientation approach is also extended to include the customer-based brand equity approach, which states that consumers ultimately decide which brands provide more value than others. This approach attempts to assess potential sources for brand equity by measuring consumer mindset or brand knowledge, i.e. all the thoughts, feelings, perceptions, images, experiences, and so on that become linked to the brand in the minds of consumers. Consumer-based brand equity occurs when the consumer has a high level of awareness and familiarity with the brand so that it holds a strong, favourable and unique association in his mind.

Another approach to brand valuation is the Brand Asset Valuator (BAV), which measures the value of a brand along four dimensions: 'Differentiation', 'Relevance', 'Esteem' and 'Knowledge'. Differentiation and Relevance build up to 'Brand Strength'. Esteem and Knowledge are used to calculate 'Brand Stature'. It is not only a research tool but also a brand concept that has been tested many times and is constantly being updated. Data gathered in BAV show that brands are created as a result of the development of four main dimensions as mentioned above, which characterize the image existing in customers' perceptions.

Brand valuation is especially important in resource allocation in business investments, brand investments, measuring return on brand investments, organizing and optimizing the use of different brands in the business according to their respective economic value contribution. It also contributes to assessing co-branding initiatives according to their economic benefits and risks to the value of the company's brand; deciding the appropriate branding after a merger according to a clear economic rationale; managing brand migration more successfully; managing portfolios of brands across a variety of markets and optimizing brand performance; and finally, where appropriate, communicating the economic value creation of the brand to the capital markets in order to support share prices and obtain funding.

The trend for non-financial key performance indicators is through narrative reporting. The criteria used by the IPA for narrative reporting are: concise; comprehensive; material; cohesive; strategic; forward looking; explicit; comparative; comparable over time. Narrative reporting should also be credible and reliable.

🔓 Key terms

Brand assets: the sources of influence of the brand. These are: customer loyalty, perceived high quality, strong brand associations, the promoter and the country of origin of the brand.

Brand earnings: calculated by multiplying the role of branding index by intangible earnings.

Brand equity: a set of assets and liabilities linked to a brand, its name and symbol that add to or subtract from the value provided by a product or service to a firm and/or to a firm's customers. It is also referred to as a brand asset which is built over time.

Branding index: the percentage of intangible earnings that are generated by the brand.

Brand financial: a way of defining brand equity or a firm's brand asset in financial terms.

Brand financial value: measured at the level of earnings before interest and tax (EBIT).

Brand measure: includes economic measures such as price, market share and asset value, and image measures such as personality, attitude and values, which underline a brand performance model.

Brand strength: measured in terms of market share.

▶

Brand valuation: a way of recognizing the value of brands as intangible assets on companies' balance sheets and offering some information about companies' brand equity.

Brand value: the profit potential of the brand, and also the economic value or price customers attach to a brand, as well as the beliefs customers have about a brand. It is the net present value (NPV) of the forecast brand earnings, discounted by the brand discount rate. The NPV calculation comprises both the forecast period and the period beyond, reflecting the ability of brands to continue generating future earnings.

Comparables: the value creation of brands in the same category that can be compared to provide cross-checks.

Cost-based brand valuation: a method of valuing brands. Depending on the time frame chosen, assets can be valued either on the basis of historic cost or replacement cost. The historical cost is about the resources that have already been invested in the brand. The replacement cost is based on the estimated cost of building a brand today from scratch.

Customer-based brand equity: the differential effect that consumer brand knowledge has on their response to brand marketing activity. Thus, according to a customer-based brand equity perspective, the indirect approach to measuring brand equity attempts to assess potential sources for brand equity by measuring consumer mindset or brand knowledge.

Discounted cash flow: a method of measuring the value of the brand by the present worth of the net economic benefit to be received over the life of the brand. This approach takes into account the amount of the income stream that can be generated by the brand, the assumed duration of income stream and the assumed risk associated with the realization of the forecast income. There are three ways to evaluate the brand under this method: royalties, premium profit and excess earnings.

EBIT: earnings before interest and tax.

EBITA: earnings before interest, tax and amortization.

Excess earning: a way of calculating the increase in profit or cash flow attributable to the brand. These cash flows are then projected over the useful life of the brand, usually over a ten-year period using a discounted cash flow analysis.

Financial brand equity: (see Simon and Sullivan, 1993) a method of separating the brand value from other assets of a company. The firm's total brand equity can be measured by subtracting the estimated economic (not just book) value of tangible and non-brand intangible assets from its total stock market value.

Income-based brand valuation: takes the value of the earning stream credited to the brand V to be equalled to the net income of the brand I (i.e. all outflows minus all inflows) over the capitalization rate R reflecting all business, economic and regulatory risk associated with the brand. As such, $V = I/R$.

Intangible earnings: brand revenue less operating costs, applicable taxes and a charge for the capital employed.

Market-based brand valuation: a method that calculates a brand value from a company's stock market capitalization or market value.

Momentum accounting: this approach suggests a brand's 'momentum' is the rate at which it generates sales and that the accounting system should focus attention in a disciplined way on changes in this momentum from period to period. The aim is for all such change to be fully accounted for in terms of 1) general dissipation of momentum, in relation to tangible asset depreciation, and 2) the impact of specific marketing activities by the firm and its competitors.

Narrative reporting: non-financial key performance indicators; the criteria for best reporting are: concise; comprehensive; material; cohesive; strategic; forward looking; explicit; comparative; comparable over time. Narrative reporting should also be credible and reliable, so these two criteria should be included in the IPA's framework.

NOPAT: net operating profit after tax.

Premium pricing: in the premium price method, the value is calculated as the net present value of future price premiums that a branded product would command over an unbranded or generic equivalent. However, the primary purpose of many brands is not necessarily to obtain a price premium but rather to secure the highest level of future demand.

? Discussion questions

1 What is the relationship between the following terms: brand awareness, brand equity, brand share and brand value?

2 Is there a difference between brand value and brand valuation? If so, explain your answer.

3 Discuss the relevance of brand equity in the strategic brand management context.

4 Explain the rationale of brand valuation. What benefits does it bring to the organization and its audiences, the shareholders, the customers?

5 Compare and contrast the underlying philosophies in the financial and behavioural approaches to brand valuation.

6 Discuss the pros and cons of each of the financial methods to evaluate brand assets such as the cost-based, market and income-based methods.

7 Explain the problems in finding one right brand valuation method.

8 Explain what 'momentum accounting' means.

9 Discuss the relevance of the customer-based brand equity approach to brand management today.

10 Discuss why it may be difficult to evaluate a mature brand using the cost-based approach.

Projects

Brand audit project

You will form brand management teams consisting of three to four students to work on this project. Your assignment is to pick a brand from the list of Business Week Top 100 brands and conduct a brand audit. To choose your brand go to www.businessweek.com.

The analysis will be based entirely on information from public secondary sources and company websites, as well as your own professional experiences and insights. Specifically, you will assess the brand planning, value and growth of your chosen brand by addressing these questions:

1 *Brand planning assessment.* How would you characterize the positioning of your brand? What have been the key marketing activities that have made the most contribution to the success of that positioning? Where are there the greatest opportunities to further enhance that positioning?

2 *Brand valuation assessment.* How has your brand built brand resonance? How do you assess the value of the brand to the company?

3 *Brand growth analysis.* How would you critique your brand's architecture? What is good and bad about its hierarchy? How does it fit into a broader brand portfolio? How well has it been expanded into new markets or channels? How would you judge its growth strategy?

4 What are the sources of brand equity?

5 Make recommendations concerning how to build and manage equity for the brand chosen. After summarizing current and desired brand knowledge structures, you should outline creative and relevant directions for management of your chosen brand, providing justification where appropriate using relevant concepts.

MINI CASE 2.1: AMERICAN EXPRESS: MANAGING A FINANCIAL SERVICES BRAND

American Express is known worldwide for its charge cards, travellers' services and financial services. As it grew from a nineteenth-century express shipping company into a travel services expert by the mid-1900s, American Express became associated in the minds of consumers with prestige, security, service, international acceptability and leisure. As the company grew, it expanded into a variety of financial categories, including brokerage services, banking and insurance, and by the late 1980s, American Express was the largest diversified financial services firm in the world. The company encountered difficulty integrating these broad financial services offerings, however, and this fact, combined with increased card competition from Visa and MasterCard, compelled American Express to divest many of its financial holdings in the early 1990s and focus on its core competencies of travel and cards. By the end of the 1990s American Express was again seeking to broaden its brand to include select financial services in order to achieve growth. Beyond the challenge of integrating these services, American Express faced a number of issues in the 2000s, including a highly competitive credit card industry, a slowing economy and a sluggish travel industry.

Questions:

1 What elements and characteristics comprised the equity in the American Express brand in the 1960s? In the 1980s?

2 How would you currently characterize the American Express brand?

3 Evaluate American Express in terms of its competitors. How well is it positioned? What are its points-of-parity and points-of-difference in its different business areas? How has it changed over time? In what segments of its business does American Express face the most competition?

4 Evaluate American Express's integration of its various businesses. What recommendations would you make in order to maximize the contribution to equity of all of its businesses' units? At the same time, is the corporate brand sufficiently coherent?

MINI CASE 2.2: THE PROCESS OF BRAND VALUATION

To capture the complex value creation of a brand, a company must take five key steps, which are: market segmentation, financial analysis, demand analysis, competitive benchmarking and brand valuation calculation.

First, the company must split the brand's markets into non-overlapping and homogeneous groups of consumers according to applicable criteria such as product or service, distribution channels, consumption patterns, purchase sophistication, geography, and existing and new customers. This refers to market segmentation. The brand value in each segment and the sum of the brand values in all the segments constitute the desired value of the brand.

Second, the company must identify and forecast revenues and earnings from intangibles generated by the brand for each of the distinct segments determined in the market segmentation stage. Intangible earnings are defined as brand revenue less operating costs, applicable taxes and a charge for the capital employed.

Third, the company is to conduct a demand analysis. The brand valuator needs to assess the role that the brand plays in driving demand for products and services in the markets in which it operates, and determine what proportion of intangible earnings is attributable to the brand measured by an indicator referred to as the 'role of branding index'. This can be done by first identifying the various drivers of demand for the branded business, then determining the degree to which each driver is directly influenced by the brand. The role of branding index represents the percentage of intangible earnings that are generated by the brand. Brand earnings are calculated by multiplying the role of branding index by intangible earnings.

Competitive benchmarking involves determining the competitive strengths and weaknesses of the brand to derive the specific brand discount rate that reflects the risk profile of its expected future earnings (this is measured by an indicator referred to as the 'brand strength score'). This also includes a structured evaluation of the brand's market, stability, leadership position, growth trend, support, geographic footprint and legal protectability.

The final step is brand value calculation. Brand value is the net present value (NPV) of the forecast brand earnings, discounted by the brand discount rate. The NPV calculation comprises both the forecast period and the period beyond, reflecting the ability of brands to continue generating future earnings.

Questions:

1 Explain what 'intangible earnings' means.
2 What is the brand index for?
3 Explain what the brand strength score means.

		Year 1	Year 2	Year 3	Year 4	Year 5
Market (units)		250 000 000	258 750 000	267 806 250	277 179 469	286 890 750
Market growth rate			4%	4%	4%	4%
Market share (volume)		15%	17%	19%	21%	20%
Volume		37 500 000	43 987 500	50 883 188	58 207 688	57 376 150
Price ($)		10	10	10	11	11
Price change			3%	2%	2%	2%
Branded revenues		375 000 000	450 871 875	531 963 725	621 341 172	625 326 631
Cost of sales		150 000 000	180 348 750	212 793 490	248 536 469	250 130 653
Gross margin		225 000 000	270 523 125	319 190 235	372 804 703	375 195 979
Marketing costs		67 500 000	81 156 938	95 757 071	111 841 411	112 558 794
Depreciation		2 812 500	3 381 539	3 989 878	4 660 059	4 689 950
Other overheads		18 750 000	22 543 594	26 599 186	31 067 059	31 266 332
Central cost allocation		3 750 000	4 508 719	5 319 837	6 213 412	6 253 266
EBITA (earnings before interest, tax and amortization)		132 187 500	158 932 336	187 524 263	219 022 763	220 427 638
Applicable taxes	35%	46 265 625	55 626 318	65 633 492	76 657 967	77 149 673
NOPAT (net operating profit after tax)		85 921 875	103 306 018	121 890 771	142 364 796	143 277 964
Capital employed		131 250 000	157 805 156	186 194 304	217 469 410	218 864 321
Working capital		112 500 000	135 261 563	159 595 118	186 402 351	187 597 989
Net PPE		18 750 000	22 543 594	26 599 186	31 067 059	31 266 332
Capital charge	8%	10 500 000	12 624 413	14 895 544	17 397 553	17 509 146
Intangible earnings		75 421 875	90 681 606	106 995 227	124 967 243	125 768 819
Role of branding index	79%					
Brand earnings		59 583 281	71 638 469	84 526 229	98 724 122	99 357 367
Brand strength score	66					
Brand discount rate	7.4%					
Discounted brand earnings		55 477 916	62 106 597	68 230 515	74 200 384	69 531 031
NPV (net present value) of discounted brand earnings (years 1–5)		329 546 442				
Long-term growth rate	2.5%					
NPV of terminal brand value (beyond year 5)		1 454 475 640				
BRAND VALUE		1 784 022 082				

TABLE 2.3 Sample brand value calculation

END OF CHAPTER CASE STUDY: NIKE INCORPORATED

Nike Incorporated is the world's leading supplier of athletic shoes, apparel and sports equipment, based in Oregon. It has revenues in excess of 16 billion USD in 2007, and employs over 30 000 people worldwide. Founded in 1964 as Blue Ribbon Sports (BRS) by Bill Bowerman and Philip Knight, and officially becoming Nike, Inc. in 1978, the company takes its name from Nike, the Greek goddess of victory. Nike markets its products under its own brand as well as Nike Golf, Nike Pro, Nike+, Air Jordan, Nike Skateboarding, Team Starter, and subsidiaries including Cole Haan, Hurley International, Umbro and Converse. In addition to manufacturing sportswear and equipment, the company operates retail stores under the Niketown name. Nike sponsors many high-profile athletes and sports teams around the world, with the highly recognized trademarks of 'Just do it' and the Nike 'swoosh' logo.

The company operated as a distributor for a Japanese shoemaker, making most sales at track meets out of Knight's car. The company's profits grew quickly and, in 1966, BRS opened its first retail store, on Pico Boulevard in Santa Monica, California.

The company's first self-designed product was based on Bowerman's 'waffle' design in which the sole of the shoe was inspired by the pattern of a waffle iron. By 1980 Nike had reached a 50 per cent market share in the United States athletic shoe market, and the company went public in December of that year. Its growth was due largely to 'word-of-foot' advertising rather than television ads. Nike's first national television commercials ran in 1982 during the broadcast of the New York Marathon.

Nike produces a wide range of sports equipment, from track running shoes to shoes, jerseys, shorts, baselayers etc. for a wide range of sports including track & field, American football, baseball, tennis, Association football, lacrosse, basketball and cricket. Nike positions its products in such a way to appeal to a youthful, materialistic crowd. It is positioned as a premium performance brand. However, it also engineers shoes for discount stores like Wal-Mart under the Starter brand.

In an effort to target the low-end athletic goods market, Nike also purchased the parent company of the Starter athletic clothing brand in 2004 for $43 million and, in 2007, the sports apparel supplier Umbro, known as the manufacturer of the England national football team's kits, for £285 million.

Nike sells its product to more than 25 000 retailers in the US and in approximately 160 countries in the world. Nike also sells its own products at nike.com, which allows customers to design shoes and delivers them direct from the manufacturer to your house. Nike sells its products in international markets through independent distributors, licensees and subsidiaries.

Nike's marketing strategy is an important component of the company's success. Nike lures customers with a marketing strategy centring around a brand image which is attained by a distinctive logo and the advertising slogan: 'Just do it', and promotes its products by sponsorship agreements with celebrity athletes and professional teams. Nike has signed top athletes in many different professional sports, like Romanian tennis player Ilie Nastase and distance-running legend Steve Prefontaine. Besides Prefontaine, Nike has sponsored many other successful track & field athletes over the years, such as Carl Lewis, Jackie Joyner-Kersee and Sebastian Coe. However, it was the signing of basketball player Michael Jordan in 1984, with his subsequent promotion of Nike over the course of his storied career with Spike Lee as Mars Blackmon that proved to be one of the biggest boosts to Nike's publicity and sales. Nike is also the official kit sponsor for the Indian cricket team for five years, from 2006 to 2010. Nike uses websites as a promotional tool to cover these events.

However, Nike's extensive use of advertising and other media has caused several controversies that have gathered substantial publicity. In one incident, consumer activist Marc Kasky filed a lawsuit in Quincy Sanford, California, regarding newspaper advertisements and several letters Nike distributed in response to criticisms of labour conditions in its factories. Kasky claimed that the company made representations that constituted false advertising. Nike responded that the false advertising laws did not cover the company's expression of its views on a public issue, and that these were entitled to First Amendment protection. The local court agreed with Nike's lawyers, but the California Supreme Court overturned this ruling, claiming that the corporation's communications were commercial speech and therefore subject to false advertising laws.

In another incident, Nike had to pay $250 000 to Capitol Records Inc., which held the North American licensing rights to the Beatles' recordings, for the right to use the Beatles' rendition of 'Revolution' for a year. Nike later discontinued airing ads featuring 'Revolution' in March 1988. Then, in 2004, an ad about LeBron James beating cartoon martial arts masters in martial arts offended Chinese authorities, who called the ad blasphemous and insulting to national dignity. The ad was later banned in China. In early 2007 the ad was reinstated in China for unknown reasons.

Questions:

1 What are the brand image and sources of equity for the Nike brand? How transferable are these associations?

2 Are sponsorships and endorsements vital to Nike's business? For instance, what effect would Nike becoming an official sponsor for the Olympics have on the company's relationship with consumers?

3 How important is 'fashion' to Nike? Is it a performance apparel company or a fashion company? What is more important for Nike when it enters a new market like China? Fashion or performance?

4 Should Nike do anything different to defend its position now that Adidas and Reebok have joined forces?

5 Critique Nike's current marketing efforts. What is good and what is bad about them? What would you do differently and why?

References

Farquhar P. H. and V. Rao (1976), 'A balance model for evaluating subsets of multi attributed items', *Management Science*, Vol. 22, No. 5, pp. 528–39.

Kapferer, J.-N. (2004), *The New Strategic Brand Management*, London: Kogan Page.

Keller, K. L. (2003), *Strategic Brand Management: Building, Measuring, and Managing Brand Equity*, 2nd edn, Upper Saddle River, NJ: Prentice Hall.

Keller, K. L. and Aaker D. A. (1992), 'The effects of sequential introduction of brand extensions', *Journal of Marketing Research*, Vol. 29, No. 1, pp. 35–50.

Leuthesser, L. (ed.) (1988), *Defining, Measuring and Managing Brand Equity: A Conference Summary*, Cambridge, MA: Marketing Science Institute.

Light, L. and Morgan, R. (1994), *The Four Wave: Brand Loyalty Marketing*, New York: Coalition for Brand Equity, 11.

Pickton, D. and Broderick, A. (2005), *Integrated Marketing Communications*, Harlow: Pearson Education.

Pitta, D. A. and Katsanis, L. P. (1995), 'Understanding brand equity for successful brand extension', *Journal of Consumer Marketing*, Vol. 12, No. 4, pp. 51–64.

Rao, V. R., Mahajan, V. and Varaiya, N.P. (1991), 'A balance model for evaluating firms for acquisition', *Management Science*, Vol. 37, No. 3, pp. 331–49.

Simon, C. J. and Sullivan, M. J. (1993), 'The measurement and determinants of brand equity: a financial approach', *Marketing Science*, Vol. 12, No. 1, pp. 28–52.

Srivastava, R. K. and Shocker, A. D. (1991), 'Brand equity: a perspective on its meaning and measurement'. Cambridge, Mass: Marketing Science Institute, working paper #91–124.

Further reading and online sites

Anderson, P. L. (2005), 'New developments in business valuation', in *Developments in Litigation Economics*, eds P. A. Gaughan and R. J. Thornton, Burlington: Elsevier, 2005.

Anonymous (2004), 'Valuation methodologies don't always translate well for corporate branding', *Marketing News*.

Arnold, D. (1992), *The Handbook of Brand Management*, London: Century Business.

Bahadir, S., Cem, B., Sundar G. and Srivastava, R. K. (2008), 'Financial value of brands in mergers and acquisitions: is value in the eye of the beholder?', *Journal of Marketing*, Vol. 72, No. 6 (November).

Barwise, P. (1993), 'Brand equity: Snark or Boojum?', *International Journal of Marketing Research*, Vol. 10 (March), pp. 93–104.

Costa, R. and Evangelista, S. (2008), 'An AHP approach to assess brand intangible assets', *Measuring Business Excellence*, Vol. 12, No. 2.

Eagle, L., Kitchen, P. J., Rose, L. and Moyle, B. (2003), 'Brand equity and brand vulnerability: the impact of gray marketing/parallel importing on brand equity and values', *European Journal of Marketing*, Vol. 37, No. 10.

Farquhar, P. H. and Ijiri, Y. (1993), 'A dialogue on momentum accounting for brand management', *International Journal of Research in Marketing*, Vol. 10, pp. 77–92.

Farquhar P. H. and Rao, V. (1976), 'A balance model for evaluating subsets of multi attributed items', *Management Science*, Vol. 22, No. 5, pp. 528–39.

Fischer, M. (2007), 'Valuing brand assets: a cost-effective and easy-to-implement measurement approach', Marketing Science Institute, working paper [07–107].

Hall, E. (1993), 'The rise and rise of name dropping', *Marketing Week*, January, 22.

Ijiri, Y. (1988), 'Momentum accounting and managerial goals on impulses', *Management Science*, Vol. 34, No. 2, pp. 160–66.

Keller, K. (1993), 'Conceptualizing, measuring, and managing customer-based brand equity', *Journal of Marketing*, January, Vol. 57, pp. 1–22.

Kim, H. B., Kim, W. G. and An, J. A. (2003), 'The effect of consumer-based brand equity on firms' financial performance', *Journal of Consumer Marketing*, Vol. 20, No. 4.

Pappu, R., Quester, P. G. and Cooksey, R. W. (2005), 'Consumer-based brand equity: improving the measurement – empirical evidence', *Journal of Product & Brand Management*, Vol. 14, No. 3.

Perrier, R. (ed.) (1997), *Brand Valuation*, 3rd edn, London: Premier Books.

Punj, G. N. and Hillyer, C. L. (2008), 'A cognitive model of customer-based brand equity for frequently purchased products: conceptual framework and empirical results', *Journal of Consumer Psychology*, Vol. 14, No. 1–2, pp. 124–31.

Reilly, R. F. and Schweihs, R. P. (1999), *Valuing Intangible Assets*, New York: McGraw-Hill.

Roslender, R. and Hart, S. J. (2006), 'Inter-functional cooperation in progressing accounting for brands: the case for brand management accounting', *Journal of Accounting & Organizational Change*, Vol. 2, No. 3.

Salinas, G. (2009), *The International Brand Valuation Manual – A Complete Overview and Analysis of Brand Valuation Techniques and Methodologies and their Applications*, Wiley-VCH, April.

Schultz, D. E. (2005), 'Measuring unmeasurables', *Marketing Matters*, May/June.

Seetharaman, A., Zainal, A. B. M. N. and Gunalan, S. (2001), 'A conceptual study on brand valuation', *Journal of Product & Brand Management*, Vol. 10, No. 4, pp. 243–56.

Weston A., Suchy, D. P. and Ahya, C. (2006), 'Fundamentals of intellectual property valuation: a primer for identifying and determining value', *American Bar Association Section of Intellectual Property Law*, published by American Bar Association, ISBN 1590314301, 9781590314302.

Wood, L. (2000), 'Brands and brand equity: definition and management', *Management Decision*, Vol. 38, No. 9, pp. 662–69.

Wyner, G. A. (2001), 'The trouble with brand equity valuation', *Marketing Research*, Vol. 13, No. 4 (Winter).

Brand Building and Business Building

Chapter overview

This chapter examines the relationship between building a brand and building a business. It argues that, although one comes before the other, the backbone of a successful brand is a successful business. However, a successful business cannot be sustained long term without a successful brand. In this chapter the factors for building a successful business are examined. Business management models are described and discussed in relation to brand building. The main thrust of the chapter is therefore that successful brand building is based on good business models, sound strategy and decision-making by senior managers, as well as innovations and providing more valued added for customers. In Part 1 of this book, Chapter 2 studied brand equity and brand valuation. This chapter has a direct link with Chapter 4, whose focus will be on the alignment between business management philosophy and strategy, and branding philosophy and strategy, which are part of the corporate-based view of branding.

After completing this chapter, you should be able to

- ❖ Examine the business environments of brands

- ❖ Examine the different business management models such as the classic business model, the business revenue model and the modern business model

- ❖ Discuss the components of successful business building

- ❖ Discuss the strategic implications of business building in brand building

- ❖ Apply the management models of business building to brand building

- ❖ Identify the critical components of successful brand building

Introduction

If you ask any businessman whether a company has a successful brand without a successful business, his answer would be no. It is patently obvious that you cannot have a brand leader on the back of a bad business. The brand is meant to bring you good business, and the better the brand, the more profitable and healthy the company's balance sheet is going to be. As at the beginning and throughout the book, we learn that brands ultimately bring the buyer to the seller by differentiating his products from that of competitors and help to retain the former and sustain the business. The next question is: can we build a successful business without a brand? The answer is again no. Although some companies have done well without a brand they have come to realize or are about to realize that they now need a brand or they are going to need one. It depends on a company's objectives how it wants to grow and how success is determined. For many companies faced with today's intense competition and globalization, the brand is the only thing that will keep their businesses functioning in the long term and give them a competitive advantage. As Chapter 4 will show, branding is important to all kinds of companies. Many of the big brands are now to be found in the water, gas and electricity companies, public services and transport, e.g. Yorkshire Water and Powergen, as well as small traders and contractors. However, strong brands take a long time to build and there are basic rules to be observed: a brand starts with a quality product or a USP, then advertising and promotions resources are required to build it. Not all companies will have the resources for this. Although branding is important to businesses, not all of them will have the resources to develop a brand and sustain it. Some principles of business management can also be applied to brand building, because there are similarities in terms of the business environments that a company director and a brand manager face, such as customers, employees, partners (e.g. in the context of strategic brand alliance), stakeholders, economics, technology and social environments. As a result, both company directors and brand managers have at least three common vocabularies: manage, adapt (to change) and look out for opportunities. This chapter will deal with business management models and how these can be applied to brand building. In other words, it will look at the strategic orientation of brand building deriving from business management principles.

The basics of brand building

What are the requirements for building a brand?

- Financial resources.
- Personnel resources.
- A clear differentiation or a USP.
- Quality and an innovative product.
- Advertising and promotions resources.

As stated, not all companies will have these kinds of resources and therefore not all companies will be able to develop, build and sustain a brand. Examples are small companies, small traders, contractors and those that operate in the non-profit sector.

Doyle (1990) has suggested that there are four levers for developing successful brands: quality, service, innovation and differentiation. Furthermore, he maintained that quality and service as opposed to advertising was the way to create successful brands (see Chapter 5).

There are eight factors that make it difficult to build brands:

1 Pressure to compete on price.

2 Proliferation of competitors.

3 Fragmenting markets and media.

4 Complex branding strategies and brand relationships.

5 The temptation to change identity/executions.

6 Organizational bias against innovation.

7 Pressure to invest elsewhere.

8 Pressure for short-term results.

Furthermore, as competition becomes more intense, companies face challenges to adjust their brands to match the changed expectations of their customers. Brand positioning can help in building the companies' brand superiority in the minds of their customers (see Chapter 5).

The classic business model

A business model converts innovation to economic value for the business. The business model spells out how a company makes money, by specifying where it is positioned in the value chain. It draws on a multitude of business subjects including entrepreneurship, strategy, economics, finance, operations and marketing. Based on the 'value-added' model of Michael Porter (1980), a business model describes how a business positions itself within the value chain of its industry and how it intends to sustain itself – that is, to generate revenue. This idea also forces management to look at its operations from the customer's point of view.

The components of a business model

Osterwalder's (2004) conceptualization describes a business model as consisting of nine related business model building blocks (see Figure 3.1).

Other authors, such as Marc Fetscherin and Gerhard Knolmayer (2004), suggest that a business model is made up of five components: the product, the consumer, the revenue, the price and the delivery. In between these two models, a business model can also be considered in terms of the following six components (Chesbrough and Rosenbloom, 2002):

1 *Value Proposition* is a description of the customer need, and the solution that addresses the need that customers have.

2 *Market Segment* is the group to target. Different market segments have different needs.

3 *Value Chain Structure* The firm is seen as a chain of value-creating activities. The firm's position and activities in the value chain and how the firm will capture part of the value that it creates in the chain is important.

4 *Revenue Generation and Margins* are concerned with how revenue is generated (sales, leasing, subscription, support, etc.), the cost structure and target profit margins.

5 *Position in the Value Network* relates to the identification of competitors and complementary organizations, and any network effects that can be utilized to deliver more value to the customer.

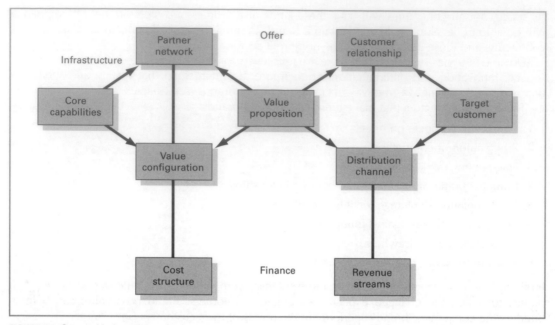

FIGURE 3.1 Osterwalder's model

6 *Competitive Strategy* describes how the company attempts to develop a sustainable competitive advantage and to use it to improve its competitive position in the market.

The business model vs the revenue model

While the term 'business model' describes the method of doing business, such as positioning the company in the value chain, customer selection, products and pricing, a revenue model lays out the process by which a company actually makes money, by specifying how it is going to charge for the services provided.

Revenue is a US business term for the amount of money that a company receives from its activities in a given period, mostly from sales of products and/or services to customers. It is not to be confused with the terms 'profit' or 'net income' which generally mean total revenue less total expenses in a given period. In Europe (including the UK) the term is 'turnover'.

Revenue is basically 'price × quantity' (the price for one, times the number, or the price per kg times the mass in kg, etc.), accumulated over all goods; if the price per unit varies with the quantity, then for each price per unit this calculation is carried out, and the results are obtained. Net revenue (revenue − returns) is used when sales returns are a factor in the business.

Revenue, like all income statement accounts, can only be presented in terms of a period – for example, the revenues a company earned between 1 January 2005 and 31 December 2005. Alternatively, one could express it in terms of the following examples: 2005 revenue, Q1 (1st quarter) revenue, or March revenue. This time span is in contrast to a balance sheet account, which would be given as of the date of the statement. To simply say that a company earned revenue of $5 million without giving a period is meaningless (although stating that a company has $5 million cash certainly has meaning). Internally, companies break revenue down by operating segment, geographic region and product line.

Revenue is a crucial part of any financial analysis. A company's performance is measured to the extent to which its asset inflows (revenues) compare with its asset outflows (expenses). Net income is the result of this equation, but revenue typically enjoys equal attention during a standard earnings call. If a company displays solid 'top-line growth', analysts could view the period's performance as positive even if earnings growth or 'bottom-line growth' is stagnant. Conversely, high income growth would be compromised if a company failed to produce significant revenue growth. Consistent revenue growth, as well as income growth, is considered essential for a company's publicly traded stock to be attractive to investors.

Revenue is used as an indication of quality of earnings. There are several financial ratios attached to it, the most important being price/sales, gross margin, and net income/sales (profit margin). Companies also use revenue to determine bad debt expense using the income statement method. Price/sales are sometimes used as a substitute for a price to earnings ratio when earnings are negative and the P/E is meaningless. Though a company may have negative earnings, it almost always has positive revenue. Gross margin is a calculation of revenue less cost of goods sold, and is used to determine how well sales cover direct variable costs relating to the production of goods. Net income/sales, or profit margin, is calculated by investors to determine how efficiently a company turns revenues into profits.

Business models that are optimized to reduce the upfront investment, that accelerate the revenue/receivables cash inflow, that obtain cogent and reliable customer feedback often and earlier, and that take other measures to reduce the investment risk all have a higher probability of business success.

Modern business models

The old business models no longer work. The reason is the new business environment in which companies operate (see Chapter 10), which is characterized by speed and complexity. In the mid-1990s a variety of aggressive strategies were developed and were rated according to their marketing assertiveness, risk propensity, financial leverage, product innovation, speed of decision-making, and other measures of business aggressiveness. Some business planners have also started to use a complexity theory approach to strategy (Axelrod, 1999; Holland, 1995; Kelly and Allison, 1999). Complexity can be thought of as chaos with a dash of order. Chaos theory deals with turbulent systems that rapidly become disordered.

Today's market leaders will have the following three features in their business strategy: visionary growth strategies, winning organization and people, and relentless innovation. While companies are still greatly concerned with cost structure, maximizing operational effectiveness and business process re-engineering, they have shifted their focus to issues such as how to build capabilities for faster growth, how to attract and retain the best people, how to develop leaders at all levels in the company, how to manage knowledge effectively, how to become a true learning organization, and how to be more effective global corporations. The new business model must, therefore, have a much sharper focus on the basics of what ultimately creates value, such as people, knowledge and coherence. It should foster the creation of value and ensure that each piece of the business contributes to system-wide value. It should also go beyond the workplace and the interface between government and business, and look into building a favourable social climate within and around the company, as well as providing customers with more value-added (MVA), which goes beyond simplifying customers' interactions with the company to delivering solutions to customers' problems. The principle of MVA is similar to a ladder with the company's product at the bottom and the solution to the company's customers' problems at the top. The more help companies provide their customers to fill that gap, the more value they add to them, which differentiates them from their competitors, who may still be scrambling around at the bottom of the ladder.

Another type of business model is the strategic response model. The competitive importance of a strategic response model lies in a firm's ability to respond to market changes faster than competitors in correcting product mistakes, refining product successes and emulating competitors' product successes. A strategic response model of a company is a useful perspective to use in viewing the totality of a single-business firm (or a new division of a firm) when market strategy is to be temporarily the dominant strategic policy.

In the late 1980s the impact of information technology in competing in markets through new products emphasized the importance of the 'response time' capabilities in companies to aggressively create market share, e.g. Toyota. Time was thus used strategically as a sustainable competitive advantage, and companies that adopted such strategies were called 'fast cycle companies'. Speeding up the response time of companies to meet changes in customer needs and the economic environment required more than simply working faster. It required working differently and thinking about why it takes time to respond, whether responses are correct, and how to respond more quickly and correctly. The sustainable competitive advantage gained from attention to time was through satisfying customers better and faster. Fast-cycle companies develop new products sooner than competitors, process customer orders into deliveries more quickly, are more sensitive to customer needs, and make decisions on how to add value in their products/services to the customer faster than competitors (Betz, 2002).

A strategic innovation model provides a perspective for optimizing both short-term resources and long-term sales by rationalizing the use of profits and capital to implement innovation. Innovation may be in physical as well as in information technologies. The following model adopted from Jennings and Haughton, reflects to some extent, the fast cycle company model above.

Moving with speed: the four components concept

1 *Thinking fast:* anticipating the future, spotting trends before others, challenging assumptions, and creating an environment that encourages people to come up with the best ideas.
2 *Making quick decisions:* being flexible, having no bureaucratic structures, shuffling portfolios, reassessing everything, and matching the decision to the consequence.
3 *Get the product to the market fast:* getting the product to the market faster through removing in-built speed-breakers, abandoning traditional visions and missions, getting vendors and suppliers operating on your timetable, and building virtuous circles of speed.
4 *Sustaining speed:* maintaining velocity through working on your business, persisting with growth, being ruthless with resources, building a scoreboard that measures activity, staying financially flexible, proving the maths, institutionalizing innovation, and staying close to the customer.

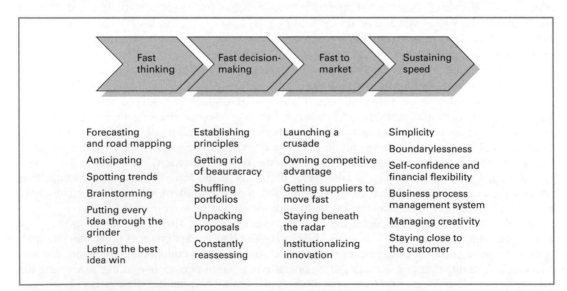

FIGURE 3.2 Fast thinking – sustaining speed

Applying business management models to building brands

Business models can be applied to brand-building situations, because a business environment is similar to the environment in which a brand manager operates. That is to say, the basic principles or rules underpinning business models can be used in brand-building situations. These include value proposition, market segment, position in the value network and competitive strategy (cf. the six components of the business model, mentioned above). With regard to value proposition, a brand must provide customers with solutions that customers will value. With market segmenting, a brand must meet different market needs and position itself in the value network to deliver more benefits or values to the customer. Finally, competitive strategy can be seen from a long-term perspective which is reflected in companies working to have a sustainable brand in order to improve the competitive position of the brand in a given market.

Modern business models emphasize three elements: visionary growth strategies, human resource and innovation. In a brand-building context, the firm's employees are one of the focal points (cf. internal branding and strategic brand management in Chapter 4). The whole company contributes to the building of the corporate or the brand. With regard to innovation, see the section on 'Innovation and branding' below.

As mentioned above, the new business model has a much stronger focus on the basics of what ultimately creates value: people, knowledge and coherence. Knowledge can be seen in the context of obtaining or acquiring market information and managing market intelligence, which includes collecting and interpreting data to give the company a better picture of the market. Coherence refers to a coherent company structure, which underlines successful brand management (see Chapter 4). In the past businesses had a functional or departmental structure. Nowadays the emphasis is more on a cross-functional teams structure. Brand managers are seen to be working more with other departments such as production, accounting/finance, etc. to ensure consistent brand delivery (see Chapter 9) to the customer, and possibly also having a seat on the board in the future (see Chapter 4). This is supported by the concept of 'total branding'. Successful brand management may also be guided by the principles of business success, which require it to be proactive, leading, innovative and venturing. These qualities are exhibited in a number of leading brands in many markets.

Brand building is based on sound business strategy and decision-making

Brand building is based on sound business strategy and decision-making by senior management. First, one cannot create or build a brand without first building a business. Many companies attempt to build a brand by throwing money into multi-million-dollar, mass advertising, brand-image campaigns. These companies fail to realize that the business is their brand (see the Starbucks story in the Branding Brief 3.1 below). Second, brand building is about business building through the generation of higher revenues and profits, which in turn will lead to greater shareholder value and a stronger brand. In order to generate higher revenues and profits, companies must go back to the business models and improve the functionality of a product, the quality of services offered, or enhance the customer's experience among others, to build a strong customer base. Marketing principles, which state that the purpose of a business is to satisfy customers' needs/desires, must also precede brand building.

Brands are built on the basis of a clear business strategy and of rigorous implementation of the 5Ps – product, price, place, promotion (or communication) and people. For example, Coke's success is based on three factors: *product availability* – Coke can be found everywhere in the world; *pricing accessibility* – Coke in India and China for instance, are sold for the same price as tea; and *product attractiveness*, which is a communication issue (Kapferer, 2004). On the other hand, Starbucks' success relies on sourcing, high product quality (using the highest-quality coffee beans), and creating a need for a new product (in this case new taste and flavour) and a comfortable environment for the customer.

Breaking the rules and acting fast

The four components of the 'fast' company model (see above) also correspond to how a brand leader usually develops. The brand leader usually starts with an innovation that succeeds or a product that captures a new trend or lifestyle. It then attempts to get to the market first, by removing in-built speed-breakers and getting vendors and suppliers operating on the company's side. To maintain momentum it then institutionalizes innovation and stays close to the customer, creating a gap between itself and incoming competition, then quickly reaches critical size in the market.

More value-added (MVA)

In branding terms, value added means that a company must provide more than customers' expectations. This can mean providing more value in either the concrete or the abstract value of the brand. A brand that is innovative, that excites and reflects a new lifestyle, will give more value to customers than a brand whose attraction is based on price only. Packaging and price can be both concrete and abstract values of the brand, because they may reflect a lifestyle also. For example, Starbucks reflects a lifestyle, while iPod is innovative and trendy for young people.

Innovation and branding

Innovation today is 'much more than new products'. Innovation means also 'reinventing business processes and building entirely new markets that meet untapped customer needs'. The ubiquity of the Internet and the globalization of business encourages the generation of new ideas. Innovation is then 'selecting and executing the right ideas and bringing them to market in record time' (*BusinessWeek*). An example of a highly innovative company in the consumer market is Apple. According to the *BW*/BCG 2007 survey, top managers believe Apple is the most innovative company in the world (see Table 3.1). Apple is one of the Top 20 innovators of the Innovation Index. It has a glorious history of innovation, beginning with the first Apple computer in 1976, followed by Graphical User Interface (GUI) along with the popular Macintosh introduced in 1984; the reliable PowerBook introduced in 1991; the PDA named Newton that created a new industry of handhelds in 1993; the new millennium revolution beginning with the iMac in 1998; the new iBook hot on the heels of the iMac in 1999; the iPod that put the oomph into MP3 players and essentially changed music as we know it in 2001; iTunes software and Music Store service that changed the music industry business model and made it easy for fans to listen to and buy music piecemeal in 2003; the iPod mini; iPod (U2 Special Edition); iPod Photo in 2004; iPod Shuffle; iPod Nano; iPod with Video and Mac Mini in 2005; the new iMac with Intel core Duo processors; and the new MacBook with Intel processors in 2006.

The iPod is Apple's best innovation, however, and some people believe it drives Apple to becoming the number one innovative company.

Introduced in 2001, the iPod has an outstanding design, easy-to-use interface, superb performance, and offers an experience like no other. Apple assumed the world's number one innovative company position and held it again in 2006 in large part due to the exponential growth of the iPod, aptly called the 'iPod phenomenon'. iPod has become associated with personal status and is a symbol that speaks of cool, hip, polished and different. What began as a new product quickly became a revolution. iPod is by far the best commercial innovation the world has seen in the past few years. Apple one-upped the iPod design innovation by creating new innovations in its business model with the launch of the iTunes online service enabled by strategic partnerships with the music, TV and movie industry (Source: creativityandinnovation.blogspot.com, 2006).

There are a number of factors that make iPod so successful: simple and elegant design that makes it extremely easy to use, with exceptional sound, video and imagery, providing an amazing

EXHIBIT 3.1 The iPod is Apple's best innovation

experience. The flexibility provided by the iTunes software and service allows us to download any music and video with the click of a button from any computer or the Internet to our iPod. The available accessories from wireless headsets, to remote controls, beautiful skins, acoustic speakers and connectors mean iPod music and videos can be taken anywhere at home, in the car, in the office, on the plane and even in the shower.

The main reasons for Apple's success lies in the fact that the company uses design thinking to create products/services that meet the hitherto unmet needs of consumers. Add to this its ability to create desire for products no one ever knew they wanted; to target, create, saturate and dominate a market sector; to stay ahead of the curve all the time; its willingness to be different (e.g. iPod, iTunes, iPhone, Macintosh, OSX), always developing new products for new markets that may be copied by Microsoft and others. Apple has great ideas and a history of developing hit, consumer-friendly products, or introducing meaningful and useful innovations for the mass market. It has maintained leadership in new product development from the first personal computer (Lisa – before the Mac) to iPods, and now mobile phones (*BusinessWeek*, May 2007).

BusinessWeek/Boston Consulting Group (BCG) recently announced the world's Top 50 innovative companies for 2008; 17 of the Top 20 innovators of the Innovation Index are included in the Top 50 innovative companies of the world by *BusinessWeek*/BCG. This is a testament to the Innovation Index methodology and process.

Understanding the values of the target market

Not all clients are alike. Different brands can coexist in the same sector because they address the value of different target markets. This is also why companies build brand portfolios to reflect the different segments of the market. Within the portfolio each brand may also be competing with itself (see Chapter 9).

Rank	Company	HQ Country	HQ Continent	Revenue Growth 2004–07 (in %)	Margin Growth 2004–07 (in %)	Stock Returns 2004–07 (in %)	Most Known for its Innovative … (% who think so)
1	APPLE	US	North America	47	69	83	Products (52%)
2	GOOGLE	US	North America	73	5	53	Customer Experience (26%)
3	TOYOTA MOTOR	Japan	Asia	12	1	15	Processes (36%)
4	GENERAL ELECTRIC	US	North America	9	1	3	Processes (43%)
5	MICROSOFT	US	North America	16	8	12	Products (26%)
6	TATA GROUP	India	Asia	Private	Private	Private	Products (58%)
7	NINTENDO	Japan	Asia	37	4	77	Products (63%)
8	PROCTER & GAMBLE	US	North America	16	4	12	Processes (30%)
9	SONY	Japan	Asia	8	13	17	Products (56%)
10	NOKIA	Finland	Europe	20	2	35	Products (36%)
11	AMAZON.COM	US	North America	29	-11	28	Customer Experience (33%)
12	IBM	US	North America	1	11	4	Processes (31%)
13	RESEARCH IN MOTION	Canada	North America	56	-1	51	Products (37%)
14	BMW	Germany	Europe	6	-5	11	Customer Experience (40%)
15	HEWLETT-PACKARD	US	North America	10	17	35	Processes, Business Models, and Customer Experience (27% each)
16	HONDA MOTOR	Japan	Asia	12	6	14	Products (40%)
17	WALT DISNEY	US	North America	6	14	7	Customer Experience (63%)
18	GENERAL MOTORS	US	North America	-2	NA	-11	Products (55%)
19	RELIANCE INDUSTRIES	India	Asia	31	-7	94	Business Models (31%)
20	BOEING	US	North America	9	32	21	Products (63%)
21	GOLDMAN SACHS GROUP	US	North America	30	6	28	Processes and Business Models (33% each)
22	3M	US	North America	7	5	3	Products (45%)
23	WAL-MART STORES	US	North America	10	-2	-2	Processes (48%)
24	TARGET	US	North America	11	3	0	Customer Experience (67%)
25	FACEBOOK	US	North America	Private	Private	Private	Customer Experience (51%)
26	SAMSUNG ELECTRONICS	South Korea	Asia	2	-14	8	Products (42%)
27	AT&T	US	North America	43	6	23	Customer Experience (33%)
28	VIRGIN GROUP	Britain	Europe	Private	Private	Private	Customer Experience (47%)
29	AUDI	Germany	Europe	11	11	41	Products (50%)

30	MCDONALD'S	US	North America	7	-7	25	Customer Experience (42%)
31	DAIMLER	Germany	Europe	-11	37	28	Products (35%)
32	STARBUCKS	US	North America	23	-2	-13	Customer Experience (60%)
33	EBAY	US	North America	33	-37	-17	Business Models (28%)
34	VERIZON COMMUNICATIONS	US	North America	12	0	9	Services (41%)
35	CISCO SYSTEMS	US	North America	20	-5	12	Products (35%)
36	ING GROEP	Netherlands	Europe	7	4	11	Services (41%)
37	SINGAPORE AIRLINES	Singapore	Asia	9	5	20	Customer Experience (55%)
38	SIEMENS	Germany	Europe	1	21	22	Products (41%)
39	COSTCO WHOLESALE	US	North America	11	-5	14	Customer Experience (46%)
40	HSBC	Britain	Europe	12	-1	4	Services (39%)
41	BANK OF AMERICA	US	North America	12	0	0	Customer Experience and Services (23% each)
42	EXXON MOBIL	US	North America	11	7	25	Processes (50%)
43	NEWS CORP.	US	North America	4	4	4	Business Models (47%)
44	BP	Britain	Europe	14	-5	11	Processes (42%)
45	NIKE	US	North America	8	-1	14	Customer Experience (43%)
46	DELL	US	North America	7	-12	-17	Business Models (37%)
47	VODAFONE GROUP	Britain	Europe	7	-21	15	Business Models (33%)
48	INTEL	US	North America	4	-10	6	Products (53%)
49	SOUTHWEST AIRLINES	US	North America	15	9	-9	Customer Experience (50%)
50	AMERICAN EXPRESS	US	North America	3	1	3	Customer Experience (35%)

TABLE 3.1 The top 50 innovative companies in the world; Apple is number one for the fourth year in a row

Branding Brief 3.1: Building the business creates the brand

Source: Extract taken from Moore, J., 'Tribal Knowledge: Business Wisdom Brewed from the Grounds of Starbucks Corporate Culture' (September 2006), pp. 3, 4 & 6 (http://tinyurl.com/BuildingTheBusiness).

Starbucks never sought to create a brand. The company was too busy being a business to try to be a brand.   Starbucks was too busy building a viable and profitable business to think about something as seemingly trivial as branding. Starbucks was too busy sourcing and roasting the highest-quality coffee beans to think about branding. Starbucks was too busy educating customers on how and why they should appreciate a stronger, bolder cup, a more flavourful cup of coffee to think about branding. Starbucks was too busy creating a comforting and welcoming place for people to relax to think about branding.

Because Starbucks was busy working on and working in the business, they built a business of which the by-product was the creation of a strong brand.

Starbucks teaches us that rarely, if ever, can you sprinkle magical branding dust to create an endearing and enduring brand.

But that doesn't stop companies from trying. Instead of spending money to improve the functionality of a product, the quality of services offered, or enhancing the customer's experience, many companies will attempt to build a brand by throwing money into multi-million dollar, mass advertising, brand image campaigns.

These companies fail to realize that your business is your brand.

Starbucks Tribal Knowledge tells us you cannot create a brand before you create a business. Your business creates your brand. Your brand should never create your business.

Branding Brief 3.2: How to build a successful brand

Source: BBC News 24

Building up a successful, well-known brand name can seem an impossible dream for a small business

Such ubiquitous branding appears the sole preserve of the giant multinationals with their multi-million-pound advertising budgets.

Yet as marketing expert Simon Edwards explains, creating an enduring brand isn't just about money.

Instead, at the core of any successful brand has to be a quality product, and that is within reach of any small firm.

Question

Ana Stamenkovic, England

'I am interested to know if you feel it is really viable for small businesses to build brand names that are recognized by the consumer, without having access to huge marketing budgets?

'For example in industries such as the jewellery industry where it is dominated by small designers and family companies, aren't we in danger of reaching a saturation of brands, and furthermore can a small enterprise really carry the cost of brand building?'

Answer

Simon Edwards, marketing director at Cobra Beer

'Here's the bad news. Most markets have been saturated for a very long time and everyday, even more companies try to break into these markets.

'The principles of branding have been put together to try to help establish a company in a crowded market and to help it compete and grow.

'But you don't need huge marketing budgets to start building an enduring brand. In fact you don't need any marketing budget at all.

'Building an enduring brand starts long before you spend money on advertising and promotion – it starts with your product and or service – what can you offer customers that your competitors can't? What can you do operationally that will make your customers want to work with you?

'Examine every point at which your company operates and try to find ways of doing it better. Look at all the competing products and make sure yours is outstanding. It is this collective aspect of your company that will establish its identity.

'Giving your company a name is not branding. Giving your customers a reason to want to remember your name is.'

Branding Brief 3.3: Brand building – first step to reinventing marketing

Source: ANA Marketing Musings, 7 February 2006

While brand building has long been the mantra of marketers, the fundamental meaning of this term has radically changed. No longer are soft measures like 'brand awareness', 'brand preference' and 'intention to buy' acceptable. Brand building from the CEO's perspective is about business building – generating higher revenues and profits, which in turn will lead to greater shareholder value.

To achieve these lofty goals, brands not only need to be built, they must also be continuously reinvented to remain relevant to ever-changing consumer needs and desires.

Brand reinvention begins with innovation. Innovation that continuously refreshes the brand in ways that speak to consumers one-to-one and build long-term appeal and trust.

The iPod is an amazing example of innovation. It has totally reinvented the way music is acquired, played and enjoyed. In fact, industry analysts are now talking about the 'halo' effect of the iPod. They're predicting that continued sales of iPods to Windows PC owners will eventually translate into increased Mac sales. And they're beginning to see a steady stream of first-time Mac buyers at the Apple retail stores. That's the power of innovation to build brands and business!

Of course, innovation not only drives new brand introductions – it also drives the reinvention of existing brands. Here's a fabulous example:

Motorola has engineered a remarkable business turnaround by reinventing its brand and approach to marketing. In the early 1990s, Motorola owned 46 per cent of the mobile handset market. But that leadership dramatically eroded against strong competitors like Nokia. By 2001, the company's share had plummeted to just 14.5 per cent.

New CEO Ed Zander and CMO Geoffrey Frost – who sadly died last year – led a remarkable reinvention of the Motorola brand – driven by off-the-chart innovation.

Positioning Motorola as 'wickedly cool and compelling', they made a highly focused, strategic investment in a new kind of marketing. Among their steps was to permeate the micro-culture of trend-setting Hollywood. They established a Motorola office in Tinseltown and courted the 'alpha techno-geeks' who love to have the latest, greatest gadgets.

Motorola products subsequently began appearing in films and TV shows – not as the result of paid product placement, but because the brand had penetrated the living, breathing celebrity community. Of course, marketing fabulously innovative products – like the amazing RAZR – was the foundation of the strategy. And the buzz built fast.

Now you might think that this kind of innovation only applies to consumer products. Not true – just ask the marketers at General Electric.

Although GE markets consumer products like light bulbs and home appliances, the lion's share of its revenues come from business products and services like jet engines, plastics, power generation and medical equipment. For decades, the company's brand identify was tied to its 'We bring good things to life' tagline – a remarkably durable slogan for a difficult-to-describe conglomerate.

But CEO, Jeffrey Immelt, and chief marketing officer, Beth Comstock, recognized that the GE brand needed reinvention for the future. At General Electric, marketers and marketing were charged with a most unusual and dynamic objective – to change the direction of the company. Mr Immelt wanted marketing and business strategies interwoven to optimize synergy and productivity. And they did just that with the spectacularly successful platform of 'Imagination at Work'.

More than just a tagline, Imagination at Work is a promise to the marketplace and an internal cultural commitment to drive organic growth through innovation. In typical GE style, the company supported its new theme with rigorous training programmes and a new enterprise-wide process that challenged managers to develop five new ideas, each with the potential to grow revenue by $50–100 million.

Today, some 80 growth projects are now 'in plan' and being funded. These efforts encompass technology innovation, product commercialization, growth expansion and value creation. It's not easy for a mega-company to grow year-over-year. But GE is consistently doing just that. Its 2004 revenues rose nearly 14 per cent over 2003 – that's over $18 billion of growth in one year! Brand reinvention driven by continuous innovation is surely a key reason why!

Conclusion

The strategic orientation of brand building deriving from business management principles has been examined in this chapter. Several business management models have been described and applied in the context of brand building. This is the author's attempt to link strategic brand management to organizational management theory, and is also a new approach to treating brand management which has rarely been looked at in the branding literature.

In this chapter I argue, first, that some principles of business management can be applied to brand-building situations, because a company director and a brand manager face similar business issues such as customers, employees, partners (e.g. in the context of strategic brand alliance), stakeholders, economic, technology and social environments. Second, brands are built on their business models and therefore customers and environmental influences are unique to each brand. So, we need to look at the business model of that brand.

A business model describes how a business positions itself within the value chain of its industry and how it intends to maintain that position so as to generate revenue. Brand building is based on a similar principle: the brand needs to position itself in the value chain of its industry or product market or product category, so as to sustain itself in generating revenue in the long term. The six components of the business model are: value proposition, market segment, value chain structure, revenue generation and margins, position in the value network and competitive strategy. With regard to value proposition, a brand must provide customers with solutions that they will value. With reference to market segment, a brand must meet different market needs. Position in the value network to deliver more benefits or values to the customer, while competitive strategy can be seen from a long-term perspective. This is reflected in companies working to create a sustainable brand in order to improve the competitive position of the brand in a given market.

The modern business model emphasizes three elements: visionary growth strategies, human resource and innovation. In the brand-building context, a firm's employees are one of the focal points of brand building (see Chapter 4, which deals with internal branding and strategic brand management). That is, the whole company contributes to the building of the corporate brand. Successful brand management may also be guided by the other principles of business success, when the requirement is to be proactive, leading, innovative and adventurous. These qualities are exhibited in a number of leading brands in any market.

It also has a much stronger focus on people, knowledge and coherence. It fosters the creation of value, and ensures that each piece of the business contributes to system-wide value. Knowledge can be seen in the context of obtaining or acquiring market information and managing market intelligence, which includes collecting and interpreting data to give the company a better picture of the market. Coherence refers to a coherent company structure, which underlines successful brand management (see Chapter 4). In the past businesses had a functional or departmental structure. Nowadays the emphasis is more on cross-functional team structure. Brand managers are seen to be working more with other departments, such as production, accounting/finance, etc. to ensure consistent brand delivery (see Chapter 9) to the customer and possibly to those with a seat on the board as well (see Chapter 4). This is supported by the concept of 'total branding'.

It also goes beyond the workplace and the interface between government and business, and looks to build a favourable social climate within and around the company. In order to succeed in today's market, brand building should create value not only for the customer but also for the company and its employees and the social community or society at large. This relates to the role of corporate social responsibility and the ethical orientation of brands (see Chapter 9).

Other business models, such as 'the fast company model', are similar to how a brand leader usually develops. The brand leader usually starts with an innovation that succeeds or a product that captures a new trend or lifestyle. It then attempts to get to the market first, by removing in-built speed-breakers and getting vendors and suppliers operating on the company's side. To maintain momentum the brand then institutionalizes innovation and stays close to the customer, creating a gap between itself and incoming competition, then reaches critical size rapidly in the market. The MVA (more value-added) concept in branding demands that a company must provide more than customers' expectations, and is similar to the new marketing principle of meeting, satisfying and delighting customers. That could mean either providing more value in terms of the concrete or abstract value of the brand, such as a brand that is innovative, that excites and reflects a new lifestyle, which will give more value to customers than a brand that is based on price alone.

🔑 Key terms

Classic business model: describes how a business positions itself within the value chain of its industry and how it intends to maintain itself to generate revenue. This model has six components: value proposition, market segment, value chain structure, revenue generation and margins, position in the value network, and competitive strategy.

Modern business model: based around growth strategies, competitive strategy, revenue model, value proposition, market segments and value chain structure. It focuses on the basics of what ultimately creates value – people, knowledge, and coherence. It fosters the creation of value and ensures that each piece of the business contributes to system-wide value. It also goes beyond the workplace and the interface between government and business, and looks into building a favourable social climate within and around the company.

MVA: is about giving customers much more than what they ask for by anticipating their needs, wants and desires. The focus of this concept is to provide customers with solutions to their problems before they even ask for them, or to give them what they want before they even know what they want. This will distinguish a company from its competitors. As they say: 'It's not the big that eat the small … it's the fast that eat the slow.'

Revenue: a US business term for the amount of money that a company receives from its activities in a given period, mostly from sales of products and/or services to customers. It is not to be confused with the terms 'profit' or 'net income' which generally mean total revenue less total expenses in a given period. In Europe (including the UK) the term is 'turnover'.

Revenue model: lays out the process by which a company actually makes money by specifying how it is going to charge for the services provided.

? Discussion questions

1 Do leading brands make the best products? Discuss.
2 Draw up a business model for a high-tech company of your choice. Explain the elements in that model.
3 Faced with a new competitive situation, which parts of the business model should companies modify?
4 In which sector(s) do you think brands are most important?
5 What are the functions of brands in the fmcg (fast moving consumer goods) sector?
6 Examine the business environment of a small firm and discuss how brands can develop in such an environment.
7 What are the main components for successful business building?
8 Discuss the strategic implications of business building in brand building.
9 Identify the factors of successful brand building.
10 Compare and contrast the classic business building model with the modern business building model, and discuss this in relation to brand building.

✎ Projects

1 Research the history of Jacob's Creek, the Australian wine brand. Find out what were the ingredients for success for this wine when it was launched in the UK mass market.
2 Discuss the business model of cola drinks and compare the different brands' strategies in this category.
3 Can you identify the differences in the brand-building model for luxury goods and non-luxury goods? Support your answer with examples.
4 Find out the cost of advertising and promotions, then work out which one would have a greater impact on profits for a small jeweller.
5 Find out whether advertising will help increase sales for commodities such as milk and fruit.

MINI CASE 3.1: A CASE STUDY IN BRAND BUILDING

Source: Elizabeth M. Lloyd (2005)

Cathay Pacific Airways partners with leading international brands, creating online campaigns that encourage users to interact with the ads

All marketers wishing to delve into international markets should learn from Cathay Pacific Airways' online brand-building techniques. The airline's approach towards reaching its audience by building online partnerships with leading brands such as Universal McCann, CNN, Yahoo! and ZUJI.com has made it one of the major online marketers in Hong Kong and across the Asia Pacific region.

It is no surprise why earlier this year Cathay Pacific was named Hong Kong's leading company by the *Asian Wall Street Journal* in its annual 'The *Asian Wall Street Journal* 200'. Additionally, just last week, Cathay Pacific received two awards in the Yahoo! Emotive Brand Awards for 2004–2005. The airline carried off the Top Emotive Brand award in the Airline category, and was one of seven companies named overall Top Emotive Brand winners. The Yahoo! Emotive Brand Awards polls the portal's Hong Kong users on brands that most appeal to them. Some 184 companies across 17 categories were nominated. More than 700 000 people voted online.

Cathay Pacific and Universal McCann Asia Pacific

In September 2004 Cathay Pacific along with its advertising agency of record, Universal McCann Asia Pacific, developed a comprehensive integrated media plan for a new branding campaign called 'People & Service'. The online component allowed Cathay Pacific to engage users in a way that is not possible for print, TV or radio. According to Catherine Ho, senior communications planner on the Cathay Pacific Central Team, Universal McCann Asia Pacific, 'The benefit of online for this campaign is that it allowed us to "dial up" audience interaction, which included a competition on the little things that Cathay Pacific has done for you in addition to running integrated branding communications online.'

It is evident that the campaign was successful due to its degree of interactivity. For the 'People & Service' campaign, rich media ads ran on all major Hong Kong portals, including atnext.com, orisun.com and msn.com.hk. According to Ho, there was a high degree of acceptance of the rich media creative:

- More than 99 per cent of viewers watched the ad without closing it.
- The ad was viewed completely by the audience (ad duration was about nine seconds).
- Viewers interacted with the ad and used one-third of the display time to play with it.
- Post-impression conversions proved 50 per cent more effective than the standard online ad.

Cathay Pacific and ZUJI.com

Earlier this year, Cathay Pacific partnered with ZUJI.com, Asia Pacific's most comprehensive online travel portal. This partnership allows Cathay Pacific's services to be marketed to ZUJI's online member base exceeding one million travellers, and to advertise in countries such as Singapore, Hong Kong, Taiwan, Korea and Australia, as well as other markets. Additionally, ZUJI offers marketers a wide array of opportunities to reach more than 28 million internet users throughout Asia Pacific, which means that Cathay Pacific has an online presence on the most visited portals on the World Wide Web in each ZUJI market, including (as of November 2004):

- Yahoo! (in Australia, Hong Kong, Singapore and Korea)
- MSN (in Singapore and Korea)

- ninemsn 'Getaway Travel' (the #1 online portal in Australia)
- AsiaOne (a premier news portal in Singapore)
- Expat Express (in Singapore)
- Taiwan Top Tours (part of the China Times' Travel Service section for Taiwan domestic itineraries)
- Naver.com (in Korea)
- Korean Air (in Korea, providing for 'Honeymoon' and 'Woman' travel portals).

Cathay Pacific and CNN

To coincide with the airline's launch of the only twice-daily direct service from Hong Kong to New York in May 2004, Cathay Pacific and CNN teamed up for an exclusive 'Be the first to know' online marketing programme. Targeting business travellers in Asia Pacific, the 'Be the first to know' online contest offered participants a chance to win a unique trip to New York.

According to William Hsu, vice president of CNN advertising sales, Asia Pacific: 'Cathay Pacific is one of our longest-standing media partners in Asia. With our solid understanding of their business and marketing objectives, we were able to add a new dimension with this targeted online program to reach the frequent business travellers in the optimum environment of CNN's online properties.'

Cathay Pacific and Yahoo! Canada

In July 1998 Cathay Pacific teamed up with Yahoo! Canada to develop an interactive traffic-building promotion. Yahoo! Canada and Cathay Pacific Airways developed a customized, interactive contest, giving Yahoo! Canada users the chance to win the trip of a lifetime – a month-long adventure for two to 18 selected Asian cities. The contest was designed to promote and draw qualified consumers to Cathay Pacific's new CyberTraveler online travel newsletter, which offers timely information on travelling in Asia, exclusive low fares, and promotions to hundreds of registered users throughout Canada.

'Cathay Pacific's Canadian CyberTraveller program is a new online initiative,' says Peter Langslow, VP Canada of Cathay Pacific. 'The customized, online promotion with Yahoo! Canada offers us an ideal solution to attract Canadian travellers and internet users of all ages. Cathay Pacific leads the way in service excellence and schedule frequency to Asia from Toronto and Vancouver, and now we have our product in front of Yahoo! Canada's vast audience.'

It is evident that Cathay Pacific is committed to the online channel. By continuing to partner with top leading international brands and creating online campaigns that encourage users to interact with the ads, Cathay Pacific is more than just an airline; it is a perfect example of what a brand marketer in the internet generation should be.

Elizabeth M. Lloyd is the Director of Corporate Marketing for Netblue, Inc., an online direct marketing company based in Silicon Valley. Previously, Lloyd was the director of marketing for opt-in email provider, NetCreations, in New York City. Prior to NetCreations, Lloyd was responsible for the PR department of ValueClick, Inc.

Questions:

1 Discuss how online branding has contributed to the success of Cathay Pacific Airways' business.

2 Evaluate the different marketing communications that can be used in the airline and travel business. Which, in your opinion is the best method for marketing travel products?

MINI CASE 3.2: LEVERAGING THE BRAND: HALLMARK CASE STUDY

Source: Branding Strategy Insider, 11 January 2008. © Brad VanAuken

As I look back on my tenure as Hallmark's chief brand advocate I'd like to share a few observations that may help you build your brand.

In the early to mid-1990s, an ever-increasing share of greeting card sales occurred in the mass channels. Wal-Mart alone was projected to achieve a 20 per cent share of the total greeting card market by the year 2000. Three brands accounted for the vast majority of sales in these channels: American Greetings, Gibson and Ambassador – Hallmark's flanker brand. The sale of Hallmark branded greeting cards accounted for no more than 20 per cent of the overall market. Hallmark branded products were sold primarily in Hallmark card shops and select chain drug stores. Hallmark's corporate share of greeting card sales was 39 per cent including all brands (Ambassador, Shoebox, etc.).

At the same time Ambassador brand sales were becoming an ever-increasing proportion of Hallmark's overall corporate sales, Ambassador's margins were eroding due to increased retailer leverage over manufacturers and heightened mass channel competition. This trend of a less and less profitable brand becoming a larger and larger share of corporate sales was not acceptable. We knew that more sophisticated contract negotiations and sales term innovations would not be enough to halt or reverse this negative trend. We had to do no less than change the rules of the game itself.

After some thought, we knew our only hope was to unleash the power of the Hallmark brand in the mass channel. But, that was tricky and unpopular as we did not want to undermine the success of the Hallmark card shops and chain drug stores – channels that were our 'cash cows' and to which we felt a strong loyalty.

(We conducted the most extensive research in Hallmark's history to assess the impact of pursuing this strategy on Hallmark card shop and chain drug store sales – which turned out to be minimal. Nevertheless, prior to the launch of this strategy, we fortified the viability of these two channels through extensive store consolidation, marketing, merchandising, systems and standards improvements, most notably through the development of the Hallmark Gold Crown programme. And, we expended great efforts to quantify and communicate the equity and power of the Hallmark name to the mass channel retailers. In fact, one mass channel retailer believed in the power of the Hallmark brand so much that it refused to switch to one of our competitor's brands in return for $100 million in sales term.)

Some salient information to help you understand the strategy: Hallmark's primary competitors had significantly reduced their costs by reducing their internal marketing research and creative development capabilities. They leveraged Hallmark's resources in this area (Hallmark employed over 700 artists and writers and 70 marketing researchers at the time) through well-constructed systems of emulation. All mass channel (non-Hallmark) brands had raised prices faster than inflation for a number of years, due to the apparent lack of price sensitivity for greeting cards (until the major price thresholds of $2 and $3 were surpassed) and the pressures applied by retailers for ever increasing year over year sales productivity gains. In fact, while over 65 per cent of Hallmark branded cards were priced under $2, 89 per cent of competitive mass channel brand's cards were priced over $2.

Competitors used their lower cost structures and higher product prices to fund ever accelerating sales terms. They placed their bets on rich sales terms buying distribution with major mass retail chains, which was in fact what was occurring. (Greeting card manufacturers negotiate multiple year contracts with mass channel retailers in which they receive most or all of a retailer's business for a specified minimum floor space and number of stores for a specified period of time. In return for that privilege, they pay substantial sales terms.)

▶

Despite the fact that mass channel share was increasingly based upon which brand could write the biggest check, Hallmark was betting on the fact that it could change the rules by introducing the power of brand equity to the mass channel. After all, Hallmark is the only greeting card brand widely recognized by consumers. (It had unaided top-of-mind awareness of nearly 90 per cent and Shoebox – a tiny little division of Hallmark – was the only other greeting card brand with significant top-of-mind awareness or preference.) Hallmark's product also was superior (validated by rigorous market research) and Hallmark products were priced lower than any other major competitive brand.

Compare this with what I was fond of saying about Hallmark's primary competitors to rally the internal troops around this strategy, 'Would you rather be our competitors with overpriced, no name, inferior products?' If Hallmark could align consumer price perceptions with reality (Hallmark was perceived to be 'expensive' by consumers), I knew we could win with this strategy. Our competitors (both public companies, one of which consistently touted quarter over quarter revenue and profit increases) were locked into multiple-year retailer contracts with very high sales terms. They would not be able to reduce prices without severely affecting their revenues, profits and stock prices.

I could devote at least several posts to the nuances of this strategy, but suffice it to say, that Hallmark's static 39 per cent greeting card market share increased to 42 per cent with increased profitability in the first two years after we implemented this strategy. Since then, Hallmark's share has steadily grown to 55 per cent in a few short years. Unleashing the power of the Hallmark brand in the mass channel resulted in substantial market share and profitability gains for Hallmark without taking away from the success of the card shop and chain drug store channels. (Hallmark card shops achieved consistent month over month sales increases for at least three years during this period, validating my held belief that the added marketplace exposure to the Hallmark brand would have a positive impact on all channels carrying Hallmark products.)

Questions:

1 Discuss whether the addition of the brand to the mass channels has had any impact on Hallmark's existing GC network of stores.

2 What is the advantage of one retail format over another? Is it value (price, value-added services), convenience (hours, location, breadth of offering), the shopping experience itself (entertainment), its self-expressive nature (brand as a badge), or something else?

END OF CHAPTER CASE STUDY: KELLOGG'S

Source: The Times 100

Building a brand in order to sustain its life cycle

Introduction

Kellogg's All-Bran has a long and distinguished history. Like many other famous products, however, it is important from time to time to re-energize its life cycle.

While All-Bran continues to be a powerful *brand*, a number of other high fibre *brands* made by Kellogg's have not had the promotional support or sales of the All-Bran brand. Kellogg's has therefore sought to support these other fibre products by associating them with the *masterbrand* All-Bran.

Kellogg's has looked to raise *consumer* interest by creating a family of fibre-based cereal brands focused around the All-Bran banner in order to create a powerbrand structure. These bran products have now been marketed as a family. This has added extra strength to each separate product. The decision to create the powerbrand was a *strategic* change, made at a high level. It involved managers at Kellogg's planning for the long *term* future. It also needed heavy resource commitments, e.g. to finance and market the initiative.

The *product life cycle* is the period over which it appeals to *customers*. The cycle can be illustrated in a series of stages showing how consumer interest, and hence sales, has altered over time.

For example, a company like Kellogg's is continually developing new product lines, which it then market tests. For many of these products, test *marketing* will indicate that the product might be popular for a short while and then interest would quickly fizzle out. Such product ideas are screened out (eliminated), because their product life cycle would look like the following:

The typical life cycle of a product can be illustrated by a curve that rises steeply, as interest in the product increases. The sales performance rises from zero (when the product is introduced to the market) before rising steadily.

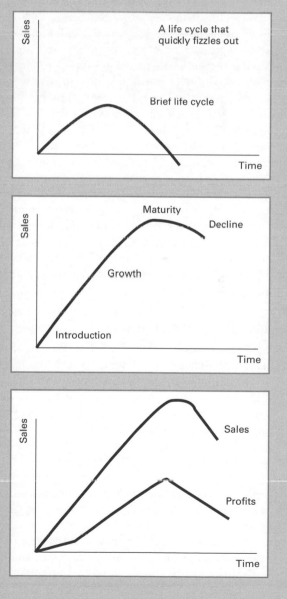

Initially the product will grow and flourish. However, as new competitors come into the market and as excitement falls about the product, then the product enters a new life cycle stage termed *maturity*. If the product is not handled carefully at this stage we may then see saturation of the market and the onset of a decline in interest.

At each stage in the life cycle there is a close relationship between sales and profits so that, as organizations or brands go into decline, their profitability decreases.

A product's life cycle may last for a few months or for more than a century. It all depends on how good the product is originally, how easy it is for competitors to emerge and how good a firm is at keeping its own product relevant and attractive to *consumers*.

To prolong the life cycle of a brand or product an organization needs to use skilful marketing techniques to inject new life into the product.

Preparing to make a strategic change

Before committing *resources* to creating the family of All-Bran *brands*, Kellogg's needed to conduct research to discover whether a change was worth making and the nature of these changes. This involved carrying out a SWOT analysis to identify:

- **S**trengths of the All-Bran brand.
- **W**eaknesses.
- **O**pportunities existing in the market.
- **T**hreats – e.g. from competitors.

All-Bran's product life cycle

Kellogg's created All-Bran as a product and the fibre sector of the cereal *market* in the 1930s. From then onwards the product experienced steady growth with the *company* injecting regular promotional spends to support product *development*. The most spectacular growth was in the 1980s with widespread publicity for the 'F' Plan Diet from nutritionists and health experts. This diet had an impact similar to that of the Atkins Diet in recent years. Following this, the Kellogg's 'bran' range has been moving into a more mature stage:

Because the product is mature, Kellogg's has looked to re-*brand* a range of fibre cereals in order to inject renewed growth and interest. The company has run a £3 million campaign that urges *consumers* to re-appraise these products. Large *investment* was needed to support the *strategy* and to evaluate the consumer response.

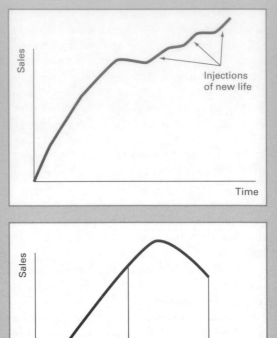

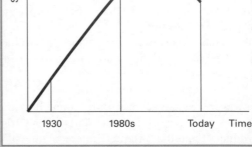

Identifying the benefits

Kellogg's needed to identify the *benefits* that would result from any changes it made. An important advantage related to managing the product range. Kellogg's identified which of its existing fibre based products offered the best present and future prospects and decided to concentrate on those. This simplification made it easier to manage the *product portfolio*. Managers could concentrate on the common elements of the chosen range and focus *marketing* activity on them. This action produced management and *marketing economies of scale*, rather than production economies – the complexity of manufacturing individual products has not been reduced. The smaller *brands* were pulled together into the All-Bran range.

Kellogg's *market research* showed that, in choosing a cereal product, *consumers* place high priority on taste. Although they want a healthier cereal, it still must taste good. So Kellogg's decided to develop new 'tastier' products under the single All-Bran umbrella, such as Bran Flakes Yoghurty.

Pulling a range of fibre products together under a single brand also made it easier to communicate with the target audiences through a shared communication plan.

Research and promotion

Research

Before proceeding with the change, Kellogg's carried out some detailed *market* research with *consumers* to discover their thoughts and feelings.

There are two main approaches to market research:

1 qualitative

2 quantitative.

Qualitative research involves working in detail with a relatively small number of consumers, e.g. observing and listening to them talking in small groups in which they discuss the *brand*, products, packaging, advertising ideas, etc. This qualitative research helped to assess consumers' perceptions, e.g. by giving them pictures of possible new packaging and letting them give their views on the *benefits* of the product and reasons why they use fibre-based cereals. The qualitative research helped Kellogg's to develop the concept of a family of fibre *brands*. The advertising and promotional materials with which the consumer groups worked were very similar to the end promotions that Kellogg's wished to communicate.

Once the *qualitative market research* was complete it was possible to test the concept through *quantitative research*. This involved using questionnaire and survey approaches with a much larger sample of *targeted* consumers to estimate the impact on sales if these changes were put into market.

Promotion

The market research revealed several matters that Kellogg's needed to address when alerting the public to changes in the brand family.

1 Some consumers might find the act of placing a range of separate products under the All-Bran brand confusing. The *solution* was to ensure that packs clearly display both the power brand name (All-Bran) and also the product name (e.g. Bran Flakes). To maintain continuity, it was vital to use consistent type fonts and colours from the old packaging, as well as introducing the flash 'new name, same great taste'. To support consumer understanding of the new range, the back of each pack featured a range sell detailing the different attributes of each of the products in the range. This allowed consumers to make purchase decisions on the basis of taste and the amount of fibre they require in their diet.

2 Research showed that consumers see cereals as a 'natural product'. This is a strong selling point. It makes it vital to feature the ingredients on the packaging. This is because the All-Bran range can be seen as part of a daily healthy diet. For example, the latest addition to the All-Bran range, the delicious Bran Flakes Yoghurty, *claims* to promote users' inner health by providing 17 per cent of daily fibre needs.

3 To give the campaign maximum impact, Kellogg's carefully coordinated television and radio advertising, PR and in-store promotions. These encouraged consumers to try out and reappraise the revamped products. For example, in September 2004, Kellogg's introduced the All-Bran 'Feel Great in a Fortnight' Challenge. This campaign was designed to make the brands benefit more relevant to consumers. Adopting the 'feel great' message moved the brand away from the outdated 'keeps you regular' message and into the feel good territory of better inner health. This promotion featured on 8 million packs and on the All-Bran website. It used William Shatner, best remembered from *Star Trek's* Starship Enterprise! The challenge invited consumers to eat one bowl of any of the cereals in the All-Bran range for two weeks

and see if they could feel the benefit. It focused on the fact that high-fibre diets may help people to feel lighter and more energetic as well as aiding the digestive system.

Conclusion

If a business wants to make a product's total sales grow, it must carefully consider how best to extend its life cycle. By creating the powerbrand 'All-Bran' and providing the right sort of well researched promotional support, Kellogg's has been able to inject renewed vigour into a family of related products. Through appropriate promotional activities and more relevant messages, Kellogg's has re-awakened *consumers*' interest in products that can play an important part in developing a healthy diet in a health-conscious world. Regular campaigns of promotional activity are helpful in enabling all organizations to sustain their own life cycle and those of their *brands* and products. It is early days in evaluating the success of the *marketing* activity supporting All-Bran but the signs are good.

Questions:

1 Why did Kellogg's engage in marketing research before deciding how to inject new growth into Special K?

2 Special K Red Berries is a variant of Special K; why was it important to check that the two products were not competing in a major way?

3 Why was it important to create marketing plans for Special K that fitted with production plans?

4 How did the development of Special K Peach and Apricot extend the brand still further?

5 What was the significance of the Special K bar in injecting further dynamism to the product life cycle?

6 Did the development of variants – Special K Red Berries, Special K Peach and Apricot, and Special K bars – destroy the market for the original Special K product in the UK?

7 How has the extension of the Special K brand been a global success story?

8 Is it possible to continually extend a brand to increase the life cycle of a product?

References

Axelrod, R. and Cohen, M. H. (1999), *Complexity: Organizational Implications of a Scientific Frontier*, New York: The Free Press.

Betz, F. (2002), 'Strategic business models', *Engineering Management Journal*, March.

Chesborough, H. and Rosenbloom, R. (2002), 'The role of the business model in capturing value from innovation: evidence from Xerox Corporation's technology spin-off companies', *Industrial and Corporate Change*, Vol. 11, No. 3, pp. 529–55.

Doyle, P. (1990), 'Building successful brands: the strategic options', *Journal of Consumer Marketing*, Vol. 7 (Spring), pp. 5–20.

Fetscherin, M. and Knolmayer, G. (2004), 'Focus theme articles: business models for content delivery: an empirical analysis of the newspaper and magazine industry', *International Journal on Media Management*, Vol. 6, Nos 1 & 2, September, pp. 4–11.

Holland, J. (1995), *Hidden Order: How Adaptation Builds Complexity*, Reading, Mass: Addison-Wesley.

Kapferer, J.-N. (2004), *The New Strategic Brand Management – Creating and Sustaining Brand Equity Long Term*, Kogan Page: London.

Kelly, S. and Allison, M. A. (1999), *The Complexity Advantage*, New York: McGraw-Hill.

Nussbaum, B. (2007) 'Why Apple is No.1 innovation' – The BW/BCG Survey, posted in May 2007, *BusinessWeek*.

Osterwalder, A. (2004), 'The business model ontology – a proposition in a design science approach', thesis.

Further reading and online sites

Axelrod, R. and Cohen, M. H. (1999), *Complexity: Organizational Implications of a Scientific Frontier*, New York: The Free Press.

Barney, J. (1991), 'Firm resources and sustainable competitive advantage', *Journal of Management*, Vol. 17, 1.

Betz, F. (2002), 'Strategic business models', *Engineering Management Journal*, March.

Bower, J. and Hot, T. M. (1988), 'Fast-cycle capability for competitive power', *Harvard Business Review*, Vol. 66 (November–December), pp. 110–18.

Christensen, C. M. and Overdorf, M. (2000), 'Meeting the challenge of disruptive change', *Harvard Business Review*, Vol. 78, (March–April), pp. 67–76.

Holland, J. (1995), *Hidden Order: How Adaptation Builds Complexity*, Reading, Mass: Addison-Wesley.

Kapferer, J.-N. (2004), *The New Strategic Brand Management – Creating and Sustaining Brand Equity Long Term*, London: Kogan Page.

Kelly, S. and Allison, M. A. (1999), *The Complexity Advantage*, New York: McGraw-Hill.

Leifer, R., McDermott, C., O'Conner, G., Verzer, R., Petres, L. and Price, M. (2000), 'Radical innovation: how mature companies can outsmart upstarts', Harvard Business School Press.

Markides, C. (1999), 'A dynamic view of strategy', *Sloan Management Review*, Vol. 40, Spring, pp. 55–63.

Porter, M. E. (1980), *Competitive Strategy: Techniques for Analyzing Industries and Competitors*, New York: The Free Press.

BBC News 24

Branding Strategy Insider

E-Coach 'The Tao of Business' by Vadim Kotelnikow

The Times 100

CHAPTER 04

Brands as Strategic Assets – Moving Up the Corporate Agenda

Chapter contents

Chapter overview

The origin of brand valuation, as discussed in Chapter 2, lies in the fact that brands are a valuable asset to companies when there is a question of buying and selling, from one owner to another. Brands were then valued in the instances of sale, merger or takeover. One of the key rationales for brand valuation is, therefore, to show that a brand exists, and that it contributes some value to the company and customers. This value varies depending on the brand's strength. Following on from Chapter 2, this chapter examines the strategic role of brands as part of the business strategy, and representative of the company's core values and belief. Therefore, they should be managed at the corporate level. The chapter employs a qualitative approach starting with a review of the academic literature followed by an examination of practices in several industries to determine to what extent companies across industries adopt this strategic view of brands. Comparisons between small and large companies will be made and conclusions reached. As part of the broad area of the strategic implications of branding, Chapter 2 examined brand equity and brand valuation, and Chapter 3 brands and business building by comparing brands and business models. This chapter is a continuation of Chapters 2 and 3, and is the last chapter to deal with the broad area of the strategic implications of branding. Part 2 will examine the area of creating and sustaining brand equity.

❖ LEARNING OBJECTIVES

After completing this chapter, you should be able to

❖ With reference to the specific literature, discuss how branding evolves from a marketing issue to becoming a strategic concern for the boardroom

❖ Compare and contrast the different notions of strategic branding such as the corporate-based view of brands and brand-based strategy

❖ Discuss the role of senior management and/or the CEO as brand custodian in the company

❖ Examine the benefits of corporate-based view and brand-based strategy from an industry perspective and across various industries

❖ Appreciate why brands need to be managed at the corporate level, faced with environmental threats, and discuss these threats

❖ Discuss the different reasons why brands need to be managed at the corporate level for various industries, mainly retailing, services and manufacturing, by identifying the different environments and actors in these industries

❖ Examine brand management models for different industries

❖ Discuss brand development in SMEs and the role country of origin plays in SME branding

❖ Examine the relationship between the brand leader and the CEO of a company

Introduction

Traditionally, branding and brand management have been seen as activities that belong in the realm of marketing, and marketing communications. For instance, brands have always been considered important in the fast-moving consumer goods (fmcg) industry, but even in this sector branding and brand management have often been regarded as part of marketing communications and the marketing mix, which have been managed by marketers and advertising agencies. However, there are signs that brands are transcending their role in marketing to become more an issue of mainstream business strategy for some organizations, and have become a key strategic issue for senior management and boards. This shift in strategic thinking as far as brands are concerned, originates from 1990s views of brands as strategic assets that an organization owns. This chapter starts with a review of the academic literature, and will look at some evidence from the industry perspective via a cross-industries examination. Comparisons will be made between large and small companies.

Brands as strategic assets – a review of the literature

Since the late 1980s a body of literature has appeared to suggest that brands should be seen as part of the firm's strategic assets rather than just a marketing issue. Blackett (1993), for instance, has described brands as 'the engine of profit' for most consumer businesses, and has referred to the well-documented trend towards brand valuation that began in the mid-1980s (see Chapter 2) when Reckitt & Colman, a British fmcg producer, put £127 million worth of brand assets on its balance sheet after its acquisition of another household goods manufacturer, Airwick Co. Ward and Perrier (1998) have also reported that brand valuation is taking place in other industries, such as consumer electronics and retailing, while Leinert and Leinert have drawn attention to the importance of top-management involvement in and support for the role of brand management in the big three US automobile industry manufacturers, Ford, General Motors and Chrysler, in a very competitive automobile industry.

Others have gone further in proposing a corporate-based view of brands (e.g. Balmer, 1995, 1998, 2003; Hatch and Schultz, 1997; Mosmans and Van der Vorst, 1998; Hankinson and Hankinson, 1999; Gray and Balmer, 2001; Davis, 2002). They argue that brands are the key strategic instruments and drivers, which are at the heart of a business' competitive position in an industry, and also form the basis for long-term competitive advantage based on successful relationships with customers.

In particular, Rubinstein (1996) argues that branding goes beyond communications and should be regarded as an integrated business process. Furthermore, brand management should be embedded in the whole company and should not be seen solely as a marketing department role. Values and corporate culture become important elements in such cases (De Chernatony, 1999). Ind goes one step further and suggests that the branding concept can be directly applied at the corporate level: 'A corporate brand is more than just the outward manifestation of an organisation – its name, logo, visual presentation. Rather it is the core of values that defines it.' Corporate branding becomes the strategic direction for an organization's activities, providing consistency through the connection between positioning, communication and staff working style/behaviour (De Chernatony, 1999).

Simoes and Dibb (2001) confirm there is an emphasis in the academic literature and, on the basis of three company case studies, that the brand concept is being spread and embedded in the whole organization, and that the brand expresses the company's core values and beliefs. In this case, the brand becomes the corporate brand. Branding is also seen as a powerful resource for creating shareholder and long-term value, and allows business performance and long-term strategy to be viewed simultaneously.

Mosmans and van der Vorst (1998) further advance that firms should shift from brand strategy, which refers to as 'a concept that drives the business', and as 'an integrated marketing idea' to brand-based strategy, which plays a critical role in selecting and maintaining a strategic direction for a firm. Strategic decisions should be driven by the brand, which is a central focus of a firm. The rationale for this is that as the brand becomes known it can form a relationship between the seller and buyer, and what they expect from one another. This makes the brand very important as a catalyst in the formation of strategy. Brands serve as strategic reference points, as they identify, give dimension to, signify, structure and stabilize the interaction between supply and demand in a business.

In a brand-based strategy, the brand functions as a directional framework that facilitates the process of strategy formation. The brand forms the selection criterion with respect to the capabilities of the company and the environment (Mosmans and van der Vorst, 1998: pp. 105–6). At the centre of the brand-based strategy, the seller must be market orientated and engage in a dialogue with his customers. He must develop brand ownership with the consumer so that there is co-ownership. In this case, buyers also make proposals for strategic alternatives. The dialogue with customers often leads companies to change to completely different products and services. For instance, consumers need banking but do they need banks? Retailers with strong brands use these to enter financial services.

To return to the argument that brands are seen more and more as a boardroom issue, Capon et al. (2001) suggest that senior management should take responsibility for the custodianship of brands; and Aaker (1996) suggests that the development of a brand strategy should be concurrent with the development of a business strategy. There is also evidence to show that the brand-orientated approach of corporate strategy would furnish firms with a sustainable edge over their competitors in terms of achieving growth and expansion.

Brands as strategic assets – an industry perspective

For many companies, brands have usually been managed by marketers, often with the help of outside consultancies and advertising agencies. However, in recent years, there seems to have been a growing awareness and/or recognition among senior managers of the strategic role of brands. Accordingly, researchers report that:

> In leading companies, the CEO is taking the role of brand custodian. Branding is no longer seen as being solely the responsibility of transient brand managers; [b]ut, it is positioned as the fulcrum of a company's relationship not only with its customers but also, with its own staff. (De Chernatony and Dall'Olmo Riley, 1999)

This was also echoed with Sir Allen Sheppard (1994), then Chairman and CEO of Grand Metropolitan plc (now Diageo plc), a British-based fmcg group:

> At Grand Metropolitan, we believe our brands to be our most valuable assets. Our businesses in food, drinks and retailing are all about consumer brands. We use brands to add value to our food and drink products and to our retail outlets, encouraging consumer loyalty and confidence. This in turn, allows us to earn enhanced profits, which benefits shareholders and staff alike. (Anonymous researcher, 2006)

> Brands are the core of our business. We could, if we so wished sub-contract all the production, distribution, sales and service functions and, provided we retained ownership of our brands, we would continue to be successful and profitable. It is our brands that provide the profits for today and guarantee the profits for the future. (Anonymous researcher, 2006)

Traditionally, branding has played an important role in the consumer goods industry for a good reason – the difficulty in achieving significant and long-term differentiation simply through product development and innovation, which can usually easily be copied by competitors. Nowadays, however, there is a realization that brands are important not just as marketing tools for consumer goods, but also because they can also be key strategic assets in themselves. Similarly, this view seems to emerge in other sectors where historically branding has not been seen as so important, such as consumer durables, services, engineering, high-tech and non-profit, as well as e-business.

In the automobile industry, for instance, Per Gyllenhammer, then CEO of Volvo, said in 1993: 'Our most important asset is the Volvo trademark' (Anonymous researcher, 2006). More recently, Jeff Bezos, founder of amazon.com, a leading Internet retail brand, has been quoted as saying: 'Brand names are super important online' (Anonymous researcher, 2006); and, in 1999, Robert Pittman, President of America Online, put it simply: 'First and foremost, consumers look for brands' (Anonymous researcher, 2006).

Lately, brand management has also come to be seen as a boardroom issue, particularly when brands are badly publicized and, in extreme cases, have brought the company down with them. This problem is found across industries. The most recent and most publicized stories refer to the Martha Stewart and Enron cases. Before the news broke of the financial scandal concerning Martha Stewart (the person), the Martha Stewart brand was one of America's strongest, with a Brand Keys index of 120. Following her conviction, the index fell to 62, lower than even Enron. The MS corporate brand name was used across a large array of businesses and had been an asset until the bad news broke. Then the disgrace affected the whole range (Laforet and Saunders, 2005). Arthur

Andersen, Enron's accountants, faced a similar problem on a global scale. Their corporate name which was used across the world had helped them serve global clients, until the partnership's involvement in Enron's collapse. The failure of the company in America made Arthur Andersen untouchable in all of its markets.

Meanwhile, in the fmcg industries, Coca-Cola Beverages suddenly faced declining sales all across Europe when a number of Belgian consumers became sick after drinking contaminated Coke; Perrier had faced a similar problem a few years earlier when some consumers found traces of benzene in its premium-priced mineral water, and Nike is still having trouble shaking off the image of running sweatshops in Asia – a problem it shares with Manchester United, the world's favourite soccer team (Laforet and Saunders, 2005).

So, a firm's reputation has the same risk and returns as its financial situation. A survey by a US insurance company of 2000 public and private companies proves this. It found reputation risk to be the single biggest business hazard (Aon, 2001). In the Information Age, the Internet is the second development that has awakened companies to reputation risk from pressure groups or disgruntled customers. Successful brands like Arthur Andersen and Martha Stewart may increase returns, and many companies turn to corporate or house brands, because of the communications and financial benefits of a shared reputation (Laforet and Saunders, 1999); however, risk always accompanies returns (Laforet and Saunders, 2005).

Corporate branders like Kellogg's and Nestlé, which use their corporate names to endorse their range, face reputation risk across their whole business if bad news hits. In contrast, Unilever and Mars' use of mono brands gives firebreaks that can limit reputation loss across a whole business. Unilever benefited from this when it launched Omo Power in the Netherlands, Persil Power in the UK and Skip Power in France. These powerful detergents contained a catalyst that dissolved clothes along with dirt (Laforet and Saunders, 2005, citing Kotler, Armstrong, Saunders and Wong, 2001).

The brief overview of the literature above suggests that brands are being looked at in a strategic light by both academics and senior management. In the following sections, we will see to what extent this is actually happening in practice, and how this trend is prevalent across industries as the literature tends to imply.

The following is based on a recent study investigating to what extent the strategic view of brands is being sought out in practice and across industries. The exploratory study used semi-structured interviews with ten consultants at leading British branding and design consultancies. The objective of the study was to gather a range of opinion to determine whether this perceived trend of branding was becoming a strategic and boardroom issue, by reflecting on consultants' experience of working with clients over the last ten to fifteen years. The consultants were chosen on the basis of their experience of working at a senior level with a range of clients in different sectors over a period of time, which would give a wider and more objective view of industry practice. The consultants held senior positions and had experience of working with a variety of client organizations for at least ten years.

Interviewees were asked four broad questions:

1 What if any, have been the main changes in client companies' attitudes towards brands and brand management over the last ten to fifteen years or so?

2 Has brand management become a more senior management or board level issue, rather than just a marketing issue for client organizations over the last ten to fifteen years?

3 Do managers in these companies now view brands and brand management as key, strategic issues for the organization?

4 Do you detect any significant differences in attitudes towards the importance of branding and brand management between different industry sectors such as fmcg, financial services, durables, non-profit and e-business?

In answer to question 1, the results of the study indicated that companies' attitudes towards brands/brand management had changed significantly over the last ten to fifteen years. It is now more common for brands to be considered at more senior management level than in the past. This is reflected in companies spending more money on branding and involving the consultancies more. The whole branding and visual design industry is going up the food chain, and companies' desire to differentiate themselves from others has led them to think more strategically about brands.

Other possible reasons for this shift in attitudes are the growing emphasis on brands, particularly on the part of fmcg manufacturers, and the increasing power of retailers and own-labels. Another reason is the difficulty in differentiating products in many consumer markets, which are becoming ever more crowded and competitive. Although this is not a new issue, markets are becoming even tougher as innovation is more easily copied, and 'lock out' of competitors simply by product development and innovation is getting harder to achieve.

There is also a growing emphasis on corporate branding: that is, the company as a brand. For example, a major European fmcg producer has recently begun to show its corporate logo more prominently on products, whereas five years or so ago only the product brand was displayed. The aim here is to move the brand from being what was described as: 'a meaningless corporate monolithic to actually standing for something which gives the business a vision and drive' (Anonymous researchers, 2006).

The new emphasis on corporate branding is also identified by the study as a major trend that is reflected in communications with stakeholders, including retailers, shareholders and employees. Corporate reputation has also been confirmed as something much more important nowadays than in the past. One of the growing key issues now is how companies can create loyal fans of the company.

In answer to question 2, the study showed the overall picture is mixed and that, not all companies embrace the idea of branding fully. There are leaders and followers in this area. Some are ahead while others are doing it for the first time. There seems to be a gap between thinking and implementation, possibly because branding is not always fully understood by some board members, and it could be because some organizations do not have a marketing director on the board, although this is changing. Even with marketers on the board, they may not always be empowered or are distanced from the implementation of brand strategy.

In answer to question 3, the study indicated that there is a strong awareness of the strategic role of brands at a senior level. This is thanks to the financial values that have been attributed to brands since they were first placed on balance sheets in the 1980s. However, most CEOs go quickly through financial measures, like profitability or earnings per share or whatever it is, before they talk about brands, but companies now also realize the link between brands and financial performance.

Concerning the issue of whether companies show any tendency towards focusing their whole corporate strategy around brands, the results of the study suggest that up to now no organizations have gone that far. Taken to the extreme, a whole business strategy built around brands could lead a corporation to outsource most or all of its non-core activities and move towards becoming a virtual corporation. No companies were found to be going down this route to any significant extent.

In answer to question 4, it was found that, in practice, some industries have been slower to adopt branding/brand management than others. Branding often comes to the fore when a company finds a new competitor in its space. The results of the study also indicated that in services such as banks, branding is now considered very seriously. Growing awareness of branding also takes place in sectors which develop new client bases, such as non profit organizations, high-tech industries and professional services like law and accountancy firms. However, the adoption of branding in some of these seems to be more advanced than in others.

The importance of branding in communicating with investors and other various groups of stakeholders in a new high-tech business is reflected in this interviewee's statement:

We've been doing some work with a technology start up – it's a company that doesn't even have a product yet, but we've been talking about the brand and recognizing that the perceptions of a relatively small number of people are critical to success of its initial public offering. It needs to communicate rationally and emotionally and be coherent about what makes it different. Ten years ago, for a high-tech start up, the brand would be the last thing they would be thinking of. More and more people realise they have to communicate with all the stakeholders in a business. (Anonymous researchers, 2006)

In the case of services, the brand is even more important than the goods, owing to the intangibility that characterizes services. One of the most problematic aspects associated with service brands is that consumers have to deal with intangible service offerings. De Chernatony and McDonald (1998) argue that financial service providers must realize that brands hold greater importance for service companies than for tangible products. This is because consumers have no tangible attributes with which to assess the brand, and because it is harder to communicate the values of service brands.

Branding has also become increasingly important within the UK financial services industry. Companies operating in the industry used to enjoy a relative position of power, being able to target a relatively small market and yet still make significant profits. However, more recently pressure has been brought to bear from a consumerist and governmental stance, resulting in financial service firms looking carefully at the type of business they transact and the related margins. Another reason is that financial products are increasingly difficult to differentiate, so branding is a way of creating differentiation and building a competitive advantage for the firm concerned.

The financial service brand is based entirely on the way the company does things and on the company's culture, which means that the whole company contributes to building the corporate brand. This is due to the inseparability that characterizes services, which means that the service provider becomes an integral part of the service delivered to the external customer. Subsequently, customers' perceptions of the brand depend mainly on individual interactions with staff, so there is a need to ensure consistency in the quality of service delivery (Papasolomou and Vrontis, 2006). Essentially, there is a need to build the service brand on the basis of a clear competitive position, which in turn must be linked to the corporate strategy. This is what the UK retail banking industry was trying to do, by launching an IM programme throughout their branch networks.

Branding is also found to be important in industries such as engineering and high-tech, but more recently also in the petroleum industry. According to industrial commentators, most of the petroleum companies operating in the domestic market have focused on branding as a means to increase their fuel sales – that is, by branding the products sold in their own filling stations. It is estimated that a branded product will increase sales by 10 to 20 per cent against a non-branded product. In the petroleum industry, the branding of a petroleum product is equivalent to an improvement in its quality (Petrescu, 2007). With respect to high-tech industry, technological superiority is no longer an adequate basis for differentiating products. Brand identity and customer-orientated benefits will determine a product's success, and branding provides identification, so that a product is more than its technical specifications. Given technical specifications, most manufactured products can be treated as commodities, while consumers will respond to brands.

Pettis presents six steps for defining, creating and managing brand equity for technology-based products:

1 Identify the questions that need to be answered and define the problem(s) to be solved.
2 Conduct qualitative and quantitative research to understand fully who the customers are, how they perceive the brand and competitive brands, and the buying process.
3 Define the brand, which includes positioning, brand associations, brand naming, brand symbol, graphic identity, taglines and brand personality.
4 Develop a brand strategy and marketing communications plan to apply the brand definition to all customer relationships.
5 Create and execute an integrated marketing communications programme.
6 Manage the brand continuously and track it through research to grow, maintain and leverage brand equity.

Brands as strategic assets – small vs large company perspectives

An academic perspective

SMEs (small and medium-sized enterprises) branding is a new field in branding research and is still at the exploratory stage. Due to their resource limitations and the owner/manager's strong influence on decision-making, small firms' behaviour follows different patterns from that of their large counterparts. It is, therefore, important for academics to study SMEs' brand management in its own context. SMEs often craft their marketing strategies through networks.

The firm's values are communicated through business and social encounters, which are part of SMEs' daily routine, and adapt their message to each particular audience and situation (Spence, 2006). Branding in SMEs is often misunderstood. It is generally thought to consist of the development of logos and advertising campaigns. In fact, the entrepreneur's/owner's personality goes beyond that of its products and services. This is in sharp contrast to the systematic approach used by their larger counterparts. Some researchers have pointed to the importance of producing a strong positioning statement attached to the brand, and the difficulties in doing so.

Benefits of and barriers to brand development in SMEs

Having a strong brand enables companies not only to distinguish their product from those of the competition, but to create customer loyalty and confidence in their performance, exert greater control over promotion and distribution of the brand, as well as commanding a premium price over the competitors, all the while improving the valuation of the business. Although branding is not synonymous with growth, and many small business owners do not want to transform their companies into large corporations, there is a need for constant renewal just to maintain a company. If people no longer buy a product, it soon becomes obsolete. Similarly, if there is a problem with product recall, the strength of the brand allows companies to go back to their audience and work through the problem with them. It can only bring enhanced value and longevity to the business. It enables SMEs to stay ahead of the competition, and competition will always be there, no matter how small a niche market a company operates in. Therefore, the benefits of branding and brand management for SMEs are clear. Just as with with large businesses, SMEs have to deal with increasingly intense competition. Branding will allow SMEs to gain a competitive advantage over their competitors through differentiation, customer retention and price premium, as well as by making things right by their customer, enhancing value to the company, and allowing them to remain in the business for as long as they can or wish to.

The barriers perceived to branding/brand management in SMEs are: time, human and financial resources to conduct the branding activities. The unavailability of these resources forces firms to concentrate on what they can do best in daily operations. This short-term focus becomes an obstacle for them in developing a long-term branding strategy. Many SMEs perceive investments in business assets, including advertising, information technology and training, as costs and, therefore, have never fully invested in them.

SMEs' approach to decision-making, marketing and branding

Marketing in SMEs is performed through networking, which is a natural way for entrepreneurs to communicate with their clients, suppliers and various stakeholders to build trust and to swap favours. Marketing by networking is based on people-orientated activities, is informal, often discreet, interactive, interchangeable, integrated, habitual and can either be passive or proactive (Gilmore et al., 2001). Studies point out several advantages and positive aspects typical of SME businesses in the execution of their marketing, such as flexibility, speed of reaction and an eye for (market) opportunities.

Entrepreneurs position themselves strategically in networks, which provide the firm with a competitive advantage or with scarce resources (Spence, 2003). Entrepreneurs tend to follow their intuition rather than go through a systematic planning process to reach their goals. Although entrepreneurial marketing activities seem haphazard and informal, successful entrepreneurs are moved by a vision, which determines the nature of the firm's main activities and direction, while tactics are more likely to be adapted to market circumstances.

This vision is transmitted to the public through the leadership abilities of the entrepreneur, who needs to cultivate his image to the same extent, if not on the same scale, as the CEOs of large corporations (Spence, 2006, citing Filion, 1991). His image will reflect the firm's values and therefore will have an impact on the brand. Creating a passion for the brand throughout the company is important for brand recognition, and this has to be initiated by the entrepreneur him/herself (see Krake's brand development model below).

Brand development in SMEs

Krake (2005) suggests that brand development in SMEs is influenced first and foremost by the entrepreneur's personality. The company structure and the position of brand management influences the marketing activities and messages communicated. The market in which the company operates also has an effect on brand development/brand management in SMEs. The available budget affects marketing activities to bring about brand recognition. Communicating a brand is rarely a problem for a small business, but the difficulty lies in establishing a clear positioning and personality for the organization, and little help is available in this area for small firms (Spence, 2006, citing Inskip, 2004).

Figure 4.1 shows how brands are developed in SMEs.

- *I Beginning and underprivileged brands.* In this quadrant, brands/companies have just been set up, have not yet managed to create awareness, and awareness of brand management needs to grow before it can be given a greater role. These are the beginning brands. Then there are brands/companies that have been in existence for longer, but have not succeeded in gaining name recognition or set up a bigger role for brand management within their organization. They do not behave in an entrepreneurial fashion, they fail to embed the idea of brand recognition within their organization and they make little or no budget available for such a concept. Such brands will probably stay in the same position in the model for the next ten years. These are the underprivileged brands.

- *II Emerging brands.* The building of a brand takes time. Brand recognition is not something that happens by itself. Making a brand recognizable demands that a conscious effort is made to achieve such recognition. In this quadrant, the owner makes everyone within the organization

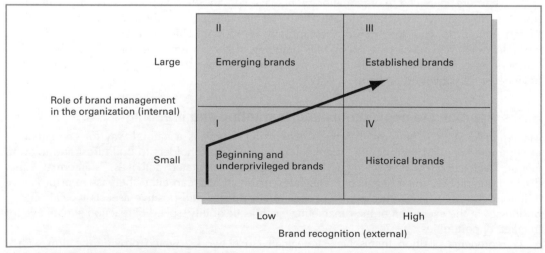

Source: Krake (2005), *Journal of Product & Brand Management*, Vol. 14, No. 4.
FIGURE 4.1 Brand Development Model for SMEs

aware of the need for this, gears the organization to it and makes the budget (however difficult this may be) available for it. In this regard, his/her own role as a publicist is also extremely important. The brands in this quadrant are known as the 'emerging' brands. It is probable that a brand beginning in quadrant I will need to pass through this quadrant as it grows into an established (quadrant III) brand.

- *III Established brands.* If the owner and the organization of an SME are determined to build up a strong brand and do actually attain such an objective, then their brand can be considered an established brand. They have attained a high degree of brand recognition, which they can maintain, and now they need to build on this to create as much brand equity as possible. In short, it is possible to reap the benefits of this success and extend it in the future.

- *IV Historical brands.* In this quadrant lie the brands that have managed to create a reasonable to large degree of brand recognition, despite the fact that there was little structural support for such an achievement within the organization. They are the exceptions that, owing to events in the past, have attained this favourable position. The actual type of product probably has much to do with this. These are middle-sized companies that, due to a striking product or a historical background have managed to build up an enormous brand recognition without actually having paid much attention to it. That is why brands in this quadrant can be labelled 'historical' brands.

Wong and Merrilees (2005) have also identified some stages of brand development in SMEs, which they refer to as 'the ladder of SMEs brand orientation', moving from minimal brand orientation, to embryonic brand orientation, to integrated brand orientation (see Figure 4.2). According to these authors, most SMEs will be on the lower steps of the ladder.

Minimalist describes a company with a low-key marketing emphasis across the board, low brand distinctiveness and orientation, as well as low brand performance.

Embryonic refers to a stronger marketing emphasis but not on branding. Branding is informal or seen as optional in this type of company. Promotional tools are also narrow. Word-of-mouth is used. Brand distinctiveness is low to medium; brand orientation and brand performance is medium.

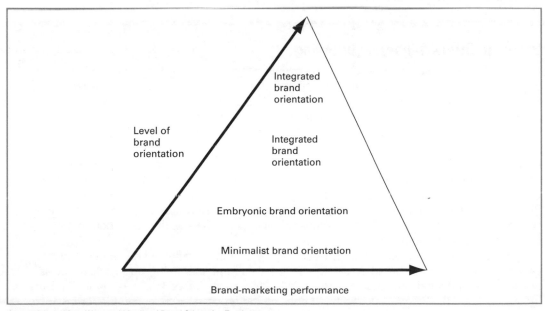

Source: Adapted from Wong and Merrilees' Brand Orientation Typology.
FIGURE 4.2 Brand orientation in SMEs

Integrated means a stronger marketing and branding emphasis, either informal or formal. Branding is not an option and wider promotional tools are being used. Brand distinctiveness is medium to high; brand orientation and brand performance is high.

Brand management and country-of-origin (COO) effects

Given SMEs' limited knowledge and know-how in branding and brand management, Spence (2006) suggests that SMEs would benefit from the role COOs play in SMEs' strategies to build strong brands and leverage their brand equity. That is to say, combining an SME's brand with that of the COO of the products could provide a multiplier effect and increase SME's visibility and credibility, especially in foreign markets. Furthermore, the synergy of COO and branding would be very important for small companies with limited resources.

Spence's study assesses the extent to which four consumer-product SMEs in Monaco use COO (i.e. Monaco's image) as part of their brand image to determine the strategies used to develop brand equity, and concludes that branding combined with COO could be of benefit to the country itself and the products and services it exports, thanks to the 'halo' effect which is produced.

The four firms investigated used the COO effect to enhance their impact, especially on foreign consumers, and in the case where these brands are exported to developing countries such as Asia and the Middle East, where the European origin has an appeal or to countries in which it is not well known. Three out of four firms studied worked on the assumption that Monaco has a positive global image, and that this image can be transferred to how consumers in the world perceive its specific competencies to design/manufacture some product categories.

Furthermore, when the brand is exported how consumers perceive Monaco and how its image influences product evaluation is of critical importance in the case of conspicuous consumption in developing countries such as Jordan and some Asian countries. In these countries, imports from developed countries generally carry symbolic meanings of fashion and status, and consumers tend to display their wealth and success by purchasing imports. Developed countries generally tend to be seen as better off than developing countries in terms of design, technology, skills and product quality. This is what the four SMEs studied tried to emphasize in their brand positioning.

Spence also finds that brand equity is transmitted through an integrated strategy including a clear vision for the brands from the company's executives, strong relationships with distributors, agents and retailers, and their presence at targeted trade shows.

Branding Brief 4.1: Internal branding

Brands are about products or services. The people behind those products and services are an important element of any brand strategy. What kind of conversation would one expect with a Coca-Cola customer service rep? How does one picture Nike's corporate HQ? Would one be troubled by a Ford dealer who prefers to drive Nissan cars? Unless employees act consistently with the brands they represent, any other branding activity can suffer. Employees bring a brand to life; they are its ultimate custodians.

Communicating the brand values to staff requires the same methods as external marketing. Companies need to segment their internal population just as they would their external audience, and communicate appropriately. Wal-Mart, for instance, uses mass media in its internal branding. Its television adverts featuring greeters in store are as much about demonstrating appropriate behaviour to the company's own employees as they are about promoting the store to the general public.

The best form of communication is leadership by example. Staff need role models and will be more likely to adopt brand values if they see their superiors living up to what they say. Naturally rewards and remuneration can provide incentives for certain behaviours, and the incorporation of the brand values with HR policies and processes is essential. BP, for instance, runs its Helios Award scheme, which honours projects and work that embody the company's brand values (green, innovation, performance and progressive).

Now in its third year, the number of nominations for the award far surpasses expectations. Employees take it seriously.

Human resource departments must also consider how their recruitment will uphold brand values. Of course, even with the best selection procedures, some employees simply don't want to know. This is particularly true when companies implement internal brand alignment for the first time.

Virgin is one company that has always recognized the importance of its people. Its attitude is demonstrated in its brand manual. Yet the process of creating and maintaining brand culture in the workplace is a difficult and delicate process.

Branding Brief 4.2: The future of brands

Source: Adapted from Interbrand

Further brand management considerations

In maximizing and sustaining the value of brands in the future there needs to be more focus on:

- *Understanding the value and value drivers of a brand.* As can be seen from the Samsung case, a focus on brand value and measuring performance on the basis of the brand value added can build momentum and create sustainable growth. It is also crucial management information for mergers, acquisitions and divestments, which will continue in the future as markets shake out and consolidate. Few mergers currently deliver long-term shareholder value, largely because of overemphasis on financials and practical operations. Greater focus on brand value would help mergers succeed as well as generating real organic growth.
- *Clarity of brand positioning.* Clarity of vision, values and positioning overall are often given insufficient attention in practice. The majority of corporate and brand visions are interchangeable, bland and viewed with cynicism. In an over-communicated world, lack of clarity will substantially reduce effectiveness and efficiency, and complex brand and sub-brand structures without a real audience rationale will reduce this still further. Clarity of strategy is also one of the leading criteria by which companies are judged.
- *Brands as total experiences, and as central organizing principles, rather than just products and logos.* The success of experience-based brands at building deeper customer relationships at the expense of solely product-based brands argues strongly for every brand to think about its total chain of experience – from visual identity to advertising, product, packaging, PR, in-store environment – and increasingly round-the-clock presence and availability online. Technology will provide the opportunity to build an even greater sensory experience into brands through touch, smell and sound. Whatever emerges, distinctive value can and will need to be added at every stage of the experience, or at the very least, not lost.
- *More compelling and more imaginative expressions of a brand's identity and brand communications.* Senior executives may not feel entirely comfortable in this area, but the ability to break through brand proliferation and communications clutter depends on imaginative and innovative creative expression. In the developed world, audiences are knowledgeable and savvy about marketing, and will increasingly edit out communications that they find boring or irritating. Imagination will need to be applied not just to the creative message, but also to the medium. Product placements in editorial, and appropriate sponsorship of events, programmes and computer games will become more important. In particular, young people around the world have high expectations from brands, and are increasingly difficult to reach and satisfy.

- *The need for internal and external operations to be aligned – and transparent.* In an all-seeing digital world, and in a sharper business environment where employees at all levels can be ambassadors or saboteurs for the company's reputation, there really will be no hiding places any more. Organizations will have no choice but to be transparent in their dealings and fulfil their promises, or to have transparency forced on them. On a more positive note, numerous studies have confirmed that investment in a company's employees, and their good treatment, translates into significantly better customer satisfaction. Customer satisfaction and loyalty are, and will be, the drivers of long-term sustainable brand value.
- *Rigorous legal protection around the world.* It is estimated that 9 per cent of world trade is counterfeited. Although international law is increasingly being upheld, even in the previous counterfeiting capitals of the world, it is likely that while there are still brands to copy, there will be willing makers and buyers of copies. Brand owners must use the full weight of the law, quickly and publicly, to prevent value loss and degradation. Brand valuation, which can demonstrate how much economic loss might be attributed to passing off, is an effective way of supporting cases such as these.
- *Corporate social responsibility as a core corporate responsibility.* Corporate social responsibility (CSR) seems to be an overused buzz term in too many organizations today, and a whole new industry has grown up around it. Although good intentions may be there, all too often organizations look at CSR as an insurance policy, or a more sophisticated form of cause-related marketing, rather than as core to their operations.

Many responsible companies produce elaborate CSR reports, including social and environmental performance. However, it is necessary to ask whether the basic principle of separate reports is the right one, or whether there should be a more integrated and central way of dealing with these issues in the future if we are going to have the kind of world we would all want, or at least to mitigate the pessimistic scenarios of environmental destruction and terrorism breeding in areas of poverty and exclusion that we might all fear.

For those who would say, 'But what has this to do with business and brands?' the fact that brands have the power to change people's lives and indeed shape the world we live in is not a fanciful notion, but a demonstrable fact. Brands have extraordinary economic power, often transcending national governments, and are able to connect with people's lives, behaviour and purchases across borders. If there are those who say that business's only concern should be to make a profit then, this would not only to be missing the point about CSR at its basic level – that CSR, by definition, demands more than the profit motive – but also missing out on opportunities for brand leadership in the future. From more than 3000 studies of brands around the world, leadership is the characteristic most closely correlated with the strongest long-term value.

Any brand seeking to succeed and to be most valuable in the future will need to think and behave like a leader: at the basic levels of product and service distinction, and at the more emotional levels of creativity, values and core social contribution.

The future of brand leadership

It is appropriate, from time to time, for governments, businesses and indeed any organization to ask themselves what they are there for. Procter & Gamble recently restated its core purpose of improving the lives of its consumers. Samsung talks about creating superior products and services and 'contributing to a better global society ... to the prosperity of people all over the world – a single human society'. The UK government published its quality of life indicators in 1999 in answer to challenges on how to create a more sustainable society.

It is easy, but probably not helpful, to be cynical about these kinds of statements. Ironically, one of the brakes to progress on environmental and social issues for companies has been a fear that their actions will be interpreted cynically. Although the stick is an important incentive for companies not to misbehave, opinion-forming media might think sometimes about the carrot of encouragement for corporations trying to do the right thing and struggling to balance the interests of shareholders, consumers and the public at large.

This balancing act also leads on to discussions about how businesses (and indeed governments) are measured and rewarded, as well as how to truly measure the wealth and well-being of society in general. A recent study by the Future Foundation concluded that the increase in wealth and possessions in the UK was poorly correlated with happiness, and the UK government's Sustainable Development Commission found the same in its study of prosperity. While it is easy to sit in the wealthy West and philosophize about these things when people in developing countries are dying through lack of basic services, it does nevertheless raise questions about the goal of development. Will our prioritizing of economic success in preference to any other be as appropriate in the future, in either developed or developing countries?

There are several references to alternative, more broad-based measurement systems for business and society in this book. These would give a broader base to the priorities of CEOs and governments.

It would, of course, be better for organizations to take an active lead in setting standards in different markets. What can be termed a 'leader brand' is not a brand leader in the old-fashioned sense, reflecting scale and muscle alone; rather it reflects a newer, restless and agenda-setting leadership across all areas of philosophy and operations, inside and out. Leader brands also need to take it upon themselves to explain the wider benefits of branding, and increasingly show sensitivity to local cultures, so that they continue to have licence to operate (and hopefully be welcomed) in even the most difficult parts of the world. As discussed throughout, brands can be uniting influences, and powerful social and economic developers. It is important for all brand owners and influencers to manage their brands well, and as a discernible force for good, and to ensure that they help people understand the benefits in a more informed way.

The balance of this book has been quite unashamedly 'pro logo', but there is a conditional 'pro' here. Brands will continue to succeed if they deserve it, and since the future of brands is the future of sustainable business and fundamental to developments in society, it is important to us all to see that they do.

Branding Brief 4.3: Successful steps to global brand leadership: the role of the CEO

The primary objective of boardrooms is to build and sustain shareholder value, and deliver competitive returns to shareholders. At the same time, branding is a very effective catalyst for better leadership and helps the boardroom to drive a shared vision throughout the organization.

The boardroom must manage by metrics, and balance short- and long-term perspectives and performance. The growing emphasis on brand strategy to drive shareholder value and competitiveness will move up the boardroom agenda and become one of the most prominent value drivers in Korea in this century.

The most important factor for building strong Korean brands is the mindset of the Korean CEO and boardroom. Branding is a boardroom discipline and successful brands can be built only when the boardroom, led by the chairman and the CEO, understands, appreciates and commits to treating branding as a strategic discipline and devotes the resources at the company's disposal to support the brands in a continuous manner.

Conclusion

According to the literature, the way companies think about brands is changing and evolving, as brands are viewed more as strategic assets rather than simply marketing tools. Recent research confirms this, by showing that there is a distinct trend towards branding moving up the corporate agenda over the last decade, and that brands are now taken more seriously by top management. However, some companies are at an earlier stage in their awareness and understanding of the strategic role of branding than others. This also varies according to industry sectors. In some sectors, while brands are seen as important, they are not captured at top management level, nor have they moved significantly towards being part of the corporate strategy or the centre of the business, while the notion of 'custodians of the brand' suggested by academics is somewhat overstated.

Overall, branding has been shown to be a very important strategic issue for many companies in many industries, if not all companies and all industries. The various academic models of branding and brand management that have been developed, and illustrated above, suggest that branding is different in different industries and contexts. There exist different models of brand management for different industries. Brand management is also very specific to each company and the market in which it operates.

To successfully manage brands, companies must first understand their industry and the market they operate in, as well as their own aims and objectives, in terms of how they want to grow and compete. To sum up, there is recognition across the board that branding and brand management are necessary for all businesses, and that brands are a company's strategic asset. However, brands are not always well understood by board members, which can result in bad brand management. It is, therefore, vital that a marketing executive sits on the board.

🔑 Key terms

Brand-based strategy: views brands as a catalyst in the formation of strategy, serving as strategic reference points as they identify, give dimension to, add significant structure, and stabilize the interaction between supply and demand in a business. At the centre of the brand-based strategy principle, the seller must be market orientated and engaged in a dialogue with his customers. He must develop brand ownership with the consumer so that there is co-ownership. In this case, buyers also make proposals for strategic alternatives. The dialogue with customers often leads companies to change to completely different products and services.

Brand orientation: refers to companies having some kind of branding activities.

Brand strategy: 'a concept that drives the business' and 'an integrated marketing idea'.

Corporate-based branding: brands are seen as key strategic instruments and drivers, which are at the heart of a business's competitive position in an industry, which also forms the basis for long-term competitive advantage based on successful relationships with customers.

Corporate brand: defined by the company's core values, beliefs, its name, logo and visual presentation.

Corporate branding: often refers to the company as a brand. Corporate branding also gives a strategic direction for an organization's activities, providing consistency through the connection between positioning, communication and staff working style/behaviour.

Embryonic: refers to a stronger marketing emphasis but not on branding. Branding is informal or seen as optional in this type of company. Promotional tools are also narrow. Word-of-mouth is used. Brand distinctiveness is low to medium; brand orientation and brand performance are medium.

Integrated: refers to a stronger marketing and branding emphasis, either informal or formal. Branding is not an option and wider promotional tools are used. Brand distinctiveness is medium to high; brand orientation and brand performance are high.

Internal branding: aligning the company's culture and its employees to act consistently with the brands they represent.

Minimalist: refers to a company with a low-key marketing emphasis across the board, low brand distinctiveness and orientation, as well as low brand performance.

Discussion questions

1 Compare and contrast how branding can be applied in the non-profit organizations as opposed to branding in an fmcg company.
2 In your opinion, why are brands seen as more important in some industries than others?
3 What are the main factors required for a company to consider branding?
4 Can you think of any cases in business where branding does not apply?
5 What are the main pillars of successful brand management in your opinion? Give examples to support your answer.
6 Compare and contrast how brands should be managed in a high-tech versus non-high-tech company? Based on the model(s) above, draw up your own models for these two cases.
7 Are there any similarities between branding in services and branding in business-to-business?
8 Give examples of companies that fall in each of the quadrants in the model of brand development in SMEs in Figure 4.1.
9 Give examples of companies that fall in each of the brand orientation stages in Figure 4.2.
10 What are the main differences between brand management in SMEs and in large companies?

Projects

1 Research the underlying causes of the failure of Dasani's launch in Europe (a bottled mineral water brand made by Coca-Cola) and suggest how Coca-Cola, the company, could have managed it better.
2 Can you identify the possible differences in brand orientation between family and non-family businesses, based on two case examples?
3 Compare and contrast your findings with a friend's.
4 Research and discuss how brand reputation risk can be measured, using a case company.
5 Discuss with a company executive of your choice the future of brands, where brands are going, how they should be managed and what to look out for, then write a summary report of approximately 1000 words on that subject.

MINI CASE 4.1: HOW CLOSELY IS THE CEO LINKED WITH THE COMPANY'S BRAND?

Research says that a CEO's reputation accounts for up to 50 per cent of the company's overall reputation. CEOs are part of a company's brand equity. Hans Snook carved out his name and brand with mobile phone company Orange. Richard Branson is the fun-loving, astute entrepreneur; Virgin is not scared to enter new markets to provide good service with a smile.

But does a company's brand flow from the personality of its leader, or does a CEO have to be shaped and moulded to fit the brand?

'The personality is one aspect of the CEO brand, but the brand is bigger', says Leslie Mayer, president and CEO of Mayer Leadership Group. 'You leverage strengths of personality in order to reach critical business success factors. The brand is the connection between the person and the business.'

'Leadership branding is important,' explains Karen Lam, president of Compass International. 'With the recent corporate crises people are becoming cynical about CEOs – there's a crisis of integrity. The CEO brand communicates what the company stands for to shareholders and customers and is a way to inspire employees to do the job they're meant to do.'

'The brand begins with the CEO's personality,' continues Lam. 'It starts with who they are, their style. Beyond that it's values, things they hold dear, why they turn up for work and so on. Finally, it's understanding what the market needs from them and how they can have a resonance with their market. It's about how they relate to customers, shareholders and employees.'

'It seems to me,' says Mayer, 'that the CEO brand is not an external face. It is the face of the culture of the organization. People see the CEO as the representative of the corporate brand on the outside and their own brand on the inside.'

Lam argues that the external and internal faces are inseparable. 'I don't see division between them. The brand straddles both. The CEO puts a face on the company and what it stands for, inside and out.'

Lam employs a similar storytelling approach when helping her clients to define their brands. She uses archetypes – the classic themes and stories found in art, literature, music and business. If CEOs can identify with one or two archetypes – explorer, warrior, sage, 'real guy', to name a few – they immediately see how to behave more consistently, thus making a greater impression.

But does any CEO walk into the office thinking, 'I am a warrior!' and then start acting like one? 'The danger is when you become a stereotype,' says Lam, recognizing the fine line between archetypes and stereotypes. 'As a brand you want to stand for something clear and consistent. As a human being you want a balance between consistency and diversity.'

Questions:

1 What is the main thrust of this debate?

2 Explain why the image of the CEO/owner is important to a company's image, especially when the company is small.

3 Are there any differences in how a CEO's image is managed compared with how a company's image is managed?

MINI CASE 4.2: INTEL: A CASE IN CORPORATE BRANDING

Intel is one of the most successful technology companies to have a balance of innovation and reliability. For example, after the launch of the Pentium chip, customers discovered some faults which were potentially devastating. Fortunately, with good crisis management, Intel regained its position of trust and high-quality performance in consumers' minds.

The company has shown how a power positioning approach can solve the problems of consumer technophobia, with its famous 'Intel Inside' campaign. Intel's position is based on authenticity, quality and performance, supported strongly by consistent global campaigns. The Intel Inside logo is placed on all print advertising, print and point-of-sale merchandising, shipping cartons and packaging, and is used by world brand and OEM computer manufacturers. Supported by explanatory communication material, it has to a large extent succeeded in allaying the fears of consumers who are doubtful of the performance of critical and complicated product they do not understand. However, the introduction of the Intel 'Bunny people' in astronaut-type attire in an attempt to humanize and add personality to the product has not been so successful, being perceived by many as cold and impersonal.

Intel has developed individual product brands, such as the Pentium and Pentium II range. The reason for this is that a name like Pentium (derived from the Greek word *penta* meaning five and alluding to the fifth generation of X86 computer chips) is a kind of shorthand, which better summarizes product benefits. Pentium II is positioned as a high-performance product aimed at corporate and end users. A 'no frills' product range called 'Celeron' has been introduced, endorsed by the parental name, but meant for a different audience; it is positioned around value, compatibility and quality. Despite this, Celeron's initial offering has not had a good start.

It remains to be seen whether Intel has really understood the needs of different market segments, and whether or not the cheaper product can hold true to the position and associations that Intel has so single-mindedly projected over the last few years. Also, if consumers will perceive the move as a riskier alternative, and even if it will devalue the position of the higher price existing products. In the worst scenario, the different products might cannibalize each other's sales, and generate customer confusion. Intel intends to introduce more branded chips, and careful education of the consumer in this highly complex market will be essential to negate customer confusion and achieve successful brand positioning.

Questions:

1 Discuss the threats to corporate branding of a high-technology product such as Intel.

2 Can you suggest a best possible brand architecture (or structure – see Chapter 6) for Intel?

END OF CHAPTER CASE STUDY: BRANDING NOT-FOR-PROFITS

Not-for-profit organizations are well placed to become powerful brands. People working in these organizations are driven by the conviction of their work and the importance of the views they express and generate. This passion is a fine basis on which to build a brand. More than a single message, logo or catchphrase, the brand is the platform on which the motivation behind the organization's work may be articulated, and the significance of its work may be appreciated.

Building institutional credibility through the brand is thus in the interest of the organization, especially with the marked downward trend in unrestricted gifts. If consistently managed, the brand is a useful symbol of historical credibility and future strategic direction, to coherent ends that are specific and compelling enough to inspire the confidence of funders.

Despite the multiple benefits of a strong institutional identity, of which effective development is but one, many not-for-profit organizations shy away from brand building. The goals of business are often regarded as antithetical to those of the not-for-profit sector. The lack of resources is another major reason cited. Most small and medium-sized organizations do not even have designated development professionals on staff; often one person will multi-task along a range of support activities including marketing, audience development, communications, development and education. Another perennial reason offered by not-for-profits is the difficulty in justifying to funders expenditure on building the brand.

These concerns are valid, though misdirected. A designated brand manager is not a prerequisite to effective brand building. Institutional identity should be the concern of every member of the organization, starting from the top. Board directors need to contribute their personal insight and influence toward building an intellectually and ethically sound organization. The executive director should ensure that all programmes and activities deliver on the organization's mission in form as well as in content. This coherence would also help him or her to better represent the organization to key constituents.

Successful brand management does not necessarily rely on the creation of new roles, but in the coordination of functions across the organization to meet strategic ends. The artistic director and development director need to view each other as partners in the growth of the organization, rather than as colleagues responsible for separate and distinct jobs. The lobbyist, analyst and outreach coordinator must stay cognizant of how the work of each supports the other. The researcher's cogent remarks at a conference, when accompanied by a paper acknowledging funder support, help the development director build relationships.

Investing in brand building should not be regarded as cosmetic. It lays the foundation for collaboration, it streamlines organizational goals, and it directs efforts towards institutional credibility and distinction.

Questions:

1 Summarize the reasons why not-for-profit organizations may not believe branding is for them.

2 How is branding different for not-for-profit organizations compared with traditional branding in fmcg companies?

3 What are the main factors mentioned in the case that would make not-for-profit organizations a candidate for branding?

4 What are the main pillars of branding in not-for-profit organizations?

5 What are the benefits of branding for not-for-profit organizations?

References

Aaker, D. (1996), *Building Strong Brands*, New York, NY: The Free Press.

Anonymous researchers (2006), 'Brand as strategic assets – moving up the corporate agenda?'.

Aon (2001), 'Reputation is the no. 1 risk – and is much bigger than many believe', Aon Limited, August.

Balmer, J. (1995), 'Corporate branding and connoisseurship', *Journal of General Management*, Vol. 21, No. 1, pp. 22–46.

Balmer, J. (1998), 'Corporate identity, corporate branding and corporate marketing: seeing through the fog', *European Journal of Marketing*, Vol. 35, No. 3/4, pp. 248–91.

Balmer, J. and Greyser, S. (2003), *Revealing the Corporation: Perspectives on Identity, Image, Reputation, Corporate Branding and Corporate-Level Marketing*, London: Routledge.

Blackett, T. (1993), 'Brand and trademark evaluation – what's happening now?', *Marketing Intelligence and Planning*, Vol. 11, No. 11, pp. 260–72.

Capon, N., Berthon, J. P., Hulbert, J. and Pitt, L. (2001), 'Brand custodianship: a new primer for senior managers', *European Management Journal*, Vol. 19, No. 3, pp. 215–27.

Davis, S. M. (2002), *Brand Asset Management: Driving Profitable Growth Through Your Brands*, USA: Jossey Bass.

De Chernatony, L. (1999), 'Brand management through narrowing the gap between brand identity and brand reputation', *Journal of Marketing Management*, Vol. 15, pp. 157–79.

De Chernatony, L. and Dall'Olmo R. F. (1999), 'Branding in the service sector', *Financial Times*, 'Mastering Management', The Reader, 4.

De Chernatony, L. and McDonald, M. (1998), *Creating Powerful Brands in Consumer Service and Industrial Markets*, Oxford: Butterworth-Heinemann.

De Chernatony, L. and Segal-Horn, S. L. (2003), 'The criteria for successful services brands', *European Journal of Marketing*, Vol. 37, No. 7/8.

Gilmore, A., Carson, D. and Grant, K. (2001), 'SME marketing in practice', *Marketing Intelligence and Planning*', Vol. 19, No. 1, pp. 6–11.

Gray, E. and Balmer, J. (2001), 'The corporate brand: a strategic asset', *Management in Practice*, Vol. 4, pp. 1–4.

Hankinson, P. and Hankinson, G. (1999), 'Managing successful brands: an empirical study which compares the corporate cultures of companies managing the world's top 100 brands with those managing outsider brands', *Journal of Marketing Management*, Vol. 15, No. 1/3, pp. 135–55.

Hatch, M. and Schultz, M. (1997), 'Are the strategic stars aligned for your corporate brand?', *Harvard Business Review*, February, pp. 128–34.

Ind, N. (1996), *The Corporate Brand*, London: Macmillan.

Krake, F. (2005), 'Successful brand management in SMFs: a new theory and practical hints', *Journal of Product & Brand Management*, Vol. 14, No. 4.

Laforet, S. and Saunders, J. A. (1999), 'Managing brand portfolios: why leaders do what they do', *Journal of Advertising Research*, Vol. 39, No. 1, January/February.

Laforet, S. and Saunders, J. (2005), 'Managing brand portfolios: how strategies have changed', *Journal of Advertising Research*, Vol. 45, No. 3, pp. 314–27.

Mosmans, A. and Van der Vorst, R. (1998), 'Brand-based strategic management', *Journal of Brand Management*, Vol. 6, No. 2, pp. 99–111.

Murray, S. (2003), 'Reputation risk: big PR to companies'aid', *Financial Times*, 20 September.

Papasolomou, I. and Vrontis, D. (2006), 'Building corporate branding through internal marketing: the case of the UK retail bank industry', *Journal of Product & Brand Management*, Vol. 15, No. 1.

Petrescu, R. (2007), 'Petrol derives revenues worth 1bn euros from foreign sales', at http://www.Zf.ro

Rubinstein, H. (1996), '"Brand first" management', *Journal of Marketing Management*, Vol. 12, No. 4, pp. 269–80.

Simoes, C. and Dibb, S. (2001), 'Rethinking the brand concept: new brand orientation', *Corporate Communications: An International Journal*, Vol. 6, No. 4, pp. 217–24.

Spence, M. (2003), 'International strategy formation in small Canadian high-technology companies – a case study approach', *Journal of International Entrepreneurship*, Vol. 1, No. 3, September, pp. 277–96.

Spence, M. (2006), 'SME branding and country of origin effects', *Academy of Marketing Conference*, London, 4–6 July.

Wong, H. Y. and Merrilees, B. (2005), 'A brand orientation typology for SMEs: a case research approach', *Journal of Product & Brand Management*, Vol. 14, No. 3.

Further reading and online sites

Balmer, J. M. T. (2008), 'Identity based views of the corporation: insights from corporate identity, organisational identity, social identity, visual identity, corporate brand identity and corporate image', *European Journal of Marketing*, Vol. 42, No. 9/10.

Bernstein, D. (2003), 'Corporate branding – back to basics', *European Journal of Marketing*, Vol. 37, No. 7/8.

De Chernatony, L. and Cottam, S. (2008), 'Interactions between organisational cultures and corporate brands', *Journal of Product & Brand Management*, Vol. 17, No. 1, pp. 13–24.

Graeme, M. and Hetrick, S. (2006), *Corporate Reputations, Branding and People Management*, Oxford: Butterworth-Heinemann.

He, H.-W. (2008), 'Corporate identity/strategy interface: implications for corporate level marketing', *European Journal of Marketing*, Vol. 42, No. 1/2.

Leitch, S. and Richardson, N. (2003), 'Corporate branding in the new economy', *European Journal of Marketing*, Vol. 37, No. 7/8.

Macrae, C. (1996), *The Brand Chartering Handbook*, Harlow: Addison-Wesley.

Roll, M. (2005), *Brand Strategy – How Asia Builds Strong Brands*, New York: Palgrave Macmillan.

Roll, M. (2006), 'New paradigm for the Asian boardroom – brand equity', *Journal of Business Strategy*, Vol. 27, No. 6.

Tarnovskaya, V., Elg, U. and Burt, S. (2008), 'The role of corporate branding in a market driving strategy', *International Journal of Retail & Distribution Management*, Vol. 36, No. 11.

Tsai, Shu-pel (2008), 'Corporate marketing management and corporate-identity building', *Marketing Intelligence & Planning*, Vol. 26, No. 6.

Wong, H. Y. and Merrilees, B. (2008), 'The performance benefits of being brand-orientated', *Journal of Product & Brand Management*, Vol. 17, No. 6.

Are brands on the corporate agenda?, at http://www.brandstrategy.co.uk/issues/2006/July/Are_brands_on_the_corporate agenda_/Browse.view

The business case for corporate ethics, at http://www.ethicalcorp.com

Branding and the New Asia: an interview with brand strategist Martin Roll, at http://www.emorymi.com/rolls.html

Branding – the strongest value driver for New Asia, at http://www.venturerepublic.com/resources/branding_the_strongest_value_driver.asp

The third way: corporate design, at http://www.computerarts.co.uk/in_depth/features/the_third_way_corporate_design

The increasing importance of branding, at http:www/brandfinance.com/uploads/pdfs/ayntka_brands_tax%20planning.pdf

PART 2

Managing Brands – Creating and Sustaining Brand Equity

Brand Identity and Positioning

Chapter contents

Chapter overview

This chapter starts with an explanation of the four brand components: brand identity, brand image, brand position and brand equity. Each of these is then examined in turn. The make-up of brand identity, its system and facets, including brand personality, are discussed. Next, the concept of brand image and its dimensions are examined. The chapter also sets out the details of how a brand image can be built and managed over time through the concept of strategic brand-image management. Next, the chapter turns to brand positioning definition and its role in the marketing mix. It discusses the brand positioning process, positioning decisions and criteria for successful positioning, as well as brand positioning strategies and perceptual mapping techniques. The issues of consistencies between brand identity and brand image are also highlighted and discussed via the systematic process of brand integrated communication. Finally, brand equity building is examined through the traditional brand-building model and the contemporary model of building brands in competitive markets. This chapter is the first in Part 2 of the book, focusing on the theme of creating and sustaining brand equity. Chapter 6 will cover the concept of brand architecture or brand structure, and the management of brand portfolios.

❖ *LEARNING OBJECTIVES*

After completing this chapter, you should be able to

❖ Understand the branding components, the make-up of brand identity, its system and facets

❖ Examine the concept of brand personality and brand image

❖ Discuss how brand managers can ensure consistency of brand identity and brand image

❖ Understand how a brand image is built

❖ Evaluate the different means of building a brand image

❖ Discuss how brand image can be managed over time, based on the concept of strategic brand image management

❖ Understand the role of brand positioning in the marketing mix

❖ Study the process of brand positioning and positioning decisions

❖ Examine the criteria for successful positioning

❖ Discuss and apply the different positioning strategies to brand positioning

❖ Utilize a perceptual map to study brand position in the marketplace

❖ Explain how brand message is communicated and the impact of market feedback on brand image

❖ Study the concept of IBC and its process

❖ Discuss the factors contributing to successful brand building and those impeding it

❖ Discuss the composition of Aaker's brand building model and the PCDL model

Introduction

Part of brand management is to manage the activities of branding, which include developing a brand identity, brand image, brand personality and brand positioning then selecting appropriate communication programmes to communicate these, and managing customer feedback through brand tracking. Developing a brand identity is also core to brand equity building (see Chapter 2), through the establishment of a clear and consistent brand identity that resonates with customers, differentiates the brand from competitors, and represents what the organization can, and will, do over time, at the same time linking brand attributes with the way they are communicated so that they can be easily understood by the customers. Part of brand equity creation consists of brand positioning. Brand positioning has a number of benefits including helping in purchase selection and reducing customers' search time for a product. It also helps differentiate a company's value claim from that of its competitors. Brand positioning aims at developing brand messages in such a way that customers will perceive the brand in the way the marketer desires in relation to competitors, so that it will enjoy a fair amount of sustainable competitive advantage in the market.

There are two issues in brand positioning: the customer's perception of the brand in relation to the competitor's position; and the dimensions of brands as perceived by customers. Brand managers and advertising professionals spend a huge amount of resources and effort on maintaining and managing the position of a brand in the customer's mindset. Brand positioning must accord with the customer's perceptions and not go against them. What people inside the company perceive as 'improvements' often only cause confusion in the minds of prospective buyers. Thus, brand positioning and brand identity are the very tools of brand creation and are central to branding. In this chapter we will examine: the brand identity system, the dimensions of brand image, principles of image formation, brand image building, strategic brand image concept management, the role of brand positioning in the marketing mix, brand positioning as a 'process', brand positioning strategies, perceptual mapping, brand identity and brand image, the integrated brand communications process and brand message communication, as well as Aaker's model of building a strong brand and the PCDL model.

The four components of branding

Apart from being a 'name, symbol, design or mark that enhances the value of a product beyond its functional purposes' (see Chapter 1), a brand is a complex entity in the mind of the consumer. As stated above, there are four key components to the brand concept: brand identity, brand image, brand positioning and brand equity.

Brand identity is the unique set of functional and mental associations the brand aspires to create or maintain. These associations represent what the brand should ideally stand for in the minds of customers, and imply a potential promise to customers. It is important to keep in mind that the brand identity refers to the strategic goal for a brand, and is aspirational from the brand owner's point of view; while *brand image* is what currently resides in the minds of consumers.

Brand positioning is the process by which companies try to create an image or identity in the minds of their target market for their brand. It is also the 'relative competitive comparison' the companies' brand occupies in a given market, as perceived by the target market. Advertising helps to communicate and convey what the brand stands for to the target audience. Brand positioning helps in communicating the brand message, and sets forth the communication objectives such as the types of message and theme that appeal to the target market. Companies that present a cohesive, distinctive and relevant brand identity can create a preference in the marketplace, add value to their products and services, and command a price premium which leads to the creation of brand equity, which in turn is an asset to the firm (see Chapter 2). In the following sections we shall look at brand identity, brand image and brand positioning in more detail. *Brand equity* has already been discussed in Chapter 2.

Brand identity

Apart from the above brief definition of brand identity, Aaker (2002) also defined it as: 'a unique set of brand associations that the brand strategist aspires to create or maintain'. An image was how brands were perceived and an identity was how brands aspired to be perceived. Brand identity is the key component of branding. According to Aaker, central to successful brand building is the understanding of how to develop a brand identity.

Brand identity system

Aaker has suggested developing brand identity as being of great importance for branding strategy. The brand identity system consists of twelve dimensions organized around four perspectives:

1 The brand as product, such as product scope, product attributes, quality/value, uses, users, country of origin.

2 The brand as organization, such as organizational attributes, local versus global.

3 The brand as person, such as brand personality, brand-customer relationship.

4 The brand as symbol, such as visual imagery/metaphors and brand heritage.

To achieve maximum brand strength, the scope of brand identity should be broad rather than narrow, the thrust should be strategic rather than tactical, and there should be an internal as well as external focus to brand creation. Broad brand-identity perspectives help the strategist consider different brand elements and patterns that could help clarify, enrich and differentiate an identity.

Brand identity provides a value proposal to the customer, which may constitute functional, emotional and self-expressive benefits. Brand identity can be implemented through brand-identity elaboration, brand positioning, brand-building programmes and brand tracking. Brand-identity elaboration is a set of tools designed to add richness, texture and clarity to the brand identity. With a clear and elaborated identity, the implementation task turns to brand positioning – the part of the brand identity and value proposition that is to be actively communicated to the target audience, as discussed below. With the brand position and brand identity in place, a brand-building programme could then be developed.

Brand identity elements

Brand identity comprises the following elements.

■ *Name*: the name of an organization and/or product offering. Depending on the brand strategy and architecture, names could be descriptive (of functions or places), eponymous (named for some person), suggestive (recognizable and relevant), arbitrary (a known word taken out of its normal context) or fanciful (unique fabrications).

■ *Logo*: a company's or product's logo can be thought of as its 'flag' – distinctive, memorable, and signalling value and allegiance in the brand it represents. Types of logos include logo marks (graphic symbols), logotypes (symbol and name combined in a specific arrangement) and word marks (consisting primarily of type, focused on typographic style and emphasizing the name rather than graphic symbolism).

■ *Tagline*: often referred to as a 'slogan', the tagline is a short verbal phrase that can serve a number of purposes such as providing descriptive information to define the company's business or the product's function. It can define the kinds of customers the company or product serves, or the benefit it provides. It can inject 'attitude' to express a distinctive personality and approach to the world. The tagline typically has a predefined spatial relationship to the logo.

■ *Design system*: the organized system that creates companies and their brands recognizable and repeatable 'visual identity'. This includes a distinctive colour palette, typography (or typefaces), secondary graphics (these are characteristic graphic objects that pull together layouts and also specific styles of illustrations and/or photos) and structural grids, which determine the distinctive arrangement of elements in different design applications.

Brand identity facets

According to Kapferer (2004), brand identity has six facets. The first is the *brand physique*. This includes tangibles like the appearance of the brand, such as the shape of the Coke bottle, the purple packaging of Cadbury, the trademark of Mercedes-Benz.

Next there is the *brand personality*. Based on the premise that brands can have personalities in much the same way as humans, brand personality describes brands in terms of human characteristics. Brand personality is seen as a valuable factor in increasing brand engagement and brand attachment, in much the same way as people relate and bind to other people. Much of the work in the area of brand personality is based on translated theories of human personality, and uses similar measures of personality attributes and factors. Alt and Griggs (1988), for instance, looked at how to measure brand personality, using a psychometric and a factorial model. They examined the 'salient' human, personality characteristics that discriminate between brands, which go together to make up a brand's personality, and measured these characteristics consistently and reliably across a range of brands. These researchers also believed that they could develop a brand personality inventory analogous to a human personality test. Apple is probably one of the companies best-known for having a clearly defined personality. There is a certain techno-geek charm, an underdog mentality, but also a sense of fun, high quality and a bit of cheekiness. There are five facets of brand personality:

1 Sincerity (down to earth, honest, wholesome and cheerful).
2 Excitement (daring, spirited, imaginative and up to date).
3 Competence (reliable, intelligent and successful).
4 Sophistication (upper-class, charming).
5 Ruggedness (outdoorsy, tough).

The third facet of brand identity is *brand culture*. It is the part of the brand from which it draws inspiration. For example, German engineering is used for Mercedes, Californian innovation for Apple and capitalism for American Express.

The fourth facet is the *brand relationship*. This refers to the brand's ability to connect with people so that it can sometimes be seen as a lover or confidante. Compare Apple's personality with that of IBM, which has a much more 'strictly business' personality. IBM's marketing evokes a sense of efficiency and getting a job done. It connects with different people in a different way, but both IBM and Apple are playing to their core audience.

Brand reflection is the fifth of the brand identity facets. This is about who is perceived to use the brand. For example, Nike is seen to be used not only by sporty but also trendy youngsters.

The last of the brand identity facets is the *self-image*. The brand speaks to the consumer self-image. Consumers often buy brands to reflect their own image and identity. Going back to the examples of Apple and IBM, in both cases Apple and IBM have clearly defined who they are and given their customers something to identify with. That connection results in a stronger customer–client relationship, and not only more sales for the company, but a happier customer as well.

To be effective, a brand identity needs to resonate with customers, differentiate the brand from competitors, and represent what the organization can and will do over time. When a brand faces aggressive competition in the marketplace, the brand personality and its reputation help it distinguish itself from competing offerings. This can result in customer loyalty and achieve growth. A strong brand identity that is well understood and experienced by the customers helps in developing trust which, in turn, results in differentiating the brand from the competition. A company needs to establish a clear and consistent brand identity by linking brand attributes with the way they are communicated, which can be easily understood by the customers. Research shows, however, as brands become more homogeneous, consumers are making brand choices more on the basis of brand personality than identity (Heylen et al., 1995).

Corporate identity

The notion of corporate identity is linked to the corporate brand concept; in fact, the two terms are used interchangeably in the literature. The concept of identity as explained above embraces the characteristics that distinguish one person or object from another. Applying this abstract idea to corporations suggests that each organization has its own personality, uniqueness and individuality (Bernstein, 1984; Gray and Balmer, 1998). The concept of corporate identity is holistic in that 'it articulates the corporate ethos, aims and values and presents a sense of individuality that can help to differentiate the organisation within its competitive environment' (Riel and Balmer, 1997, p. 355). For example, McDonald's uses three main values – consistency, cleanliness and cheerfulness – to establish its mission of being 'number one in the fast food industry'. A strong identity is very important for transmitting a consistent internal and external image among stakeholders (see the works of Hatch and Schultz, 1997; Gray and Balmer, 1998; Simões and Reis, 2000) turning into a valuable asset (Anson, 2000).

Branding Brief 5.1: Bran identity – a cereal ad that simulates human excretion

The spot

A construction worker in a hard hat and orange vest stomps through a busy site with a box of All-Bran cereal, enumerating the problems he has 'staying regular'. As he extols the benefits of the All-Bran ten-day challenge (that's eating the cereal 'once a day, for ten days'), a variety of visual metaphors play out behind him: a steel I-beam is pulled out from a gap in a wall; some strategically placed barrels roll off a flatbed parked directly behind our narrator's derrière; a dump truck pulls up and unloads a ton of bricks. The spot ends with an image of brown bran shards, as an announcer says: 'The All-Bran Challenge. Do it. Feel it.'

The visual puns in this ad are bold and disgusting. Advertisers have long tended to avoid direct references to the scatological when promoting products for gastrointestinal tracts. For example, toilet paper is squeezed or rubbed on faces to demonstrate its softness; adult nappy ads show pensioners engaging in tennis matches; and elaborate digital renderings of pulsating stomach linings evoke the effectiveness of digestive medicines. Today, companies go beyond euphemism, as in recent ads: consider the rise of brand icons like the Charmin bears (who ably answer the old question about what bears do in the woods) and the Kandoo frog, a character created by Pampers to promote its brand of flushable wipes. These characters are very frank and forthcoming about wiping their behinds, but even these ads stop short of actually simulating human excretion.

Brand image

Brand image is defined as 'consumer perceptions of a brand' and is measured as 'the brand associations held in consumers' memory'. A brand is less likely to have one brand image than several, though one or two may predominate. The key in brand image research is to identify or develop the most powerful images and reinforce them through subsequent brand communications. The term 'brand image' gained popularity as evidence began to grow that the feelings and images associated with a brand were powerful purchase influencers, through brand recognition, recall and brand identity. It is based on the proposition that consumers buy not only a product (commodity), but also the image associations of the product, such as power, wealth, sophistication and, most important, identification and association with other users of the brand. In a consumer-led world, people tend to define themselves and their Jungian 'persona' by their possessions.

According to Sigmund Freud, the *ego* and *superego* control to a large extent the image and personality that people would like others to have of them. Good brand images are instantly evoked, are positive and are almost always unique among competitive brands. They are usually evoked by asking consumers the first words/images that come to their mind when a certain brand is mentioned (called 'top of mind'). When responses are highly variable, non-forthcoming or refer to non-image attributes such as cost, it is an indicator of a weak brand image. Brand image can be reinforced by brand communications such as packaging, advertising, promotion, customer service, word-of-mouth and other aspects of the brand experience.

To measure brand image one can either use and adapt an existing list of brand associations (e.g. Aaker's brand personality list) or start from scratch, by eliciting brand associations measuring the strength of these associations. The outcome of this is a shortlist of the positive and negative associations consumers have with the brand, ranked by strength. It is useful to report the average strength of each association with the brand and the strength of the association with competing brands, and to do this for each target segment, e.g. brand users and users of competing brands. To be effective, a brand image must be well planned, nurtured, supported and vigilantly guarded (Knapp, 2000).

The dimensions of brand image

Brand image is known to have two dimensions: functional and symbolic. Swartz (1983) suggested that, as consumers strive to project an appropriate image through the various products they own and use, marketers would seek understanding of symbolic consumer behaviour. In symbolic consumer behaviour, interest lies in investing the role of products as 'messages' or non-verbal communication permitted by the user/owner. Attention then needs to be paid to differentiating the message.

Swartz's study used a 2x4 factorial design to test the hypothesis that different brands elicit different interpretations by the persons exposed to them. Her study showed that individuals have different interpretations for different brands of the same product. She concluded that the extent of functional differences between brands of the same product is minimal: 'message differentiation' was presented as a viable product-differentiation strategy; message differentiation involves distinguishing one brand from another on the basis of message communicated by the use/ownership of the brand. Such a strategy centres round the effective use of advertising to assist the target market in making the desired interpretations of the brand, and the management of the elements of the marketing mix to ensure that consistent messages about the brand are being communicated. Regarding the dimensions of corporate image, Spector (1961) suggested the most common attributes associated with a corporation's image are: dynamic, cooperative, businesswise, character, successful and withdrawn.

Principles of image formation

According to Nelson's (1962) seven principles of image formation, people are not exclusively rational creatures. They respond to situations in ways that appear to them to protect their self-images. One needs to determine the various images and reference points or anchorages that already exist in the minds of a particular group or society. If an image appears stable, and if reference groups surrounding the individual continue to support the image, both internal and external forces opposing the image will be resisted. If an image is marked by doubt, uncertainty or insecurity, one can utilize additional means for creating further doubts, or present the new image in a form which will dispel anxiety or doubts. Place the desired image in the most favourable setting. If at all possible, clothe the new image in the already accepted values which people hold. Finally, to stimulate development of a new image, one must attract the attention of large numbers of potential consumers.

Brand image building

Image building represents what potential buyers register and retain about the company or its branded products/services, from all sources of communication. These 'brand promise' communications form the first impressions received by potential buyers and can also reinforce the perceptions of current buyers.

A brand image can be built via integrated marketing communications (IMC), also known as 'total communication'. These include advertising, sales promotions, sponsorship activities, the Internet, and direct mail such as letters, brochures, catalogues or videos. Brand image is also built through consumers' direct contact, information received about a brand, in stores at the point of sale; through articles or stories they read in the media; or through interactions with a salesperson. The challenge is to understand how to use the various IMC tools to make such contacts, and deliver the brand message effectively and efficiently.

Advertising can be used to create brand images and symbolic appeals, which is a very important capability for companies selling products and services that are difficult to differentiate merely on their functional attributes. For example, since 1980 Absolut has used creative advertising to position its vodka as an upscale, fashionable, sophisticated drink, and differentiate it from other brands. Its advertising strategy has been to focus attention on two unique aspects of the product: the Absolut name and the distinctive shape of the bottle.

Public relations (PR) helps to build a stronger brand image, through getting the public to understand a company and its products. It allows the company to tell its story in a thorough and authentic way. It also helps the company achieve 'transparency', which is what customers demand in today's economy. Working to generate positive media coverage is a big part of PR. Stories in the media are like third-party testimonials, and people are more likely to believe what they read in a news story than in an advertisement.

Regarding design and packaging, the role of design is to develop visual communications that can enhance the company, and its brand image and identity; while the role of packaging is to develop and reinforce the core brand attributes, as per the long-term brand strategy of the company and the heritage the brand enjoys with its customer. Packaging can be updated to keep the overall brand image potent with existing customers, while attracting a new generation of consumers. However, extensive research must be done before packaging is developed to reveal the brand's chief assets. While some assets are overt, others might be dormant or remain undiscovered. Packaging can thus directly communicate brand values and create an emotional connection with the consumer. It can also strengthen brand identity and brand image, and give clear, concise and consistent communication hierarchies that effectively communicate with the customer.

In fmcg, distribution also helps in building the brand image. It is obvious that a very strong brand like Coca-Cola will need an excellent distribution network to reach its customers. This is the problem it faced in India a few years ago, where the marketing was able to generate demand but the distribution network was not strong enough to meet it, resulting in devaluation of Coca-Cola's brand equity in India to some degree.

Distribution can be an attractive alternative route to connect to customers who face myriad choices and crowded shop shelves. Customers today are demanding and view shopping as entertainment rather than a chore. Many companies are reinventing their distribution models to reach out to more likely customers using direct customer contact and point of purchase. There is a need to shift emphasis from mere reach or availability to reaching consumers with a three-way convergence based on product availability, brand communication and higher levels of brand experience. An example would be, say, a cosmetics company like Revlon opening up salons in Asian markets, and Revlon beauty advisers providing information and advice to shoppers with in-store promotions and sampling.

In self-service stores like supermarkets customers are also able to physically handle the brands before buying them, and this offers scope for impulse purchases, which was not the case until a few years ago in Asian markets for instance, where most of the stores were small family concerns. Live demonstrations of the benefits of brands can be undertaken at supermarkets and this can further strengthen brand image.

Culture is also the basis of brand image building. The brand perception is an important factor in taking any decision regarding brand image building for any type of product category. The perceived personality of a brand can be shaped by marketers via 'transferring cultural meaning' into it in various ways, such as by associating the brand in communications with an endorser or place that already possesses the personality or meaning considered strategically desirable for that brand.

Strategic brand image concept management

Park et al. (1986) presented a normative framework, termed 'brand concept management (BCM)', for selecting, implementing and controlling brand image over time (Figure 5.1). Their framework consists of a sequential process of selecting, introducing, elaborating and fortifying a brand concept. This concept can guide positioning strategies and, hence, the brand image at each stage. The method for maintaining this brand image linkage concept depends on whether the brand is functional, symbolic or experiential. Maintaining the linkage would enhance the brand's market performance.

Branding Brief 5.2: Temporal tips on corporate identity, brand identity and brand image

Source: Adapted from BrandingAsia.com; http://www.temporalbrand.com/

It is important to distinguish between corporate identity, brand identity and brand image. Corporate identity is concerned with the visual aspects of a company's presence. When companies undertake corporate identity exercises, they are usually modernizing their visual image in terms of logo, design and collaterals. Such efforts do not normally entail a change in brand values so that the heart of the brand remains the same. Unfortunately, many companies are sometimes led to believe by agencies and consultancy companies that the visual changes will change the brand image. But changes to logos, signage and even outlet design do not always change consumer perceptions of quality, service and the intangible associations with the brand.

Such changes can also reassure consumers that the company is concerned about how it looks. Brands do have to maintain a modern look. But the key to successfully effecting a new look is evolution, not revolution. Totally changing the brand visuals can give rise to consumer concerns about changes of ownership, or possible changes in brand values, or even unjustified extravagance. If there is a strong brand personality to which consumers are attracted, then substantial changes may destroy emotional attachments to the brand. People do not expect or like wild swings in the personality behaviour of other people, and they are just as concerned when the brands to which they have grown used exhibit similar 'schizophrenic' changes.

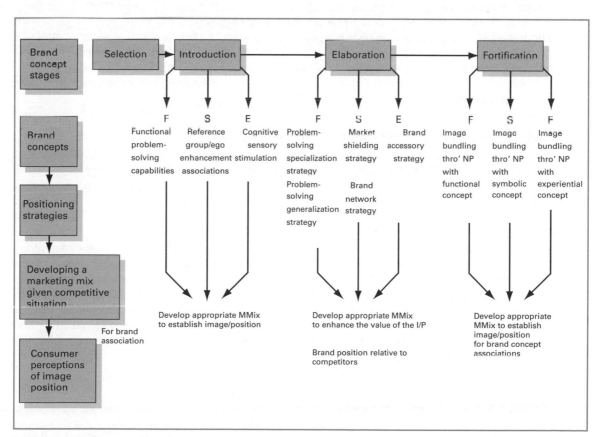

FIGURE 5.1 Brand concept management

If the intention is to substantially improve the standing of the brand, then corporate identity changes can be accompanied by widespread changes to organizational culture, quality and service standards. If done well, and if consumers experience something new and improved, then the changes will have a corresponding positive effect on brand image.

Brand identity is the promise that a company makes to consumers. It may consist of features and attributes, benefits, performance, quality, service support and the values that the brand possesses. The brand can be viewed as a product, a personality, a set of values and a position it occupies in people's minds. Brand identity is everything the company wants the brand to be seen as.

Brand image, on the other hand, is the totality of consumer perceptions about the brand, which may not coincide with the brand identity. Companies have to work hard on the consumer experience to make sure that what customers see and think is what the companies want them to.

Brand positioning

Brand positioning is the 'market space' a brand is perceived to occupy in the mind of the target audience. The term 'positioning' was coined in 1969 by Jack Trout in the paper 'Positioning is a game people play in today's me-too market place', which was published in the journal *Industrial Marketing*. It was then expanded into his ground-breaking first book (with Ries), *Positioning: The Battle for Your Mind* (Ries and Trout, 1986). It is the aggregate perception the market has of a particular company, product or service in relation to its perceptions of the competitors in the same category. It will happen whether or not a company's management is proactive, reactive or passive about the ongoing process of evolving a position. However, a company can positively influence the perceptions through enlightened strategic actions. All strong marketing communications programmes need to focus on only a few messages to achieve better impact in an increasingly noisy environment. The brand positioning is the part of the brand identity that companies decide to actively communicate to the market.

The role of brand positioning in the marketing mix

Segmenting, targeting, positioning (STP) are seen in Kotlerian marketing theories as sequential processes, each adding to the next, and culminating in the positioning of the brand. Segmenting is about breaking up a mass market along meaningful dimensions into relevant and actionable groups. Targeting concerns itself with choosing a group that is reachable, and has the required volumes and/or strategic importance. Positioning is about attaching a permanent meaning and relevance to the product in the mind of the consumer. It tells the consumer what role the brand plays in his or her life. It convinces the consumer to choose the company's brand over competitors' brands. Brand positioning is, therefore, the value delivery mechanism of the brand. It determines what kind of value the brand will deliver and how. Different positioning for a brand means that the value to the customer is different. When a brand is repositioned, it is clearly trying to redefine its value to the consumer. There are two distinct processes involved in the oft-misunderstood concept of positioning. The first is identifying the position, which involves exploring, understanding and mapping the consumer's mind and selecting the space to occupy. The second is achieving the chosen position, by engineering the elements of the marketing mix. Better value can be delivered to the consumer by improving both of these processes.

Brand positioning as a 'process'

According to Keller, positioning is a process of identifying and establishing points of parity and difference, to establish the right brand identity and to create a proper brand image. Positioning can be a process through which it can lead to a specific brand image and personality in the minds of the target audience. Kotler defines brand positioning as an act of designing the company's offer and image so that it occupies a distinct and valuable place in the minds of the target market. Brand positioning is, thus, a process through which the brand manager identifies the desired position in the customer's mind, and develops strategies to reach and strengthen the brand at that position in relation to competitors.

Positioning decisions

The brand manager must make the following decisions about brand positioning: first, he must decide what the space is going to look like and what the most important dimensions in the category are; second, what the other products in that space are and where are they; finally, what are the gaps or unfilled positions in the category, which dimensions are most important, and how these attitudes differ by market segment, as well as what position he wants the brand to have.

Criteria for successful positioning

Ideally the objective of brand positioning is to make people feel that there is no substitute for the brand. Successful positioning is based on physical product differences and good marketing communications. There are six criteria for successful brand positioning:

1 *Relevance*: means a brand having a clear vision and a concise meaning. Examples are Disney, Microsoft and Ralph Lauren. Disney's success is measured by no less than 610 per cent growth in the last decade, according to its most recent annual report. Walt Disney was a visionary. His vision for the Disney Company was not to crank out cartoons or build theme parks, but 'to make people happy'. Virtually everyone in the developed nations of the world is crystal clear about what the Disney brand stands for – imagination, wholesomeness, fun. Microsoft products are for ordinary computer users, not techno-geeks. The Microsoft brand enables people to leverage the power of computing to work better, have fun and fulfil their aspirations. Its advertising asks users, 'Where do you want to go today?' The company is a giant, but a friendly one, one that puts a high priority on being simple, contemporary, approachable, hip and even low-tech, albeit that attribute may seem counterintuitive in the context of a technology business. Finally, with regard to Ralph Lauren, the brand and the man's clothing is positioned as the choice 'for people who care more about looking good than being fashionable'.

2 *Distinctiveness*: as mentioned above, Disney, Microsoft and Ralph Lauren are all distinctive brands, which are positioned to fulfil a particular need and/or in a specific way, that differentiate them from their competitors. If a brand lacks distinctiveness, it will be forced to compete on price or promotion.

3 *Coherence*: there is a need to have a coherent positioning, which is reflected in coherent communications. For example, a brand is positioned as a premium brand, but is unavailable in exclusive or high-image stores. As a result, the brand image is diluted. Take Snapple, a strong brand brought down by fuzzy thinking. A few years ago, Snapple was earning $516 million a year. In 2008, it lost $100 million. In its glory days the brand was touted as 'the best stuff on earth', and the sales figures showed that people bought into that. Then Quaker bought the company and disaster ensued. Among other things, Quaker systematically dismantled the brand's quirky, off-centre image. It fired Wendy, 'the Snapple lady', gutting a campaign that had helped build the brand and boost market share. Then, it stopped advertising on the Rush Limbaugh and Howard Stern radio shows in favour of a more mainstream media approach. Finally, it approved a new ad campaign with the slogans, 'We Want to Be No. 3' (i.e. behind Coke and Pepsi) and 'Threedom=Freedom'. No one seemed to know exactly what the Snapple brand stood for any more. Quaker finally called it quits and sold the floundering beverage brand to Triarc for $300 million – $1.4 billion less than it had paid for it.

4 *Commitment*: companies need to stay committed to the positioning of their brand in the market, in the face of competitors' threats and appeal to a specific market segment. Too often

brands appear to break loose from their original vision. In search of short-term profits, they try to appeal to more than one market segment (brand stretching or extension – see Chapter 7), and lose track of what they are about and what they stand for. Nevertheless, the experiences of Virgin, Disney, Nike and Ralph Lauren underscore the point that companies can success-fully operate in multiple markets, provided they do not lose sight of what the brand means and what its parameters of relevance are, and stay committed to the original brand positioning in the markets they serve; in other words, stay true to their *brand essence* (see Key terms). Thus, Richard Branson made his entry into the business world through the record business, but his foray into significant brand recognition came from Virgin Airlines. The company then rapidly expanded into a sort of crazy quilt of unrelated businesses: megastores, clothing, soft drinks, insurance, mutual funds, cosmetics, bridal services.

5 *Durability*: the positioning of the brand is built in the consumer's mind over a period of time. When brands are launched, they do not succeed overnight, but take time to achieve a domi-nant position in the market.

6 *Clarity*: the positioning of the brand should be clear so that it can be easily communicated and quickly comprehended. Clarity in brand communication should facilitate information processing and consumer comprehension, and help in building a strong brand position in the market.

Brand positioning strategies

Although successful brand positioning depends on how effectively the brand is being communi-cated, other elements of the marketing mix such as pricing, packaging, labelling, distribution and product features play a vital role in brand positioning success. There are many ways in which a brand can be positioned. These are discussed below.

A brand can be positioned according to its unique attributes or unique selling proposition (USP), which is the simplest form of brand positioning. Alternatively, it can be positioned according to product features, such as colour, size, shape, or taste and smell, which are also known as 'pseudo-physical' characteristics, and customer benefits, which are advantages that promote the well-being of the user. Brands can also be positioned on the basis of corporate brand name, which represents quality and value, or brand endorsement. This strategy is used in the case of line and product extensions.

Of course, brands can be positioned in terms of usage, occasion and time. For example, many fmcg are positioned in this way. Thus, some foods, household and personal care products (to mention just a few) are positioned in terms of usage, occasion and time. Another typical fmcg brand positioning is by price–value. In developing countries, if the brand is positioned as high value at a low price, it has the highest likelihood of success in these markets. Price–quality positioning has its problems as well as opportunities. Companies are constantly under pressure to upgrade the quality by lowering the price. It is also difficult to upgrade the brand in the 'ladder' when it is positioned as 'good value for money', as it may always be associated with its original image and product-class category. Other ways in which a brand can be positioned are by single use or application, or by multiple uses, or on the basis of market segmentation.

In positioning by segmentation, brands can be positioned according to different criteria such as demographic, which is concerned with age, gender, income, education, social class, race, life cycle/stages, religion, race, etc. For example, cosmetics, beauty treatments and clothes typically target teenagers, young adults and more mature customers differently; while cigarettes, perfumes and cars are often positioned on a gender basis. Brands can also be positioned by implicitly or explicitly referring to competitors. Implicitly referring to competitors is done through the use of metaphors, packaging references or catch-line references. This positioning strategy can be applied only if the competitor is well known, and the identification with those associations must be strong enough to achieve instant customer recognition. Explicitly referring to competitors can be done through comparative advertising. For example, Tesco directly compares its prices with those of its competitor Asda and other low cost–value supermarkets in its advertising.

Finally, brands can be positioned in terms of non-functional or abstract value, based on sensory system, social value, self-esteem, conditional and epistemic values, as well as through the use of cultural symbols and brand personality. For example, advertising for Lynx body spray is based on masculine sensory appeal to young females. Products like fashion, beauty products and personal care products such as shaving cream are positioned on the bases of social value, self-esteem, and conditional (as in situational and epistemic) value, i.e. creating a novelty among current users of competing brands.

Branding Brief 5.3: Beware – tinkering marketers

Source: Branding Strategy Insider.com

Not too long ago reports had Peter Brabeck, the departing CEO of Nestlé, putting the company on a diet.

He discovered that the food maker was churning out 130 000 variations of its brands – and 30 per cent weren't making any money. He has launched an aggressive plan to jettison weaker brands and simplify the organization. It's bye-bye to low-carb Kit-Kats and lemon cheesecake-flavoured chocolate (can you imagine?).

Nestlé faces a predicament that haunts many companies that have acquired other companies, to a point that its subsidiaries are almost impossible to manage. When you're into dog food, chocolate, baby food, ice cream, coffee and on and on, you can easily see the problem.

But what's even worse is that these mega-companies end up with hundreds of marketing people sitting around cooking up new ideas that aren't very good ideas. Or they sit around and try to figure out how to improve things. They just can't stop tinkering. What top management fails to understand is that the road to chaos is paved with improvements.

In all my years in the business, I've never seen a marketing person come into a new assignment, look around, and say, 'Things look pretty good. Let's not touch a thing.'

On the contrary, all red-blooded marketing people want to get in there and start improving things. They want to make their mark. Just sitting there wouldn't feel right.

When a company has offices full of marketing people, you've got to expect endless tinkering with a brand. It's how they keep from getting bored.

Someone on the Prell shampoo brand said, 'Hey, why don't we add a blue Prell to our line of green Prell?' Of course, this ignores the consumer perception that if it isn't green, it can't be Prell.

Bad idea.

At McDonald's someone said, 'Hey, let's take advantage of the pizza trend and add McPizza to the menu!' Of course, this ignores the consumer perception that hamburger joints can't know much about making pizza.

Bad idea.

Someone at Anheuser-Busch said, 'Hey, why don't we add dry and ice beers to our line-up?' Of course, this ignores the consumer perception that beer is usually wet and not served over ice.

Bad ideas.

Someone at Volkswagen said, 'Let's introduce a $60 000 automobile called the Phaeton.' Of course, this ignores the fact that in America, a Volkswagen has no prestige as a brand.

Bad idea.

At Bic, the marketing people, because Mr Bic is still around, are busy putting the brand on everything they can think of – such as pens, lighters, razor blades, panty-hose, perfume and even sailboards.

Bad ideas.

Someone at Heinz, the king of ketchup, figured out that it should also be in mustard. And, to save money, let's use the same-shape bottles. People thought it was yellow ketchup.

▶

Bad idea.

Someone at Daimler-Benz figured out that luxury cars aren't enough. Buying Chrysler would give them a wide range of vehicles to sell everywhere.

Very bad idea.

And of course, you can't leave out the endless and painfully expensive tinkering with logos.

Xerox, one of the great logo designs of all time, decided to change its logo and have the big letter 'X' break up in pieces to signify going digital. This was unfortunate, for at about the same time, the company ran into serious financial problems. All the new logo said to people was that Xerox was disintegrating. Luckily, a new CEO and smarter heads prevailed, and Xerox went back to the original logo.

Positioning has to line up with the perceptions in the mind, not go against them. What people inside the company perceive as 'improvements' often only cause confusion inside the mind of the prospect.

In positioning, once you've gotten a brand up to altitude, your watchword should be 'steady as she goes'. A brand can only stand for one thing in the mind; the more things you try to make it stand for, the more the mind loses focus on what you are. Endless variations give marketing people something to do while they do long-term damage to a brand or a company.

Perceptual mapping

Perceptual mapping is a technique that determines a brand's position in relation to competitors on various dimensions. Brands can be positioned against competing brands on a perceptual map. A simple perceptual map shows the positioning of brands on two dimensions on the basis of price and quality (see Figure 5.2 below). It represents consumer perceptions in two-dimensional space, and enables the brand manager to find out the relative positioning of his brand compared with competitors.

Other perceptual maps are based on a variety of dimensions, and/or focus on multiple features of the brands. They help in identifying the underlying dimensions that differentiate consumer perceptions of one brand positioning, compared with another, often that of competitors. Multi-dimensional scaling is a method used to develop perceptual maps. Other techniques used for building perceptual maps include hierarchical clustering, multi-discriminant analysis, profile mapping and conjoint analysis. Figure 5.3 is an example of a perceptual map of car brands based on multiple features and price.

FIGURE 5.2 Two-dimensional perceptual map

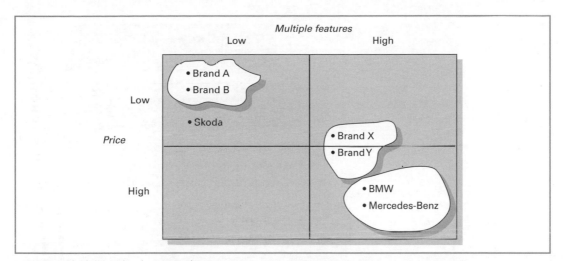

FIGURE 5.3 Multi-dimensional perceptual map

Brand identity and brand image

A company may promote, or position and advertise, in an attempt to develop its brand identity and brand image, but along the way communication can become fragmented. A gap between brand identity and brand image can cause major concerns with the overall brand. The target audience may lose interest, sometimes there are conflicting impressions and misinformation, or the brand message may be missed entirely. Accordingly, companies have to work hard on the consumer experience to make sure that what customers see and think is what companies want them to. This leads us to the next section, on how brand message should be communicated on the basis of the integrated brand communications model described below.

Integrated brand communications

Integrated brand communications (IBC) is a systematic process that helps build a successful brand-communications programme. It enables the company's brand to be promoted more effectively, so it is aligned with its market's needs and the company's business objectives. IBC also focuses on the understanding of the role of brands within the business model, and determines how brands can help grow and sustain the business. There are ten steps to building a successful IBC programme, as Figure 5.4 demonstrates.

Step 1 starts with understanding the role the brand plays in the business and how IBC helps in securing greater loyalty across the business. If necessary, audits are conducted for business strategy, customers, employees and key stakeholders to determine the value of the brand.

Step 2 looks at what factors contribute to the brand value by quantifying objectively the return on investment of funds used to build and promote the brand, and determining the overall effectiveness of the integrated communications programme, by measuring the relative change in brand value from assessment period to assessment period.

Step 3 identifies the target market and designs a brand strategy that connects with the audiences who drive the success of the business, together with a communications plan to connect with those contributing to or influencing the business success.

Step 4 defines unique value propositions on three bases: a) that these are distinguishable from competitors' propositions; b) that they must be credible; and c) that they have the 'stretch' to grow with the business as it evolves.

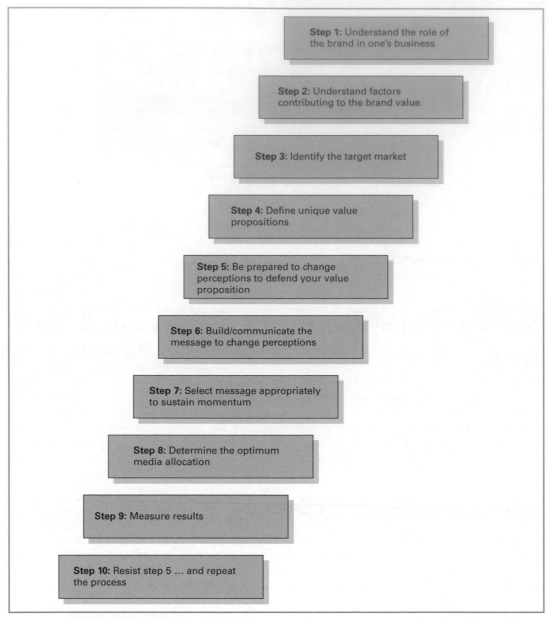

Source: Based on Ray's IBC at Brandchannel.com

FIGURE 5.4 Steps in building a successful integrated brand communications (IBC) programme

Step 5 makes preparations to change consumers' perceptions and to defend the company's value proposition. This is especially important where the company faces questions of credibility. It must change the way its targets think about the company's brand value to them.

Step 6 builds the messages to change consumers' perceptions accordingly. Here the company must have a compelling message which can deliver the value proposition to the target market in order to generate communications success.

Step 7 complements the messages with the most appropriate delivery vehicle. Individualized communications meet the needs of the audience better. Advertising and PR are powerful awareness-building tools. High-touch media such as collateral, direct and interactive are better for relevance, and instilling a clear sense of differential value and a sense of relevance (Ray @ brandchannel.com).

Step 8 is about determining the optimal media mix to optimize the power of the message with a limited budget.

Step 9 assesses the results by measuring the effectiveness of messages and media, and return on investment. The ROI must be judged relative to all competing investments.

Step 10 examines opportunities for improvement – for example, in the messages, the targets, budget allocation and assessment tools.

Brand building

Aaker's model of building a strong brand

Aaker (2002) suggested that the key to successful brand-building is to understand how to develop brand identities, to know what the brand stands for, and how to most effectively express that identity. Aaker's brand-building model (see Figure 5.1) evolves around developing the brand identity system, brand value proposition, and brand–customer relationship and implement these through brand position, execution and tracking. Brand positioning demands the active communication of the brand identity and value proposition to the target audience. The next step involves media selection and the development of communication programmes to be monitored at the brand tracking stage. Doyle (1990) suggested that there were four levers for developing successful brands: quality, service, innovation and differentiation. Furthermore, he maintained that quality and service, as opposed to advertising, was the way to create successful brands. Aaker, by contrast, recognized eight factors that make it difficult to build brands:

1 Pressure to compete on price.

2 Proliferation of competitors.

3 Fragmenting markets and media.

4 Complex branding strategies and brand relationships.

5 The temptation to change identity/executions.

6 Organizational bias against innovation.

7 Pressure to invest elsewhere.

8 Pressure for short-term results.

The PCDL model

The PCDL model (see Figure 5.6) is different from the traditional models of brand building, in that it applies to brand building in competitive markets. As competition intensifies, companies face challenges to adjust their brands to the altered expectations of their customers. Positioning brands according to the factors that customers prioritize can help in building companies' brand superiority in the minds of those customers. The model also suggests that consistency in integrated communications and messages along the brand-identity dimensions targeted towards customers are critical to the success of brand-building efforts, by delivering a consistent, self-reinforcing brand image. Companies need to ensure that the brand remains strong even during difficult times and offers value that is consistent with the brand promise. The four stages suggested in the PCDL model – **P**ositioning the brand, **C**ommunicating the brand message, **D**elivering the brand performance, and **L**everaging the brand equity – can enable companies to build strong brands.

Brand positioning – the brand can be positioned through its features/functions, tangible/intangible attributes, benefits.

Brand message can be communicated through advertising campaigns focusing on themes or sometimes using celebrities; or events and shows.

Brand performance delivery – focuses on products/service performance, and customer care. Brand equity can then be leveraged through line/brand extension, ingredient branding, co-branding, brand alliances and social integration.

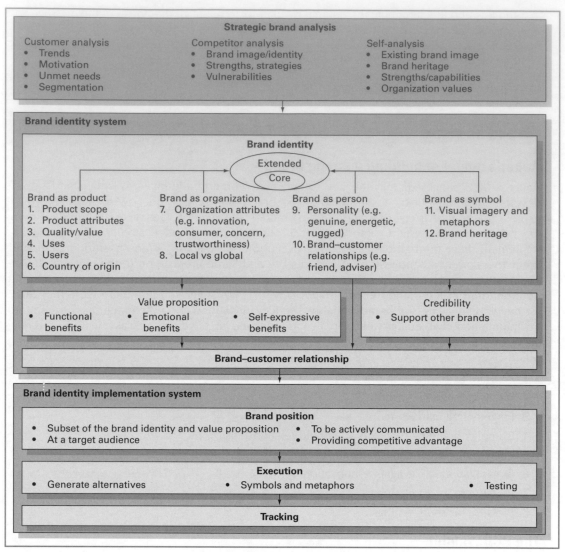

Source: Aaker, D. (2002).
FIGURE 5.5 A model of building a strong brand

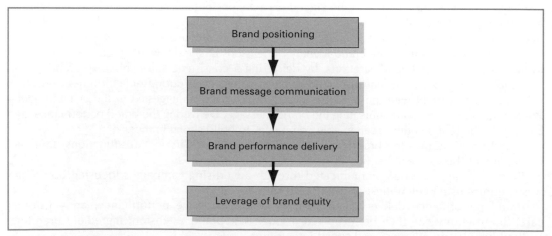

FIGURE 5.6 The PCDL model

Brand attributes	Archies	Boroline	Dabur Vatika
Positioning the brand			
Positioning	Feelings and emotions	Value for money	Premium quality, pure coconut oil
Brand associations	Greeting cards and soft toys Gift items for youth	Antiseptic skin cream 'Haathiwala cream'	Coconut hair oil White and green bottle
Communicating the message			
Promotion	Radio, TV, FM channels, cable and satellite channels, Hollywood Movies, Hindi movies (Bollywood)	Newspapers, magazines, radio, outdoor advertising, festivals, sponsorship of cricket and football matches	Sponsored events and shows, music awards, TV show
Campaign	'The most special way we are' Focused on sentiments, feelings, and emotions	'Combining modern chemistry and the science of ancient Indian Ayurveda' Trust of generations of consumers	'Values of youthfulness and natural beauty' Featuring modern, young, multi faceted, confident, and achievement-driven women celebrities
Social cause	Tie-up with NGOs (Help Age India, Child Relief and You, etc.)	'Save Trees' campaign, financial assistance to patients requiring heart surgery	'Vatika Super Model India 2001' and 'Vatika Zee Sangeet Awards' to recognize the talent in society
Delivering the performance			
Product focus	Advancing social expressions, and products at different price points	'Guard and cure against dry skin problems'	'Benefits of natural products in a single pack'
Distribution coverage	'Archies Gallery' stores, organized franchising	Availability at retailer level	Easy accessibility at retailer level
Leveraging the brand equity			
Brand extension	Key chains, wide range of stationery, gift items, etc.	Hair care products, detangling shampoo, and pain balm	Cream conditioning shampoo, anti-dandruff shampoo, fairness face pack

Source: Ghodeswar, B. M. (2008).
TABLE 5.1 Brand-building characteristics

Conclusion

Brand identity is one of the components of branding. It is the unique set of functional and mental associations the brand aspires to create or maintain. These associations represent what the brand should ideally stand for in the minds of customers, and imply a potential promise to customers. Brand identity is what brand owners want their brands to be, while brand image is what currently resides in the minds of the customers, i.e. what customers perceive the brands to be. Brand positioning is the 'market space' a brand is perceived to occupy in the mind of the target audience and is the part of the brand identity that companies decide to actively communicate to the market. It is also a process through which the brand manager identifies the desired position in the customer's mind, and develops strategies to reach and strengthen the brand at that position in relation to competitors. Brand positioning helps in communicating the brand message and sets forth the communication objectives, such as type of message and themes that appeal to the target market. Companies that present a cohesive, distinctive and relevant brand identity can create a preference in the marketplace, add value to their products and services, and command a price premium that leads to the creation of brand equity, which is an asset to the firm.

The brand identity system is a concept that is central to brand equity building. It consists of twelve dimensions organised around four perspectives: the brand as product, as organization, as person and as symbol. Brand identity can be implemented through brand identity elaboration, brand position, brand-building programmes and brand tracking. Brand identity is determined by its physical appearance, personality, culture and ability to connect with people; how the brand is perceived to be used by its reflection of the consumer self-image. All these are known as brand identity facets. To be effective, a brand identity needs to resonate with customers, differentiate itself from competitors, and represent what the organization can and will do over time. Thus, brand identity has to be consistent with its brand image, i.e. what companies want their customers to see and think of the brand is consistent with what their customers perceive the brand to be. A brand image has two basic dimensions – the functional and the symbolic; a corporate image has many dimensions – dynamic, cooperative, businesswise, character, successful and withdrawn. Brand image can be built through IMC, but the challenge lies in the application of different IMC tools to deliver the brand message effectively and efficiently. Advertising can be used to create brand images and symbolic appeals. PR allows the company to tell its story in a thorough and authentic way, and helps the company achieve 'transparency'. Design and packaging can develop visual communications to enhance the company's brand image and brand identity. Packaging can develop and reinforce the core brand attributes. Distribution also helps in building the brand image, as does culture. The perceived personality of a brand can be shaped by marketers via 'transferring cultural meaning' into it in various ways. Brand image can be strategically managed over time, using a sequential process of selecting, introducing, elaborating and fortifying the brand.

Brand positioning is a process through which the brand manager identifies the desired position in the customer's mind, and develops strategies to reach and strengthen the brand at that position in relation to competitors. Positioning decisions include deciding in which product market to compete, identifying the target market to which the brand would have the desired meaning, finding out where the brand stands in the customer's mind in relation to competitors, using a perceptual map, and what set of brand benefits and attributes need to be built for successful positioning. A brand can be positioned in several ways: by unique attributes or USP, or in terms of product features and customer benefits. It can be positioned on the basis of corporate brand name, or in terms of usage, occasion and time, as well as by price–value. These positioning strategies are often used by fmcg companies, although there are some pitfalls with price–value positioning. A brand can also be positioned by segmentation, implicitly or explicitly referring to competitors; or in terms of non-functional/abstract value, based on sensory system, social value, self-esteem, conditional and epistemic values, as well as through the use of cultural symbols and a brand personality. A successful positioning is carefully monitored and enhanced through effective brand communications, so that the brand can maintain a distinct and unique position in the consumer's mind. The IBC process focuses on the understanding of the role of brands within the business model, and determines how brands can help grow and sustain the business.

Developing brand identity is the core of brand equity building, knowing what the brand stands for, and how most effectively to express that identity. However, as competition intensifies, companies must try to adjust their brands to match the changed expectations of their customers. Positioning the brand according to the attributes that customers prioritize can help in building the companies' brand superiority in the minds of their customers, as can delivering consistent brand message and offering value that is consistent with the brand promise even in difficult times, and by delivering the brand performance through customer care programmes, then leveraging the brand equity.

🔐 Key terms

Brand culture: the part of the brand from which it draws inspiration.

Brand essence: the major features that shape the brand and form its distinctiveness; otherwise known as an articulation of the 'heart and soul' of the brand. It is the description which defines a brand and its guiding vision. It must always be present, from production to communication.

Brand identity: a unique set of brand associations that the brand strategist aspires to create or maintain.

Brand image: consumers' perceptions of a brand measured as the brand associations held in consumers' memory.

Brand mantra: a short expression explaining the brand positioning and core brand values; a particularly valuable instrument for conveying the meaning of the brand.

Brand personality: describes brands in terms of human characteristics.

Brand position: the part of the brand identity and value proposition that is to be actively communicated to the target audience.

Brand positioning: the 'market space' a brand is perceived to occupy in the mind of the target audience, and the part of the brand identity that companies decide to actively communicate to the market. It is also a process through which the brand manager identifies the desired position in the customer's mind, and develops strategies to reach and strengthen the brand at that position in relation to competitors.

Brand promise: the essence of the benefits (both functional and emotional) that customers can expect to receive from experiencing a brand's products/services, which reflects the heart, soul and spirit of the brand (Knapp, 2000).

Brand reflection: who the brand is perceived to be used by.

Integrated brand communications (IBC): focuses on the understanding of the role of brands within the business model, and determines how brands can help grow and sustain the business.

Perceptual mapping: a technique that determines a brand position in relation to competitors on various dimensions. Thus, brands can be positioned against competing brands on a perceptual map.

Strategic brand image concept management: consists of a sequential process of selecting, introducing, elaborating and fortifying a brand concept. This concept can guide positioning strategies and hence the brand image at each stage. The method for maintaining this brand image linkage concept depends on whether the brand is functional, symbolic or experiential.

❓ Discussion questions

1 What brands are associated with the following taglines?
   a) You deserve a break today.
   b) Be all that you can be.
   c) Just do it.
   d) It's the real thing.
   e) Where's the beef?

?

  f) It takes a tough man to make a tender chicken.

  g) We try harder.

2 Explain the meanings of brand identity, brand personality, brand image, brand essence, brand promise and brand mantra, and their relationships.

3 Referring to Trout's positioning concept, explain what key decisions a brand manager must take to achieve successful positioning.

4 Discuss how culture can be the basis of brand image building. Give examples.

5 Discuss the pros and cons of each of the brand positioning strategies. Support your answer with examples.

6 What is/are the most important aspect(s) in brand message communication? What are the potential problems that occur in customer feedback that have an effect on the company's brand image? How should managers overcome these problems?

7 Explain what fragmenting markets and media means, and how these impact on brand building.

8 Discuss the possible reasons for brand repositioning. How will you be able to separate repositioning strategies from confused positioning situations?

9 'The most effective brand positioning is by consumer benefits.' Discuss. Are there any situations where this approach would not work? Support your answer with examples.

10 Discuss the strategies for delivering a brand performance as identified in the PCDL model.

Projects

1 Devise a message appeal and select the best communication media for a yoghurt brand, based on its brand positioning, which you have to determine. Explain your rationale.

2 Do a search of advertisements, magazines and other communication media to find out eight brands (two each) that are positioned in terms of:

  a) Unique value proposition.

  b) Product features and consumer benefits.

  c) Corporate identity.

  d) Category-related usage.

3 Conduct a mini market survey to find out consumers' perceptions of the following banks: NatWest, Lloyds TSB, HSBC and Barclays. Then use a perceptual map to describe their brand positioning according to customers' perceptions.

4 Apply the IBC process to devise an IBC programme for a brand of your choice.

5 Develop a new concept for either an existing consumer product or entirely new product of your choice, and design a brand communication message for that product.

MINI CASE 5.1: VOLKSWAGEN: CHANGING PERCEPTIONS AND POSITIONING – STRETCHING A BRAND

Source: Branding Asia.com

Volkswagen (VW) is a famous international brand name that has traditionally been associated with the mass market, its most famous model being the Beetle. Indeed, it is currently exploiting nostalgia with the new Beetle retro-model. However, not content with sticking to the categories where it enjoys success, the company is also attempting to move into the prestige and luxury car segments dominated by established brands like Mercedes and BMW.

Its first venture into this market segment is with the new Passat V6 Syncro, which is out of the price range of the typical VW buyer. Evidently, other models are planned at higher-level segments and prices. Even though VW owns Audi, Bentley and Lamborghini, among other brands, many people are sceptical that it can stretch its own brand upwards, when consumer perceptions still associate the VW-branded cars with smaller and less prestigious vehicles.

Its 'badge value' (brand associations) would not appeal to customers of BMW, Mercedes or even Audi. Additional problems arise when consideration is given to the fact that other brands such as Volvo and Toyota's Lexus are also shifting their position to target the prestige market, which demands performance, luxury and marque. VW acknowledges the issues but says it will give customers more product. But is product what the luxury car owners are really buying? More likely, according to research, it is status, prestige and self-expression that determines their decision, and VW will need to do a considerable amount of consumer perception management and distributor education to successfully bring any of its VW-branded models into that league.

Questions:

1 Explain what luxury branding is.
2 What are the positioning or repositioning strategies at VW's disposal when moving into the prestige and luxury car market segments?

MINI CASE 5.2: DELL COMPUTER

Source: Permission granted by Rob Ludlow, www.nifty-stuff.com

Even before entering his teens Michael Dell strove for greatness, and by the age of 18 he had dropped out of college and created the beginnings of what years later would become the US leader in PC sales, the Dell Computer Corporation. How did Dell reach the top? Was it Michael Dell's tenacity and great entrepreneurial skills that made the climb possible, or were there other factors involved? Can the company sustain its position? What are the key strategic issues, both internal and external, that the company must evaluate in order to achieve a sustainable competitive advantage that will lead to above-average returns and therefore produce greater shareholder wealth?

Strengths: Dell Corporation needed more than luck, bumping into walls, and other less-effective strategies to achieve its position in the market. The company experienced growth in both revenue and net income between 1985 and 2000, and has achieved an average of 6.4 per cent net profit margin. Dell's primary core competency and strength was the fact that Michael Dell pioneered the system of buying computers in a 'built-to-order' system as opposed to that of inventory-based systems. This provided the company with the ability to decrease its costs considerably by virtually eliminating the holding costs associated with inventory, and the costs of discounting older or less popular items. Dell's just-in-time system also allows for faster response to changes in technology and computing innovations. It is first-mover advantage in this new system of production that propelled the company forward and gave it its strongest competitive advantage.

Dell has also been able to develop other strategic advantages throughout the years. For example, Dell has an incredible relationship with its vendors. The company develops very strong relationships with a few key suppliers, and requires that these suppliers be and remain at the top of their game. Dell has 'virtually integrated' the suppliers of its supply chain in such an effective and efficient manner that it seemed as though these vendors were just another extension of the Dell Corporation. Parts are provided just-in-time to the point that the exact number of items needed are delivered daily, and in a few cases even hourly. Also, Dell has also taken great strides in lowering, and in some cases eliminating, many of the costs associated with service of its products. The primary tools have been the development of Internet-based help databases and systems that 'self-heal' in cases of software problems. Another strength: Dell was exceedingly effective at communicating with its customers, and interpreting the results of that communication. Also, Dell has moved into the server market very aggressively and effectively. Finally Dell has strong management and superior brand name awareness and recognition.

Weaknesses: fortunately the Dell Corporation isn't hindered by too many internal weaknesses. Michael Dell has stated that the biggest challenge that he sees is the ability to obtain qualified individuals who will facilitate the development of a stronger hold in the international market.

Threats: though Mr Dell isn't concerned about his company's ever-increasing competition, he should be. Competitors will continue to see the decrease in the margins they receive from retail sales and costs associated with carrying inventories. These competitors, specifically the large companies such as Compaq, HP and Gateway, will continue to see the gold at the end of Dell's rainbow and will pursue it. While Dell is ahead of the game in the US, its biggest competitor, Compaq, is not far behind and still has domination internationally. Competitors will continue to develop similar 'built-to-order' systems and some may even find the secrets to Dell's success. Another threat is the fact that the personal computer market is becoming mature and saturated in the US. In general the PC market has many of the characteristics of an industry to avoid, i.e. a large number of small competitors and a small number of large competitors, low costs for customers to switch brands, frequent new product introductions, entry barriers low, and weak margins!

Opportunities: Dell has a few opportunities that will provide the means by which to continue its ability to create value for its shareholders. The international market has great potential for exploitation, specifically in China and South America. While PC growth in the US has slowed, growth internationally is expected to continue at a high growth rate. There is also opportunity for diversification into other areas where Dell's expertise and brand name will add value to the process. The prospects in the server market should also prove to show great growth potential.

Conclusions: within the past few years Dell has continued to experience growth, but some markets where Dell is active have become mature and saturated. Key strategic issues must be taken into account when devising a strategy for Dell to continue to achieve above average returns.

Questions:

1 What makes Dell successful?

2 What is the Dell's brand positioning? What is its brand essence compared with IBM and Microsoft?

3 What are the key strategic issues Dell must take into account in order to continue to achieve good returns?

4 How would you apply the PCDL model to build a brand like Dell, in a saturated and competitive market such as the PC market?

END OF CHAPTER CASE STUDY: WHAT'S WRONG WITH SLIM-FAST BEING SLIM? WHERE IS THE MISSING LINK?

In 1977 Daniel Abraham introduced a product that has been helping procrastinators get ready for bikini season ever since. The brand's promise is ingeniously summed up in its own name – Slim-Fast. But somewhere along the way Slim-Fast appears to have lost sight of its largest asset and become just … slim.

Unilever, Slim-Fast's parent company, is blaming it for a near 21 per cent fall-off in profits. By its very name, Slim-Fast promises that its customers will not only lose weight, but lose weight in a hurry. Yet, the only evidence that the brand is conscious of the second part of this promise is on its website, where a small tease tells us that we can 'lose up to 10 lbs by December 24th'. Meanwhile, all other Slim-Fast ads fail to capitalize on this differentiator.

Slim-Fast's diets are based on eating fewer calories than the body burns, thus spurring the body to use fat stores, which results in weight loss. It's maths a five-year-old can do. The Atkins diet is radically different in claiming that the way in which the body breaks down certain calories makes all the difference. But this is all so technical, isn't a diet a diet? Don't we all just want to lose weight? No and yes.

While the dieter of one to two decades ago may have been fooled or clueless about how the body loses weight, today's obsessed dieters know a staggering amount about the difference between a fat calorie and a carbohydrate calorie. As Slim-Fast scrambles to introduce new products such as soup, and releases scientific studies claiming healthier benefits than the Atkins diet, odds are that nobody will be fooled.

For so many years we have known Slim-Fast to be the impatient dieter's choice. A sudden re-brand like this will simply lead the savvy to ask the obvious question: 'Is it fast, or is it healthy?' Even the dimmest dieting bulbs among us are far too sceptical and battle-scarred to believe that both might be possible. Simply put, Slim-Fast is reversing on decades of brand building because it got spooked, breaking one of the cardinal rules of long-term branding.

Atkins, as well as the other recent fads, such as the South Beach Diet and The Zone, all lack a strength that Slim-Fast is known for: speed.

Slim-Fast could position itself to take advantage of another recent fad that is gaining attention in the mainstream media, like the possibility that eating a low-calorie diet may slow ageing. It is a plain, simple concept that anyone can process: lose weight fast and slow ageing.

Questions:

1 What is wrong with Slim-Fast?

2 What is confusing about Slim-Fast's brand positioning?

3 What is its brand promise, brand value and brand essence?

4 What should the Slim-Fast brand message be?

5 How would you apply the IBC process to help grow and sustain Slim-Fast?

6 Can you identify the gap between Slim-Fast's brand identity and brand image, i.e. what the company wants the customers to feel about the brand and how the brand is actually perceived?

References

Aaker, D. (2002), *Building Strong Brands*, London: Simon & Schuster UK Ltd.

Alt, M. and Griggs, S. (1988), 'Can a brand be cheeky?', *Marketing Intelligence & Planning*, Vol. 6 No. 4, pp. 9–16.

Anson, W. (2000), 'Corporate identity – value and valuation', *Corporate Reputation Review*, Vol. 3 No. 2, pp. 164–8.

Balmer, J. M. T. (1995), 'Corporate branding and connoisseurship', *Journal of General Management*, Vol. 21 No. 1, pp. 24–46.

Bernstein, D. (1984), *Company Image and Reality: A Critique of Corporate Communications*, Eastbourne, UK: Holt, Rinehart & Winston.

Doyle, P. (1990), 'Building successful brands: the strategic options', *Journal of Consumer Marketing*, Vol. 7 (Spring), pp. 5–20.

Ghodeswar, B. M. (2008), 'Building brand equity in competitive markets: a conceptual model', *Journal of Product & Brand Management*, Vol. 17, No. 1, pp. 4–12.

Gray, E. R. and Balmer, J. M. T. (1998), 'Managing corporate image and corporate reputation', *Long Range Planning*, Vol. 31, No. 5, pp. 695–702.

Hatch, M. J. and Shultz, M. (1997), 'Relations between organizational culture, identity and image', *European Journal of Marketing*, Vol. 31 No. 5/6, pp. 356–65.

Heylen, J. P., Dawson, B. and Sampson, P. (1995), 'An implicit model of consumer behaviour', *Journal of the Marketing Research Society*, Vol. 37, No. 1, pp. 51–67.

Knapp, D. (2000), *The Brand Mindset*, New York: McGraw-Hill.

Nelson, P. (1962), 'Seven principles in image formation', *Journal of Marketing*, Vol. 26, No. 1, (January), pp. 67–71.

Park, C., Whan, B., Jaworski, J. and MacInnis, D. J. (1986), 'Strategic brand concept-image management', *Journal of Marketing*, Vol. 50 (October), pp. 135–45.

Ries, A. and Trout, J. (1986), *Positioning: The Battle for Your Mind*, New York, NY: Warner Books.

Simões, C. and Reis, M. (2000), 'Crafting corporate image for a market-driven corporation: a Brazilian case', in *Marketing in a Global Economy Proceedings, Buenos Aires*, American Marketing Association, Chicago, IL, pp. 328–35.

Spector, A. J. (1961), 'Basic dimensions of the corporate image', *Journal of Marketing*, Vol. 25, No. 6, (October), pp. 47–51.

Swartz, T. (1983), 'Brand symbols and message differentiation', *Journal of Advertising Research*, Vol. 23, No. 5, pp. 59–64.

Trout, J. (1969), 'Positioning is a game people play in today's me-too market place', *Industrial Marketing*, Vol. 54, No. 6 (June), pp. 51–5.

Van Riel, C. B. M. and Balmer, J. M. T. (1997), 'Corporate identity: the concept, its measurement and management', *European Journal of Marketing*, Vol. 31, No. 5/6, pp. 340–56.

Further reading and online sites

Alsem, K. J. and Kostelijk, E. (2008), 'Identity based marketing: a new balanced marketing paradigm', *European Journal of Marketing*, Vol. 42, No. 9/10, pp. 907–14.

Anson, W. (2000), 'Corporate identity – value and valuation', *Corporate Reputation Review*, Vol. 3, No. 2, pp. 164–8.

Balmer, J. M. T. (1995), 'Corporate branding and connoisseurship', *Journal of General Management*, Vol. 21, No. 1, pp. 24–46.

Balmer, J. M. T. (2008), 'Identity based views of the corporation: insights from corporate identity, organisational identity, social identity, visual identity, corporate brand identity and corporate image', *European Journal of Marketing*, Vol. 42, No. 9/10.

Bernstein, D. (1984), *Company Image and Reality: A Critique of Corporate Communications*, Eastbourne, UK: Holt, Rinehart & Winston.

Collins, M. (2002), 'Analyzing brand image data', *Marketing Research*, Vol. 14, No. 2, pp. 33–6.

Francoeur, B. (2004), 'Brand image and Walt Disney: a qualitative analysis of magical gatherings', *Journal of Undergraduate Research*, VII.

Ghodeswar, B. M. (2008), 'Building brand identity in competitive markets: a conceptual model', *Journal of Product & Brand Management*, Vol. 17, No. 1, pp. 4–12.

Gray, E. R. and Balmer, J. M. T. (1998), 'Managing corporate image and corporate reputation', *Long Range Planning*, Vol. 31, No. 5, pp. 695–702.

Hatch, M. J. and Shultz, M. (1997), 'Relations between organizational culture, identity and image', *European Journal of Marketing*, Vol. 31, No. 5/6, pp. 356–65.

He, H.-W. (2008), 'Corporate identity/strategy interface: implications for corporate level marketing', *European Journal of Marketing*, Vol. 42, No. 1/2.

Hofsted, A., van Hoof, J., Walenberg, N. and de Jong, M. (2007), 'Projective techniques for brand image research: two personification-based methods explored', *Qualitative Market Research: An International Journal*, Vol. 10, No. 3, pp. 300–9.

Kaikati, J. G. and Kaikati, A. M. (2004), 'Identity crisis: the dos and don'ts of brand rechristening, marketing management', Vol. 13, No. 1 (January–February), pp. 45–9.

Kapferer, J. (2004), *The New Strategic Brand Management,* New York: Kogan Page.

Keller, K. and Richey, K. (2006), 'The importance of corporate brand personality traits to a successful 21st century business', *Brand Management*, Vol. 14, No. 1/2, September–November, pp. 74–81.

Muzellec, L. and Lambkin, M. (2005), 'Does Diageo make your Guinness taste better? An empirical assessment of the effect of a corporate rebranding on corporate and product brand personality', reputationinstitute.com.

Rajagopal, P. (2006), 'Brand excellence: measuring the impact of advertising and brand personality on buying decisions', *Measuring Business Excellence*, Vol. 10, No. 3.

Simões, C. and Reis, M. (2000), 'Crafting corporate image for a market-driven corporation: a Brazilian case', *Marketing in a Global Economy Proceedings, Buenos Aires*, American Marketing Association, Chicago, IL, pp. 328–35.

Trout, J. (1969), 'Positioning is a game people play in today's me-too market place', *Industrial Marketing*, Vol. 54, No. 6 (June), pp. 51–5.

Van Riel, C. B. M. and Balmer, J. M. T. (1997), 'Corporate identity: the concept, its measurement and management', *European Journal of Marketing*, Vol. 31 No. 5/6, pp. 340–56.

CHAPTER

06

Brand Architecture

Chapter contents

Chapter overview

This chapter explains what brand architecture or brand structure consists of, what vertical and horizontal hierarchy of brands means, and discusses the management of brand portfolios and product relationships. It also examines issues of brand leverage and the problem of brand dilution. It discusses the different branding approaches used on product packs, such as corporate branding, endorsement, dual branding, standalone and furtive brands – examples are drawn mainly from the fmcg sector – and the rationale behind each branding approach. It asks how to choose an appropriate brand strategy and examines international brand structure. Finally, it looks at the environmental pressures on branding, discusses where brands are going, the latest strategies and future trends. This is the second chapter of Part 2, which covers the theme of how to create and sustain brand equity. Chapter 5 was concerned with brand identity and positioning. Chapter 7 will deal with brand extension.

❖ LEARNING OBJECTIVES

After completing this chapter, you should be able to

- ❖ Appreciate the concept of brand structure

- ❖ Understand how the brand portfolio is managed

- ❖ Contrast the management of a single brand identity with the management of a bundle of identities in a portfolio of brands

- ❖ Understand the rationale behind brand leverage

- ❖ Examine the process of brand relationship optimization

- ❖ Examine the problems of brand leverage and brand dilution, and how to overcome these

- ❖ Design a strategic balance brand portfolio

- ❖ Understand the impact of brand name strategies on consumer choice of a product

- ❖ Select an appropriate branding approach according to the product market context

- ❖ Examine the growth of brand licensing and strategic alliance in branding

- ❖ Examine brand structure in international markets, its context and relevance, and the differences between those in domestic markets

Introduction

As marketing becomes more targeted, competition more intense, globalization prevails and company mergers and acquisitions become ever more common, brands have become more complex. Brands are owned by other brands which, in turn, are owned by another set of brands. Since each party tries to leverage and maximize its own brand, managers are now looking for ways to optimize relationships among brands. They do not focus on managing a single brand only, but also on links between brands within the company and its associated organizations. This is what is known as the 'management of brand portfolios'. Throughout this chapter we will examine how a brand portfolio is managed, what branding strategies are appropriate for each business context, and the notion of brand structure or brand hierarchy in international markets.

The management of brand portfolios and product relationships

From single brand management to brand portfolio management

In 1933 Joan Robinson noticed that several identical brands of a certain article might be sold claiming different qualities under names and labels which were designed to persuade richer and more snobbish customers to separate themselves from poorer (and less snobbish) customers. Since then, branding has become a central marketing issue and a corporate strategy (as opposed to being a trademark stamped on goods) as companies try to include it in their balance sheets and/or make major acquisitions to get it. There are a number of reasons why branding and brand management are of interest to academics and practitioners, and induce them to write about it.

- A brand provides functional benefits and added value for customers.

- It guides the integration of the marketing mix, and provides an anchor for marketing tactics and strategy in a turbulent environment.

- In consumer durable markets where variants of products are only on the market for a short time, the brand is essential for retaining consumer confidence and recognition.

- In an attempt to increase the perceived value, companies added brands to their balance sheets. Rank Hovis McDougall was a leader in this and, in late 1988 added over $1 billion worth of brands to its balance sheet, and in so doing tripled its recorded shareholders' funds overnight. Arthur Young and Company (1989) found that 25 per cent of the companies it surveyed included some amount for brand names or intellectual property in their accounts.

- Brands are a major reason for making acquisitions. In 1988 the acquisition of such brand names as Kit Kat, Quality Street, Smarties, Rolo and Yorkie was the reason for Nestlé paying six times the book value of its Rowntree acquisition (Laforet and Saunders, 1994).

These factors explain why over 400 articles and books were found to be written on branding. The main focus of the 1980s regarding brands was takeovers. Many thought the only way to have a successful brand was to buy one. Many felt the development of new mega-brands would be impossible in the future and money would be better spent on acquisitions than on research and development. The fact that six to seven out of ten new products failed strengthened the argument that takeovers made more sense than trying to develop new successful brands. It was during this period that many brands began to suffer. With the changing management associated with takeovers and acquisitions, brands failed to maintain a clear image in the consumer's mind. Consumers were becoming confused about what a brand represented. The high turnover of brand managers coupled with a preoccupation with short-term earnings has led to inconsistencies with brand equity. Some have felt that brands themselves were doomed because of years of inconsistent advertising and agency management, generic marketing, look-alike advertisements, undistinctive products and the proliferation of promotions (Rooney, 1995). As a result, the early literature on branding concentrated mainly on brand building (e.g. Doyle, 1989), brand equity building (e.g. Aaker, 1991; Baldinger, 1990), brand loyalty analysis (e.g. Bayus, 1992; Grover and Srinivasan, 1992), brand value measures through price trade-offs (e.g. Blackston, 1990) and brand valuation (e.g. Barwise et al., 1989).

It has been said that there are many advantages to investing in a brand name and company name simultaneously. The thrust for companies in the 1990s was not towards new brands but on strengthening and expanding those which already existed (Rooney, 1995, citing Baumn, 1990). The focus of branding in the 1990s was to create mutually beneficial situations; finding the right brand mix for the consumer while generating adequate sales and profits was a challenge for marketers back then. This trend was reflected in the number of authors writing about it (e.g. Aaker and Keller, 1990; Nielsen, 1984; Smith and Park, 1992; Wernerfelt, 1988). The main reasons for brand extensions (see Chapter 7) include acting as a signal for new product quality, offering economic returns, and short-term gains in perceived quality and brand recognition.

Companies also became more interested in making use of their existing brand names for brand extension and umbrella branding (see below). Corporate identities and brands began being offered together. For example, in the automobile market the joint venture between Honda and Rover to produce their respective Legend and Stirling marks resulted in their pursuing opposed branding strategies. While Rover extended its luxury Rover brand name across their whole range, Honda chose to establish an independent Acura division focusing upon a performance- and quality-sensitive segment of the car market. In the household sector, there was Lever Brothers' extension of Persil into the dishwashing liquid market and Nestlé's use of Nestlé Rowntree brands such as Aero (an aerated chocolate bar) in desserts. In academic literature, terms such as sub-brand, nested branding, umbrella and family branding began to emerge. Consequently, managing a bundle of corporate and brand identities became more important than managing a single brand entity, and this topic has been examined and researched until recently.

The strategic balance of brand portfolio management

Recent research (e.g. Chalain, 2006) shows how the combination of brands within a portfolio is a key factor for company development, growth and risk management. First, brand portfolios are the result of a process which is divided into three phases:

1 Characterized by brand accumulation, then transition and reduction of brands.
2 Organization of relationships between brands takes place.
3 Brand portfolios are developed and used as a strategic tool to gain competitive advantage and as a planning model, i.e. the way the company plans and develop itself for the next year.

Therefore, brand portfolios deal with both the internal and external environments. They represent a company's multiple competencies and a way of managing complexity. Brand portfolios also help sustainable competitive advantage at the brand-level competencies as well as managing transition.

According to the Chartered Institute of Marketing (2003), brand portfolio management influences a number of areas such as R&D and marketing resources, cost efficiency, growth, leverage and clarity. First, R&D and marketing expenditure needs to be allocated to areas where the best returns can be obtained. For instance, companies often focus on a few high-potential or drive brands that have scale, strong and distinctive messages or a unique selling proposition (USP), to see whether they can grow and how they can grow (interview with United Biscuits manager, 2004).

One of the ways companies might decide to grow these is by sub-brands. For example, in 2001 United Biscuits decided to extend its Hula Hoops brand. It varied the hoops by making bigger and smaller ones in addition to the standard size. The new hoops retained the core essence of hoops, but at the same time helped position different segments of the market to meet different needs. Thus, the company managed to take hoops into different formats, building the Hula Hoops brand scale and increasing its brand visibility with consumers.

Second, in terms of cost efficiency, synergy is created within the company's brand portfolio. Strong associations not only benefit all the brands, but are also cost efficient in creating economies of scale in both production and manufacturing and communications.

Third, as far as growth is concerned, six ways are identified in which portfolio management could enhance growth:

1 Clear prioritization of future focus by major market.
2 Prioritization by brand and product.
3 Concentration of expenditure on priority market, brands and products.
4 Operational cost savings through simplified business.
5 Disposal of brands that don't fit.
6 Gap filling by product development and acquisition.

Fourth, with regard to leverage, leveraging brands makes them work harder. A proper portfolio analysis can highlight which brands are best suited to being extended. Finally, clarity: clarity of product offerings is needed, to underpin a consistent brand identity with all stakeholders.

Other authors suggest how a portfolio of brands can be optimized using a five-step approach. First, managers decide on the brands to review. Second, they shortlist all of the brands and analyse each one's contribution to the company. Third, they assess the brands according to current market performance (traction) and future prospects (momentum). Fourth, the brands are classified along those three dimensions (contribution, traction and momentum), allowing managers to identify both challenges and opportunities. The process enables companies to sort their brands into different categories: *power* (a brand that needs to be defended ferociously and deployed judiciously), *sleeper* (a brand that with a little fast tracking can build into a power brand), *slider* (a valuable brand that has lost momentum, is slipping backwards and needs immediate intervention to prevent meltdown), *soldier* (a solid brand that contributes quietly without the need for much management attention), *black hole* (a brand that sucks up resources and may or may not ever pay out), *rocket* (a brand that is on its way to power-brand status), *wallflower* (a small, underappreciated brand with very loyal customers, often under-priced and under-marketed), and *discard* (a brand that should have been mothballed years ago). Last, the objectives for each individual brand are tied together into an overall plan, which will include any changes to the roster, brand architecture and resource allocation (Hill et al., 2005).

The problems of brand leverage

Brand extension is one of the most commonly practised techniques in branding, which is reflected in the number of authors writing about it (Interbrand, 1990), followed by empirical studies (Laforet and Saunders, 1994). Many organizations have attempted to extend a popular, successful brand into new markets. In some cases this has been very effective, while in others it has been disastrous. An operator who wants to extend a brand into new markets should make sure the link is obvious. In other words, it should be obvious to consumers why a company is using the brand name on a new product. It is dangerous to use a name where it does not fit. If an organization truly knows what the brand means to its customers, it will also know what it does not mean. If the product and the brands do not mesh, customers will not buy (Rooney, 1995).

There are many examples of organizations which have overextended their brands, some at the expense of the core brand. Others have extended their lines in a way that has radically altered the personality of the core brand. These are the main dangers associated with brand extensions. However, there are some very good reasons to extend that lead to profits and success. Currently, it is much harder to build new successful brands than to defend old ones. There are also many failures associated with new product introductions. When a company uses a brand name that has already been established, some risk associated with new products may be eliminated (Rooney, 1995). For more discussion on brand extension and brand dilution, turn to Chapter 7.

Brand structure

Brand-naming strategies

Before any concept of brand structure/brand hierarchy, or what practitioners refer to as 'brand architecture', was developed there was no set of ground rules concerning brand-naming strategy. Marketing textbooks and anecdotal literature use a series of terms such as super branding, corporate branding, corporate endorsed, dual branding, family branding, blanket family names, separate family names, standalone brands and free branding, multi-brand strategy, nested brand names, brands and sub-brands to describe various brand types used on fmcg packaging, i.e. by consumer goods manufacturers. These terms were given very little formal definition and varied with the people using them.

Corporate branding used to be referred to as 'superbranding'. This is the use of the corporate name to apply across a company's product-class category or product line. Superbranding, as Murphy (1987) suggested, is a form of umbrella branding whereby a corporation borrows the equity it has accrued at great expense in its corporate name and applies it to a new product or line. Honda, Dole, Bird's Eye, Stouffer's, Del Monte and Levi Strauss are the companies which have achieved superbrand status over the years. The superbrand identity, as Murphy suggested, may be used alone with a description such as Honda Power Equipment or as an endorsement for another line bearing its own separate brand identity, as in Stouffer's Lean Cuisine frozen entrées, or Pillsbury

Hungry Jack biscuits. In either case, the new product borrows heavily from the equity already built into the superbrand or corporate identity. Corporate branding is also known as 'companies that have all their products labelled with their corporate brand'. Corporate brands are a means whereby the company itself becomes the end product. Corporate names have also been seen as similar to family names, though this should not be taken to mean that a family name is automatically derived from the name of the company (Roberts and McDonald, 1990). The most noticeable explosion of corporate brands is in the service sector. McDonald's and Marriott have led the way. The financial services sector and retailers have equally been working hard to build up the brand strength associated with long-standing, fast-moving consumer goods (fmcg). It is standard practice in industrial or business-to-business markets for any branding to take place at the corporate level.

It is common to see a corporate brand endorsing a product brand. This is known as 'corporate endorsement' or 'corporate endorsed products', where a corporate name is used in conjunction with a product brand name. Buday (1989) asserted that the established corporate or family name provides necessary consumer reassurance from its parent, while the product brand name distinguishes the brand extension. This also often happens at the end of a TV advertisement when the corporate logo suddenly appears in the corner, or on the back of a package where the corporate brand is displayed to identify the company that owns the brand.

In the case of family branding and blanket family names, 'family brands' is a general term, referring to product items that have the same basic brand name (Pride and Ferrell, 1977). Ann Page is a family brand name which is used on many Ann Page food products. Gerber also uses its name on all baby items, and its products are differentiated according to whether they are food or non-food items. This technique allows the owner to promote all product items when promoting the family brand, whereas a blanket family name implies that the firm uses part or all of its name across a range of products that are not necessarily related by type, function or application, e.g. Dunhill and Canon. Another example is SmithKline Beecham. Before its merger with GlaxoWellcome it used to use part of the company's name, Beecham, as a blanket family name for many of its household products. The danger in the corporate blanket approach is that it works only up to a point, because it can inhibit the development of sub-brands, i.e. product brands aimed at different targets. Small brands are, however, often forced to adopt this approach at the expense of the individual brand. For them the corporate blanket is a means of saying 'I exist' over and over again. Retailers adopt this approach. If the core values associated with the brand can be applied to other markets, then the established brand identity can often take the brand into those markets. Lucozade is an example of successful brand-stretch through packaging. The original design was accentuated to pick up the flavour of new, albeit closely related, markets: sport, light, etc. A more radical brand extension, that of the confectionery brand Mars into the ice-cream sector has also made use of the same key visual equities, the brand name, logo style and colours.

Not only do companies want to label all their products under the corporate name, many of them try to stretch brands by launching more variants under a single brand name or identity, thus creating families of brands. The early literature refers this to as 'separate family names strategy'. This practice is often found where one company sells across the quality or applications/functions range using separate family names, e.g. consumer and industrial markets. This may also be a result of mergers and acquisitions, where the parent company gains control over a former competitor and thereby secures access to another family or set of family names. Where this is the case, the acquisition and maintenance of a large number of family names is usually scrutinized and subject to subsequent rationalization. There is a point at which a host of family names under the control of one parent company becomes dysfunctional, e.g. British Leyland's Austin Mini and Morris Mini.

Another brand type mentioned in the early literature is individual brand names' strategy (Roberts and McDonald, 1990). This is also known as 'free branding' or 'standalone product branding' (Aaker, 1991), which is not trading off an existing name. Product branding refers to the adoption of individual brand names for each product and each product positioning, i.e. one name, one proposition – for example, Tide, Bold, Dash, etc., all brands belonging to Procter & Gamble. Unlike the family name these are not extended to a family of products. Another term for the individual brand names strategy is the 'multi-brand strategy', which is the development by a particular seller of two or more brands that compete with each other. Procter & Gamble was the pioneer of this strategy. Following the phenomenal success of its Tide detergent brand introduced after World War II, another brand, Cheer, was introduced in 1950. Cheer took some sales away from Tide but the combined sales volume was larger than if Procter & Gamble had sold only Tide. Procter & Gamble subsequently introduced other brands of detergent, each launched with a claim of different special power and ingredients. Other manufacturers in the soap and other fields began to follow this strategy.

'Nested brand name' is a term used by Aaker (1991), to refer to brand names which are developed within brand names. Aaker also suggested that firms used these to develop associations and as a platform for new growth. The terms 'brands' and 'sub-brands' mentioned above are similar to Aaker's notion of nested brands. Sub-brands are widely accepted by academics and practitioners. This term is also found in the area of retail banking. The practitioner's definition of sub-brands is when more than one brand name is used on a product pack, the sub-brand appears less prominently. The name on the pack does not refer to any brand type in particular.

Corporate and brand identity

The emergence of dual brands and/or endorsed structure appears most commonly in the fast-moving consumer goods, retail financial services and retailing sectors. For a while Nestlé Rowntree pursued a branded approach, e.g. Mars, but Nestlé's name began to appear on the independently branded Kit Kat in the late 1990s. In contrast, in retail financial services and retailing the use of corporate endorsement is quite common. In financial services, this tendency was growing towards the end of the 1980s, with products like Lombard NatWest, Midland Montague and Lloyds Abbey Life (Saunders and Watters, 1993), while in the 1990s retailers like Sainsbury's and Tesco also used similar strategy as their manufacturers' counterparts, with products like Sainsbury's Novon (a washing-powder product) and Tesco La Femme (a range of costmetic products).

The application of dual branding among practitioners was strongly reflected in the literature. The issue of complex branding strategies was raised by Hall in 1992, although before that Cowley (1991) suggested that there might be a number of identities besides the corporate one surrounding the brand identity, or that there might be a range of levels of open corporate endorsement. Hall also noted the rise of corporate endorsement in 1993. Olins (1989) and Murphy (1987) tried to develop frameworks describing brand structures. Much of their work had its origin in design, where the interplay between corporate identity and the branding approach is evident. In 1994, using their empirical study of 400 leading manufacturers' brands, Laforet and Saunders proposed a brand hierarchy that came closer to actual practice than Olins and Murphy's early frameworks. This was followed by Douglas's international brand structure as described below.

Brand hierarchy

In 1989 Olins proposed three approaches to structure corporate identities: the monolithic, the endorsed and the branded. *Monolithic structures* have the organization using one name and one visual style throughout. In this case, what is a corporate identity to the company is a brand to the consumer. Kellogg's, British Airways and Shell all tend to follow this approach. *Endorsed structures* have the corporate identity used in association with the name of subsidiaries whose visual styles can be quite diverse. Industrial companies like General Electric Company and Hawker Siddeley tended to do this. Although ICI has had many strong brands, such as Dulux paints, it seeks to endorse this with its corporate identity with corporate advertising linking the brands. A while ago, Lever ran a press campaign linking its products, and simultaneously introduced a Lever flash on the front of its household products. *Branded identities* have products under totally different brand names and visual styles. Procter & Gamble, Mars and Allied Lyons tend to fall into this category.

Arnold (1992) suggested further that branding can occur at any of the following levels: a brand, a company, a range of products or an individual product line. Often, however, the decisions seem to be taken without reference to branding principles, and questions need to be asked about the possible confusion of objectives. Arnold also insisted that a company which inserts its corporate logo on to a set of perfectly strong but distinct brands within its portfolio risks confusing the consumer. Thus, according to the early literature, the levels where branding occurs can be presented as shown in Figure 6.1.

In the tier structure, each level aims at one audience at a time; the corporate aims at the shareholders, the City and employees. The corporate divisions (D) are the manufacturing units. The brands aim at the consumer. This is considered a well-defined structure which separates the corporate functions and the brands' (B) functions. However, in practice there are always overlaps. For instance, some companies, such as General Electric, at one time had problems in presenting themselves and their products to their customers without confusing the numerous identities they had. As GEC expanded, it took over the old AEI and English Electric companies and with them a multiplicity of companies and brands. Neither AEI nor English Electric had been successful in rationalizing companies, companies' names, brands and brand names, which was one of the

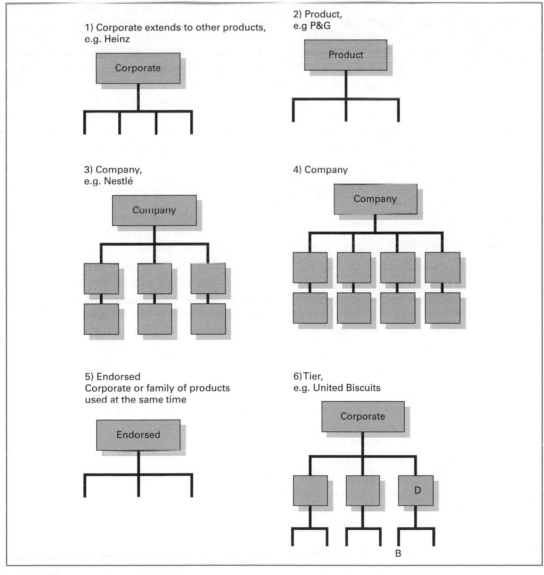

FIGURE 6.1 Levels where branding occurs

reasons why both companies fell into the lap of GEC. GEC had made an attempt to extract the benefit from a whole variety of company and brand names, many of which had had considerable significance and goodwill in the past, but the effect was unsuccessful. It also wanted to use the best of its existing stock of names in such a way as to retain customer loyalty. However, at the same time, it wanted to reduce the number of names and to associate them as much as possible with GEC. All of which is fine, but what emerged did not make much sense, because the names now contained within GEC had differing traditions and backgrounds that meant very different things to customers, agents and employees. However, at the time, they were being thrown together in a way which made them meaningless.

With regard to Olins' (1989) system of identity, it misses some of the complexities of brand structures. One omission is the predominance of nested branding mentioned above, used extensively by the Pet Foods division of Nestlé. For instance, within the Friskies range, there exists the straight Friskies products and the more luxurious Gourmet range. Murphy's (1987) four-level system of corporate identities recognized some of this complexity through corporate-dominant systems, brand-dominant systems, balanced systems and mixed systems. The corporate, brand and balanced systems were close to Olins', but the mixed system recognized the extent to which companies varied the corporate and brand names depending upon the appropriateness of the endorsement that the corporate identity can bestow on the brand.

Olins' and Murphy's systems of corporate identity were challenged by Laforet and Saunders' 1994 study on complex brand structures. Using a content analysis of 400 brand packages from leading grocery suppliers to two main British supermarkets, these authors had demonstrated that types of brand names can be grouped as a series of levels according to their breadth of use and relation to the corporate name. At the highest level is a corporate brand name that covers all a firm's products and at the lowest a virtual brand name that identifies a variant of a brand. These brand types were used singly or in combination, and often with a description of the product. Six brand types were identified:

1 *Corporate brand name*: as mentioned above, companies like Shell, Kellogg's and Heinz use their company names across virtually all their product range.

2 *House brand names*: diversified companies sometimes use the names of divisions (or houses) to promote products in different markets, or even segments. For example, Quaker did this with Fisher-Price toys, Ford with Jaguar, and GM with Opel and Cadillac.

3 *Family brand names*: as mentioned above, these are names used as an umbrella of a family of products. They differ from house names in being devoid of any relationship with the brand name and company structure. Sometimes they are a family of products that once belonged to an acquired company, such as Nestlé's Carnation Coffee Mate, condensed milk, etc. They are often the result of brand leverage where a strong mono-brand name is used to launch related brands. Some long-guarded mono brands had been extended in this way. These included Mars' countline extensions (Mars, Snickers, Bounty, etc.) to iced confectionery and Unilever's introduction of Persil dishwashing liquid.

4 *Mono brand names*: mono brand names are the dominant form used by many leading marketers, such as Procter & Gamble (Ariel), SmithKline Beecham (Tabasco sauce), etc. As brand leverage or extension is taking place, the mono brand names do not appear alone. For instance, in the mid-1990s Unilever used to add a Lever flash to the front of its household products and Nestlé added its name to Kit Kat, Rolo, etc.

When more than one brand name appears on a pack, the least prominent one is termed *sub-brand*. For example, in the case of Nestlé and its product brand Crosse & Blackwell Branston Pickle, Crosse & Blackwell is a family brand because it appears across a family of products, while Branston Pickle is a brand. However, Crosse & Blackwell is called the sub-brand because of its size on the package.

5 *Virtual brand names*: occasionally virtual brand names appear as suffixes used to identify variants of a brand or as a qualifier to a brand name. For instance, Nestlé's Pet Foods division has

Friskies Gourmet and Friskies Gourmet A La Carte. These are two distinct products differentiated by the addition of the virtual brand name 'A La Carte' to the Friskies Gourmet name. The virtual brand name exists only as part of a derived brand name.

6 *Description*: it is usual to describe a variant of a brand with a description, e.g. Batchelors Cup-a-Soup oxtail or Knorr beef stock cubes. However, virtual brand names and descriptions are not just alternative ways of describing variants since Friskies Gourmet A La Carte needs 'with Seafood'.

The content analysis of brand packaging showed that more than 50 per cent of these were mixed brands using a combination of mono, corporate, house and family brand. Of these, most (38.5 per cent) were dual brands but 13.5 per cent were endorsed. Thirty-two per cent of the products used a brand-dominant style although many of them were furtive. Each of the companies studied used almost all of the branding styles, but the most frequently used devices were the mixed-brand and the brand-dominant approaches. House names appear more often than the corporate identities, but the majority of companies (65 per cent) chose not to identify themselves sometimes.

A grid (Figure 6.2) showed how individual products were branded. The vertical axis gives the type of brand names used, and the horizontal axis the prominence given to each one – for example, Friskies Gourmet A La Carte with Seafood, in which Gourmet A La Carte is shown prominently along with a description of the pet food. In this case, Friskies, the house brand, appears on the front of the package but in a distinctly smaller typeface. The identity of Nestlé, which owns the brand, is not revealed. Nestlé's Friskies Gourmet A La Carte with Seafood was a rare complicated example. In contrast, some branding was very direct, e.g. Mars bar, where only the corporate name and description were used. In a way, this brand grid helps conceptualize a brand hierarchy. At the top of the *brand hierarchy* is the corporate name, e.g. Nestlé. Next level is the house name, e.g. L'Oréal (a division of Nestlé). Then comes the family name or super brand name, e.g. Friskies, followed by the mono brand name, i.e. product brand name, e.g. Gourmet, virtual name and product description, e.g. A La Carte with Seafood.

Table 6.1 shows the occurrence of brand types, i.e. the number of times a brand type showed on the pack in the sample surveyed, and the percentages of companies that employed these brand types.

Brand hierarchies, or *brand structures,* is a concept that attempts to illustrate the many levels and combinations of brands (or brand types) used on product packs, as shown in Figure 6.3. Laforet and Saunders (1994) have identified three major patterns of corporate brand structures: corporate dominant, mixed brands and brand dominant.

Brand type	Brand strength				
	Prominent (4)	Inferior (3)	Endorsed (2)	Disclosed (1)	Undisclosed (0)
Corporate					Nestlé
House					
Family		Friskies			
Mono	Gourmet				
Virtual	A La Carte				
Description	with Seafood				

FIGURE 6.2 Brand grid

Brand style	Products (%)	Companies* (%)
Corporate dominant		
Corporate brands	5	20
House brands	11	65
Mixed brands		
Dual brands	38.5	95
Endorsed brands	13.5	50
Brand dominant		
Mono brands	19	75
Furtive brands	13	65

*Percentages do not add up to 100% because almost all firms use more than one strategy.
TABLE 6.1 Occurrence of brand types

Brand architecture refers to the way in which a company organizes, manages and launches a brand in the market. Brand architecture is an external entity of a business strategy that supports business goals and objectives. There are three common types of brand architectures:

1 *Corporate dominant*: within this structure, two sub-types of structures were identified – the corporate and house brand structures. The house structure is more common than the corporate one (see examples of Quaker and Mars above). This structure exists following company mergers and acquisitions.

2 *Mixed brands*: within this structure are the dual brand and endorsed structures. The dual-brand structure is where two brand names show roughly equal prominence on product packs. According to the authors above, this is the most common form of branding (see Table 6.1), and was used by most of the firms studied. Endorsed brand structure is where house, family or mono brand names have almost equal prominence on product packs. Many large diversified companies such as ICI and 3M have this structure.

3 *Brand dominant*: This structure recognizes that there are the single brand structure on one hand, and the furtive brand structure on the other. For example, Procter & Gamble and Mars adhere to this approach. Most of the companies using this approach do not display their corporate name or logos on the front of the product pack, but these usually appear in the company's address on the back of the product pack. Furtive brand structure is similar to the single or mono brand structure, except that the corporate name is not disclosed anywhere on the product pack, e.g. Flora's package does not say it is made by Van Den Bergh.

Rationale

Corporate brands are used when companies operate in a tightly defined market. This simple brand structure also reflects firms' organic growth. This has kept their markets close and helped avoid the brand clutter and diversification that acquisitions can produce. History (i.e. how companies started or where the brands came from) and tradition also influence the use of corporate brands. Many leading brands have held their market position for many years, with their names traceable back to the origin of their company. Company and brand were then one, and some of these relationships remain. Many corporate brands, including Nestlé chocolate and Kellogg's cornflakes, are therefore associated with long-term ownership of the brand. Emerging firms usually have strong leaders who impose their personality and name on their business. In these businesses, tradition dictates the use of corporate names that are deeply embedded in the company's past (Olins, 1989). It is unthinkable

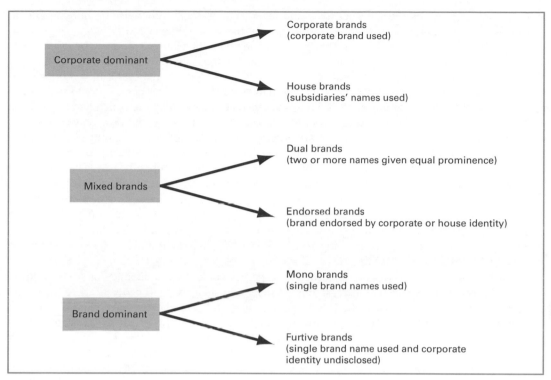

FIGURE 6.3 Brand hierarchy

that Sir Adrian Cadbury would not use his family name on new products, such as Cadbury's Time Out.

Company structures equally reflect brand structures. The fundamental concern with organizational structure is the degree of centralization and decentralization (Ind, 1990), both geographically and across products. Companies with many subsidiaries, such as BAT and Unilever, are in quite a different position to companies with close parental links, such as Mars. In centralized companies there is more chance of standardization, so corporate dominant structures are more likely. Conversely, highly decentralized companies, such as Glaxo, retain no control of their logo and allow international subsidiaries to develop their identities. Olins (1989) suggests that in these decentralized companies, where controls are weak, brand-dominant structures occur.

House branding is more common than corporate branding, and occurs when a diversified company has divisions that operate in tightly defined markets. It also appears when acquisitions are made and a subsidiary is given some independence. The divisional structure that the house names represent allows the subsidiaries to focus on their own business and can give them a promotional advantage. The houses can develop independent identities that can benefit the range of products they market. House branding occurs because product ranges are incompatible or because different segments are being targeted. United Biscuits could probably market dog biscuits using one of its many house names, but the association would probably not help sales for human consumption. Segments may also need to be treated separately. The National Westminster Bank has branches in most British high streets, but Coutts, its personal banking service for the wealthy, has a separate network.

Mixed brands occur for corporate and marketing reasons. Even where the branding is consumer driven, corporate history has a great influence. The popularity of brand extensions and the use of brand leverage mean that many new products are launched as mixed brands (Aaker and Keller, 1990). Mergers and acquisitions give companies reasons for mixed branding. It has been said that the acquiring company obtains a rich archive of brand heritage that can be used to bolster flagging lines. The Rover group did this when attaching the sporty MG name to Metro and Montego sedans.

Acquisitions can also expose avenues for brand leverage that would otherwise be uneconomic to pursue, such as Nestlé's use of the Aero confectionery name on desserts and drinks.

Mixed brands can also be transient. The leverage of an established family brand can be used to help in launching a new product. If successful, the family brand name is then slowly removed so the family brand and new mono brand can have their own firm identities. Another reason for mixed branding is standardization. After an acquisition, firms may wish to associate related products or try to standardize names internationally. For example, Mars did this across Europe with Snickers, which had been called Marathon in some markets. For a while, both names were on the package, but now only one is.

It has been argued that shareholders are the target when a corporate identity is used as an endorsement. Sometimes it is done to convince shareholders of the value of an acquisition. It can also be used to transfer the glamour of top brands to an unexciting company name. There are clear risks in doing this. An unappealing corporate identity can add clutter and reduce the appeal of a mono brand. There is a danger of consumers responding negatively to the revealed omnipotence of a large corporation or corporate mishaps affecting many products (e.g. the use of the Martha Stewart corporate brand name across a huge array of businesses was an advantage until the bad news of the financial scandal concerning Martha Stewart the person; following her conviction, the company's index fell from 120 to 62).

Dual brands occur not necessarily because companies could gain economies of scale in advertising and promotions but also to increase market share and shelf space to generate more sales. This is consistent with an ACNielsen study (1984), which suggests that brand extensions offer no economic return in the long term and, with Smith and Park's (1992) study on the effects of brand extensions on market share and advertising efficiency. The latter shows that the strength of the parent brand is related positively to the market share of brand extensions but has no effect on advertising efficiency.

Mono brands occur when a company has a wide range of products. Diversification explains this structure. Furthermore, it has been argued that the use of mono or single brands also allows companies to target different target markets and differentiate brands, and gives consumers the perception of wide choice. This is used in shopping goods where the knowledge that some products, e.g. Cardhu, Lagavulin and Talisker malt whisky, are all made by the same firm adds nothing to their value. Similarly, mono brands, with different names in different countries' markets, reduce the international mobility of products and thus allow prices to fit local markets.

Furtive brand structure increases the opportunity for differentiating or isolating brands. It can occur because a company like Unilever's divisional structure gives house names rather than the corporate identity on packaging. In other cases there may be ethical but unappetizing connections between products like Mars confectionery and Pedigree pet food. The isolation provided by furtive brands can reduce the impact of adverse publicity. Some matters can be out of a company's control, such as saboteurs and activists tampering with food products. Usually 'scares' are linked to one brand but, if family brand names are involved, an adverse public reaction can affect others (Laforet and Saunders, 1994).

How to choose an appropriate strategy

It would seem appropriate that companies operating in several markets should adopt a family branding strategy (or use the super brand name) to cover products in the same category. The risk of brand dilution is reduced and economies of scale can be achieved. Established family brand names will help support new product launches and induce product trial.

It will also pay to adopt a corporate endorsed approach in the long run at least, for those operating in a homogeneous market. However, it does not pay to use a corporate branded or corporate endorsed approach when the company is small or less well known, as the company's name does not mean much to the consumer. It pays to use individual brand names instead. It would be more important in this case to improve sales rather than market share. The standalone brand approach would, therefore, reduce the risk of brand dilution.

Elasticity of the brand will be an issue in brand leverage as this will increase in the future. If the brand, whether a corporate, super or product brand name, does not bring any benefits to the company in terms of competitive leverage and benefit transfer, and to the consumer in terms of perceptual values, perceptual fit and brand trust, it is not worth using it as an endorsement to another brand. Perceptual fit implies the consumer must perceive the new item to be consistent with the parent brand. Competitive leverage means the new item must be comparable with or superior to other products in the category. Benefit transfer means the benefit offered by the parent brand is desired by consumers of products in the new category. Perceptual values are concerned with the values that consumers perceive in the extended product, whether it is price, quality or reflecting a new lifestyle that is relevant to the consumer. Brand trust is a relatively new concept in brand extension. In the literature, trust involves brand credibility – in brand extension acceptance and performance satisfaction. Credibility includes truthfulness, fair-mindedness, sincerity, concern for customers, similar values (as the parent brand), confidence, competence, expert standing and reputation. Performance satisfaction is concerned with personal experience, usage history, fulfilling expectations, quality consistency, experience of peers, quality level and dependability (Reast, 2005).

Managers interviewed insisted that competition in the market was as a result of companies using dual brands and endorsed brand approaches. Most often it was thought that companies tended to put logos indiscriminately on their product packs in the hope of increasing any product associations between the new product and the parent brand or shared brand heritage between two brands – the old and the new – to save advertising costs in building brand awareness. Companies often failed to think through the role of each brand identity and the benefits that brands might bring to each other. Companies should take a more systematic approach to dual branding or mixed branding, by asking themselves the following questions:

1 What brands does the company have?
2 What market does the company operate in?
3 What product market does the company operate in?
4 What is the target market?
5 How does the company want to position itself? What is the company's philosophy?
6 What is the company's view of supporting brands?
7 Are new brands justified? Can the company afford it?
8 If not, how can drive brands be selected (see United Biscuits' strategy above)?
9 What are the components of the identity and what is the role of each identity?
10 What is the role each brand plays and how can it work with other identity components?
11 What is the target market and how does the company maximize the message in that target market?

The drawbacks of dual brands and mixed brands are:

■ Brand dilution can take place if there are problems with the new brand. If that is the case, in a corporate endorsed situation, it can damage corporate reputation.

■ Customer confusion may surpass their value in terms of association benefits. Various associations within the product class or range may confuse customers.

■ The use of a corporate brand name to endorse a weak brand would not be of any help. It may help to reassure first-time purchasers, but may not add credibility and may reduce consumer perceptual quality.

Unless there is image consistency, personality, quality, value, product attributes of the endorsed or dual brand, multiple brand names should not be used across product class categories. Sub-brands (or product brand names) should be used in targeting different customer segments of the market. It is also argued that brand names with higher consumer utility extend better than those with lower consumer utility (Rangaswamy et al., 1993). Therefore, it would help if the corporate name, divisional name and super brand name is one with high consumer utility. Narrow brand names such as Campbell have advantages over broader brand names such as Heinz for extensions that are highly similar. However, broader brand names have advantages over narrow brand names for extensions that are moderately similar to the brand's current products (Boush and Loken, 1991).

There are other implications apart from choosing the right branding strategy for product packs. First, firms that consider adding a corporate identity to their product brands should also consider the value or costs of adding this and try to balance the sales generated from it. Second, companies should pay attention to how they should manage brand transition, which is a situation where companies use dual branding to eventually move towards single brands.

International brand structure

There is at the present time a need for firms to coordinate and integrate their marketing activities across markets. This is due to globalization, companies setting up or acquiring other companies or entering into alliances across national boundaries. An important part of a business's international marketing strategy is its branding policy in international markets. The main purpose of branding in international markets is to define the firm's identity and its position in these markets via an explicit international brand structure. Here, the firm has several choices:

- Use the same brand name in different countries.
- Leverage brand strength across boundaries.
- Maintain local brands to meet local customers' preferences.
- Choose a brand structure or architecture that suits, i.e. either corporate/house or product-level brands or some combination of the two (Douglas et al., 1999).

According to Douglas et al., there are several issues related to international brand structure, which make it very complex. First, there are different levels of branding within the firm that need identifying; then there is the number of brands at each level as well as their geographic and product market scope. The number of levels refers to corporate, house/product business and product. Another issue is how these should be used in conjunction with each other. Then, there is the question of how to manage brands that span different geographic markets and product lines, as well as who should have custody of international brands and be responsible for coordinating their positioning in different national or regional markets, as well as making decisions about use of a given brand name on other products or services. A further issue is, if the company expands through acquisition or strategic alliances, how the brand structure of different merged firms arises. Finally, the question to be considered is how far should branding be integrated or standardized across countries.

Douglas et al.'s (1999) developmental framework of international brand structure revealed three major patterns of brand structure: corporate-dominant, product-dominant, and hybrid or mixed structure. This is consistent with Laforet and Saunders' 1994 findings of firms operating in domestic markets but, with large variations within a given type of structure depending on the firm's administrative heritage and international expansion strategy as well as the degree of commonality among product lines or product businesses. These structures were also continually evolving in response to the changing configuration of markets or as a result of the firm's expansion strategy in international markets.

Corporate-dominant structure was found among only a few of the companies studied. These were business-to-business organizations with a heavy emphasis on corporate branding, or a relatively narrow and coherent product line. Other cases included consumer goods companies focused on a global target segment, whose objective was to establish a strong global identity for the brand rather than respond to local market conditions. The corporate logo and visual identification (e.g. Apple and Nike) played a major role in defining the corporate brand image worldwide.

Product-dominant structure was common among American firms who had expanded internationally by leveraging individual brands (e.g. P&G's brands such as Camay or Pampers). The reason why this structure exists is, first, because of acquisition. Companies expanded through acquiring national companies with a number of local brands, in addition to their own global and regional brands. Second, these were well-established traditional brand names known for their quality and reliability. Third, this structure allows products to be tailored to local preferences, and product innovation was quite low. There were few potential synergies from harmonizing brands across borders.

A large number of companies had *hybrid brand structures* with a combination of corporate and product brands. For example, Coca-Cola used the Coca-Cola name on its cola brand worldwide, with product variants such as Cherry Coke, Coke Lite or Diet Coke, and caffeine-free Coke in some, but not all, countries. In addition, Coca-Cola has a number of local or regional soft drink brands, such as Lilt in various fruit flavours in the UK, TabXtra, a sugar-free cola drink in Scandinavia, and Cappy, a fruit drink in eastern Europe and Turkey (Douglas et al., 1999). In other instances, companies use the corporate name for some product businesses, but not others. For instance, Danone used the Dannon/Danone name on yoghurt worldwide, on bottled water in the US and on cookies in eastern Europe. Danone also owns the Lu and Jacob brands which are used on biscuits in Europe and the US, and three other bottled water brands: Evian, sold worldwide, Volvic and Badoit, only sold in France, as well as Kronenbourg and Kanterbrau beers, and Vivagel and Marie frozen foods in Europe. Other companies had different brand architectures for different product divisions. For example, Unilever had a global brand in its personal products division. The yellow fats division consists mostly of local brands with some harmonization in positioning or brand name across countries, while the ice-cream division had a combination of local and global product brands such as Magnum, Cornetto and Solero. These were endorsed by a country or regional house brands such as Walls and Algida, and all shared a common logo worldwide.

Rationale

Douglas et al.'s (1999) study suggested that international brand structure is determined by three main features: firm-based factors, product market characteristics and market dynamics. While it is argued that the firm's history shapes its brand structure, market dynamics and the growth of economic and political integration as well as rising media costs create pressures to harmonize branding across countries to achieve economies of scale and scope.

Firm-based factors relate to a firm's organizational structure, its expansion strategy, the mode of expansion (this refers to acquisition, organic growth or entering strategic alliances to broaden the geographical scope of the firm's operations), the importance of corporate identity, and the diversity of its product lines and product divisions.

Product market characteristics relate to the nature of the product market(s) in which the company operates and how this influences its brand structure. Whether there is a homogeneous market or a global consumer group that shares similar interests and needs, global brands may be used. The degree of market integration – whether the same competitors compete in these markets – and the cultural embeddedness of the product; for instance, food is often culturally embedded and there is more likely to be a demand for local brands. All these factors will affect international brand structure.

Market dynamics will have an effect on how brand structure evolves in international markets. It has been argued that, in the context of international markets, if political and economic barriers between countries were removed, together with regulatory change, opportunities for branding harmonization would result in fewer brands. The integration of markets and the growth of regional and global media also help international or global brands to increase cost-effectiveness and reinforce brand strength. Advances in global communication technology and retailing internationalization would further facilitate the growth of international branding and global brands. Finally, consumer mobility (the movement of customers across national borders through travel) means that the development of a global identity would be enhanced, with resulting synergies created through this global presence.

Corporate endorsement and brand extension in international markets

It has been found that, increasingly, complex brand structures at the corporate and product level are beginning to emerge in international markets. Typically, corporate endorsement of product brands occurs on one hand and, on the other, strong brands are leveraged across countries and product categories. The reasons for the shift in corporate endorsement are, first, the consumer's need for product quality and reliability reassurance. Second, potential cost savings can be generated through promotion of a global corporate brand rather than multiple single brands. Third, this will enhance corporate image and visibility. For example, Cadbury uses the Cadbury name on all its confectionery products, in conjunction with product brands such as Dairy Milk, Wispa, etc. A house brand is also sometimes used in the international market (e.g. Unilever's ice-cream division had a combination of local and global product brands such as Magnum, Cornetto and Solero. These were endorsed by a country or regional house brands such as Walls and Algida, and all shared a common logo worldwide).

The prominence and role of the corporate brand or logo varies from country to country (e.g. Douwe Egbert uses the Friesian lady logo on its coffee in all countries, but the size of the lady and the positioning statement vary from country to country; in Spain, for example, the positioning emphasizes the richness of the coffee and the master brewer, in the UK its continental taste, and in Holland the association with family and comfort are featured). The reason for extending strong brands across product lines and across countries is economies of scale and sharing of brand values and brand strength, and also to take advantage of existing consumer loyalty or awareness (e.g. Danone uses the Danone name to market biscuits in Eastern Europe, in order to leverage customer familiarity with the name; similarly, Nestlé's Maggi brand, used on sauces and seasonings, had high recognition in eastern Europe and so was extended to frozen foods rather than the Findus brand used elsewhere in Europe) (Douglas et al., 1999).

To conclude, global trade continues to increase and change rapidly. As international markets evolve, companies need to consider how to modify their brand structure or architecture and look towards rationalizing brands and improving efficiency as well as harmonizing brand strategy across product lines and international markets. It seems limiting the number of strategic brands across countries enables firms to consolidate and strengthen their position as well as enhancing brand strength. In the light of new market conditions effective management of international brand structure is cruical to maintaining firms' position and strengthening key brands in international markets.

Environmental pressure on branding

In 2000 Aaker and Joachimstahler predicted a trend from single brands, through endorsed and sub-brands, towards corporate branding structures. The reasons for this were said to be emerging market complexities, competitive pressures, channel dynamics and globalization. However, companies' adoption of multiple brands, their aggressive brand extensions and complex sub-brand structures confused the market even more. Therefore, in order to overcome these problems, these authors argued for a simpler and cost-effectively leveraged corporate brand structure to be put in place of a standalone brand structure.

Conversely, the efficiency of 'pooling' and 'trading' strategy also points to a financial gain from using brand names together, as Petromilli et al. (2002) have suggested. 'Pooling' captures more shelf space and market share through the deployment of single brands to differentiate products. Simultaneously, two or more brand names used together would 'trade off' each other's brand values. Furthermore, the need for brands to be in the market quickly led companies to stretch existing brand names instead of launching new brands that would take longer to establish. Using a combination of brands together means that each sub-brand (name) gains from the 'pooling' effect and benefits from 'trading' on the halo effect of master brand associations, and also saves time. Therefore, mixed brands are suggested in place of other structures.

However, Kapferer (2001) suggested that single brands were becoming more common as companies de-capitalize. There are three reasons for this:

1 The use of market segmentation and differentiation to create barriers to cannibalization and to avoid distribution channel conflicts.

2 De-capitalization is a logical response as markets fragment into increasingly small segments.

3 Companies turn to the single brands after failing to find the synergies anticipated from corporate branding.

A number of companies use a single-brand strategy to grow vertically in a highly segmented market (Laforet and Saunders, 2005). Vijayraghavan (2003) argued that, in intensely competitive markets, single brands offer more character and allow better positioning than other brand structures. The drivers of this trend are increasing market segmentation, falling customer loyalty and competitively priced alternatives. He further commented that, in price-sensitive markets, value-for-money brands such as own-labels were often volume pullers. In these segments umbrella branding did not help and conflicted with the umbrella brand's use in less price-sensitive segments. Pierce and Mouskanas (2002) also noted that individual or single-brand names within a portfolio became more powerful when they were interrelated. They then suggested that successful companies should concentrate on a small group of powerful brands.

The broader business environment also pushes companies away from corporate brands and towards standalone identities or single brands. With anti-globalization movements, global brands attract protesters as well as customers. Anti-globalization authors such as Naomi Klein and critics of fast food nations such as Eric Schlosser have in some way turned activists against the wider market of big labels and corporate brands in particular (Laforet and Saunders, 2005). For instance, in Europe Cadbury, a corporate brand that uses its corporate name across its product range, is targeted in the 'obesity debate' rather than Mars, which mainly uses individual brand names (Mesure, 2004, in Laforet and Saunders, 2005). Furthermore, the use of the Internet by pressure groups can spread criticism of companies in seconds. Another pressure on corporate brands comes from the risk of reputation loss. As has been observed, sometimes limiting the use of a corporate brand is about controlling risk (Nelson, 2002), while negative publicity about a brand does not necessarily do damage to the parent brand if a strong visual and nomenclature link has not been established. The need for precise product positioning and limiting risks suggests an increase in the use of individual or single brands (Laforet and Saunders, 2005).

Other threats to branding are, first, threats from own-labels in some areas, especially in the frozen and chilled sectors. Second, people have become more visually inclined and time pressured. Product packaging (see Chapter 12) is sometimes better retained in the consumer's mind than brand names due to its powerful visual elements. Third, consumers are also influenced by price or value for money, especially in the food area, where own-labels dominate national brands. Nowadays, there are only a few brands that are important to consumers: that is, there are very few brands that they cannot do without. This probably explains why six to seven out of ten new product launches fail, so that more products have become me-too products, i.e. have incremental improvements. In addition, in order to keep costs down, brand deletion is very common among fmcg companies. Thus, companies get rid of those brands that are in decline. Many companies also operate in very fast-moving industries and often have no time to think of strategies. Instead, they just focus on the day-to-day running of the business so that there is not always consistency in the branding strategies deployed by firms. This poses a threat to brands and branding in general.

New brand strategies

There has been a significant change in strategies in the past ten years. The results of Laforet and Saunders' (2005) study indicate that, compared with ten years ago, companies today deploy more branding styles and approaches, and there has been a decline in corporate brands. Of the companies surveyed, 61 per cent used a mixed branding approach compared with 53 per cent in 1994 (Table 6.2).

There is a certain fuzziness surrounding the use of mixed, endorsed and dual-brand structures. Endorsed brands are now more complicated (Table 6.3). Family or super brands are used

	Products		Companys[a]	
	1994	**2004**	**1994**	**2004**
Brand style	%	%	%	%
Corporate dominant				
Corporate brands	5	3	20	20
House brands	11	6	65	40
Mixed brands				55
Dual brands	39	35[b]	95	
Endorsed brands	14	26[b]	50	
Brand dominant				
Mono brands	19	26	75	100
Furtive brands	13	6	65	50

[a] Percentages do not add up to 100% because all firms use more than one strategy.
[b] Double branding is used on 19% of products surveyed, triple branding is used on 12% of products surveyed, and composite branding is used on 1% of products surveyed.

TABLE 6.2 Occurrence of branding styles, 1994–2004

in conjunction with a product brand instead of the corporate or the house brand, as previously (e.g. Cadbury Schweppes, Kellogg's, Procter & Gamble, Mars, United Biscuits). Similarly, mixed brands used to be associated with a vertical hierarchy of brands where, for example, a family brand name would appear with a product brand name. Dual branding is now more complicated. The relationship between brand names appearing on a dual brand is horizontal, i.e. product brand names have equal prominence on packs. Take, for instance, Cadbury's Dairy Milk Crunchie, where Dairy Milk and Crunchie, which are two product brand names, have equal prominence in typeface on packs, while Cadbury is a corporate name also featured on the same pack.

The mixed structures include both the endorsed and dual-brand styles appearing simultaneously on product packs. There are also two new approaches:

1   A collection of powerful brands is used in a combined format to communicate parts of a product or act as ingredient signifier, e.g. Bisc and Bounty. Companies hope that using Bounty in conjunction with Bisc will signify to consumers the coconut taste contained in the brand

Corporate branded	Corporate name (endorsing a product brand)
	House brands
Endorsed+	Corporate name (endorsing a product brand)
	House name (endorsing a product brand)
	Family/super brand name (endorsing a product brand)
Dual brand	Corporate, house, family brand + product brand
	Product brand 1 + product brand 2
Multi-branded	Endorsed multi-brand (i.e. family endorsing two product brand names)
	Triple brand (corporate name + brand 1 + brand 2)
Branded	Mono brand
	Furtive brand

TABLE 6.3 Emergent brand structures

1994	2004
Mixed corporate branded Cadbury Schweppes,** Heinz, Kellogg's**	*Mixed corporate branded* Heinz
Mixed house branded Associated British Foods,* Northern Foods, Unigate,** United Biscuits,** Rank Hovis McDougall*	*Mixed house branded* Associated British Foods,* Northern Foods, Rank Hovis McDougall*
Mixed family branded Quaker, Kraft General Foods	*Mixed family branded* Quaker, Kraft General Foods
	Family brand dominant United Biscuits,** Uniq**
Mixed corporate endorsed Nestlé, Colgate Palmolive, SmithKline Beecham**	*Mixed corporate endorsed* Nestlé, Colgate Palmolive
Mono branded Allied Lyons,** Mars,* Unilever,** Procter & Gamble,* Reckitt Benckiser,** CPC, Dalgety	*Mono branded* Procter & Gamble,* Mars,* GSK**
	Brand dominant Allied Domecq,** Reckitt Benckiser,** Unilever**
	Corporate dual brand dominant Cadbury Schweppes,** Kellogg's,** Gillette, Sara Lee

* Moderate changes; ** significant move.

TABLE 6.4 Brand styles by strength/usage compared for 1994 and 2004

Bounty. As far as consumers are concerned, they know what to expect. Another example is Cadbury's Dairy Milk Crunchie, a combination of several brand names, which gives a stronger signal to the consumer than Cadbury's Dairy Milk with honeycomb pieces.

2 The licensee and licensor brands appear in a combined format on product packs (e.g. McVitie's Snickers flapjack). The ultimate goal is shared branding. Thus brands can feed off each other and use each other's values and goodwill. Similarly, stronger communications can be achieved with the consumer in terms of trust and immediate awareness of the new product. On the other hand, many of the dual brands were transient as companies changed from using one brand name to another (e.g. Whirlpool-Philips). Dual brands were also a result of short-term profit making (e.g. Maltesers Teasers from Celebrations were launched at Christmas).

Laforet and Saunders' study showed that few manufacturers remained constant in their overall brand strategies over the past ten years. Some have switched their brand strategies altogether (Table 6.4). Mergers and acquisitions and companies' restructuring activities were part of the change in strategies, while environmental factors such as consumption trend, competition and transition have further impacted these. Spreading risks and moving away from corporate branding are part of today's branding rationale.

The growth of brand licensing

Brand licensing is a contractual permission to use a brand in association with a defined product, for a defined period of time, in a defined territory. Licensing is the process by which a brand/property owner extends a trademark or character from its principal environment onto products of a completely different nature.

How can licensing boost business?

Licensing trademarks for business purposes has existed for many years, and consumers are buying more licensed products and brand names now than ever before. Licensing can benefit businesses in the following ways. It can:

- Expand the product portfolio.
- Drive new revenue streams through licensing opportunities.
- Increase the brand's global awareness.
- Inspire customer loyalty and build brand equity.
- Fuel valuable promotional and retail partnerships.
- Make the brand more lifestyle orientated.

Licensed products offer opportunities to create differentiation and provide a direct line into consumer consciousness. Nowhere is this more evident than on the high street, where cartoon characters have become fashion statements and fashion chains are offering licensed home wares and stationery. In supermarkets, the cereal aisles are enlivened by licensed character promotions and cereal brands score success on other breakfast products. In specialist retailers you find high-price-point licensed collectibles, and designer goods that use classic iconography to strike a balance between familiarity and cutting-edge product design. Licensing can thus transform a product, boost sales and build a brand. Partnerships are at the heart of all licensing deals, and the parties involved in licensing are increasingly becoming more closely entwined. Licensors deal directly with the retailer, the licensing agent, the licensee or a sales promotion agent (Brand Licensing Europe, 2007).

In today's marketplace there are several reasons for companies to use brand licensing, especially in the fmcg sector. First, due to the power of large distributors and pressure to generate brand value and increase brand strength, brand leverage is taking a different form from the usual extension of brands within a company's brand portfolio. Large companies look for extensions that go beyond their own competencies and to partnering with other companies to market new, brand-enhancing, revenue-generating products that appeal to the consumer. Examples of brand licensing are Walkers adding the Marmite brand into crisps and McVitie's recently licensing its brand to Mars Snickers in flapjacks.

According to the manager of United Biscuits, which owns McVitie's:

> By licensing the brand you bring all the awareness – we do not have to explain what the brand stands for. It is much more cost effective way to stretch the brands into different areas and we get the recognition that Mars built.

In other words, the reasons for the company to license its brand to Mars were: to have brand saliency with the consumer; to show how big its company is; to increase the company's global awareness and its expertise in areas other than biscuits; and to increase revenues more cost effectively. The second reason for brand licensing is the sharing of brand heritage and mutual benefits for both the licensee and licensor. McVitie's has expertise in flapjacks, whereas Mars has expertise in chocolate confectionery but not in flapjacks, and vice versa (as United Biscuits' manager says, to 'get the recognition that Mars built'). Third, the decline of broadcasting and the fragmentation of communication and distribution channels increases the cost of branding. With corporate brands declining, brand leverage is sought in other ways (Laforet and Saunders, 2005).

Brand licensing – more than product extension?

The effect of brand licensing in the marketplace goes beyond extending the company's core competencies, but this can result in a change of perception and direction for the brand. According to branding experts, brand licensing can be much more than product extension. It is an attitude extension it does not have much to do with the products the company makes, but with the attributes that the brand is seen to possess:

Attitude → Belief → Consumption

Brand extensions can succeed because the new product deepens the meaning of the brand and extends its attitude in a way that leads to increased consumption (Bass at Brandchannel.com). Fit and added value are two essential ingredients for successful brand extensions. Fit ensures that the brand is extended within the domain of the parent brand, i.e. the new brand is extended into a related product category or range of the parent brand, and leverage is the added value of the new extended brand (e.g. Kellogg's Rice Krispies).

For brand licensing to work, the following questions must be asked to ensure that fit and added value exist in licensed brand extensions: What is the strategic benefit of licensing? What are the target product categories? How is the licensing strategy related to the brand strategy? Before adopting brand licensing, the company's capabilities and resources should also be examined. For instance, does the company have experience in drawing up and negotiating licence agreements? What is the current new product development process? Is the company prepared to carry out technical inspections of licensees? What support will the company offer to licensees? In terms of resources, are key decision-makers available to develop a licensing strategy and approve potential licensees? Does the company have a budget for developing a licensing strategy (Bass at Brandchannel.com)?

According to Bass, the current trend in fmcg is that the owner usually waits until a suitable opportunity is presented to him. The main barriers to brand licensing are often internal, such as the company's bureaucracy and approval process. Furthermore, although brand managers do recognize the benefits of brand licensing, few are motivated to spend the time to generate royalties, which is rarely fed back into the marketing budget, and fewer still have a long-term licensing strategy.

The most important contributing factor to the success of a licensed brand extension is the quality of the manufacturer. The brand owner needs to target potential licensees and develop tools to assist them to implement a brand extension. A licensing agent can help to brainstorm opportunities, scope the market and develop opportunities that might otherwise stall or run out of momentum. The riskiest alternative is to do nothing.

Branding Brief 6.1: The role of confectionery brand extensions

Source: Lyla Adwan, Euromonitor International, 17 March 2003

The benefit of extending known brand names into other markets is threefold. In the first instance, it builds brand awareness, making the confectionery product more likely to be the subject of an impulse purchase. Second, use of known brands practically guarantees the success of the new product, where a totally new brand might fail. Finally, and perhaps most important, brand extensions guarantee revenues when confectionery sales are traditionally slack, such as in hotter weather, or under threat from competing product formats.

Mars spearheaded the confectionery brand extension policy into ice cream, setting a precedent which has been avidly followed by companies such as Nestlé and Cadbury Schweppes, while the latest developments in 2002 and 2003 include extensions into cake bars and biscuits.

Mars led the way with ice cream

At the forefront of confectionery brand extensions, Mars' ice cream portfolio mirrors that of confectionery, with Mars, Galaxy/Dove, Snickers, Bounty and Twix all commonly found in the ice-cream cabinet, as well as sugar brand Starburst.

This policy offers Mars significant potential economies of scale, particularly in relation to advertising and promotional investment. There is a major emphasis on encouraging impulse purchase, which ideally suits the promotion of the Mars range, although 2001 witnessed a shift in focus with the launch of several bulk brands. Chocolate confectionery brands fit well within the recent premiumization and more indulgent nature of bulk ice creams.

Cadbury has also extended many of its confectionery products such as Flake, Bourneville, Crunchie and Refreshers into impulse ice cream. Nestlé, on the other hand, which has been aggressively developing its overall ice cream business, has been slower at promoting its confectionery brands, although Kit Kat does appear in an impulse ice cream format.

Cake bars and chilled desserts popular

Mars also teamed up with United Biscuits in the UK to develop its Galaxy and Milky Way brands into individually wrapped cakes, while Cadbury Schweppes offers its Fudge brand as a cake, and builds on the equity of the Dairy Milk brand for its Mini-Rolls.

Nestlé, however, avoided cakes, preferring brand extension into chilled desserts, making use of its substantial dairy expertise. This is one of the few sectors where Nestlé pipped Mars to the post in terms of product development, having launched Milkybar, Rolo and Smarties desserts long before Mars' tie-up with Eden Vale to develop Galaxy, Milky Way and Bounty in the UK.

Biscuits are latest extension

In 2003 both Mars and Nestlé extended some of their confectionery brands into biscuits. The filled/coated sweet biscuit market is forecast to grow considerably faster than the countline market between 2002 and 2007. As health and wellness issues become more important, consumers view even indulgent biscuit varieties as less unhealthy than countlines, making this a key sector of interest for confectionery manufacturers.

Mars' Bisc& range includes biscuits topped with M&M's, Twix, Mars and Bounty, while Nestlé has launched biscuit versions of Milkybar and Smarties. Mars' product, in a similar fashion to Cadbury cake bars, are individually wrapped items available in multi-packs, designed to take advantage of snacking and lunch-box trends. By contrast Milkybar biscuits come in a traditional paper tube, while Smarties biscuits are in a stand-up pouch. Thus both are targeted more at in-the-home consumption and sharing trends, reflecting a difference in strategy among the confectionery market leaders.

Brand awareness, where next?

Nestlé has also been very keen to develop and extend brands within the confectionery market in order to respond to growing consumer sophistication by segmenting brands along age and gender lines. While Kit Kat Chunky cannibalized Kit Kat sales, brands like Milkybar have been extended within confectionery in order to widen the consumer base, rather than just splitting sales. Thus Milkybar Munchies are labelled 'For Adults' while Milkybar Choos are aimed at very young children.

The company has gone even further with its number two core confectionery brand Smarties, using tie-ups with companies like Ritter Sport and Haribo in Germany to launch tablets and jelly-filled Smarties at the end of 2002. White and milk chocolate tablet bars followed in the UK at the start of 2003. While Smarties may have lagged behind in terms of product development over 2001 and most of 2002, Nestlé is now trying to update the brand's image by increasing the formats in which it is available within confectionery, in addition to extending the brand into biscuits. This is on top of moves made in 1998 and 2000 into the chilled desserts and ice-cream markets.

Further development for Smarties could be used to revitalize Nestlé's declining packaged cake sales such as Yes in Germany, or could be used to leverage the company's expertise in children's breakfast cereals.

For Nestlé, as indeed for all confectionery manufacturers, the key to brand extensions is maintaining interest and increasing usage occasions without cannibalizing the core product. Whether manufacturers respond to this challenge by segmenting the brand along age lines, or whether they extend it into new markets depends on the maturity and development of the market the brand is located in.

Thus in the same way that flavour variations are often country-specific, so are brand extensions, highlighting the importance of local knowledge within the context of a global marketplace.

Branding Brief 6.2: Brand licensing

Source: Based on Retail Space Invaders: private label forces fmcg to develop brand licensing strategies – Adam Bass

Quantum leap extension

Until the introduction of the Trade Marks Act in 1994, allowing your brand to appear on a product emanating from another company would have potentially risked invalidating your registered trade mark. The Act effectively allowed a trade-mark licensing regime to exist and now, of the ten most popular classes covered by new trade mark applications at OHIM (the European Community trade mark office), eight are typical merchandising and/or licensing classes.

Using licensing to extend into new categories opens up a broad range of possibilities, leveraging decades of equity to establish an advantage over comparably recent and disposable private labels. A single product brand like Marmite, for example, has carefully harnessed the expertise of external manufacturers to exploit gaps in their product portfolio: Marmite Flavoured wafer-thin cheese biscuits helped the brand cross over into an aristocratic setting, satisfying a consumer need that, with turnover of £1m, would not have justified investment from its owner, Unilever.

Extension through licensing is not to be confused with product improvement or the targeting of new consumer segments through pack size or flavour variations. Improvements in response to technical innovation and new trends like 'low-carb' or 'organic' maintain brand equity but fog up the marketing atmosphere, raising consumer expectations about the speed of delivery of new products.

Only extension through licensing can deliver the sort of quantum leap that takes Evian into moisturizing lotion or Bisto into Yorkshire puddings. Because of the interest from own-label manufacturers looking for growth by exploring licensing opportunities, a licensing strategy is an essential requirement for today's brand managers.

Creating a strategy

To create a licensing strategy, a brand manager should first think about running an ideation session, either with consumers or internally. This will help to identify as wide a range of potential extensions as possible which can then be explored by a licensing agency. The ideation session should explore all opportunities no matter how far fetched because the licensing agency will invariably focus attention on the most commercially viable options.

Once the core categories have been identified, the licensing agency can carry out a research and scoping exercise that will gather data about the core target categories, establish fit with the brand and develop initial contacts. After presenting potential licensees with a brand outline, the licensing agency can gauge response and add detail to the initial concepts.

With the initial concepts fleshed out, the licensing agency should then work to align interests between suitable parties to reach an appropriate licensing contract and help to deliver product and packaging that leverage the brand equity in the new category and achieve the sales and distribution outlined in the contract. Additionally the agency should help to manage the ongoing relationships whilst ensuring coordination between current and future licensees so that retailers receive a consistent message about the brand.

Without a strategy in place, the brand owner is dependent upon snap judgements in response to enterprising manufacturers pursuing a vague interest in licensing, with no one prioritizing a target list of categories or coordinating efforts to reach an agreement.

From a straw poll of around 200 UK brand owners contacted over the last four years, it's surprising how only a handful of UK companies have a licensing strategy or an in-house licensing department. With US brands and trademarks generating $34.2 billion worth of licensed product sales in 2003 and the increasing power of private label, this sector is set to grow radically in the UK.

Branding Brief 6.3: Unilever

Source: Adapted from the company's website: www.unilever.com/brands/hpc/

From sumptuous soups to sensuous soaps, their products all have one thing in common. They help you get more out of life.

Home and personal care

As a leader in world markets including home care, skin and hair care, deodorants and anti-perspirants, Unilever's products meet people's diverse requirements to clean and care for their homes, their clothes and themselves. It is growing its biggest brands through innovative product development and compelling brand communications. Each of these brands has enormous potential to meet the changing needs of consumers through a variety of products that fulfil the brands' promise. At the same time, they also have the potential scale, profitability and international appeal needed to be world leaders. Yet while each is a global brand, some are known by different brand names in different markets. For example, Sunsilk is called Sedal or Seda in Latin America, while Rexona is Degree in North America and Sure in the UK.

In many parts of the world Unilever leads the home care market, with brands including Cif, Comfort, Omo, Skp and Suggle. It's a position it has secured by understanding that household products have to be as diverse as the people who use them. So as well as developing tablets for the most sophisticated washing machines, for example, Unilever also produces low-cost soap bars for people that wash their laundry in river water.

In personal care, its skin care brands include Dove, Lux and Pond's. Unilever also has leading oral care brands including Signal, antiperspirant/deodorant brands including Rexona and Axe, and a wide range of hair care products under its Dove, Sunsilk and Suave brands.

Food brands

Unilever is one of the world's leading food companies. Its passion for understanding what people want and need from their food – and what they love about it – makes Unilever's brands a popular choice.

Unilever Bestfoods is one of the world's leading food companies. Its passion for understanding what people want and need from their food and what they love about it, makes its brands a trusted part of people's lives. It is committed to adding vitality to people's lives by ensuring its products taste great and can form part of a healthy balanced diet.

- Healthy choices – its success is based on making healthy food the easy and enjoyable choice. World-class nutrition and health expertise enables it to provide options that can help people stay healthy, and look good and feel good all at the same time. The benefits of brands such as Slim-Fast and Flora/Becel Proactiv are recognized by the medical profession and all Unilever Bestfoods brands include good-for-you choices that can form part of a balanced diet.

- Natural and fresh – everything in its frozen foods range uses the best-quality, fresh ingredients, which are rapidly frozen. 'Fresh freezing' locks in all the nutritional value and taste, without artificial colourings, flavourings or preservatives. It's all part of the company's aim to help consumers feel good and get more out of life.
- Fun, indulgent and refreshing – the company puts more fun into a healthy balanced diet with Heart brand ice creams, including Magnum and Cornetto. Fruit flavoured ices from Solero, and the Lipton range of tea and soft drinks brings refreshment with natural vitality.
- Food you can trust – whatever people love about food, we aim to make sure they can trust us to source, make, distribute and market our brands in a way that's good for them and the world we share.

Conclusion

Intense competition, market complexities, globalization, mergers and acquisitions, multiple and aggressive brand extensions have left companies with an increasingly complex brand portfolio to manage. Furthermore, in order to increase consumer response, and ultimately sales, profitability and market share, companies have mixed matched brand names from and within the brand portfolios. In the early days a number of terminologies were used to describe these brand activities, such as nested branding, family or umbrella branding, super branding, blanket family names, brand and sub-brand, corporate endorsed, etc. However, one way to keep brands under control is to create a hierarchy of names, called brand architecture or brand hierarchy or brand structure.

Olins and Murphy suggest three major systems of corporate identities: the monolithic, the endorsed and the branded structure; and/or the corporate dominant, balanced/mixed system and the brand dominant. However, Laforet and Saunders find that firms rarely adhere to one approach and there are complexities in the brand approaches used. This complexity surrounds the mixed and dual brand approaches used, and there exists a vertical and horizontal relationship between brands. Laforet and Saunders' empirical findings show in detail how companies' brands portfolio are deployed. Types of brand names can be grouped as a series of levels according to their breadth of use and relation to the corporate name. At the highest level there is a corporate name that covers all a firm's products, and at the lowest a virtual brand name that identifies a variant of a brand. Six brand types have been identified: corporate brand name, house (or a company's division) brand name, family brand names (or super brand), mono brand names, virtual brand names, and description. These are used singly or in combination. The brand structure is described in terms of the corporate dominant structure (which has two sub-structures: corporate and house brand), the mixed brands (includes dual and endorsed sub-structures) and brand dominant (includes single and furtive sub-structures). Laforet and Saunders' recent research also finds more fuzziness surrounding the mixed brand structure. In some areas of fmcg, such as snacks, more dual brand names are used and the relationship among brands is more horizontal (see their new typology of brand structures).

A number of reasons have been identified for the brand structure used, among which are: mergers and acquisitions; history; strategic associations; symbiosis; increased brand visibility and saliency with consumers; acting as brand ingredient and taste signifier; transmitting strong signals to consumers; increasing consumers' curiosity and reducing the chance of their becoming bored with a brand that appears in only one format; helping to attract non-users of the core brand; short-term benefits; the decline of broadcasting and fragmentation of communication and distribution channel; the increased cost of branding; economies of scale; reinforcing the brand as expert; maximizing consumer trust; extending a brand that reflects a change in lifestyle or demographic; multiple markets; product positioning; and limiting and controlling reputation risk.

A further study examines international brand structure, showing three major patterns of brand structures: corporate-dominant, product-dominant and hybrid or mixed structure, similar to the findings of firms operating in domestic markets, but with large variations within a given type of structure depending on the firm's administrative heritage and international expansion strategy, as well as the degree of commonality among product lines or product businesses. International brand structure is driven by three main factors: firm-based characteristics, product-market characteristics and market dynamics.

Companies are facing new pressures from emerging market complexities, channel dynamics, competition from global players, changes in consumption trends, lifestyle choices and transition. These pressures are reflected in a switch of brand strategies used in the past ten years. Laforet and Saunders' recent research finds that few companies have remained constant in the brand approaches they use, and some have switched their brand strategies altogether. Among the factors mentioned above, spreading risks and moving away from corporate branding to brand licensing are part of today's branding rationale.

To conclude: the management of a portfolio of brands is substantially different from the management of single and individual brands. Brand portfolios are the result of a process which is divided into three stages. Phase 1 is characterized by brand accumulation, then transition and the reduction of brands. In Phase 2 organization of relationships between brands takes place; followed by Phase 3, where brand portfolios are developed and used as a strategic tool to gain competitive advantage and as a planning model, i.e. the way the company plans to develop itself for the next year. Therefore, brand portfolios deal with both the internal and external environments. They represent a company's multiple competencies and a way of managing complexity. Brand portfolios also help sustain competitive advantage in terms of brand-level competencies, as well as helping to manage transition.

Finally, this chapter questions what has been said about brands and how they can be managed. Branding can be political and historical-based as well as market-based. The chapter questions what has been said about building and buying brands. Companies might buy brands, but how do they use them? It questions the role of corporate and brand identities, and how companies should use these to avoid brand dilution and customer confusion. Firms who are considering adding a corporate identity to their product brands should first consider the value or costs of doing this, and try to balance these with the sales generated from it. The chapter examines how companies manage transitions where companies use dual brands in the short term and move towards single brands in the long term.

🔑 Key terms

Brand association: the association that consumers make with a brand or a product. Usually it is symbolic or at the abstract level. It also refers to brand image association. For example, Cadbury is associated with purple colour, but also with quality and the paternal feeling that the company's employees have about it.

Brand dilution: when a brand is overstretched into an unrelated product category and loses its original association – e.g. if Cadbury were to extend in the cereal product market, it might dilute its brand image as a fine chocolate maker. Not many consumers would associate Cadbury with cereals.

Brand elasticity: brand stretchability, i.e. the extent to which it can be leveraged to another product category.

Brand extension: brand leverage or a brand that extends to a related or unrelated product category. For example, Cadbury launching a new product that carries the Cadbury name and the new product (or the extension) name, e.g. Cadbury's Dairy Milk is a brand extension of Cadbury; or if Cadbury tries to extend into the cereal market, which is unrelated to its original product category – confectionery, e.g. Cadbury's Crunchie cereal bar (this is a fictitious name).

Brand hierarchy: a brand structure in which brand names are visualized as a hierarchy with the company or corporate name on top, then the division or house name, the family name, product brand name and product description at the bottom. This is a concept developed by Laforet and Saunders in 1994 to explain how brand names are being deployed by fmcg companies. This also refers to the branding approaches or brand strategies companies use.

Brand leverage: see **brand extension**.

Brand licensing: a contractual permission to use a brand in association with a defined product, for a defined period of time, in a defined territory. Licensing is the process by which a brand/property owner extends a trademark or character from its principal environment onto products of a completely different nature.

Brand portfolios: a portfolio of brands that companies accumulate as they grow. This could be through mergers and acquisitions. Chailan (2006) refers to these as the result of a process which is divided into three stages. Phase 1 is characterized by brands accumulation, then transition and reduction of brands. Phase 2 – organization of relationships between brands takes place. Followed by Phase 3, where brand portfolios are developed and used as a strategic tool to gain competitive advantage and as a planning model.

Brand structure: see **brand hierarchy**.

Corporate branding: the use of the corporate name on all the company's products, e.g. Kellogg's and Cadbury use their name on all their product range.

Corporate dominant structure: corporate branding and house or division branding whereby the corporate name and the house or division's name are used across the company's product range.

Dual branding: corporate endorsement and family or super branding, i.e. when the corporate name is used to endorse a product brand name, and when a family brand name or super brand name is used in conjunction with a product brand name, e.g. Friskies Gourmet A La Carte (Friskies is a super or family brand name used across Nestlé pet food).

Family branding and blanket family names: using a family brand name across a product range. Family brand is a general term, which refers to product items that have the same basic brand name. Anne Page is a family brand name which is used on many Ann Page food products. Blanket family name implies that the firm uses part or all of its name across a range of products that are not necessarily related by type, function or application, e.g. Dunhill and Canon.

Free branding: corresponds to using individual product brand names.

Furtive brand: a single-product brand name whose corporate name is not disclosed on the back of the product. This often happens because companies want to hide their identity, in particular when operating in conflicting product markets like food and pet food.

House brand name: using the division or a company's subsidiary name across a product range.

Hybrid structure: a mixed structure with a combination of corporate and product brand names.

Mixed brand: a combination mix of brand name approach used by a company across its product range that could take the form of corporate endorsement, family brand, division brand and product brand used altogether.

Mono brand name: similar to individual product brand name or single or mono brand name.

Nested brand name: brand names used within brand names.

Product dominant structure: a company that uses an individual product brand name in all its product range.

Sub-brand: when more than one brand name appears on a pack, the least prominent one is termed sub-brand.

Super branding: family branding, i.e. using a family brand name across a product range.

Umbrella branding: corporate branding or family branding.

Virtual brand name: suffixes used to identify variants of a brand or a qualifier to a brand name, e.g. Friskies Gourmet A La Carte. A La Carte is a virtual brand name. It exists only as part of a derived brand name.

? Discussion questions

1 Choose two market leaders in two different industries. Contrast their branding strategies and brand portfolios.

2 Choose two market leaders in the same industry. Contrast their branding strategies and brand portfolios.

3 What are the main aspects you consider when designing a branding approach for any company?

4 If you were a brand manager, what questions would you ask yourself to help guide effective and consistent brand decisions? For capitalizing on new business opportunities such as overseas expansion?

5 Explain the pitfalls of brand extension and how to overcome these.

6 Discuss the rationale behind a single brand approach compared with a corporate brand approach.

7 Examine the branding approach you would use in the context of a business-to-business sector. Explain any differences compared with the fmcg sector.

8 Discuss the brand associations you have for the following three products: Nestlé Kit Kat, Ford Jaguar and Cadbury's Marathon cereal bar.

9 Following question 8, which one of the brand approaches will not work?

10 Discuss how the 'No Logo' movement (Klein, 2000), and related anti-globalization and anti-Americanization movements constitute a major crisis for brand managers today.

Projects

1 Examine the process of brand optimization for a company of your choice that wants to expand abroad.

2 Take a look at ten products sold in supermarkets, report on the branding approaches used on their packaging (e.g. corporate name, product name, company's subsidiary name, family brand name, etc.), then answer question 3 below.

3 Conduct a small market survey to find out consumers' opinions about the different branding approaches observed earlier. Which ones do they prefer, and do these mean anything to them?

4 Examine the growth of brand licensing in recent years across three industries of your choice. Can you explain the reasons for this occurring?

5 Search for a company case that recently made an acquisition or merged, examine its brand portfolio and design a strategic brand portfolio for this company.

MINI CASE 6.1: NEW LIFESTYLE TRENDS CALL FOR A NEW RESPONSE FROM THE FOOD INDUSTRY

Source: Adapted from *Irish Jobs Column*, 2003

The food industry in Ireland is worth £10 billion a year, with exports topping £5 billion, and it continues to be the country's most important indigenous industry. The Irish food industry employs 40 000 people and is made up of about 700 small to medium-sized companies. Eight of the top ten Irish-owned exporting companies are in the food and drink businesses. The Irish food and drink industry, however, must innovate and adapt to consumer trends and demands. People have less time than ever before and require more convenience foods and ready meals.

The rise in the consumption of convenience foods in the form of ready-to-eat meals is set to continue. According to research by Teagasc, the food research agency, 'micro-waveability' is the single biggest factor affecting consumers' decisions to buy such products. Microwaveable products now account for 18 per cent of all new products as consumers are spending less time cooking – down from several hours a day in the 1950s to just 20 minutes a day today.

Until Marks & Spencer came along, ready meals were called 'TV dinners' and regarded as a poor substitute for the real thing. While consumers viewed ready meals as expensive, the majority of the participants in the Teagasc survey purchased them on a weekly basis. People today want to eat fast, but they want it to taste good. Chilled products were seen to be of better quality, but frozen products were purchased in greater quantities due to their prolonged shelf life.

The UK market for ready meals is worth £1.5 billion a year, between frozen and chilled products, and represents a big opportunity for Irish food companies. While per capita consumption of ready meals in Ireland is only about one-third that of the UK, the market is growing rapidly, especially for chilled products.

According to Bord Bia, it is expected that Ireland's prepared consumer food sector will continue to grow. 'Expansion in the number of women working, loss of cooking skills, reduced household size and increased disposable income are certain to lead to an expansion in the market for ready meals,' according to Teagasc. Enhanced awareness of health and diet, a growing number of vegetarians as well as increased interest in ethnic and international foods would further drive demand. Teagasc is developing a 'food lifestyles model' for food manufacturers to develop a better understanding of consumer behaviour and attitudes to food purchase and consumption.

Question:

1 Identify new lifestyles and explain how these changing lifestyles create growth opportunities in the snack food market.

MINI CASE 6.2: CADBURY SCHWEPPES' NEW HORIZON

Source: Eric Combelles, Euromonitor International, 30 October 2003

After a series of acquisitions conducted throughout 2002 and at the beginning of 2003 (Dandy, Kent and Adams) Cadbury Schweppes is now in a position where restructuring its food business is a must. The company announced it is planning to cut 10 per cent of its workforce (5500 employees worldwide) over the coming three years across its business units.

Cadbury claims some of the savings will be used to promote products in regions where it does not hold a leading position. What are these regions? What are the products the company will promote?

Market and position review

In 2002 Cadbury ranked fourth in the global confectionery market. This was based on strong sales stemming from western and eastern Europe, Africa and the Middle East as well as Australasia. Cadbury enjoys double-digit percentage shares in each of these regions. Asia-Pacific, and both Latin and North America are thus obvious targets for the company, where its market shares orbit a meagre 2 per cent in value terms. Moreover, Euromonitor forecasts firm value growth for confectionery in Latin America and Asia-Pacific between 2003 and 2008. But are these two regions the only targets for Cadbury?

The company's range of products covers all three confectionery sectors, namely chocolate confectionery, sugar confectionery and gum, each offering something different to its diverse portfolio. Chocolate confectionery cannot boast a healthy image, but does benefit from a large indulgence factor. Companies market premium products in an attempt to fuel value sales but volumes remain generally stable. Sugar confectionery is cheap and profit margins are low, which forces companies into the production of high volumes, including the production of private label.

Gum, on the other hand, is the only sector that has shown higher value than volume growth between 1998 and 2003. The sector is also expected to do so over the next five years, a fact that has formed the basis of Cadbury's recent acquisition strategy. This stems largely from functional gum which allows manufacturers to add value through product development. In a context where multiple grocers continue to put pressure on prices, functional gum offers attractive profit margins. Moreover, the production of gum requires advanced technology that belongs to just a few companies located in Asia, America, Europe and North Africa, and these companies have prevented multiple grocers from introducing private-label alternatives.

Region potential

In western Europe gum offers the greatest potential, with retail sales expected to outstrip growth in chocolate and sugar confectionery by at least three times. Here competition is limited to Perfetti van Melle and Wrigley, and Cadbury's newly strengthened gum portfolio, including brands such as Stimorol, Hollywood, Trident and V6 as well as Clorets and Chiclets, is now able to mount an effective challenge. In fact, the acquisition of Adams sees it go into number two spot from a much lower base just a couple of years ago.

In eastern Europe, where the health trend has yet to reach western levels, chocolate confectionery continues to drive growth. Cadbury is expected to develop its sales further while implementing its cost-saving programme. Ultimately profit margins are expected to rise.

The biggest obstacle in North America is the agreement linking Cadbury with Hershey for the distribution of chocolate confectionery. Cadbury might opt to focus purely on gum. The dominance of Wrigley makes this a uniquely tough environment, but the acquisition of second player, Adams, now provides a solid platform on which to mount a sustained challenge.

Gum is forecast to outperform both chocolate and sugar confectionery in Latin America, and Adams' leading position in the region provides Cadbury with an instant foothold. In Asia-Pacific all sectors are expected to perform equally well and shares are up for grabs for companies investing wisely.

The new horizon

The restructuring is part of a longer-term strategy being implemented to challenge its rivals and especially the world's biggest confectionery player, Mars Inc. Having identified the underlying changes taking place in the market, with consumer preferences shifting from traditional confectionery (chocolate and sugar) towards modern trends (functional food and other healthy food), Cadbury has embarked on a programme of acquiring key gum companies.

The next step will see the closure of factories, likely to take place all over the world and which has already started in Manchester and Chesterfield, UK, but also in Australia where Cadbury operates 16 plants. Expected savings will be diverted to supporting key brands in its portfolio in order to become the world's number one confectionery company.

Reactions on the stock market have not all been positive for Cadbury, with its shares losing value as analysts still think the recent acquisitions were too expensive. Cadbury aims to achieve its objectives by cutting costs and generating sufficient cash from its key brands for continued support and investment.

Questions:

1 What are the product strategies and communication strategies that Cadbury Schweppes could use to enhance the level of differentiation between its subsidiaries?

2 Explain, in your opinion, how Cadbury Schweppes could have acted differently in order to respond to changing consumer preferences?

3 Are there any other strategies it could have employed instead of acquisitions followed by restructuring the company?

4 Design a brand architecture for Cadbury Schweppes.

5 Should Cadbury Schweppes choose a different brand architecture for its overseas markets?

END OF CHAPTER CASE STUDY: BRAND STRATEGY POSITIONS PRODUCTS WORLDWIDE

Source: Based on Jan Willem Karel, *Journal of Business Strategy*, May/June 1991

During the mid-1980s Whirlpool Corporation (W) faced a critical strategic decision. The company had been highly successful as a US producer of major home appliances. However, demographics, the economic outlook and the competitive environment in the US, where five large, well-funded competitors battled for market share, clearly pointed to limited growth opportunities there.

This realization led to a thorough review of W's options. Further integration, diversification and financial restructuring were analysed and considered, but rejected in favour of global expansion in the home appliance business.

A detailed analysis of the worldwide major appliance business revealed a significantly different picture than in the US. The world market for major appliances of about 180 million units was growing rapidly, especially in western Europe (the largest market) and in Asia. Though appliances differed in configuration from region to region, the technologies and skills needed to design, build and market them in any location worldwide were basically the same.

At the same time, corporate growth could be fed not only by market unit sales growth but also, by the anticipated consolidation of appliance companies in Europe, South America and Asia. The economies of scale to be gained through global operation, such as sourcing of parts and development of new products, clearly pointed to continued industry consolidation in Europe and other areas of the world – much like that already experienced in the US. The end result would likely be the emergence of a few large, committed companies dedicated to serving a global major home appliance industry.

The competitive dynamics and emergence of EC 1992 led W to choose to expand in Europe first, with full recognition that, at some point, the company also would need an Asian presence. Though alternatives were considered, the preferred expansion vehicle was a joint venture (JV) with NV Philips, which was willing to sell an interest in its $2 billion major appliance business.

The Philips JV – named Whirlpool International BV (WIBV) – had one significant complication. Philips was unwilling to sell its brand name, the second-best recognized brand in Europe, under which a substantial portion of its major appliance business was conducted. How could the business done under the Philips brand name be transferred to another name or group of names?

Fortunately, there was evidence that this could be successfully accomplished. In fact, the best case study was internal to W. During the 1960s, the corporation established the W brand and grew it to the number-two market position in the US by 'dual branding' product as RCA W. This dual-branding process established the precedent and provided the confidence that a brand transfer could be accomplished with the Philips name.

A small group of European and US managers was commissioned by W Chairman Dave Whitwam to determine the strategy, timetable and resources that would be needed to position the W brand in Europe. After carefully defining its mission, the group set about gathering data regarding market shares, consumer perceptions, competitive brand positions and anticipated market dynamics.

Dual-branding strategy

There was clearly no single key to success from the strategy, but a host of sensitive factors and judgemental issues required evaluation and consideration. Perhaps most significant was the realization that the brand-transfer program had to be a process – one that could be empirically tested and adjusted as new intelligence and competitive reactions were taken into account. A discussion of the key elements of the strategy follows. First, be aggressive. As the largest manufacturer of major appliances in the world, W certainly did not need to be apologetic about the brand transfer – or about using the W name as the ultimate repository of the Philips brand business. Extensive studies of W, including its 'odd' spelling and difficult pronunciation in certain European languages, were not necessarily negative. Its uniqueness, as well as the dynamism of the world and the inherent value of investing in the brand and company name simultaneously, offered many advantages.

The ability to start with a clean slate (with a name virtually unknown to European consumers) also had advantages over trying to reposition one of the existing European brand names that W had acquired as part of the JV with Philips.

Second, capture the hearts and mind of the W European employees and of the European trade. Clearly, if the European organization didn't understand how it stood to benefit – that all of the knowledge and resource of W were behind the brand transfer process – the programme could easily fail. Getting the programme introduced correctly was of paramount concern.

Two major meetings were scheduled to introduce the dual-branding programme: one in Milan, Italy, on 5 November 1989, for WIBV staff and one in Cannes, France, two months later for the trade. The November meeting drew 540 of WIBV's top managers from around the world and served as a kind of dress rehearsal for the presentations and staging of the January 1990 event. Following the Milan meeting, a comprehensive communication package outlining the strategy went out to the rest of the WIBV organization.

While the first priority was briefing WIBV people, most of the energy and anticipation focused on the trade. Cannes represented the apex of the year-long effort. In the hour-and-a-half-long presentation, several audio-visual treatments centred on the meeting's theme of '1+1=3'. Speeches by W senior managers were translated simultaneously into eleven languages. Itineraries and literature about the JV were also translated and packaged in personalized binders. And the trade was treated to a preview of a new television advertising campaign that shortly would be telecast throughout Europe.

The next morning dozens of the trade media gathered at a hotel in nearby Nice for a press conference (again with simultaneous translations) followed by personal interviews with Whitwam and senior management within WIBV. That afternoon, Whitwam and the team flew to London to meet with European business and financial press to review the strategy.

By all accounts, dealers were upbeat about the event and supportive of the strategy, although a few remained cautious. The media generated some 180 stories in Europe alone, most lauding W for its move and explaining what the W name brought to the branding equation.

The dual-branding campaign and the presentations for the staff, trade and media were launched, with a full realization that there was only one chance to get it right and that some WIBV people, especially those with a long history with Philips, were initially wary about the implications of tampering with such a well-known and well-respected brand name. Thus, the theme of '1+1=3' was selected. It said to the trade that the value of the two parts, W and Philips, was greater than their sum.

The result of extensive market research is what 'licensed' this positive and aggressive approach. It indicated the approach would work. But there was no way to know what to expect from the dealers whose business depends on the draw of the Philips brand.

It's one thing to prove to the trade that the company was going about this in the proper manner, basing its decisions on hard and thorough market data. But dealers also wanted to know what new things the JV would bring as competitive advantage.

There was plenty to tell them, but an equally important message was to let them know that whatever was implemented would depend ultimately on what was relevant for their country and market. This reinforced another theme: WIBV intended to think global but act local. While the company now enjoyed a broadened global perspective through its association with Whirlpool, WIBV management realized it could win only by meeting the needs of its various local markets.

Therefore, a third element in the strategy was the commitment to make the W brand more valuable than the Philips brand so that the brand transfer could be accomplished with the minimum amount of risk. This caused the team, with the lead taken by the key country managers in Europe, to develop an extensive list of added values that ran the gamut from special sales incentives to improved stocking and distribution of spare parts to totally new products.

Those value-added benefits attracting the greatest interest, however, included the promised introduction of multiple consumer helplines modelled after W's consumer assistance lines in North America and the possibility of dealer and consumer financing options through Whirlpool Financial Corporation International (WFCI).

Both the helpline concept and the WFCI financing are novel to the various European markets. The complexity of these markets and the various national regulations necessitate that these be implemented on a country-by-country basis. Language and cultural differences require that the helplines also be country-based and not pan-European markets.

Some of these things will take more time to put in place than others, but considerable progress has been made. In the UK, for example, a consumer helpline has been launched. And WFCI is offering financial packages to retailers, including extended payment terms and financing of display stock and inventory.

Because the idea of the brand transfer brought out strongly held opinions and was new to all managers, a fourth element of our strategy was to base brand transfer decisions on the results of extensive quantitative research. Several simultaneous and ongoing research projects were initiated both to help position the W brand vis-à-vis competitive brands and to monitor weekly (throughout the duration of the brand transfer process) the brand recognition and buying preference related to the W name. This research, along with guidelines established in the original proposal is what is determining the timing for various tactical and, funding decision and it will continue to do so throughout the programme.

The JV agreement with Philips that created WIBV stipulates that W may use the Philips brand name only until 1999. So a final element of the dual-branding strategy involved deciding when to drop the use of the Philips brand name. The decision was to do so on a country-by-country basis (not across Europe at the same time) and to do so only when research showed that recognition of and buying preference for W branded appliances within a country had reached predetermined target levels.

Cultural considerations

Perhaps the media campaign followed naturally from the previously mentioned strategic elements. Whirlpool International's media blitz, however, did break long-standing conventions within the European advertising industry. Traditionally, what appeals to the French won't play well to the Germans or to the English, so advertising has been culturally sensitive. But for a variety of reasons, WIBV wanted to consolidate its advertising under a single pan-European advertising campaign and under a single agency, Publicis FCS International, and to base its approach on hard data from detailed market research.

It wasn't easy. Various proposals were favoured or rejected along country lines as expected. But when all the research was in, one particular approach – a simple, informational commercial introducing Philips and Whirlpool – elicited a positive response from consumers in every country where it was tested. The commercial is being aired with positive reactions throughout Europe and it's also putting the W brand name on the map.

The advertising programme to support the introduction of Philips–Whirlpool dual branding, the first pan-European advertising campaign for the major home appliance industry, received extensive testing in four countries before its launch. In-depth interviews were conducted with 900 housewives to check the campaign's objectives.

After just six months of dual-brand advertising in Europe, the campaign is meeting its objectives:

- There is a significantly high spontaneous awareness of the new dual-branding programme and association of Whirlpool with Philips.

- Simultaneously, the spontaneous level of awareness for Philips appliances was maintained.

- In five countries, the campaign scored significantly higher than targeted. In addition to these five countries, expected levels were achieved in two countries. An insufficient total was reached in only one country and corrective action is already under way.

- Results attained in German- and Latin-language-speaking countries proved that the pronunciation of 'Whirlpool' is not an obstacle.

Questions:

1 What are the cultural considerations the case study refers to? Give examples.

2 What should the advertising programme objectives of the Philips–Whirlpool brand be?

3 Can you think of similar examples of dual branding?

4 What is the strategy to be adopted for a corporate branded company which acquires or merges with another company?

5 Research Whirlpool or Philips corporations and their brand portfolio, then design an international brand architecture for either company.

6 What are the considerations a corporate branded company should take into account when going global? Compare and contrast these with an individually branded company.

References

Aaker, D. A. (1991), *Managing Brand Value: Capitalizing on the Value of a Brand Name*, New York: The Free Press.

Aaker, D. and Keller, K. (1990), 'Consumer evaluations of brand extensions', *Journal of Marketing*, Vol. 54, No. 1, pp. 27–33.

Aaker, D. and Joachimstahler, E. (2000), *Brands Leadership*, New York: The Free Press.

ACNielsen Co (1984), 'Extending brands', *The Nielsen Researcher*, April.

Arnold, D. (1992), *The Handbook of Brand Management*, London: Century.

Arthur Young and Company (1989), *The Arthur Young Report on Brand Valuations: Practical Implications for Australian Business*, Sydney, Australia: Arthur Young and Company.

Baldinger, A. (1990), 'Defining and applying the brand equity concept: why the researcher should care', *Journal of Advertising Research*, Vol. 30, No. 3, RC2–RC5.

Barwise, P., Higson, C., Likierman, A. and Parsh, P. (1989), *Accounting for Brands*, London: The Institute of Chartered Accountants and the London Business School.

Bayus, B. (1992), 'Brand loyalty and marketing strategy: an application to home appliances', *Marketing Science*, Vol. 11, No. 1, pp. 21–37.

Blackston, M. (1990), 'Price trade-offs as a measure of brand value', *Journal of Advertising Research*, Vol. 30, No. 4, RC3–RC5.

Boush, D. M. and Loken, B. (1991), 'A process tracing study of brand extension evaluation', *Journal of Marketing Research*, Vol. 28 (February), pp. 16–28.

Brand Licensing Europe, 2007.

Buday, T. (1989), 'Capitalizing on brand extensions', *Journal of Consumer Research*, Vol. 5, No. 4, pp. 27–30.

Chailan, C. (2006), 'In search of a well-balanced brands portfolio: the L'Oréal – Bodyshop case', in the proceedings of the 2nd Annual International Colloquium on the Dynamics of Brand, Corporate Identity & Reputation in the Knowledge Economies, 7–8 September 2006, Manchester Business School.

Cowley, D. (1991), *Understanding Brands*, London: Kogan Page.

Douglas, S. P., Craig, C. S. and Nijssen, E. J. (1999), 'International brand architecture: development, drivers and design', Intbrand.html.

Doyle, P. (1989), 'Building successful brands: the strategic options', *Journal of Marketing Management*, Vol. 5, No. 1 pp. 77–95.

Grover, R. and Srinivasan, V. (1992), 'Evaluating the multiple effects of retail promotion on brand loyal and brand switching segments', *Journal of Marketing Research*, Vol. 29, No. 1, pp. 76–89.

Hall, J. (1992), 'Support for brand new perspectives', *Marketing*, 14 May.

Hill, S., Ettenson, R. and Tyson, D. (2005), 'Brand portfolio renewal', *Sloan Management Review*, Vol. 46, No. 2, London: Kogan Page.

Ind, N. (1990), *The Corporate Image*, London: Kogan Page.

Interbrand (1990), *Brands: An International Review*, London: Interbrand.

Kapferer, J. N. (2001), *(Re) Inventing the Brand*, London: Kogan Page.

Klein, N. (2000), *No Logo*, New York: Picador.

Laforet, S. and Saunders, J. A. (1994), 'Managing brand portfolios: how the leaders do it', *Journal of Advertising Research*, Vol. 34, No. 5, Sep/Oct, pp. 64–76.

Laforet, S. and Saunders, J. A. (2005), 'Managing brand portfolios: how strategies have changed', *Journal of Advertising Research*, Vol. 45, No. 3, pp. 314–27.

Murphy, J. (1987), 'Branding: the game of the name', *Marketing*, 23 April.

Nelson, S. (2002), 'Corporate brand and packaging design', at http://www.findarticles.com/p/articles/mi_qa4001/is_200210/ai_n9119373/print.

Olins, W. (1989), *Corporate Identity*, London: Thames and Hudson.

Petromilli, M., Morrison, D. and Million, M. (2002), 'Brand architecture: building brand portfolio value', *Strategy & Leadership*, Vol. 30, No. 5, pp. 22–28.

Pierce, A. and Mouskanas, H. (2002), 'Portfolio power: harnessing a group of brands to drive profitable growth', *Strategy & Leadership*, Vol. 30, No. 5, pp. 15–21.

Pride, W. and Ferrel, O. C. (1977), *Marketing: Basic Concepts and Decisions*, Boston: Houghton Mifflin.

Rangaswamy, A., Burke, R. R. and Oliva, T. A. (1993), 'Brand equity and the extendibility of brand names', *International Journal of Research in Marketing*, Vol. 10, pp. 61–75.

Reast, J. D. (2005), 'Brand trust and brand extension acceptance: the relationship', *Journal of Product & Brand Management*, Vol. 14, No. 1, pp. 4–13.

Roberts, C. and McDonald, M. (1990), 'Alternative naming strategies: family vs individual brand names', *Management Decision*, Vol. 27, No. 6, pp. 31–6.

Robinson, J. (1933), *The Economics of Imperfect Competition*, London: Macmillan.

Rooney, J. A. (1995), 'Branding: a trend for today and tomorrow', *Journal of Product & Brand Management*, Vol. 4, No. 4, pp. 48–55.

Saunders, J. and Walters, R. (1993), 'Branding financial services', *International Journal of Bank Marketing*, Vol. 11, no. 6, pp. 32–9.

Schlosser, E. (2001), *Fast Food Nation: The Dark Side of the All-American Meal*, New York: Houghton Mifflin.

Smith, D. and Park, C. (1992), 'The effects of brand extensions on market share and advertising efficiency', *Journal of Marketing Research*, Vol. 29, No. 1, pp. 296–313.

Vijayraghavan, K. (2003), 'Fmcg firms relearn marketing strategies', *New York Times*, April.

Wernerfelt, B. (1988), 'Umbrella branding as a signal of new product quality: an example of signalling by posting a brand', *Rand Journal of Economics*, Vol. 19, No. 3, pp. 458–63.

Further reading and online sites

Brandchannel.com

Harish, R. (2008), 'Brand architecture and its application in strategic marketing: the example of L'Oréal', *Icfai Journal of Marketing Management*, Vol. 7, No. 2, pp. 39–51, May.

Morgan, N. A. and Lopo, L. R. (2009), 'Brand portfolio strategy and firm performance', *Journal of Marketing*, forthcoming.

Muzellec, L. and Lambkin, M. (2008), 'Corporate rebranding and the implications for brand architecture management: the case of Guinness (Diageo) Ireland', *Journal of Strategic Marketing*, Vol. 16, No. 4, September, pp. 283–99.

Nijssen, E. J., Craig, C. S. and Douglas, S. P. (2001), 'Executive insights: integrating branding strategy across markets: building international brand architecture', *Journal of International Marketing*, Vol. 9, No. 2, pp. 97–114.

Uggla, H. (2006), 'The corporate brand association base: a conceptual model for the creation of inclusive brand architecture', *European Journal of Marketing*; Vol. 40, No. 7/8, pp. 785–802.

Varadarajan, R., DeFanti, M. P. and Busch, P. S. (2006), 'Brand portfolio, corporate image, and reputation: managing brand deletions', *Journal of the Academy of Marketing Science*, Vol. 34, No. 2, March, pp. 195–205.

CHAPTER

07

Brand Extension

Chapter overview

Central to good branding practice is creating a brand that people value enough to buy and re-buy. These brand values or images can then be used to extend or leverage new products in the same product class or in a different product category, which can be targeted to the same customers or new ones. For the firm the main benefit of brand leverage or brand extension is cost reduction, as compared with developing and launching a completely new product. To the customer the benefit of brand extension is immediate product recognition through a familiar brand name and packaging which saves time on product search and buying decisions. Brand extension can also have long-term advantages, in that brand equity can be built and sustained. However, these are counter-balanced by a number of problems.

This chapter deals with these issues and those mentioned above. It starts with a definition of brand extension, types and strategies, and the benefits and risks of brand extension; what is required to extend into a new product category and to gain consumer acceptance of the brand extension; the key success factors of brand extension; how we assess the scope for brand extension; what are the issues involved in extending into a mature versus a new market; how brands can be linked and how they interact; brand dilution, and the distancing techniques to overcome risk of brand dilution; the planning process of brand extension; and, finally, the effects of brand extension strategies on brand equity. This chapter is part of the broad theme of managing brands – creating and sustaining brand equity, which is also a central topic of this book. Chapter 6 was concerned with brand architecture, and the management of brands and product relationships. Chapter 8 will focus on managing brands across a life cycle.

❖ LEARNING OBJECTIVES

After completing this chapter, you should be able to

- ❖ Understand and appreciate the importance of brand extension

- ❖ Understand the rationale for and the factors influencing brand extension

- ❖ Discuss the options for brand extension

- ❖ Differentiate between vertical and horizontal extension, as well as upscale and downscale extension

- ❖ Discuss the conditions for category extension

- ❖ Evaluate the criteria for consumer acceptance of brand extension

- ❖ Understand the theory underlying consumer brand association

- ❖ Evaluate key success factors of brand extension for different types of brand extension

- ❖ Discuss the concepts of brand linkage, brand relationship and brand symbiosis or shared benefits

- ❖ Discuss when to extend a corporate brand or a product brand

- ❖ Examine issues relating to extending into a mature market and a new market

- ❖ Understand when brand extensions do not work, the problem of brand dilution and how to overcome this; understand how distancing techniques work

- ❖ Examine the possible effects of brand extension on brand equity

- ❖ Follow a systematic procedure to carry out brand extension and assess the scope for brand extension

Introduction

Consumer goods manufacturers have it very tough these days. From complying with government regulations, to meeting price demands from retail customers, profit margins are shrinking. Brand leaders such as Procter & Gamble have multi-billion-dollar budgets at their disposal to fund R&D, and to develop and launch new products. For other companies it is becoming more difficult to compete when they are faced with rising transportation, logistics, advertising and other costs in developing new products. The pressure of cost reduction has led to companies leveraging their brands more and in different ways, since brand extensions are often seen by managers as a safer and more economical way of offering an exciting new product. Extensions of popular brands cause less disruption to the overall business and less strain on manufacturing capabilities. Consequently, these companies have learned to work with the brands they have, and have tried to use different ways of linking and connecting brands to create powerful images and meanings for the consumer, so gaining their attention through immediate product recognition of the parent brand.

However, further pressured by new market trends and the need for short-term profits, many of these companies have extended beyond their core businesses and have often contradicted their core brand values by creating more brand confusion. This tension is reflected in a change of focus from product quality, value, reliability and popularity to qualities that are becoming more important for today's consumers like health, fitness, beauty and environmental friendliness. For instance, Coca-Cola is working with L'Oréal to create a beauty product that targets active and image-conscious women over the age of 25; while PepsiCo is also finding some brand contradictions in Whole Foods, strangely called Fuelosophize. These examples show how far some companies are prepared to move away from their traditional markets and value propositions to keep up with new market trends and increase sales. This chapter will look at brand extension strategies, their benefits and risks, and their effect on brand equity in the long term. It will examine the best ways of conducting a brand extension, as well as other issues already mentioned in the chapter overview above.

Perspectives on brand extension

The practice of brand extension in general is related to the extension of brand names, since a brand name represents a collection of concepts which consumers learn to associate with a particular product. The nature of these associations is often of considerable interest to managers, when contemplating the extension of a brand name across several products. An analogy for brand extension is umbrella branding (see Chapter 6), a term which means 'the practice of labelling more than one product with a single brand name'. This approach is commonly used by multi-product companies. Corporate branding, corporate endorsement and family branding are brand extensions, by which a brand name is either extended across all the company's products (i.e. corporate branding) or a product class (i.e. corporate endorsement), or a product category (i.e. family branding) (see Chapter 6).

A brand extension strategy is defined, as 'any effort to use a successful brand name to launch a product modification or additional products' (Kotler, 1972). In the case of product modifications, it is commonplace – for instance, in the detergent industry – to talk about 'brand X', then the 'new improved brand X', then the 'new brand X with additives'. The definition of brand extensions also covers the introduction of new package sizes, flavours, models, and so on. More important, a successful brand name is often used by companies to launch new products. For example, after Quaker Oats' success with Cap'n Crunch dry breakfast cereal, Quaker used the brand name and cartoon character to launch a line of ice-cream bars, T-shirts and other products. Many other companies, such as Kellogg's, Nestlé, etc. in the breakfast cereals market, also use brand extension to cover a variety of new products that may not find distribution without the strength of the Kellogg's or Nestlé name. However, while the brand extension capitalizes on the parent brand, it must create its own niche and it must establish its own brand loyalty.

The rationale of brand extension

Brand extensions represent an opportunity for firms to use the equity built up in the names of existing brands to enhance marketing productivity. Also, because of the dramatic increase in media costs, the more extensive and aggressive use of promotions by established firms, and the cost and difficulty of obtaining distribution, firms are using established brand names to facilitate entering new markets. Another advantage of brand extension is the protection against own-labels or store brands. Firms that lose the advantage of brand extension or brand leverage within the trade can run into serious trouble. For instance, drug makers face eroding market shares from less expensive generics. Designer labels compete vigorously against an increasing number of popular house brands in clothing and department stores. Large supermarket chains push their own premium store brands aggressively (see Chapter 11). Brand extensions have been found to attract not only existing customers, but also new ones. Consumers with low to moderate loyalty towards the parent brand, those who have less exposure to the parent brand, and non-users are more likely to be receptive to changing their brand loyalties and to try the new brand extension. Therefore, brand extensions can bring new customers to the company, thereby increasing sales even further.

Choice of brand extension

A company has a choice of two types of brand extension: a (product) line extension and a (product) category extension. A line extension refers to an existing brand name that is being extended to a product in one of the firm's existing categories. For example, Coca-Cola's line extensions include Classic Coke, Diet Coke, Caffeine-Free Coke, Cherry Coke, Coke Vanilla and other soft drinks. Often a line extension involves a different flavour or ingredient, a different form or a different application for the brand. To some extent, this is similar to Kotler's earlier definition of a brand extension strategy, which involves partly launching product modifications. Line extension is used to target a new market segment within the same product category as the parent brand. A category extension refers to an existing brand name which is extended to a new product category and which enables the brand name to enter a completely different product class. Examples are Jello frozen pudding pops, Bic disposable lighter, Cracker Jack gourmet popping corn, Ivory shampoo, and many others.

Vertical and horizontal extension

Brand extension strategy comes in two forms: horizontal and vertical. In a horizontal extension, an existing brand name is applied to a new product introduction in either a related product class, or in a product category completely new to the firm (see Scheinin and Schmitt, 1994). A vertical brand extension, on the other hand, involves introducing a brand extension in the same product category as the parent brand, but at a different price point and quality level (see Keller and Aaker, 1992; Sullivan, 1990). There are two options for a vertical extension: the brand extension is either introduced at a lower price and lower quality level than the parent brand – known as step-down; or at a higher price and quality level than the parent brand – step-up. In a vertical brand extension, a second brand name (i.e. the new product brand name) or descriptor is usually introduced alongside the parent brand name, in order to demonstrate the link between the brand extension and the parent brand name.

Benefits and risks of line and category extension

The potential benefits of line and category extension include immediate name recognition, and the transference of benefits associated with a familiar brand. Thus, brand extensions are attractive to firms that face high new-product failure rates, because they provide a way to take advantage of brand name recognition and image to enter new markets. More specifically, the leverage of a strong brand name can substantially reduce the risks associated with introducing a product into a new market, by providing consumers with the reassurance and knowledge about a familiar and established brand. The use of established brand names, as in the case of line extension, to access new markets is also based on the increasing recognition that some brands have built a loyal consumer and trade franchise, can command premium prices and, as a result, enhance the overall value of the firm that owns them. Furthermore, brand extension can decrease the costs of gaining distribution, and/or increase the efficiency of promotional expenditures.

The brand extension decision is often strategically critical to an organization. Although an extension is a way to exploit perhaps the most important asset owned by a business, it also risks decreasing the value of that asset. The wrong extension can create damaging associations that can prove expensive, or even impossible to change. If the wrong judgement is made, substantial time and resources are lost and other market opportunities may be missed. An extension can weaken the parent brand in the original category. Risks come not only from a new product failure, but also from the success of a category extension (Farquhar, 1990). Many of the dangers of overextending a brand name and advice against category extensions have been mentioned in classic literature such as Ries and Trout (1986).

There is a potential risk of brand dilution (as discussed below) if the new line extension fails to satisfy customers, so that their attitude towards other extensions in the same line, as well as towards the parent brand itself are affected. Another risk of brand dilution may arise from the intra-brand competition within the same category between the core or parent brand, and the extended brand. To avoid intra-competition, differentiation between products is a must. Although the products are inevitably similar, since they belong in the same product line, they must be sufficiently distinguishable not to compete with one another as much as they would with competitors' brands.

Branding Brief 7.1: Are brand extensions good or bad? How can companies improve market share by brand extension?

Source: Fireix.wordpress.com

Companies tend to leverage strong brand awareness by extending it to product variants in the same product line (e.g. a different size, flavour or colour) or different product categories, as long as the essence of the brand you are leveraging fits the new product.

So, when adding new products to your portfolio of offerings, you will need to consider both the fit of the product and the brand. The brand extension should be logical from a customer perspective

In technology products you will need to consider that the promise of quality carries over to your brand extension. You might want to consider how brand extensions work with other products in the portfolio or other products marketed by the company.

The product's brand is not established before the first purchase of the new product. Thus, the brand concept, extended well, can provide immediate customer attention, help associate existing brand strengths to the new product and eventually help the new product to be sold briskly, thus gaining market share.

There are certain risks associated with brand extensions. The new product may be perceived as significantly different from the original product and would eventually cause confusion in the marketplace. If the new product fails, there could be negative impact on to the core brand.

So, before you develop a brand extension, you might want to consider how far a brand can be extended before it dilutes its identity with customers. What market segment are you targeting the brand extension to? You might want to consider a flanker branding strategy instead. If there are significantly different value propositions, you might want to use separate branding.

Conditions for extending a brand into a new product category: perceptual fit, competitive leverage and benefit transfer

There are three conditions for extending a brand into a new product category: perceptual fit, competitive leverage and benefit transfer. *Perceptual fit* implies that consumers must perceive the new extension to be consistent with the parent brand. *Competitive leverage* means the new extension must be comparable with or superior to other products in the category. *Benefit transfer* means the benefit offered by the parent brand is desired by consumers of products in the new category. Aaker and Keller (1990) also suggested that the success of a brand extension depends on assumptions about consumer behaviour on the following three points:

1 Consumers hold positive beliefs and favourable attitudes towards the original brand in memory.

2 These positive associations facilitate the formation of positive beliefs and favourable attitudes towards the brand extension.

3 Negative associations are neither transferred to nor created by the brand extension.

As regards the longer-term business outcome of brand extensions, brand extensions may offer no economic return, since short-term gains in perceived quality and recognition are potentially counterbalanced by brand dilution (see Smith and Park, 1992). Doyle (1989), however, suggests that there are four brand extension options which a company can adopt:

1 If the brands appeal to the same target market segment and have the same differential advantage, they can safely share the same company name or range name.

2 If the differential advantage is the same but the target market differs, the company name can be extended because the benefit is similar.

3 If a company has different differential advantages, it should use separate brand names. Some synergy can be found if the brands appeal to the same target market, by using the same company name with separate product brand names.

4 If both the target customers and the differential advantages are different, then using unique brand names is the most appropriate strategy.

This will also be discussed in more detail in the section on extending with a corporate name, family name or product brand name, below.

Criteria for consumer acceptance of brand extension

The evidence to date suggests that consumer acceptance of a proposed brand extension is most likely to be positive if:

1 The parent brand has high perceived quality; the brand name often affects consumer perception of product quality and is also an influencing factor in consumer purchasing decisions.

2 There is a good perceived fit between the parent brand (and its category and the company) and the proposed extension (product and category). The closer the fit between parent and exten-

sion brand, the greater the chance of securing positive sales benefit for the parent brand from the launch of the extension. Fit comprises two dimensions: similarity between the product category of the parent brand and its extension (product category fit); and similarity between the image of the parent brand and its extension (brand image fit).

3 Perceived expertise refers to consumer perception of the company's ability to produce the extension, especially when it extends into an unrelated product category (e.g. a grocery retailer extending into financial services).

4 To a lesser extent, the extension is not regarded as too easy to make.

5 Brand reputation and perceived category risk.

Perceived fit is the most complex of these factors. Assuming a reasonably high-quality parent brand, it is also the main determinant of the extension's acceptance and perhaps of the risk that the extension may dilute (see below) the equity of the parent brand. The perceived fit depends on the consistency between the perceived attributes of the parent brand and those of the proposed extension. Attributes include both specific product features and more abstract or emotional image variables. A brand whose image is based on abstract attributes like prestige, style or durability may be more extendible than one with strong associations with specific product features like stain resistance of a particular colour or flavour. Other aspects of fit include consumer perceptions of the firm's ability to supply the extension, and whether the extension is a close substitute for the parent brand (or in some cases, a complement to it), as mentioned above.

Where the parent brand already covers more than one product or variant (e.g. Coke, Diet Coke, Caffeine-Free Diet Coke), it may be useful to explore the extent to which consumers perceive a proposed extension as 'typical' of the brand. For a given quality parent brand, there is a close relationship between consumers' attitudes towards the extension and their perception of how well it typifies the brand.

There is an inverted U-shaped relationship between how long a consumer takes ('response latency') to decide whether a brand extension exists and its typicality. In Boush and Loken's (1991) study, verbal protocols showed that subjects evaluating a 'close' category extension (e.g. canned soups to canned fruit, calculators to cameras) considered a larger number of specific attributes than when evaluating either a line extension in the parent category or an extension into a more distant category (e.g. canned soups to cereals, calculators to refrigerators).

Branding Brief 7.2: In brief: Kellogg's improbable brand extension

Source: Underconsideration.com/brandnew

Kellogg's has licensed its numerous characters to be produced by a store called Under The Hood. As is evident from the photo above, and as you can see on the website, the clothing line is meant to be hip, cool and lend the wearer enough street cred to avoid getting beaten up when cruising the mean streets of the urban environment. Is this a smart brand extension by Kellogg's? or just a desperate one? Heck, maybe it's genius.

Brand reputation and perceived category risk

Categorization theory holds that people organize objects or information into categories. This enables them to process and understand their environment to the extent that a person perceives an object to be a member of a category, or the components of the category, so that affect and beliefs are then transferred to the object. When faced with a brand extension, consumers initially categorize the extension by assessing the suitability of its membership in a category that contains a product that has a brand name as an identifiable label. This categorization process is said to influence consumer choice of a brand. If the core brand associations (see types of brand association, below) are transferred to the extension, consumers will perceive the extension as fitting with the new category and hence will accept it.

There are eleven types of brand associations:

- Product attributes
- Intangibles
- Customer benefits
- Relative price
- Usage/application
- User/customer
- Celebrity person
- Lifestyle/personality
- Product class
- Competitors
- Country/geographic area (Aaker, 1991).

For a consumer product, the brand association often results from the company's image, product image and user image. Each of these three images can be divided into two types of association: the perception of utilitarian and functional attributes, like speed or ease of operation; the perception of soft or emotional attributes, like providing fantasy, or being trustworthy. The type of brand association includes product category, usage situation, product attributes and customer benefits.

Broniarczyk and Alba's (1994) study of the influence of brand-specific association – that is, an attribute or benefit that differentiates a brand from competing brands in brand extension – revealed that these dominate the effects of brand affect and category similarity, particularly when consumer knowledge of the brand is high. Studies that look at the influence of parent brand knowledge on brand extensions indicate that consumers are less likely to include an unfamiliar parent brand in their consideration set of the brand's original category and, thus, are less likely to purchase it. Similarly, other studies found that extensions into categories more similar to the original brand tend to be more readily accepted, and that brand reputation influences consumer adoption of brand extension (see Hem et al., 2003).

Laforet (under review) also found that consumers purchase a brand that is best known in a specific product category and its subsequent extensions in that product category, because of their strong association with the original category. Cadbury, for instance, is the most preferred brand in the confectionery market among British consumers. Laforet's study showed that consumers would not buy Cadbury if it extended in the cereal market. This suggests that Cadbury is so strongly associated with its original chocolate product category that its name cannot be associated with cereal products. Cadbury is also seen as the leading brand in the chocolate product market in the UK. The extent to which a brand is associated with a product category also depends on its target market. For example, in the cereal market, Nestlé is the most preferred brand among British households. Nestlé is found to influence choice among British households. Subsequently, its extension into the cereal market is accepted (Laforet, under review). Thus, perceived category risk is one of the factors influencing consumer acceptance of brand extension.

Key success factors of brand extension

Factors contributing to the success of line extension

There are a number of factors contributing to the success of line extension: the parent's brand strength and its symbolic value; early entry timing; a firm's size; distinctive marketing competencies; and the advertising support allocated to the line extension. For instance, in the cigarette industry it has been found that the cannibalization effects of line-extension activity were limited, and line extension into earlier sub-categories would have helped the parent brand. Furthermore, normally, even with cannibalization, the incremental sales generated by the extension seem to be reason enough to make a line extension strategy viable. In addition, consumers need to feel trust and have favourable attitudes towards the core brand for the extension (either line or category) to be successful. Such beliefs and attitudes are known as 'brand associations', as mentioned above, and serve to differentiate one brand from another.

Factors contributing to the success of category extension

Successful extension of a brand, particularly into diverse categories, can reduce the effects of fit on subsequent extension. Although a single aberration in performance may not harm a brand immediately, failure to manage quality variance (referring to managing quality across all products affiliated with a brand) is likely in the long run to reduce brand strength directly (i.e. it has a negative effect on consumers' confidence in and favourable evaluation of the brand extension), and negates the potentially favourable effects of adding products to a brand. Consequently, one of the keys to successful category extension is that companies gradually extend a brand into more diverse product categories, while maintaining a high degree of quality consistency across products.

Another key success factor is whether the brand extension fits with the core or parent brand, and whether it is consistent and congruent with the latter. Companies often use their own perception of the parent brand as the benchmark to determine if a brand extension fits with the parent brand's image and category (see above). These perceptions are very often different from customers' perceptions and may lead to a failed extension. As a result, the brand can be misaligned in the consumers' minds. So, companies must, first of all, examine the consumer perspective. Second, they must be prepared for a potential response to brand damage. They must also follow the right steps and ask the right questions before extending a brand, as discussed in the section below.

Assessing scope for brand extension

There are a number of criteria to consider in assessing scope for brand extension:

- Strength of the parent brand (e.g. core brand personality and values, brand reputation/quality, credibility)
- Target market
- Extendibility
- Transferability
- Brand breadth
- Product category risk
- Creating new meanings
- Market-related factors.

A particularly critical strategic issue for companies is deciding what set of associations they want to have, such as personal, lifestyle and customer type. The introduction of brand extensions generally should not be reliant on market-related factors like changes in consumer needs, and competitive positioning. It should also be congruent with the core brand's personality and values.

Before companies decide to extend a brand they should assess the *strength of the core brand*, in terms of its personality and values, reputation, quality and credibility across product categories; whether the core brand is a corporate brand, or in a product category, or in a target market; whether the core brand is not a corporate brand. If the core brand has all the attributes mentioned above, consumer adoption of the new extension is the most likely. If it is not, then companies need to think about its *extendibility*, *transferability* and *breadth*, and decide on the *product category* and the *target market* they want to extend the brand into or aim at. Companies also need to make decisions about whether they want to develop *new meanings* to the extension or not. That will depend on *market-related factors*.

The more abstract the brand association, the more the scope for brand extendibility. Unless the brand is able to add something intangible such as general qualities rather than functionality to the product, extending the brand to other product categories will be difficult. Brands tied to a particular set of associations are also found to be risky for extension. The brand manager must try to link the core brand with a set of associations which are flexible and provide a platform for current positioning and subsequent leverage. The bigger the gap in perceptions between the parent brand and the extension, the bigger the communication challenge. In that case the only link between the parent and the extension lies in the brand image and identity.

Companies need to present the extension in such a way that the consumer buys the idea of the extension by referring to the essence of the core brand. The success of brand extension relates to the whole of the core brand, rather than to obvious overlaps in terms of features of the target market. The brand essence represents the brand value, not the price or inherent product attributes.

Transferability is defined as the extent to which a brand is perceived as able to make a product in another product class or category. The perceived expertise of the manufacturer to make the extension product has a direct impact on the evaluation of brand extensions. The brand breadth serves to describe whether a brand is wide or narrow. A wide brand like Heinz or Sony may be more extendible than a narrower brand like Campbell's or Black & Decker, although in the long run, it is the extension that determines the breadth, not vice versa (Boush and Loken, 1991; Keller and Aaker, 1992; Loken and Ward, 1987).

Extending into a mature vs a new market

In a saturated market established brands become so dominant that newcomers and own-labels struggle to compete. For new brands, it is much tougher to break into a saturated market. For own-labels, to overcome this fierce competition with established brands they would have to offer an extra-special product line, or compete on price or promotions, or rely on impulse buying. For established brands, it has not been easy either, since in order to keep up with new consumption trends, many have had to extend into unfit product categories and as a result have contradicted their core brand values. Examples of this are: Coca-Cola extending into vitamin-enhanced water, Heinz into organic ketchup, Procter & Gamble's extending the Mr Propre brand from a floor-cleaning agent into a detergent, and Oil of Olay extending into vitamins.

Companies' strategies have also become cyclical as their brand portfolios have grown larger with mergers and acquisitions, and this has created confusion. They have had to drop some brands and have gone back to being small, or to using a standalone brand instead (e.g. Virgin with Zavvi). Similarly, when a company grows too rapidly or too widely, the brand starts losing strength, focus and relevance for its core customers. Companies should have a plan and work out a strategy before considering a brand extension. This involves taking and following a number of correct steps, and asking the right questions (see 'Brand extension procedure', below), as well as finding out what their customers want, as often companies extend brands without a clear sense of what the brands mean to consumers (e.g. Isuzu's attempt to become a car company, when it only had credibility as a truck and SUV maker). Examples in the fmcg market are Nestlé and Coke. Nestlé is a corporate name but it is also a product brand name, and people can relate to that. So, it is logical for Nestlé to use its corporate name across a wide range of product categories. By contrast, Coca-Cola should not use Coke and water, for instance, as this combination would not work, and it may be better for it to keep its product brands and use another name for water. This is why consumer studies are important to companies considering brand extensions.

Companies also need to play to their strengths when extending brands. For example, Sainsbury's is one of the leading supermarkets in Britain and was known for offering good-quality products, before it was overtaken by competitors such as Asda and Tesco, which offered goods at a lower price. To keep up with the competition, Sainsbury's lowered its prices and, as a result, its brand image was diluted.

Brand extension remains a complex area, and the issue of brand extension deserves further research. First, not all brands that are extended into unrelated or unfit product categories fail (see Figure 7.1). Second, the reason for brand extension failure is not necessary linked to product category, for example, Coca-Cola with Dasani and Oil of Olay with vitamins. These brands have been extended into unrelated product categories: one succeeded and the other failed. In Coca-Cola's case, the reason for failure was ethics, bad marketing and the problem associated with extending in a mature market. Coca-Cola's extension into mineral water with its Dasani brand failed because Dasani made a false claim that it was pure water from the source when, in reality, it was tap water. Dasani's marketing was also wrong in terms of pricing (it was charged at a high price because of the claim) and promotions (Coca-Cola spent too much on advertising for this brand), as well as the fact that the brand was extended into a market dominated by a number of leading brands such as Evian and Volvic. Oil of Olay's extension into vitamins was successful because it was extended into a less mature market with fewer dominant brands. It might also be argued that Oil of Olay's brand extension has remained with its core brand value, which is beauty. The Coca-Cola's case highlights the fact that the failure of brand extension was more than product category risk.

Extending a brand in recession

In the current economic climate new product launches of any type will be on the decline. Brand extensions carry a higher risk than line extensions, because they need marketing support to educate consumers in the new category. However, if well conceived and in the right category, they can have lasting power. In this economic climate consumer risk-taking is likely to be limited, except maybe towards lower-cost brands. A brand extension in a way demands risk-taking, particularly in a product category with which consumers are unfamilar. Also, if the brand itself is not strong, the brand extension is likely to be weak. Furthermore, brand extensions cannot insulate brands from decline, especially nowadays. The only thing that successful brand extensions offer in this environment beyond what any new product offers is 'the opportunity to bring a brand back into the consumer's consciousness', according to E. M. Tauber, a brand extensions guru. Brand extensions offer something new that consumers can associate with the brand and make it more exciting. Getting it right the first time is crucial, because early success with a target audience can help with future extensions. Brand extension is a strategy that should continue to serve brands well. Despite the economic downturn, it creates an opportunity for firms to expand their business and make profits, in related and unrelated product markets.

Extending with a corporate brand, family brand or product brand

Figure 7.1 shows that there are a number of criteria for extending a corporate name. First, a corporate name can be extended if the corporate name is also a product brand name to which consumers can relate, or if the corporate name is familiar to the consumers and is perceived as expert, or is perceived as having unique attributes in the area into which it is being extended; also, if the product or purchase is a public necessity, or public luxury, and the core brand values are the same in the product category into which it is extended. In these instances, it is likely that positive brand associations between the corporate name (or the core brand) and the extension will occur, which will lead to possible purchase.

To extend a brand name that is not a corporate name, it will be best if the brand name is an established one, and that it is extended into the same product category. Only in this way can positive brand associations result between the core brand and the brand extension (categorization and familiarity theory). If there is product fit between the core brand and the extension in terms of brand image, value, personality, identity, quality and expertise; and if the core brand values and core brand essence are the same in the brand extension, we say there is mutual brand symbiosis (i.e. shared brand values between the parent brand and the extension). Consequently, this will lead to a purchase. On the other hand, if a brand is extended into a remote product category or is unknown in that product category, few brand associations are likely to occur between the core brand and the extension. Even if there is product fit between the core brand and the extension, there may be no symbiotic branding (see the left-hand third of the second box in Figure 7.1). Because the brands do not benefit from being associated with each other, and since there is no brand association, it will not lead to a purchase. With a low-involvement product, which is extended in a market where brand switching is high and where the core brand is not an established brand, even if there is product fit between the core brand and the extension, the likelihood for that brand to be purchased is also low.

To produce positive consumer attitudes towards the brand extension and influence purchase, companies can use advertising to promote source credibility or to create a good product/usage experience. The favourable experience will then determine subsequent purchase. Companies can also focus on communicating the core brand essence. In a case where the core brand is extended into a remote product category, in order to have positive consumer attitudes towards the extension, companies can communicate the core brand essence, image and identity, using all the relevant cues, as consumers will need a large amount of information in this instance.

If an established brand is extended into an unfit product category or in a product category that can undermine the parent brand's reputation and image, negative brand associations between the

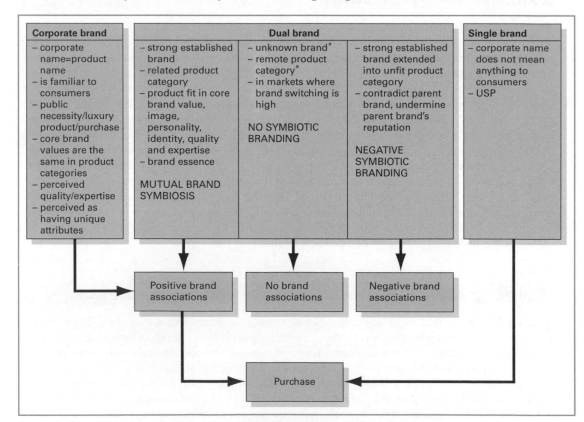

Source: Taken from Laforet (under review), 'Brand names on packaging and its impact on purchase preference'.

* Refer to strategies discussed above for this case.

FIGURE 7.1 Contexts for extending and using a corporate, dual and single brand, brand associations and their influence on purchase

core brand and the extension are most likely to emerge. Thus, there is negative symbiotic branding (see the right-hand third of the second box in Figure 7.1) where there is a negative effect, when the two brands are used together. This will not lead to a purchase. So, when extending into a remote product category, it may be better to use single-product brands (Laforet and Saunders, 1994). Single brands should also be used when the corporate name does not mean anything to consumers. Single brands which have a USP will usually be selected.

Brand bundling and brand bridging

Brand bundling, also known as 'cross-branding', is a strategy for fortifying a company's brands through association with other companies' brands. This strategy requires fewer upfront resources, and is adopted by companies who are less inclined towards building their own brand.

Product complementarities are a form of brand bundling which often appears in the form of ingredient branding. For example, Intel contributes towards enhancing the brand value of Compaq machines in the global market. Ingredient branding can add value to the host company's products and enhance the primary brand. There is, however, a risk of products not being shared equally by all participating brands under the brand bundling strategy. Also, when using this strategy companies must be mindful of the secondary associations created by other companies' brands. The benefits to companies are as mentioned above. In addition, cooperative branding also allows customers to gain benefits from promotions offered by these brands with a single purchase or service transaction. For example, people using Tesco's petrol station can win air miles from a number of international air tour operators.

The brand bridging strategy uses the parent brand to endorse a new brand in a remote product category. It is a similar concept to corporate endorsement (see Chapter 6). Once the endorsed brand or the new product is sufficiently strong in the targeted product market, the core brand fades away: hence, the temporary use of the core brand serves as a stepping stone for the company to build competency for new brands. However, there is a chance that the parent brand might be diluted, as there is a limit to which it can be stretched. Brand bridging may fail, when the core brand and the endorsed brand are too far apart in the consumer's mind.

Figure 7.2 summarizes the brand extension types mentioned above.

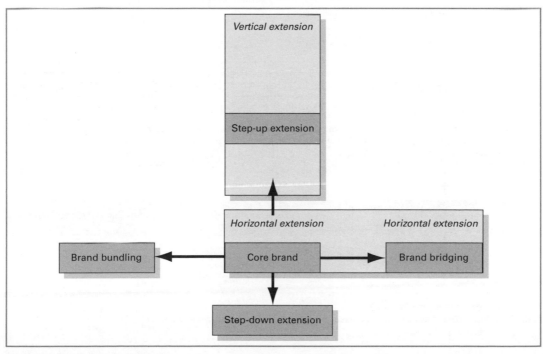

FIGURE 7.2 Brand extension typology

Brand linkage

There are two types of brand linkage which can take place between a company's brands, or between a company's and a partner's brands. Figures 7.3 and 7.4 describe these situations. The first illustrates brand symbiosis, referring to the mutual benefits shared between the brands of a company. The second shows the interaction matrix, which describes the relationship between a company's brands and includes partners' brands.

Brand symbiosis

See the section above on 'Extending with a corporate brand, family brand or product brand' for an explanation of Figure 7.3.

The brand relationship and interaction matrix

The brand relationship interaction matrix in Figure 7.4 is extracted from Rajagopal and Sanchez's analysis on brand architecture, and relationships within product categories. This matrix illustrates the types of business relationship involved, whether close or distant, and the linkage between the brands, which is either strong or weak. The close brands are those owned by the company, and the distant brands are independent brands that are not connected with the parent brands.

Transaction I is characterized by strong brand linkage and close business relationships. Here, strong formal control is exerted, often through ownership. Interaction is often supervisory in nature. The supervisory and advisory form of relationship II is characterized by strong brand linkage and distant business relationships. Control is informal and weaker than when the business relationship is close. Interaction is advisory: for example, a manufacturer's provision of a merchandising service to a retailer. The interactive and cooperative brand environment can be explained in terms of weak brand linkage and close business relationships. Here the control is strong but, the linkage between the brands is weak. Interaction between the businesses is cooperative (e.g. joint management seminars and information sharing). Quadrant IV of the matrix describes a weak brand linage and distant business relationships. The control and interaction are based on market conditions. Such interaction tends to be transactional (e.g. sales calls by employees of one business to another and alliances).

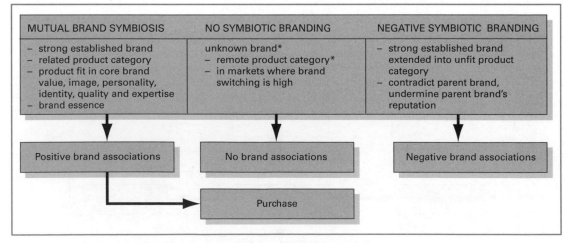

* Refer to strategies discussed above for this case.

FIGURE 7.3 Mutual brand symbiosis, no symbiotic branding and negative symbiotic branding

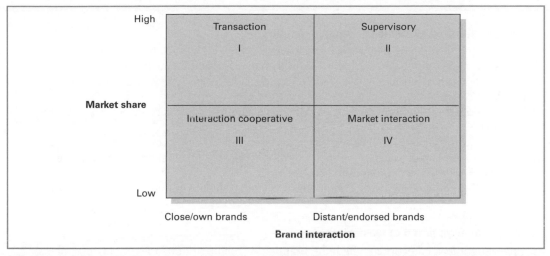

FIGURE 7.4 Brand interaction

Brand dilution

While there can be significant benefits in brand extension strategies, there can also be signifi-cant risks, resulting in a diluted or severely damaged brand image. Poor choices for brand extension may dilute and deteriorate the core brand, and damage the brand equity. Most of the literature focuses on consumer evaluation and positive impact on the parent brand. In practice, the failures of brand extension are more frequent than the successes. Nevertheless, on the evidence of past research, brand extensions whether successful or unsuccessful do not perceptibly dilute the parent's equity in the short term. Some dilution of belief about a specific brand attribute ('gentle') was found in one study, when subjects were told that the brand would be extended to a new product rated low on that attribute (see John and Loken, 1992). This is an extreme case, but it suggests that even a less extreme inconsistency might in the long run lead to dilution of trust and preference – and that in terms of longer-term business outcomes of brand extensions, brand exten-sions may offer no economic return.

Brand extensions also raise the long-term risk of negative image spillover from any widely publi-cized problem linked to the same brand name, for example product tampering, etc. Sullivan (1990) found positive spillover to other models from Jaguar's first major model change in 17 years, and negative spillover (i.e. when information about one product affects the demand for other products with the same brand name) from the Audi 5000's widely publicized (alleged) problem with 'sudden acceleration'.

Branding Brief 7.3: Exploring brand extension

Source: Brandingstrategyinsider.com © Brad VanAuken

Successful brand extensions – some examples

- Jell-o (pudding, pudding snacks)
- Crayola (markers, pens and paints)
- Dole (pineapple juice, fruit juice, fruit salad, fruit juice frozen fruit bars)
- Ivory (soap, dishwashing liquid, gentle care detergent)
- Woolite (fabric wash, carpet cleaner spray)
- Arm & Hammer (toothpaste)

Question: For each brand, what was the transferable core brand association that made a successful extension possible?

Unsuccessful brand extensions – some examples

- Bic perfume (leveraging the 'small disposable pocket items' association)
- Levi's tailored classic suits – What is Levi's primary association (casual clothes)?
- Campbell's spaghetti sauce – Why didn't 'tomato sauce' transfer from Campbell's soups to spaghetti sauce?
- McDonald's Arch Deluxe (for adults) – What is McDonald's primary association (fast food for kids)?
- Bayer 'Aspirin-free' – What is Bayer's primary association (aspirin)?
- Volvo 850 GLT sports sedan – What is Volvo's primary association (safety)? What is a primary proof point (boxy armoured car styling)?
- Or, an all-time favourite, New Coke – What is Coke? 'It's the real thing' with its long-time secret formula.

The most common brand extension problems

- Extending into a category in which the brand adds nothing but its identity (its products or services are not significantly different from current products or services in the category).
- Extending through opportunistic brand licensing without regard to impact upon the brand.
- Extending into lower (and sometimes higher) quality segments.
- Not fully understanding brand benefit ownership, transfer or importance.

Over-extending brands

In a recent edition of *The Brand Management Newsletter* we asked: 'When is a brand over-extended? What does it look like? What are early warning signs?' Here is what some of our readers had to say:

- A brand is over-extended when its iterations are no longer valid to its customers.
- When is a brand over-extended? Brand over-extension occurs when a brand's identity does not cause an emotional response – which develops into a desire to make a purchase – to the public. Additionally, brand over-extension is the result of a brand's inability to evoke a clear vision of the product's function in the public's mind. When I see a well-made Coke commercial, I am reminded that I have not had a Coke – not just any 'ole soda – in a while.
- What does it (brand over-extension) look like? Brand over-extension looks like an undervalued product. A product that is everywhere but undervalued is over-extended. When the public dismisses the function of the product, the product becomes as unique as dirt.
- What are the early warning signs? Editors misuse brands by allowing the use of the words Kleenex and Xerox to be used as nouns instead of adjectives. When editors disregard your identity, they are teaching the masses to disregard your product.
- A brand is over-extended when its employees can't immediately and succinctly say what it stands for when asked.
- A brand is over-extended when all you can say about it is 'It is the quality innovative leader in the categories in which it operates. It offers its customers assurance.'
- A brand will be over-extended when profit-driven business units have the freedom to enter new categories with the brand name without the input and direction of a brand equity oversight mechanism.
- You know you are in trouble when the person heading up your brand licensing department doesn't have a strategic bone in his or her body and is compensated primarily for the incremental profits that he or she generates.

Distancing techniques

Distancing techniques are the means through which the brand extension is positioned closer to, or further away from the core brand. A variety of linguistic and graphical distancing techniques can be used in advertising, sales promotion, and on packaging. Graphical distancing techniques involve manipulating the size of the core brand name in order to position the brand extension an appropriate distance from the core brand. Graphically downplaying the core brand name by making it smaller, or even non-existent, implies that greater distance is being put between the core brand and the brand extension. Making the core brand name larger implies that there is a closer association between the core brand and the brand extension.

Linguistic distancing techniques use words to manipulate the distance between the core brand and the brand extension. One type of linguistic distancing technique involves presenting a new brand extension identifier, in order to give the extension its own unique identity. This new identifier can be used alone, or in tandem with the core brand name. A second type of linguistic distancing technique involves using possessive forms, or modifiers to connect the core brand name with the brand extension name (e.g. 'a division of', 'brought to you by', 'from'). Linguistic and graphical distancing techniques can be used simultaneously for greater effect (Kim and Lavack, 1996).

Distancing and parent brand evaluation

According to Aaker (1991), distancing the parent brand name from the brand extension is particularly useful for protecting the parent brand in vertical extension situations (see above). It is important that the price/quality positioning of the original parent or core brand image remain relatively unaffected and unharmed by the introduction of a vertical brand extension. One way of reducing the risk to the core brand image is to introduce a vertical brand extension that is distanced from the core brand.

The use of brand extension names affects consumer perceptions of how closely brand extensions are linked to each other and to the parent brand. For example, the Audi 5000 received negative publicity due to a problem it had with sudden acceleration. These negative perceptions spilled over on to the Audi 4000 because of the close degree of brand name linkage between the Audi 4000 and the Audi 5000. However, these negative consumer perceptions affected the Audi Quattro to a much lesser degree because the degree of association between the Quattro and the Audi brand name was smaller (Sullivan, 1990). Fortunately, the Quattro was distanced further from the Audi core brand through the use of a linguistic distancing technique (i.e. a unique brand extension identifier).

Distancing and step-up brand extension

From the point of view of the step-up brand extension, it is better to be further away from the core brand, in order to avoid being associated with the core brand's lower level of quality. If firms choose to introduce step-up vertical extensions, then they should put a maximum amount of distance between the core brand and the step-up extension. This greater distancing will be beneficial to the core brand image, as well as to the image of the new step-up brand extension (Kim and Lavack, 1996).

In the automobile industry it has become common practice for car manufacturers introducing a new upscale automobile to give it a completely new brand name (i.e. maximal distancing). This has certainly been the case in the upscale new car introductions of Acura, Infiniti and Lexus (from the makers of Honda, Nissan and Toyota respectively). In these three cases, entirely new luxury brand names have been introduced. The reason for avoiding a closely linked brand extension strategy is a desire to separate clearly or remove the new upscale luxury brand from the more pedestrian and utilitarian existing brand. In this way, the new luxury brand is not tainted by the lower quality of the existing utilitarian brand, and the existing utilitarian brand is not harmed by perceived inadequacies it may suffer in comparison to the new luxury brand introduction.

Distancing and step-down brand extension

The impact of distancing on step-down brand extensions is exactly the opposite of the effect found for step-up extensions. It is generally advised to position the extension close to the core brand so that it can benefit from being associated with the superior quality of the core brand. There is also a trade-off that exists when introducing step-down extensions. Greater distancing is beneficial for the core brand, but is less effective for the brand extension. Closer links are detrimental to the core brand, but are beneficial for the brand extension.

Finally, the decision to use distancing should be related to the strategic goals of the company (i.e. whether to focus resources on maintaining the core brand, or whether to concentrate on the newly introduced brand extension). If maintaining the core brand image is highly important, then distancing techniques should be used when introducing a vertical brand extension. However, if the potential for capturing new market segments with the brand extension is deemed to be a more profitable strategy in the long run, the brand extension should be closely linked to the core brand (Kim and Lavack, 1996).

Brand extension procedure

To start with, a brand manager must ask the right questions before extending a brand, such as: What are the company's objectives? Do we want to go head to head with competitors or not? Who are our competitors? If we use existing brands, how are we going to achieve what we want to achieve? Would a corporate name generate more positive associations to the brand extension? How well do customers relate to the corporate name? Would it be better for us to use single brands? What new meanings do we want to create for the extension, if any? Who is our target market? What are the current fads, trends?

Three types of research are required for the four stages of the brand extension process, below.

1 The first type of research is an internal type and is conducted at the initial stage of the brand-extension process. This answers the first two questions above. It requires communication between the brand manager and the managing director or marketing director or another member of the senior management team to discuss the company's objectives. The brand objectives should be aligned with the company's objectives.

2 The second type of research is external, to find out who the company's competitors are, as this will help to establish whether they are extending into a mature or new market. In which case, different strategies must be adopted (see Figure 7.1 and above).

3 The third type of research a brand manager must conduct is related to investigating which brand strategy/type will be more effective and beneficial to the company in terms of generating sales – that is, if the company's objective is to increase sales. At the same time, the manager must decide whether he wants to create new meanings to the extension to suit the target market and/or to suit the current fads and market trends. Then, he will need to find out whether new meanings would be compatible with the core brand, otherwise distancing techniques may be employed. The manager also needs to find out other market-related factors concerning the industry they operate in. This stage also corresponds to assessing the scope for brand extension (see above).

4 The last step in this process is deciding whether to go ahead with the brand extension or not, after gathering all the facts and going through all the above steps.

Figure 7.5 summarizes the steps in the brand extension procedure.

Effect of brand extension strategies on brand equity

As mentioned above, brand extension can dilute the brand equity in the long run (see the section on 'Brand dilution', above), if the fit between the original parent brand and the extension is low. The initial brand equity and perceived image fit have a positive influence on consumers' attitudes towards

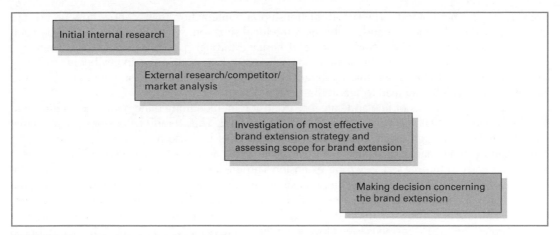

FIGURE 7.5 Steps in the brand extension procedure

the extension, which along with initial brand equity in turn affects the brand equity after the extension (Buil et al., 2006). Thus, companies must make every effort to increase brand equity, consumer perception of fit and positive attitudes towards the extension, to protect brand equity after the extension.

Nevertheless, brand extension can also have positive effects on brand equity in the long term. Some research shows that when category similarity is high, the parent brand is reinforced, i.e. the brand name accessibility and aspect accessibility are increased. When category similarity is low, the parent brand is diluted, i.e. the brand name accessibility and aspect accessibility are decreased. Thus, some studies suggest that successful brand extensions help strengthen product category dominance, build brand equity and brand loyalty. Multiple brand extensions also help to reinforce the parent brand as expert in a product category and therefore strengthen its dominance in that category. Once established, the brand can command premium price and generate repurchase.

Conclusion

Brand extensions represent an opportunity for firms to use the equity built up in the names of existing brands in order to enhance marketing productivity. Also, because of the dramatic increase in media costs, the more extensive and aggressive use of promotions by established firms, and the cost and difficulty of obtaining distribution, firms are using established brand names to facilitate their entering new markets. Other advantages of brand extension include the protection offered against own-labels and bringing new customers to the firm.

Brand extension can be carried out via line extension or category extension. Line extension is concerned with extending a product in the same product class of the core brand. Category extension is about extending a product in a different or unrelated product category – than that of the core brand. A vertical brand extension involves introducing a brand extension in the same product category as the parent brand, but at a different price point and quality level, either at a higher price and quality (known as step-up extension), or at a lower price and quality (known as step-down extension). A horizontal extension takes an existing brand name and applies it to a new product in either a related product class or in a product category completely new to the firm.

Other brand extension strategies that can be used by firms are brand bundling and brand bridging. Brand bundling, or 'cross-branding', is a strategy for fortifying a company's brand through associations with other companies' brands. This is good when companies have limited resources, or require different expertise to produce the product, e.g. ingredient branding. Brand bridging strategy uses the parent brand to endorse a new brand in a remote product category. Once the endorsed brand or the new product is sufficiently strong in the targeted product market, the core brand fades away. The temporary use of the core brand serves as a stepping stone for the company to build competency for new brands. The brand relationship and interaction matrix show how brands are strategically linked. Mutual brand symbiosis is the ideal situation, where two brands feed off each other, and share benefits of brand values and heritage through positive associations. There are situations where there is no symbiotic branding, where two brands do not gain any benefit by being associated with each other; negative symbiotic branding is when the extension contradicts the core brand's value, which may lead to brand dilution.

The potential benefits of line and category extension include immediate name recognition and the transference of benefits associated with a familiar brand. Thus, brand extensions are attractive to firms that face a high level of new product failure rates because they provide a way to take advantage of brand name recognition and image to enter new markets. However, brand extensions also carry some risks. The wrong extension can create damaging associations that can be expensive, or even impossible to change. An extension can weaken the parent brand in the original category. Risks come not only from a new product failure, but also from the success of a category extension. Brand extension can dilute the brand equity in the long run, if the fit between the original parent brand and the extension is low. However, when category similarity is high, the parent brand is reinforced. Therefore, brand extension can also have a positive effect on brand equity.

Brand extensions also raise the long-term risk of negative image spillover from any widely publicized problem linked to the same brand name – for example, product tampering. To overcome brand dilution, distancing techniques may be used by positioning the brand closer to or further away from the parent brand. A variety of linguistic and graphical distancing techniques can be applied in advertising and sales promotion, and on packaging.

Successful category extension rests on three conditions: consumer perceptual fit, competitive leverage and benefit transfer. Perceptual fit implies that consumers must perceive the new extension to be consistent with the parent brand. Competitive leverage means the new extension must be comparable with or superior to other products in the category. Benefit transfer means the benefit offered by the parent brand is desired by consumers of products in the new category. Factors contributing to the success of line extension are: the parent brand strength and its symbolic value, early entry timing, a firm's size, distinctive marketing competencies, and the advertising support allocated to the line extension. For consumers to accept the new extension, the parent or core brand must be perceived fit, of quality, expert in the product category and product class into which it extends, and perceived as not easy to make.

Because of its risks, brand extension needs to be planned. The planning process for brand extension consists of four steps or stages. These are: conducting initial internal research, to align the brand extension's objective with the company's objective; analysing the external environment by conducting a competitor/market analysis to find out what they are doing and who are the competitors, etc; investigating the most effective brand extension strategy and assessing scope for brand extension; making the decision as to whether to extend or not, and how.

🔓 Key terms

Benefit transfer: the benefit offered by the parent brand is desired by consumers of products in the new category.

Brand association: how brand meanings are derived. For a consumer product, the brand association often results from the company's image, product image and user image. Each of these three images can be divided into two types of association. One is the perception of utilitarian and functional attributes, like speed or ease of operation. The other relates to 'soft' or emotional attributes, like providing fantasy or being trustworthy. Types of brand association include product category, usage situation, product attributes and customer benefits.

Brand breadth: refers to how wide or narrow a brand is. A wide brand that is often used across a whole product range or category (i.e. a corporate or a family brand) is more extendible than a narrower brand, like a product brand or single brand.

Brand bridging: brand bridging strategy uses the parent brand to endorse a new brand in a remote product category. Once the endorsed brand or the new product is sufficiently strong in the targeted product market, the core brand fades away. The temporary use of the core brand serves as a stepping-stone for the company to build competency for new brands.

Brand bundling: also known as 'cross-branding', this is a strategy for fortifying a company's brand through associations with other companies' brands. Product complementarities are a form of brand bundling. Product complementarities often appear in the form of ingredient branding.

Brand dilution: brand dilution happens when the parent brand's image is diluted or severely damaged, which can lead to its brand equity deteriorating in the long term. See also **Negative symbiotic branding**.

Brand essence: the core value of the brand, e.g. Oil of Olay's brand essence is beauty.

Brand extension: strategy defined as 'any effort to use a successful brand name to launch a product modification or additional products'.

Brand extension procedure: the process of brand extension, which involves four stages: initial internal research, external research/competitor/market analysis, investigation of the most effective brand extension strategy and assessing scope for brand extension and, finally, making a decision about the brand extension.

Brand linkage: how brands can be linked together either between companies' brands or partners' brands to maximize consumer brand associations to influence choice. There are two types of brand linkage: **brand symbiosis**, and **brand relationship and interaction**.

Brand relationship and interaction: the brand relationship and interaction matrix illustrates the types of business relationship involved, whether close or distant, and the linkage between the brands, which is either strong or weak. The close brands are those owned by the company, and the distant brands are independent brands that are not connected with the parent brands.

Brand-specific association: often companies like to give their brand a specific attribute or benefit that differentiates a brand from competing brands. This is called brand-specific association. However, many fmcg products have little differentiation among them because of market maturity.

Brand symbiosis: or symbiotic branding, takes place when two brands feed off each other and mutual benefit can be shared between them. These benefits can be reflected in the brand values, image, brand heritage, etc.

Categorization theory: this holds that people organize objects or information into categories. This enables them to process and understand their environment to the extent that a person perceives an object to be a member of a category, the components of the category, and affect and beliefs are then transferred to the object. This categorization process is said to influence consumer choice of a brand.

Category extension: the extension of a product in another product category unrelated to the core or parent brand.

Competitive leverage: when the new extension is perceived as comparable or superior to other products in the category.

Cooperative branding: similar to **brand bundling**, or cross-branding.

Distancing technique: the means through which the brand extension is positioned closer to, or further away from, the core brand.

Extendibility: the extent to which a brand is 'stretchable' in meanings and associations. The more abstract the brand association, the greater the scope for brand extendibility. Unless the brand is able to add something intangible like general qualities rather than functionality to the product, extending the brand to other product categories will be difficult.

Graphical distancing technique: this involves manipulating the size of the core brand name in order to position the brand extension an appropriate distance from the core brand.

Horizontal extension: takes an existing brand name and applies it to a new product in either a related product class or in a product category completely new to the firm.

Image spillover: an image or the information about a brand or a core brand, whether positive or negative, can spread and affect other brands in the whole product range.

Line extension: the use of an existing brand name on a product in one of the firm's existing categories. Often a line extension involves a different flavour or ingredient, a different form or a different application for the brand.

Linguistic distancing technique: using words to manipulate the distance between the core brand and the brand extension.

Negative symbiotic branding: when a well-known brand is extended into an unfit product category that contradicts its core brand value there will be negative symbiotic branding between the core brand and the extension, which may lead to brand dilution.

No symbiotic branding: there is no symbiotic branding when two brands cannot take advantage of being associated with each other.

Perceptual fit: when the consumer perceives the new extension to be consistent with the parent brand.

Response latency: the amount of time a consumer takes to decide whether a brand extension exists and its typicality (see Boush and Loken, 1991).

Step-down extension: a form of vertical brand extension whereby the extension is introduced at a lower price and lower quality level than the parent brand.

Step-up extension: a form of vertical brand extension whereby the extension is introduced at a higher price and quality level than the parent brand.

Transferability: the extent to which a brand is perceived as capable of making a product in another product class or category.

Vertical extension: involves introducing a brand extension in the same product category as the parent brand, but at a different price point and quality level.

? Discussion questions

1 How do you define brand extension? Discuss the relevance of brand extension in the context where the brand value is being leveraged.

2 Explain what vertical and horizontal extension are, their benefits and risks.

?

3 Why do you think companies go for more and more extensions (e.g. Cadbury's Dairy Milk, Cadbury's Dairy Milk Crunchie)?

4 Explain what brand bundling and brand bridging mean.

5 Discuss the contexts in which there are brand symbiosis or shared benefits between two brands, and where there is no symbiotic branding and only negative symbiotic branding. What is negative symbiotic branding similar to?

6 Explain why line extension is potentially more risky than category extension. Give five examples of successful and failed line extensions in the global market, and explain the reasons for their success or failure.

7 Brand extension can be seen as a tactical move for a firm since it involves incremental changes in products, as opposed to developing completely new products. Can you make a brand extension more strategic for a firm like British Gas?

8 What are the key ingredients for successful brand extension in: i) fmcg, ii) services? Support your answer with examples.

9 Explain what category dominance is. What are the potential benefits and pitfalls of a leading brand when it is extended in: i) a related product category, ii) an unrelated product category?

10 Discuss the implications for a small brand to extend in: i) a mature market, ii) a new market. What are the most effective communication strategies for the small brand when extending in these markets?

Projects

1 Brand extensions often carry potential risks for the corporate brand, but some corporate brands have successful brand extensions. Explain the factors contributing to their success for three British corporate brands in any sector of your choice.

2 Follow the systematic procedure mentioned in this chapter to carry out a brand extension, and assess the scope for brand extension for a new fictitious brand and an old brand of your choice.

3 Conduct a consumer survey to find out consumer perceptions of brand extensions with different kinds of distancing techniques.

4 Conduct telephone interviews with five company executives in fmcg to find out which brand extension strategies have been most/least used and why. Ask them whether there are any substitutions for brand extension.

5 Conduct a consumer survey to find out consumer perceptions and acceptance of controversial brand extensions such as Oil of Olay's extension into vitamins, Coke into vitamin-enhanced water, Heinz into organic ketchup, etc.

MINI CASE 7.1: DOING IT THE VIRGIN WAY!

Source: Adscovery, 9 September 2006

There's not a single marketing magazine or blog out there which has not sung praises of the Virgin brand. And the more I read about Virgin and Sir Richard Branson, the bigger fan I become of both – the brand and its chief. While all the big airlines are going down, Virgin is still thriving. And it's not only in the airline business, Virgin Active, its European health-club chain, Virgin Mobile USA, the brand's extension into the cell phone business, and many other ventures by Branson are doing great globally. So what's the secret recipe? Well taking a close look at the brand activities makes it very clear ... for Virgin, customers come first and there's no compromising there. Virgin doesn't give a crap what market research says or what the trend is in the industry, if the customer wants it, Virgin will have it.

Sir Richard Branson is a true visionary. What he thought and implemented two decades ago is now slowly attracting followers – people should be having fun when spending their money. He gives great importance to customer satisfaction. And how does he do that? A really simple concept – *'put yourself in the customer's shoes and think is this the way I want to be treated if I were the customer?'* Most of the innovations which he brought in his business were based on his own experiences as a customer. Flying in any major airplane was, and is, a really lack-lustre affair. You are tied to your seat for the whole time, everyone around doing their own stuff and feeling really relieved when the flight is over. The same was the experience with Branson. So when he came up with Virgin Airlines, he made it a real party airline ... Virgin has fun-loving attendants, stand-up bars and massages and nail treatment onboard! When all the airlines are showing movies to the customers as per their (the airlines') choice and schedule in the seatback video screens, Virgin went a step further and gave customers the right to choose from the library of on-demand videos. Any market research would have negated the expensive services Virgin provides onboard, but just because customers want them, Virgin provides them, and they thrive.

If you think Virgin just got lucky in the airline business, look elsewhere. Virgin had the same customer focus in its brand extensions and that helped them blossom in those industries as well. It provided customers pay as you use plans for its health clubs in Europe, Virgin Active, instead of locking them into contracts. The customers loved it and Virgin Active became successful. Virgin Mobile USA provided its customers with prepaid cards with no service agreements and contracts. Result – a more than 4 million customer base. Both are great examples of customer focus. We can see a pattern in Virgin's way of doing business – enter an industry where customers are not satisfied by the existing services, think of yourself as the customer and look for pain-points, keep the focus deep on customer needs and strive to provide them with satisfaction.

Moral of the story – take a look at whatever business you are in and ask yourself, if I were the customer, would I be happy and satisfied? If the answer is no, plan and implement changes. If the honest answer is yes, you are set to succeed the Virgin way!

Questions:

1 Can you identify the Virgin brand's core values?

2 What are the key success factors of Virgin's brand extensions?

3 Can you think of any other British corporate brands that have successfully extended across product categories?

MINI CASE 7.2: SNACK SECTOR OFFERS OPPORTUNITIES FOR HEALTHY BRAND EXTENSIONS

Source: Adapted from NutraIngredients.com/news

The burgeoning UK snack market is creating opportunities for food makers to develop profitable extensions of established brands with healthy credentials, according to market analysts Datamonitor.

But the brands need to have a healthy image, the company warns. Nestlé's new cereal bar, available in two flavours, will be sold under the low-fat yoghurt brand Ski. The company has also recently launched a yoghurt drink under the same brand, called Ski Stopgap, to be marketed as a healthy breakfast alternative and on-the-go snack.

Both extensions are aimed at developing the Ski brand's snacking credentials, however, it is this latest move that is the most significant. Nestlé is now developing the brand beyond the dairy sector into an area where Nestlé has already been unsuccessful. It was only in April 2003 that Nestlé withdrew the Rowntree Fruitsome cereal bar, less than a year after its launch. (according to the Datamonitor report).

Launched by the company's confectionery division, the Fruitsome bar suffered because it did not create the perception of being a healthier alternative to confectionery.

But Nestlé can hope for better things from the Ski cereal bars, according to Datamonitor:

Our research shows that of all mealtime occasions that consumers skip, breakfast is the most common. And a bar is the perfect alternative. (Daniel Bone, Datamonitor analyst)

When consumers skip meals they tend to experience feelings of guilt, and look for something healthy.

Strong growth in the UK's cereal bar category – estimated at around 20 per cent year on year – has been driven by the presence of some established, trusted names. 'Kellogg's pioneered the market with its NutriGrain bar, which benefited from the well-known, widely trusted brand,' said Bone. He added, however, that while cereals generally have a more positive image than many other foods, bars have suffered as consumers became aware that many are, in fact, high in salt, sugar and fat. Nevertheless, the products do meet the two 'mega-trends' influencing today's consumer purchasing patterns, added Bone.

Using established brands with already well-known health credentials could well be the ace card for manufacturers and retailers seeking to capitalize upon the booming and increasingly health-focused UK snack market in the next five years (according to Datamonitor). 'Opportunities appear to be particularly strong for trusted dairy and cereal brands,' it adds.

Questions:

1 Explain the reasons why Nestlé's new cereal bar failed.

2 Compare and contrast the brand value of Kellogg's NutriGrain and Nestlé's new cereal bar. What does Kellogg's NutriGrain have that Nestlé's new cereal bar does not?

3 What are the problems of extending in a mature market? What do companies have to be aware of most?

4 What are the potential threat(s) to Nestlé's corporate brand with such an extension?

END OF CHAPTER CASE STUDY: BRANDING WITH NO FEAR – A CASE OF BRAND PROLIFERATION IN THE HOTEL INDUSTRY

Source: Extract from © Hilton Hotels Corporation; © Home Towne Suites

There are about 50 individually branded hotels in the world. The market is segmented by hotel type – economy, midscale, extended stay, upscale, and luxury hotels. In recent years, the number of brands in each category has skyrocketed. In the category of the extended-stay segment alone, there are over 30 different brands, three of the brands listed in the survey illustrate the dilemma: Homestead Suites, Homewood Suites, and Home-Towne Suites. How can a consumer possibly differentiate one similarly named brand from another?

This is just one aspect of the branding problem. The larger hotels seem to spawn brands whenever the mood strikes. The problem is getting worse. Not only is it hard to create the critical mass necessary to make these brands relevant, but these new hotel brands have to create a very distinct identity and then deliver the matching experience to have any chance of resonating in the mind of the consumer.

How did the hotel market become so brand-ridden? There was a time when such venerable brand names as Hilton, Sheraton and Marriott were all a consumer needed to know to make a decision about where to stay. That changed dramatically with the era of consumer choice and market segmentation. Just as cola and toothpaste brands have proliferated, so have lodging brands.

While one can still stay at a branded 'Marriott Hotel', one can also stay at JW Marriott Hotels and Resorts, Courtyard by Marriott, Residence Inn by Marriott, Fairfield Inn by Marriott, TownePlace Suites by Marriott, and SpringHill Suites by Marriott.

Consistent quality may be one of the biggest challenges facing hotel brands. According to the *Wall Street Journal* only one chain out of nine, was considered 'outstanding'.

Individual hotels are capitalizing on the lack of brand differentiation, by creating unique personalities and targeting niche segments that larger chains may be unable to efficiently service, at an exorbitant price tag. The big chains are responding to the boutiques by offering their own 'select-service' upscale properties, and their association with these different names – Hotel Indigo (InterContinental), aloft (W Hotels/Starwood), Cambria Suites (Choice).

Hotel industry observers see a number of trends emerging that may result in an influx of even more brands, with the emphasis on specialization. But with so many hotel brands to choose from, travellers may well become confused, frustrated, or even immune to brand differentiation. So, when it comes to new hotel brands, will consumers be checking in … or checking out?

Questions:

1 What are the hotels' brand strategies?

2 'Loyalty programmes may be seen as a substitute for quality of experience.' Do you agree with this statement? Why, or why not?

3 What are the hotels' brand extension strategies?

4 Explain what the era of consumer choice and market segmentation is about. How does it affect hotels' brand strategies?

5 Are there any differences between brand extension types used in the hotel industry compared with the fmcg industry? If so, what are they? Can you draw up a brand structure (or architecture) of any hotel in the case study?

References

Aaker, D. A. (1991), *Managing Brand Equity*, New York, NY: The Free Press.

Aaker, D. A. and Keller, K. L. (1990), 'Consumer evaluations of brand extensions', *Journal of Marketing*, Vol. 54, pp. 27–41.

Boush, D. M. and Loken, B. (1991), 'A process-tracing study of brand extension evaluation', *Journal of Marketing Research,* Vol. 28, pp. 16–28.

Broniarczyk, S. M. and Alba, J. W. (1994), 'The importance of brand in brand extension', *Journal of Marketing Research*, Vol. 31, May, pp. 214–28.

Buil, I., Martinez, E. and Pina, J. M. (2006), 'The effect of brand extension strategies on brand equity', Academy of Marketing, 2nd Annual International Colloquium on the Dynamics of Brand, Corporate Identity & Reputation in the Knowledge Economies, Manchester Business School, Manchester, UK.

Doyle, P. (1989), 'Building successful brands: the strategic options', *Journal of Marketing*, Vol. 5, No. 1, pp. 77–95.

Farquhar, P. H. (1990), 'Managing brand equity', *Journal of Advertising Research*, Vol. 30, No. 4, pp. 7–12.

Hem, L., de Chernatony, L. and Iversen, M. (2003), 'Factors influencing successful brand extensions', *Journal of Marketing Management*, Vol. 19, No. 7–8, pp. 781–806.

John, D. R. and Loken, B. (1992), 'Diluting beliefs about family brands: when brand extensions have a negative impact', in Marketing Science Institute, Report No. 92–122.

Keller, K. L. and Aaker, D. A. (1992), 'The effect of sequential introduction of brand extensions', *Journal of Marketing Research*, Vol. 29, (February), pp. 35–50.

Kim, C. K. and Lavack, A. M. (1996), 'Vertical brand extensions: current research and managerial implications', *Journal of Product & Brand Management*, Vol. 5, No. 6, pp. 24–37.

Kotler, P. (1972), 'A general concept of marketing', *Journal of Marketing*, Vol. 36, No. 2, New York.

Loken, B. and Ward, J. (1987), 'Measures of attribute structure underlying product typicality', in *Advances in Consumer Research*, Vol. 14, eds M. Wallendorf and P. Anderson, Provo, UT: Association for Consumer Research, pp. 22–26.

Ries, A. and Trout, J. (1986), *Positioning: The Battle for Your Mind*, New York, NY: Warner Books.

Smith, D. C. and Park, C. W. (1992), 'The effects of brand extensions on market share and advertising efficiency', *Journal of Marketing Research*, Vol. 29, pp. 296–313.

Sullivan, M. (1990), 'Measuring image spill-overs in umbrella branded products', *The Business Journal*, Vol. 63, No. 3, pp. 309–30.

Further reading and online sites

Aaker, D. A. and Keller, K. L. (1990), 'Consumer evaluations of brand extensions', *Journal of Marketing*, Vol. 54, pp. 27–41.

Aaker, D. A. and Keller, K. L. (1993), 'Interpreting cross-cultural replications of brand extension research', *International Journal of Research in Marketing*, Vol. 10, No. 1, pp. 55–9.

Bridges, S. (1992), 'A schema unification model of brand extensions', in Marketing Institute, Report No. 92–123.

Carter, R. E. (2008), 'Friend or foe: the impact of line extension advertising and perceived quality on parent brand sales', Louisville College of Business Research, Paper No. 2008-04, at http://ssrn.com/abstract=1140847.

Colucci, M., Montaguti, E. and Lago, U. (2008), 'Managing brand extension via licensing: an investigation into the high-end fashion industry', *International Journal of Research in Marketing*, Vol. 25, No. 2, pp. 129–37.

Czellar, S. (2003), 'Consumer attitude toward brand extensions: an integrative model and research propositions', *International Journal of Research in Marketing*, Vol. 20, No. 1, March pp. 97–115.

Grime, I., Diamantopoulos, A. and Smith, G. (2002), 'Consumer evaluations of extensions and their effects on the core brand: key issues and research propositions', *European Journal of Marketing*, Vol. 36, No. 11/12.

Iversen, N. M. and Hem, L. E. (2008), 'Provenance associations as core values of place umbrella brands: a framework of characteristics', *European Journal of Marketing*, Vol. 42, No. 5/6.

Kumar, P. (2005), 'Brand counterextensions: the impact of brand extension success versus failure', *Journal of Marketing Research*, Vol. 42, No. 2, pp. 183–94.

Kumar, P. (2005), 'The impact of cobranding on customer evaluation of brand counterextensions', *Journal of Marketing*, Vol. 69, No. 3.

Laforet, S. and Saunders, J. (1994), 'Managing brand portfolio: how the leaders do it', *Journal of Advertising Research*, Vol. 34, No. 5, pp. 64–76.

Liao, S.-H., Chen, C.-M. and Wu, C.-H. (2008), 'Mining customer knowledge for product line and brand extension in retailing', *Knowledge Management News & Resources*, Vol. 34, No. 3, pp. 1585–2230 (April), esp. 1763–76.

Mininni, T. 'How far will brand extensions stretch?', Marketing Profs, at https://www.marketingprofs.com.

Nijssen, E. J. and Hartman, D. (1994), 'Consumer evaluations of brand extensions: an integration of previous research', in Bloemer, J., Lemmick, J. and Kasper, H. (eds), Proceedings of 23rd European Marketing Academy Conference, Maastricht: European Marketing Academy Conference, pp. 673–83.

Park, C. W., Milberg, S. and Lawson, R. (1991), 'Evaluation of brand extensions: the role of product feature similarity and brand concept consistency', *Journal of Consumer Research*, Vol. 18, September, pp. 185–93.

Rangaswamy, A., Burke, R. R. and Oliva, T. A. (1993), 'Brand equity and the extendibility of brand names', *International Journal of Research in Marketing*, Vol. 10, No. 1, pp. 61–75.

Sheinin, D. A. and Schmitt, B. H. (1994), 'Extending brands with new product concepts: the role of category attribute congruity, brand effect, and brand breadth', *Journal of Business Research*, Vol. 31, No. 1, pp. 1–10.

Sheinin, D. A., Dubé, L. and Schmitt, B. H. (2008), 'Derivative beliefs and evaluations', *Journal of Product & Brand Management*, Vol. 17, No. 7, pp. 453–62.

Shine, B. C., Park, J. and Wyer Jr, R. S. (2007), 'Brand synergy effects in multiple brand extensions', *Journal of Marketing Research*, Vol. 44, No. 4.

Smith, D. C. and Park, C. W. (1992), 'The effects of brand extensions on market share and advertising efficiency', *Journal of Marketing Research*, Vol. 29, pp. 296–313.

Sullivan, M. (1990), 'Measuring image spill-overs in umbrella branded products', *The Business Journal*, Vol. 63, No. 3, pp. 309–30.

Sunde, L. and Brodie, R. J. (1993), 'Consumer evaluations of brand extensions: further empirical results', *International Journal of Research in Marketing*, Vol. 10, No. 1, pp. 47–53.

TippingSprung, Branchannel.com 'Top brand extensions', atwww.brandchannel.com/paers_review.asp?sp_id=1222.

Völckner, F. and Sattler, H. (2006), 'Drivers of brand extension success', *Journal of Marketing*, Vol. 70, No. 2.

What's your brand mantra? 'Innovation and brand extensions', at http://brand.blogs.com/mantra/2006/08/innovation_and_.html.

Yu, H. X. (2008), 'Consumer innovativeness and consumer acceptance of brand extensions', *Journal of Product & Brand Management*, Vol. 17, No. 4.

CHAPTER

08

Managing Brands across a Life Cycle

Chapter overview

Previously, we have seen how brands can be created, for example through the development of a brand identity (Chapter 5), and managed and sustained through brand building and leverage options (Chapters 6 and 7). As part of the broad theme of managing brands – creating and sustaining brand equity – this chapter focuses on how brands are managed across a life cycle. Although, some might argue that a brand does not have a life cycle, since, unlike a product that can grow, mature and decline, a brand is supposed to live on for ever. However, this is not always the case, as only those that are well managed can do so. Given this perspective, the brand life cycle follows the same pattern as a product life cycle (PLC). The only difference between a product and a brand is that, while all products go through the same life cycle, not all brands have the same life cycle. Some brands will never decline; others will, if they are not well managed. Furthermore, an industrial brand may not have the same life cycle as an fmcg brand. Also, a brand is an abstract concept and it can be viewed from several different perspectives. The brand life cycle is viewed from those perspectives and, therefore, there may be more than one brand life cycle. This chapter starts with describing what a PLC is. Then, it discusses the brand life cycle debate, and explains the difference between a PLC and a BLC. Next, it introduces the BLC models from three perspectives, and how brands should be managed across these life cycles. The chapter explains again in detail the BCM, which was mentioned in Chapter 5 – that is, how brands/brand image are managed over time. Through the case studies, other strategies of managing brands across the life cycle are also examined. Chapter 9 will concentrate on corporate and brand reputation building.

❖ LEARNING OBJECTIVES

After completing this chapter, you should be able to

❖ Distinguish between a product life cycle and a brand life cycle

❖ Appreciate why a brand life cycle is not as straightforward a concept as a product life cycle

❖ Understand that brands can have many life cycles and that not all brands have the same life cycle

❖ Understand how to boost an underperforming brand, and revitalize and manage brands in crisis which are part of managing brand life cycles

❖ Study how brands develop and the stages of branding

❖ Study the stages of a brand life cycle

❖ Manage brands across their life cycle

❖ Understand what membership experience is and how to create that in a brand

❖ Discuss the stages at which brands are seen as being, from instrumental to symbolic to terminal, and the implications for companies

❖ Discuss the stages from being a trademark, to experience, corporate and global brand, and how to manage brands in each of these stages

❖ Be aware of the barriers facing global brands

❖ Study how to manage global brands

❖ Apply the concept of brand image management for brands across industries

Introduction

As mentioned before, every product goes through a life cycle, after which it will die. Similarly with brands: if they are not well managed they will follow suit. Companies are under pressure to build, manage and sustain their brand equity through each of the brand-evolving stages, by constantly revitalizing brands, improving their performance and managing them in crisis. These are among the most important duties of brand managers and central to brand management. Managing brands across their life cycle is a complex task for the brand manager. It involves a good understanding of the environmental factors that affect the brand at each of the stages of its life cycle. From the market perspective, it is about knowing what the market wants and needs at each of these stages. From the company's and brand's perspectives, it is about finding out how companies can best deploy the marketing mix to meet consumers' needs and to meet the company's objectives, as well as the brand's objective, which is to grow and sustain that growth. Managing brands across their life cycle is a complex task that requires the ability to manage resources and to use creativity and innovation in order to operate successfully in a dynamic and changing environment.

This chapter focuses on the product life cycle and brand life cycle concepts, as well as models of managing brand across the life cycle adopted from academic literature and practitioners' models.

The product life cycle

In classical marketing we learn that a product has a life cycle, which is based on four stages: introduction, growth, maturity and decline (see Figure 8.1).

At the introduction stage, primary demand is created by building awareness, interest, trial and acceptance of the product. In the growth stage selective demand is created through market penetration. At this point the main concern is with persuading the mass market to choose the brand, and with expanding users and usage of the product. The maturity stage consists of reinforcement and revitalization, defending or amending the brand position, as well as checking the inroads made by the competition. Often at this stage product changes or modifications take place. The purpose is to enhance sales by improving the product's basic functionality, via 'new and improved' versions. Many fmcg companies adopt this strategy. Procter & Gamble frequently promotes 'new and improved' versions of many of its brands; Crest, for example, continually modifies its product through quality improvements. P&G has also done the same thing over the years with Pampers and LUVs. Ultra Pampers is a quality improvement that simply makes the disposable nappy more absorbent. Similarly, personal computers are undergoing rapid advances in which significant new functions are constantly added. Adding new benefits to the product is an alternative viable strategy adopted also in this case.

Alternatively, modifying the augmented product to extend growth and maturity, services can be added where none existed before: adding new products (NPs) to the same product line through line extensions, e.g. Crispy M&M's or Smokey Red Barbecue; or finding new markets and market segments for existing products – for example, expanding geographically, or targeting ethnic groups and repositioning to different markets. Promoting added consumption, and changing the marketing mix are among other strategies adopted at the maturity stage of the PLC. For example, products can be repositioned to different markets by changing the brand's image or personality – for example, Miller High Life and Marlboro cigarettes repositioning to the 'heavy half'. The image was changed to fit better with the masculine themes associated with the higher-consumption beer market – the male, blue-collar segment. Then there is promoting added consumption in existing markets – for example, Nabisco promotes its Knox gelatine as a food supplement that can strengthen fingernails; or changing the marketing mix in the way the brand is promoted. Changes can also be made to the product's price and its distribution channels.

In the decline stage the product is 'harvested' by reducing the expenditure undertaken during the previous stages. Harvesting also means finding ways to cut production and marketing costs to the bare bones, by eliminating unprofitable distribution channels. This stage is, thus, characterized by preparations for removal, milking the brand for all possible remaining profits, then, finally, discontinuing the product or selling it to another firm.

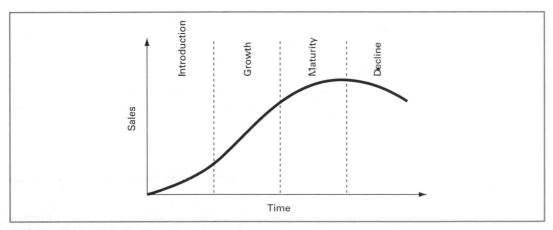

FIGURE 8.1 Product life cycle curve

Branding Brief 8.1: How has Snickers managed the brand's product life cycle over the years?

By differentiating its product through various ad campaigns and by creating various product lines, Snickers has managed its brand's product life cycle.

Product lines:

1   Snickers Crunch
2   Snickers Almond
3   Snickers Marathon Bar.

Ad campaigns:

1   Hungry, Why Wait, Grab a Snickers
2   Snickers, It's only good if you eat it
3   Bring Joy to the World (*guy with the guitar sings a song*).

Is there such a thing as a brand life cycle (BLC)?

Arguments against the BLC

Some people believe that brands do not have a life cycle. In fact, numerous studies have shown that many brands that were leading the market years ago are still in that position. For instance, David Mercer once tested the PLC concept with 929 brands spread across 150 fmcg markets in the UK and concluded that the 'life cycle' of the brand leaders is indeed more stable, and much longer, than some of the previous work might have suggested. Mercer's research indicates that the average length of life, for the brands in the wide range of fmcg markets investigated, considerably exceeds two decades.

Unlike a product, a brand may go through its life cycle and then be replaced by a newer version, since the old one is obsolete. The brand would live on and continue through the growth or maturity stage, because the new version would keep it from becoming obsolete. Brands can be kept vital and growing, and tired brands can be revived. Old brands can be leveraged to new growth through a process of some kind.

Similarly, specific branded products may 'die' from obsolescence or changing consumer tastes, but brands can be rejuvenated with new products and services. Except for a few consumer-related markets, such as ethical pharmaceuticals, the brand is tied to a physical product in such a way that the changes in formulation determine its life. With well-conceived strategies, programmes and tactics, a brand can be kept relevant to consumers and last almost indefinitely. RCA, for example, began its life as the Radio Corporation of America. By transforming itself as new technologies replaced radio, the brand has maintained a leadership position. Today, the Kodak brand is being transferred to electronic imaging systems as chemical-based photography nears the end of its life cycle. Examples of brand longevity are fairly common: Lipton brand tea is still popular today and, in fact, has outlasted the British Empire. Other long-lived brands include Bass Ale (1777), Baker's Chocolate (1789), Ivory Soap (1881) and Coca-Cola (1886).

Nevertheless, without careful management, brands can follow the general pattern of a product life cycle, i.e. moving through introduction, growth, maturity and decline stages in a relatively rapid fashion. Well-managed brands, however, can prosper almost indefinitely.

Arguments for the BLC

Some people believe brands have a life cycle, and that 'the brand life cycle is that of the sum of the products under that brand name'. Brands have life cycles, but once they mature, only the good ones can stay around for a very long time, referring to what Mercer found earlier. If a product is a person's body, the brand is its soul; it can live for ever.

Life cycles can be iterative with sub-life cycles. They can also be iterative, or become sub-life cycles. Many big-name brands constantly refine themselves using iterative life cycles. For instance, in the impulse confectionery market in the UK, the three major manufacturers, Mars, Cadbury and Nestlé, have launched 'limited edition' brands. These have the effect of attracting interest to the category. Thus, a product brand or service brand may have a series of short life cycles. This may occur where the product or service is used for a short time only, and the target market itself is constantly changing. For example, baby food manufacturers gain and lose consumers all the time. This means that there are always opportunities for new consumers as 'established' buyers move out of the market. In this case there cannot be one life cycle, but instead a whole series.

There are practical questions concerning the extent to which a brand life cycle, based on the PLC model, helps marketers to know when their brand is in decline and when it is time to cut marketing budgets. Perhaps the brand is experiencing just a slight decline before a dramatic increase in another growth period, or maybe there is a levelling-off of sales with no more peaks and valleys, just perpetual maturity. This approach has also been criticized for its non-scientific way of measuring and pinpointing an exact location in a life cycle as well as not being directly linked with profitability, and there may be other approaches that are better predictors of the brand's longevity, such as brand valuation (see Chapter 2) and customer equity. Customer equity – in simple terms, the lifetime value of all of a brand's customers – may be a much more accurate indicator of how much longer a brand is likely to live if the company maintains the status quo. (For more on the topic see Rust, Zeithaml and Lemon, 2000.) The more equity a brand has, relative to its competitors, the longer it will live irrespective of its chronological age. If a brand has weak equity, its managers know they need to change marketing inputs to make it healthy again and prolong its life.

Nevertheless, companies use the brand life cycle based on the PLC model, along with other indicators, to avoid falling into the decline phase. For example, since its introduction of the iPod, Apple has rolled out products and services, on a fairly regular basis. IBM, on the other hand, saw the signs, and the diminishing sales. While the brand remains very much intact, the business has changed completely. It no longer sells 'machines' and is restructuring to sell 'management'. Thus, although there are limitations to using the BLC that derives from the PLC model, this approach enables us to understand the way a company innovates and introduces new products and services to market.

The following BLC models developed by academics and practitioners do not necessarily follow the PLC concept. These models are not based on growth or profitability of the brand per se, but instead the focus is on the customer experience with the brands, and how these evolve and are managed in a number of stages. As well as showing how a particular brand should be positioned and its relation to the company's overall strategy, these models enable companies to look at their corporate strategies, portfolio of brands and products in a meaningful way.

The BLC models

There are three very different views of a brand life cycle. First, brands are seen as evolving in stages: first, from the customer perspective; second, from the brand's perspective; and, finally, from the company's perspective. The following describes these BLC perspectives, and the management of brands across the life cycle as seen from these three perspectives.

The five stages of a brand life cycle

The following is adapted from consulting agency Benson.

There are five stages of the brand life cycle, beginning with the brand definition and then progressing through four distinct customer experiences. Each of the following stages has both a short- and long-term impact on how customers view the brand.

1 The brand definition.
2 The awareness experience.
3 The buying experience.
4 The using and service experience.
5 The membership experience.

There are two aspects of this brand life cycle that should be highlighted at the outset: first, brands live in the minds of their customers. The implication here is that companies do not own a brand, they are merely its captain and steward. Therefore, companies should view their brand from the perspective of the customer's experience, until it is eventually renewed or retired. Second, although success at each brand life cycle stage varies widely, every brand that generates even a single customer travels through stages 1 to 4. By contrast, stage 5, the membership experience, is reserved for brands that generate such intense loyalty that customers actually integrate them into their personal identities. However, long before any membership experience can exist, brands must create clear definitions that can be embraced by their primary target customers. It should also be noted that some brands are better than others at certain stages; some brands never mature through the full five-stage life cycle, and seem stuck in the equivalent of adolescence or early adulthood.

Defining the brand

The first step in a brand's life cycle is its creation. Brands are not products, nor are they services. Brands represent a promise to fulfil a customer need. The promise may be utilitarian, such as a clean, pressed shirt from the dry cleaner, or it may be emotional, such as the comfort provided by Volvo's commitment to safety. A company constructs a brand promise based on the following:

■ Defining the primary target customer for the product or service. These are the people who will experience the company's brand most directly and intimately.

■ Defining the product or offering in terms of features, capabilities or skills for the company's primary target customer, and identifying the requirements to meet the customer's needs. The offering describes the product or service based on its unique characteristics and defines the capabilities required to deliver the promise.

■ Defining the benefits the brand provides to its customers. For example, when you choose to shop at Staples, you get informed sales support, a deep and intelligent selection of product choices, a competitive price and, most important, no hassles. When you purchase a Sony DVD player, you expect it to work when you plug it in and for several years thereafter. The benefit component clearly articulates what customers receive for their time and money. It is the value the brand provides.

■ Choosing how to deliver the brand promise. Although many people consider this to be simply marketing communication, it is more accurately viewed as the customer's awareness experience.

The awareness experience

Brands live in the minds of the customer. To get into the customer's mind typically requires an appreciation of and empathy with the emotional benefits of the brand – for example, will it help me sleep better at night? Will it say positive things about me to others? Does it make me feel accomplished or successful or happy?

There are several methods and channels available for establishing awareness among the primary target customers. These include broadcast media, print advertising, direct mail, direct email, billboards, store locations, public relations and direct sales. These are the most common, although some are better than others at targeting customer segments efficiently.

Brand awareness can be measured through brand recall and brand recognition. It is the criterion against which all other brands in the category are measured. An example of brand recognition would be if I say the word 'Sony', and you recognize who they are, and can name one or more of their products and services. Brand awareness means that customers understand and may desire the brand. The brand could appeal to them both emotionally and intellectually, so that they know why they could prefer it over competing brands. It also means that they believe in the promise of the brand, a promise that they understand from advertising, through word of mouth, and from observing others who have bought, and are using and enjoying the brand.

However, brand awareness is not the end goal. The goal is to create awareness, and secure a buying commitment and a customer relationship. To complete the customer acquisition successfully, companies must follow a compelling awareness experience with a seamless and fulfilling buying experience.

The buying experience – the first moment of truth

In the buying experience the company engages the customer, and she considers whether the brand promise is worth the cost. It is a moment of truth, a dividing line that separates prospects from customers. The company's brand needs to excel at moving people from the prospect stage to the customer stage, or the company's brand's life cycle will be short. Many factors can impact on the brand-buying experience. Is the product available in the right colour and the right size? Can the store employees or account managers answer your questions and facilitate or validate your choice? Is it priced appropriately? Customers expect to find the brand in the retail store, on the Internet, through a call centre, or through a sales representative. Wherever and whenever they buy their preferred brand, be it Caterpillar or Polo, they want to have a consistent and positive buying experience.

The using and service experience – the other moments of truth

The using and service experience of brands are yet two more moments of truth, two opportunities to keep the brand promise. The first of these is the using experience. In the buying experience, a retailer or channel partner can provide support and guidance and ensure a positive experience, helping the customer through any difficulties he may encounter. By contrast, there is typically little or no support in the home or the work environment, to ensure that when the customer plugs it in that it will start and start every time.

We expect the brands we use to provide both functional and emotional benefits. The functional benefits range from the model, colour and size ordered, to the durability, stability and performance of the product. If we ordered the 'Special Deluxe Model' we expect an additional set of features to provide us with extended capability and shelf life. The emotional benefits we expect from the brand range from safety and confidence to the signals of quality and prestige that the brand communicates to others. Both products and services need to be engineered to ensure positive and consistent using experiences.

The service experience is the third moment of truth for the brand. It often has a profound impact on the customer relationship, and determines whether repeat purchases occur and whether word-of-mouth is positive or negative. Successfully fulfilling expectations in customer service can be as critical as the using experience, and should be anticipated as part of your brand definition activity.

The membership experience

When brands obtain a certain level of awareness and are recognized or recalled by the target market, and when customers want to be affiliated with the brand, it achieves a new status. That new status is the membership experience. The exclusivity and the privileges of membership are valued by the customer. They recognize the brand as being strong, favourable and unique. They enjoy sharing experiences with other owners of the brand.

Membership status is desired by every brand, because it induces repeat purchase, with referral-generating, discount-forgoing and premium-paying customers. The customer goes out of his or her way to purchase the brand even when another more convenient and competitive brand will meet the same need. Apple Computer has achieved this status. Starbucks, the Harvard Business School, Intel, Caterpillar, BMW, Disney, McDonald's and Wal-Mart have also attained this status. The customer is proud to say that they purchase and use the brand. They display it. It is a source of identification. It is a sign of quality and a source of comfort. The brand is seen as a best friend and as a leader in its category.

After stage 5 is when a brand loses its meaning and relevance. When this occurs, the brand steward has two choices: either rejuvenate or retire. If rejuvenation is chosen, the cycle starts fresh by reinvigorating the brand promise to realign its meaning and relevance with customers' evolving needs. If retirement is chosen, then the company must harvest the last of the brand's equity and invest its resources in other brands (Benson and Kinsella, 2009).

Key questions for brand and marketing executives to ask about their brands:

- What does your brand need to do at each stage of its life cycle to be successful?
- Can your company's capabilities meet all of the requirements to fulfil your brand promise?
- What company capabilities can you leverage to exceed expectations and which new capabilities need to be developed?
- How well are your current brands performing at each stage of their life cycle?
- At which life cycle stage are you falling short of your brand promise, and how can you fill the gap?

The Goodyear model

In academic literature, McEnally and de Chernatony's (1999) Goodyear model focuses on the evolving nature of *branding* over time, rather than on the strategic design of brand concepts at particular times, and for particular brand launches. Rather than tracing an actual brand over time, Goodyear's is a conceptual model of the possible stages that a brand might go through (Figure 8.2).

Stage 1: Unbranded goods

In the first stage, goods are treated as commodities and most are unbranded. This stage is usually characterized by an excess of demand over supply. It is most closely approximated by developing

Stage of branding		Time	Type of value
Stage 6	Brand as policy		
Stage 5	Brand as company		Terminal
Stage 4	Brand as icon		Symbolic
Stage 3	Brand as personality		
Stage 2	Brand as reference		
Stage 1	Unbranded	Time = 0	Instrumental

Source: McEnally and de Chernatony (1999).

FIGURE 8.2 Illustration of the branding process over time

economies and the former Soviet bloc countries, and is rarely seen in developed economies. Producers make little effort to distinguish or brand their goods, with the result that the consumer's perception of goods is utilitarian.

Stage 2: Brand as reference

In the second stage, competitive pressures stimulate producers to differentiate their goods from the output of other manufacturers. Differentiation is achieved primarily through changes in physical product attributes (gets clothes cleaner). Consumers' memory networks expand beyond recognition of the basic product category to include other product information in order to evaluate goods on the bases of consistency and quality. They begin to use brand names based on their image of the brand as an heuristic device in decision-making. Even so, consumers primarily value brands for their utilitarian value. Utilitarian values are described as instrumental, because they enable consumers to reach certain ends, and as enjoyment, which is pleasure derived from owning or using the object.

Stage 3: Brand as personality

By this stage, differentiation among brands on rational/functional attributes becomes exceedingly difficult as many producers make the same claim. Therefore, marketers begin to give their brands personalities. An example is Ivory soap. By creating the personality of the caring mother, the marketer injects emotion into the consumer's learning and valuing process. Doing so brings the brand closer to the consumer through an emotional bond, as mothers who want to be perceived as caring use Ivory soap.

In the previous two stages there was a distinction between the consumer and the brand. The brand was an object at some distance and was removed from the consumer. Incorporation of personal characteristics into the brand makes it more appealing to consumers, who are more likely to affiliate with brands possessing desirable personalities. Thus, the personalities of the consumer and the brand begin to merge, and the value of the brand has become self-expression.

Social constructionism explains the symbolic nature of brands. All individuals share in a process of transmitting, reproducing and transforming the social meaning of objects. As consumers, individuals within a social group interpret marketer-sponsored information such as advertising, and use brands to send signals to others about themselves. Other individuals interpret these signals to form images of and attitudes towards the brand's user. If the user does not get the anticipated reaction, he or she may reconsider use of the brand. This process of decoding the meaning and value of brands, and using brands correctly is active involvement of the consumer in the brand's image.

Stage 4: Brand as icon

In this stage, the brand is 'owned by consumers'. They have extensive knowledge about the brand – frequently worldwide – and use it to create their self-identity. An example is the Marlboro cowboy, who is recognized around the world. The cowboy is rugged, a man against the odds, but he is not crude or lacking in sophistication. Consumers who want to be perceived as strong, rugged or loners might smoke Marlboro cigarettes. The cowboy is a symbol or icon of a set of values.

To be well entrenched in the consumer's mind, the icon must have many associations, both primary (about the product) and secondary. For example, Air Jordan shoes have primary associations with Michael Jordan's athletic prowess, and secondary associations with the Chicago Bulls and winning. The more associations a brand has, the greater its network in the consumer's memory and the more likely it is to be recalled. Thus, management of these brands must continually find associations that strengthen the iconic stature of their brand.

Stage 5: Brand as company

This stage marks the change to postmodern marketing. Here, the brand has a complex identity, and there are many points of contact between the consumer and the brand. Because the brand equals the company, all stakeholders must perceive the brand (company) in the same fashion. The company can no longer present one image to the media and another to shareholders or consumers. Communications from the firm must be integrated throughout all of their operations.

Communication is not, however, unidirectional. It flows from the consumer to the firm, as well as from the firm to the consumer so that a dialogue is established between the two.

In stage 5 consumers become more actively involved in the brand-creation process. They are willing to interact with the product or service, in order to create additional value. Examples of this are the use of ATM machines and patronage of stores such as IKEA. In the ATM example, the consumer adds value to the banking process, by determining when and where consumers will be, when problems occur in the co-development of services. Do staff perceive the involvement of consumers as threats? Are consumers willing to pay a premium for the brand as policy?

The Mootee brand life cycle model

This brand life cycle model was developed in the mid-1990s by Mootee, a Japanese branding practitioner, to help companies understand how a particular brand should be positioned and its relation to the company's overall strategy. This was based on his extensive study of US and European companies and their brands in different categories. This model enables companies to look at their corporate strategies, portfolio of brands and products in a meaningful way.

This BLC model suggests that all brands evolve through four stages. Most of them start as a *product brand*, and then some are transformed into a *service brand*. Over years of brand-building effort and market presence they gradually become either a *category brand*, which is defined as having leading market share within a category; or a *personality brand*, which establishes a strong brand personality that consumers identify with; or an *experience brand*, which goes beyond traditional service and product excellence with a strong sense of uniqueness. Another type of brand is an *ingredient brand*, which is actually a co-brand since it coexists together with others who might be responsible for physically manufacturing products or delivering the service. Ingredient brands usually serve the purpose of providing additional trust or confidence, and often signify the use of an exclusive or proprietary technology. Examples include Lycra, Polartec, Gore-Tex, Windows, Intel, Dolby and Oracle; and Windows and Intel, which are independent IBM ingredient brands. After being extremely successful, these brands become cash-generating trademarks. They will then sometimes be moved up one level and become a *corporate brand* (the brand name becomes the corporation) or a *global brand*, expanding geographically to become a global dominant leader. These different stances illustrate the major strategic choices required by each corporation, namely the optimum level at which a brand should be positioned to capture and create shareholder value. Companies can sometimes successfully move brands to different strategic levels to become the leading brand if that brand is very successful.

It should be noted, however, that some categorizations are not mutually exclusive. A brand can be both a global brand and a personality brand (Virgin) or a global brand and an ingredient brand (Intel). The model suggests that the ultimate goal for all companies is to have a global brand. A strong global brand is a powerful weapon and many studies suggested the most valuable brands are all global (see Figure 8.3).

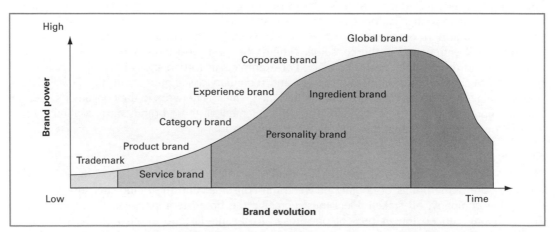

FIGURE 8.3 Idris Mootee's brand life cycle model

Branding Brief 8.2: Top five mistakes in managing high-tech brands

Source: http://www.design4brand.com/articles/article-04.php © Dan Berne

High-technology brands offer a unique set of challenges and opportunities. The goal of high-tech branding is essentially the same as that for packaged and other consumer goods: to create a compelling association between the company's products (including services) and customers. Brands shape customer perceptions. They add value to the bottom line by creating clear customer advantage, thereby enhancing profitability. Then why do so many high-tech firms struggle with creating a coherent brand strategy?

Here are five common mistakes companies make when developing and managing their brands.

Mistake 5: Not knowing how your brand is performing

Tracking brand performance is tricky; there's no doubt about it. And getting quantitative results are a challenge for traditional brand measurement techniques. You've got basically three ways to measure how well your brand strategy is working. First, there's looking at your short-term sales. Did your marketing mix model increase sales and/or higher-end profits? Second, is brand loyalty increasing your customer-based brand equity? Do customers come back to you and recommend you to others? Thirdly, does your brand provide bottom-line value, in terms of present/future value, discounted cash flows, or other forms of shareholder gains? Any of these measurements takes time and resources. Choose one and follow through.

Mistake 4: Believing the brand is not important to high-tech business customers

Maybe you think customers buy on emotional appeal when it comes to lipstick and cell phones. But what about ERP software or multi-function printers? How does brand impact those purchase decisions? In many ways, it's due to where the product category sits on the Technology Adoption Life Cycle. Let's look at the different emotional jobs that the brand must do in two different parts of the life cycle. For the visionary in the Early Adopter stage, the brand must help the customer feel, 'I'm the one around here who really thinks out-of-the box. I'm willing to take risks to achieve breakthrough results.' For the pragmatic buyer in the Bowling Alley stage, the brand must help the customer feel 'I've made a safe choice and a smart buy. I'm of value to my company because I know how things really work around here.' Knowing this, which of your product design and promotional elements would you change?

Mistake 3: Leaving the brand strategy solely to the marketing department

Branding is often equated to a set of logos, messages and advertising. But these are not the most effective tools for building high-tech brands. Unfortunately, most R&D folks assume brand is something those Marketing guys do after the product is done. In truth, brand strategy should also impact every phase of product development and customer support. While Marketing can lead the brand-strategy effort, other departments should help create the strategy and design the key brand elements, from features and design to sales materials. For example, if the brand needs to communicate best-in-class ease of use, then the user-interface and sales support process should embody that brand attribute, as well as the colour and layout of the sales brochure. It all needs to come together.

Mistake 2: Having a sloppy brand architecture

Does your product portfolio make sense to you, your channel, and to your customers? Do your brands and sub-brands break along customer lines? Technology? Business segments? Or all of the above? If customers cannot distinguish between two sub-brands in terms of what they offer, then why spend money on developing and marketing both of them? Every sub-brand and product line should have a clear role in your portfolio, whether it's to gain share, acquire niche profitability, or serve as a firewall. It's not enough for the architecture to distinguish brand names and numbering schemes. An uninformed stranger should be able to look at your brand portfolio architecture and say, 'I get it', without having to sit through an hour-long PowerPoint presentation. If not, you are confusing yourselves, your channel and your customers.

Mistake 1: Managing the brand for the short term

Brands build value over time, but sustaining the brand story and maintaining investments year after year is a daunting effort for most high-tech firms. It's easy to see how it happens. The players come and go. VP's of Marketing are typically measured in quarter-to-quarter results, whether by market share or overall earnings per share. It's often easier to measure the investments in your brand (money spent) than the long-term, and intangible, returns. But short-term tactics, such as price promotions and frequent brand persona changes, only serve to dilute the brand. And this short-term thinking can lead to the 'price-promotion doom loop'. Your quarterly results are soft, you drop price to make up the volume, while reducing your brand budget. Great. You've gained volume for the next quarter, but your competitors respond and you've reset the expectations of the brand value in your customers' minds. And you're back to another quarter of soft results, ready to drop price again.

Do any of these common mistakes ring a bell?

A coherent brand strategy can address each and every one of the above mistakes. Let design4brand help you avoid these and maximize your brand value.

Branding Brief 8.3: Brands, many lives?

Source: Martin Payne at poolonline.com (http://www.poolonline.com/archive/issue12/iss12fea5.html)

One of the issues facing brands today and in the future is the apparent shortening of the 'product life cycle'. While many brands continue to lead their markets after many years, others have short life cycles and are frequently designed with this in mind. Brands either live or die. They can innovate and evolve or they can be designed for a short life. The Loop's Brand Positive research programme has uncovered some of the reasons why life cycle theory should now be revisited to ascertain how brands are being developed for short lives.

Strong brands remain strong

Numerous studies have shown that many brands that were leading the market years ago are still in that position, which makes it difficult for a challenging brand to overtake them. The ability to extend the life cycle or, possibly, the effective marketing of these brands has meant that the life cycle, in its purest form, does not exist. The brand must remain relevant in an ever-changing marketing environment. It must continue to provide consumer value.

Market leaders have an in-built advantage that makes it easier for them to survive than number two or three brands. For example, some of the factors that tend to favour leading brands are:

- It is easier for them to gain and maintain distribution.
- They tend to be more profitable and this feeds back into communications, research and development budgets.
- They have a higher level of consumer awareness.
- They can maintain higher promotional budgets.
- They can speak with a different voice to the consumer.

Moreover, these brands have been highly active in ensuring that their life cycle is continually renewed. Nescafé, for example, has maintained its position as the UK's leading instant coffee brand through frequent updating. This has extended the brand beyond the core Nescafé coffee into variants such as Espresso and Cappuccino as well as different bean types and, most recently, an organic variant. However, while the brand remains modern and relevant, the core brand values do not change and this is the key to its endurance.

The constantly changing brand

The alternative way to retain a brand's freshness is to keep changing it. This may be more relevant in a marketplace which is experiencing rapid change so that the brand can reflect and exploit this by exhibiting new traits. As previously noted, this could also be a method of catching the consumer's attention: in the impulse confectionery market in the UK, for example, the three major manufacturers Mars, Cadbury and Nestlé have launched 'limited edition' brands. These have the effect of attracting interest to the category. Gerber Foods is recognizing the seasonal nature of fruit through its Spring 2000 UK launch of Ocean Spray Cranberry Seasons. This new product has a seasonal life and is replaced with the change of seasons.

Target market issues

A product or service may have a series of short life cycles. This may occur where the product or service is used for a short time only and the target market itself is constantly changing. For example, baby foods manufacturers gain and lose consumers all the time. This means that there are always opportunities with new consumers and 'established' buyers move out of the market. In this case, there cannot be one life cycle but a whole series. Other areas that are time-dependent include toys. Look at the longevity of brands such as Barbie that has been a best-selling toy for generations of girls.

Globalization and rapid communications shorten time cycles

Outside factors that impact on a brand mean that it can often be advantageous to look outside the home country for areas of development. This works two ways and cross-border marketing means a much greater level of competition.

The Internet has been a significant inflection point here as it enables the rapid dissemination of ideas and development of products around the globe. In effect, it acts to shorten the life cycle in many categories. High-profile dotcom failures will not just be the result of unstable business models or poor management, but could also fall victim to the fact that simple ideas based on open-technology standards can easily be copied.

The dynamics of innovation

Innovation is, by its very nature, only short term. To be innovative, a company or brand must strive for constant leading-edge development, thereby ensuring that it remains ahead of its competition or develops new categories that it can exploit before the competition reaches parity. At this stage the genuinely innovative company must be launching version 2.0 or moving into the next market. This is all the more apparent in fast-moving markets or in sectors where there is intense competition.

However, the fast pace of development may often cause the product or service development to encounter problems that result in the launch date having to be postponed. While this itself may not be an issue, there is a potential for consumer confusion, or even negative publicity, as the communications programme may already be underway. Recent examples here are the launch of its Internet banking arm Intelligent Finance by the Halifax bank, where advertisements had to be taken in the press to explain that there were technical problems with the service and, even more recently, Barclays' announcement of security flaws in its online banking.

While in this type of environment early publicity may be necessary to ensure that consumers wait for the product or service rather than opting for a competitor, there is danger in launching a product or service that does not yet exist or does not function correctly. Any ensuring publicity could be viewed as a necessary risk.

Nevertheless, innovation is crucial. To put it simply, it is more effective to make your own product obsolete before your competition does. It is important to be developing future versions of a product or service so that the product life cycle is restarted and competitors are always playing catch-up.

More lessons from the information technology sector

As marketing moves away from mass marketing towards customization and, ultimately, personalization, the life cycle may help to address different target markets in turn. This theory is popularized in Geoffrey Moore's series of best-selling books on IT marketing, but there is no reason why this strategy cannot be applied to other categories. Geoffrey Moore's 'bowling alley' approach refers to picking off different market segments, one at a time while all the time continuing to build critical mass for the product and focusing marketing resources. It helps the product shift from early adopter to early majority status and move away from 'the chasm'. This may be achieved by the recognition that the life cycle varies for each different group of consumers. Product development and marketing communications can thus be organized to suit the target segments.

Summary

The current and future brand marketing environment is becoming more competitive and the pace of change is accelerating. One approach to harnessing this for the company or brand's benefit is to revisit life-cycle theory and undertake development on a short-term basis. This could include the recognition of different product life cycles for different consumers or different target segments. There is no shame at all in launching a product or service that can be copied by competitors, but continual updating is vital to always stay one step ahead. The product launch date could be viewed as the start of the development process, not the culmination.

The Loop's Brand Positive™ Knowledge Development Programme has recognized that identification and application of life cycle theory is becoming a key to future marketing development. This feeds into a range of solutions such as Horizon™, Blackjack™ and Bedrock™ that can be offered to clients to address brand-evolution issues. These impact across different time scales through the short, medium and long terms.

Brand concept management

(See also Chapter 5.)

Taking a strategic long-term approach, Park, Jaworski and MacInnis (1986) developed a framework called brand concept management (BCM), which is concerned with selecting, implementing and controlling brand image over time to enhance market performance. The framework consists of a sequential process of selecting, introducing, elaborating and fortifying a brand concept. This then guides positioning strategies and the brand image at each of these stages. Three types of brand concepts are developed, which are based on consumer needs, namely *functional, symbolic* and *experiential*.

1 A brand with a *functional concept* is one that is designed to fulfil immediate consumption needs.

2 A brand with a *symbolic concept* is one that fulfils internally generated needs like self-enhancement or ego identification.

3 A brand with an *experiential concept* is one that fulfils internally generated needs for stimulation or variety. This refers to brands that fulfil experiential needs and provide sensory pleasure, variety, and/or cognitive stimulation.

Once a broad needs-based concept has been selected, it can be used to guide the positioning strategy through the three management stages of *introduction, elaboration* and *fortification*. In the *introductory stage* of BCM a set of activities are designed to establish a brand image/position in the marketplace during the period of market entry. During the *elaboration stage*, positioning strategies focus on adding value to the brand's image so that its perceived superiority relative to the competitors can be established or sustained. In the the *fortification stage*, the aim is to link an elaborated brand image to the image of other products produced by the firm in different product classes. The specific strategy implemented at the three different stages depends upon the initial concept type. Below is an example of brands from each concept type and the implication for long-term brand management.

The BCM model suggests a continuity of interaction with the brand and an increasing array of choices, as it goes from the introduction to the elaboration and fortification stage. The three different concepts provide clear brand positioning, and the successive stages help increase consumer loyalty and involvement with the brand (Table 8.1). Each concept helps a brand build a consistent and unambiguous long-term relationship with the consumers. However, the success of a brand concept

Concept introduction	Concept elaboration	Concept fortification
Brand with a functional concept	*Vaseline Petroleum Jelly*	
1869 Vaseline Petroleum Jelly introduced to the market as a lubricant and a skin balm for burns	Problem-solving generalization strategy. Produce usage extended to multiple usage situations: preventing nappy rash, removing eye make-up, lip balm	Vaseline health and beauty-related products: Vaseline Intensive Care Lotion Intensive Care Bath Beads Vaseline Constant Care Vaseline Dermatology Formula Range of Vaseline Baby Care Products
Brand with a symbolic concept	*Lenox China*	
Almost a century ago, the Lenox Company introduced a line of fine china	Market shielding concept. A tightly controlled marketing mix to preserve the status quo	Lenox Crystal Lenox silver-plated Hollowware Candles Jewellery
Brand with an experiential concept	*Barbie Doll*	
The Barbie Doll was introduced to the market in 1959	Brand accessory strategy. Accessories like outfits, houses, furniture, cars, jewellery for Barbie, Ken	Barbie Magazine Barbie Game Barbie Boutique

TABLE 8.1 Brand concept management

does still depend upon such factors as the effectiveness and efficiency of positioning efforts, and the competitive environment.

Even a brand whose image has been managed successfully can decline if the brand concept ceases to be valued by the target customers and the market trends in a particular category shift significantly. For example, Jiffy Pop popcorn, meant to be cooked over a stove, became obsolete following the ubiquitous usage of the microwave oven. Jiffy Pop eventually introduced Microwave Jiffy Pop, but not before it was too late to save the brand. A single brand can also fulfil more than one type of need. For example, travelling first-class with a premium airline could fulfil both symbolic needs as well as experiential ones, thereby making a single brand concept insufficient as a basis for long-term brand strategy. Despite these criticisms, BCM is still one of the most elaborate frameworks for long-term brand management.

Brands can also be revitalized and boosted if underperforming, through a number of strategies (see Mini cases 8.1 and 8.2 and the End of chapter case study) so that brands do not follow the same life cycle as a product. This leads naturally on to the next section, on brand revitalization.

For more on this topic see Chapter 5.

Brand revitalization

Even the biggest and best brands eventually lose their appeal, since new competitors can outdo them in terms of features and price, new channels of distribution may emerge, or new technologies may erupt and disrupt. Alternatively, customer cultures and lifestyles may shift to alter a brand's saliency; there is no brand immune to these forces. Nevertheless, the loss of appeal of the brand does not have to be permanent thanks to brand revitalization. Nowadays, because of the heavy investment of new product development, companies seem to be interested in the revitalization of diminishing brands more than ever before.

Aspects of brand revitalization

Brand revitalization is about seven things: increasing usage; finding new uses; entering new markets; repositioning the brand; augmenting product/services; making existing products obsolete; extending the brand (based on Aaker, 1991).

Increasing the usage among current customers may be the simplest thing to implement, because it is easier and costs less than changing the brand image or repositioning. Usage can be increased in two ways – by increasing the level (i.e. how much the brand is used) or by increasing the frequency of consumption (how often the brand is used).

To find new uses for the brand, thorough marketing research must be carried out into how the brand is used. Then, and only then, can all the ways in which the brand is used be determined, and additional ones explored and eventually given prominence. Entering new markets may be a way to gain additional growth for the brand.

Sometimes the brand positioning and image have to be changed fundamentally by improving the strength, favourability and uniqueness of brand associations. The positive associations which have been created earlier need to be strengthened and any negative associations neutralized. To fully revitalize the lost brand equity, additional positive associations often need to be created to reflect the changes in market conditions. Augmenting the product is another aspect of brand revitalization. This is essentially the same thing, and deals with gaining brand equity by creating points of difference (Aaker, 1991). Also, brand elements (e.g. the name or logo of the brand) need to be changed as part of the repositioning to convey information of the change to customers.

Sometimes revitalization requires re-branding a company from the top down. This can include a refurbishment of the logo, trademark and trade dress to revamp the entire corporate brand image. Sometimes it involves updating the brand's products and specific product attributes with better, more in-demand features. Revitalization may also require repackaging for a fresher, more contemporary brand look to appeal to new generations of consumers. A successful example of corporate revitalization is Samsung. In the mid-1990s Samsung Electronics' chairman and senior management decided that Samsung would no longer provide commodity electronics products to the world's retailers, including Wal-Mart, but would focus instead on developing innovative product design and stake its own claim to become a global brand. As a result, the company focused on product innovation and brand-design strategy, and saw a meteoric rise in sales and brand value in a few short years (Mininni, www.brandchannel.com).

Making existing products obsolete is another way to revitalize the corporate brand. Brand meanings can be clarified if the company chooses to concentrate on a clearer selection of market offerings, thus helping the desired brand associations to form in the minds of consumers. Extending the brand can be controversial, especially at the corporate level. Undoubtedly, many companies have managed to move from one product class to another by making use of their established brand name. So, if by extending the brand to another product class helps to create or shape brand associations and image, then it is indeed a plausible way to revitalize a brand. Indeed, research into the area suggests that upscale extensions may very well be effective (Munthree et al., 2006).

Brand revitalization process

There are three stages in the brand-revitalization process: brand visioning, brand orientation and brand implementation (Merrilees, 2005). *Brand visioning* is the reformulation of the brand, where distinctive features and values are emphasized, and the competitive positioning of the brand mapped out. *Brand orientation* is the process of making the brand the central and coordinating element of marketing strategy. *Brand strategy implementation* is the final phase of brand revitalization, where the brand strategy is implemented through the marketing mix.

Conclusion

Unlike products which are known to have a life cycle from introduction to growth, maturity and decline, brands are not seen to have a life cycle as such, owing to their long-lived nature. They could live on and continue through the growth or maturity stage. If well managed, brands can be kept vital and growing, and tired brands can be revived. The brand life cycle (BLC) may be viewed from three perspectives: the consumer's, the brand's and the company's. From the consumer's perspective, the brand life cycle begins with the brand definition, then progresses through four distinct customer experiences: awareness, buying, using/service and membership. Each of these stages has both short- and long-term impacts on how customers view the brand. This BLC concept suggests that brands live in the minds of their customers and thus implies that companies do not own brands, but are merely their captain and steward. This concept also holds that every brand that generates even a single customer travels through stages 1 to 4. By contrast, stage 5, the membership experience, is reserved only for brands that generate such intense loyalty that customers actually integrate them into their personal identities. However, long before any membership experience can exist, brands must create clear definitions that can be embraced by their primary target customers. It should also be noted that some brands are better than others at certain stages, while some brands never mature through the full five-stage life cycle, seemingly stuck in the equivalent of adolescence or early adulthood.

The Goodyear model views brand life cycle from the brand's perspective. It describes how brands evolve through six stages. In the first stage, goods are treated as commodities and most are unbranded. Producers make little effort to distinguish or brand their goods. In the second stage, competitive pressures stimulate producers to differentiate their goods from the output of other manufacturers. Here, the brand is served as a reference; consumers begin to use brand names in decision-making. In the third stage, differentiation among brands on rational/functional attributes becomes exceedingly difficult as many producers make the same claim. By creating a personality for the brand, the marketer hopes to achieve differentiation. In the fourth stage, the brand is an icon, i.e. is owned by consumers. Consumers have extensive knowledge of the brand, and use it to create their self-identity. In the last stage of this BLC, the brand is equal to the company. All stakeholders must perceive the brand (company) in the same fashion.

The Mootee brand life cycle model suggests that all brands evolve through four stages. From the product brand where most brands start as a product, then some are transformed into a service brand and become either a category brand, i.e. the leader in their product category, or a personality brand with which consumers can identify. Or they may become an experience brand, which goes beyond traditional service and product excellence with a strong sense of uniqueness. After being extremely successful these brands become cash-generating trademarks. They will then sometimes be moved up one level and become a corporate brand (the brand name becomes the corporation) or a global brand, expanding geographically to become a globally dominant leader.

Brand concept management (BCM) takes a strategic long-term approach to managing brands over time. The framework consists of a sequential process of selecting, introducing, elaborating and fortifying a brand concept. This then guides positioning strategies and the brand image, at each of these stages. In the *introductory stage* of BCM a set of activities is designed to establish a brand image/position in the marketplace during the period of market entry. During the *elaboration stage*, positioning strategies focus on adding value to the brand's image so that its perceived superiority relative to competitors can be established or sustained. In the *fortification stage*, the aim is to link an elaborated brand image to the image of other products produced by the firm in different product classes. Apart from BCM, brands can be revitalized and boosted if underperforming, through a number of strategies, so that brands do not follow the same life cycle as a product. This is also known as *brand revitalization*, which is concerned with: increasing usage; finding new uses; entering new markets; repositioning the brand; augmenting product/services; making existing products obsolete; and extending the brand. The three stages in the brand-revitalization process include brand visioning, orientation and implementation

---

🔐 Key terms

Brand as company: where there is a need to focus on corporate benefits to 'diverse' consumers. Integrated communication strategy is essential through-the-line.

Brand as icon: where consumers 'own' the brand; brand taps into higher-order values of society; advertising assumes a close relationship; use of symbolic brand language; often established internationally.

Brand as personality: brand name may be 'standalone'; marketing support focuses on emotional appeal; product benefits; advertising puts brand into context.

Brand as policy: refers to company and brands aligned to social and political issues. Consumers 'vote' on issues through companies; consumers now 'own' brands, companies and policies.

Brand as reference: brand name is often the name of the maker; name used for identification; any advertising support focuses on rational attributes; name over time becomes guarantee of quality/consistency.

Brand evolution/brand life cycle model: a brand starts as a trademark or a product brand then is transformed into a service brand. Through years of brand-building efforts, the brand becomes either a category brand which is defined as having leading market share within a category; or a personality brand, which establishes a strong brand personality with which consumers can identify; or an experience brand, which goes beyond traditional service and product excellence with a strong sense of uniqueness. After being extremely successful, the brand sometimes moves up one level and become a corporate brand, i.e. the brand name becomes the corporation, or a global brand, expanding geographically to become a global leader.

Brand image concept management: see Chapter 5.

Brand life cycle: brands are said to evolve in six stages from being a trademark, to being a product brand, a service brand, then category brand, personality brand or experience brand, then from corporate to global brand. Sometimes they can also be referred to as a five-stage process: the first consists of determining who the brand is for, what benefits it gives, how it is going to deliver its promise; the second consists of developing the awareness experience; the third, the buying experience; the fourth and fifth, the using/service and membership experience, respectively.

Brand revitalization: the process aiming to keep the brand fresh, vital and relevant in the contemporary market (Merrilees, 2005) by recapturing lost sources of brand equity or obtaining new ones.

Five stages of a brand life cycle, the: the five stages of a brand life cycle consist of, first, defining the brand by determining who it is for, what offerings it should have, what benefits it provides to its customers and how it is going deliver its promise. Create the awareness experience through marketing communications or communication media; brand awareness is measured through brand recall. Then, create the buying experience, the using experience and the membership experience. The buying experience corresponds to what is called 'the first moment of truth'. This is concerned with the brand delivering its promise, and giving customers consistent and positive buying experiences. The second moment of truth is the using and service experience. The using experience relates to functional and emotional benefits that brands provide, and the service experience relates to the customer relationship. The membership experience refers to when customers want to be affiliated with the brand.

Product life cycle: A product has a life cycle which is based on four stages: introduction, growth, maturity and decline.

Unbranded: refers to commodities; packaged goods; major proportion of goods in non-industrialized context; minor role in Europe/US; supplier has power.

? Discussion questions

1 Some people believe that, unlike products, brands do not have a life cycle because they are supposed to live for ever. Do you agree with this argument? Support your answer with examples.

2 What are the main differences between a product life cycle and a brand life cycle?

3 Some people explain branding in terms of development stages, while others try to conceptualize the life cycle of brands. Why do you think it is difficult to pin down a life cycle for brands compared to that of products?

4 'Not all brands develop in the same way. This explains why there is no single brand life cycle, but several.' Do you agree with this statement? Support your answer with examples.

5 Using business examples, discuss how and why some brands have many lives while others have a shorter life cycle.

6 Explain the advantages/disadvantages of positioning/repositioning strategies based on examples of fmcg firms.

7 Explain how the concept of brand-image management is a step further than positioning/repositioning strategies.

?

8 Discuss how globalization and rapid communications shorten product life cycle. Give examples from various industries.

9 What are the main barriers facing global brands and their management?

10 It has been said, there is a process, a discipline and a way of thinking that increases the odds of discovering ways to leverage old brands to new growth. Can you explain what this process or discipline or way of thinking is?

Projects

1 Can you draw up a product life cycle for an industrial product, an fmcg and a service product of your choice? What conclusions do you come up with?

2 Compare and contrast the brand life cycle of any Nestlé product with a less famous brand in the same area.

3 Conduct a short interview with a high-street bank branch manager. Ask him/her to discuss the benefits and drawbacks of using a PLC in their industry.

4 Apply the Goodyear model to any products of your choice.

5 Discuss ways of leveraging old brands to new growth with an fmcg brand manager.

MINI CASE 8.1: MANAGING MATURE BRANDS

In addition to influencing perceptions and choice of a mature brand, a brand manager may encourage consumption of the brand through the following:

■ *Ensuring awareness at the point of consumption.* Consumers need to be aware of the brand's various usage situations, such as breakfasts or morning snacks. The brand must also be on the top-of-one's mind and convenient when the consumption decision is being made. Campbell's Soup, for instance, schedules its radio advertisements to be broadcast just prior to lunch and dinner. Furthermore, it instructs radio stations to broadcast specially developed 'Storm Spot Ads' during inclement weather.

■ *New uses.* A point-of-purchase display can offer ideas for new uses of the brand, along with tear-off recipes.

■ *Larger packages.* These can encourage greater usage with many categories of foods, beverages and household cleaners. The larger the package size the greater the volume of a brand a person will consume.

■ *Price promotion.* Directly decreasing a brand's price similarly increases usage volume. Although this can be accomplished through shelf-price reductions, such promotions are unlikely to impact on usage volume if the consumer does not recall having bought the item on sale when using it.

■ *Need for variety.* Increasing usage must be weighted against the possibility of user satiation.

■ *Adopting revitalization strategies.* The customer, the brand's market share and the company's competitive strengths influence what revitalization strategies should be used with a particular brand.

■ *Redefining a company's share of its target market.* A high-share brand should focus on strengthening perceptions of the brand and on accelerating its use. A low-share brand should place a greater emphasis on simply encouraging choice. Medium-share brands may need to employ strategies based on all three (perceiving, choosing and using), in order to attract new consumers.

■ *Defining one's market.* A niche brand such as Healthy Choice may have a 16 per cent share of the total canned soup market, but it may also have a 58 per cent share of the premium soup market. If it wants to define its market as 'all soup users', it needs to invest in 'choosing strategies'. If it wants to define its market as 'premium soup users', it needs to invest in 'perceiving and using' strategies.

■ *Analysing tactical trade-offs.* After defining the target market, tactical options can be analysed on the basis of effects on margins, effects on brand image and speed of implementation. Each revitalization option necessitates different trade-offs.

Questions:

1 Discuss consumer purchasing behaviour with regard to mature products.

2 Using the PLC, explain whether there are any strategies other than those mentioned in the case study that companies could adopt when the product reaches maturity.

3 Discuss the segmentation scope for mature products.

MINI CASE 8.2: BUILDING BETTER BRANDS – BRAND LIFE CYCLE MANAGEMENT, MYTH OR REALITY?

Source: Rebecca Robin at Brandchannel.com

Building and maintaining distinctive, recognizable brands has never been more crucial. Faced with fewer blockbusters in the pipeline, increasingly crowded therapy areas and the onslaught of more savvy and aggressive generic entrants, pharmaceutical companies are recognizing the need to take a more strategic and rigorous approach not only to developing and maintaining new brands, but also to maintaining and evolving established brands for maximum competitive advantage.

Managing the life cycle of a brand has historically meant maximizing marketing investment for launch and sustaining a level of investment through peak, only to let the brand go from boom to bust as patent expiry looms. To what extent are we missing out on improving return on investment (ROI) by failing to optimize opportunities at every stage of the brand's life cycle – from development and pre-launch, through peak and maturity, up to and beyond patent expiry? Are we still paying lip-service, in some cases, to the notion of brand equity? Or, in recognizing the value afforded by strong branding, can we begin to realize the value in the developing best practices for brand life cycle management?

Certainly, pharmaceutical companies are more versed in brand than ever before; but at the long-term level of implementing and leveraging brand, there appears to be something missing in translation. The question for debate is: brand life cycle management, myth or reality?

Laying the foundations

Optimizing the opportunity for the brand comes down to maximizing and maintaining the key brand variables – positioning, personality, brand name and identity. Establishing clear and strategic foundations, therefore, is fundamental to underpinning the development of any brand. The blueprint of great brands can be seen to meet four key criteria:

1 *Relevance.* Understanding the existing brand dynamics of the therapy area, the unmet needs in the market, the hearts and minds of both prescriber and patient target audiences, is crucial to determining the relevance of the window of brand opportunity.

2 *Credibility.* The paradigm shift in patient power has created a compelling push-pull dynamic, which has forever changed the way in which a pharmaceutical brand is brought to market. Brand cues and communications, therefore, need to be taken into consideration and be credible across all target audiences. Brands need to speak the patient's language as much as the prescriber's language.

3 *Differentiation.* It is vital that the branding foundations being put in place are defined for differentiation vis-à-vis the future brand context, as much as the current brand context.

4 *Stretch.* Ultimately, those branding foundations should be sufficiently flexible, to accommodate changes in the market and for the post-patent life of the brand.

However, are we opening that window of brand opportunity far enough? Getting the branding right will never compensate for a poor product; but getting the branding wrong, or failing to unlock the true potential of a brand, can make the difference between good brand recognition and loyalty and great brand recognition and loyalty – thus impacting on the bottom line in terms of the difference between good ROI and great ROI.

Increasingly, companies should think about ways in which they can start to take ownership of 'white space' around the brand in the lead-up to launch, leveraging branding that shapes the perspective of the market. This might include anything from branding a new class of drugs, to branding, or indeed, re-branding a condition.

Leveraging the power of language surrounding the brand can play a critical role in helping to shift mindsets and influence behaviour. Recent examples of this include the transition from 'urinary incontinence' to 'overactive bladder' and, of course, the migration from 'impotence' through 'erectile dysfunction', to the acronym ED. Such an approach to early-stage brand development, however, necessitates a rethink about when the branding process begins and about developing best practices for branding.

In the not so distant past, pharmaceutical companies had a tendency to operate by taking the rising stars of the pipeline to market in cruder terms – a trademark was secured, an advertising campaign rolled out and a brand was born. Clearly, we have progressed light years from those dark days. Yet, for global brands to become a more effective and efficient, long-term commercial reality, an approach to brand-building must be adopted that is as much inside-out as outside-in.

Despite substantial progress having been made 'outside-in' in a better understanding of and engagement with the dynamics of a rapidly changing market, with an increasingly enfranchised end-user – are we, nevertheless, missing opportunities for our brands by not understanding the role of brand 'inside-out'? Is the external window of opportunity for the brand being undermined by lack of internal buy-in and integration of brand within the organization, by insufficient structures and systems to ensure that branding begins at the 'right' time? A clear understanding of brand and a well-entrenched framework for brand development is a basic, but crucial platform for ensuring that the brand is optimized for launch.

For example, carrying out the legal, linguistic and regulatory due diligence required to secure the global brand name alone is becoming increasingly challenging and time-consuming. Starting the brand development process too late can be a make or break point when it comes to hitting launch on time. Equally, having a clearly defined brand in place pre-launch means nothing unless it is rolled out consistently and effectively across all manifestations and touchpoints of the brand, ensuring that brand messaging and communications are clear and consistent – from advertising, PR and sales-aids, down to use of colour and intagliation on the product itself. Clarity of brand proposition and consistency in communicating that proposition are the watchwords of good branding. With global brands fast becoming a strategic imperative, companies have to move equally fast to make them a reality.

As centres for excellence in drug discovery are developed, so we need to see the equivalent in terms of commercialization and brand optimization. Indeed, AstraZeneca is one of the pioneers in the entrenching of brand within the organization and in translating brand awareness into brand reality. Product strategy and licensing (PS&L) groups are centralized, global commercial constellations within the organization.

Sir Tom McKillop, chief executive of AstraZeneca, describes the centralized role of the company's PS&L group as: '... the nerve centre for product positioning and how we think about products, how we transfer the learning from one country to another'.* Critically, there needs to be greater consensus within companies on the branding of products – from a fundamental understanding of why brand matters, to practical issues of when the brand development process should start, who is responsible for that process and how it is going to be implemented.

Brand maintenance

Optimizing opportunity for the brand is something that should never go out of focus throughout the life cycle of the brand. While considerable time and investment are deployed in creating and developing a brand in the lead-up to launch, important consideration needs to be given to maintaining and managing the opportunity for that brand following the launch. Faced with faster and newer entrants to the market, how do you ensure that your market-leading brand does not fall victim to pretenders to the throne?

Again, the holy grail of Relevance, Differentiation, Credibility and Stretch should be applied continually to check and monitor the health of a brand. As the market changes, brand managers need to be proactive in pre-empting and responding to those changes, anticipating and accounting for new competitors and laying the foundations for new indications and formulations. The essence of brand life cycle management, therefore, increasingly needs to take the form of brand 'guardianship', with responsibility for managing, maintaining and extending the potential of that brand throughout its life cycle.

As much as systems and structures need to be in place to determine and develop the brand opportunity, these systems and structures should be established with a view to the long-term management of brand life cycles. Novartis has implemented such a structure around therapy areas. According to Jean-Jacques Garaud MD, senior vice president/global head of clinical R&D at Novartis: 'The teams in therapy areas have the responsibility of looking at the strategy aspect of given brands and products. Beneath that, we have international product and brand teams that are involved in the further development of the drug. There is an organization around life cycle ...'.**

Building brand life cycle management into the fabric of a company necessitates a concomitant change in our approach to the value of brands in the industry – no longer with a sense of resignation in the face of patent expiry, but with a clear and strategic vision for the long-term, commercially viable potential of that brand. Brands are by no means and can never be a panacea for better products coming to market with improved benefits, nor, for generic entrants offering a cheaper alternative. Brand equity, however, can play a considerable and substantial role in helping to maintain a premium position and, ultimately, in slowing erosion of sales and market share by subsequent entrants.

Extending the brand

Managing the life cycle of a brand means anticipating and preparing for brand 'after-life'. Line extensions, innovative methods of delivery, next-generation products are fast becoming the new 'after-lifeblood' of the industry. Let's not forget the importance of the one element that will remain constant throughout the life cycle of a brand: the brand name.

Positioning, packaging and communications are all subject to variance and change but the brand name will endure. A great name encapsulates the brand, ignites consumer recognition, helps define personality, and differentiates from competitors in the marketplace. As the first public act of branding, the brand name can be leveraged to create awareness and start to build product pull. Equally, in seeking to extend the life of existing brands, equity that has been established in a brand name during its on-patent life can provide a solid platform for line extensions, new indications and new formulations.

Equity in the brand name, therefore, should not be underestimated, as companies seek to maximize ROI by evolving and extending established brands – whether through new formulations, new dosage forms or drug delivery systems. Consider, for example, Avandia, whose 'verbal equity' has been leveraged successfully in the subsequent evolutions of the brand, in the forms of Avandamet and, more recently, Avandaryl – a balanced blend of the equity of the brand names Avandia and Amaryl.

As equity in the brand name can be leveraged, so can equity in the brand identity as a whole, including the visual components of the brand, such as use of colour and shape. AstraZeneca's 'purple pill' migration from Prilosec to Nexium can be seen to have become a benchmark example of this within in the industry. While on-patent life is subject to expiry, trademarks are renewable – a fact often neglected by brand managers. All forms of intellectual property, therefore, from patent, to trademark and 'get-up' should be protected vigorously.

Nor should equity in the corporate brand be underestimated. For the most part, the corporate brand in the pharmaceutical industry is a blank canvas, whose added-value, whose benefit proposition is yet to be articulated in the hearts and minds of prescribers and patients. One could envision customer loyalty becoming considerably deep-rooted to a company that has built up a reputation around developing brands that are 'senior-friendly' (for example, through proprietary delivery systems or innovative forms of packaging), or to a company that has established a level of excellence in customer service. Once clearly defined and effectively articulated, corporate brands could start to create a new level of endorsement, of brand life cycle added-value.

Conclusions

Branding represents a real competitive advantage, but the question remains as to whether we are making the most of that advantage. Ultimately, brands in the pharmaceutical industry are the means by which the science is translated into a commercially viable reality. A good product will always be a good product, but with other good entrants to market, an integrated, consistent and sustained approach to developing and managing strong, distinctive brands will be what helps to translate a good product into a great brand. In the worst of times (in the struggle for share of voice, in the battle against brand exclusivity and in the engagement with the entry of generics), brands can afford us the best of times.

We are witnessing change slowly, but surely, with companies starting to embed brand at a more fundamental level within their organizations. We are beginning to see some companies instill best practices in brand development, in terms of Standard Operating Procedures, that specify critical endpoints and benchmarks from the initiation of early-stage branding to the finalization of a ready-for-launch brand. A select few are now starting to make the transition of applying those principles to the entire life cycle of the brand. However, the inherent brand mindset within the industry is fundamentally one of managing the life of a brand, rather than managing a brand for life.

The industry, as a whole, still has a way to go to shake off the shackles of traditional approaches – to evolve from the way it's always been done to the way it can be done. However, this will only happen when we fully accept that brands, which have long been powerful wealth creators in every other industry, can have real and long-term value in the pharmaceutical industry. Brands are valuable assets, but only if developed, managed and maintained as such. As long as we continue to see the product life cycle in terms of the beginning of the end – as long as we continue to limit our perception of innovation to drug discovery – brand life cycle management will, for many companies, remain a myth.

Only when we recognize the value of maintaining, extending and evolving a brand, will we succeed in keeping our most valuable assets, brand new, and in making brand life cycle management a reality.

Source: MedAdNews, September 2003: 'Can a drug live forever?'
**Source: MedAdNews*, July 2003: 'Company of the Year: AstraZeneca/Exclusive Interview with Sir Tom McKillop'.

Questions:

1 Can you relate the brand life cycle for pharmaceutical products to any of the brand life cycle models in this chapter?

2 How different is the brand life cycle of pharmaceutical products to that of non pharmaceutical products?

3 What are the issues in managing pharmaceutical products?

4 What does the transition from 'urinary incontinence' to 'overactive bladder', and the migration from 'impotence' through 'erectile dysfunction' mean?

5 What does the author mean by 'an approach to brand-building must be adopted that is as much *inside-out* as *outside-in*'?

6 What are the barriers faced by pharmaceutical brands?

END OF CHAPTER CASE STUDY: INJECTING NEW LIFE INTO THE BRAND LIFE CYCLE

Source: The Times 100

The Polo® name and image are reproduced with the kind permission of Société des Produits Nestlé S.A.

The Polo mint is a British institution – 'The mint with the hole'. Everyone is familiar with Polo and can clearly distinguish the brand from other products. The pack has its own distinctive colour and shape.

As with most established brands, there comes a time when they need a bit of a facelift to inject new life into them. Markets are in a constant state of change and the life of a product is the period over which it appeals to customers. The product life cycle charts the life of the product from its launch until its eventual decline. In the course of time rival products come along and begin to take away some of a brand's market share. It is at this time when the enlightened business will take stock and make sure that it wins back its prime position. The Smarties brand offers a classic example of this in recent times.

In the late 1980s M&M's moved into a market which had been dominated by Smarties for a long time. Fortunately the warning signals were recognized and new life was injected into the brand by bringing out blue Smarties, 'Gruesome Greenies' Smarties and other extensions to the brand. The net effect was to revitalize it.

So, if a firm wants to revitalize the life cycle of a product or brand, it is essential to invest in its development. This means not only putting a lot of work into the product before it is launched. Once it is on the market, it is also necessary periodically to inject new life into the product.

Injecting new life can be done in a number of ways, including:

■ Changing the product to better meet the needs and wants of consumers.

- Using price to influence market share, e.g. change prices relative to those of the competition.

- Altering patterns of distribution, e.g. by making the product more widely available.

- Changing the style of promotion, e.g. by creating brand awareness through advertising and promotions which show the additional benefits of new aspects of a product.

Mint competition

Polo has traditionally been the market leader in mints in the United Kingdom. However, during the late 1980s and early 1990s this position was slipping. We can see this decline by looking at the Index of Polo Sales from 1986 to 1993. Instead of making sense using sales figures, it is sometimes useful to use an index. Index numbers in this context use 1980 as a base year and then other figures are expressed as a percentage of this.

Polo's problem was that it had gradually lost its value as a product in the eyes of consumers. When this happens it affects the position of a product in the marketplace. This was as a result partly of strenuous competitive activity, partly because of a lack of innovation in the Polo brand itself and partly because advertising had not bound people sufficiently to the brand.

Competitors such as Trebor Extra Strong Mints, Trebor Mints, Trebor Spearmints and Softmints had fought hard to win a share of the market from Polo. Instead of consumers primarily associating mints with Polo, they were choosing from a variety of mints.

Polo's response to these trends was decisive. The key problem was that the brand had not been developed and so it was starting to be seen as predictable. To regenerate sales volume and rejuvenate brand interest, three new Polo variants were added to the range in 1994 and Polo was relaunched as Polo Original.

Extensive market research was carried out before the relaunch. The objectives were to:

- Revitalize the brand.

- Rejuvenate the total sales of Polo.

- Broaden Polo within the consumers' repertoire – i.e. offer consumers a range of different types to select from to create trade interest in the brand. Retailers are always keen to stock products for which there is a lot of interest, and hence demand.

The new flavours were selected as a result of market research because:

- Spearmint is a very popular growing market.

- Strong provides direct competition with Trebor's Extra Strong Mints.

- Sugar Free is a small but growing market which is becoming increasingly appealing to figure-conscious consumers.

- At the same time all these mint variants support Polo's core brand values of being 'hard, smooth, round hole mints'.

Target markets

As the market for mints has grown it has also become more diverse. In the past there was only one Polo which was targeted at the general public of mint eaters. There tended to be a single message which was put over through advertising and promotion to this market. Selling to a single market in this way is called 'undifferentiated marketing', i.e. you sell the same product, at the same price, through the same distribution channels, with the same advertising and promotion to an undifferentiated target group.

The new strategy involves widening and deepening this market by using differentiated marketing. This enables the company to alter ingredients of the marketing mix such as where and how it advertises its products, the outlets it sells its products in, and gives it the flexibility to charge different prices for the variants of this where appropriate.

To extend the total market for Polo mints each of the products needs its own 'marketing mix' which enables it to be focused at the appropriate target market. For example, Sugar-free Polos have been advertised in the women's press, while the Spearmint and Strong Polos have been advertised through posters and more recently in TV adverts.

Developing a distinct message

In developing Polo through differentiated marketing it has been necessary to do two things.

1 It has been essential to stress the core strengths of Polo.

2 It has been necessary to create the character of the variants in their own right.

The Polo's core strengths which have needed to be stressed are:

1 Its unique physical form – it is this which distinguishes Polo most tangibly from other mints.

2 Polo's 'friendly' reputation, built up over many years through humorous advertising.

3 The core strengths had to continue to be a key part of all Polo advertising. However, in addition to these core strengths it is also important to draw out the distinct characteristics of the variants. Polo has established these as being:

- Polo Original – the original and best taste.

- Polo Spearmint – the younger trendier mint.

- Polo Strong – a smooth strong taste.

- Polo Sugar Free – the sugar-free mint with a hole.

A success story

The Polo strategy of differentiated marketing in order to extend the Polo brand has been a success both in terms of the overall brand, and for the three variants. Significantly, the size of the overall mint market has grown.

Polo has regained its supremacy as the UK's number one mint. The total mint market grew by £6 million to £207 million in 1994, and this increase continued in 1995. In 1994 market growth was largely a result of the spearmint and sugar-free sectors stimulated by the new Polo variants. By stocking Polo, retailers were able to increase their total mint sales rather than simply substituting sales of one mint brand for another.

By April 1995 Polo Spearmint had captured 4.3 of all mint sales, Polo Strong had 1.7 and Polo Sugar Free had 1.5. Of course it is early days and the marketing mix will now need to be carefully applied to ensure that the new mints are provided to consumers at the right place, the right time and the right price with the appropriate advertising and promotional mix to appeal to their lifestyles

The Polo goes from strength to strength

The Polo case study provides us with an interesting and exciting example of the way in which an innovative company can retain market leadership for its products. The Polo mint is just one element of the overall portfolio of sweets and confectionery products produced by Nestlé Rowntree.

The art of successful marketing is knowing when and how to make changes to highly successful products. Polo has been a successful product for many years. Its continuing success will depend upon further innovation and change which is taking place to make a good brand an even better brand.

Questions:

1 Using any brand life cycle models mentioned in the chapter, describe where in this brand life cycle the Polo is.
2 How should Polo be managed within the brand life cycle above?
3 Compare Polo's brand life cycle to those of its main competitors.
4 What is the Polo brand personality and brand essence?
5 Discuss how the Polo brand image should be managed over time, using BCM.

References

Aaker, D. A. (1991), *Managing Brand Equity*, New York, NY: The Free Press.

Benson, J. and Kinsella, B. (2009), 'Is your brand going to graduate or be stuck in adolescence?', at www.Benson.consulting@rcn.com.

Blattberg, R. C. and Neslin, S. A. (1990), *Sales Promotion: Concepts, Methods, and Strategies*, Englewood Cliffs, NJ: Prentice-Hall.

Chandon, P., Wansink, B. and Laurent, G. (2000), 'A congruency framework of sales promotion effectiveness', *Journal of Marketing*, Vol. 64, No. 4, pp. 54–66.

McEnally, M. and de Chernatony, L. (1999), 'The evolving nature of branding – consumer and managerial considerations', *Academy of Marketing Science Review*, Vol. 1999, No. 02, at http://www.amsreview.org/articles/mcenally02-1999.pdf.

Mercer, D. (1997), *New Marketing Practice – Rules for Success in a Changing World*, Harmondsworth: Penguin Books.

Merrilees, B. (2005), 'Radical brand evolution: a case-based framework', *Journal of Advertising Research*, Vol. 45, No. 2, pp. 201–10.

Park, C. W., Jaworski, B. J. and MacInnis, D. J. (1986), 'Strategic brand concept-image management', *Journal of Marketing*, Vol. 50 (October), pp. 135–45.

Rust, R. T., Zeithaml, V. A. and Lemon, K. N. (2000), *Driving Customer Equity: How Customer Lifetime Value is Reshaping Corporate Strategy*, New York: The Free Press.

Wansink, B. (1996), 'Does package size accelerate usage volume?' *Journal of Marketing*, Vol. 60, No. 3, pp. 1–14.

Wansink, B. and Huffman, C. (2001), 'Revitalizing mature packaged goods', *Journal of Product & Brand Management*, Vol. 10, No. 4, pp. 228–42.

Wansink, B. and Park, S. (2000), 'Comparison methods for identifying heavy users', *Journal of Advertising Research,* Vol. 40, No. 4, pp. 61–72.

Further reading and online sites

Andrews, M. and Kim, D. (2007), 'Revitalising suffering multinational brands: an empirical study', *International Marketing Review*, Vol. 24, No. 3.

Anonymous author(s) (2007), 'Brand survival: do brands really last forever?', *Strategic Direction*, Vol. 23, No. 3, pp. 10–12.

Berry, N. C. (1988), 'Revitalizing brands', *Journal of Consumer Marketing*, Vol. 5, No. 3, pp. 15–20.

Evans, J. R. and Lombardo, G. (1993), 'Marketing strategies for mature brands', *Journal of Product & Brand Management*, Vol. 2, No. 1, pp. 5–19.

Ghosh, A. K. and Chakraborty, G. (2004), 'Using positioning models to measure and manage brand uncertainty', *Journal of Product & Brand Management*, Vol. 13, No. 5.

Groucutt, J. (2006), 'The life, death and resuscitation of brands', *Handbook of Business Strategy*, Vol. 7, No. 1, pp. 101–6.

Liss, D. (2002), 'Fire drill: preparing for crisis', at brandchannel.com.

Logman, M. (2007), 'Logical brand management in a dynamic context of growth and innovation', *Journal of Product & Brand Management*, Vol. 16, No. 4, pp. 257–68.

Munthree, S., Bick, G. and Abratt, R. (2006), 'A framework for brand revitalization through an upscale line extension', *Journal of Product & Brand Management*, Vol. 15, No. 3.

Stockmyer, J. (1996), 'Brands in crisis: consumer help for deserving victims', *Advances in Consumer Research*, Vol. 23, pp. 429–35.

Wansink, B. and Huffman, C. (2001), 'Revitalizing mature packaged goods', *Journal of Product & Brand Management*, Vol. 10, No. 4.

CHAPTER

09

Building Brand and Corporate Reputation

Chapter contents

Chapter overview

This chapter examines the principle of corporate and brand reputation building, which is a new area of branding. It explains what this means, introduces the notion of corporate social responsibility, discusses recent research and illustrates with examples from various industries. This chapter is the last chapter on the topic of 'Managing brands – creating and sustaining brand equity'. Previous chapters have covered the management of brand identity and positioning, brand architecture, brand extension and managing brands across the life cycle, in Chapters 5, 6, 7 and 8 respectively.

❖ LEARNING OBJECTIVES

After completing this chapter, you should be able to

❖ Explain why there is a need to build brand and corporate reputation

❖ Explain the meanings of brand and corporate reputation in business

❖ Discuss and apply the process of reputation building to build branding and corporate reputation across industries

❖ Examine the role of communications in building and maintaining corporate reputation; in particular, discuss the model of total corporate communications developed by Balmer and Gray, and its implications for successful corporate reputation building

❖ Explain how corporate reputation is measured

❖ Discuss what drives CSR and how it is applied across industries

❖ Examine the effects of reputation on firm performance

❖ Discuss the meanings of brand and corporate reputation from the consumer perspective (to include the influence reputation and CSR have on consumer satisfaction and forgiveness), and compare/contrast with corporate views

❖ Explain what competitive intelligence means and its implications in the management of corporate reputation

❖ Examine corporate reputation in international markets

Introduction

Brands are increasingly seen as having an organizational interface as well as merely a marketing context. Nowadays there is a need for the non-marketing functions to back the brand up at all levels within the organization. Financial scams and failure to comply with ethical production norms can harm the brand by demonstrating that it does not live up to what it professes or promises to customers. Brands are also under constant pressure to deliver ever greater returns to their investors and to shoulder responsibility for employees' morale, the environment and the wider communities. With brands being called upon to play the role of ambassador for the organization, it is important that companies ensure that brand values are never compromised and are consistently maintained over time and space. These are the issues of brand reputation building and one of the focuses of this chapter. The second focus of this chapter is on corporate reputation building.

The outline of this chapter is as follows: first, we look at the challenges facing modern brands, and the context for brand and corporate reputation building. We explain the meanings and definitions of brand and corporate reputation and the role of corporate reputation in building and sustaining the corporation's most valuable asset. Second, we introduce a reputation model and discuss its implications for building brand and corporate reputation. We also look at the role of communications in building brand and corporate reputation. We discuss the issues involved in corporate reputation measurement, and others stemming from the latest research in the field. We look at the effects of corporate reputation on firm performance and its influence on consumer satisfaction and forgiveness. Corporate reputation is also examined from the consumer perspective. The notion of corporate social responsibility (CSR) is introduced, examples of relevant industries that adopt CSR are illustrated, and the reasons behind CSR adoption discussed. Competitive intelligence, corporate reputation and corporate reputation in international markets are all included in the last part of the chapter.

Context for brand and corporate reputation building

The dilemma facing modern brands

Anti-globalization activist and writer Naomi Klein, in her book *No Logo* (2000), accuses big brands and corporations of being led mainly by greed, exploiting the world's citizens and the environment. Other writers also note that bullying, domineering and corrupt practices by brands are not uncommon (Kompella, 2003). For example, some big brands use their size to crowd smaller players out of the market or to damage the environment, to exploit employees or to cheat consumers. These are rogue or socially irresponsible brands.

Bad brands share a number of common features with other modern brands: first, they opt for short-term profits at the expense of the sort of long-term brand-building activities which contribute to companies' long-term benefit, and create brand values for the consumer which could, in turn, increase their loyalty. Second, they fail to build relationships with customers and to understand what they expect. Third, they also fail to react quickly to the unfavourable reports that are spread about them. This is part of their failure to understand what reputation risk is, how it manifests today and how it can be managed. Each of these problems is discussed below.

Driven by short-term gains and profitability, companies do not take time to build brand equity through creating brand values and instilling in customers that compelling desire to purchase the brand, which is seen as the primary focus of branding in providing an emotional reason for purchase. Instead, consumers are persuaded to buy through discounts, rebates and contests. Companies' passion for short-term gain is also reflected in their incessant pursuit of cheaper production costs: moving their factories to cheaper foreign countries and laying off thousands of their workers while maximizing profits. This behaviour is detrimental to the well-being of the workforce as well as to product quality, among other things. The better long-term options would have been re-engineering the business to become the world's lowest-cost producer or investing in new product development and value-added marketing. The surer path to profitable market share growth is the latter, since it has been proved that customers will pay more if they feel that they are receiving additional value with the higher price (Asacker, 2006).

Building relationships with customers has never been more demanding. Nowadays customers have high expectations of brands and their virtues, especially, from highly trusted brands. A recent study by Jennifer Aaker et al. (2004) found that the more trusted brands run a greater risk of offending customers than the more exciting ones. Highly trusted brands are also sincere ones – those with 'traits of nurturance, family-orientation and traditionalism', whose relationship strength and satisfaction are characteristic of sincere personalities (Snyder, 2003) – for example, Hallmark and Cadbury. Exciting brands are those which 'are built around qualities of energy and youthfulness' – for example, Yahoo! and MTV. Aaker et al. found that sincere brands enjoy stronger relationships than exciting brands until something bad happens (e.g. they fail to deliver on a promise to customers, whatever it may be). The sincere brand finds it harder to recover despite apologies, and attempts to make amends to its customers; for the exciting brand this is less of a problem (Snyder, 2003). This situation demands that companies take into account customer expectations of them when building and managing corporate reputation.

Internet development and negative word-of-mouth mean that companies are now more exposed than they used to be.

All of the above-mentioned factors have brought reputation risk into the limelight, and brand and corporate reputation have been the subject of much recent research as well as becoming the focus of attention for many companies' boards of directors, as companies have begun to realize that their reputation carries the same risks and returns as their financial situation. For instance, Barclays Bank formed a Brand and Reputation Committee that puts reputation on a par with financial and operational risk (Laforet and Saunders, 2005, citing Maitland, 2004), and a recent survey by an American insurance company of 2000 public and private companies shows reputation risk as the single biggest business hazard (Laforet and Saunders, 2005, citing Aon, 2001).

Three types of risk

Clearly, if brands have value they can lose value. Strong brands can go off course and fall apart. As discussed above, the risks most companies have faced are strategic missteps. According to *Fortune* 1000, during the mid- to late 1990s companies often lost their market value for strategic and brand-related reasons

There are three types of risk: brand equity, reputation and marketplace. *Brand equity risk* arises in turning the brand into a commodity or differentiating it from its competitors. Companies do this to themselves when they compete only on price. Brand equity risk can also be caused by brand misalignment – for example, when the promise a company projects is different from its customers' actual experience of its products or services. Or when a company grows too rapidly or broadly, the brand starts losing strength, focus and relevance for its customers, core and new alike (this is also one of the pitfalls of brand extension). *Reputation risk* involves losing the brand quality and trust built over time, if something suddenly goes wrong (see the Coca-Cola and Perrier examples previously mentioned). *Marketplace risk* reflects changes in the economy, industry or marketplace such as a decline in consumer demand for a company's products or services.

Definitions and meanings of brand and corporate reputation

A number of definitions of reputation are given in the literature, ranging from the simple to the complex. Brand reputation is concerned with both tangible and intangible perceptions of what it is 'good at' (Leiser, 2003). Reputation is what consumers think of the company, its products and its services. It embraces wider audiences such as the supply chain, the shareholder and society at large. A good reputation is a prime requirement for a successful organizational brand (Knox, 2004).

Another definition of reputation is 'the estimation of the consistency over time of an attribute of an entity' (Herbig and Milewicz, 1993; Milewicz and Herbig, 1994). According to the authors, this estimation is based on the entity's willingness and ability to perform repeatedly an activity in a similar fashion. Reputation is an aggregate composite of all previous transactions over the life of the entity; it is a historical notion and requires consistency in an entity's actions over a prolonged time for its formation. Thus, a firm will lose its reputation if it repeatedly fails to fulfil its intentions as stated through market signals. A market signal is the information conveyed by firms to tell the market or its competitors and customers its intentions, commitments or motives. A firm that does not fulfil its marketing signals will lose its reputation, which could prevent the firm from sending signals effectively later on (Milewicz and Herbig, 1994: pp. 40–41).

Perceived quality and credibility underpin reputation. If consumers perceive that a company's products are of high quality over time, that company will develop a reputation for high-quality products and can command premium prices for those products. Credibility is the belief in a company's intentions at a given moment in time; it is the extent of the trust or confidence in the company actually carrying out its intentions. In other words, a company is credible only if it does what it says it will do – for example, whether to believe the product claims made by a company's advertising or made by a vendor. Credibility is also time sensitive in that the credibility perceived today can differ significantly from credibility perceived at a different time. Credibility exists when one can confidently use past actions to predict future behaviour (Milewicz and Herbig, 1994).

To achieve credibility for high quality, a company must first develop a reputation for producing and delivering quality products. A product warranty or guarantee will provide credibility to a potential user, only if it is substantial enough to be extremely costly to a manufacturer if the product were to fail (Milewicz and Herbig, 1994). A one-month guarantee for a watch has little value to the buyer because of the low expected cost to the company issuing the warranty. However, a two-year guarantee gives better value to potential buyers because of the large amount of money at stake if the product fails. A firm that fails to honour this guarantee to its customers loses its credibility. To regain this credibility, it must again pay the high costs of reputation building. Once a reputation is established, the firm has every incentive to maintain that reputation, because a firm with a good reputation owns a valuable asset in the goodwill generated by its brand names, corporate logos and customer loyalty.

Reputation-building model

A user demonstrates the credibility of the firm's current brand signals by using the firm's current reputation and credibility to predict the quality of the good produced by the firm. The credibility of a firm increases if its actions agree with its statements, and its credibility decreases if its actions and pronouncements are inconsistent. There are four types of credibility transactions (CT):

1 *True positive* is when the company says it will do something and then does it.

2 *True negative* is when a firm indicates it will not do something and then does not do it.

3 *False positive* is when a firm indicates it will do something or take some action, and then fails to do so.

4 *False negative* is when a firm says it will not do something, and then goes ahead and does it.

A false positive or false negative is also known as a 'mixed signal' – that is, signalling one intention, then contradicting the signal by doing something else. A CT compares what a firm signals through its public announcements, statement of intent and press releases with its actual performance (Milewicz and Herbig, 1994). This is then fed back to establish credibility and reputation. Note, however, that what is negative for the firm may not be negative for the consumer – for example, a price drop may be seen as negative for a company but positive for consumers.

As mentioned above, a mixed signal damages a firm's credibility, and repeated mixed signals result in the complete loss of credibility. Inconsistent mixed signals will erode a firm's reputation. However, consistent mixed signals will eventually establish a reputation of a sort. If a company consistently gives a false positive and fails to deliver on its promises, it will establish a poor reputation. Conversely, if a company always provides superior products, regardless of the signal given, it will eventually develop a reputation for high quality (Milewicz and Herbig, 1994). To achieve credibility, a company must first develop a reputation, and it often takes many CTs before a reputation can be established. Credibility is therefore built over a period of time. The more consecutive positive CTs, the higher the positive reputation; the more consecutive negative CTs, the higher the negative reputation. On the other hand, repeated inconsistent mixed signals will give the firm 'no' reputation.

Managing corporate and brand reputation

Implications of the reputation model for building brand reputation

Brand reputation is most significant when there is little differentiation among competing products or services, for example in commodities markets or banking products. Brand reputation here refers to the trust in what the brand promises to deliver, and that these promises are acknowledged by buyers/users, which in turn leads to the first purchase and, possibly, second purchase. If,

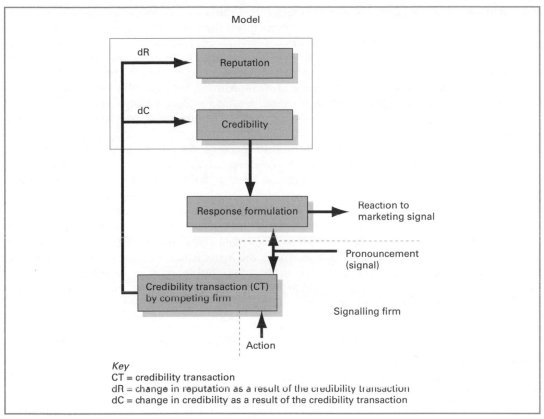

Source: Milewicz and Herbig (1994)

FIGURE 9.1 Model of reputation building and destruction

however, companies fail to deliver what the brand promises, the second purchase will not happen. Subsequently, constant attention to the product or service must be paid in order to maintain an established reputation over the longer term. Reputation and credibility are two important components in brand reputation. Buyers tend to use brand names as signals of quality and value, and often gravitate to products with brand names they have come to associate with quality and value. Brand names can also be repositories for a firm's reputation. High quality on one product can often be transferred to another product via the brand name (Herbig and Milewicz, 1995).

Reputation and new products

Reputation and credibility are the starting points of the brand-extension process. However, the reputation of the core or parent brand is not entirely carried over to the new product extension, because of the consumer's perception of the fit between the core brand and the extension product (see Chapter 7). Therefore, companies need to signal the core brand quality and how it fits with the product extension. The customer who tries the product or brand extension will assess whether these are true. If the signals are fulfilled, credibility will follow, enhancing the reputation not only of the brand extension, but also of the core brand. Milewicz and Herbig's model of reputation building (see Figure 9.1) shows little difference between building a brand reputation and corporate reputation building, which is much more complex, as discussed below.

Corporate reputation

The way companies are perceived has a huge impact on their performance, and that reputation is undoubtedly linked to the success of a business. Managing corporate reputation is concerned with managing the company's image among a broad range of stakeholders: financial analysts, journalists, employees, clients or customers, competitors, shareholders, suppliers, opinion leaders and category experts. These stakeholders directly or indirectly influence company success. An organization's key to survival in a competitive marketplace is attracting and retaining support from these constituencies. CEOs see corporate reputation as a valuable intangible asset. A good reputation encourages shareholders to invest in a company. It helps to attract good staff, retains customers and some argue that it improves overall returns for the company. However, the latter has not been empirically proved because of disagreements among researchers in the measurement of corporate reputation.

Research shows companies with a more positive reputation project their core mission and identity more consistently than those with a lower reputation. These companies communicate information not only about their products, but also about a range of issues relating to their operations, identity and history. There are two perspectives to reputation management: the marketing perspective, which is based on the primacy of customer value and the view that the brand is a strategic resource for the business; the organizational perspective, by contrast, views branding as an organizational tool that must be managed so as to create alignment between the internal culture and the external image of the organization. Today the focus is more on the latter, which is also known as a bottom-up (customer value) approach as opposed to a top-down approach, focusing on a company's vision and strategy, i.e. strategic rather than tactical. This leads to our next point on the company's role in building and sustaining corporate reputation.

Corporate reputation building – the organization's role in sustaining the most valuable corporate asset

In order to develop and build a corporate reputation, corporate behaviour needs to be carefully controlled. This requires organizations to concentrate in five areas: strategy, responsibility, accountability, integration (Capozzi, 2005) and measuring the company's efforts. In terms of *strategy*, companies must have a total view of the organization and understand the needs of its stakeholders. *Fostering responsibility* within the company means having a central vision of its reputation, and involving the CEO as lead champion managing and implementing this reputation across departments throughout the entire organization. *Accountability* means companies are responsible for the outcomes of their business efforts, and these can be measured in terms of impact and influence. 'Impact' is measured by how effectively and efficiently companies deliver a message to an audience. 'Influence' relates to the measurement of each communication effort, so that each discipline can take responsibility and credit for its role in the outcome. These measures can be applied to every facet of a company's communication effort – from marketing PR programmes, to CEO counselling, to crisis avoidance. *Integration* means harmonizing the interactions and relationships with stakeholders through integrated marketing communications (IMC) or total communication. *Measuring the company's efforts* involves evaluating the company's impact and influence. Impact refers to measuring how effectively and efficiently the message is delivered to the targeted audience. Influence is concerned with measuring the outcome of all the company's communications efforts. However, measuring corporate reputation is not a straightforward task, as can be seen below.

Role of communications in building and maintaining corporate reputation

Communications make a firm transparent, and enable shareholders to appreciate the way a firm manages its operations, thus improving the firm's reputation. Modern corporate communications are regarded as an important tool of corporate strategy, focusing on IMC – the integration of management, organizational and marketing communications, known as the 'total corporate communications' approach (Balmer and Gray, 2000). This approach operates at three levels:

1 Primary communications, which are those concerned with products and services, behaviour towards employees and employees' behaviour towards other stakeholders. These should present a positive image of the company and set the stage for a strong reputation.

2 Secondary communications are more formal and work through advertising, PR, graphic design, sales and promotions. These should be designed to support and reinforce the primary communication.

3 Tertiary communications include word-of-mouth, media interpretation and spin, competitors and spin. These should be positive and will succeed in building a superior reputation if the first two stages of corporate communication are properly conceived.

Total corporate communication does mean that everything an organization says, makes and does is seen to communicate. Consistent performance on the three levels of communications will help build corporate reputation over time.

Other authors emphasize the strategic importance of stakeholder communications and recognize the important role of senior management in the adoption of corporate communications to enhance corporate reputation, as discussed above. Similarly, integrity and credibility are the pillars of

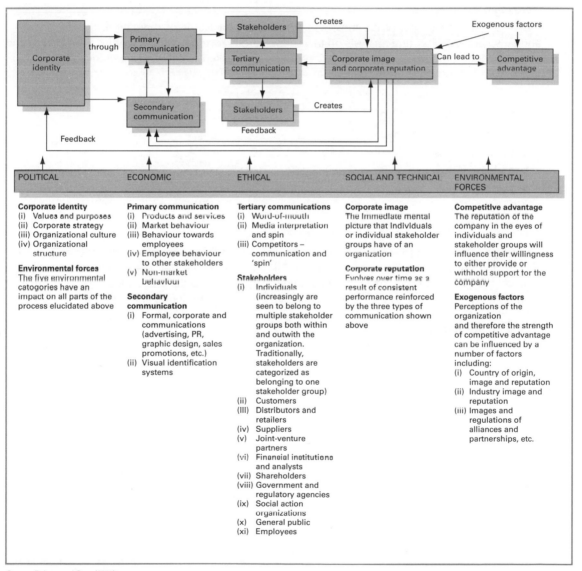

Source: Balmer and Gray (2000)

FIGURE 9.2 Model of total corporate communications

strategic communication. Measures and processes for the improvement of corporate communications will result in the successful building of corporate reputation.

Measuring corporate reputation

Key elements of corporate reputation

Most people agree that the key elements on which corporate reputations are based are *image* (how others see us), *identity* (how we see ourselves) and the *desired identity* (how we want others to see us). Measuring corporate reputation is about measuring the gap between image and identity. It involves aligning the *internal and external stakeholders'* perceptions of a firm.

Measures of corporate reputation

Ranking measures

Ranking by media is one of the most widely accepted measures of reputation. *Fortune*'s AMAC annually surveys CEOs and analysts on their views about *Fortune* 500 companies (from 1984) and *Fortune* 1000 companies (from 1995). Respondents are asked to rate a competitor's reputation in terms of *eight* key attributes of reputation:

1 *Financial soundness.*
2 Long-term investment value.
3 Use of corporate assets.
4 Innovativeness.
5 Quality of the company's management.
6 Quality of the company's products and services.
7 Ability to attract, develop and keep talented people.
8 Acknowledgment of CSR (Chun, 2005).

The advantages of using these key attributes is that they provide comparable data over an extended period of time and over the sample size. The disadvantages are that companies are assessed in terms of their financial performance even though reputations should not be judged on performance alone. The 'soft asset' of corporate reputation can be difficult to define and measure.

Brand equity scales

This method of measuring corporate reputation is by using the brand equity concept. Using this method, researchers attempt to measure the soft asset or intangible aspect of corporate reputation. For example, one study attempts to measure the corporate reputation of a beverage company through the following 12 criteria:

1 Quality of the product.
2 Advertising levels.
3 Sponsoring activities.
4 Conducting factory tours.
5 Long-established traditions.
6 Highly regarded employment with firm.
7 Well-trained employees.
8 Well-known products.
9 Strong management.
10 Costs of advertising.

11 Soundness of the company.

12 Profitability.

The problem with this type of measurement is that different researchers and managers might have different views of brand equity.

Image measures

This technique derives from that used to measure store or corporate images employing Likert or semantic differential scales, Fishbein models, multi-dimensional scaling and open-ended questions. The dimensions used are:

1 Store appearance – clean, decor, uncluttered displays.

2 Service – checkout, helpful, friendly.

3 Product mix – wide selection, brand names, quality.

4 Price – good value, reasonable prices, special offers.

Identity measures

Balmer and Soenen (1999) suggest a method to measure the interface between actual identity (e.g. values, history, structure) and desired identity (e.g. visions) using interviews, observation, history audit and focus groups. Other researchers explored the relationship between identity and image from a senior management perspective. Nine factors were examined: region, type, ownership, size, information processing structure, strategy, image, type of identity and strength of identity.

Other methodologies suggest, for instance, one way to measure corporate reputation is to produce composite reputation scores for companies based on the weighted average of specific perceptions – for example, on CSR, quality of management, innovation, employee treatment. The weighting tends to be based on the relationship between specific dimensions and a measure of overall opinions or something similar (Page and Fearn, 2005).

Another method is to assess which dimensions of corporate reputation are the most important by relating different corporate perceptions to in-market brand equity to show what really counts to consumers (Page and Fearn, 2005). Consumers' overall opinion of the corporation is recorded and an assessment made of the corporation's behaviour based on 14 criteria. Also recorded are consumers' awareness and usage of and opinions about the branded products or services that each corporation makes or owns, and their knowledge of the link between each brand and the corporation; also attitudes towards corporations and CSR issues (this question helps the researchers to identify different groups of respondents and understand how serious consumers are about these issues). The key measure of in-market brand equity is the percentage of category buyers who 'bond' with each brand. This measure has been shown to relate to in-market sales and actual consumer purchasing. Consumers who bond with brands are more loyal, spending significantly more on that brand than others in the category.

The third way of measuring corporate reputation is by making the identity and self-image of the firm the crucial point of contact between the firm itself and its various stakeholders – that is, by finding out how the company wants to be perceived in terms of its identity and self-image through its communications to stakeholders, and what is the stakeholders' actual perception of the company on those aspects. Some researchers also suggest that this interface should be studied as it is the 'moment of truth' for the firm if it wishes to align the image held by the individual stakeholder with the image projected by the firm. First, customers' attitudes to the product/service provided by the company are examined to gauge the current key drivers of customer value. Then the current and desired competitive positioning of the firm are matched with the key drivers of customer value, utilizing a customer value monitor (Knox et al., 1999) to assess the company's capabilities in respect of these value drivers. This process serves to highlight the gap that exists between the current brand positioning and the positioning desired to meet the vision outlined in the managing strategy for the firm. This gap relates to the reputation and performance of the firm. Clients' views of the firm can clarify whether the firm has been positioned, for instance, as a holistic, all-service organization or as an expert in specific niche areas (Bickerton, 2000).

Finally, a word of warning: apart from the advantages and disadvantages mentioned above, generally it is recognized that subjectivity plays an important role in the assessment of reputation. There is also a lack of theoretical basis for its assessment. For further discussion on some of the issues and methods involved in assessing corporate reputation, refer to Bromley (2002).

Brand vulnerability assessment

As well as finding out how the company and its brands are perceived by consumers and the stakeholders alike through reputation measurement, companies can also assess the vulnerability of their brands. Essentially, companies can conduct an analysis of their brand to determine what risks it faces and if these are serious. This process involves an examination of the company's brands' potential risks among its key stakeholders such as customers, employees, the financial community, influencers and regulators, as well as competitors. It is concerned with identifying the external risks – financial, legal, strategic, personnel-related, technological, political and environmental. The impact of catastrophic occurrences such as storm, malice, theft and accident may be covered by insurance. The brand might be eroding or there might be brand damage affecting various internal and external constituencies. There might be a risk to the brand posed by a problem with key customers, partners or suppliers, and action may be required. Next, a plan for risk management and for a response to possible brand damage must be adopted. It should include a communication plan to keep everyone concerned fully informed and properly reassured, as goodwill can be an effective barricade against short-term brand erosion in a crisis (Lippincott, 2007).

Effects of reputation on firm performance

Relationship between corporate reputation, brand equity and sales

Some research shows there is little relationship between corporate reputation and consumer brand equity and that, although a bad reputation makes building brand equity difficult, a good reputation does not guarantee strong brands (Page and Fearn, 2005). For reputation to count, first, the consumer must have heard of the company and be able to link the products it makes with that company. Second, consumers must think about it during the brand decision-making process, and most of the time they do not. As discussed above, the study claims most consumers do not think about CSR when they are shopping, and price plus reputation often carry more weight than just reputation.

Customer satisfaction, loyalty and profitability

Reputation is found to be positively correlated with satisfaction and loyalty, but no such relationship was found between satisfaction and loyalty. Reputation was measured by asking 100 executives to rate their own company on six criteria:

1 Offering good services.
2 Having a long-term perspective.
3 Adjusting to the needs of customers.
4 Being inventive.
5 Competence.
6 Overall reputation.

However, despite the popular view that satisfaction links a firm's reputation to profitability, the association of reputation, satisfaction and financial performance has not been empirically studied (Chun, 2005). Links between customer satisfaction and the image of an organization have also been under-researched.

Employee satisfaction and retention

The interaction between customer and employees as part of the service on offer is very likely to affect customer satisfaction, give rise to repeat business and enhance a firm's reputation. Well-motivated employees stay with the company longer and get to know their customers better. This leads to still better service, builds still greater customer satisfaction, and further improves relationships and company profits. Similarly, repeat customers tend to be pleased with the value they receive and their satisfaction is a source of pride and energy for employees. The service outlet with the highest customer retention can have the best employee retention because happy employees give better service to the customer and create customer satisfaction and loyalty. Happy employees and happy customers are crucial to organizational effectiveness.

Corporate social responsibility (CSR)

Corporate social performance is defined as a business organization's configuration of principles of social responsibility, processes of social responsiveness and policies, programmes and observable outcomes as they relate to the firm's societal relationships (Wood, 1991: p. 693). CSR associations reflect the organization's status and activities with respect to its perceived societal obligations. CSR associations are often unrelated to the company's ability to produce goods and services (Brown and Dacin, 1997).

Research shows that corporate social responsibility and, to a lesser extent, environmental responsibility are likely to pay dividends, and that corporate social performance (CSP) appears to be more

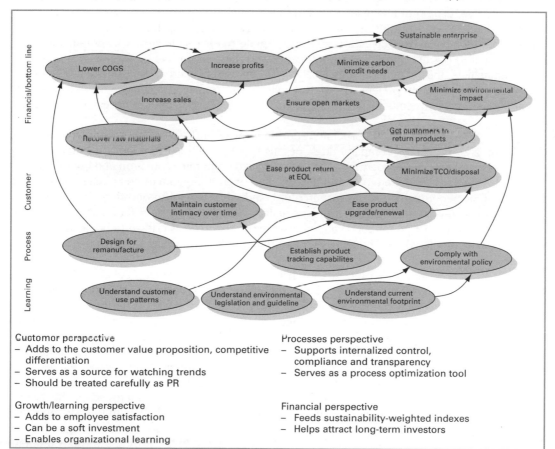

Customer perspective
– Adds to the customer value proposition, competitive differentiation
– Serves as a source for watching trends
– Should be treated carefully as PR

Processes perspective
– Supports internalized control, compliance and transparency
– Serves as a process optimization tool

Growth/learning perspective
– Adds to employee satisfaction
– Can be a soft investment
– Enables organizational learning

Financial perspective
– Feeds sustainability-weighted indexes
– Helps attract long-term investors

FIGURE 9.3 Sustainability scorecard

highly correlated with accounting-based measures of corporate financial performance than with market-based indicators. It also shows that organizational effectiveness is a broad concept encompassing both financial and social performance. Companies are likely to adopt CSR voluntarily because of the cost–benefit analysis of a firm's investment, in some industries especially. Also, companies can integrate sustainability matters into all areas of their overall balanced scorecard, as shown in Figure 9.3. As the most widely recognized performance management methodology, the balanced scorecard manages and tracks performance across four areas of the business: the customer, the processes, the company's growth and learning, and the financial perspective.

Corporate performance is defined as a company's financial viability or the extent to which a company achieves its economic goals. Corporate financial performance (CFP) measures include measures of internal resources utilization, such as ROA or ROE, and market return or sales growth. Corporate social performance measures include social audits, charitable contributions and reputation indices.

Although research has not established that there was a direct impact of CSP or CSR on CFP, it reveals that companies are not penalized for having a high corporate social performance. Thus, managers can afford to be socially responsible. Furthermore, it might help if those managers who believe that CSP is an antecedent of CFP were to actively pursue CSP because they think the market will reward them for doing so. Managers can use CSP as a reputational lever, and be aware of the attention of third parties, regardless of whether they are market analysts, public interest groups or the media. In fact, social audits in and of themselves are only moderately beneficial. A company that is high in CSP may benefit especially from receiving public endorsement from government agencies such as the Environmental Protection Agency or Occupational Safety and Health Administration. As some suggest, the key to reaping benefits from CSP is a return from reputation (Orlitzky et al., 2003).

The positive relationship between CSP and CFP is now also widely recognized, and companies are more likely to pursue CSP as part of their strategy for attaining high CFP. It has also been argued that successful executives are able to integrate market strategies with non-market strategies in order to position their firm for optimal effectiveness. There are also guidelines as to how firms can achieve this integration strategically in a number of different areas, involving the news media, activists, social movements, legislatures, ethics, etc. Social performance may also increase unintentionally, as firms emulate others that are experiencing high financial success (Orlitzky et al., 2003).

In the context of brand and corporate reputation, many businesses first encounter CSR when their brand is in trouble. A company does, or fails to do, something that lands it in the CSR hot seat. In such cases, poor CSR performance poses a risk to corporate reputation and brand; but CSR is now moving from the sphere of brand risk to brand opportunity. Smart companies are realizing that good CSR performance can be a source of brand advantage. The question now is not how companies can protect their brands from reputation debacles, but how they can build brands aligned with strong CSR performance and global citizenship. Trust is critical to brand success, but trust is in short supply when it comes to CSR, and that presents an opportunity for brand owners and their agencies.

Similarly, the search for responsibility has now moved from an ethical niche into the mainstream. Early leaders, like the Body Shop and Ben & Jerry's, promoted environmental, social and economic responsibility alongside their products. Today we have BP re-branded as moving 'Beyond Petroleum', while Toyota runs messages about green cars and sustainable mobility in its 'Today, Tomorrow, Toyota' campaign, and BASF promotes its contribution to saving energy.

The new emphasis being put on business agendas for CSR, global citizenship and sustainable development has huge implications for the commercial communications sector. Values have been shifting, especially in the industrialized world, from a focus on material prosperity to one increasingly emphasizing quality of life. 'Consumers are increasingly interested in the "world that lies behind" the product they buy. Apart from price and quality, they want to know how and where and by whom the product has been produced.' As a result, the concept of the *triple bottom line* (economic, social and environmental) has gained a footing in the business world. Corporate reporting and communication has expanded into new areas.

The economic bottom line embraces such issues as employment and other issues for local communities. The social bottom line measures progress in areas such as diversity (e.g. age, gender and race) and working conditions. The environmental bottom line sums up a company's ecological footprint, in terms of the energy and raw materials used, and the emissions and waste produced.

Sector breakdown	No. companies adopting CSR in 2006
Accountants & Consultants	9
Aerospace & Defence	3
Automobile & Parts	2
Banks	10
Beverages	3
Chemicals	1
Construction & Building Materials	9
Diversified Industrials	1
Electricity	5
Engineering & Machinery	2
Food & Drug Retailers	3
Food Producers	5
Gas, Water & Multi utilities	8
General Retailers	7
Government	2
Insurance	6
Leisure & Hotels	4
Media & Entertainment	4
Mining	3
Oil & Gas	3
Personal Care & Household Products	2
Pharmaceutical & Biotechnology	3
Real Estate	7
Speciality & Other Finance	4
Steel & Other Materials	1
Support Servioos	13
Technology Hardware & Equipment	3
Telecommunication Services	2
Tobacco	3
Transport	6

Source: Business in the Community Environment Index 2006

TABLE 9.1 Adoption of CSR across industries

There are also growing numbers of objective standards that give an assessment of a company's CSR performance, such as FTSE4Good, the Dow Jones Sustainability Index or AA1000. CSR reporting has become a growth industry. For example, a range of developments consolidated into the Global Reporting Initiative (GRI), launched in the US but now based in Amsterdam (www. globalreporting.org). Although many companies start off on the defensive, many also recognize CSR as a growing opportunity. This is demonstrated by its adoption across sectors as diverse as insurance, pharmaceuticals and telecommunications (European Association of Communications Agencies).

Adoption of CSR across industries

According to the Environment Index 2006 Survey, two in five companies link staff pay to environmental objectives and targets; 66 per cent of companies ask suppliers to provide information on their environmental performance; 85 per cent of companies manage their impacts through an Environmental Management System (EMS) (see Table 9.1). Of these, 75 per cent have it independently certified, but only two in five companies have ISO 14001 (or equivalent) certification. Seventy-eight per cent of companies publicly reported performance on climate change in 2006 and 66 per cent did so on waste; 22 per cent of companies also showed continuous improvement in performance on waste over the past three years and 37 per cent chose to report on water consumption. The next most popular choices were resource use at 18 per cent and biodiversity at 13 per cent.

Branding Brief 9.1: Yorkshire Water's investment in environmental management

Source: Based on Yorkshire Water's presentation at University of Sheffield Management School in 2006

Yorkshire Water is one of the ten largest water and sewerage companies in the world. It serves a population of 4.7 million. It is the biggest landowner in the region. Yorkshire Water invests £1 million in the environment every day.

It supplies 1.24 billion litres and treats 1 billion litres of wastewater each day. It treats the water that leaves the house and returns it, once it has been cleaned, back to the river. The scale of this task is mind blowing.

Yorkshire Water operates 85 Water Treatment Works, which prepare the water for public use, and 656 Waste Water Treatment Works, which clean the waste and return it back, safe and clean, to the environment.

There are 140 'large' reservoirs, i.e. 25 mega litres or bigger, which are governed by Reservoir Safety legislation, comprising impounding reservoirs, clear water tanks, service reservoirs, etc. In addition to this, Yorkshire Water has some 600 or so smaller reservoirs and tanks. Enough pipe work to circle the Earth.

Many of the pipes were constructed in the nineteenth century and are still in use today. Yorkshire Water's job is to maintain these in good working order and continually improve them for future generations to protect public health, the environment and public water supply.

Water is a heavily regulated industry; although Yorkshire Water is a private company, it provides a very public service.

There are three official regulators: an economic one, an environmental one and a water quality one. The Office of Water Services, or Ofwat, is the economic regulator. Every five years Ofwat decides what Yorkshire Water's future investment programme should be, and tells it by how much it should raise or lower prices to fund it.

The Environment Agency is the environmental regulator. Yorkshire Water works with it to ensure that it takes water from and returns it to the environment in a sustainable way.

The Drinking Water Inspectorate monitors the quality of the UK's tap water. Yorkshire Water also works very closely with the Health & Safety Executive which is responsible for protecting the safety and well-being of Yorkshire Water's employees and contractors.

Businesses are taking environmental management ever more seriously because of legislative compliance, public and stakeholder relations (business image), competitive advantage (cost-savings, tendering), environmental protection. So businesses are increasingly using EMS tools.

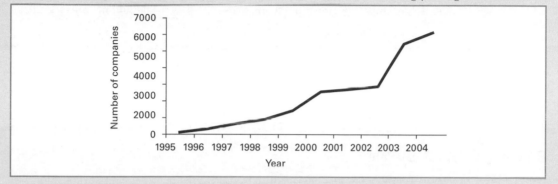

Uptake of ISO 14001 (UK)

Yorkshire Water gained certification to ISO 14001 (1996) in April 2004. It has company-wide certification and ten-month implementation period. SGS external auditors – six-monthly surveillance visits and Yorkshire Water is certified to ISO 14001 (2004) in May 2005.

Key Elements of Yorkshire Water Environment Management are: Environmental Policy. Over 1000 environmental aspects identified; approx 100 main pieces of legislation identified; numerous environmental objectives and targets; management review team; training and auditing.

The benefits of ISO 14001 for Yorkshire Water are: a tool to introduce environmental efficiencies into the business; improved environmental benchmarking scores; increased competitive advantage for commercial bids; reduced fees for IPC applications/EA earned autonomy; improved process control/environmental monitoring; fuller understanding of business's total impact; assurance that impacts are identified and managed; a driver for reduction of raw materials and consumables; improved public image and 'green credentials'; increased workforce environmental awareness which reduces risks.

Yorkshire Water's investment in environmental management is to gain other competitive advantages, including customer choice; be seen to be green; energy efficiency; carbon management and life-cycle analysis. Thus, CSR has an effect on Yorkshire Water's triple bottom line in that it helps it to combine the successful running of a business with addressing its role in society or the community.

Yorkshire Water's CSR programmes include:

- Cool Schools, which has been the Yorkshire Water flagship campaign since it was launched in July 2002. It was launched in response to concerns from local health and education experts about the damaging effect dehydration was having on children's mental and physical well-being. Yorkshire Water launched Cool Schools to address this. Since it was launched it has installed more than 1000 free water coolers in more than 500 primary schools across Yorkshire.
- Volunteering.
- Be Cool, Save Water.
- BAP.
- Advisory Panel.
- Pee-O-Meters.
- Fun campaigns with a serious message about health and value for money.

Yorkshire Water's impact on society

It provides society with much more than just high-quality water and sewerage services. Through its various community programmes it is committed to making a real difference to communities across the region. Yorkshire Water was nominated as the most efficient water company. It has been the first company to achieve four 'A' ratings for efficiency. Eighty per cent of customers believe it plays a key role in protecting the environment, while 70 per cent agree that it has improved the quality of Yorkshire's coastal bathing areas and rivers.

Branding Brief 9.2: DuPont

DuPont is an example of a multinational using CSR-based advertising to develop and position the corporate brand.

The company's research found that most people, including investors, customers, consumers and employees, did not fully understand what DuPont did, or how often it affected their lives. The goal of the campaign was to highlight its achievements in creating products that safely meet the basic human needs of health, food and shelter.

Ruhrgas AG, founded in 1925, is Germany's biggest natural gas supplier and marketer, selling not directly to consumers but to 18 regional gas suppliers and a few city-owned companies.

Its campaign presented natural gas as the energy source of the future, emphasizing its environmental friendliness, comfort and reasonable cost. The signature is 'Voll im leben', or 'Life to its fullest', with natural gas an obvious part of this daily life.

Yet, a recent survey for the World Economic Forum (WEF) shows there is still a dramatic lack of trust in democratic institutions and large companies across the world.

The European advertising and communication sector faces a great challenge and opportunity, helping clients rebuild the trust lost in recent years. Marketing and corporate affairs will no longer be completely separate functions, but will need to work more closely together.

Communicating messages about environmental and product performance benefits can lead to double-messaging that does not work. There is a need to learn how to communicate these things and to grow brand value in a new environment, while still selling product.

International organizations are also looking at the commercial communications sector with great expectations. For example, UNEP's Advertising and Communication Forum is a broad initiative which aims to use communication skills and techniques to promote sustainable consumption patterns, promote products, services and campaigns that foster sustainable consumption and pursue best practice in environmental management.

The European Association of Communications Agencies (EACA) is working closely with UNEP to create greater understanding of CSR issues by encouraging audiences to recognize and understand the issue of sustainability; developing an agency Code of Ethics, joining the Global Compact, developing and promoting case histories with sustainable features; making CSR/sustainability one platform for EACA's annual European advertising effectiveness awards, creating a communications toolkit for governments to assist them in addressing social and environmental challenges, and publishing a guide to CSR for agencies.

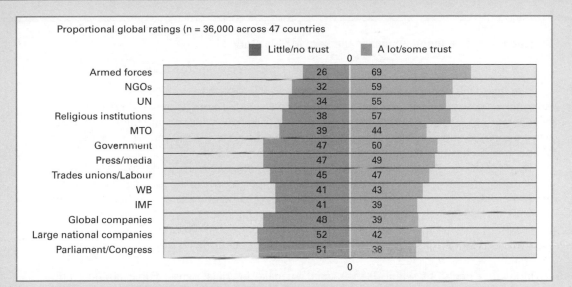

Proportional global ratings (n = 36,000 across 47 countries

■ Little/no trust   ■ A lot/some trust

	Little/no trust	A lot/some trust
Armed forces	26	69
NGOs	32	59
UN	34	55
Religious institutions	38	57
MTO	39	44
Government	47	50
Press/media	47	49
Trades unions/Labour	45	47
WB	41	43
IMF	41	39
Global companies	48	39
Large national companies	52	42
Parliament/Congress	51	38

Source: European Association of Communications Agencies
Trust in institutions to operate in society's best interest

More broadly, there is no shortage of high-level backing for CSR activity. There's the UN's Global Compact, for example, which has engaged leading businesses around the world to pledge improved responsibility. And the European Business Campaign 2005 on CSR aims to mobilize 500 000 business people and stakeholders. Among its milestones is a marathon of major CSR conferences throughout Europe, culminating in a 'business Olympics' in 2004 to raise awareness.

The EU has also become involved. The European Commission issued a 'Communication' in summer 2002 which stressed the voluntary nature of CSR but also its importance in achieving the EU objectives of building a successful and inclusive economy. It rejected the European Parliament's call for mandatory CSR reporting, but has set up a 'Stakeholder Forum' to continue dialogue on the subject. With all this high-level activity, CSR has become impossible to ignore. Businesses will have to respond (European Association of Communications Agencies).

Branding Brief 9.3: Shell and M&S case stories

Shell – 'profits and principles'

In 1997 Shell made a public commitment to CSR. Since then the company has worked to turn this commitment into reality on the ground, aiming to integrate the concept into business activities with commitments to reduce greenhouse gas emissions and invest in renewable resources.

But the company says it felt misunderstood; many people didn't seem to understand its principles and practices well enough. So a new ad campaign was developed to illustrate Shell's approach to solving problems and meeting CSR challenges. This corporate campaign focuses on the Shell brand, rather than a particular product.

Staying green in a tough economic climate: M&S's story

Source: adapted from *Harvard Business Review*, HBR Green, Sir Stuart Rose, 2008

Despite the tough consumer climate and the reaction to M&S sales results, it is sticking to Plan A to make M&S carbon neutral and send no waste to landfill from its operations by 2012. The plan extends to sustainable raw materials sourcing, sets new standards in ethical trading, and helps people leading healthier lives. Plan A could cost around £200 million over five years, although M&S has not actually done a hard cost–benefit analysis.

There are compelling commercial – as well as moral – reasons to do so. Take the early results it's generating. The M&S 'Wash at 30' campaign, which encourages consumers to wash their clothing at a lower temperature than used to be considered the norm, has saved an estimated 25 000 tons of carbon dioxide. It has reduced CO_2 emissions by an additional 55 000 tons by switching 23 per cent of electricity to renewable resources. Towards its goal of zero waste to landfill, 75 per cent of the construction waste from the M&S store refurbishment programme is now recycled.

Individual decisions within Plan A need to make financial sense. For example, various initiatives – recycling clothes hangers, reducing packaging, and encouraging reusable carrier bags instead of plastic – are saving M&S millions of pounds, reducing landfill waste and decreasing electricity consumption. Progress against Plan A is closely monitored because M&S regularly consults with a wide range of NGOs. The plan has also gained NGO recognition and was recently awarded the World Environment Center gold medal for sustainable business practices. The company has a series of key public reporting dates with NGOs so that it can take their recommendations and ask for help. M&S has also deliberately tied Plan A reporting to its financial reporting schedule so that its stakeholders know when to expect to hear.

Marks & Spencer is holding firm in its commitment, but will others be able to? Or will green agendas be relegated to 'nice to have' not 'need to have' for companies struggling in tough economic times? What specific green ideals are most important for a company to not abandon when times are tough?

CSR associations and consumer product evaluations

Consumers' cognitive associations of a company (i.e. corporate associations) can be a strategic asset source of sustainable competitive advantage (Brown and Dacin, 1997). Influencing these corporate associations is an important strategic task. Companies spend great sums of money each year on corporate advertising, corporate philanthropy, sponsorships, cause-related marketing and image (brand or company or store image) studies. However, the outcomes of companies' actions to enhance corporate associations are difficult to ascertain. Brown and Dacin's research shows what consumers know about a company can influence their evaluations of, or reactions to, the companies' products. Their study found, more specifically, that a reputation based on a company's abilities may have a greater impact on both specific product attribute perceptions and the overall corporate evaluation than a reputation for social responsibility. This is to some extent consistent with Page and Fearn's (2005) study on corporate reputation from the consumer's perspective.

Page and Fearn show that what matters most to the consumers is fairness towards consumers, corporate success and leadership rather than public responsibility. Consumers want good business practice but when it comes to brand strength and purchasing, personally relevant factors are more important to them. Thus, despite consumers' overt concern for ethical behaviour, most consumers seem to care more about how fair companies are to them, and how good their products and services are, rather than how fair they are to workers or the environment. Therefore, pushing a corporate social responsibility (see below) agenda to consumers does not reap the best rewards. Ethical brands that do not result in a price increase or lower quality are likely to be more successful. Nevertheless, consumers do expect public responsibility, especially if there are overtly ethical brands in the marketplace. Being perceived as the 'bad guy' will cause damage to a company's reputation.

For companies not under overt pressure on ethical issues, communications campaigns that push the ethics of a company to consumers will not yield most rewards, since ethical behaviour is expected. Maintaining a strong reputation for leadership, innovation, success and fairness to customers will have a much stronger direct effect on brand equity and sales than ethics. Being seen to fail or, worse still, to rip consumers off, is of much more direct relevance to consumers and will have stronger effects on businesses (Page and Fearn, 2005). Finally, for some companies, corporate reputation and ethics count for more than they do for others. For example, in the water industry, being ethical and environmentally friendly counts for more with the customer than in the footwear industry, because the water supply and its processes have a more direct impact on the environment than the shoes.

Corporate associations have also been found to exert dual influences on evaluations of new products both through their effect on product attribute perceptions and the overall evaluation of the company. CSR associations appear to exert an influence on product evaluations through their influence on corporate evaluation. The results of these studies indicate that consumers can and will use corporate associations as the basis for inferences about product attributes that are not known prior to purchase. Therefore, through developing good corporate associations, companies can leverage what consumers know about a company to compensate for what they do not know and cannot evaluate about a product. CSR associations have been found to have a significant influence on consumer responses to new products. Brown and Dacin's research shows that negative CSR associations can ultimately have a detrimental effect on overall product evaluations, whereas positive CSR associations can enhance the product evaluations – although no direct impact of CSR on purchases has been found.

Influence of reputation, CSR and satisfaction on forgiveness

New research shows that socially responsible brand values have an effect on forgiveness both directly and indirectly – that is, indirectly through the reputation of the company and via satisfaction. Thus, socially responsible brand values can increase both the reputation of the company and satisfaction with it, and lead to an increase in tendencies towards forgiveness.

To conclude, CSR is neither a fad nor an optional extra. The interest in it is reflective of a deeper change in the relationship between companies and their stakeholders, including consumers. Healthy business requires a healthy community and should be contributing to its creation and maintenance. The public increasingly wants to know about the companies that stand behind the brands and products presented to them; and to use their consumer power to reward good companies and punish bad ones. It is vital for research to monitor the ever-shifting background of different audiences' needs and criteria for judging companies. For companies, three kinds of measure are needed: a summary reputation measure, appropriate image dimensions and benchmark comparisons. Communications make a difference. MORI's studies of journalists reveal a close correlation between the rating of companies' press relations and overall favourability towards them. This tells us that coverage of a company in the business pages, for instance, is as strongly influenced by the company's communications effectiveness as by its business performance (Lewis, 2001). That's why it is all the more important to get press relations, investor and customer relations right. Campaign recall is one way to measure the impact of communications and their success.

Consumer nationalism and corporate reputation in international markets

According to Wang (2005), consumer nationalism has a critical impact on corporate reputation in the global marketplace. Consumer nationalism is an expression of one's national identity that makes individuals favour or reject products from other countries. It is a form of consumer activism which includes consumer resistance activities encompassing a wide range of social issues (e.g. apartheid in South Africa, various corporate environmental and labour practices). Consumer nationalism is similar to the concept of consumer ethnocentrism (see Chapter 13). Consumer ethnocentrism focuses on consumer relationships based on the discrimination between 'us' and 'them'. These strong feelings of antipathy that consumers have towards foreign countries would negatively affect their purchasing behaviour. Regardless of product attributes such as price and quality, consumers' bias and discrimination, expressed through their loyalty to their country, consumer nationalism or consumer ethnocentrism, are directed towards either products from certain countries or all foreign products.

Consumer nationalism manifests itself in focusing on events that would involve conflicts in international relations, foreign policy or in the political arena, or on economic issues such as trade and other cross-border business activities. These events develop their focal power to capture consumers' attention and imagination, to transform themselves into an issue linked to an international (i.e. foreign) corporation concern and, eventually, to mobilize consumers to express their national identity in their consumption intentions and choices (Wang, 2005). Many players are involved in such events – news media, advocacy groups, governments, other international corporations, etc. – with the mass media usually serving as the battleground for the shaping of such crises.

Wang identifies four factors which might cause international corporations and their brands to be at risk of consumer nationalism: national association, familiarity/visibility, likeability and magnitude. With *national association*, the stronger the international brand's perceived national association, the more vulnerable the brand becomes to consumer nationalism. In the case of *familiarity/visibility*, Wang asserts that the more visible the international brand is to consumers, the greater the likelihood that it will become the target of consumer nationalism. With *likeability*, the more consumers like the international brand, the more difficult it will be for them to express consumer nationalism, if they discover that they dislike the perceived parent country of the brand. With regard to *magnitude*, the more competitive the marketplace, the greater the likelihood that international brands will become targets of consumer nationalism.

Wang also argues that, when consumer nationalism occurs, the most likely damage will be to corporate reputations. In the aftermath of such incidents, companies may suffer financial loss, i.e. a drop in sales and profit margins but, more important, they may see damage to their corporate reputation as a result of the volume of negative publicity they have received. Constant bad publicity in the form of consumer nationalism and criticism will cast a shadow over international brands and dilute their emotional appeal, hence posing a major threat to their corporate image and reputation in the host country. For instance, American companies suffer from mistrust in many parts of Europe because of former President Bush's administration's foreign policies (*The Enquirer*, online, 2004). Erosion of a company's brand image and that image's emotional power will not only diminish its own competitive advantage, but also empower its competitors. However, it has been suggested that such impact can often be short-lived and brands may soon rebound when the nationalistic movement is over.

Competitive intelligence and corporate reputation

Recent research emphasizes the importance of the emergence of social media or user-generated media, for the management of corporate reputation and as a way in which firms can monitor stakeholders' online conversations to anticipate reputation risks and information crises. Monitoring systems on the Internet and elsewhere can help protect corporate reputations from information crises, as opposed to firms once monitoring traditional mass media (e.g. press, radio and TV) to manage their reputations. These used to play an intermediary role between the different groups of stakeholders for information exchange. The Internet in particular is now changing the role of intermediary.

Stakeholders can now express their opinions about a firm's actions by using newsgroups,

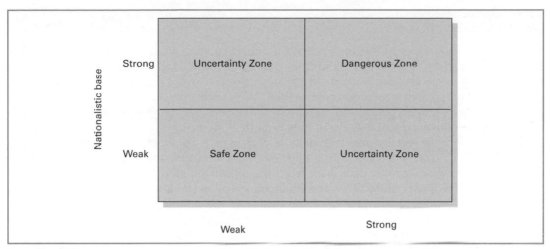

Source: Wang (2005)
FIGURE 9.4 Identifying hot spots for consumer nationalism

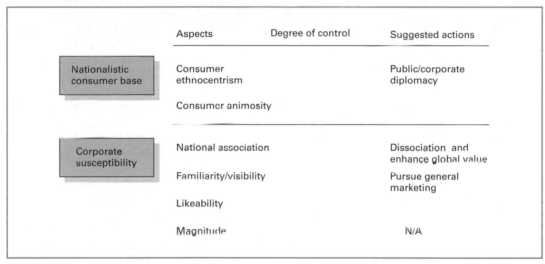

Source: Wang (2005)
FIGURE 9.5 Protecting against consumer nationalism pre-crisis

creating and writing blogs, posting videos and podcasts, etc. Users of such sources can be customers and stakeholders as well as activists, who have no hesitation in using them to spread messages concerning a firm's activities. Several examples have been reported and referred to as the 'Kriptonite' case (Chazaud, 2006). Activist groups, such as environment protectors or consumer associations, use buzz marketing and other new practices to broadcast their evaluation of a firm's actions in the fields of social responsibility and environmental issues. Chazaud's research shows how user-generated content media may impact on a reputation and initiate an information crisis that could damage a firm's reputation. He argues that competitive intelligence practices such as monitoring systems can help an organization to manage its online reputation by protecting it from information risks and by detecting some opportunities to enhance its reputation. This involves identifying active sources, detecting links between different communities to reveal stakeholder networks, determining the importance and the veracity of monitored information and deciding who in the firm will receive the results of this monitoring process. In addition, watching online conversations and opinions emerging from social media can help organizations to protect their corporate reputation.

Conclusion

Increasingly brands are seen as going beyond a marketing context and becoming ambassadors for the organization. They represent what the organization stands for. Brands are under constant pressure to deliver greater and greater returns to their investors, to take responsibility for employees' morale, the environment and wider communities. With such roles to play, it is important that companies ensure that corporate and brand values are never compromised and are consistently maintained over time and space so as not to infringe their reputation.

The perception of quality and credibility underpins any corporate reputation. To achieve credibility for high quality, a company must first develop a reputation for producing and delivering quality products, which can be done over time. The reputation-building model states that a user determines the credibility of the firm's current brand signal by using the firm's current reputation and credibility as a means of predicting the quality of the goods produced by the firm. The credibility of a firm increases if its activities conform to its public statements, while its credibility decreases if its actions and pronouncements are inconsistent. Four types of credibility transactions exist: true positive (when a company says it will do something and subsequently does it), true negative (when a company says it will not do something and subsequently does not), false positive (when a company says it will do something or take some action and then reneges) and false negative (a company says it will not do something and reverses itself by going ahead and doing it). A false positive and a false negative are known as 'mixed signals'. A mixed signal decreases a firm's credibility; repeated mixed signals result in a complete lack of credibility; and inconsistent mixed signals will erode a firm's reputation. If a company consistently gives a false positive and fails to deliver on its promises, it will be left with a poor reputation. Conversely, if a company always provides superior products, regardless of the signal given, it will eventually develop a reputation for high quality. To achieve credibility, a firm must first develop a reputation. It often takes many credibility transactions before a reputation can be established.

Reputation and credibility are important in brand reputation. Buyers tend to use brand names as signals of quality and value, and often gravitate to products with brand names they have come to associate with quality and value. Brand names are thus repositories for a firm's reputation. High quality in one product can be transferred to another product via the brand name. Reputation and credibility are the starting points of the brand-extension process. Brand reputation is most significant when there is little differentiation among competing products or services. Company-reputation building is more complex than brand-reputation building. Corporate-reputation building concentrates on five areas: strategy, responsibility, accountability, integration and measurement. In terms of strategy, the company must have a total view of the organization and understand the needs of its stakeholders, fostering responsibility within the company by having a central vision of reputation and involving the CEO as lead champion to implement it across departments. Integration involves harmonizing the interactions and relationships with stakeholders through IMC or total communication. Measuring means to evaluate the strategy's impact and influence.

Communications play a very important role in corporate reputation building. They make a firm transparent, enabling shareholders to appreciate the way a firm manages its operations, which then facilitates a better reputation for the company. There are three levels involved in corporate communications: primary communications, which are concerned with products and services communications; secondary communications, which are concerned with advertising, PR, graphic design, sales and promotions, and are designed to support primary communications; and tertiary communications, which include word-of-mouth, media interpretation, competitor communication and spin. Total corporate reputation is concerned with everything an organization says, makes and does. Consistent performance on these three levels of communication will help build corporate reputation over time. Stakeholder communications and the role of senior management in corporate reputation are two other important aspects.

Corporate reputation is measured in terms of companies' ranking, or brand equity scale, and measurements of image and identity. There is little empirical evidence to show a relationship between corporate reputation and firm performance. Some research shows little relationship between corporate reputation and consumer brand equity. A poor reputation makes building brand equity difficult, but a good reputation does not guarantee strong brands. Reputation is found to be positively correlated with satisfaction and loyalty, but no relationship was found between satisfaction and loyalty, although recent research does show that brand personality and reputation affect brand identification, which in turn affects brand loyalty.

As well as constantly assessing their reputation, companies should also assess potential brand risk among their key audiences such as customers, employees, the financial community, influencers and regulators, as well as competitors, identifying external risks such as financial, legal, strategic, personnel, technological, political and environmental. Where the brand is already being eroded, the effects of brand damage on various internal and external constituencies and risks to the brand posed by problems with key customers, partners or suppliers should also be determined. A plan for risk management and potential response to brand damage must then be adopted via a communication programme to keep all citizens fully informed and reassured, as goodwill can be an effective barricade against short-term brand erosion in a crisis.

Corporate social responsibility (CSR) is a business organization's configuration of the principles of social responsibility, processes of social responsiveness and policies, programmes and observable outcomes as they relate to the firm's societal relationships. There is no evidence that CSR has a direct impact on corporate performance or on corporate reputation, and there are some contradictions in the latest research findings, although some research indicates that CSR is likely to pay dividends and appears to be more highly correlated with accounting-based measures of corporate financial performance (CFP) than with market-based indicators. One piece of research shows that what matters most to consumers are fairness and corporate success and leadership rather than public responsibility. For companies not under overt pressure on ethical issues, communication campaigns that push the ethics of a company to consumers will not yield the best rewards since ethical behaviour is taken for granted. Maintaining a strong reputation for leadership, innovation, success and fairness to customers will have a much stronger direct effect on brand equity and sales than ethics, while another report suggests that socially responsible brands have an effect on consumer forgiveness.

A phenomenon that can have a severe effect on corporate reputation in the global marketplace is known as 'consumer nationalism'. Research identifies four aspects of how international corporations and their brands might be at risk of consumer nationalism: national association, familiarity/ visibility, likeability and magnitude. With national association, the stronger the international brand's perceived national association, the more vulnerable the brand becomes to consumer nationalism. In the case of familiarity/visibility, research shows that the more visible the international brand is to consumers, the greater the likelihood that it will become the target of consumer nationalism. Likeability means that the more consumers like the international brand, the more difficult it will become for them to express consumer nationalism, if they discover that they dislike the perceived parent country of the brand. With regard to magnitude, the more competitive the marketplace is, the greater the likelihood that international brands will become targets of consumer nationalism. When consumer nationalism does arise, the greatest damage is likely to be to corporate reputation. In the aftermath of such incidents, companies may suffer financial loss – i.e. a drop in sales and profit margins – but, more important, they will experience damage to their corporate reputation as a result of the volume of negative publicity they have received. There are ways companies can protect themselves from consumer nationalism in international markets, by avoiding the hot spots of consumer nationalism and by protecting against consumer nationalism pre-crisis.

Research shows how competitive intelligence practices such as monitoring systems can help an organization manage its online reputation, by protecting it from information risks and by detecting some opportunities to enhance its reputation: identifying active sources; detecting links between different communities to reveal stakeholder networks; determining the importance and the veracity of monitored information; and deciding who in the firm will receive the results of this monitoring process. In addition, watching online conversations and opinions emerging from social media can help organizations to protect their corporate reputation.

🔒 Key terms

Brand equity scales: corporate reputation is measured in terms of intangible aspects such as quality of the product, advertising levels, sponsoring activities, conducted factory tour, long-established traditions, highly regarded employment with firm, well-trained employees, well-known products, strong management, cost of advertising, the soundness of the company, and profitability.

Brand identification: the logo is the most common form of the brand identification, and it is also one of the basic tools of communication and advertising.

Brand reputation: the credibility that the brand promises to deliver and the fact that these promises are acknowledged by buyers/users, which in turn leads to the first, and possibly second, purchases. It is also concerned with both tangible and intangible perceptions of what the brand is 'good at'.

Brand risk: the threatened loss of value due to a change in people's perceptions about the company. These changes in perception can impact on the demand for a company's products and services and, in the worst case scenario, its licence to operate.

Competitive intelligence: both a process and a product. The process of competitive intelligence is the action of gathering, analysing and applying information about products, domain constituents, customers and competitors for the short-term and long-term planning needs of an organization. 'The product of competitive intelligence is the actionable output ascertained by the needs prescribed by an organization' (Wikipedia).

Corporate financial performance: measured in terms of internal resources utilization, such as ROA or ROE, and market return or sales growth.

Corporate reputation: what consumers think of the company, its products and its services. The perception of quality and credibility underpins reputation. If consumers perceive a company's products to be of high quality over time, that company will develop a reputation for high-quality products and can command premium prices for its products.

Corporate reputation measures: there are several ways of measuring corporate reputation: by ranking, by brand equity scales, by assessing image and identity, composite reputation scores, customer value monitor, and many more.

Corporate social performance: measured by social audits and charitable contributions or reputation indices.

Corporate social responsibility (CSR): a concept whereby organizations consider the interests of society by taking responsibility for the impact of their activities on customers, employees, shareholders, communities and the environment in all aspects of their operations. This obligation is seen to extend beyond the statutory one to comply with legislation. It sees organizations voluntarily taking further steps to improve quality of life for employees and their families, as well as for the local community and society at large (Wikipedia).

Credibility transactions: the four conditions mentioned in Milewicz and Herbig's reputation model: 1) True positive refers to when the company says it will do something and subsequently does it; 2) true negative refers to when a firm indicates it will not do something and then does not; 3) false positive: when a firm indicates it will do something or take some action and then fails to do it; 4) false negative is when a firm says it will not do something and contradicts itself by going ahead and doing it.

Customer value monitor: companies must understand when, why and how customers react to products, services and price changes, and use that information to improve relations with their customers through value-managing internal functions and processes. Thus, companies must monitor what customers value in companies and their products on a regular basis and try to satisfy what they value most.

Identity measure: a method of measuring the interface between actual identity (e.g. values, history, structure) and desired identity (e.g. visions) using interviews, observation, history audit and focus group.

Image measure: uses Likert or semantic differential scales, Fishbein models, multi-dimensional scaling and open-ended questions. For example, the dimensions used are: 1) store appearance – clean, decor, cluttered, displays; 2) service – checkout, helpful, friendly; 3) product mix – wide selection, brand names, quality; 4) price – good values, prices, specials.

IMC: a management concept that is designed to make all aspects of marketing communication such as advertising, sales promotion, public relations and direct marketing, work together as a unified force, rather than permitting each to work in isolation.

Leverage: brand leverage, or brand extension or brand stretching, is a marketing strategy in which a firm marketing a product with a well-developed image uses the same brand name in a different product category. Organizations use this strategy to increase and leverage brand equity (Wikipedia) (see also Chapter 6).

Market signal: information conveyed by firms to tell the market or its competitors and customers its intentions, commitments or motives.

Ranking measure: ranking by media is one of the most firmly established measures of reputation. *Fortune*'s AMAC annually surveys CEOs and analysts on their views about *Fortune* 500 companies (from 1984) and *Fortune* 1000 companies (from 1995).

Sustainable development: a socio-ecological process characterized by the fulfilment of human needs while maintaining the quality of the natural environment indefinitely. The linkage between environment and development was globally recognized in 1980, when the International Union for the Conservation of Nature published the World Conservation Strategy and used the term 'sustainable development' (Wikipedia).

Virtual pressure groups: an online interest group or lobby formed by like-minded people who seek to influence public policy to promote an interest. Pressure groups exist in all modern pluralist democracies and have sprung up on all sides. Some defend producer interests. In response, others press for consumer concerns or push for broad policies such as protection of the environment. The proliferation of some pressure groups is so extensive, their size so large and their organization so sophisticated, that they virtually constitute another arm of government. Virtual pressure groups are those pressure groups which form and communicate with each other online.

? Discussion questions

1 In your opinion, what has changed in audiences and communication channels today?
2 Discuss environmental, economic, social and technology developments in the past ten years, and the impact of these on a) consumers; b) companies.
3 What is the role of business and communication?
4 What are the communication and media tools available for companies today?
5 What are the main characteristics of corporate communications?
6 Explain the main methods of measuring corporate communication.
7 What are the major consequences of brand reputation loss? Support your answer with examples.
8 Explain how companies can build reputation through branding.
9 a) Give examples of consumer nationalism manifestations and events in the UK or abroad.
   b) Discuss what multinational companies can do to protect themselves against nationalistic advocacies in international markets.
   c) How should governments react in consumer nationalism crises in their country?
10 Explain what brand risk is and how it can be assessed.

Projects

1 Research and present your information on how a developing country of your choice tackles the subject of corporate social responsibility.
2 Contrast these with a western country of your choice.
3 Investigate how corporate social responsibility is managed in one small and/or medium-sized company of your choice. Compare and contrast these with one large company.
4 Using one of the measures of corporate reputation mentioned in this chapter, devise a set of questions and conduct a mini-survey with ten or more customers of an insurance company of your choice, and ask them the reasons why they chose the company's services. Find out their rating against these, and assess the company's brand equity, image and identity, etc.
5 Conduct interviews with one or two executives of a company of your choice. Find out how they manage corporate reputation in their company. Do they have a formal strategy for handling reputation risk? What are the resources available? Ask them to discuss any obstacles in managing corporate reputation and how they overcome these? Could you suggest how they can overcome these obstacles?

MINI CASE 9.1: COMPANIES IN CRISIS – WHAT *NOT* TO DO WHEN IT ALL GOES WRONG

Source: Reprinted by permission of Mallen Bakker, http://www.mallenbaker.net/csr/crisis03.html

Exxon Mobil and the *Exxon Valdez*

Many companies have faced a crisis during their history, whether due to external forces beyond their control, through their own failings or management problems, or a combination of the two.

Only a few, however, come to personify corporate irresponsibility through one pivotal event. Such a one is Exxon's experience with the *Exxon Valdez*.

What happened. In 1989, the *Exxon Valdez* oil tanker entered the Prince William Sound on its way towards California. In spite of the fact that the weather and sea conditions were favourable and the Bligh Reef clearly marked on the maps, the ship ran aground and began spilling oil. Within a very short period of time, significant quantities of its 1 260 000 barrels had entered the environment. At the moment of the collision the third mate, who was not certified to take the tanker into those waters, was at the helm. The probably cause was established that the Captain and many of the crew had been drinking alcohol in considerable quantities.

What did the company do? According to most observers, too little and too late. The action to contain the spill was slow to get going. Just as significantly, the company completely refused to communicate openly and effectively. The Exxon Chairman, Lawrence Rawl, was immensely suspicious of the media, and reacted accordingly.

Shortly after the accident had taken place, and the world's media had piled in to begin extensive coverage, a company spokesman pointed to the existence of procedures to cover the eventuality – procedures which the TV shots showed were demonstrably failing. When asked if Rawl would be interviewed on TV, the response was that he had no time for that kind of thing.

Meanwhile the operation on the ground was getting nowhere fast. Around 240 000 barrels had been spilled, with another million still on the ship. During the first two days, when calm weather would have allowed it, little was done to contain the spillage. This spillage spread out into a 12-square-mile slick. Then the bad weather struck, making further containment almost impossible.

After more than a week, the company was still giving no ground on the request for better communication. The media clamour became so hostile that eventually Frank Iarossi, the Director of Exxon Shipping, flew to Valdez to hold a press conference. It was not a success. Small pieces of good news claimed by the company were immediately contradicted by the eyewitness accounts of the present journalists and fishermen.

John Devens, the Mayor of Valdez, commented that the community felt betrayed by Exxon's inadequate response to the crisis, in contrast to the promises they had been quick to give of how they would react in exactly this eventuality.

Eventually, Rawl deigned to go onto television. He was interviewed live, and asked about the latest plans for the clean-up. It turned out he had neglected to read these, and cited the fact that it was not the job of the chairman to read such reports. He placed the blame for the crisis at the feet of the world's media. Exxon's catastrophe was complete.

Cost and benefit The consequences for Exxon of its two-pronged disaster – the spill and its environmental consequences, alongside its disastrous communications – were enormous. The spill cost around $7 billion, including the clean-up costs. Of this $5 billion was made up of the largest punitive fines ever handed out to a company for corporate irresponsibility.

The damage to the company's reputation was even more important, and more difficult to quantify. However, Exxon lost market share and slipped from being the largest oil company in the world to the third largest. 'Exxon Valdez' entered the language as a shortcut for corporate arrogance and damage.

Questions:

1 Explain how Exxon handled the crisis. Discuss in terms of its systems, ability to move quickly once the problem had occurred, leadership, etc.

2 What were their major pitfalls?

3 How could they have handled the situation better?

MINI CASE 9.2: LEVI'S TAKES ITS ETHICAL ASPIRATIONS INTERNATIONALLY

Levi Strauss & Co. was founded in the 1850s by a European immigrant. The company tailored its first jeans from tent canvas in response to California gold miners' complaints that trousers just could not take the abuse of panning nuggets and staking claims. The company is private having been taken through a leveraged buyout in the 1980s.

Levi's enjoyed a stream of record sales and earnings from 1989–1993. Its 1993 sales earned Levi's the number 90 position in the *Fortune* 500. The following year, however, the company dropped to number 193. Levi's slowdown was attributed to new product development and distribution. The company estimates it lost at least $200 million in sales by its delay in developing wrinkle-free slacks (the fastest-growing segment of the men's pants business). Levi's also takes two to three times as long to replenish its supply of pants for major retailers compared with the ten days achieved by competitors. Despite this, it remains a strong company with a reputation for high-quality clothes, and an impressive brand name.

Levi's mission is not only to make a profit but also, make the world a better place in which to live. It is committed to diversity, recognition, and related compensation and reward systems, empowerment and ethical practices.

Levi's aspiration statement has also been applied to international contracting. In the 1980s, a little publicized incident involving the working conditions of its Saipan contractor caused Levi's management to name a committee of top executives to review the company's dealings with its suppliers. In 1992, following three years of work, the committee's guidelines for contractors were adopted, covering employee working conditions, labour relations, environmental impact and regular inspection for compliance – the first such code adopted by any MNC. Following its code, the company terminated business relations with 30 businesses and demanded changes from 120 others around the world. When it was found that a contractor in Malaysia employed under-age children, Levi's and the contractor found a solution that allowed the children to continue to contribute to their families' support. Levi's also withdrew from China in response to what it considered 'systemic labour inequities' in the apparel sector in China. The work schedule required 12-hour days plus overtime, with only two days off each month, for pay below the legal minimum of 12 cents an hour, and poor safety conditions in factories, which have resulted in dozens of employee deaths.

Questions:

1 Levi's has taken the position that a company should not only be profitable but should also make the world a better place to live. Do you agree or disagree with this philosophy? Explain your position.

2 Levi's strategy is a combination of globalization (selling a standardized product in multiple markets) and national responsiveness (modifying its products to be responsive to the tastes of local markets). How is Levi's able to pursue both of these strategies simultaneously?

3 Why did Levi's leave China? Is this decision part of the firm's overall social responsibility philosophy or did the company overreact to the situation?

4 If you were advising the company, what conditions would you set up as prerequisites for it to re-enter the Chinese market?

END OF CHAPTER CASE STUDY: AMWAY

Source: The Times 100 Business Case Study

Meeting global responsibilities by caring for communities

Introduction

Successful businesses do more than simply provide goods and services for customers. They also make a real contribution to the communities in which they operate.

Successful ethical enterprises:

- Create employment and job security.
- Provide products that give consumers good value for money.
- Contribute to creating a more caring and cared-for community, and hence a better world.

Amway provides a good example of a business that recognizes its wider responsibilities. It is one of the world's largest direct sales companies. Amway works with around 3 million independent business owners (IBOs) in more than 80 countries. These IBOs are the link between Amway and the final consumer. They are also Amway's links with citizens and communities across the globe.

As well as its business aims the company has a range of social aims that are part of a 'Global Cause Programme'. These are outlined below.

The world's most respected companies recognize that being a good corporate citizen means supporting causes that matter to the communities in which they operate. This is why Amway Europe has created links with the United Nations Children's Fund (UNICEF). UNICEF is a global champion for children's rights. It seeks to make a lasting difference and improve children's lives.

The United Nations Convention on the Rights of the Child sets out the right of all children to reach their full potential. It is the foundation of UNICEF's work. Working with UNICEF, Amway has launched an exciting pan-European fundraising campaign for children. It recognizes the importance of building good working relationships with UNICEF's National Committees in each market in order to roll out fundraising programmes to Amway's IBOs and their customers.

Direct selling and supply chain

A supply chain contains a set of links that bring finished products to end consumers. As a direct selling company, selling consumable products directly to consumers and bypassing the traditional 'retail' or 'high street', Amway has its own distinct chain, placing a strong emphasis on IBOs, who are able to focus on individual customers and their needs.

Amway manufactures the majority of its own-brand products at its manufacturing plant in Ada, Michican. It then distributes these directly to the IBOs through a centralized warehouse in Venlo, Netherlands. Having signed a contract to work within Amway's Rules of Conduct and Code of Ethics, IBOs are trusted to operate flexibly within a 'self-regulatory' environment. They develop direct supply channels and sell products to friends and customers that they know or meet.

Amway's supply chain is different from a more conventional supply chain that normally sells goods to final consumers through retail outlets. Amway's way of working depends on building lasting connections with the end consumer. Feedback provided by consumers and IBOs helps to shape future changes in products and the service provided.

As a global company, Amway has built up a strong regional structure around regional affiliates such as Amway UK and the Republic of Ireland. Operating through the regional structure, affiliates are responsible for:

- Forecasting (ensuring stocks are sufficient to meet demand).
- Customer service.
- Efficient distribution: ensuring products reach IBOs on time and in top condition.
- Product promotion and IBO support, e.g. supplying brochures to IBOs.

Getting the image right is vital in a business that relies on building relationships with individuals and the wider community. IBOs often sell directly to friends and it is essential to provide high-quality, value-for-money products with a 100 per cent satisfaction guarantee. Amway spends time, money and effort on creating an appropriate design and appearance for Amway products. It also develops campaigns that support the business and social aims of the company.

Growth

Growth is a major driving force for global businesses. It has to be. Standing still is not a viable option in a world in which competitors are growing by building new links in new countries and markets. Growth brings advantages known as 'economies of scale'. These advantages include being able to spread advertising and marketing costs over much greater volumes of output. This results in lower unit costs and more competitive prices.

Economies of scale include spreading costs over a larger output.

By expanding globally, Amway can increase its scale of operations. This leads to:

- Increased sales and profits for Amway.
- Increased sales and profits for IBOs.
- Better quality and a wider, cheaper product range for final customers.

To achieve these benefits Amway continues to expand into new markets such as eastern Europe and Ukraine. Amway regularly seeks to develop new products in line with market research aimed at finding out what customers want.

In order to attract IBOs and new affiliates, Amway needs a strong brand image. Corporate social responsibility (CSR) is vital to any company seeking to build its image. CSR refers to the role that a company plays in meeting its wider commitments as a citizen. Such commitments include supporting worthy causes and always acting in an ethical, honest way. Because Amway operates in many different markets worldwide and with a range of affiliates and IBOs, it has to devise and communicate its plans for CSR activities very carefully.

Recently, Amway has produced its 'One by One – Global Cause Program'. The plan is clear and robust, and is helping to maintain Amway's reputation with all its stakeholders.

Developing a global strategy

In the same way that Amway has a global strategy for producing, distributing and marketing its products worldwide, its strategy for promoting CSR is also global. Amway defines a global cause as 'a social issue affecting many people around the world engaged in a struggle or a plight that warrants a charitable response'. The company recognizes that as a successful enterprise it must build its business based on the principles of 'relevance, simplicity and humanity'.

Amway's vision is 'helping people live better lives'.

Developing the Global Cause Program:

- Helps Amway to bring this vision to life.
- Declares what the organization stands for.
- Builds trust and respect in Amway brands.
- Establishes corporate social responsibility as a high priority.

Amway developed its Global Cause Program in 2002. It is the result of extensive research. This involved studying relevant issues and holding discussions with organizations involved in providing help to the needy and underprivileged in communities worldwide.

Some research was primary research, e.g. interviewing potential partners. Other research was secondary, e.g. examining published sources about global trends in poverty, lack of educational opportunities.

From the outset, Amway established some clear objectives. These were to:

- Build loyalty and pride among IBOs and employees.
- Enhance Amway's reputation as a caring organization.
- Make a real difference to human lives.

Further research indicated that people linked to Amway had a clear favourite area for the Global Cause Program to cover. They wanted it to develop initiatives concerned with children and the family. They felt that there are millions of compelling reasons to focus on helping children, including for example:

- Amway is a business owned by and operated by families.
- Children are the world's future.
- Children embody hope.
- With children it is possible to make a lifelong difference.

Research showed that:

- Half of the world's poor people are children.
- Every year 12 million children die before their fifth birthday.
- 540 million children live in crisis situations.
- Over 125 million children have no access to basic education.
- Even in the most developed countries some children are left behind.

Research also showed, however, that children's needs differ from one part of the world to another. Amway therefore recognizes that if its Global Cause Program is to have maximum impact it will need to be tailored to the specific needs of particular regions and areas.

Developing a European strategy

Amway's global campaign for children is called 'One by One'. This illustrates the idea of making a difference in children's lives one step at a time. The campaign is part of an umbrella cause to improve the well-being of children worldwide. The campaign name and logo are colourful, cheerful, optimistic and hopeful.

The European part of this strategy involves working with UNICEF, which is already an existing partner. Because of its excellent work with children, UNICEF was the logical choice.

The campaign fits comfortably with Amway's global strategy but is also tailored to meet local needs. At the end of 2004 Amway's European businesses donated 500 000 euros to UNICEF for UNICEF projects. This money was raised through three initiatives:

1 Selling UNICEF Christmas and other greetings cards.
2 Making donations in multiples of 69p (1), £3.45 (5), and £11.72 (17) when placing orders for goods.
3 Direct donations.

In January 2004 Amway activated a three-year contract to sell an exclusive range of Christmas products through European affiliates. The programme includes a commitment to raise 500 000 euros for UNICEF by the end of August each year.

Conclusion

Amway's 'One by One' campaign provides a good example of the way in which businesses can make a difference in the communities in which they operate. Research showed that Amway's stakeholders are committed to activities which better the lives of families and children. The company has therefore been able to formulate a plan and a well-targeted programme to harness the commitment of its people to help others and create a more prosperous world. By working with UNICEF it is partnering one of the world's most highly regarded children's organizations. Together they are able to help children enjoy a better future.

Questions:

1 What do you understand by the term corporate social responsibility (CSR)?

2 Explain two actions that Amway and its IBOs are currently taking that involve CSR.

3 Analyse the key ingredients in Amway's CSR strategy. Show how the strategy is designed to translate the vision into practical steps on the ground.

4 Recommend ways in which Amway could enhance and develop its impact on making every child matter.

References

Aaker, J., Fournier, S. and Brasel, S. A. (2004), 'When good brands do bad', *Journal of Consumer Research*, Vol. 31 (June).

Asacker, T. (2006), 'When companies run out of ideas, bad things happen to brands', Brandchannel. com.

Balmer, J. M. T. and Gray, E. R. (2000), 'Corporate brands: what are they? What of them?', *European Journal of Marketing*, Vol. 37, No. 7/8, pp. 972–97.

Balmer, J. M. T. and Soenen, G. B. (1999), 'The acid test of corporate identity management', *Journal of Marketing Management*, Vol. 14, pp. 69–92.

Bickerton, D. (2000), 'Corporate reputation versus corporate branding: the realist debate', *Corporate Communications: An International Journal*, Vol. 5, No. 1, pp. 42–8.

Bromley, D. B. (2002), 'Comparing corporate reputations: league tables, quotients, benchmarks, or case studies?', *Corporate Reputation Review*, Vol. 5, pp. 35–50.

Brown, T. J. and Dacin, P. A. (1997), 'The company and the product: corporate associations and consumer product responses', *Journal of Marketing*, Vol. 61 (Jan), pp. 68–84.

Capozzi, L. (2005), 'Corporate reputation: our role in sustaining and building a valuable asset', *Journal of Advertising Research*, Vol. 45, No. 3, pp. 290–3.

Chazaud, N. (2006), 'Reputation et Internet: de nouveaux enjeux pour les entreprises', *Le Mensuel de Université*, No. 13 (Feb).

Chun, R. (2005), 'Corporate reputation: meaning and measurement', *International Journal of Management Review*, Vol. 7, No. 2, pp. 91–109.

Herbig, P. and Milewicz, J. (1993), 'The relationship of reputation and credibility to brand success', *Journal of Consumer Marketing*, Vol. 10, No. 3.

Herbig, P. and Milewicz, J. (1995), 'To be or not to be … credible that is: a model of reputation and credibility among competing firms', *Marketing Intelligence and Planning*, Vol. 13, No. 6, pp. 24–33.

Klein, N. (2000), *No Logo*, New York: Picador.

Knox, S. (2004), 'Positioning and branding your organisation', *Journal of Product & Brand Management*, Vol. 13, No. 2, pp. 105–115.

Knox, S. D., Maklan, S. and Thompson, K. E. (1999), 'Pan-company marketing and process management', *Irish Marketing Review*, Vol. 12, No. 1, pp. 36–45.

Kompella, K. (2003), 'Chennai chatter – what's wrong with brands these days?', Brandchannel.com.

Laforet, S. and Saunders, J. (2005), 'Managing brand portfolios: how strategies have changed', *Journal of Advertising Research*, Vol. 45, No. 3, pp. 314–27.

Leiser, M. (2003), 'Strategic brand value: advancing use of brand equity to grow your brand and business', *Interactive Marketing*, Vol. 5, No. 1, pp. 33–9.

Lewis, S. (2001), 'Measuring corporate reputation', *Corporate Communications: An International Journal*, Vol. 6, No. 1, pp. 31–5.

Lippincott (2007), 'Brand risk management: why brands are becoming more valuable and more vulnerable', at www.lippincott.com/insights/a–brandriskmanagement.shtml.

Milewicz, J. and Herbig, P. (1994), 'Evaluating the brand extension decision using a model of reputation building', *Journal of Product & Brand Management*, Vol. 3, No. 1, pp. 39–47.

Murray, S. (2003), 'Reputation risk: big PR to companies', *Financial Times*, 30 September.

Orlitzky, M., Schmidt, F. L. and Rynes, S. L. (2003), 'Corporate social and financial performance: a meta-analysis', *Organization Studies*, Vol. 24, No. 3, pp. 403–41.

Page, G. and Fearn, H. (2005), 'Corporate reputation: what do consumers really care about?', *Journal of Advertising Research*, Vol. 45, No. 3, pp. 305–13.

Snyder, B. (2003) 'Highly trusted brands run more risk of offending customers', at http://www.gsb.stanford.edu/news/research/mktg_goodbrands.shtml.

Wang, J. (2005), 'Consumer nationalism and corporate reputation management in the global era', *Corporate Communications: An International Journal*, Vol. 10, No. 3, pp. 223–9.

Wood, D. J. (1991), 'Corporate social performance revisited', *Academy of Management Review*, Vol. 16, pp. 691–718.

Further reading and online sites

Anonymous author(s) (2003), 'Coca-Cola stumbles in Belgium: response time is critical in crisis brand management', *Strategic Direction*, Vol. 19, No. 5, pp. 23–5.

Barnett, M. L., Jermier, J. M. and Lafferty, B. A. (2004), 'Corporate reputation: the definitional landscape', at www.coba.usf.edu/barnett/CRR%20Proceedings%202004.pdf.

Coombs, W. T. and Holladay, S. J. (2006), 'Unpacking the halo effect: reputation and crisis management', *Journal of Communication Management*, Vol. 10, No. 2, pp. 123–37.

Dezenhall, E. and Weber, J. (2007), 'Damage control: why everything you know about crisis management is wrong', *Portfolio*, ISBN 1591841542, 9781591841548.

Eberl, M. and Schwaiger, M. (2005), 'Corporate reputation: disentangling the effects on financial performance', *European Journal of Marketing*, Vol. 39, No. 7/8, pp. 838–54.

Enquirer, The at www.enquirer.com/editions/2004.

European Association of Communication Agencies (2003), 'Communicating corporate social responsibility', at www.responsiblepractice.com/english/insight.

Factiva Insight: Reputation Intelligence, at www.factiva.com.

Jaques, T. (2008), 'When an icon stumbles: the Ribena issue mismanaged', *Corporate Communications: An International Journal*, Vol. 13, No. 4, pp. 394–406.

Klein, J. and Dawar, N. (2004), 'Corporate social responsibility and consumers', *International Journal of Research in Marketing*, Vol. 21, No. 3, pp. 203–17.

Manning, L. (2007), 'Food safety and brand equity', *British Food Journal*, Vol. 109 No. 7, pp. 496–510.

Neville, B. A., Bell, S. J. and Mengüç, B. (2005), 'Corporate reputation, stakeholders and the social performance–financial performance relationship', *European Journal of Marketing*, Vol. 39, No. 9/10.

Paraskevas, A. (2006), 'Crisis management or crisis response system? A complexity science approach to organizational crises', *Management Decision*, Vol. 44, No. 7, pp. 892–907.

Power, J., Whelan, S. and Davies, G. (2008), 'The attractiveness and connectedness of ruthless brands: the role of trust', *European Journal of Marketing*, Vol. 42, No. 5/6, pp. 586–602.

PART 3

The New Business Environment

CHAPTER 10

The New Competitive Environment and Branding

Chapter contents

Chapter overview

This chapter analyses the new competitive environment and its impact on branding. The rise of technology, the Internet, the fragmentation of the media and the challenges of modern markets will all have an impact on brand strategy. It discusses the nature of competitive branding and strategic brand alliances, and how environmental forces affect companies around the world. Chapter 9 examined the principle of corporate and brand reputation building in response to environmental threats. Chapter 11 will cover competition from own-labels as part of the broad topic on competing in the new business environment.

❖ LEARNING OBJECTIVES

After completing this chapter, you should be able to

❖ Describe the different environmental forces and how these affect businesses in general

❖ Examine the new competitive environment and how it influences brand strategy

❖ Explain in detail the notions of market convergence, market entry timing, distributors' power and channels evolution, competitive branding

❖ Examine the changes in consumer markets, and discuss the impact on brand strategy and brand communication

❖ Discuss companies' response to globalization

❖ Apply knowledge on environmental issues to solve branding problems

Introduction

Marketers must create competitive advantage by constantly adapting to and setting off change. To stay ahead of competition, companies must adapt to market changes and are likely to be more successful if they are more aware of the forces shaping market behaviour and possess insights that enable them to develop sustainable competitive advantages. The challenges brand managers face are the evolving needs of buyers within a market populated by global competitors and the opening-up of territorial markets. They must also deal with the fuzziness of product–market boundaries caused by increased deregulation and competitive initiatives, which have resulted in the creation of new products/services and the lowering of costs; as well as the increasing pace of technological change, resulting in the strengthening of the power and independence of the channels of distribution, together with pressure from investors and factors contributing to blurred market boundaries. In this chapter these environmental forces will each be examined as well as the implications for brand strategy, brand communication and strategic alliances; but, first, the drivers of change and an overview of today's competition are described.

Drivers of change

Economic factors

Changes in economic circumstances can be as global as the economic crisis initiated by OPEC in the 1970s, or as localized as a small town hit by a plant closing. Firms that anticipate economic change and identify the constituents through which that change will be applied are better placed to adapt goals and action plans. Examples of economic factors include unemployment rates, price levels, inflation rates and interest rates. Personal income, savings rates, employment levels and price-level trends can have dramatic effects on the attractiveness of a firm's products or services.

Ecological factors

Ecological factors – once on the fringes of business concern – are becoming increasingly important (e.g. water pollution, ozone depletion, global warming). Many natural resources are not renewable, so the rate of consumption becomes a major issue for firms dependent on the resource. Industrial pollution remains a problem for society. Responsible stewardship of the environment is a business issue.

Political/legal factors

Firms are affected directly and indirectly by political/legal influences at all levels of government (federal, state and local). In addition to serving as regulatory bodies, governments also represent a major factor in the private sector through fiscal policy. Taxation and government spending can represent both opportunities and threats, depending on the nature, timing and position of the impacted enterprise. Fiscal policy can have dramatic impacts on the overall economic climate of the firm.

Social factors

The social climate in which business operates has systemic implications for firm success and the demand for goods and services. Businesses exist to satisfy the needs and wants of society. On a micro level, it is clear that public wants and needs can significantly determine the effectiveness of a given firm's strategy.

Demographic research is designed to assess population characteristics as they relate to market potential and threats. An ageing population, for instance, represents a distinct opportunity for a firm selling generic products. Increases in the number of single households represent many opportunities for firms selling household products.

Similarly, data on consumer buying habits allow firms to reposition their marketing channels or alter their advertising mix. Changing consumer awareness and concomitant market responses might call for changes in product quality or positioning. Consumer perceptions of the quality of Japanese-made products, for example, have improved so dramatically since the 1960s that Japanese companies now have a perceptual advantage of perceived quality as opposed to an earlier disadvantage. Perceived quality differentials have been reversed in many industries, so that some manufacturers must now compete on the basis of price rather than quality.

Special trends and fads also have major implications for product/market choices. The social factors include ageing population, communication changes, education for all, fears, future households, holistic well-being, literacy, personal productivity and population distribution.

Technological factors

Electronics, bioengineering, chemicals and medicine are a few of the fields in which major technological change has created new business opportunities. In some cases entire industries have emerged, such as generic engineering, bringing with them new opportunities and new threats. In other cases, technological changes within industries have brought new forms of product competition, e.g. micro technologies in electronics that require openness to new applications. Other technological process changes – as in the use of robots in automobile manufacturing – have led to different competitive advantages in production costs and product quality.

Firms subject to technological obsolescence or intent on maintaining some form of technological leadership must stay abreast of technological innovation and, as far as is possible, forecast future technological change and its potential for acceptance. Some firms may be more severely or more rapidly affected than others. Technological innovation is a key factor for success in many industries, and must be monitored and forecast aggressively. Therefore, sensitivity to the techno-logical environment is a primary component of successful strategic planning.

Overview of today's competition

Today's intensive competition introduces a whole new set of competitive conditions. No longer is it possible for a company to develop a competitive advantage that will allow it to compete comfortably in an industry segment over a period of time. Competitive pressures are too strong and competitive conditions are changing too rapidly. The criteria for success are:

- *To understand* the customers even more intimately than the customers do themselves. It is about designing and delivering products and services to meet unique customer needs. Customers are also smart. No longer is it possible simply to produce a product or service and expect to sell it to the customer. They are more knowledgeable thanks to the wider avail-ability of information. They know what they want, and expect quality, good service and quick responses. They know who the competitors are. They understand the options open to them. Customers will make informed buying decisions.

- *Quality capability*. World-class quality is an absolute requirement for entering the competitive environment. Companies that cannot consistently meet or exceed customer expectations will not even be considered. Furthermore, poor quality adds costs and reduces value to the cus-tomer. Customers will not tolerate such added costs as repairs, delay or inconvenience.

- *Speed*. Companies must have zero wait time. Customers expect delivery of products and serv-ices just-in-time and exactly when they want them.

- *Cost*. Customers expect world-class quality products and services, and they expect all of this at minimum cost. Sophisticated customers understand competitive conditions and will not overpay for a product or service.

- *Innovation*. Innovation is the core capability a company must have to compete effectively. To continually meet changing customer needs, to offer the best products and services at the lowest costs most rapidly, companies must continually innovate and sustain innovation in the long term. Continuous development of new products and services is necessary to meet changing customer demands. Continuous improvement and, sometimes, re-engineering of processes is necessary to improve speed and quality while lowering costs. As Porter (1990) noted, innovation is the way companies can obtain a competitive advantage. Whether it is innovation that results in a new product design, a new production process, a new marketing approach or a new way of conducting training, innovation and sustained innovation are the keys to long-term success.

- *Competition* has implications for preparing brand managers for the future. To start with, brand managers can be proactive by focusing on customers. They need an understanding of the business and the environment in which business operates, as well as a proactive orientation. The importance of adapting to external dynamics is increasing and will continue to grow in the years to come. Environmental turbulence is not a passing phenomenon. The volatile environment of many organizations challenges management systems in general and brand management in particular.

How do the above reflect in brand management? The combination of potential economic benefits and consumer interest suggests that managers should think carefully about brands from a strategic perspective. This view is compounded by evidence which shows that most successful brands are the outcome of several years of investment and strategic planning (Simões and Dibb, 2001).

The fastest-moving companies today plan on a continuous basis rather than an annual one, and use business scorecards to map their performance in each area of the action plan from total business to individual performance level.

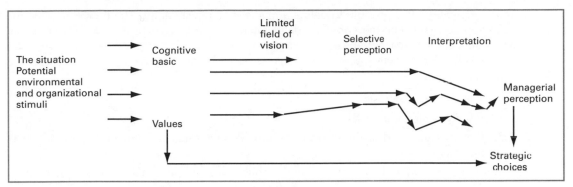

Source: Adapted from Stahl and Grigsby (1992)

Source: Adapted from Stahl and Grigsby (1992)

FIGURE 10.1 A model for bounded rational strategic decision-making

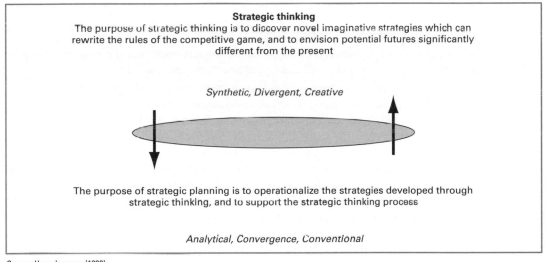

Source: Heracleneous (1998)

FIGURE 10.2 Strategic thinking and strategic planning

What are the implications of strategic planning for brand management?

Traditional elements of a brand plan would include:

- *Brand vision (long term)*. The brand vision is usually a high aspiration or stretch statement about where the managers want the brand to end up. They usually involve taking over the world, or at least a number of markets. Remember to define the market the company is in, in a wider context, e.g. 'We are not in yoghurts, but in the human health and happiness business'.

- *Brand mission (mid-term)*. Mission statements classically should be the *4Ms*:

1 meaningful (credible)

2 motivating

3 measureable

4 memorable.

When did you last remember your mission statement? One of the great mission statements of all time was 'Get the Cat', when Komatsu targeted its company on beating Caterpillar in the heavy earth-moving market.

- *Market definition*. It is possible to define a market in any way at all. The trick is to keep the definition constant until the company deliberately decide to change it. The GE rule is that when the company reaches 40 per cent market share, it needs to redefine its market so that it now only has 10 per cent – a recipe for aggressive market-share growth.
- *Situation analysis*
  1 Market size and forecasts.
  2 Market dynamics and trends.
  3 Market structure and share of trade at supplier, intermediary and end customer level segmentation.
  4 Brandscape (own and competitor brand architectures and performance, brand definitions, comparative brand strategies, brand competencies).
  5 Market attraction vs brand competency chart.

  End-customer segmentation should be defined in terms of demographics, behaviour, situation and needs/values.

  The brandscape is developed to understand in depth the role of each competing brand. This might well culminate in a 'conversion chart' which depicts each brand's customer base by segment, and the extent to which their customers are committed, satisfied or not.

  Market attraction vs competency chart is the classic McKinsey portfolio planning chart which shows the attraction of each market segment to the company's brand and brand power within each segment, with the size of each bubble depicting the size of each opportunity in sales, profits or lifetime value.

- *Alternative scenarios for the next two to five years*. Most markets will not be operating in quite the same way in two years' time, especially with the growth of e-marketplaces and Internet-based competition. Scenario planning can help identify potential futures that will at least test the company's current market model.
- *Key programmes and their goals*. Increasingly, brands require focused, larger-scale investments to maintain and build their competitive position. Picking out two or three critical programmes tells the rest of the organization where the focus is.
- *Brand objectives and change analysis* (what will have to be done differently). Objectives should be measurable. The reason for the change analysis is to highlight what has to be done differently.
- *Brand action plan and component plans* (new brand development, new product development, customer relationship management, channel plan, etc.). The action plan provides the detailed activities that need to take place. The component plans provide more detailed information on specific areas within the brand plan, such as the new product development programme, the contribution of e-CRM activities or the advertising plan.

Final remark: the fastest-moving companies today plan on a continuous basis rather than on an annual one.

Alternatively, the company could start the brand planning process with the following questions:

- *Where are we now?* This involves four steps:
  1 Assessing the current value of the brand using one of the brand valuation methods discussed in Chapter 2. Note that size alone cannot be the sole yardstick of brand equity; customer commitment is also important.
  2 Conducting a customer analysis. Be warned that most segmentation analyses focus on describing different groups of consumers without reference to the real marketing issues. There is a need for better understanding of the customer's relationship with a brand in building stronger brands. Here, brand managers must also be aware that people have varying need states, and additional factors may further complicate the picture.

3 Carrying out a market analysis. Here, brand managers must try to identify the patterns of competition within and across product classes.

4 Conducting a competitive analysis using SWOT analysis or a more advanced method (see Walton, 1999).

■ *Where could we be?* This consists of market or consumer gap analysis, setting objectives, targeting and positioning. Gap analysis involves analysing current market offerings to assess the extent to which they meet customer demands. Setting objectives includes setting advertising and promotions objectives and others. Brand managers need to evaluate how these affect brand performance in general. For targeting and positioning, refer to Chapter 5.

■ *How do we get there?* This is about planning and briefing, execution, the use of integrated marketing communications, pre-testing, media planning and budgeting (see World Advertising Research Center (WARC) for strategies for each of these aspects).

■ *Are we getting there?* This is about tracking and measuring, brand and marketing activities, as well as conducting sales analysis (see WARC) articles on 'How to use targets and norms in advertising tracking', 'How to track customer satisfaction', and 'Advertising: short-term and long-term effects').

Globalization and greater openness of markets

Global competition has entered many markets. For instance, in the 1980s unrivalled Japanese competitors had many successes in the motorcycle and consumer electronics markets because of their quality and reliability. In the 1990s the grocery business had competition from low-cost retailers from the Scandinavian and continental European multinationals, such as Unilever and Nestlé. It is foreseen that in the near future competition is likely to come from China and India.

It is clear to many people today that China is poised to take over the world's manufacturing. This phenomenon is also known as 'Chinacosm'. Manufacturing workers outside China are being displaced on a large scale, and Mexico is losing jobs to China. In addition, a significant share of manufactured goods is sourced in China. Wal-Mart for instance, buys more than $12 billion worth a year from China and provides a direct outlet for Chinese-manufactured goods into the US, which most economists agree has contributed to low US inflation. India has seen the emergence of a new force in high-tech competition originating from a firm called Wipro, which is situated in Bangalore. By 2004, 17 000 engineers were expecting to take on projects for such clients as Home Depot, Nokia and Sony. Wipro is competing with Accenture, EDS, IBM and the big accounting firms. For brand managers, one of the ways to thrive on competition is by attacking them at home.

Branding Brief 10.1: Protecting your trademark far from home

Source: Cassiano Golos Teixeira, 26 September 2005, at Brandchannel.com

The power of a brand in the market is directly related to the legal protection of the trademark. Therefore, any company that desires to be competitive and maintain or improve its own image in the market must adopt an international intellectual property (IP) strategy in order to have a strong trademark. There are uncountable cases of companies that, before launching a product or even a name, do not make a deep clearance of their trademarks, identifying earlier trademarks that may be confusingly similar. So far, there are even more cases of companies that, after the clearance, forget that a strong trademark must not only be new and distinct, but must also be maintained so worldwide. Many times the consequences of not having an effective IP strategy arises only when the first shipment of goods to a foreign country is blocked in the alien port due to the existence of a similar registered trademark by a competitor. The problem is that covering foreign trademark regions may be costly and, many times, impossible.

One would say that the best international strategy is to file trademark applications in all countries immediately, before any deal. But is this worthwhile? Indeed, notwithstanding the legal advantages of such an option, in most cases this is a utopian ideal, especially for small and medium-sized enterprises or for the low-gross-profit products of large enterprises, which simply don't have the resources to acquire a full trademark worldwide.

Many countries have means in their legislation to avoid unfair registrations. For instance, the Brazilian Industrial Property Law of 1996 provides that every person who, in good faith on the priority or filing date, has been using an identical or similar mark in Brazil for at least six months to distinguish or certify an identical, similar or alike product or service shall have the right of preference for the registration. In other words, a person who has been using a trademark in Brazil for at least six months has priority registration if there should enter a competing, similar mark (not yet registered) on the market.

Although, if it is not easy to enforce a prior used trademark by such legal means, it would be even harder or impossible if the prior user does not know that a further application has been filed. Another point: even if you have an application or a registered trademark, you must be proactive, enforcing it against other applications or counterfeiters. But if you don't know what your potential competitors or counterfeiters are doing worldwide, what can you do? Nothing – just lose your corporate identity among uncountable similar trademarks. But do not forget, in some countries (for example, Switzerland, which is not party to the European Community Trademark system), there prevails a first-to-file system where protection for prior users is very restricted. Therefore, in the determination of the intellectual property strategy of a trademark, it is very important to consider many factors, such as the intended life cycle of the brand, potential consumer markets, and potential producers' and counterfeiters' countries, among others. Choose the strategy that best fits your business plan budget. In this manner, the best practice that should be included in all strategies would be: watch out!

Strategic alliances

As a result of globalization, domestic firms seek alliances with foreign competitors, in particular in the automobile industry. Given shrinking margins and profits at home, companies search for greater opportunity abroad by teaming up with foreign competitors. For instance, Cereal Partners Worldwide, a joint venture of General Mills and Nestlé, has substantial market share outside North America, at the expense of Kellogg's.

To survive, companies have to share costs and risks, but also knowledge, distribution and capital via strategic alliances that will stretch organizational capabilities and change the nature of brand management. Examples are Apple and Sony combining their design and manufacturing skills to produce the popular Powerbook. Sony and Nintendo have combined hardware and software capabilities to take on Sega in the market for video games distributed on CD-ROM, and Nike relies on DuPont to design air-tubes that provide bounce in the soles of its Air Jordan basketball shoes, and manufacturers in Asia to deliver the product.

Strategic alliances with certain suppliers, distributors and even with former competitors are a key to firms' future competitive strength. The idea is that unknown producers try to form an alliance with well-known retailers to take advantage of the latters' reputation in order to create a favourable association for the unknown brand. Other firms have combined brand names through brand alliances to increase consumer response.

For instance, a wide variety of products now contain branded ingredients, such as Diet Coke with NutraSweet or IBM personal computers with Intel chips. Others have used multiple brand names to communicate co-branded product variants. Examples are Special K frozen waffles by Eggo (both Kellogg's brands), Bisc& Bounty (Mars brands), Cadbury's Dairy Crunchie Bubbly (all

Cadbury brands) and Nestlé's Milky Bar Munchies. Co-branding extends to alliances between the complementary brand names of independent producers, for example, Ford's Citibank MasterCard.

Collaboration with competitors

Alliances between manufacturers with complementary skills or between manufacturers, their suppliers and distributors are natural, however there are reasons for even direct competitors to collaborate. Global challenges encourage domestic competitors to form alliances and create pressure for change in monopoly and antitrust regulation to make the alliance feasible. For example, the IBM–Apple–Motorola partnership was forged to develop the next generation of power PCs, and eroded the dominance of Intel and Microsoft. Global alliances may provide a way of weakening monopoly and antitrust restraints.

Branding Brief 10.2: Lenovo lining up to buy IBM's PCs? Chinese company faces challenges in potential deal

Source: Adapted from Rex Crum, CBS.MarketWatch.com, last update: 4:11 pm ET, 3 December 2004

Its name certainly doesn't carry the recognition of Dell, Hewlett-Packard or Apple Computer, but China's Lenovo Group could climb up the personal-computer food chain if it buys IBM's PC business.

Lenovo, which sells low-margin PCs in China under the Legend brand, is reportedly negotiating for IBM's PC business for as much as $2 billion.

Lenovo's Legend line is still relatively unknown outside China, and research firm Gartner Group pegs the company's share of worldwide PC shipments at 2 per cent, placing it in ninth place between Gateway, Inc. and Apple. IBM holds third place, behind Dell and H-P, with a 5.6 per cent market share.

But Lenovo has made strides in the PC market and is expected to boost its worldwide 2004 shipments by more than 30 per cent from 2003, to 3.7 million units, according to Gartner. Lenovo is expected to increase shipments faster than the 25 per cent rate forecast for Dell, Inc.

'It has been no secret that Lenovo has been looking to expand beyond its core geographical markets', said Prudential Equity analyst Steven Fortuna in a research note. '[A] move of this nature could allow the company to scale its business and compete more effectively on a worldwide basis.'

Buying IBM's PC business would give Lenovo more credibility and status in the industry, but questions remain about how PC makers can consistently make profits in what is viewed as a commoditized business. Dell is known for squeezing out costs through to widespread adoption of industry-standard technologies, and Dell is the only PC company to have maintained profitability over recent years.

'It could be a good deal for Lenovo, but it might not be,' said Simon Yates, an analyst with Forrester Research. 'They've made their name in China with low-end PCs, but they don't have the high-end market presence yet. In the end, it will come down to how they do against Dell and H-P.'

Rob Enderle, of Enderle Group, said that while he believes IBM could sell its PC business, he doubts Lenovo will go through with a deal due to the realities of trying to retain the strength of IBM's retail efforts. 'It would provide them with legitimacy in the market and the resulting products would do well in retail,' Enderle said. 'But they would still lose most of the existing IBM-connected business over time and would still need to rebuild a retail channel to even get this benefit and shelf space.'

Product design for the global market

There are two options or more. One is standardization, in that brand managers need to have product designs containing features important to all markets and standardize these across markets. Economies of scale from a single global design may be enough to lower prices and/or increase promotion in each market to offset a lack of features. Two is adaptation, i.e. products would need to have features that satisfy local requirements. Three, brand managers can have flexible product designs that have options that can be added to a basic design that satisfies local requirements.

Branding Brief 10.3: Branding and hip-hop culture

Hip-hop was once seen as an urban phenomenon, but is now the one uniform force in the American marketplace. Previously seen as a niche strategy, nowadays 'urban marketing' expands across the entire youth demographic.

Hip-hop culture is a pop phenomenon that largely arose through cable television and the Internet. Americans are now exposed to regional tastes and styles in weeks and months, which used to take years to reach them. At its core, hip-hop sprang from the inner cities. From Run-DMC in Hollis, Queens, to NWA from South Central Los Angeles, the music grew from economic inequality and socio-cultural frustrations. However, what started as a New York/Los Angeles/ Philadelphia art spread to artists from all corners of America. Being exposed to the music not only allows local artists to take this sound and regionalize it but, more important, expand the culture, making it a palatable strategy for corporations across the country.

While hip-hop culture was being embraced by mass American culture, suburban whites became members of the culture despite not having anyone with whom they could truly relate. Apart from MC Serch of 3rd Bass and Vanilla Ice, white America had little to offer in terms of hip-hop talent. Enter Eminem, the ultimate catalyst for the proliferation of the culture. His entrance was the pinnacle of white immersion into hip-hop. The success of Eminem helped clear the final obstacle.

Perhaps the most crucial reason for the mass acculturation of hip-hop goes beyond the music. Societal shifts made it easy to be a part of hip-hop culture without owning a Jay-Z or Fat Joe record. The fact that companies like Mountain Dew and the US Army stand behind this 'street promotion' indicates American acceptance of this culture.

In the end, cultural consumption leads back to corporate acceptance and ways to use the culture for market capitalization. Companies staying culturally relevant now see hip-hop as the answer to all of their problems. While in some cases this has been a stop-gap solution, the effect of invigorating hip-hop into the brand is self-evident. If Reebok has painted itself into a corner, choosing now to be a lifestyle brand rather than a sports brand, you cannot argue with its current success. From slumping sales with pitchmen like Shaquille O'Neal and Steve Francis, the brand has made a dramatic positioning shift in recent years. With Jay-Z and 50 Cent replacing athletic stars as lead pitchmen, the brand has never been hotter.

Openness of markets

Deregulation has led to increased competition from traditionally defined product–market boundaries. For example, banks and credit unions are now in competition for credit card use with non-financial companies, such as retailers and manufacturers. These companies use their established relationships with customers to penetrate the credit market. Conversely, banks have gone into partnership with airlines and telecommunication companies to tempt credit-card users with frequent-user miles. On a larger scale, NAFTA opened free trade between North American countries, as did the EU between most countries of Europe, including eastern bloc countries in regions such as the Balkans.

The effects of deregulation are felt in many industries, varying from telecommunications to healthcare and transportation. The effects are intense competition and reduced prices and margins. Competitive forces, though, often precede deregulation. These are both cause and effect. The challenge for brand managers is to adapt proactively to market changes brought about by deregulation.

Technological change impact

Technological change is affected by the globalization of markets. Globalization means larger markets for technology products and a greater need to coordinate management activities over distance and time. Computer-aided design, manufacturing, engineering, software engineering and associated approaches have reduced dramatically the time required to develop, design, test and manufacture new products, while at the same time reducing costs and improving quality. Information technology, when used with flexible manufacturing systems, can reduce order-fulfilment cycles and inventory requirements. Thus, technology can be leveraged to gain competitive advantage. A discussion of the impact of technology on brand management follows.

Product innovation

Innovative products offer greater functionality at lower costs and can displace existing products, providing opportunities for new entrants that many not otherwise have been available. Innovations sometimes also provide additional opportunity for complementary products: for instance, simplified programming devices for VCRs. Technology can be used to differentiate a company's products and warn off me-too products.

Private labels, for instance, have been able to capture high market share in some mature fmcg categories such as paper towels, jams and jellies. Manufacturer-branded goods have also been able to overcome competition by innovation in similar categories like detergents, soft drinks and razors. Innovation is part of a corporate strategy to sustain competitive advantage. Examples are 3M, DuPont and Gillette. Brand managers need to think creatively in mature and stable product markets and in terms of services, imagery, distribution (e.g. direct mail) and pricing (e.g. frequent flyer plans) all of which can create differentiation.

Market convergence

Technological advances have sometimes blurred boundaries between product markets. For example, airlines, hotels and car rental agencies share the same reservation system. Multimedia computer applications combining sound, pictures and text use similar data-handling mechanisms as AT&T's picture phones. These explain acquisitions, for instance AT&T's purchase of NCR, as well as alliances between American Airlines, Marriott and Hertz, which often result in joint promotion and advertising of brands.

The challenges to brand managers include: how to utilize skills from one product market in another; assembling and managing the skills of several partners in developing and marketing new products and services; and managing joint promotions and ensuring that partner brand strategies do not adversely affect their own brands.

The search for defensible competitive advantage has also extended the boundaries of existing product categories. Sometimes new or hybrid categories are created: examples are cereal bars, disposable cameras, and portable telephones and multimedia combining computer and music systems. As a consequence, these have allowed brand managers to tap into new markets and use these as an opportunity to increase sales. Many firms also realize the added value a recognized ingredient or component brand name can have in terms of further influencing and establishing their brand presence in the consumer market.

Market entry timing

Companies with shorter product-development cycles close in on potential markets faster. Speed is more important in harvesting the best customers and the early adopters who are willing to pay more. Brand managers can make it more difficult for customers to turn to other providers and, thus, gain a strategic advantage. A pioneer has the advantage of setting the standard to which others are compared, and acquires a reputation for innovation. This reputation can have a positive influence on product trial and faster diffusion. Shorter order-fulfilment cycles and mass customization enable brand managers to take advantage of market segmentation while keeping control of costs.

Distributors' power and channels evolution

In the past products moved in a loosely coupled fashion from manufacturers to wholesalers and retailers to the final consumer. The levels of distribution and supply now see the importance of system-wide coordination to improve operating efficiencies. Relationship management captures this new awareness of the symbiotic, inter-organizational requirement for delivering customer value. Conflict with a distribution channel can now be a potentially fatal obstacle to the success of the brand, while increased competition has changed the geography of product market boundaries. The scope for distribution has broadened through the globalization of markets. The difficulty now lies with brand creation and maintenance in global markets.

As the relationship between producers and distributors has intensified, the power of retailers has increased. Thanks to new forms of retailing, such as warehouse stores and office product depots, the emergence of sophisticated information technologies and logistical support, manufacturers have lost much of the control they once held over the ways their brands are marketed through the distribution system. The rapid diffusion of the electronic scanner has contributed to the shift in information power from manufacturers to retailers.

Retailers have gone into direct competition with manufacturers by offering private labels as good-value-for-money brands. As a consequence manufacturers with a lower price-quality position have been losing ground (see Chapter 11). In addition, some retailers have begun to move upstream in quality through attractively packaged private-label brands designed to offer greater value than the national brand.

Brand managers are faced with new choices to compete or join by producing for the retailer's private label. Otherwise they may be forced to concentrate only on flavours or varieties with which the private label does not want to compete. Distributors who can develop bonds with consumers can play manufacturers off against one another. Market research information is vital for brand managers in dealing with distributors. Retailers also use trade promotion at the expense of consumer advertising budgets. Brand managers can wean trade customers from promotions through 'everyday low price' and other strategies.

Changes in consumer markets

Competition exposes consumers to new information and product/service alternatives that have the potential to influence their tastes and preferences. Producers have also learned more about what is being offered by competitors and what prospective buyers would purchase, and have adapted their offerings accordingly. As far as brand managers are concerned, the challenge to them is to understand the dynamics of changing markets and manage brand associations effectively. As a result of retailers' everyday low-price strategy they have added further value to their product lines, sometimes to a degree that cannibalizes their own product range. To brand managers, such market moves have meant the development of new products with different price levels.

Shifts in socio-demographics have also provided opportunities for new products, e.g. snacks on the go and pre-packed lunches. Singles and lone-parent families are on the increase; equally the female head of household is no longer the gatekeeper and arbiter of family tastes and preferences. A great deal of family shopping is now done by teenagers and men, and more two-income families are eating out. Branded consumer goods are gradually declining and some restaurant chains are having to produce supermarket versions of their products, e.g. frozen food. As a result, brand managers are able to develop growth strategies in related industries – for example, PepsiCo's expansion into fast-food chains, like Pizza Hut and KFC.

Market fragmentation is reflected in the growing differences in taste that accompany cultural and economic diversity, such as concern for the environment, and the value of time, health and nutrition. The rise of cable, with its myriad channels, and the consequent decline of network television, is a response to the increasing fragmentation of audiences, but it also makes it more expensive for firms to reach potential customers. However, global communication networks promise greater homogeneity in international tastes and preferences. For instance, CNN, MTV and some BBC channels now reach over 120 million viewers worldwide on a daily basis.

The challenge for brand managers is to provide an orchestrated message to customers, distributors and other target groups in the form of 'one voice marketing'. Although not new, IMC is driven by feasibility of direct marketing activities, fragmented media, more sophisticated and efficient telecommunications and increased reliance on sales promotions relative to advertising. Each of these has made the development of a strong and consistent brand image more difficult to achieve.

Competitive branding

To gain competitive advantage, brand management must first have a sound internal environment and a sound company structure. People within the company must ensure continuity in, and respect for, the brand's intangible attributes once they have been defined.

Brands must become the CEO's responsibility or a boardroom issue (see Chapter 4). Brand managers must not be the only people responsible for brand policy. The whole company should be involved: financial, accounting, technical and legal managers as well as managing directors should all participate in its development. It will be brand managers who will be working in cross-functional teams and will report directly to senior management, rather than the marketing department, as it once was.

As a given brand can now be linked to several different technologies, produced by different business units and marketed by different sales teams, a company will need a flatter hierarchical structure with a brand marketer, a brand marketing manager in charge of the brand's overall management and a marketing director in charge of the coordination of the large brands.

Also, to compete effectively, companies need to capitalize on driver brands and trim down brand portfolios, since these are often problematic and costly to manage. Owing to mergers and acquisitions in fmcg especially, as companies pursue expansion and growth, they find themselves faced with a plethora of local brands, product or product-line brands, and company brands (see Chapter 6).

In many cases this capitalization has put an end to the proliferation of brands and product names. To capitalize successfully on brands, companies must retain the best-known brand names and transform them into umbrella brands. The basis of competitive branding is brands that can be sustained through innovation and those that address diversity in fragmented markets.

In addition, companies must maintain consistency in brand identity. They must not be tempted into chasing short-term profits by extending brands through licensing, at the expense of the brand's intrinsic identity.

Also, gaining competitive advantage by reducing the brand portfolio is one thing, but reducing a brand to only one product can often mean shrinking brand equity. This can jeopardize the brand because eventually every product and every brand will die. It has been shown that brand extension helps to increase brand equity.

Competitive branding is equally about focusing on long-term benefits rather than short-term profits. Therefore, companies should not be too hasty in producing for retailer's own-labels for short-term profit at the expense of long-term gain. They must try to strike a balance between these two areas. Producers of well-known national brands should not produce retailers' own-labels. Similarly, they should use the same technology as that used by their competitors. In many cases, it has been shown that companies that do not produce own-label brands are more profitable than those that do.

To succeed in the future, brand managers must attract customers regularly and repeatedly with innovations that are consistent with brand values but, at the same time, surprising and enticing. Trend spotting will be important. They must develop customer loyalty by focusing on quality and price, which are consistently maintained for existing consumers. Sustainable growth and ethical commerce will be sources of strength for the brand. Direct relationships with consumers will be important and brands will have to be much more evident at the contact point with customers, and omnipresent.

Cause branding and social marketing

The integration of social issues with business practices is also a fundamental part of today's business strategy. Using cause associations, leading companies can position their brands for the future. Companies such as ConAgra Foods, Avon and Timberland have made social commitments central to the way they conduct their businesses, as well as being a core component of their corporate reputation, brand personality and organizational identity.

Particularly when companies find it hard to compete on innovations and advertising in a saturated marketplace, strategic cause programmes provide companies with valuable leadership and differentiation strategies, as well as enhanced brand equity and credibility, greater reach, and significant resources and relationships. Strategic cause initiatives such as breast cancer, literacy, human rights and famine help companies meet bottom-line objectives and make a substantial long-term impact on these critical social issues at the same time. Corporate cause initiatives also engage employees, customers, partners, community members and others in taking collaborative action on the issues most important to them and their communities. Non-profit partners add value to the programme, enhance credibility and secure the company's leadership position within the issue. In return, non-profit organizations gain enhanced brand equity, public awareness, committed relationships, and additional money and resources. For example, ConAgra's Foods Feeding Children Better is the US's largest corporate initiative dedicated to ending childhood hunger. ConAgra Foods' partnership is with America's Second Harvest, the US's largest domestic hunger relief organization with a national network of more than 200 regional food banks and food rescue organizations. America's Second Harvest brings credibility to ConAgra Foods' programme and has a national and local impact on hunger; and for America's Second Harvest, a substantive partnership with a respected corporation helps this non-profit organization to build institutional credibility and raise funds to support and expand its programmes nationally in the US (Cone et al., 2001).

New creative media and branding

According to DM Business Intelligence in 2004 new media gained over 41 per cent of market share compared with traditional media. New media include such things as 3G, interactive TV, web TV and ATM marketing. Since the 'users' of the media are subscribers, it means that advertisers can target specific needs based on their 'opt in' profile. For example, an ATM machine user comes up and his profile says he has young children. The bank can target him for products intended for college savings. A man in his forties would receive an ad for income return allowance (IRA) and retirement investment. A 'dinky' (dual income, no kids yet) would get a 'growing your net worth' ad. Similarly, 3G, interactive TV and web TV have this capability since they are also subscriber based. The real impact on branding will be through segmentation. In the mass market, fine-tuning segmentation can be very expensive and time-consuming. In these media, in place of extensive market research, the consumers themselves have provided the information needed for segmentation; and given that the media enable companies to customize by user, personalized profiting and branding can be established for them. By contrast, other media, such as print ads, TV ads, etc., throw out a theme and hope someone who identifies with that theme first actually sees it, and then actually relates to it. The success of new media branding can be determined by the audience interacting with it.

New media can have an impact on branding strategies in the following ways:

1 *By impacting on processes*. For example, in the communication planning process, media planning used to start only once the creative idea was in place. Today because of the new media, some creative ideas are born out of the media themselves. Hence corporations are rethinking their procedures and are trying to integrate media thinking at the beginning of the communication process.

2 *By impacting on the brand's associations*. A brand needs to come alive and be consistent in its multiple avatars across media.

3 *New media can have an impact on brand evolution*. New media allow the brand to change/adapt faster than old media, because they are more interactive and it is easier to get quick feedback on new initiatives.

4 *They impact on the world the brands live in*. Media agencies are now hiring behaviour experts to add value to their media learning. Soon both the creative agency and media agency will have account planning functions instead of planners focusing only on creative product.

5 *New media impact on brand strategy by changing society*. They make consumers more aware and informed, and therefore more difficult to convince unless genuine value is offered.

6 *They make it possible for customers to 'own' the brand*. New media allow the consumer to co-create the brand thanks to interactivity (MarketingProfs, 2005).

One of the problems with new media, however, is that they are increasingly putting branding in the hands of consumers. They have empowered consumers to share their opinions and influence behaviour more than ever before. It is estimated that more than 24 million blogs were launched in 2004. Using the Internet, blogs, websites, forums, etc., consumers can publish anything that is on their mind. This can benefit companies as well as destroy them. If a company has a great product or service that everyone likes, 'word of mouse' advertising can literally make a brand overnight. On the other hand, if the product or service does not deliver on its promises, or the company behaves badly in terms of, say, labour relations or environmental policy, never mind the mainstream media catching the story, Internet bloggers can make or break a brand overnight (MarketingProfs, 2005).

How environmental forces affect companies around the world

LEGO

For many of today's parents, the world-famous LEGO brand brings back happy childhood memories. Although the product format and range which LEGO offers are now much more extensive, the creative imagination they are designed to capture remains the same. This interest in creative imagination has formed the cornerstone of LEGO's branding. The company's website describes this philosophy and explains the continual search for new ideas that allow LEGO to live up to its positioning statement: 'Creativity unlimited ... Just imagine'.

> Our vision is for people all over the world to experience positive, happy associations every time they see a LEGO logo, see a LEGO element or hold it in their hands. Imagination, exuberance, spontaneity, self-expression, quality – these are some of the words we wish to link with the LEGO name, together with values like development, concern for others and innovation. (www.lego.com)

The history of the LEGO brand goes back more than 60 years. Originally, the LEGO name was derived from the Danish words *Leg Goldt* (play well). After recognizing the opportunities for new plastic materials in the 1950s, the company began manufacturing the forerunners of today's LEGO bricks. Before long, the business was enjoying international success. This success was to be long-lived, with LEGO recently being voted 'Toy of the century' (www.lego.com). A powerful and instantly recognized global brand has been a key feature of this success. LEGO has worked hard to establish this brand through a number of routes. The group organizes its business into four main categories: the core business of play materials, family attractions, lifestyle products and media. In each of these categories the brand is clearly and consistently applied. At the heart of LEGO's business are its play materials. Here the LEGO brands feature across a plethora of offerings. In order to cater for a target age range of 0 to 16 years, the company has split its offerings into nine different product programmes. These include LEGO PRIMO and LEGO DUPLO sets aimed at 0 to 5 year olds. The 4 to 9 year age range can enjoy, among others, LEGO BASIC and the ZNAP vehicle/monster transformation sets. Older LEGO customers can collect LEGO TECHNIC or investigate LEGO MINDSTORMS, a revolutionary new microchip-based system.

In the family attractions area of its business, LEGO has developed a number of theme parks in Denmark, the UK and the US. UK-based Legoland Windsor is typical. Here the LEGO brand is in evidence throughout the park, from the buildings and rides, which are enveloped in LEGO camouflage, to the recreation of famous landmarks in LEGO bricks and the retail outlets which provide the opportunity to test or buy the full range of LEGO products. Meanwhile LEGO Lifestyle, the third of LEGO's business categories, with its range of licensed children's wear, games, bed linen and cosmetics, also enhances the LEGO brand. The company's final business category, media, fosters LEGO's commitment to innovation and new ventures, with a range of software, videos, books and music.

LEGO's commitment to its brand does not end with the products on sale to customers. Recently the company has created an extensive website and online shop. Now consumers can do everything from the comfort of their own homes, from perusing the latest LEGO designs to purchasing theme park tickets.

From such case study analysis it is clear that the outcome of branding is beneficial to both parties. Brands allow the consumer to identify the product that best serves his/her psychological and physical needs. In addition, when an organization develops a brand, it is differentiating the supply and, through communication, is enhancing its position in the market(s). This, in turn, enables the business to gain consumers' loyalty.

The success of world-renowned toy manufacturer LEGO is linked both to physical brand attributes, such as the simple and distinctive basic LEGO brick, and to psychological aspects, such as the company's commitment to fostering creative imagination.

McDonald's and Burger King are paradigmatic examples of two companies operating in the same line of business, yet trying to transmit different identities. In this way, brands are turned into touchstones – powerful strategic assets which aid organisational existence and survival. As the second example shows, for McDonald's the benefits can be measured by the speed of international expansion which the company has enjoyed.

McDonald's

The golden arches of McDonald's are a familiar sight to burger lovers around the world. This international giant competes by offering a fast, efficient service of good-value, quality food items through conveniently located restaurants. McDonald's uses its huge marketing budget to ensure that its brand is one of the most advertised and best known in the world. Throughout the world most consumers have seen an advertisement or billboard promoting the McDonald's brand. Many have also engaged in the McDonald's experience, visiting their local restaurant to enjoy a Big Mac, Quarter Pounder or fries. Whenever they encounter McDonald's, these consumers also come face to face with the brand: in and outside the restaurant, on burger wrappers, and on the packaging for fries, napkins and cups.

There are good reasons behind McDonald's efforts to establish its brand in consumers' minds. In particular, the strength of the brand has allowed the company to enjoy rapid international expansion, much of which is based on franchising, where McDonald's offers enthusiastic entrepreneurs the opportunity to own and run their own restaurants. Franchisees pay a fee either to lease or buy a new or existing McDonald's restaurant, which they then run. For McDonald's this helps to reduce capital outlay, while still ensuring the benefits of expansion. For the franchise holder, the power of the McDonald's brand provides the potential for a successful business venture. The company's successful record of franchising all over the world would not be possible without the brand to back it up.

Communication with external publics has played an important role in the development of the McDonald's brand. Traditionally, the branding literature was primarily concerned with how this external communication of the brand was handled. However, as organizational management becomes more challenging, a change is taking place in how branding is viewed. Instead of simply seeing the brand from an external angle, the concept is also being considered from an internal perspective (De Chernatony, 1999). The rationale is that it is insufficient to merely create position and communicate the brand. Instead, total consistency in branding is needed from the very outset of the production process to the marketing of the final product/service.

In the literature there is general agreement on the need to embed the 'brand spirit' in all company activities (Rubinstein, 1996). Staff and employees now have a major role in this process as important players in conveying the brand message, i.e. they become part of the brand reality. For example, one of Virgin's branding foundations is the way the company handles and motivates people (Macrae, 1999). This approach emerges naturally from how the organization operates, and helps the business to develop a coherent product and service delivery. In some circumstances the brands that are created are a source of vital strength and competitive advantage. However, in order to achieve this aim, branding needs to be more than just a marketing activity. Indeed, as the brand orientation and total brand management concepts suggest, the branding perspective is shifting towards a business philosophy in which the entire organization is involved.

As these cases show, leading brands are responsive and react to environmental dynamics by focusing on their employees and the people in the company, creating value for customers and shareholders. In responding to environmental forces, Tiley (1999) also defends a total brand-management approach based on the total quality management concept, which consists of three elements: the embodiment of meaning, eloquent communication, and response to change. Tiley agrees with De Chernatony (1999) that the meaning of the brand should be embedded in all actions of the company. In contrast to Porter's (1985) value-chain approach, which locates sales and marketing at the end of the chain, Tiley (1999) argues that in order to create value, the brand must be evident at every stage in the chain, from the processing of raw materials to the final product. Communication, which follows on from the brand-building process, must be coherently and effectively transmitted wherever there is contact with the various publics. As Tiley (1999, p. 191) observes, 'We believe that branding alone is not enough. It can only deliver lasting value when the brand informs the configuration of the business. Brands which keep their promises keep their consumers.' This approach to total brand management is seen to be followed by brand leaders such as Nike and Coca-Cola.

The above examples are taken from Simoes and Dibb (2001).

Conclusion

Economic factors have dramatic effects on the attractiveness of a firm's products or services. Ecology is a business issue. Many natural resources are not renewable, so the rate of consumption becomes a major issue for a firm that is depending on a resource. Responsible stewardship of the environment is also a business issue. Firms are affected directly and indirectly by political/legal influences at all levels of government. For instance, fiscal policy can have dramatic impacts on the overall economic climate of the firm. The social climate in which business operates has systemic implications for firm success and the demand for goods and services. Social trends and fads have major implications for product/market choices. Major technological change has created new business opportunities. The use of robots in automobile manufacturing has led to different competitive advantages in production costs and product quality. Technological innovation is a key factor in success in many industries, and it must be monitored aggressively.

Today's intensive competition introduces a whole new set of competitive conditions, and the criteria for success are based on quality capability, speed, cost and innovation (to include product innovation and strategic planning). Managers should think carefully about brands from a strategic perspective. Faced with global competitors, brand managers must attack them at home and form strategic alliances. Strategic alliances formed with suppliers, distributors and even with former competitors are key to a firm's future competitive strength. Combining brand names through brand alliances will also increase consumer response. Designing products for global markets will be an important part of brand managers' activities. They must have flexible product designs that have options which can be added to a basic design that satisfies local requirements.

Deregulation has led to increased competition from traditionally defined product–market boundaries. The challenge for brand managers is to adapt proactively to market changes brought about by deregulation. Technological change will reduce the time required to develop, design, test and manufacture new products, while reducing costs and improving quality. Technology can be leveraged to gain competitive advantage. Market convergence can also blur the boundaries between product markets. The challenges to brand managers will be how to utilize skills from one product market into another; assembling and managing the skills of several partners in developing and marketing new products and services; managing joint promotions; and ensuring that partner brand strategies do not adversely affect their own brands.

To succeed in the future, brand managers must attract customers regularly and repeatedly with innovations that are consistent with brand values, but are at the same time surprising and enticing. Trend spotting will be important. So will developing customer loyalty by focusing on quality and price, which are consistently maintained for existing consumers. Sustainable growth and ethical commerce will be sources for strengthening the brand. Direct relationships with consumers will be important since brands will have to be much more evident at the contact point with customers and omnipresent. To gain competitive advantage, brand management must also have a sound internal environment and a sound company structure. Competitive branding is based on the whole company getting involved in brand-policy development. Employing 'cause' programmes strategically will also provide companies with valuable leadership and differentiation strategies, enhanced brand equity and credibility, greater reach, significant resources and relationships. These programmes will engage employees, customers, partners, community members and others in taking collaborative action on the issues most important to them and their communities. Finally, companies can take advantage of the new creative media which will enable personalized profiling and branding, and will have a great impact on the branding processes, brand associations, brand evolution, media learning value, societal change and co-creation between consumers and companies, thanks to its interactivity. However, the danger of new media is consumer empowerment: a brand can be made or broken overnight by Internet bloggers.

Key terms

Brand plan: mainly the brand vision (long term), brand mission (mid-term), market definition, situation analysis, brand objectives, change analysis (what will have to be done differently) and brand action plan.

Chinacosm: China's dominance of the world of manufacturing.

Competitive branding: focusing on the long-term benefits not the short-term profits, which involves the whole company getting involved in developing a brand policy. Also capitalizing on driver brands, building brands that can be sustained through innovation and working on brand–identity consistency.

Distributors' power and channels evolution: as the relationship between producers and distributors has intensified, the power of retailers has increased. Because of new forms of retailing such as warehouse stores and office product depots, the emergence of sophisticated information technologies and logistical support, manufacturers have lost much of the control they once held over the ways their brands are marketed through the distribution system. The rapid diffusion of electronic scanners has contributed to the shift in information power from manufacturers to retailers.

Globalization: companies operating in many international markets, and coming to be known as multinationals. Also refers to competition coming from multinationals.

Indiacosm: India's dominance of the world in high-tech industries.

Market convergence: blurred boundaries between product markets due to technological advances.

Market entry timing: it is known that speed is more important in harvesting the better customers and the early adopters who are willing to pay more.

Market fragmentation: differences in tastes and preferences because of cultural and economic diversity. This provides scope for differentiation.

Openness of markets: deregulation has led to increased competition from traditionally defined product–market boundaries. The challenge for brand managers is to adapt proactively to market changes brought about by deregulation.

Strategic alliances: formed by companies to share costs and risks, and also knowledge. This will stretch organizational capabilities and change the nature of brand management.

Technological change impact: computer-aided design, manufacturing, engineering, software engineering and associated approaches have dramatically reduced the time required to develop, design, test and manufacture new products, while reducing costs and improving quality. Information technology, when used with flexible manufacturing systems, can reduce order fulfilment cycles and inventory requirements. Technology can be leveraged to gain competitive advantage.

? Discussion questions

1 Using PEST (political, economic, social and technological) analysis, identify and analyse how these environmental forces affect an industrial brand.

2 What aspects of brand management will be most affected by technology changes? Discuss.

3 Discuss the meaning of market and media fragmentation and 'pluralism' in society. How do these affect brand management?

4 In what ways does strategic planning benefit brand management?

5 What is competitive branding?

6 Discuss Figure 10.1. How does this model apply to brand management?

7 How do cultural factors affect branding?

8 Can you explain what global, regional and local brand management is about? Discuss the branding decisions with regard to each of these three contexts.

9 What is strategic brand alliance? Discuss its advantages and disadvantages.

10 What does market convergence mean for a medium-sized company? How can the company take advantage of this to manage its brand effectively?

✎ Projects

1 Find out from the academic management literature what the concept of total quality management (TQM) means; apply this to brand management. Write a report of approximately 500 words, addressed to your managing director and describing how you would apply TQM to brand management.

2 Research three new products which have recently being taken off the market. Reflect on the reasons why these innovations failed.

3 Extreme sports, online chat rooms, vegetarianism ... Can you predict what will be the next trend?

4 Corporate social responsibility is a major theme for modern businesses and is one of the bases of competitive branding. Go to your local grocery store and select five different ecological products. How are they presented in the store? Reflect on the way these products are regarded.

5 Keep a record of five to ten advertisements you see in posters, on television, etc. How often are environmental issues mentioned in these ads?

MINI CASE 10.1: IMPACT OF SUSTAINABLE DEVELOPMENT ON BRANDS

From Ford Motor Company to the City of New York, many organizations are concerned with implementing 'sustainable development' guidelines. Others are more worried about implementing 'real' business plans or restructuring into leaner, more efficient organizations. For these companies, it is business as usual until a costly crisis occurs and forces the changes upon them.

Around 2001, fast food and obesity started to be mentioned in the same breath. The US Surgeon General then reported that obesity could be linked to some 300 000 deaths and US$117 billion in healthcare costs annually. While many factors, such as genes and lack of exercise, can contribute to excessive weight gain, a gigantic disaster may reasonably be looming over the $110 billion industry. As this could badly hurt profits and brand equity, hamburger restaurants such as

McDonald's and Wendy's have been refocusing their marketing strategies on healthier dishes and lifestyles.

The perfect storm could still unfold, however. The latest sign of it is the speed at which Hardee's Monster Thickburger has become the centre of a crisis. Just a day after Monster's roll-out, the gargantuan burger was already joke material on American late night shows, and was promptly commented on in countries as far afield as Britain, France, Spain, Australia and Japan. 'A Monster on your plate! To hell with the health risks of unbridled obesity,' exclaimed an article in Canada (where Hardee's burger is not sold).

While its fast-food rivals have been busily polishing their image in the public opinion, CKE, the parent of Hardee's, actually sees the media attention as a marketing benefit. Although this PR strategy might prove to be a terrific crisis-management spin, it is doubtful that bad taste will be a differentiation factor in a category called 'junk food'.

The impact of unsustainable development is not obvious for everyone as, by definition, it slowly affects the next generation over a long period of time. Yet, indicators are pointing to the fact that humankind is going to face major environmental challenges during the course of this century.

In our own businesses, there are reasons to be optimistic. If there is a downside to ugliness, there is only an upside for corporate and marketing strategies deploying sustainable business development principles, as sustainable development fits squarely into modern financial theories. Besides the communication effort of marketing, there is also an opportunity for investors' relations to leverage such a policy among its audience.

Questions:

1 Explain what sustainable development means. Give examples of best practice in sustainable development in companies.

2 Discuss the issues of sustainability and branding.

3 How does sustainability contribute to the branding 'triple' bottom line?

MINI CASE 10.2: FEED BRANDING – PODCASTS, RSS, RINGTONES AND DIGITAL RADIO

In 2004 GM used a podcast to help introduce its 2005 vehicle line-up. Microsoft soon followed suit; now dozens of companies use podcasts as part of their branding mix.

Such podcasts represent the first wave of an emerging trend called 'feed branding', which also includes RSS feeds, ringtones and digital radio. Podcasts are 'radio' programmes or other broadcasts uploaded to Apple's iPod and other MP3 players. Subscription-based RSS feeds relay updated content from news sites or blogs. About 10 to 15 per cent of such feeds now carry advertising, but that percentage will increase rapidly. Ringtones are customizable sounds on mobile phones. Digital radio uses satellites to transmit content-specific ads or even images to accompany disc jockeys or songs.

Podcasts can easily be created with the Garage Band software that comes with every Mac, which means that they are often as niche as a blog. But more sophisticated companies are developing broadcast-quality programmes on specialized topics, and sponsoring programmes with wide appeal, like soap opera sponsorships during radio's heyday and the earliest days of TV. A few even have advertising, comparable to 30-second radio commercials, usually at the beginning and end of the podcast.

Consumers can listen to podcasts at their convenience, which reduces distractions and increases receptivity. One disadvantage, however, is a lack of measurement. Because the podcasts are listened to away from the computer, real-time tracking is impossible. Podcasts have other branding applications as well. Since audiences can be away from a TV, PC or other equipment, podcasts will be used more frequently (and be more effective) than video cassettes and their descendants.

Business applications include supplying sales forces and prospects with product, usage or other information, establishing corporate communication networks for dispersed locations, facilitating knowledge capture, allowing meetings to be recorded and shared, and even providing guidance for new employees.

RSS feeds, available through numerous aggregators or advanced browsers like Firefox, eliminate the need to cruise favourite websites or blogs for updated information. Small firms that have experimented with RSS advertising have reported results that are 20 to 30 per cent better than with email ads, with CTRs hitting an impressive 10 per cent. Ring/ring-back tones, also known as audio or sonic branding, can also be considered part of feed branding. The Crazy Frog ringtones have already swept the UK and are a fast-emerging fad in the US.

Finally, digital radio is also threatening to rewrite some branding rules. In addition to offering cable-like access to hundreds of channels, digital radio lets listeners pause, rewind and time-record high-quality broadcasts. Additionally, relevant information such as artist and album information can be transmitted.

Question:

1 Explain how feed branding changes the world of communications, and how it benefits consumers.

END OF CHAPTER CASE STUDY: BRAND MANAGEMENT FOR THE NEXT MILLENNIUM

Source: Extract from Lippincott Mercer, James Bell, Senior Partner

When the big ball comes down in Times Square on 1 January, a lot of seemingly far-sighted company and product names, like 20th Century Fox, 20th Century Funds and Gateway 2000, will become anachronisms.

Aside from that, what will a new millennium mean in the world of branding? While we all secretly hope for a clean slate to more and more, larger organizations are managing and promoting their existing brand assets, rather than undertaking wholesale branding change and overhaul. Begin a new century, probably very little – except for a three-month media frenzy and a lot of expensive parties – will be different. In fact, some of the trends now emerging will take hold, especially in the area of brand management, naming, and graphic design. Here are some of our predictions.

Brand management: stay the course, matey

More and more, larger organizations are managing and promoting their existing brand assets, rather than undertaking wholesale branding change and overhaul. Companies that re-engineered, downsized and globalized in the late 1980s have begun to see the fruits of their labours: rapid international growth and soaring stock prices. Most of these companies have fairly well-established names, logotypes, and brand images – at least in their home market – that require at most minimal tinkering.

But growth and expansion can come with two bad side effects: brand fragmentation and dilution. Wider geographies, decentralized reporting structures, and acquisitions have put tremendous pressure on organizations trying to project a consistent and coherent image and identity around the world. With the proliferation of media channels, there are more and more 'reinterpretations' of the brand, many of which are based on a fundamental misunderstanding of the core brand definition and attributes. As a result, the visual elements such as signage, packaging and the overall marketing look and feel – along with naming practices – have begun to vary, then unravel.

Thankfully, far-sighted organizations have addressed this problem by establishing brand policies and guidelines, and instituting training and compliance programmes. Such programmes are not implemented by a dressed-up platoon of logo cops enforcing nuisance laws, but by committed senior management teams helping employees better understand the underlying value of managing a proven business asset. And these programmes usually support the communication of the brand's uniqueness and value proposition. Citibank and IBM are good examples of organizations which have set up the appropriate organizational structures, mechanisms and procedures for managing their brands in the 100 plus countries where they do business.

The explosion in company intranets has been beneficial in establishing and maintaining consistency and coherence in brand management. Many companies can now communicate with their far-flung employees directly, interactively and constructively, providing clear brand definitions and positioning platforms, naming and graphic guidelines, design templates, and other tools for managing their brand on an ongoing and global basis. With the brand (vs pure product) now a widely accepted and proven business asset, this is rarely an exercise of proselytizing to an empty auditorium.

Questions:

1 Identify the major environmental forces mentioned in the case study.

2 How do these external forces affect brand management for large companies in this case?

3 How does technology influence the company's internal and external environments?

4 What brand policies does the author refer to in this case study?

5 Identify the effects of globalization for companies in this case study.

6 Explain what brand fragmentation and dilution mean here.

References

Cone, C., Phares, L. and Gifford, C. (2001), 'Leveraging cause branding to effect social change: the convergence of cause branding and social marketing', *Social Marketing Quarterly*, Vol. 7, No. 3.

De Chernatony, L. (1999), 'Brand management through narrowing the gap between brand identity and brand reputation', *Journal of Marketing Management*, Vol. 15, No. 1–3, pp. 157–79.

Drejer, A., Olesen, F. and Standskov, J. (2005), 'Strategic scanning in a new competitive landscape: towards a learning approach', *International Journal of Innovation and Learning*, Vol. 2, No. 1, pp. 47–64.

Heracleous, L. (1998), 'Strategic thinking or strategic planning?', *Long Range Planning*, Vol. 31, No. 3, pp. 481–87.

Macrae, C. (1999), 'Brand reality editorial', *Journal of Marketing Management*, Vol. 15, No. 1–3, pp. 1–24.

Porter, M. E. (1985), *Competitive Advantage: Creating and Sustaining Superior Performance*, New York: The Free Press.

Porter, M. E. (1990), *The Competitive Advantage of Nations*, New York: The Free Press.

Power, D. 'General external environmental analysis', at http://planningskills.com/passwordzone/lecturenotes/unit5.html.

Rubinstein, H. (1996), 'Brand first management', *Journal of Marketing Management*, Vol. 12, No. 4, pp. 269–80.

Schocker, A., Srivastava, R. K. and Ruekert, R. W. (1994), 'Challenges and opportunities facing brand management: an introduction to the special issue', *Journal of Marketing Research*, Vol. 31, pp. 149–58.

Simões, C. and Dibb, S. (2003), 'Rethinking the brand concept – new brand orientation', *Corporate Communications: An International Journal*, Vol. 6, No. 4, pp. 217–24.

Stahl, M. J. and Grigsby, D. W. (1992), *Strategic Management for Decision Making*, PWS Kent Publishing Company.

Tiley, C. (1999), 'Built-in branding: how to engineer a leadership brand', *Journal of Marketing Management*, Vol. 15, No. 1–3, pp. 181–91.

Walton, P. (1999), 'Marketing rivalry in an age of hyper-competition', *Market Leader*, No. 4, Spring.

World Advertising Research Center (WARC), at www.warc.com.

Further reading and online sites

Corcoran, I. (2007), *The Art of Digital Branding*, US: Allworth Communications, Inc.

Cova, B. and Pace, S. (2006), 'Brand community of convenience products: new forms of customer empowerment – the case "My Nutella The Community"', *European Journal of Marketing*, Vol. 40, No. 9/10, pp. 1087–105.

Hastings, G., *Social Marketing: Why should the Devil have all the Best Tunes? The Potential: Why Should the Devil Have All the Best Tunes?*, Oxford: Butterworth-Heinemann.

Marketing Profs (2005), 'How does new media impact on brand strategy', at www.marketingprofs.com/ea/qst_question.asp?qstid=10088.

Media; culture, graphical at http://www.ilo.org/public/english/dialogue/sector/sectors/media.html.

Nair, B. (2004), 'Corporate branding in a competitive international environment', at http://www. brandchannel.com/papers_review.asp?sp_id=606.

Parsons, P. J. (2007), 'Integrating ethics with strategy: analyzing disease-branding', *Corporate Communications: An International Journal*, Vol. 12, No. 3, pp. 267–79.

Rodrigue, C. S. and Biswas, A. (2004), 'Brand alliance dependency and exclusivity: an empirical investigation', *Journal of Product & Brand Management*, Vol. 13, No. 7.

Chapter contents

Chapter overview

According to practitioners, today there are few brands that consumers must have in their shopping basket. Consumer studies further showed that brand switching is high in fmcg. Previously, national brands (or manufacturer brands) used to control distribution channels, and store brands (or retail brands) used to be perceived as cheap and of low quality. The proliferation of me-too products in the marketplace has undermined national brands' ability to innovate even further. Few brands are perceived as giving real value to the consumer, either functional or symbolic. There is also a lot more choice on offer and shopping behaviour has changed. The shopper is less involved with the product and more economical with time. They want to be able to find the brand they want there and then, and shopping decisions are often made in store. They are also easily bored. Thousands of products are launched a year per company, whether it is merely an update or a completely new product just to maintain brand loyalty. This is the dilemma facing many national or manufacturer brands.

The changing nature of competition is reflected in the power passing to the retailer, who can produce in bulk, is able to keep costs low and therefore can dictate price. As well as providing more choice, the retailer need no longer be known for producing for the low end of the market.

As part of the theme of competing in the new business environment, Chapter 10 examined new environmental pressures and the challenges of modern markets impacting on branding. This chapter discusses competition from own-label or retail (or store) brands, by examining the growth and changing nature of retail brands; why retailers have a retail brand and how retail brands grow in the long term. It examines the building of a retail business and retail brand, discusses retail brand extensions and looks at the impact of retailer brands on consumer choice. It analyses the competition between manufacturers and retailers – how manufacturers can overcome low-cost competition from retailers and defend against own-label imitations. Chapter 12 will focus on packaging design and branding for the consumer.

❖ LEARNING OBJECTIVES

After completing this chapter, you should be able to

❖ Explain what a retail or store brand is

❖ Examine and discuss the differences between a retail brand and a manufacturer or national brand, in terms of their strengths and weaknesses

❖ Discuss the issues with retail brand extension from the consumer's and company's perspectives

❖ Examine the benefits of retail brands in a business sense

❖ Examine how a store brand is built, sustained and grown

❖ Examine and discuss the reciprocal effects between store brands and store image

❖ Examine the key opportunities and threats facing retailers

❖ Discuss the nature of competition between manufacturers and retailers

❖ Discuss the impact of store brands on consumer choice

❖ Discuss the strategies to overcome own-label, low-cost competition and imitation

Introduction

In the days when national brands (or manufacturer brands) used to control distribution channels, store brands (or retail brands) used to be perceived as cheap and of low quality. Now, however the proliferation of me-too products in the marketplace has undermined the national brand's ability to innovate further. Few brands are perceived as giving real value to the consumer. Furthermore, consumer studies have shown that brand switching is high in fmcg. There is also a lot more choice on offer and shopping behaviour has changed. Shoppers are less involved with the product and more economical with their time. They want to be able to find the brand they want whenever and wherever they want, and shopping decisions are often made in the store. They are also easily bored. Thousands of products are launched by any one company each year, whether it is an updated version or a completely new product, merely to maintain brand loyalty. This is the dilemma facing many national or manufacturer brands.

Since the late 1980s/early 1990s, store brands have been set to dominate national brands, particularly in the UK and in the supply chain. The changing nature of competition has shifted decisively in the retailer's favour in terms of cost and quality control, physical distribution, management of shelf space, technological advances and innovation. Furthermore, retailers have also begun implementing differentiation and repositioning strategies by promoting themselves across a wider range of product categories and higher-quality products at competitive prices (Burt, 2000; Veloutsou et al., 2002) since the mid-1990s. Retailers have adopted more product lines and in virtually every product class (Burt, 2000). For instance, Sainsbury's offers 8000 store brand lines. The question regarding the extent to which retailers can extend into new unrelated product categories under their store brand has been raised, because retail brand extension carries huge risks with thousands of products appearing under an umbrella brand name (see Chapter 6). However, a retail brand does bring many benefits to the retailer, such as bargaining power, locked-away profit and many more, provided that the retail brand is built around a successful retail business in the first place. These are among the issues that this chapter will examine, together with opportunities presented to store brands and the threats facing them.

Just like any other brands, retail brands need to be built to last. This chapter will look at how a retail brand can be sustained and grown, not forgetting the issue of retail brand versus manufacturer brand. The competition between these two is examined in more detail. The chapter also examines the strategies manufacturer brands could use to fight off own-label competition. The consumer perspective is also explored, as is how this impacts on choice.

The growth and changing nature of retail brands

Before the end of World War II the manufacturer's brand dominated the market scene, with the retailer wholly dependent on the manufacturer's brand and branding support to get customers through the door. After the end of the war the pattern began to change, with a shift in retail power following the introduction of the retailer's own-label. It started with Sainsbury's and Marks & Spencer, who used their own labels for 70, 80 or 100 per cent of their sales. Marks & Spencer used the St Michael label 100 per cent and Sainsbury's had sales of 70 to 80 per cent of its own labels before slipping back to 56 per cent in 1987. Over the whole retail spectrum, own-labels were steadily increasing market share from 22 per cent in 1980 to 27 per cent in 1990. This rise was helped by the inroads made by own-labels in the fast-growing multiple grocers sector in 1985. By the mid-1980s, five grocery chains held half (by value) of the whole grocery trade, with about 60 per cent in the hands of three – Sainsbury's, Tesco and Asda – by the 1990s (*The Economist*, 1993).

Own-labels rose in commodity items such as baked beans and pet foods. In the US and Spain own-labels were the first to have products like cigarettes and detergents. Own-label products account for more than 20 per cent in some European supermarkets in France and Switzerland (*The Economist*, 1993), even though France is known to be more branded than Britain, for instance. The

French own-labels have less power than the British ones. In the UK own-label tends to dominate chilled, frozen foods and ready meals – where it has two-thirds of market share, while the manufacturer brand dominates the snack, confectionery and cereals sectors.

The recession of the early 1990s gave retailers a competitive edge over the manufacturer and reinforced their position in the marketplace. The retailer was seen as a price-cutting hero, challenging American imports. Having achieved a sizeable market share in the value sector, own-label evolved to offer consumers a range of differently priced sub-brands encompassing 'value', 'organic', 'healthy', 'vegetarian', 'premium', 'child-friendly' and 'allergenic' products. Tesco's Finest and Sainsbury's Taste the Difference brands reflect retailer confidence that own-label can deliver premium as well as average value (Rani and Velayudhan 2008). The premium trend begun with food is now moving into non-food categories like clothing and homeware, and in many sectors in almost in all industries, such as furniture, automobile equipment, agricultural cooperatives and pharmaceuticals (also see 'Issues with retail brand extension', below). This steady growth is the result of a shift in control in favour of the retailer. The retailing industry enjoys low costs, high-quality products, better physical distribution and management of shelf space than its counterparts. The retail sector's technological advances and innovation are as substantial as the manufacturer's. So, will the growth of own-label restrict consumer choice? Let's look at the driving forces.

The driving forces

- *Retailer competitiveness.* Competition shifts in the retailer's favour in terms of cost and quality control, physical distribution, management of shelf space, technological advances and innovation. The retailer enjoys low costs and more high-quality products.

- *Cost and quality control.* Since retailers are able to promote in bulk, they can achieve economies of scale. They can produce cheaply in their turn, and are able to provide customers with good-value products, while still being able to achieve higher profit margins compared with the smaller manufacturers. They have been able to keep costs low and therefore to dictate price.

- *Physical distribution.* Unlike the manufacturer who needs the retailer to get his products through to the consumers, the retailer can get his products direct to the consumer through his own distribution channel. The retailer manages his shelf space effectively with the use of EPOS, which can provide the retailer with invaluable information to meet the customer's needs and demands for particular products, thus enabling him to organize his shelf space effectively.

- *Technological advances.* Retailers use EPOS or just-in-time (JIT) to cut the time it takes to get dry groceries from the manufacturer to customers from 104 days to 61 days by linking suppliers and using computers to compete with the giant discounters. There is also electronic data interchange (EDI), which is a system that sends the data captured at store level directly to the supplier. EDI enables JIT ordering, speeding up stock turnarounds, and creating close partnerships between retailers and suppliers as companies share trading data for mutual benefit (Cox and Brittain, 2004). EDI also helps the development of efficient customer response. In addition, retailers will continue to increase their competitiveness and lower operating costs by outsourcing non-core activities such as IT and facilities management, as well as using systematic intelligence in merchandising, store operations and supply-chain management to customer management and marketing. Thus, they can apply advanced analytics to achieve substantial gains in productivity and revenue growth. Zara has a fast-renew stock system. Virtual and online shopping are other areas of retail technology. With virtual shopping, users wear headsets and hold handsets to get products from the shelves as they move through the store. The products reappear in a shopping basket at the virtual checkout. Such systems are being developed by Sainsbury's. There are a number of advantages with this. For the consumer, time is saved; and for retailers, they could do without expensive outlets. Online shopping through the World Wide Web enables buyers to identify best prices, but it will not replace outlets completely, because many consumers will still want to shop in conventional environments.

■ *Innovation.* The retailer's ability to innovate is as substantial as and comparable to the manufacturer's. Sainsbury's own food development department is the biggest in the country, and it was the first to introduce products like high-price squash, vitamin-fortified milk and vacuum-packed grapefruit. More grocers are also into biodegradable or recyclable products.

At the same time, consumers' perception of manufacturers' brands has changed. In the US, for instance, consumers were in favour of the retail brand or own-label. According to a study by DDB Needham, an American advertising agency, when consumers realized that own-labels' quality had improved, many did not return to national (or manufacturer) brands. The proportion of American consumers loyal to national brands fell from 64 per cent in 1985 to 57 per cent in 1992. In the UK consumers who were willing to pay more for particular product brands has also fallen sharply since the late 1980s. This was partly due to the economic recession, during which time there was an increase in customer loyalty to retail shops.

The promotion and support for brands is too high for many manufacturers. For example, Benson & Hedges spent £10 million on promotion for its King Size cigarette; Nestlé spent £7.5 million on Whiskas advertising, while Whitbread spent £6 million for Carling Black Label. However, in reality, some companies cut their advertising budgets and increased trade promotions instead. Others such as Frito-Lay, Borden and Procter & Gamble also reduced their product lines and deleted those brands that accounted for only 2 per cent of sales, such as Puritan cooking oil and White Cloud toilet paper, which were scrapped in the 1990s. Some manufacturers spent more on advertising cereals compared with canned fish, an area in which own-labels' penetration was high. Besides advertising costs, manufacturers have to spend a lot on overheads – 23 per cent of total costs.

The retailer also stocks far fewer national brands, forcing manufacturers to conduct huge promotions under the form of trade deals and coupons, deleting and slimming their product line, matching the retailer's price and plunging into own-label production. Tesco and other big supermarket chains prefer to have just two or three brands in a product line on the supermarket shelf plus their own-labels. This is otherwise known as the battle for shelf space (see the section on 'Competition between manufacturers and retailers', below).

Does the growth of retailer brands restrict consumer choice?

Will store brands cut out national brands altogether? Many food firms say retail brands tend to hit a natural ceiling when they have a share of between one-quarter and one-third of a market. Furthermore, leading brands are often protected from the retail brand's onslaught because second-line products absorb the initial attack.

Well-established national brands will bounce back: first, by cutting prices or simply not raising them; second, by introducing new products and staying abreast of technological change. Nowadays, however, more retailers can also afford to pay for R&D. Wrigley's chewing gum is an example of a strong brand and good management. Wrigley did not raise its price on its standard five-pack of gum between 1987 and 1993. It developed its own version of sugar-free gum and devoted 90 per cent of its marketing budget to advertising and 2 per cent to promotions. As another example of a manufacturer using scientific breakthrough to make cost-cutting less painful, Unilever developed a fat substitute for margarine, got rid of an expensive raw material and, at the same time, scored a marketing hit with its customers. Genuine innovations, not just mutations of existing products or incremental innovation, will help brands keep own-label rivals at bay.

At the same time, there is increased competition among retailers themselves. In the end, retail brands are brands like any other. In the past they have avoided (except for short intervals) direct competition with each other. The situation has changed, and is now similar to that between manufacturers.

There will also be competition within the retailer's product range. Retailers, too, can provide choice by using sub-brands (see Chapter 9 and the section on 'Issues with retail brand extension', below). Examples include Boots No 7 and 17 cosmetics ranges, and Sainsbury's Green Care range of washing and cleaning products. Because retailers can extend their product range more cheaply than some manufacturers, they can provide more choice within their product range. In fact, the retailer is now behaving more and more like the manufacturer.

Finally, international retailing competition coming from France, Germany, Sweden and Norway means that choice will not be restricted for consumers. In 2003 some top 30 food retailers extended their businesses into 85 different countries. The push factors for international retailing are: saturated home markets; fierce competition; and restrictive legislation which has pushed many large European food retailers into globalization mode, including British food retailers. The pull factors are: the falling barriers to market entry, e.g. the European Union and the North American Free Trade Area; Japanese stores spreading across Asia and Europe in the 1980s and 1990s; manufacturers of goods for retailers becoming more international themselves; the emergence of strategic retail alliances in the form of joint ventures among some European food retailers; and, finally, emerging markets and convergence in consumers' taste worldwide.

To conclude, choice will exist between national brands and retail brands, and between retail brands themselves as well as within retailers' product ranges.

Issues with retail brand extension

British grocery retailers have been pursuing brand extension into traditional and non-traditional product categories, offering ranges in virtually every product class. The broader the product categories offered to a wider array of consumers, the more total turnover will contribute to retailer growth. Furthermore, when faced with increased competition within a certain category, retailers may expand their category expenditure instead of trying to steal market share from the competing national brand. However, there remains the question of the extent to which retailers can expand into new product categories under their store brand. Extending own brand into non-food products is more complicated and is unlikely to result in a Tesco's bicycle. Nevertheless, in categories where price elasticity is low, retailers either develop their own sub-brands (see Chapter 6) or purchase/license established brands that have credibility in the category (Rani and Velayudhan, 2008). Retail finance is another sector that has been the target of large grocery retailers such as Tesco, Asda and Sainsbury's, because this market offers higher returns on capital and there were fewer providers in the past.

The topics of *cross-category success* and *demand variation* have been researched by a number of academics. For instance, DelVecchio (2001) suggests five essentials for success in new categories:

1 Category complexity.
2 Quality variance reflected in consumer perceptions and the extent to which the brands competing in a category differ in terms of quality.
3 Inter-purchase time, indicating the frequency of product usage.
4 The extent to which the product is used/consumed in a public/private situation.
5 Price level.

Other researchers also suggest the number of brands operating in the category and the retail outlet through which the category is sold.

A fundamental underlying characteristic of a brand extension is the extent to which the extension is 'similar to' or 'fits' the parent brand category. The success of brand extensions depends on the transfer of parent brand awareness and associations to the extension. A greater similarity of fit is reflected in more shared brand attributes between the core brand (or the parent brand) and the extension. In other words, the core brand is seen as relevant, and consumers assume that the quality of the extension is similar to the quality of the core product. It is also argued that consumer perception of the expertise of a company can be an important factor influencing evaluations of a product extension. 'Company expertise' describes the extent to which consumers believe that a company can deliver products and services that satisfy their needs and wants. This is critical because consumer reactions to a proposed extension can affect the positive perceptions of the core brand.

Perceptual risk is a concept used by consumer researchers to explain consumer perceptions of the uncertainty and adverse consequences of buying a product or service (Dowling and Staelin, 1994). Risk varies directly with the product type and the buying situation, whether online, door-to-door or in the store. There are six forms of risk: performance, financial, physical, time, social and psychological. With regard to store brands, fewer risk types are considered relevant or tested. In a model developed by Dowling and Staelin (1994) examining the effect of risk on the level of information, three main compositions were proposed: overall risk, category risk and acceptable risk. Other researchers also listed emotional, social and psychological risks, or functional, financial and social (e.g. DelVecchio, 2001; Narasimhan and Wilcox, 1988).

Perceptual risk affects category success – the likelihood of store brands succeeding in new product categories – and the fact that their growth has been highly uneven across product categories has gained significant attention among academics and the industry. According to the literature, the variation in the store brand market shares is essentially a result of individual category differences. It has been shown that store brand buying increases when overall risk perception declines, and that effect will be magnified as category quality variance increases.

Consumers would also buy more store brands if the category has higher customer experience than search characteristics. Store brands are predicted to succeed in categories that are not complex and show relatively little variance in functional quality across the competing brands. It has also been observed that the less likelihood in the consumer's view there is of some retailers being able to produce a specific product, the more likely it is that the consumer will develop a negative attitude towards such a product under the retailer's store brand.

Similarly, it has been shown that public usage of a product reduces store brand purchase because of its the lack of 'symbolic' quality. Furthermore, when quality variance within a product category is high, it is likely that consumers will choose manufacturer brands over store brands to reduce the financial risks associated with that purchase.

Laforet (2007) further advances the subject by examining consumer fit perception, risks and trust in retail brand extension in financial services for three top British supermarkets. The author found that, when consumers know and are loyal to the store, they tend to trust the store brand extension. Whereas, when consumers do not know the store or are new to it, the questions of fit and risk arise. The findings show that fit and risk perceptions are associated with non-loyal, non-using, non-aware and non-intending-to-buy customers; whereas brand trust is perceived in brand extension among customers who are loyal store users, aware and intending to buy. Gender, age and income also influence fit, risks and trust perception. Men are more concerned with lifestyles and image, and have less confidence in the store's expertise in financial services than women. Older consumers and low-income groups are more concerned with product performance and financial risks than younger consumers and the higher-income groups.

These findings have several implications:

■ In brand extension, when the company or brand is known to the consumer, trust is transferred from the parent brand to the extended product, whereas when the company or brand is unknown to the consumer, fit and risks are perceived. This is consistent with Reast's (2005) findings, that brand trust is an important concept in brand extension and that it is related to brand extension acceptance. Laforet also suggests that a company's existing customers are more likely to accept and try the company's brand extension than are new customers.

■ The stronger the corporate brand, the higher the chance of consumer brand extension acceptance. The reverse applies for weaker corporate brands. This is consistent with research that suggests a corporate brand must be strong in order to gain product association benefits (Nelson, 2002). There were those too who found trust correlated with the size and the power of the firm – the larger being more trusted (Young and Wilkinson, 1989).

■ These have implications in terms of brand extension decision-making and implementation.

Why should retailers have a retail brand?

Locked-away profit

It has been argued that own brands allow retailers to capture part of the profit locked away by double marginalization when manufacturers use simple linear pricing. It has been shown that a retailer that is faced with a take-it-or-leave-it offer from a monopolistic manufacturer can retain some surplus by offering a store brand to consumers. Retailers can also benefit from competing with a national brand by introducing premium store brands whose quality matches or even exceeds that of national brands. Similarly, own brands are seen as a lever in manufacturer contracting (see below).

Price discrimination

Store brands allow consumers a choice of price between the retailer and the manufacturer. Retailers can exploit price discrimination among consumers through national, store and fringe brands. Such discrimination may increase total channel profits, even if there are no cost differences to the retailer in selling these three types of brands. It has been argued that retailers may want to use a store brand to discriminate between heterogeneous consumers. In other words, depending on consumer tastes, the retailer will want to set prices that induce some consumers to self-select into each type of brand. If retailer price–cost margins are higher on store brands than on national brands, the retailer may have an additional incentive to carry a store brand beyond the price discrimination incentive (Morton and Zettelmeyer, 2004).

Marginal–average cost gap

The retailer can also take advantage of the marginal–average cost gap. The fact that national brands need advertising support implies that manufacturers have average costs that are usually substantially higher than their marginal costs of production. Since in the long run manufacturers will not supply their products below average cost, the gap between the marginal and average costs of national brand manufacturers allows retailers to achieve higher per unit profits selling a store brand than selling a national brand with similar marginal costs of production. Despite this, a retailer should not aim to substitute all store brands for national brands, because the retailer depends on national brands to serve consumers who derive utility from the brand associations created by advertising. However, it is likely that the larger the fixed cost associated with supporting a national brand, the more likely a retailer is to carry a store brand (Morton and Zettelmeyer, 2004).

Economies of scale

The larger the revenues in a category, the more likely it is that a retailer will carry a store brand because of economies of scale.

Bargaining power

It has been suggested that another reason for retailers carrying store brands is the benefit of bargaining with manufacturers in a category. In other words, retailers can use store brands as part of a strategy for negotiating with manufacturers. The retailer can position the store brand to mimic the leading national brand. By improving the retailer's disagreement pay-off, the store brand decreases the incremental contribution of the leading national brand to category profits, thus allowing the retailer to improve its supply terms with the manufacturer. These terms could involve promoting sales of the store brand.

The building of a retail business and a retail brand

Building a retail business

From a strategist angle, there are three main types of strategies for a retail business:

1 Growth strategies, which require the adoption of an expansion plan that is aimed at increasing market share and profitability. This is partly determined by the economic cycle and by competitors. It is a popular approach with shareholders, management groups, suppliers and stakeholders.

2 Recovery strategies are the result of the economic cycle, which goes up and down. Companies often try to turn a loss-making business round or to retrench, by divesting non-performing parts of their business.

3 Sell-off or liquidation requires an 'exit' strategy. This happens when businesses are so badly affected by competition and economic recession that they are sold off completely (Cox and Brittain, 2004).

The value chain

The value chain describes areas where a company's critical success factors lie. In other words, it constitutes a firm's competencies which, according to Porter (1985), will give the company a competitive advantage over competitors. There are sets of activities a firm can employ to create value, resulting in increased profitability for the firm. These activities are: logistics, operations, marketing and sales, services, procurement, technology development, human resource management and firm infrastructure.

Retail strategies

Growth strategies refer to:

■ *Penetration*: the retailer aggressively seeks to increase market share. For example, Asda has won its share of the market against Tesco, Sainsbury's and smaller grocers such as the Co-op.

■ *Merchandise development*: adding new merchandise to appeal to customers and thus to increase sales. This strategy is pursued by many large retailers today, including Tesco, Asda and Sainsbury's. These retailers have moved from food retailing to clothes and now to financial services.

■ *Market development*: geographical expansion into new or existing areas, such as overseas.

■ *Diversification*: the retailer will offer new merchandise for new target customers. It is the most expensive and riskiest option, but it can bring big rewards.

Integration is another strategy retailers can adopt. Here, the retailer will seek to minimize channel conflict through the ownership of channel members via mergers and acquisitions. *Selectivity* strategy is a result of pulling out of some geographical areas and cutting down on the merchandise range to meet the needs of a more defined target market. *Productivity* is a strategy that concentrates on improving productivity with the same or fewer resources. The 80/20 rule is the aim – 80 per cent of the profit is generated from 20 per cent of the merchandise on offer.

In *developing overseas markets* there is no single formula, no best type of store and no best ownership structure. Flexibility and timing are key success factors. Flexibility during implementation is essential when selecting the store format and entry mode that best fit the company and external circumstances (Global Retail Development Index, 2003). Global retailers often use a combination of store format to limit risks – for example, hypermarket and supermarket or supermarket and discount. This depends on the retailer and region. Tesco favoured a mix of hypermarket and supermarket when entering eastern Europe. In Asia, Carrefour uses hypermarkets and discount stores. In Thailand, Tesco entered with hypermarkets, then convenience stores, and now plans to expand with a supermarket format. Ownership also varies in regions and in the implementation phase. In Malaysia, Tesco formed a joint venture with Malaysian conglomerate Sime Darby Berhad. In Turkey, it acquired 84 per cent of Turkish retailer Kipa's business (Global Retail Development Index, 2003).

The timing of the entry into a country is critical, as is the time a retailer takes to get operations up and running. For example, Sainsbury's attempted to enter Egypt in 1999, but was forced to leave in 2001 after rapid expansion. French Auchan had a similar experience as Sainbury's in Malaysia. It was forced to withdraw in 2001. Timing depends on a number of factors, such as the retailer's strategy, its capabilities, size and the competitive situation in the foreign market.

Generally, retailers have three options: quick expansion, an escalator method in which retailers alternate between periods of growth, and stable states or wait and see (Figure 11.1). For example, in 2001, French Carrefour took a wait-and-see attitude when entering Russia and China. It planned to develop a retail base through acquisition. Other retailers took different approaches – for example, Dutch Ahold quickly opened stores in the Czech Republic to take first-mover advantage, while Wal-Mart preferred the escalator approach (Global Retail Development Index, 2003). Although each retailer uses a different entry mode, all selected their overseas target markets, managed their time and were flexible in revising their strategies to exploit successes or mitigate failure.

In the quest to deliver greater value to customers and to respond to the threat from the major stores, *partnerships* have become popular in the retail industry. Many supermarkets have expanded the array of products and services offered on site by co-locating with banks, pharmacies and restaurants. Retailers also seek partners in areas traditionally considered core, such as data analysis, merchandise management and credit services. For example, Tesco and Kroger both work with dunnhumby, a firm specializing in the analysis of shopper transaction data and management

Best expansion model		Time to break even	
Fast expansion	80%	> 12 months	10%
Slow expansion	20%	12 to 18 months	70%
Wait and see	0	< 18 months	20%
Years to reach positive ROI		**Key success factors**	
> 4 years	10%	Adapted concept	60%
4 to 5 years	70%	Entry model	58%
5 to 10 years	20%	Critical size	40%
		Real estate	40%
		Human resources	20%
		Innovation	20%
		Readiness	20%
		Key performance indicators	10%
		Branding	10%
		Competitive knowledge	10%
		Timing	10%
		Flexibility	10%

Source: based on Kearney (2003)

FIGURE 11.1 Summary of interview findings

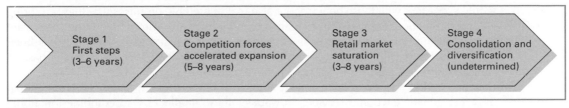

FIGURE 11.2 Stages of maturity for modern food retail markets

of loyalty programmes. Industry relationships will continue to grow and become more diverse and complex, making effective alliance management a strategically important competency (IBM Consulting, 2004).

Developing profitable new growth strategies

Profitable growth is the mission of every retailer, but it has become increasingly difficult to achieve. This is because many retailers overextend their businesses, often leading to uncontrolled growth and unsustainable results. Competition is also at its peak between retailers and manufacturers, among retailers themselves and with other more dynamic sectors such as travel, leisure, entertainment, healthcare, financial services and telecommunications. The product life cycle is further shortened and accelerates maturity leading to saturated retail markets. One way to reinvigorate the growth cycle is by getting more out of existing geography, outlets, inventory, customers and brands as well as through innovation, all of which encourage retailers to look for new ways to increase sales and profits. Second, growth can be enhanced not only through increased economies of scale but also using other advantages of scale such as market presence, product development capabilities and marketing. Third, instead of competing with fast-growing service sectors, retailers can create opportunities for themselves by redefining their businesses. For this, retailers will require changes in all areas of culture, operations, strategy and finance. The retailers who develop the capabilities to manage product and customer profitability will have the earnings to support future investment and growth, while those who focus on sales growth through geographic expansion alone will not succeed.

There are three strategies retailers must adopt to maximize profits:

1 Expand into new markets. Once these markets are saturated with outlets, retailers can sustain their earnings growth by improving the mix of products they sell, which leads to **2**.

2 Improve product selection by eliminating unprofitable products and managing product offerings. Retailers must pull unprofitable products from the shelves and avoid high-volume but low-profit customer segments.

3 Increase customer value by improving long-term relationships with customers, which requires knowing everything, from the customer base segments that are profitable down to individual names and what will make those customers interested in the retailers' offers. This is similar to relationship marketing or customer-relationship management (CRM). Retailers must also understand which customers are the most valuable to them, and what and why they buy. This allows retailers to increase the total economic profit contribution of the customer base through the use of point-of-sale data to capture purchasing information. This information will allow retailers to forecast purchase patterns and thus increase profitability and value over the lifetime of the customer relationship (Werner et al., 2004).

Building retail brands through powerful personality and emotional benefits

The building of a brand starts by defining the target customer group and its needs/expectations, and assessing how well the brand currently meets these. Next, the retailer must decide which of the benefits it can offer that will give the brand a distinctive position in the marketplace. Then, the retailer's marketing and advertising efforts should focus on creating an image around the brand that is not only consistent with these benefits, but also makes credible promises that they will bring excitement and satisfaction. Retailers must create a brand personality with which consumers want to identify, and rethink the underlying business system that is needed to deliver it. It has been shown that consumers make more frequent visits, check out larger-than-average shopping baskets or pay price premiums at the stores of brands they perceive as strong.

Traditionally, multi-category retailers have sought distinctiveness through such functional features as price, convenience and service. Nowadays, these retailers try to combine functional benefits with the emotional and relationship benefits that give a brand a true personality in the eyes of consumers. For example, Marks & Spencer's 'Your Marks & Spencer', or Boots' 'Ideas for life' and Tesco's 'Every little helps' illustrate how retailers seek to build brands around the emotional benefits of grocery shopping, combining functional benefits such as convenience, assortment and delivery services with speciality products, high-quality prepared meals and an extensive assortment of fine wines.

In reality, the consumer marketplace is also polarizing (see Table 11.1 and Branding Brief 11.2). Homogeneous markets no longer exist. On the one hand, customers seek low cost for basic goods with low emotional investment, and mega-players capture market share by delivering good value at very low prices, while on the other, customers seek greater personal value when purchasing goods with high emotional importance. As a consequence, differentiated specialists build profitable niches by delivering relevant value to targeted groups of customers. This has implications for retail branding strategies, one of which is to develop a focused distinctive brand proposition, as is discussed throughout this chapter.

Customer type	Business scope	
	Fragmented, local, disengaged	Consolidated, global, integrated
Proactive customers driven by highly personalized value systems and strong desire for authenticity	Emphasis on local flavours; thriving regional and local players; high level of innovation in products, channels, services; resurgence of intermediaries	
Individualistic super-shoppers armed with ubiquitous information access		Integrated, global supply chains; widespread failure of mid-tier retailers and brands that fail to differentiate
Homogeneous – customer focus on personal relationships and privacy. Extremely localized and gated shopping behaviours	Highly fragmented competition with no truly dominant players	
Passive – customers unaware of and uninterested in choice		Sameness sells; 70% global market share held by mega-scale competitors; generic mass-market offerings; traditional shopping channels; small niche players

Source: based on IBM Institute for Business Value analysis (2004)

TABLE 11.1 Alternative future scenarios

Branding Brief 11.1: Tesco's brand success story

Source: based on Meera Mullick-Kanwar, 'The evolution of private label branding', at Brandchannel.com, 2004

Tesco, Sainsbury's nearest rival, had been developing its offer using a different tack: carefully segmented, private-label echelons and ranges. Tesco has a value selection for cheaper commodities categories. Yet, this value brand was not manifested as the generic, store brand of the past. The critical point of difference with these products is that they are defined less by which manufacturer gave the retailer an opportunity in a certain product category, and more by what a working-class family on a tight budget would need to get by.

Concurrently, Tesco created an organics line, a kids' line and, perhaps most impressively, the Tesco Finest sub-brand. Tesco Finest started in ready meals and chilled foods, where the retailer has a natural advantage (these products are difficult to prepare and distribute). Integral to its success was its very high premium-ness. The exceptional price and quality were well received by the higher-end consumer. It was also evident that Tesco Finest was an encompassing proposition and could stretch into other categories. But rather than trying to rule the world, Tesco selectively ventured into those specific areas where it could add value.

High-end cookie tins, which are popular Christmas gifts, are a good example. Tesco was smart to recognize that manufacturers were struggling to add value in this seasonal, yet, premium playing field because branded products deemed suitable for everyday consumption dominated the category. Tesco Finest was able to compete here because, as a brand, it had more permission to extend into the premium sector. In view of that, its Tesco Finest cookie ranges have been a big success.

Underpinning Tesco's winning private-label strategy was spectacular packaging design across the entire range. For instance, Tesco Finest packaging was in silver boxes that were very premium looking, with first-rate product photography. There was also a section of the aisle dedicated to the range. It was well marketed and supported from start to finish.

Of course, Tesco was not baking its own cookies. It was sourcing them from the very manufacturers with whom Sainsbury's was looking to compete. However, Tesco was offering to buy at wholesale those products that the branded manufacturers would struggle to sell.

Branding Brief 11.2: The future of shopping: customize everything

Source: by Sara Clemence, Portfolio.com, 16 March 2009

Chris Clark is not a trend-obsessed tween or the kind of guy who lives for designer sneakers. The 37-year-old Dallas attorney is that rare person who actually just wears his running shoes for running.

Yet over the past few years Clark has bought three pairs of kicks from Nike's NikeID program, carefully customizing everything from the laces to the soles to a label with his middle name – Inslee – emblazoned on it.

'Nike is what I've always worn,' Clark explains. 'But sometimes you find a shoe that fits great and the colours in the stores are awful. I still care about how they look.'

Bespoke products have always been available to anyone willing and able to pay the price, whether for an individually tailored suit or a customized car. In recent years, one of the big shifts in retail has been giving customers the ability to design their own versions of premium products – like wedding rings, pricey handbags and Nikes – at prices that are comparable to the regular versions.

Now, without most of us realizing it, we're on the cusp of another big change. Thanks to market demands and developments in technology, we're going to be living in a user-generated world, where everything we use can (and will) be customizable. It's already happening, in ways both obvious and not.

Kleenex now has a site that lets you design your own tissue boxes for $4.99. Want your initials on M&M's? That can be had too – though at the moment for a far higher price than the regular chocolates.

We have begun customizing other products daily without even realizing it, says Joe Pine, speaker, management adviser, and author of the seminal book *Mass Customization*. Consider Facebook and MySpace pages, for example, or the applications on our iPhones.

'We're training people to get used to getting exactly what they want,' he says. 'That creates a snowball effect and they're going to start demanding it from other companies.'

In the sneaker world, there may be no greater brand contrast to Nike, with its high-tech designs and superstar spokespeople, than Keds. While the top-of-the-line shoes that Nike sells are generally priced above $100, Keds' canvas sneakers retail for around $35.

Except, that is, for the custom versions, which became available through Keds Studio in August. The shoes, on which shoppers can print any colour, pattern or image, run at $60. And in the first three months of business, Keds had 80 000 customizations, though not all translated into purchases, especially given the economic slowdown.

Keds had wanted to play in the custom space for years, says Charlene Higgins-Crawford, the company's e-commerce director of merchandising and operations. 'It's taken us a while to figure out how to do it and to find a partner that had the technology.'

Keds Studio was in part made possible by the availability of very high-quality digital printers at a price that made the results affordable. Software developments let them give customers a good – and necessary – look at what they were buying. Partnering with Zazzle, a custom printing company that handles the whole process, means the completed shoes can be shipped within just two weeks.

'It's very important to be in the custom market,' Higgins-Crawford says. 'It's not going to grow your business like crazy, but desire to have exactly what you want in the way you want it is pretty significant with our target audience.'

The same holds true across the board, Pine says. 'There's been a huge trend towards commoditization, where consumers don't care about the product, they don't care who makes it, they don't care about the brand,' he says. 'They care about three things: price, price and price. That's Wal-Mart's raison d'être.'

In that kind of market, companies are turning to user customization to distinguish themselves. When Stan Davis coined the term 'mass customization' in 1987, it was an oxymoron, Pine says: 'When I wrote my book, I said in the subtitle that it was the new frontier. It went from oxymoron to new frontier to today, when it's an imperative.'

Today the challenge is getting the price of customization down. Tomorrow it might be a new form of information overload.

As Clark says of his experience with Nike: 'It actually was almost to the point of, do I really have to pick the colour of the thread? There are almost too many choices.'

Building a store image

Store image is another important element of retail brand building and can have an impact on customer loyalty. Store image is a complex combination of tangible and intangible, or functional and psychological attributes. More specifically, store image is derived from customer functional experience/learning and the psychological feeling/attitude of a store simultaneously. In addition, the formulation process of store image involves two basic subjects: the external world, such as location, appearance, merchandise and staff, and the consumer's subjective impressions of selected elements of that world, such as information considered, information interpreted, evaluated, integrated and inference.

Nine store attributes are: location, atmosphere, price, merchandise assortment, service, advertising, sales promotion, store brand and store name. *Location* is where a store is situated in a specific geographic area. Convenience is a major consideration of customers. This translates into ease of reaching the store location, parking availability and fast checkout (Sheth et al., 1999, p. 725). The environment is increasingly recognized as a factor that has a significant degree of influence on purchase. *Atmosphere* is the combination of the store's physical characteristics such as architecture, layout, signs and displays, colours, lighting, temperature, sounds and smells, which together create an image in the customer's mind. Atmosphere communicates information about the store's service, pricing and fashionability of merchandise. Salespeople are the most important factor as they can influence customer buying behaviour through their services. It has been found that service quality directly affects both customers' attitude and satisfaction. Furthermore, staff politeness, present ability, courteousness, pleasantness, availability of credible information, knowledgeablility about the merchandise, eagerness to help customers and trustworthiness are important as customers undertake specialized, complex or expensive shopping (Sheth et al., 1999, p. 725).

Strategic focus

Retail brand building calls for management attention across the entire business system. An example is Wal-Mart. Wal-Mart keeps the promises it makes to its customers by being the lowest everyday price retailer, by stocking national brands at low prices in a down-home service environment. To ensure that the goods offered at these prices are actually available in the store, the company has developed Retail Link, an information system that informs both suppliers and store managers of each product's inventory level, order status and location in the distribution system. The electronic sharing of data permits buyers and store managers to plan precisely how to meet demand in each store. The company's senior management takes part in a teleconference that focuses on the rapid correction of lapses in supply-chain product deliveries. Wal-Mart also assures a high level of service by offering performance-based incentives to employees at every level (Henderson and Mihas, 2000).

How retail brands grow long term

Growth stages

First stage: imitating the leading brand

In this first growth stage, the retailer will try to take market share from the manufacturer (or national) brand by allocating more shelf space to its own-labels and increasing the average price of some bigger manufacturer brands. Next, the retailer will imitate the national brand, typically copying the packaging and the packaging attributes such as colour, packaging shape, key designs, name, typography, etc. of the category leaders. In this way, the retailer hopes to confuse and lead inattentive consumers primarily into selecting its own brands instead of the major national brands. Customer loyalty can then be built after product trial, i.e. once consumers have tried and been convinced that own brands are as good as national brands.

Second stage: strategic differentiation, identity creation through creating powerful brand personality, emotional values and store positioning

In the second stage the retailer's aim is to capture market share from competitors. It will then focus on differentiating its products and creating an identity both for the store and store brands by emphasizing the intangible aspects of store brands such as brand personality and emotional values, as discussed above. It then positions its store so that it is no longer centred solely on price, but on other factors such as value added, and recyclable and retail concepts. The retailer at this stage will try to improve his store image (see above).

Creating a sustainable brand

For a retailer to survive and flourish in the future, he must create a genuine sustainable brand. Senior managers must make brand building an integral part of how they think about the business. Category management and brand management must work together to fuel the marketing strategy. Product and positioning points of difference will set own brand apart in the consumer's mind. A consumer-centric approach should be at the heart of own-brand development instead of the product-centric thinking of the past. Retailers need to understand the contribution and role of own brand within their business and within the consumer's life. Own brand, communication and expression should all be developed in accordance with this thinking. When own brands are appropriately created and steered, they can become successful just like national brands, by creating a connection with consumers, drawing them into a retail store but, more important, becoming an essential, experiential and indispensable lifestyle choice that they embrace for many years to come.

More specifically, to create a sustainable brand, retailers must concentrate on the following:

■ Category management, which consists of collaboration with manufacturers in understanding and deciding how to optimize the product lines and SKUs to develop the greatest degree of category interest and excitement for consumers.

■ Understanding salient consumer needs to develop own brand proposition accordingly, based on the functional and emotional benefits, as well as committing to offer consumers multiple options and varieties with distinct attributes, benefits and price points.

■ Leveraging and creating connection with consumers. Unlike national brands, own brands are exclusively available through a specific retailer and can often transcend specific product categories because they use a consumer focus instead of a product focus as their brand foundation. A successful own brand has the capacity to strike a chord with consumers in multiple-product categories. The exclusive brands may be the reason that consumers are initially drawn into the store, but once they are there, the retailer also has the opportunity to encourage them to spend more on impulse purchases, for instance.

■ Optimize and promote synergies of touchpoints through developing a store environment, merchandising, packaging and promotional mix. Appropriately coordinated, these can create a strong and consistent brand message.

■ Creating a balance between brand messages and portfolio offerings. Design themes can help the consumer navigate the breadth of the own-brand portfolio (see Chapter 6) and appreciate its depth of expertise in different areas of the store. For example, when shopping at a chemists, the consumer's buying decision pathway in the over-the-counter cough and cold-care category is quite distinct from his or her drivers in the food category.

■ Packaging design, nomenclature and product strategy can boost the retailer's vision of the own brand promise. Branding, packaging design and sub-branding initiatives are critical tools that help to visualize and verbalize what the own brand stands for, demonstrating its expertise and differentiating it from national brands in various product categories.

■ Product quality and innovation are also a necessary functional underpinning for own-brand offerings.

In addition, to avoid losing out to mega retailers on one side and focused specialists on the other, retailers must clearly differentiate themselves through a well-focused brand proposition. It is widely recognized among industry experts that the key for retailers is to build clear and distinctive brand positioning for such parts of the business as brands, formats and even departments in the most important areas for their target customers, and to regularly monitor how they and their competitors compare with one another. Consider the following brand propositions: mass value – Asda, Netto, Aldi, Wal-Mart, etc.; problem-solver – Ikea; Homebase (home improvement); Orange or

Vodafone (communications solutions); lifestyle – Selfridges, John Lewis; opportunist – Zara, Virgin Megastores.

Competition between manufacturers and retailers

One of the concerns arising from the continuing consolidation of the grocery sector is the increase in retailers' monopoly power and their ability to pressure suppliers for more favourable and sometimes unjustified terms and conditions. This problem can be reduced by maintaining a balanced customer portfolio, although this is unlikely. As a consequence, it is a very serious matter for suppliers where the brand portfolio is limited to retailers' own brands. This is because there are few brands that consumers must have and/or want to trade off, if they can find substitutes. Consumer studies show that brand switching is high in fmcg. Some manufacturers matched up retailer's price – for example, after letting the price of its cheese rise by 45 per cent above that of its own-label rivals, Kraft cut it by 8 per cent in 1992 and has since kept its price rises in line with inflation. Another example is France's BSN, which also cut its prices, but to compensate must have had to cut costs significantly. Other manufacturers were persuaded to produce for retailers. The reasons for this are: first, manufacturers can make use of excess capacity; second, greater economies of scale can be exploited with bigger production runs; third, better relationships with retailers can be built to cut out the smaller competitors. For example, United Biscuits as well as making McVitie's and other brands became a large supplier of store brands (or own-labels). Half of its biscuits market consists of own-labels or retail brands or store brands. The same is true of Heinz and Campbell. Campbell used to stick to areas in which it does not have a dominant brand (the pickle area, where it produces store brands), while Heinz became the largest producer of own-label soups in America after it lost its market supremacy with its Campbell brand.

In the future retailers will stock one, or at most two, manufacturer's lines, progressively delisting minor brands, but creating a mega-brand umbrella inviting niches for suppliers who can offer a different, specialized proposition. This will lead to huge promotions by manufacturers, which will come in two forms: trade deals offering grocers generous slotting fees and, in some cases, failure fees if the products do not sell; and special deals that allow supermarkets to buy batches of their products at less than list price for limited periods. Where the retailer gets fees, the consumer gets coupons. However, discounts on existing brands pose a danger, because these can appear as disguised subsidies that strengthen consumer belief that branded products are no different from own-labels.

Branding Brief 11.3: New code proposed for retailer–supplier deals

Source: Adapted from FoodandDrinkEurope.com

The rules that govern agreements between retailers and suppliers could be strengthened under a new proposal by the UK's Competition Commission (CC) to protect manufacturers and others from restrictive practices.

The order would extend the Groceries Supply Code of Practice (GSCOP) and aims to ensure that suppliers do not have unfair or unexpected costs imposed on them by retailers. It is in response to the CC's inquiry into UK groceries retailing last year, which concluded that measures were needed to address its concerns about relationships between retailers and their suppliers.

The CIAA, the EU food industry trade association, has also expressed concern over alleged abusive practices by retailers in their dealings with food manufacturers, who face direct competition from increased market share of retailers' own private-label products.

Furthermore, the European Commission has noted a number of ways in which retailers could act unfairly in their dealings with manufacturers. These include cartels, purchasing agreements between competing buyers, resale price maintenance, certification schemes, tying, and single branding.

The CIAA added other claims to the list, such as chronically late payments, long payment periods for suppliers, 'forced' discounts to meet buyers' targets, and 'forced' contributions to finance mergers and acquisitions.

The new code will prohibit retrospective changes to terms and conditions, and limit the extent to which suppliers are required to pay for listings, promotions, inaccurate forecasts or customer complaints.

It will also set out a clear procedure for resolving disputes and the requirement for retailers to provide reasonable notice and commercial justification before a supplier is de-listed.

The new code would be included in all retailers' contracts with their suppliers and provide a much clearer framework. By extending to code to include other retailers, it would ensure more suppliers benefit from this protection. The new code would include all retailers with groceries turnover in excess of £1 billion per year, which would mean about ten retailers in total.

Tesco appeal

Meanwhile the CC's recommendation for the inclusion of a 'competition test' in planning decisions on larger grocery stores to prevent their dominance in local areas has been successfully challenged by Tesco.

The appeal by the supermarket giant was upheld by the Competition Appeal Tribunal yesterday on the grounds that certain considerations about how the test would work and its costs and benefits should have been explored further in the report.

Overcoming low-cost competition from retailers and defending against own-labels' imitations

The brands that survive will be those that can price competitively, have better quality and designs, offer variety or have fashion appeal, or identify with the consumer and market consistently.

Price cutting is not always an easy option. Branded manufacturers often find it difficult to match own-brand prices. In order to cut prices, manufacturers have to cut costs dramatically. For example, in order to compete with Grand Met, Philip Morris cut 8 per cent of its workforce and trimmed operations worldwide over three years (*The Economist*, 1993). On the other hand, innovation or scientific breakthroughs are better than cost-cutting (see Unilever's example above, p. 295).

With the help of suppliers, the best food brands can also innovate in packaging and design to include biodegradable and recyclable packaging, which are popular among today's consumers. Similarly, creating good value attracts consumers and legitimizes a price premium. Added value is what many consumers look for in a brand. They want not bigger, but better, brands. Good brands have a history and that history is communicated through advertising time after time. National brand manufacturers should try to work on the intangibles and create a different value system from retailers' own brands, as well as trying to reconnect with consumers, i.e. by identifying with them or creating new dreams. These then need to be reinforced through constant promotions.

Too many companies have allowed themselves to focus on retailers and not on consumers. As a result, they have slashed advertising budgets and piled up trade promotions, as mentioned above. The resulting imbalance is unhealthy for the companies that did that. However, if food manufacturers spent a relatively high proportion of their sales on advertising, they would be less likely to see own brands make inroads into their market share; yet only a handful of companies, such as Coca-Cola, have actually spent more on advertising in recent years (*The Economist*, 1993).

Other strategies that national brand manufacturers might adopt in order to compete with retailer own brands include: partnerships with retailers, in which manufacturers produce for retailers or share market information (e.g. EDI); designing new distribution channels – for example, through tele-shopping and online shopping; mergers and acquisitions, as well as overseas expansion, are among other options.

Some food groups are spending more on acquisitions in domestic and foreign markets. Nestlé and Unilever had been buying steadily. In more than a decade they have between them spent more than $22 billion on acquisitions. Takeovers and mergers can sometimes be the only way for a company to win market share without indulging in a costly price war. They are also an easy way to acquire strong brands and to strengthen weak ones. Equally, economies of scale can often help large food groups to fend off own-brand threat. In international markets, unlike soap or cigarettes, global food brands are less common, except for such giants as Coca-Cola and Kellogg's that can easily slip across borders. Differences in culture, religion and taste make food one of the hardest products to sell internationally. Global brands often have to be tailored to suit local tastes. Through acquisitions, companies can build a network of local marketers. Without the management heritage of Nestlé or Unilever, other food manufacturers will find it difficult to build a global business (*The Economist*, 1993).

One prime target for overseas expansion is the emerging countries, especially eastern European ones. This is partly because this region is growing more than the global average, with regional output growth of more than 3 per cent, and partly because most of these countries will join the European Union by 2010 (Global Retail Development Index, 2003). Russia is reported to have the most potential among European markets, with inflation forecast at 16 per cent in 2003 as opposed to 84 per cent in 1998, and GDP growth of 4–5 per cent a year. It also has the largest food market in Europe, with a population of 143 million, and an increasing spending power (US$1041 annual income in 2003). In terms of economic and political reforms, Russia is now officially recognized as a market economy by the US and EU. Thus Russia has become stronger economically.

Defending against own-brand imitations and strategically managing brands to create and deliver good customer value will help manufacturers to overcome competition with own brands. There are a number of ways to defend against own-brand imitations:

- Through innovation and regular modifications to manufacturers' packaging and product characteristics. Manufacturers must also focus on the uniqueness of their brand signs and the individuality of their packaging and products in order to make them more recognizable to consumers.

- By focusing on strategic brand drivers in the company's brand portfolios and leveraging their heritage and positive attributes in new product categories (see 'Brand extension' and 'Brand portfolio management' in Chapters 6 and 7).

- Through positioning and branding the company in the supply chain. This requires manufacturers to shift marketing from a narrow departmental approach, positioning and selling product lines more broadly to include positioning and branding their organization in the supply chain (Knox, 2004). In marketing an organization, companies must consider four ways to do this: the company's overall reputation, its product/service performance, its products and customer portfolio and its networks (Knox, 2004).

Conclusion

Retail branding is a mix of activities ranging from the strategic management of the store brand and store image to detailed decision-making, involving product assortment planning. Retail brand management is now recognized as a more complex brand and product assortment process than before, when this used to be concentrated solely on the low-cost/quality nature of the retail brand. The benefits of having a retail brand are that it allows retailers to capture locked-away profit by double marginalization, while manufacturers use simple linear pricing. Retailers can exploit price discrimination among consumers through national, store and fringe brands, and between heterogeneous consumers. Retailers can also take advantage of the marginal–average cost gap of national brand manufacturers to achieve higher per unit profits selling a store brand compared with selling a national brand with similar marginal costs of production. Having a retail brand also gives retailers economies of scale and bargaining power.

A retail business or a retail brand can be built around a number of areas, including the value chain, which describes areas where a company's critical success factors lie. Retailers can create value through logistics, operations, marketing, sales, services, procurement, technology development, human resources management and firm infrastructure, resulting in increased profitability for the firm; growth strategies through penetration to increase market share; merchandise development to increase sales; market development via geographic expansion, and diversification by offering new merchandise for new target customers. Other growth options include: integration, selectivity, productivity and overseas market development as well as partnering. Retail brands can be built around their personality and emotional benefits as well as through their store image. Store image is concerned with store location, appearance, merchandise and staff, as well as with the consumer's subjective impression of them. The building of a retail brand demands management attention across the entire business spectrum.

Retail brands grow in stages. In the first stage, the retail brand grows by taking market share from the national brand, through the retailer's allocation of more shelf space to its own-labels and increases in the average price of some national brands. The next stage is copying the national brand. Finally, there is strategic differentiation, identity creation and store positioning. To create a sustainable brand, retailers must concentrate on category management to optimize the product lines: by understanding salient consumer needs to develop their own brand proposition based on both functional and emotional benefits to the customer; by leveraging and creating connection with consumers; by optimizing and promoting synergies of touchpoints, balancing between brand messages and portfolio offerings; through packaging design, nomenclature and product strategy, product quality and innovation.

For manufacturers of national brands, their concern arises from the continuing consolidation of the grocery sector through the increase in retailers' monopoly power, resulting in suppliers capitulating to retailers' often unjustified terms and conditions. Another concern is how these manufacturers can overcome the low-cost competition from retailers and defend themselves against own-label imitations. These concerns have often led manufacturers to cut their advertising budgets and concentrate on trade promotions, which are not the best options. In order to compete with retailer own brands, a number of better options exist. These include: partnerships with retailers; new distribution channels; takeovers and mergers (these are considered an easy way to acquire strong brands and to strengthen weak ones); and overseas expansion (especially in eastern European markets). There are a number of ways to defend against own-brand imitations. These include: innovation and regular modifications to national brand packaging and product characteristics; unique brand signals and individuality in national-brand packaging and products to make them more recognizable to consumers; a greater focus on brand drivers and exploiting their traditions and expertise in new product categories; and, finally, positioning and branding the company in the supply chain.

🔑 Key terms

Bargaining power: retailers can use store brands as a tool to negotiate with manufacturers. The retailer can position the store brand to mimic the leading national brand. By improving the retailer's disagreement pay-off, the store brand decreases the incremental contribution of the leading national brand to category profits, thus allowing the retailer to improve its supply terms with the manufacturer. These terms could involve promoting sales of the store brand.

Battle for shelf space: a fiercely competitive situation between retail brand and manufacturer brand. It takes the following form: the retailer stocks fewer national brands. This leads to the manufacturer undertaking huge promotions in the form of trade deals and coupons, as well as deleting or slimming down its product line to match the retailer's price, or even resorting to producing its own-labels. Tesco and the other big supermarket chains prefer to have just two or three brands in a product line on the supermarket shelf, plus their own-labels.

Brand trust: the brand trustworthiness consumers rate in the brand extension. This is based on the company's or the core parent brand's credibility and perceived expertise in the area, especially when there is a high level of risk associated with the purchase. Brand trust, measured on two correlate dimensions – credibility and performance satisfaction – has a high influence on brand-extension acceptance.

Economies of scale: the larger the revenues in a category, the more likely a retailer will carry a store brand because of economies of scale.

Electronic data interchange (EDI): a system that sends the captured data at store level direct to the supplier. EDI enables **just-in-time** ordering, speeding up stock turnaround and creating close partnerships between retailers and suppliers as companies share trading data for mutual benefit.

EPOS: electronic point of sale data that can be collected instantly from the product's bar codes, highlighting who uses which product and when. Such customer information is highly valuable in terms of segmentation and product positioning.

Growth strategies: retail growth strategies include the following: penetration by aggressively increasing market share; merchandise development by adding new merchandise to appeal to customers and increase sales; integration through mergers and acquisitions to minimize channel conflict through ownership of channel members; selectivity by cutting down on merchandise range or by pulling out of some geographical areas to meet the needs of a target market; productivity refers to the 80/20 rule – 80 per cent profit from 20 per cent costs; developing overseas markets; partnerships with banks and other non-retail businesses.

International retailing competition: refers to competition from France, Germany, Sweden, Norway and Japan. A number of reasons explain this. The push factors are: saturated home markets, fierce competition and restrictive legislation pushed many large European food retailers into globalization mode, including British food retailers; falling barriers to market entry, e.g. the European Union and other trade blocs (the North American Free Trade Area); Japanese stores spreading across Asia and Europe in the 1980s and 1990s; supplier strategies – manufacturers of goods for retailers becoming more international themselves. The pull factors are: strategic retail alliances – since 1988 some European food retailers have formed joint ventures; emerging markets and convergence in consumers' taste.

Just-in-time (JIT): cuts the time it takes to get dry groceries from the manufacturer to customers from 104 days to 61 days by linking suppliers and using computers.

Locked-away profit: own brands allow retailers to capture part of the profit locked away by double marginalization when manufacturers use simple linear pricing.

Marginal-average cost gap: national brands need advertising support, which implies that manufacturers have average costs that are usually substantially higher than their marginal costs of production. Since in the long run manufacturers will not supply their products below average cost, the gap between marginal and average cost of national brand manufacturers allows retailers to achieve higher per unit profits selling a store brand compared with selling a national brand with similar marginal costs of production.

▶

Market polarization: refers to the market being divided into poles and extremes in terms of taste.

Multi-category retailers: those retailers that sell grocery and non-grocery products, e.g. many supermarkets.

National brand: also known as the 'manufacturer brand'.

New growth strategies: there are three specific strategies retailers can adopt: 1) expand into new markets once these markets are saturated with outlets – retailers can sustain their earnings growth by improving the mix of products they sell; 2) improve product selection by eliminating unprofitable products and manage product offerings better; 3) increasing customer value. This means improving long-term relationships with customers, which requires knowing everything from the customer base segments that are profitable down to individual names and what will make those customers interested in the retailer's offers. This is similar to relationship marketing or customer relationship management (CRM).

Own-label: another name for **retail brand**. The shift in retail power began after World War II with the introduction of the retailer's own-label. It started with Sainsbury's and Marks & Spencer who used their own labels for between 70, 80 to 100 per cent of their sales. Marks & Spencer used the St Michael label 100 per cent and Sainsbury's had 70 to 80 per cent own-label sales before slipping back to 56 per cent in 1987.

Perceptual fit: a fundamental underlying characteristic of a brand extension is the extent to which the extension is perceived as 'similar' to or 'fitting' the parent brand category. A great similarity of fit between the core brand and the extension product is reflected in more shared brand attributes between the former and the latter. Alternating the core brand is seen as relevant and the consumers infer that the quality of the extension product is similar to the quality of the core product.

Perceptual risk: consumer perceptions of the uncertainty and adverse consequences of buying a product or service. Risk varies directly with the product type and the buying situation, whether online, door-to-door or store. There are six forms of risks: performance, financial, physical, time, social and psychological.

Price discrimination: this exists between store brands and national brands and fringe brands. Retailers exploit price discrimination between these brands in order to increase total channel profits, even if there are no cost differences to the retailer in selling these three types of brands. Also, depending on consumer tastes, the retailer will want to set prices that induce some consumers to self-select into each type of brand.

Retail brand: see **Own-label** and **Store brand**.

Retail brand building: just as with any other brand, retail brand building is based on building a successful retail business by understanding the industry's nature and scope, and focusing on the value chain, growth strategies and more profitable new growth strategies. A retail brand can also be built based on its personality and emotional benefits to the customer. Its store image has a direct effect on its brand image. Retail brand building is also based on the management and coordination of its entire business (see **Strategic focus**).

Retail brand extension: a store brand name that is extended either in a new product category or line. For example, Asda and other supermarkets have brand extensions in financial services – that is, they have extended their store name into a completely new product category. However, if they had brand extensions in groceries that would be line extension. The issues with retail brand extension are: perceptual fit, perceptual risks, and perceptual risk effects on category success and brand trust.

Store brand: the use of a store name across a number of product categories, e.g. Sainsbury's offers 8000 store brand lines. Store brands represent an extensive and highly complex umbrella-branding strategy: complex, because the store image itself is more complex and dynamic than product associations. Store brands may offer hundreds of product categories and its brand attributes may not be consistent for all attributes. Store brands represent an opportunity to build store image and differentiate their stores, since store brand is also an influencing variable in consumers' purchasing decisions.

Store image: a complex combination of tangible and intangible, or functional and psychological attributes. More specifically, store image is derived from the customer's functional experience/learning and psychological feeling/attitude of a store simultaneously. In addition, the formulation of a store image involves two basic aspects: the external world such as location, appearance, merchandise and staff; and the consumer's subjective impressions of selected elements of that world such as information considered, interpreted, evaluated, integrated and inferred. Store image can have an impact on customer loyalty and influence the evaluation of store brand (i.e. the Tesco brand).

Strategic focus: one aspect of building a retail brand by companies focusing their attention across the entire business system, from stock management, consistent pricing, information system management to planning demand more precisely for each store, handling lapses in supply-chain product deliveries and managing employee performance through the use of incentives. A good example is Wal-Mart.

Sustainable brand: to create a sustainable brand, retailers must concentrate on the following: category management, which consists of collaboration with manufacturers in understanding and deciding how to optimize the product lines; understanding the salient consumer needs to develop the own-brand proposition accordingly; creating connections with consumers; optimizing and promoting synergies of touchpoints through the store environment, and the merchandising, packaging and promotional mix to create a strong and consistent brand message; balancing between brand messages and portfolio offerings; using branding, packaging design and sub-branding initiatives to help visualize and verbalize what the own brand stands for; demonstrating its expertise and differentiating it from national brands in various product categories; focusing on product quality and innovation; concentrating on a well-focused brand proposition, e.g. mass value – Asda; problem-solving – Ikea (home improvement); Orange (communications solutions); lifestyle – Selfridges; opportunist – Zara.

Uncontrolled growth: the result of retailers overextending their businesses.

Value chain: areas where a company's critical success factors lie. In other words, it constitutes a firm's competencies, which will give the company a competitive advantage over competitors.

? Discussion questions

1 What relevance does the value chain have for retailers?
2 How can a retailer develop synergies in its value chain? Give examples.

3 Explain what 'push and pull' means in marketing. What does it mean in terms of cross-border retailing?

4 Explain different terms of own branding.

5 What are the main growth options available to retailers?

6 What are the main issues in retail brand extension from the consumer perspective?

7 Compare and contrast the retailer brand and the manufacturer brand, by discussing the strengths and weaknesses of each.

8 Explain the reciprocal effects between store brands and store image. What are the implications for retailers?

9 Describe the key opportunities and threats facing retail business today.

10 Discuss the possibility that non-store retailing will eventually replace store retailing. What are the implications for logistical planning posed by the growth of non-store retailing?

Projects

1 Conduct interviews with up to 30 consumers (or students/academic staff) to find out how brand naming affects their intention to buy a) brands that use store name; b) brands that are not based on store name. Compare and contrast your findings.

2 Conduct interviews with up to 30 consumers (or students/academic staff) to find out how consumers perceive own brands and national brands in a selected product category on a number of attributes, e.g. price, quality, etc. Compare and contrast your findings.

3 Conduct interviews with up to 30 consumers (or students/academic staff) to find out how the retailer brand marketing mix impacts on consumer purchase intention, in terms of a) brand and packaging; b) price gap, as follows:

Percentage of consumers who intend to buy the retailer brand				
Brand & packaging	Price gap	−20%	−35%	−50%
Store brand (not copycat)				
Store brand (copycat)				
Private label (copycat)				
Private label (not copycat)				

Compare and contrast your findings.

4 Find out from any published data the effects of Sainsbury's Cola launch on Coke's market share before launch and after launch. Report your findings.

5 Gather information on a retailer of your choice (e.g. Marks & Spencer). Do a SWOT analysis of the company and develop a growth strategy for the company, to include a branding strategy.

MINI CASE 11.1: STARBUCKS COFFEE

Starbucks' international journey began in 1996 with the first Starbucks in Tokyo. Several store openings followed throughout Asia, where Starbucks now operates in 13 markets. In 1998, Starbucks purchased the Seattle Coffee Company in the UK, which had 60 retail locations, and built the business to 300 shops.

Starbucks now operates more than 5000 coffee houses in North America, Europe, the Middle East and the Pacific Rim. Not bad for a company that started from a single store on Seattle's waterfront in 1971. The brand was named after the coffee-loving first mate in Melville's classic novel, *Moby Dick*. The name evoked the romance of the high seas and seafaring coffee traders. Today, the coffee trading practised by Starbucks involves an entirely different kind of romance.

The business is based on repeat purchase and loyalty. Starbucks provides quality coffee in a relaxed atmosphere for those seeking a respite between home and work. Also, grab-and-go consumers can take coffee and a snack home or to the office. The ambience and service is the same everywhere. This is the vaulted Starbucks Experience, an elusive halo that competitors desire, but have trouble duplicating.

There may be slight differences between Starbucks in different countries, but they all share similarities as part of a family of stores. Starbucks in Tokyo, Vienna or Sydney basically look the same. What's also the same are the assortment of coffees and other beverages offered to discriminating customers who pay a premium for speciality blends.

But the essence of Starbucks is not about the coffee, although the coffee is great. It's about the coffee-drinking and the coffee-house experience. That observation has occurred to competing retailers, which have tried to copy the Starbucks Experience, especially in Europe where there have been coffee houses since the 1600s. The knock-offs began springing up three years ago, joining other established shops, which have also reacted.

The most important nuance is bonding with the local community. In the US, the Starbucks Foundation contributes to programmes for literacy, early learning, AIDS outreach and environmental awareness. The company has also founded a school in the Philippines and an orphanage in Korea; and in New Zealand, its programme called Lend a Hand allows store employees to work on community projects on company time.

The most important thing Starbucks must keep in mind is that no brand expands in a vacuum and every brand is rooted in popular culture. That's the difference between advertising and branding. Advertising grabs their minds; branding grabs their hearts.

Questions:

1 What is Starbucks' strategy?

2 Given your assessment of its competitive position, how should it leverage its resources and capabilities to achieve future growth?

3 Explain the comments: 'The most important thing Starbucks must keep in mind is that no brand expands in a vacuum' and 'Every brand is rooted in popular culture. That's the difference between advertising and branding. Advertising grabs their minds; branding grabs their hearts.'

MINI CASE 11.2: BOO.COM

Sources: Dave Chaffey, from original sources including Malmsten et al. (2001) and New Media Age (1999); Malmsten, E., Portanger, E. and Drazin, C. (2001) *boo hoo. A dot.com story from concept to catastrophe*, Random House, London, UK; New Media Age (1999) *Will boo.com scare off the competition?* (author Budd Margolis), New Media Age, 22 July 1999, online only

Boo hoo – Learning from the largest European dotcom failure

Context – 'Unless we raise $20 million by midnight, Boo.com is dead.' So said Boo.com CEO Ernst Malmsten on 18 May 2000. Half the investment was raised, but this was too little, too late, and at midnight, less than a year after its launch, Boo.com closed. The headlines in the *Financial Times*, the next day read: 'Boo.com collapses as investors refuse funds. Online sports retailer becomes Europe's first big Internet casualty.' The Boo.com case remains a valuable case study for all types of businesses, since it doesn't only illustrate the challenges of managing e-commerce for a clothes retailer, but rather highlights failings in e-commerce strategy and management that can be made in any type of organization.

Company background – Boo.com was a European company founded in 1998 and operating out of a London head office, which was founded by three Swedish entrepreneurs, Ernst Malmsten, Kajsa Leander and Patrik Hedelin. Malmsten and Leander had previous business experience in publishing where they created a specialist publisher and had also created an online bookstore, bokus.com, which in 1997 became the world's third largest book e-retailer behind Amazon and Barnes & Noble. They became millionaires when they sold the company in 1998. At boo.com, they were joined by Patrik Hedelin who was also the financial director at bokus, and at the time they were perceived as experienced European Internet entrepreneurs by the investors who backed them in their new venture.

Company vision – The vision for Boo.com was for it to become the worlds first online global sports retail site. It would be a European brand, but with a global appeal. Think of it as a sports and fashion retail version of Amazon. At launch it would open its virtual doors in both Europe and America with a view to 'amazoning the sector'. Note though that, in contrast, Amazon did not launch simultaneously in all markets. Rather it became established in the US before providing local European distribution through acquisition and re-branding of other e-retailers in the United Kingdom for example.

The Boo.com brand name – According to Malmsten (2001), the boo brand name originated from filmstar 'Bo Derek', best known for her role in the movie *10*. The domain name 'bo.com' was unavailable, but adding an 'o', they managed to procure the domain 'Boo.com' for $2500 from a domain name dealer. According to Rob Talbot, director of marketing for Boo.com, Boo was 'looking for a name that was easy to spell across all the different countries and easy to remember … something that didn't have a particular meaning'.

Target market – The audience targeted by Boo.com can be characterized as 'young, well-off and fashion-conscious' 18 to 24 year olds. The concept was that globally the target market would be interested in sports and fashion brands stocked by Boo.com.

The market for clothing in this area was viewed as very large, so the thought was that capture of only a small part of this market was required for Boo.com to be successful. The view at this time on the scale of this market and the basis for success is indicated by New Media Age where it was described thus: 'The $60b USD industry is dominated by Gen X'ers who are online and according to market research in need of knowing what is in, what is not and a way to receive such goods quickly. If Boo.com becomes known as the place to keep up with fashion and can supply the latest trends then there is no doubt that there is a market, a highly profitable one at that, for profits to grow from.'

The growth in the market was also supported by retail analysts, with Verdict predicting online shopping in the United Kingdom to grow from £600 million in 1999 to £12.5 billion in 2005.

However, New Media Age does note some reservations about this market, saying: 'Clothes and trainers have a high rate of return in the mail order/home shopping world. Twenty year olds may be online and may have disposable income but they are not the main market associated with mail order. To date there is no one else doing anything similar to Boo.com.'

The Boo.com proposition – In its proposal to investors, the company stated that its 'business idea is to become the world-leading Internet-based retailer of prestigious brand leisure and sportswear names'. They listed brands such as Polo Ralph Lauren, Tommy Hilfiger, Nike, Fila, Lacoste and Adidas. The proposition involved sports and fashion goods alongside each other. The thinking was that sports clothing has more standardized sizes with less need for a precise fit than designer clothing.

The owners of Boo.com wanted to develop an easy to use experience which re-created the offline shopping experience as far as possible. As part of the branding strategy, an idea was developed of a virtual salesperson, initially named Jenny and later Miss Boo. She would guide users through the site and give helpful tips. When selecting products, users could drag them on to models, zoom in and rotate them in 3D to visualize them from different angles. The technology to achieve this was built from scratch along with the stock control and distribution software. A large investment was required in technology with several suppliers being replaced before launch which was six months later than promised to investors, largely due to problems with implementing the technology.

Clothing the mannequin and populating the catalogue was also an expensive challenge. For 2000, about $6 million was spent on content about spring/summer fashion wear. It cost $200 to photograph each product, representing a monthly cost of more than $500 000.

Although the user experience of Boo.com is often criticized for its speed, it does seem to have had that wow factor that influenced investors. Analyst Nik Margolis writing in New Media Age (1999) illustrates this by saying:

> What I saw at Boo.com is simply the most clever web experience I have seen in quite a while. The presentation of products and content are both imaginative and offer an experience. Sure everything loads up fast in an office but I was assured by those at Boo.com that they will keep to a limit of 8 seconds for a page to download. Eight seconds is not great but the question is will it be worth waiting for?

Of course, today, the majority of European users have broadband, but in the late 1990s the majority were on dial-up and had to download the software to view products.

Communicating the Boo.com proposition – Early plans referred to extensive 'high impact' marketing campaigns on TV and in newspapers. Public relations was important in leveraging the novelty of the concept and human side of the business – Leander was previously a professional model and had formerly been Malmsten's partner. This PR was initially focused within the fashion and sportswear trade and then rolled out to publications likely to be read by the target audience. The success of this PR initiative can be judged by the 350 000 email pre-registrations that wanted to be notified of launch. For the launch Malmsten (2001) explains that 'with a marketing and PR spend of only $22.4 million we had managed to create a worldwide brand'.

To help create the values of the Boo.com brand, *Boom* 'a lavish online fashion magazine' was created which required substantial staff for different language versions. The magazine wasn't a catalogue which directly supported sales, rather it was a publishing venture competing with established fashion titles. For existing customers the *Look Book*, a 44-page print catalogue was produced which showcased different products each month.

The challenges of building a global brand in months – The challenges of creating a global brand in months are illustrated well by Malmsten et al. (2001). After an initial round of funding, including investment from the JP Morgan, LMVH Investment and the Benetton family, which generated around $9 million, the founders planned towards launch by identifying thousands of individual tasks, many of which needed to be completed by staff yet to be recruited. These tasks were divided into 27 areas of responsibility familiar to many organizations including office infrastructure, logistics, product information, pricing, front-end applications, call centres, packaging, suppliers, designing logos, advertising/PR, legal issues and recruitment. At its zenith, Boo.com had 350 staff, with over 100 in London and new offices in Munich, New York, Paris and Stockholm. Initially Boo.com was available in UK English, US English, German, Swedish, Danish and Finnish, with localized versions for France,

Spain and Italy added after launch. The website was tailored for individual countries using the local language and currency and also local prices. Orders were fulfilled and shipped out of one of two warehouses: one in Louisville, Kentucky, and the other in Cologne, Germany. This side of the business was relatively successful with on-time delivery rates approaching 100 per cent achieved.

Boo possessed classic channel conflicts. Initially, it was difficult getting fashion and sports brands to offer their products through Boo.com. Manufacturers already had a well-established distribution network through large high-street sports and fashion retailers and many smaller retailers. If clothing brands permitted Boo.com to sell their clothes online at discounted prices, then this would conflict with retailers' interests and would also portray the brands in a negative light if their goods were in an online 'bargain bucket'. A further pricing issue is where local or zone pricing in different markets exists: for example, lower prices often exist in the US than Europe and there are variations in different European countries.

Making the business case to investors – Today it seems incredible that investors were confident enough to invest $130 million in the company and, at the high point, the company was valued at $390 million. Yet much of this investment was based on the vision of the founders to be a global brand and achieve 'first mover advantage'. Although there were naturally revenue projections, these were not always based on an accurate detailed analysis of market potential. Immediately before launch, Malmsten (2001) explains a meeting with would-be investor Pequot Capital, represented by Larry Lenihan who had made successful investments in Yahoo! and AOL. The Boo.com management team were able to provide revenue forecasts, but unable to answer fundamental questions for modelling the potential of the business, such as 'How many visitors are you aiming for?', 'What kind of conversion rate are you aiming for?', 'How much does each customer have to spend?', 'What's your customer acquisition cost, and what's your payback time on customer acquisition cost?' When these figures were obtained, the analyst found them to be 'far fetched' and reputedly ended the meeting with the words. 'I'm not interested. Sorry for my bluntness, but I think you're going to be out of business by Christmas.'

When the site launched on 3 November 1999, around 50 000 unique visitors were achieved on the first day, but only four in 1000 placed orders (a 0.25 per cent conversion rate), showing the importance of modelling conversion rate accurately in modelling business potential. This low conversion rate was also symptomatic of problems with the technology. It also gave rise to negative PR. One reviewer explained how he waited 'eighty-one minutes to pay too much money for a pair of shoes that I'm still going to have to wait a week to get'. These rates did improve as problems were ironed out – by the of the week 228 848 visits had resulted in 609 orders with a value of $64 000. In the six weeks from launch, sales of $353 000 were made and conversion rates had more than doubled to 0.98 per cent before Christmas. However, a relaunch was required within six months to cut download times and to introduce a 'low-bandwidth version' for users with dial-up connections. This led to conversion rates of nearly 3 per cent on sales promotion. Sales results were disappointing in some regions, with US sales accounting for 20 per cent compared to the planned 40 per cent.

The management team felt that further substantial investment was required to grow the business from a presence in 18 countries and 22 brands in November to 31 countries and 40 brands the following spring. Turnover was forecast to rise from $100 million in 2000/01 to $1350 million by 2003/4, which would be driven by $102.3 million in marketing in 2003/4. Profit was forecast to be $51.9 million by 2003/4.

The end of Boo.com – The end of Boo.com came on 18 May 2000, when investor funds could not be raised to meet the spiralling marketing, technology and wage bills.

Questions:

1 Which strategic marketing assumptions and decisions arguably made Boo.com's failure inevitable? Contrast these with other dotcom era survivors who are still in business – for example, Lastminute.com, Egg.com and Firebox.com.

2 Using the framework of the marketing mix, appraise the marketing tactics of Boo.com in the areas of product, pricing, place, promotion, process, people and physical evidence.

3 In many ways, the vision of Boo's founders was 'ideas before their time'. Give examples of e-retail techniques used to create an engaging online customer experience which Boo adopted that are now becoming commonplace.

END OF CHAPTER CASE STUDY: THE LAUNCH OF THE BISC& BRAND

In general, biscuits are regarded as a runner-up to, or substitute for, 'chocolate biscuit countlines', especially by younger family members. The biscuit market is not perceived by consumers to be as exciting as the confectionery market. Masterfoods developed a strategy for the Bisc&® brand to succeed within the biscuit category, through identification of key customers, development of key message and appropriate distribution channels.

The key purchaser is found to be mums with young children between the ages of 5 and 12. The purchaser is also the key decision-maker. Her purchase of biscuits and chocolate biscuits is often in substantial quantities for all of her family. The children also had an important role in influencing the decision to purchase.

The key message of the Bisc&® brand is that these biscuits are delicious combinations that bring together the traditional biscuit world with the exciting world of chocolate, and which are suitable for both children and adults alike. The central aim of the company was to introduce the Bisc&® brand as a new biscuit product that appeals to the key purchasers and consumers, while leveraging the strength of existing established brands.

Masterfoods worked closely with key distributors in the biscuit market like supermarkets, other retailers and wholesalers. The biscuits were marketed to the general public through a variety of marketing communications including advertising on the radio, on television, in the consumer and trade press, as well as a large sampling and PR campaign. One of the big features of the PR campaign is that Bisc&® will be a sponsor of the Irish Hospice Foundation's Coffee Morning shortly after it is launched. The key slogan in the Bisc&® advertising campaign is 'You'll love them together' reflecting the unique combination of biscuit and great taste of your favourite chocolate topping.

Masterfoods has chosen to launch the Bisc&® brand in the 'everyday treats' bay of the biscuit aisle and to promote it accordingly. This is a new departure for Masterfoods as prior to the launch of Bisc&®, it competed only in the 'chocolate biscuit countlines' sub-segment with Twix® and Twix Top®. Bisc&® now brings the packaging advantages associated with the 'chocolate biscuit countline' sub-segment to the 'everyday treats' sub-segment, and thereby broadens the usage occasions of this sector.

The packaging and marketing of the product along with the price and where the brand is positioned in the biscuit aisle will be crucial to the product's success.

Questions:

1 In your opinion, why is it important to manage every aspect of a product launch? From the case study, outline four key areas you would consider important.

2 In the case of Bisc&®, why was it important for management to understand the difference between the roles of the 'purchaser' and the 'consumer'?

3 Why do marketing managers take advantage of product extensions? What is the advantage of associating or combining a new brand with four established brands?

4 You are a marketing executive promoting a new brand. In your opinion, on what shelf and where on the shelf would you want your brand to be displayed?

References

Burt, S. (2000), 'The strategic role of retail brands in British grocery retailing', *European Journal of Marketing,* Vol. 34, No. 8, pp. 875–90.

Chen, J. and Paliwoda, S. (2004), 'The influence of company name in consumer variety seeking', *Brand Management,* Vol. 11, No. 3, pp. 219–31.

Colgate, M. and Alexander, N. (2002), 'Retailers and diversification: the financial service dimension', *Journal of Retailing and Consumer Services,* Vol. 9, No. 1, pp. 1–11.

Collins-Dodd, C. and Lindley, T. (2003), 'Store brands and retail differentiation: the influence of store image and store brand attitude on store own brand perceptions', *Journal of Retailing and Consumer Services,* Vol. 10, No. 6, pp. 345–52.

Cox, R. and Brittain, P. (2004), *Retailing: An introduction,* Financial Times: Prentice Hall.

Dawar, N. and Parker, P. (1994), 'Marketing universals: consumers' use of brand name, price, physical appearance, and retailer reputation as signals of product quality', *Journal of Marketing Research,* Vol. 58, No. 2, pp. 81–95.

DelVecchio, D. (2001), 'Consumer perceptions of private label quality: the role of product category characteristics and consumer use of heuristics', *Journal of Retailing and Consumer Services,* Vol. 8, No. 5, pp. 239–49.

Dowling, G. R. and Staelin, R. (1994), 'A model of perceived risk and intended risk-handling activity', *Journal of Consumer Research,* Vol. 21, No. 1, pp. 119–34.

Economist, The (1993), 'The food industry', 4 December.

Henderson, T. A. and Mihas, E. A. (2000), 'Building retail brands', *McKinsey Quarterly,* August.

Keller, K. L. and Aaker, D. A. (1992), 'The effects of sequential introduction of brand extensions', *Journal of Marketing Research,* Vol. 19, No. 1, pp. 35–50.

Knox, S. (2004), 'Positioning and branding your organisation', *Journal of Product & Brand Management,* Vol. 13, No. 2, pp. 105–15.

Laforet, S. (2007), 'British grocers' brand extension in financial services', *Journal of Product & Brand Management,* Vol. 16, No. 2, pp. 82–97.

Malmstem, E. et al. (2001), *Boo Hoo: a dotcom story,* London: Random House.

Morton, F. S. and Zettelmeyer, F. (2004), 'The strategic positioning of store brands in retailer–manufacturer negotiations', *Review of Industrial Organization,* Vol. 24 (2 March), pp. 161–94.

Narasimhan, C. and Wilcox, R. (1998), 'Private labels and the channel relationship: a cross-category analysis', *Journal of Business,* Vol. 71, No. 4, pp. 573–600.

Nelson, S. (2002) 'Corporate brand and packaging design', at http://www.findarticles.com/p/articles/mi_qa4001/is_200210/ai_n9119373/print.

Rani, L. and Velayudhan, S. K. (2008), 'Understanding consumers' attitude towards retail store in stockout situations', *Asia Pacific Journal of Marketing and Logistics,* Vol. 20, No. 3, pp. 259–75.

Reast, J. D. (2005), 'Brand trust and brand extension acceptance: the relationship', *Journal of Product & Brand Management,* Vol. 14, No. 1, pp. 4–13.

Richardson, P. S., Dick, A. S. and Jain, A. K. (1994), 'Extrinsic and intrinsic cue effects on perceptions of store brand quality', *Journal of Marketing,* Vol. 58, No. 4, pp. 28–36.

Sheth, J. N., Mittal, B. and Newman, B. I. (1999), *Customer Behaviour: Consumer Behaviour and Beyond,* Fort Worth, TX: Dryden Press.

Veloutsou, C., Saren, M. and Tzokas, N. (2002), 'Relationship marketing: what if…?', *European Journal of Marketing,* Vol. 36, No. 4, pp. 433–49.

Werner, U., McDermott, J. and Rotz, G. (2004), 'Retailers at the crossroads: how to develop profitable new growth strategies', *Journal of Business Strategy,* Vol. 25, No. 2, pp. 10–17.

Young, L. C. and Wilkinson I. F. (1989), 'The role of trust and cooperation in marketing channels: a preliminary study', *European Journal of Marketing,* Vol. 23, pp. 109–22.

Further reading and online sites

ACNielsen (2003) The retail store as a brand, at http: www2.acnielsen.com/pubs/2003_q2_ap_retail. shtml.

Clarke, I. (2000), 'Retail power, competition and local consumer choice in the UK grocery sector', *European Journal of Marketing*, Vol. 34, No. 8.

Collins, A. and Burt, S. (2003), 'Market sanctions, monitoring and vertical coordination within retailer-manufacturer relationships: the case of retail brand suppliers', *European Journal of Marketing*, Vol. 37, No. 5/6.

Dawson, J. (2000), 'Viewpoint: retailer power, manufacturer power, competition and some questions of economic analysis', *International Journal of Retail & Distribution Management*, Vol. 28, No. 1.

Gómez, M. and Benito, N. R. (2008), 'Manufacturers' characteristics that determine the choice of producing store brands', *European Journal of Marketing*, Vol. 42, No. 1/2.

Gomez-Arias, T. J. and Bello-Acebron, L. (2008), 'Why do leading brand manufacturers supply private labels?', *Journal of Business & Industrial Marketing*, Vol. 23, No. 4.

IBM Business Consulting Services (2004), The retail divide: leadership in a world of extremes, at www. globalscorecard.net/download/retail_2010_exescum.pdf.

Solomon, M., Bamossy, G., Askegaard, S. and Hogg, M. K. (1999), *Consumer Behaviour – A European Perspective*, Financial Times: Prentice Hall.

Statt, D. A. (1997), *Understanding the Consumer; A Psychological Approach*, London: Macmillan.

Winters, A. A., Winters, P. F. and Paul, C. (2002), *Brandstand: Strategies for Retail Brand Building*, New York: Visual Reference Publications.

Wong, C. Y. and Johansen, J. (2008), 'A framework of manufacturer–retailer coordination process: three case studies', *International Journal of Retail & Distribution Management*, Vol. 36, No. 5.

Packaging Design and Branding for the Consumer

'Packaging is the expression of the soul of every product', *Peter Brabeck, Nestlé CEO*

Chapter contents

Chapter overview

Despite companies spending large amounts on research and advertising, a quick look at the average supermarket shows that most packaging in fmcg is me-too and does not stand out enough from the crowd of products displayed on the supermarket shelf. Attracting consumers through innovative packaging and product innovation will overcome competition to a great extent. Understanding what consumers need, value and are motivated to purchase is central to packaging design. Chapter 10 examined environmental pressures and the new challenges of modern markets impacting on branding strategies and communications. Chapter 11 discussed own-label competition. This chapter examines the relationship between branding and packaging design; the role of packaging in communicating values and reinforcing the brand message. It asks what consumers want from their packaged brand – functionality or interaction; how packaging influences brand choice under conditions of high involvement and pressure of time; how manufacturers overcome the dichotomy between food quality and the processed appearance of their brand packaging to engender trust in consumers. It discusses relevance and recognition issues, and how environmental issues influence consumer buying behaviour. It also discusses recent trends and the use of new technologies in packaging design to meet consumers' packaging needs. New innovative packaging design examples are illustrated. It explains how branding efforts go hand in hand with packaging design and sub-branding initiatives, how brand strategy is executed on the package, and when and how to optimize the relationships among brands by emphasizing visual cues. Chapter 13 willl focus on country-of-origin branding as part of gaining competitive advantage for some producers in the new competitive arena.

❖ LEARNING OBJECTIVES

After completing this chapter, you should be able to

❖ Explain the meaning of and relationship between branding and packaging design

❖ Explain how packaging can communicate value and reinforce the brand message

❖ Describe packaging functions and elements

❖ Identify what consumers need, want and value in their packaging by identifying their needs, values and purchase motivations, and make recommendations on how packaging designers can meet consumer expectations

❖ Discuss the issue of food quality and how packaging can engender trust in consumers

❖ Discuss consumers' concerns for food safety and how information displayed on food labels influences consumers' perception of the product and brand choice; how consumers' environmental concerns affect their buying behaviour, and the relationship between eco-awareness and food health concerns

❖ Discuss the use of various new technologies in innovative packaging design and their implications in terms of meeting consumers' packaging needs

❖ Discuss the techniques employed in executing the brand strategy on the package

Introduction

Many grocery stores carry 100 000 products or more, with thousands of new products coming on to the market every year. The incredible proliferation of new products in the marketplace, particularly in the area of natural, organic, gourmet, niche, speciality and new age, has led to manufacturers demanding more upscale, sophisticated graphics and cutting-edge new packaging.

Retail studies show that up to 85 per cent of consumer purchases are made on impulse, and is influenced by packaging, which is one of the most important factors in purchase decisions made at the point of sale (Silayoi and Speece, 2004, citing Prendergast and Pitt, 1996). According to packaging research, consumers find product packaging more memorable than advertising or promotions. In a consumer survey at Brandchannel.com, for example, colour was found to be the dominant feature, followed by package shape and brand logo.

American statistics indicate that on a per-dollar basis, packaging that expresses a brand's assets yields greater return on investment than advertising, while experts assert that package design, as part of a brand identity system, can outperform up to three advertising campaigns and more than eight promotional cycles.

In low-involvement purchases, the visual elements of the package play a major role in representing the product, and when consumers are pressured for time these will influence their buying decisions.

In an intensifying competitive environment or in a recession, where consumers compare shopping and scrutinize labels, the packaging that can convince consumers to buy the product or can guarantee product uptake will be more valuable to companies than anything else. For this and the above reasons, manufacturers are now placing more and more emphasis on packaging design. They are focusing on communicating the brand in a fast, interesting and efficient manner to achieve stand-out on the shelf, to gain consumers' attention, product recall and premium shelf space.

In the following sections the role of and relationship between branding and packaging are examined. Consumers' needs, wants and values from their packaged brand are analysed from the consumer's perspective, on the one hand, and from the manufacturer's and packaging designer's perspectives on the other. Brand packaging will be examined in terms of its functionality, interaction with consumers, and its ability to engender trust in consumers in food quality and green labelling.

Relationship between branding and packaging design

As previously mentioned, branding is regarded as a powerful mechanism that can set owners' products apart from competitors' in the mind of the consumer. Packaging, on the other hand, may be defined as: 'a critical tool that helps to visualize, verbalize what a company's brand stands for and demonstrate its expertise, and serves as point of difference in various product categories'.

Brand identity and packaging design are increasingly important components of corporate branding strategies as they contribute significantly to marketing or branding success. While marketing and advertising efforts seek to create need or demand for a product, only the package can tangibly deliver that product or brand to the consumer. The package will meet the consumer directly, and it must deliver just the right brand message to prompt a purchasing decision.

Since a brand's packaging is its most enduring and accessible brand communication vehicle, it is important that it conveys the brand message through an innovative structure and package design system. The brand's packaging must also be a synergistic part of the overall brand-expression continuum. The fundamental purpose of package design is to sell the product. Beyond its basic function (which is discussed below) of protecting the product and preserving taste, food packaging must, in effect, talk to the consumer. It must be able to tell the consumer what the product is and why it is superior to any other competitive brand.

The role of packaging

Packaging functions and elements

Logistics and marketing functions

The logistical function of packaging is mainly to protect the product during movement through distribution channels. The marketing function of packaging is that of brand communication. Packaging provides a way of conveying messages about product attributes to the consumer at the point of sale. The logistic and marketing functions are inseparable, since the package sells the product by attracting attention and communicating, as well as allowing the product to be contained, apportioned, utilized and protected.

Communicating value and reinforcing the brand message

What package designers used to say twenty years ago is still valid: you cannot make a bad product look good, but you can make a good product look better. This perception of quality is linked to value, which is the most important purchase consideration next to taste and freshness. The package's overall features can underline the product's uniqueness and originality, and reflect the product's quality. If the packaging communicates high quality, consumers assume that the product is of high quality. If the packaging symbolizes low quality, consumers will transfer this low-quality perception to the product itself. The package can also communicate favourable or unfavourable meanings about the product. It has been suggested that consumers are more likely to spontaneously imagine aspects of how a product looks, tastes, feels, smells or sounds while they look at a picture on a product package. Packaging is also one of the most important ways to communicate and continually reinforce the brand message, which will be discussed later.

Visual elements

Purchase decisions can be affected by two main features of packaging: visual and informational. The visual aspect or element consists of graphics and the size and shape of the packaging, which relate to the affective side of decision-making. Graphics includes layout, colour combinations, typography and product photography, all of which create an image of the product. Underwood et al.'s (2001) study based on a virtual reality simulation shows that packaging pictures increase shoppers' attention to the brand, especially private-label brands. This, in turn, can improve consumers' perception of the brand and influence choice. Shape and colour are very important in packaging design and billions of pounds are spent every year on packaging colour design to achieve the colour combinations that fit consumers' expectation.

Computer technology enables 3-D images to be portrayed, and colours and shapes manipulated on the screen to ascertain consumers' reactions. Consumers' identification of a product with its colour is so strong that it would be hard to imagine that they would see well-known products in a different colour other than their own (e.g. red for Kit Kat). It has been suggested that colour choice depends on the target market and the type of product sold. If the target market is men, then the products might use stronger colours: reds and blacks. If the target market is women, the colours might use softer shades of pinks and blues, and, if aimed at children, then a mixture of bright, happy, attractive colours could be the best approach.

Shape and colour also affect logo design. A 1997 study by Claessens Product Consultants showed that shape is more important than colour in logo identification. Although colour aids in logo recognition, correct identification does not depend on it. Logos appearing in different colours or in black and white are as easy to identify as logos in their actual colour combination. In their study of genetically modified product labelling, Costello et al. (2005) indicate that consumers like rounder shapes, while angular shapes reduce purchases. They suggest oval white shapes used for products containing non-genetically modified ingredients, and red angular shapes for genetically modified products as a hazard warning.

Packaging size and shape are also used by consumers as visual heuristics to make volume judgements. It has been said that more elongated packages are perceived to be larger, even when consumers frequently purchase these packages and can experience the true volume. In other words, disconfirmation of package size after consumption may not lead consumers to revise their volume judgements in the long term, especially if the discrepancy is small (Raghubir and Krishna, 1999).

Informational elements

The informational elements consist of the information provided and the technologies used in the packaging, which address the cognitive side of decisions. Product information is important, especially when consumers are engaged in high-involvement purchases. High-involvement purchases are those which consumers perceive as financially or emotionally risky. When consumers are involved with the product, they will be more attentive, and will seek information about the brand they are interested in. Highly involved consumers will evaluate message information, relying on message argument to form their attitudes and purchase intentions. In such cases, written information on the package can assist consumers in making their decisions carefully as they consider product characteristics.

The downside of packaging that gives too much information (or sometimes misleading and inaccurate information) is that it can create confusion and information overload. It has been suggested that information overload can lead to choice reduction. This applies to experienced consumers and heavy users, who tend to look at fewer brand alternatives (Mitchell and Papavassiliou, 1999). This is caused by brand loyalty and by consumers not wanting to read labels every time they buy a product. Many consumers appreciate food labelling, but are not always satisfied with their formats. This issue will be discussed later in relation to green labelling.

In the UK consumer survey data indicate that nearly two-thirds of consumers read food labels, but one-third want to see clearer labelling. Research also shows that many consumers find the format prescribed in law for voluntary and compulsory labelling difficult to use. In a recent survey, 90 per cent of respondents agreed that nutritional information panels should be laid out in the same way for all food products so that they are easy to understand quickly. Consumers' awareness of label information has increased in recent years, and also of food safety and nutritional health, in line with consumer sophistication and higher living standards. In packaged food products or fmcg (fast-moving consumer goods), purchases are often made and products picked up randomly. As a result, information on the package carries less value than in high-involvement purchases, as explained above.

The technology involved in recent innovative packaging designs is working to make products more efficiently packaged for a longer shelf life (see 'Ambient, viral and sensory branding', below), more environmentally friendly, and nutritionally responsive to each of the emerging segments of society, and to meet maximum food safety requirements. Packaging technology also conveys information linked to consumers' lifestyles. Packaging technology is very important for developing packaging, materials and processes which will enable manufacturers to survive in high-growth and competitive markets. The following sections will look at examples in fmcg.

Understanding consumers' packaging needs

Consumers' needs and purchase motivations

'Consumer behaviour discipline' states that consumers' motivations and needs affect choice and purchases. From the provider's perspective, they need to know why customers buy their products. Seeking an answer to this question requires companies to understand consumers' needs and motivations.

The principles of consumer behaviour state that there are two basic types of need that consumers seek to satisfy: utilitarian and hedonic. *Utilitarian* needs arise from the physical and tangible aspects of a product, such as its functionality and pleasing appearance. *Hedonic* are those subjective and experiential aspects that a product offers, e.g. to boost self-confidence, to provide excitement or an experience.

In psychology, *motivation* refers to the processes that cause people to behave in the way they do. Motivation occurs when a need is aroused which the consumer wishes to satisfy. Examples of common purchase motivations are: value for money; product quality; product availability (consumers liking to have the product there and then); convenience (for example, not having to travel far to get the product); service quality, especially with products that require maintenance and care; protection (from delivery of the product to back-up or after-sales service); reputation and skills (mainly complex products); products that provide an experience or life-time experience, such as leisure and travel.

There are four criteria which consumers use to evaluate a brand:

1 The information the brand package provides.

2 Whether the product provides pleasure or pain.

3 Whether the product appeals to the consumer's self-image and/or value system.

4 Whether the product protects the consumer from anxiety and from external threats.

Retail studies have found shopping motivations underpin a number of personal motives. People shop as a diversion from the routines of daily life, for self-gratification, to learn about new trends, for exercise, and for sensory stimulation (e.g. when handling merchandise, trying things on or trying them out). People shop for social experience, the pleasure of bargaining or because they enjoy the store environment. They like browsing and exploring the store's offerings, talking to sales people and spending money. Shopping is an activity that can be performed both for utilitarian and hedonic reasons. Shopping is a way of acquiring essential products as well as satisfying some important social needs.

Today, changes in consumer trends are occurring more rapidly, and consumers increasingly demonstrate unpredictability. Their choice of products often depends on mood, situation, whim, occasion and condition. Factors affecting shopping behaviour are referred to as 'antecedent states':

■ *Mood* or *physiological condition* can affect purchases and how products are evaluated. Moods can be affected by the weather or other factors specific to the consumer. A mood state can be either positive or negative, and can bias judgements of products/services in that direction. Knowledge of what people do at the time a product is bought may improve predictions of product and brand choice.

■ A *consumption situation*, e.g. entertaining friends, feeling pressed for time or being depressed. For instance, companies try to tailor their efforts to coincide with situations where people are most prone to buy.

■ *Usage context* is similar to a consumption situation but has the additional dimension of how often/how many times. Situational factors are the bases for situational segmentation.

■ *Time factors* refer to economic, psychological, social and psychological time. *Economic* time is concerned with people prioritizing things. *Social* time refers to working hours, opening hours, eating hours and other institutional schedules. *Psychological* time is about how time is experienced, e.g. psychological waiting time such as queuing.

There are different types of unplanned purchases: *pure impulse* describes buying on the spur of the moment. Other unplanned purchases can be anything from purchasing an item through *reminder* effects such as buying a product that is not on the shopping list but might be needed at the time; or purchasing an item through *suggestion* effects, such as buying a product to match with another product that we already have.

What do consumers want from their packaged brand?

From the manufacturer's and designer's perspectives, a brand package is designed to satisfy consumers' functional and emotional needs. *Functional* needs are those of convenience and ease of use, while *emotional* needs describes consumer involvement with the brand. Some have argued that the role of packaging has evolved more towards creating an emotional connection with the target consumer – through the use of language, typography, structure – while others believe user interface is crucial. All package designers want, however, is to get into the mind of the consumer. In design this translates into a number of consumer-led innovative brand packages, which are illustrated below.

In increasingly competitive environments, which are characterized by shorter development times and a greater threat from private labels, there is a need for stand-out packaging that can differentiate a brand from its competitors and provide premium value for the consumer. At one time attractive, striking packages or minimalist, high-quality gadgets used to be confined to the affluent markets (see below). Nowadays, however, value-added packaging, also known as 'smart' or 'structural' packaging – which uses materials, systems, mechanical, chemical, electrical or electronic features in combination – has been gaining more general acceptance. Here concentration is focused on conveying old-fashioned attributes like quality and value in new, cutting-edge ways, and on fulfilling consumers' desire for time-saving, ease of use and convenience, to suit their busy lifestyles.

Innovative packaging also benefits manufacturers and retailers. For the manufacturer it promotes the value of the brand, improves manufacturing efficiency and reduces the cost of goods. For the retailer, it reduces costs through the supply chain, maximizes on-shelf availability, and drives purchase and profitability.

Possible applications of smart packaging are those that: catch the eye; dispense product cleanly; monitor freshness and food quality (rather than by a printed sell-by date); help prevent errors; visually indicate readiness to eat; and confirm authenticity. There are indications in the market that consumers want something that is both smart and different. They want a product that has an aspirational design and is easy to use (e.g. steel cans now feature easy-to-open, pull-top lids and are lighter in weight; glass jars have also experienced a weight loss and have been given tamper-proof lids); is easy to dispose of; does not take up a lot of space (e.g. Kraft recently introduced a 48-ounce plastic container for its Miracle Whip salad dressing and mayonnaise which does not take up as

EXHIBIT 12.1 Portability creates new packaging forms
Kellogg's is capitalizing on portability and convenience packaging with its test-market launch of Drink 'n Crunch; Cargo Daily Lip Gloss provides small daily capsules

EXHIBIT 12.2 Differentiation via the package – water in bottle designs from plastic to glass

much room on the refrigerator door as the glass jar did), is sturdy; is reusable; and, most important, is convenient. Innovative packaging designs cater for consumer convenience at home and away from home (travel-size packages for products for use on the go, see above). According to some industry commentators, packaging has to sell the product, make an emotional connection with consumers, but user interface is still crucial as mentioned above. Packaging has to be in harmony with its contents, be user-friendly and must protect.

As far as protection is concerned, designers have combined aluminium foil and plastic film with paperboard to offer added protection and enhance product appearance. Customization is another relevant issue in packaging, e.g. single servings to meet individual needs (see below). It has been said that smart packaging also offers four ways of creating brand experience: form, format, function and feel (tactile products and sensory branding, as discussed below). In terms of form and format, smart packaging has become more sophisticated. For instance, beverage manufacturers are collaborating with design firms to produce new, irregularly shaped bottles, or bottles with multiple curves or unusually textured surfaces to have greater shelf impact. Their focus is on being both functional and beautiful.

As well as being visually appealing and meeting consumers' functional needs, the brand package must interact, communicate and create an emotional bond with the target consumer. According to design experts from Leeds University, brand packaging must be able to provide pleasure and understand consumers. Pleasure includes the physiological (equivalent to the aforementioned functional needs), the social (Starbucks encourages people to spend time in the store not just to buy coffee but spend time with others), the psychological (Gillette Mach3 Turbo represents macho men and shaving performance; it can also represent the power relationship) and the ideological (brand packages that say something about a person's ideology). 'Understanding consumers' is to do with a brand package that understands people's hopes, fears, dreams and wishes.

Branding and smart packaging

Brands have personalities and fulfil consumers' emotional needs. Packaging innovation can stimulate growth and put clear water between the positioning of the brand and its own-label look-a-like. Smart packaging has the potential to halt the erosion of brand value, outfox the counterfeiters and bring back to brands something of what made them great in the first place (Butler, 2005). It has been said that, increasingly, packaging design can make or break a product/brand. The package is the only thing that can tangibly deliver the product/brand to the consumer. Today, packaging design may be one of the most crucial factors in building brand awareness and brand equity.

EXHIBIT 12.3 Customization

The Body Shop's 'Invent Your Scent'

According to design experts, packaging can make brands great again. Dramatic forms of packaging innovation could be a way to sustain and grow brands, and to counteract private-label/counterfeit pressures. The main opportunities for brand packaging are in communication (using visual signals, graphics, colour, etc., to stand out on the shelf), improved interface (ease of use and disposability) and brand storytelling (see box). The latter is essential for brands where there is an emotional connection with the consumer. True-life stories aim to infuse products with an authenticity and uniqueness that appeals to the discriminating consumer, for whom feeling good is more important in product selection than price.

OPPORTUNITIES: BRAND STORYTELLING

Coyopa Rum

Hundreds of years ago, before Europeans landed on the shores of Barbados, legend has it there lived a people who had lightning coursing through their veins. These natives possessed a powerful energy that manifested itself through their celebrations and their songs. This spirit was called *Coyopa*. When this race of people left Barbados, the spirit remained on the island. It is a spirit that is still alive in the people of Barbados, their music, their dance, and their rum. Coyopa Rum is a full-bodied rum from the island of Barbados. Made with island sugar cane and aged ten years in oak casks, Coyopa embodies the spirit of Barbados. Coyopa has a buttery molasses aroma and a decadently rich taste.

Ambient, viral and sensory branding

Ambient branding

To continue with the subject of smart branding and packaging discussed above, *ambient products* can be kept at ambient temperature, generally have a longer shelf life and do not require refrigeration. The use of quality packaging for many products such as cereals, coffee, tea, rice and pasta helps to promote the brand and differentiate the contents. Innovative design solutions are used to boost shelf appeal with consumers, but also to keep production costs down and increase efficiency (though some may think that ambient brands are based on presentation and spin, rather than the reality of what is in the carton).

The following illustrates how ambient branding is being used in a case study at Tetra Pak, a global leader in food processing and packaging.

Tetra Pak once decided to run an information and promotion campaign in Romania about the benefits of milk processed by UHT (ultra-high temperature) technology, on the grounds that in the Romanian market only a small part of the milk consumed is processed. Tetra Pak commissioned Brandient, a brand-packaging design agency, to handle the campaign strategy and design.

Preliminary analysis with the client revealed a somewhat contradictory situation. The aseptic, carton-packaged milk preserves the natural taste and the nutritional properties for a long time. It does not require refrigeration and can be stored at an ambient temperature – features addressing all requirements of food security and consumer convenience. Nevertheless, consumers have not assimilated the technical information provided by the producer, relying instead on urban myths according to which processed milk contains preservatives or additives. Therefore, a new approach was needed in order to change this perception and to give information to consumers in a credible, memorable and appealing way. In order to overcome this communication hurdle, an animated character, the 'milk droplet', who puts a friendly and accessible face on the technical information, was developed and succeeds in conveying the message in the blink of an eye. This approach guarantees both a high impact for the delivered message and more credibility, since the animated character is perceived as a guarantee of the truthfulness of the information provided by the manufacturer. The 'milk droplet', campaign was communicated through the website, as well as through billboards, advertorials, brochures and animated commercials, and was also shown in cinema.

Viral branding

Viral branding assumes that it is consumers rather than firms that have the greater influence in the creation of brands. Many experts today recommend under-the-radar marketing, which seeds the brand among the most influential people. The basic idea is that, if the firm can convince these people to make the brand their own, and configure the brand, like a virus, to make it easy to talk about, these influencers will rapidly spread their interest in the brand to others through their social networks, in the same way as a virus is spread. Companies think going viral is the quickest and cheapest way to advertise brands. In viral branding's view, brands are no longer led by corporate activities, but rather given meaning and value on the streets by opinion-leading trendsetters, who adopt the brands and give them cachet.

In viral branding a covert public relations mode becomes the core of the branding effort. Many major ad agencies and consultancies have launched specialized groups, such as Young & Rubicam's Brand Buzz, to deliver viral branding plans to their clients.

The viral approach also assumes that it is consumers not marketers who create identity value. Consequently, identity branding has turned into a process of stealthily seeding brands with the right customers so that they will take up the brand and develop its value. The company can thus take a back seat, while consumers themselves create what the brand stands for. However, can viral branding build an iconic brand?

Simply getting people to talk about something – for example, repeating a catchphrase from an ad – is not, however, a particularly signifcant event, because mostly such talk quickly fades from memory and becomes detached from the meaning of the story. What does stay in the memory are stories that affect how people think about themselves in the world. The problem with the viral model is that it assumes that any communication is good as long as it is retold. Much more important, however, is what people remember and use symbolically in their everyday lives. This is the subject of semiotics, as discussed below.

Sensory branding

Sensory branding describes those activities or initiatives undertaken by a company to create some kind of impact on the senses of the consumer by choosing a message, propagated through a medium, which appeals to one of the *five senses* (depending on the product or service).

The primary idea of sensory branding is to create high *brand recall* among consumers. It also involves introducing the product and going beyond product marketing to play on the consumer's own faculties. The idea could also be to achieve a successful product differentiation strategy at a time when the markets are becoming crowded with products.

What sensations are triggered when you see letters crafted out of a variety of materials and then photographed? Does 'cool' come to mind? How about 'sensual'? Tactile means relating to touch or invoking the sense of touch. But tactile does not have to translate into tactless. What can't be absorbed by touch and texture must be compensated for by the visual.

Use of semiotics

Semiotics is an analytical approach grounded in the social sciences and devoted to the analysis of symbolic communication. Semiotics is some sort of code which shapes the meaning of the brand in creative execution. In this sense, brands are less about the material benefits of goods and services, than about the meanings and emotions they trigger in the hearts and minds of consumers. Semiotic not only classifies units of data by things they have in common, such as look and feel, but by the meanings they share with other units. Semiotics link the consumer world to brand associations, cultural trends and business opportunities.

Black and white ads	Ads in colour
Mode of representation: narrative prose	Mode of representation: icon
Model as the 'girl next door'	Model as 'universal goddess'
Model in medium shot looking at someone else in the image	Model in close-up looking straight into the camera
Metonymy (based on contiguity)	Metaphor (based on similarity)
Casual, realistic lifestyle	Formal, fantasy lifestyle
Concept of 'woman' as everyday women	Concept of woman as unattainable ideal, woman
Ads for American perfumes	Ads for French perfumes

TABLE 12.1 The semiotic world of luxury perfumes

Packaging and purchase decisions – how packaging influences brand choice under high involvement and time pressure

Studies of how packaging elements influence brand choice under conditions of high involvement and time pressure have demonstrated that visual package elements play a major role in representing the product for many consumers. In low involvement and when they are rushed, packaging elements influence choice to a greater extent (Silayoi and Speece, 2004). Graphics and colour are the major influences (Figure 12.1). Attractive packaging also generates consumer attention, and picture vividness has the most positive impact for products with lower levels of involvement. However, the informational element is becoming increasingly important in influencing choice. People tend to guess product performance by reading the label if they are considering products more carefully. Appropriately delivered information on packaging has a strong impact on the consumer's purchase decision. This information reduces uncertainty and creates product credibility.

Studies suggest that the visual and informational elements of packaging stimulate purchase decisions in different ways. Consumer evaluation of packaging elements changes as the perceived risk of the consumption situation increases. Visual elements such as graphics, colour, size and shape positively influence choice in the low-involvement situation. Informational elements, on the other hand, tend to play a key role in high-involvement decision-making.

Time pressure also changes how consumers evaluate products, playing a key role in high-involvement decision-making. Time pressure changes how consumers evaluate products at the point of sale, by reducing their ability to give attention to informational elements. Silayoi and Speece's (2004) study indicates that under time pressure consumers tend to make their decisions when the package comes with a distinctive appearance and contains simple, accurate and simplified information. A unique package shape may raise consumers' curiosity sooner and lead to a quick purchase decision. Package size is also indirectly related to time pressure. The study concludes that, in the face of time pressure, the visual elements will have more impact on the purchase decision than will the informational element. Consumers who are worried about saving time will pay more attention to the claims of new technology, because packaging technology is linked to convenience food products. Therefore, under time pressure packaging technology also has more positive effects on the purchase decision.

Relevance vs recognition – brands must communicate trust and comfort to anxious consumers

At the height of technological development, new brand campaigns have often stressed 'recognition' with grandiose brand messages that magnify the brand's virtues, stressing its cutting-edge nature and its limitless possibilities. In reality, tragic events such as the September 11th attack on the World Trade Center and the London bombings in July 2005 have changed people's views about

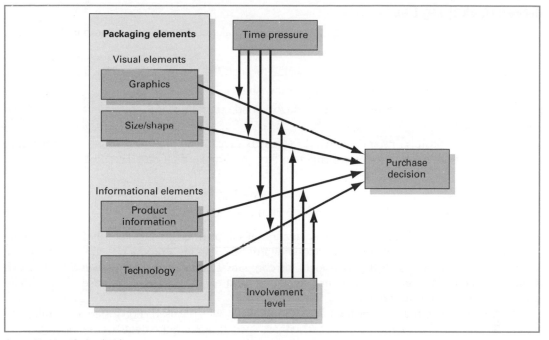

Source: Silayoi and Speece (2004)

FIGURE 12.1 Conceptual model of packaging elements and product choice

the world they live in. Some commentators suggest that these events have had a great impact on consumer values and behaviour. According to a 2001 national survey of more than 1000 American adult consumers, 46 per cent of respondents said spending time at home with family and friends is more appealing. Other activities they have also found more appealing since September 11th include eating with friends and family, cooking meals at home, shopping for food to make for family and friends, watching TV with family or friends, as opposed to doing so alone and reading books. Activities consumers identified as less appealing include planning vacations and shopping for items they do not need but would like to have (Swientek, 2001).

Consumers are focusing more on their home life to give them a sense of stability and security. Market researchers refer to this phenomenon as 'cocooning', 'burrowing' and 'fortressing'. Tragic events like those of September 11th have reminded people of such fundamental human values as family, community, security, integrity, work–life balance and authenticity. In uncertain and anxious times, many consumers seek familiarity and things of which they have had previous experience, and brands must represent what is relevant to consumers and their lifestyles. Established and trusted brands represent familiarity. These brands have been with the consumers in the past and they will be with them in the future. Consumers' trust and confidence in these brands could be related to the fact that they know what to expect.

What is also relevant today are the real values of credibility, integrity, safety and security. This suggests that the previous in-your-face attitude campaigns are now out. Attitude is being replaced by appreciation: appreciating the product, appreciating the customer, the situation or the moment. This change of attitude stresses that marketers should be more traditional, safer and less cutting edge. If this is true, marketers should focus on simple, straightforward messages and price–value relationships, since consumers have become more comparative shoppers nowadays. This sends a message to marketers to stay true to their brand persona, making it relevant to changing values and lifestyles, communicating its distinctive attributes and staying true to them.

Seven packaging tips

To summarize, here are seven packaging tips that will make customers buy a company's product:

1 Satisfy consumers' functional and emotional needs.

2 Focus on differentiation, premium and value through the use of smart packaging.

3 Understand consumers' hopes, dreams and wishes.

4 Provide specific brand experience through sound, sensation and enjoyment of innovative brand packages.

5 Understand basic consumer demands so as to save them time and money; support and make life a little easier for them; entertain them and make their day; keep them healthy and secure.

6 Communicate relevancy, trust and comfort, as well as safety and protection.

7 Tell a story that can connect consumers with the brand packaging.

A company must also find out what package attributes appeal to the customer that it is targeting. For instance, if it is a hurried housewife shopping for the company's product, then convenience of use should be at the top of its list. If, instead, the company's target market is the over-50s, they will seek convenience as well but issues such as size of print on the package and ease of use should also top the company's priority list.

Next, companies must understand how the package will be used. For instance, families no longer sit down and eat a meal together. There are special diet requirements or dieting in general in most households. It is not uncommon to serve different meals to different individuals within a household, and package sizes should vary accordingly. This also applies to people who travel frequently. They will require sample or trial-size packages.

Knowing where people shop is also important. For instance, there is a shift from traditional retailers to new and innovative store formats. The convenience store that used to be considered a low-end retailer will now have moved into larger premises that provide premium products sometimes at premium prices. Research shows that consumers no longer make one big trip to stock up, but instead make several trips a week and get just what is needed at the time. Grab-and-go cups of snack foods do not just suit travellers, they are now offered at convenience stores. Finally, companies must keep abreast of technology and focus on innovation, as well as looking for ways to combine two products into one package to save costs.

Overcoming the dichotomy between food quality and the processed appearances of packaging, to engender trust in the consumer

Despite the pretty packaging, it is often difficult to tell what the product is. It has been known for consumers sometimes to buy the package, not the brand, but better educated and higher-income consumers are said to be willing to pay more for product quality. Questions about food quality have been raised in answer to consumers' concerns about food safety. Nowadays more and more consumers want to be reassured, and they look for integrity in a food package that delivers its promise of good quality. One major security scare could be enough to persuade consumers to shop elsewhere, and manufacturers to change their packaging methods immediately or go out of business.

The advances in food processing methods and legislation are other factors that drive companies to look for ways to improve their packaging so as to engender trust in consumers. These can take the following forms:

1 Make it easier for consumers to read ingredient contents on product packs. For instance, a recent study conducted by Leeds Communication and Information Design Research Group shows six ways companies can prioritize pack information and messages so as to fit them into the limited space available. These are usability, comprehensibility, brand reflection, cohesion and differentiation, prominence and experience building.

- *Usability* means shaping the typeface to increase legibility and using colour contrast for the text and icons wherever possible. Colour can also be used to indicate low fat and high fat in products.

- *Comprehensibility* means not being over-technical with the list of ingredients, and making connections explicit – for example, why bacteria is bad in toothpaste.

- *Brand reflection* refers to the congruence between pack messages and advertising. Ideally, companies should try to be as consistent as possible in what they want the pack messages to say and the advertising messages conveyed by the brand. Otherwise, consumers might detect discrepancies between pack messages and brand's advertisements.

- *Cohesion* and *differentiation* mean that similar messages should be grouped together.

- *Prominence* refers to highlighting the most important information to make it stand out and positioning it to the best advantage on the pack. This should be done keeping in mind how products are stacked on supermarket shelves, or in the fridge or cupboard at home. Products that show the name, ingredient contents and information in the correct way will have a greater influence on repurchase.

- *Experience building* concerns user-friendly instructions, tips for healthy lifestyles, helpline information and delight factors on packs. In another study, by Rettie and Brewer (2000), it has been shown that, to maximize recall, words should be on the right-hand side of packs and pictures on the left-hand side. Their results confirm the asymmetry in the perception of packaging elements.

2 Deal with the issue of chemical migration from packaging. This can be leaching, bleeding and leaking of substances from the packaging into the food by sub-microscopic processes (Central Science Laboratory (CSL), Department for Environment, Food and Rural Affairs (DEFRA), 2005). Migration of chemicals from food-contact materials has an impact on food quality and food safety. For instance, during the packaging of fresh and processed meat poultry, when it touches the food, chemicals in the packaging can migrate to the food, so the question is how companies can improve the situation to meet EU regulations. Under EU rules, Framework Directive Article 2 states that:

> materials and articles must be manufactured so that, under their normal or foreseeable conditions of use, they do not transfer their constituents into foodstuffs in quantities which could endanger human health, bring about an unacceptable change in the composition of foodstuffs or a deterioration in the organoleptic characteristics thereof. (CSL, DEFRA, 2005)

The CSL suggests that *active packaging* could change the condition of the packed food, extend shelf life and improve its sensory properties, while still maintaining food quality. Examples of active packaging are: *absorbers*, which are scavengers of oxygen, water, carbon dioxide, ethylene, off-flavours such as amines and aldehydes; and *emitters*, which release preservatives, antioxidants, flavourings and colours. However, at the moment, this type of packaging cannot be introduced into the EU because existing legislation states that food-contact material should not trigger any chemical reactions which might change the food's taste, appearance, texture or smell, or alter its chemical composition. This applies even if the changes are beneficial (CSL, DEFRA, 2005).

Another packaging innovation is high-barrier packaging which provides good barrier properties while maintaining biodegradability. Unfortunately its new type of coating fell outside the legal definition of RCF in Directive 93/10/EEC. This meant that a new Directive on RCF had to be introduced, which allowed the inclusion of the new coatings (Regulation 14/2004/EC) and new methods of testing.

3 Retain product freshness through improved packaging. Smart packaging developed and used in the fresh-cut industry, for instance, includes indicators of time and temperature, gas composition, seal leakage, and food safety and quality. These intelligent systems alter package

oxygen and/or carbon dioxide permeability by sensing and responding to changes in temperature. Other smart films incorporate chemicals into packets placed in the packaging system, with no contact with the product; an example would be the use of O_2 scavengers with O_2 indicators.

Another type of smart film, developed with food safety in mind, is currently undergoing testing. This novel system, when incorporated into a packaging film, uses an antibody detection system to detect pathogens, and expresses a positive finding as a symbol on the surface of the package, thereby alerting food handlers to the presence of pathogens. Although this technology shows promise, it is still in its infancy and comprehensive assessments have yet to be performed. Several limitations have been suggested with this technology; for example, it would not likely be able to detect pathogens at concentrations below 10 CFU/g or cm^2 and would not detect pathogens within the product. These examples show that the industry has responded to consumers' needs by improving packaging and food quality/safety issues for consumers through innovation. Hence, there is a *technological push* on the part of the providers and designers. However, for innovations or leading-edge packaging to succeed, potential hurdles and pitfalls such as those mentioned above must be anticipated.

Branding Brief 12.1: Nanotechnology and Packaging

Source: Based on Technologies Ltd's presentation at University of Sheffield, Management School, 2006

Nanotechnologies are not new but their applications in packaging are relatively recent. They can revolutionize the packaging and presentation of goods, from the brightness of package colours and self-cleaning containers to anti-piracy applications and increased barrier protection for foods. Nanotechnologies can provide safety features when used in food packaging. They can increase shelf life, freshness, and protection against bacteria and funguses. They are ecologically sound, reducing packaging weight while increasing its robustness and biodegradability. They can also provide built-in sensors, RFDI and displays which can 'speak' to mobile phones (Wilkinson, 2006). Examples of nanotechnologies' applications are in plastic beer bottles and shelf life. Nanocor is currently producing clay-based nano composites for use in plastic beer bottles that give the contents a six-month shelf life. These plastic bottles are usually lighter in weight and less material is used, which also means lower transportation costs and better recyclability.

Nanotechnology also improves conductivity. Carbon nano fibres and nano tubes can modify a range of properties including electrical and thermal conductivity. It has been said that, in the longer term, research should concentrate on the manufacture of materials to change properties depending on external or internal conditions. For example, researchers are hoping to use the changing molecular composition of milk that is beginning to spoil to bring about a reaction with nano particles embedded in the packaging, causing the colour of the packaging to change. Other ideas include a smart ice-cream carton that would change its molecular structure to prevent heat from affecting the contents – for example, if it was left in the back of a car on a hot summer's day.

Other examples of nanotechnologies' applications are micro-thin layers of a car's paintwork, textiles, inkjet printing, home products, personal care and drug delivery; you can also find nano particles in sun cream.

How environmental issues influence consumer buying behaviour

The 1990s have been described as the decade of environmental responsibility, as evidenced by increasing consumer demand for green packaging. Those consumers want environmentally friendly packaging that recycles, degrades or burns easily. In response, packaging designers have broadened the range of available packaging. During the past few years an influx of shelf-space aseptic packages, retort hot-filled packages, film/foil pouches, multi-layer film pouches and micro-wavable plastic containers in a range of packaging configurations and made from a variety of materials have come into use, including recycled paperboard.

However, not all customers are green consumers and demand green packaging. Research conducted by Raymond et al. (2005) shows that consumers make mental links between healthy food and eco-responsibility. Their qualitative study explores household habits in families with young children in two areas: eco awareness and food-health awareness. Semi-structured interviews were conducted with 28 families, all with at least one child under three. Ten were from Bangor, North Wales, and 18 from Greater London. Issues covered in interviews were supermarket loyalty, brand loyalty, food-health awareness, eco-awareness and preference in pack design style for non-food household products.

The study's findings show that concern about food health was correlated with a sense of responsibility towards environmental issues. Positive attitudes towards these were most obvious in exploratory brand-hopping consumers. Three distinct types of households were identified:

1 *The easy-living group*: typically, lazy, habitual, self-centred, trusting in big brands, con-forming and unconcerned. They are not eager for new information and are happy with the familiar.

2 *The well-intentioned group*: they want to improve but do not always follow through. They are family-centred, can cope with changing needs, are health conscious, eco-conscious and do not trust the big brands.

3 *The eco-trendy group*: typically, energetic and informed, actively distrustful of big brands, conscientious, concerned, ethical consumers who like to be different.

The study concludes that caring about food health is linked to caring about the environment. The rise of food-health awareness might also be accompanied by a greater demand for eco-friendly packaging and products. These findings can be used to influence package design and provide an understanding of the basis of consumer preference.

How information displayed on food labels impacts on consumer perceptions of the product

Warning-label research suggests that label design characteristics and linguistic variation affect consumers' perceptions of products and, consequently, behaviour. Costello et al.'s (2005) study into the effects of food-label design and linguistic variation on hazard perception and behavioural intention looks at the impact of changes in label colour, shape, font size and wording for labels indicating genetically modified (GM) and non-genetically modified (non-GM) content on food products. These researchers show that, first, the majority of consumers are not in favour of GM foods.

The use of words such as 'may contain/contains no' on packs does not help, and varying descriptions such as 'contains GM ingredients' as opposed to 'GM organism' are not clear and tend to put consumers off. People want to be sure. Even voluntary GM-free labelling was found not to be welcomed by consumers, who looked at shape, colour and hazard. As hazard went up, sales went down. The colour red and an angular shape seemed to lower consumers' willingness to buy the product. Rounder shapes were preferred among the respondents. Costello et al. conclude that perhaps companies that sell GM products should use oval shapes and white colours, since these are neutral and preferred by respondents. The preferred pack's message would be the one that says: 'contains genetically modified ingredients'. Finally, the authors state that, unless special care is taken in the design and wording of GM and GM-free labels, manufacturers and retailers are best advised to avoid voluntary labelling as it confuses the consumer more.

The benefits of eco-labels

Eco- or social-development labels are simple, readily identifiable marks, which are ostensibly intended to indicate that a product has a lower overall environmental impact than other products in a specified product category.

First, here are some definitions and explanations of what labelling means. *Category labelling* refers to a label that conveys information regarding the product category. This is typically done through the use of certain symbols or colours. For instance, orange juice containers may have pictures of oranges and a predominance of orange colouring on the label, while apple juice containers may have pictures of apples and a predominance of green colouring on the label.

Specific product information labelling describes labels that convey information regarding a variety of product-specific attributes. For example, the label on a packet of Cheddar cheese may provide information regarding the quantity of protein, fat sugar and calcium that the cheese contains, while the label on a packet of washing powder may contain information regarding the quantity of powder required to wash 1 kg of clothes and the relative performance of the powder at different wash temperatures.

Brand labelling refers to a label that conveys information regarding the brand or the product. This is probably the most important part of the label (Robertson, 1987) because it provides the consumer with explicit information regarding several product attributes, including the performance the consumer can expect from the product, the price which the consumer would expect to pay (relative to other brands in the product category) and other product attributes which the consumer has previously learnt to expect from the brand, either from past use or from advertising.

Certification labelling might convey information regarding the certification of the product by an independent authority. Such certification is intended to enhance the consumer's expectations regarding certain product attributes. Several certification schemes exist, such as those covering reputation, expert advice, accreditation and warranties. Product certification symbol examples are the British Standards Institute's 'Kitemark', the International Wool Secretariat's 'Woolmark', and the hallmarks on gold and silver articles. The purpose of these marks is to signal to the consumer that the product has been accredited by the specified authority for the specified purpose.

There are two types of product certification: those which certify manufacturers' claims and those which certify more general concepts. *Manufacturers' claims certifications* are those such as the Woolmark and the Vegetarian Society emblem. The Woolmark, owned by the International Wool Secretariat, indicates that a garment is made from 100 per cent virgin wool. The Vegetarian Society emblem is owned by the Vegetarian Society in the UK and signifies that a product contains no meat products. *General concept certification* refers to 'safety' and 'overall product quality', and is hard to define because it relies so much on individual responses to products. One successful example is Underwriters Laboratories (UL), a private American organization which offers certification marks for product safety. In order to qualify for a UL certification mark, a product must fulfil the product safety criteria in the appropriate product category. These criteria are developed in consultation with producers and are updated regularly in order to incorporate technological innovations. The UL provides some useful basic safety information, enabling consumers to make decisions both when they are purchasing and when they are using a product. Another example is Good Housekeeping (GH), which offers a product-quality seal. This is effectively a warranty extended by GH to readers

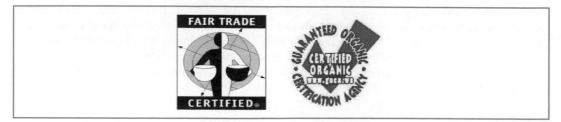

EXHIBIT 12.4 Examples of eco- and social development labels

of its magazine. GH (not the manufacturer of the product) promises to replace any product which has been awarded the seal (or to refund the value of the purchase) if the consumer is not satisfied (Kerwin, 1994).

Eco- and social development labels (e.g. Exhibit 12.4) are certification marks awarded to those products in a particular category that have met certain predefined criteria. It has been suggested that these labels might also help to improve the sales and image of labelled products, once consumers have accepted the objectivity and reliability of such environmental labels. An eco-labelling programme might encourage manufacturers to be more forthcoming about the environmental impact of their products in competition with other firms whose products bear an eco-label. They too may wish to signal their environmentally friendly behaviour to the market, by carrying out an eco audit or complying with ISO 9000 and ISO 14000. Eco-labels might equally make consumers more aware of environmental issues. Eco-labels might also help to protect the environment. However, some critics have cautioned that eco-labels may not actually improve the information available to the consumer and, at worst, may even have the opposite effect (Shimp, 1995; Wynne, 2003).

Another problem is how to develop an eco-labelling scheme. First, product category boundaries are not easy to select. Second, it is not easy to take into account all the physical effects which a product has on the environment during its life cycle. No one can accurately estimate the impacts of these effects and continuously update the eco-label product selection criteria. Some commentators also suggest that national eco-labels may become a barrier to trade, but an international eco-label might be no better.

Packaging Brief 12.2: The demand for eco-labels in Sweden

In the early 1990s Eca, one of Sweden's largest retailers, put pressure on certain major producers of consumer goods to obtain eco-labels for their products, singling out producers in the detergent and battery industries. Most of the targeted manufacturers initially refused to comply, so Eca responded by decreasing the shelf space devoted to their brands and increasing the space devoted to eco-labelled brands. Many manufacturers refused, though, to budge. Members of the Swedish Nature Federation then initiated a public campaign against products not bearing eco-labels, which would have to carry a label warning: 'I'm not eco-labelled, don't buy me.' In response, Swedish consumers, wary of being seen to be unfriendly towards the environment, reduced their consumption of these products. At this point, the targeted producers gave in and applied for eco-labels (e.g. Procter & Gamble's brand of dishwashing detergent was simply repackaged with an eco-label for the Swedish market; Duracell did the same with its range of products).

Packaging Brief 12.3: Product disposal and recycling management (WRAP and PET)

Source: Adapted from Barthel, 2005

British consumers dispose of 4.6 million tonnes of packaging waste and 5.2 million tonnes of food waste annually. Half of this packaging waste is said to originate from the retail grocery sector, which, in turn, accounted for nearly 70 per cent of £9 billion spent on packaging in the UK in 2004. As recycling rates rise rapidly, consumers are more aware of what ends up in their bins and how the products they buy are packaged. In response, retailers, manufacturers and packaging companies try to look for ways to develop packaging that can perform as well, but use considerably less material.

The Waste & Resources Action Programme (WRAP) has recently been established to work closely with retailers to develop a range of practical product designs that seek to minimize household food and packaging waste. In addition, WRAP's Materials Teams work with retailers and brands on projects to investigate the feasibility of incorporating recycled content into food grade packaging. One of the projects, the rPET (recycled PET) Project, has resulted in the relaunch of Marks & Spencer's Food To Go range, with packaging containing recycled PET. Examples of technology used: RF sealing technology, which stands for radio frequency technology, is a leak-proof seal for most thermoplastic materials including food packaging trays. The seal is stronger, more durable, increases yield, has fewer complaints and uses less material, thus results in lighter packs. Less material also means cost reduction.

Participating companies included Coca-Cola Enterprises (CCE), Marks & Spencer and Boots. The project ran large-scale trials on these companies' use of rPET in food, drink and personal care packaging. It investigated the technical, logistical and economic feasibility of using rPET. From the companies' perspective, the drivers of rPET are: cost advantages, brand enhancement, positive public relations, proven technology and that it mitigates against future mandatory systems. While, according to independent consumer research, 86 per cent of consumers felt it would be good if packaging contained recycled plastic, 74 per cent felt that the reputation of a retailer or brand would be enhanced if its product packaging were made from recycled plastic; 90 per cent felt manufacturers and retailers should get on with producing packaging containing as much recycled plastic as possible, and 70 per cent believed that, if more packaging used recycled plastic, they would be encouraged to recycle more.

Why some packaging fails – some common mistakes

Despite the efforts of manufacturers, retailers and packaging designers to improve brand packaging to meet consumers' packaging needs and demands, and to engender trust in consumers, as discussed earlier this chapter, it is accepted that not all brand packaging succeeds in the market-place. This section looks at the reasons why some brand packaging fails.

According to a design expert from Oxford University, some packaging falls at the first hurdle. Some packs have beautiful designs but are boring and fail to inspire, educate or entertain the consumer. Often these also fail to connect with the consumer and to communicate the essence of the product and its attributes. Other packaging falls at the second hurdle which, as the expert explains, is because it is difficult to read the instructions or contents on the product. The packaging is also difficult to open, and hard to dispose of and recycle.

Brand identity and packaging design

Brand identity and package design are important components of companies' branding strategies. Two main applications exist: where package design contributes to the creation of a brand identity and image for a new product or a new product line; where it contributes to the development of a logo and a package-design system for line extensions by leveraging existing brand equities, while at the same time creating distinctive imagery for a new category segment.

In the first case, brand identity and image are created from scratch. Logo design, product naming and research are usually done prior to this. Category audits are undertaken to assess the competition on the shelf. The brand assets of the new product are revealed and its brand drivers identified. Consumer-based research into brand experiences that impact on consumer perception and decision-making are assessed. For example, Unilever's Carb Options is a new line that repackages some of Unilever's popular food products, with the original brands' equities being leveraged on the new packaging as 'sub-brands'. Some of these products include Skippy Peanut Butter, Wishbone salad dressings and Ragu pasta sauces (Mininni at Brandchannel.com).

An example of the second case is Procter & Gamble's Pringles Snack Stacks products. Snack Stacks offer consumers the same Pringles in an eight-pack configuration of small plastic tubs that are linked together in a paperboard sleeve, which is ideal for lunchboxes and for those who wish to control portions. The iconic Mr Pringles character has been updated for a new generation of potato chip fans and is now a global player in the crowded snack market in 140 countries (Mininni at Brandchannel.com).

Packaging design and dual branding

In the fast-moving consumer goods (fmcg) sector especially, brands exist at many levels and in many combinations, often as a result of mergers and acquisitions, brand leverage or brand extension and the multiple markets in which companies operate. The brand hierarchy outlined in Chapter 6 and below is the best way to describe these levels and combinations of brands used. Packaging can be designed to reflect these levels and the combinations of brands on the package, as well as optimizing the relationship among brands by emphasizing visual cues. The following section is concerned with these as well as with the execution of brand strategy on the packaging and the presentation of the branding level on the packaging.

As shown in Chapter 6, the brand structure conceptualized by Laforet and Saunders in 1994 had three main levels of branding: corporate dominant, brand dominant and mixed branding.

Corporate dominant describes a situation in which corporate names or subsidiaries' names are used on product packs across all the company's products. The reason for this is history. For example, corporate branding (i.e. corporate names used on all the company's product packs) happens because of how companies started. For example, in the case of Cadbury, its corporate name has been used for generations on all its product packs. Its values have been kept and passed on from generation to generation.

However, it has been argued that companies should only use a corporate brand name across its product range if this name is very strong and easily recognized, if the product is to gain benefits from being associated with it. For instance, when Nestlé wanted to enter into low-calorie frozen food, it was felt that the Nestlé corporate brand could not extend into this category. However, its family brand, Stouffer's, could, because it had already earned a reputation for providing great-tasting, high-quality frozen food. So, the package designer placed the Stouffer's brand name prominently on the package, giving Lean Cuisine instant credibility in the trade and among consumers. Since then, Lean Cuisine has become a strong brand in its own right and, in turn, has benefited Stouffer's.

This is what is known as strategic associations, and what most companies are trying to do. This is also the main reason why some companies adopt a dominant brand approach in which a single-product brand name is used on packs; or furtive, where a single-product brand name is used, but the company's name or manufacturer name is not disclosed in the address of the pack – to keep their conflicting businesses or conflicting markets separate. For example, Mars Corporation makes confectionery products as well as pet foods and it is appropriate for the company to keep separate names for the confectionery market and the pet foods. Similarly, Philip Morris owns General Foods and Kraft, and decides that the corporate name Philip Morris should not appear on food packaging. This strategy is also used when the corporate name does not mean much to customers. An example is Aurora foods. There would be no advantage in using this name on the company's product packs because it is an unfamiliar name to the customer.

The brand dominant approach is used when companies operate in multiple markets. It allows a variety of product positioning as well as letting similar products compete in the same market. While it has been argued that a strong corporate brand may generate instant awareness and visibility for a product brand, it can also prevent the company from having similar, potentially competitive products in closely related categories. Even if the message and package design is tailored to each product and niche audience, a consumer many not easily perceive the differences between the products. For example, Unilever has taken the branded approach of letting each product develop its own personality and attributes (see below). This has allowed Unilever to have similar products compete in the same market. This is also a strategy to overcome the risk of diluting the brand (see Chapter 6).

The lesson for packaging design here would be to focus on unique brand marks and colours to establish themselves as the product brand identities that serve to differentiate the product in a similar category and are powerful enough for the consumer to see them as something special. For example, Coca-Cola established its distinctive script and bright-red colour as cues for a whole category.

Mixed branding occurs where dual brand names (a combination of corporate name or family name used with a product brand name) or endorsed brand names (a corporate name or subsidiary name used with a product brand name) appear on product packs simultaneously. The rationale behind the use of dual brand names and the endorsed approach is explained in Chapter 9. The main reasons for this are: brand symbiosis (the benefits of shared brand heritage and brand value between two brand names) and economics. Each brand can capitalize on the other's positive attributes and brand values, while still maintaining enough independence to make a strong product–brand statement.

The decline of broadcasting and the fragmentation of communication and distribution channels are increasing the cost of branding. Managers now view endorsed and dual brands as giving an economic edge over standalone (or single) brands. This provides a greater variety of positioning alternatives than if the corporate branding were the only option considered. Examples are Kellogg's Rice Krispies Treats – in this case, Treats feeds off Rice Krispies' heritage of quality and breakfast cereal, while Treats help position Rice Krispies as a product that kids enjoy.

However, the ambiguity in the use of dual branding on product packs makes decisions about how to relate corporate and product brands in a visual sense complex. This complexity demands that these brand relationships be thought through properly and not decided ad hoc. Making the wrong choice can have a detrimental effect on companies' long-term revenue and profitability. A company with multiple brands may survive one product failure, but a corporate brand intrinsically linked to only one product brand may suffer (Nelson, 2002). So, before any decisions can be made about how to use the multiple levels of branding on product packs, the company must have a clear sense of what each approach means, what each stands for, and what they mean to themselves and to the consumer. For instance, what it would mean for Mars to be identified with Maltesers, from Mars' perspective and from the customer's. Would there be any benefits in adding the corporate name Mars to the brand Maltesers? How might Mars Maltesers affect consumers' perception of Mars and Maltesers? Once these questions are answered, companies can work with package designers to determine how each level of branding should be presented on the package. For instance, sometimes the designer must discreetly add the corporate identity in the lower right-hand corner of the package front. At other times, he might have to apply the corporate brand, logo, colour, typography and illustration in an appealing and non-disruptive place.

EXHIBIT 12.5 Unilever's product range

When companies extend a brand in a related or non-related product category using dual brand names on packs (e.g. Coke Vanilla or Mars beverages), the challenge for a packaging designer is to understand when and how to optimize the relationships among brands by emphasizing visual cues such as colour, shape, logo and graphics and packaging materials. Studies show that in brand leverage, in order not to dilute the core or parent brand image, package designers must keep a psychological distance between the core brand and the product brand (Kim and Lavack, 1996).

To sum up, packaging design uses logos and styles, which encompass colours, shapes, patterns, typefaces and or symbols that may be used either separately or together to create an identity that visually represents the company, its products and its values. Over time, the link between a style and a company and its products can become so strong that all it takes is a quick look for consumers instantly to recollect the corporate brand or the product brand, depending on the brand approach used. However, the power of visual associations can create problems too (consider brand dilution with reference to Kodak).

Conclusion

Packaging design and branding go hand in hand: branding is a powerful mechanism that can set owners' products apart from competitors' in the mind of the consumer. Packaging is defined as a critical tool that help to visualize and verbalize what a company's brand stands for, to demonstrate its expertise and to serve as a sign of differentiation in a variety of product categories. It has a logistics and marketing function, which are to protect the product during movement and brand communication. Its role is to reinforce the brand message, and understand and communicate what consumers value most. Purchase decisions are affected by the visual and informational aspects of packaging. When involvement is high and time pressing, the visual elements influence choice to a greater extent. In high-involvement situations, the information on packs can reduce uncertainty and create product credibility. While time pressure changes how consumers evaluate products at the point of sale, a unique package shape may raise consumers' curiosity sooner and lead to a quicker purchase decision.

From a manufacturer's and designer's perspective, a brand package is designed to satisfy consumers' functional and emotional needs. Functional needs refer to convenience, ease of use; emotional needs describe consumer involvement with the brand. Packaging is regarded as something which can create an emotional connection with the target consumer through the use of language, typography, structure and user interface. To stand out from the crowd, nowadays, packaging must also provide added value beyond a striking appearance through revolutionary packaging. This is known as smart packaging or structural packaging and nanotechnology. The main focus of structural packaging is to reduce costs and improve manufacturing efficiency as well as provide a number of consumer benefits such as dispensing the product cleanly, monitoring freshness and guaranteeing food quality. In addition, packaging design must take into account consumers' values. Especially since September 11th, consumers' values have changed and tend to focus more on home life and security. Packaging must therefore communicate relevancy, trust, comfort and safety to these anxious consumers.

Safety is an issue which is also linked to food quality. The advances in food processing methods and legislation have driven companies to look for ways to improve their packaging in order to engender trust in consumers – such as making it easier for them to read the ingredient contents on product packs. According to research, simple warning messages such as 'contains genetically modified ingredients' are also welcome by consumers. Similarly, eco-labels can benefit both the manufacturer and the consumer in that they can help achieve sales and at the same time raise consumer awareness of environmental issues. Part of raising environmental awareness are sustainability programmes such as WRAP and PET, which aim to develop a range of practical product designs that seek to reduce household food and packaging waste.

Packaging design contributes to the creation of a brand identity and image for a new product or a new product line, and to the development of a logo and a package design system for line extensions by leveraging existing brand equities, while creating distinctive imagery for a new category segment. Packaging designers need to work with brand manufacturers, in particular those who use a combination of brand names within their brand portfolios (or dual brand and endorsed approaches) to determine how each level of branding should be presented on the package. Unique brand marks and colour created by the packaging designer can establish themselves as brand identities. They serve as product differentiators and help to see off the competition.

🔐 Key terms

Active label: gives more information about the product and how it can be used. Its purpose is to engage the consumer with the product and build a relationship with the consumer. For example, the active label on the self-cooling wine bottle tells something about the vineyard but also suggests how the consumer might want to drink the wine.

Affective side of decisions: when decisions are based on feelings and emotions rather than on reason or logic.

Brand identity and packaging design: the role of package design is to create a brand identity and image for a new product or a new product line. Also to develop a logo and a package design system for line extensions by leveraging existing brand equities, while creating distinctive imagery for a new category segment.

Brand labelling: labelling to convey information about the brand or the product. It provides the consumer with implicit information regarding the product's attributes, including the performance the consumer can expect from the product; the price which the consumer would expect to pay (relative to other brands in the product category) and other product attributes which the consumer has previously learnt to expect from the brand, either from past use or from advertising.

Brand symbiosis: by design, when two brand names are used together or simultaneously on product packs, the brand values and heritage of the established brand and the new brand or the extended brand feed off each other.

Branding and packaging relationship: packaging helps visualize and verbalize what a brand stands for, demonstrates its expertise and helps differentiate the brand from others in the same product categories.

Certification labelling: conveys information regarding certification of the product by an independent authority. Such certification is intended to enhance the consumer's expectations regarding certain product attributes. Several such certification schemes exist covering reputation, expert advice, accreditation, warranties etc. Examples are the British Standards Institute's 'Kitemark', the International Wool Secretariat's 'Woolmark', and the hallmarks on gold and silver articles. The purpose of these marks is to signal to the consumer that the product has been accredited by the specified authority for the specified purpose.

Cognitive side of decisions: when decisions are made based on reason and logic.

Eco- or social development labels: simple, readily identifiable marks, which are intended to indicate that a product has a lower overall environmental impact than other products in a specified product category.

Execution of brand strategy on the package: the presentation of branding level(s) (or brand hierarchy) on the package and/or the brand combinations used on packs.

High-involvement purchase: where the consumer is highly involved with the product often because they perceive that the purchasing risks are high. If the product is expensive or complex or technical, this means the consumer must take time to search for information about the product, compare prices and evaluate the product for suitability before a buying decision can be reached.

Low-involvement purchase: reverse of high-involvement purchase, where the consumer is not involved with the product because perceived risks are low. The product is a commodity or a frequently purchased type product, or a fast-moving consumer good (fmcg). Product evaluation does not take place before purchase. Purchases are made emotionally, often on impulse, and buying decisions take place in retail outlets or on the spot.

Nanotechnology: a form of technology that creates materials from building blocks smaller than atoms that will unleash unprecedented capabilities (material 100 times stronger than steel but a sixth the weight, 1000 miles to a gallon of fuel, car batteries the size of small torch batteries, etc.). Nanotechnology can revolutionize the packaging and presentation of goods. From the brightness of package colours and self-cleaning containers to anti-piracy applications and increased barrier protection for foods as well as safety, providing features in food packaging such as increasing shelf life, freshness and protection against bacteria and funguses.

Packaging design and dual branding: the ambiguity and the use of dual branding on product packs makes decisions about how to relate corporate and product brands in a visual sense complex. This complexity demands that these brand relationships be thought through properly and not based on ad hoc decisions. For instance, sometimes the designer must discreetly add the corporate identity to the lower right-hand corner of the package front. At other times, he might have to apply the corporate brand, logo, colour, typography and illustration in an appealing and non-disruptive place, as well as keeping a psychological distance between the core brand and the product brand, in order not to dilute the core or parent's brand image.

Packaging functions: the logistical function of packaging is mainly to protect the product during movement through distribution channels. The marketing function of packaging is that of brand communication. Packaging provides a way of conveying messages about product attributes to the consumer at the point of sale. The logistic and marketing functions are inseparable since the package sells the product by attracting attention and communicating as well as allowing the product to be contained, apportioned, utilized and protected. In terms of brand communication, packaging's function is to communicate the value of the brand and reinforce the brand message.

Packaging informational elements: information provided and technologies used in the package, which address the cognitive side of decisions. Product information is important, especially when consumers are engaged in high-involvement purchases.

Packaging visual elements: the visual aspect or element of packaging consists of graphics and size/shape of packaging, which address the affective side of decisions. Graphics includes layout, colour combinations, typography and product photography, all of which create an image for the product.

Smart packaging: packaging that (often but not exclusively) uses smart materials or devices. Smart materials are those that exhibit some kind of useful response to an external change, e.g. the material might become deformed in some way if voltage is applied. Examples of smart products are a smart kettle that uses thermochromic materials incorporated into a polymer body as a safety feature. The kettle changes colour as the water boils. Or a smart comb that uses surface roughness and other sensors to evaluate the condition and health of your hair, and provides hair-care advice. Types of smart packaging are track and trace for supply chains, security-smart packaging such as authentification of the brand owner, and consumer-smart packaging that provides product functionality.

Structural packaging: similar to **Smart packaging**.

Tactile products: products designed, through shape or form or material, to tap into consumers' touch sense.

Technological push: there is a technological push in the market when producers and manufacturers use new technology to respond to consumers' needs by improving packaging and food quality/safety through innovative packaging such as structural or smart packaging.

WRAP: Waste & Resources Action Programme, which has recently been established to work closely with retailers to develop a range of practical product designs that seek to minimize household food and packaging waste.

? Discussion questions

1 What are the problems or challenges faced by commodity marketers in general?

2 What associations do consumers have for milk? What are the implications of these associations in terms of building brand equity for and increasing the consumption of milk?

3 What are the problems or challenges faced by the CMPB (California Milk Processor Board) now that milk consumption has reached a plateau?

4 What are the implications for the branding and marketing of commodity products in developed and developing countries?

5 Discuss the advantages and disadvantages of re-branding and re-positioning.

6 Discuss the advantages and disadvantages of re-branding and re-positioning of a global brand.

7 Compare and contrast the role packaging and advertising play in consumers' buying decisions.

8 Discuss this statement: 'Packaging is more powerful in consumer brand recall than advertising.'

9 Discuss how packaging can increase consumer brand loyalty.

10 Discuss how corporate re-branding may destroy, transfer or create brand equity.

11 Discuss the possible conflicts that might arise in the case of a high-couture designer who wants to expand their business and cater for the mass market, e.g. Vera Wang wants to provide a line of clothing and handbags for Kohl's retail chain.

12 Which types of products are actively using the 'nano inside' branding?

13 Which products/manufacturing processes are most likely to create nano health hazards?

Projects

1 Create a chocolate pack for Christmas, aiming at children aged five to twelve years. The shape and structure should have a high 'novelty factor' where shelf impact and product awareness is essential.

2 Consider re-designing a real-life fmcg brand of your choice that could do with a timely make-over. You are encouraged to conduct a small survey or interviews with either consumers or managers to assist you in this project.

3 Create a brand architecture and naming strategy that would extend a real-life company's brand of your choice, without compromising the brand's integrity.

4 Design brand packaging to reflect corporate social responsibility (see Chapter 9). You may base your ideas on FairTrade brand packaging or similar.

5 According to research conducted by Landor Associates, green-motivated individuals base purchase decisions on whether or not a brand reflects green behaviour in its packaging, ingredients and corporate actions. First, explain what elements you should focus on in designing for green consumers, then design brand packaging for these consumers.

MINI CASE 12.1: KEY ELEMENTS OF GOOD DESIGN

One day Lizzie went to buy a can of soft drink. She wanted a new soft drink brand, called 'Fresh Orangi' she had seen on an ad. She stopped at the closest dairy. No Fresh Orangi. Second dairy. No. Third dairy. No. It was not until the fifth outlet Lizzie found what she wanted. And it looked great: mouth-watering packaging, good in-store presentation and icy cold. Until Lizzie pulled the top and upended it. Nothing. She tried again. Nothing. She unscrewed the lid and battled with the seal between the cap and the product. Lizzie took a gulp. Not bad. Worth traipsing across London for and appearing an idiot for being unable to open it?

So, this is a pretend example but while there is no Fresh Orangi, the tale illustrates what design is and, more importantly, what it is not. Let's start with what it is not. Good design is not the shape of a product or its container, the way it is engineered, the number of features that can be crammed into it, the way it's advertised or the act of making it look nice. Instead, commercial design is effective communication, at an emotional level. In a practical sense, this means a combination of four key factors: aesthetically pleasing, well engineered, fulfilling the function the consumer purchased it for, and aligned with the brand strategy.

Using these criteria, Fresh Orangi singularly fails on good design despite looking great. It was badly engineered as the consumer could not open it easily. Although it tasted fine, the fact most stores did not sell it meant it didn't fulfil its job to quickly quench the customer's thirst.

Design is a 360-degree package, with the consumer in the middle. Good design is all about creating a totally good experience for the consumer. Bad design is when there are negative associations; in Fresh Orangi's case: too hard to buy and too difficult to open.

The Apple Mac computer is a great example of good design. It looks good and is extremely well packaged. The computers are well engineered so they do not crash. They do what the customer wanted them to do when he bought them. They are preloaded and easy to set up, they do not tend to get viruses and the support network pretty much works. Apple Mac is all about simplicity and excellence, and it lives up to that, relentlessly.

When a company has good design criteria sorted for one product, brand extensions work better, too. The company can simply apply the same design strategies to help create success for other products. Apple's iPod is a great example of that. On the other hand, Fisher & Paykel, a company often heralded for its design, seems to fail on key design criteria. Its washing machines are whiteware's beige box equivalents. They are unremarkable and unreliable, plus their customer helpline did not seem particularly interested in their customers' problems. Thus, despite the hype, Fisher & Paykel is an engineering company that is not customer driven and has no good design.

The key to great design is having strong and well-articulated core values. Companies that have their brand strategy sorted find it easiest to consistently get design right, too. For instance, to begin with designers of Direct Broking, an online share-broking company, have worked with the company executives to identify a clear brand strategy based on the message 'Simple. Direct'. This brand driver was all about making share broking easy and accessible then, turned to the other three aspects of design: 1) Aesthetics: the website, advertising material and product information all had to look simple and direct. The designers concentrated on using basic colours and simple graphics. 2) Engineering: the designers had to make sure inexperienced investors found the company easy to find, easy to understand and easy to work with. 3) Meeting customer needs: as part of the strategy the designers removed jargon and complexity where possible, redesigned forms to make them easy to navigate and understand, and used plain English in marketing material. Finally, since launching the 'Simple Direct' positioning, Direct Broking's customer base has grown significantly.

Questions:

1 Discuss the elements of good design to meet customers' and client companies' expectations.

2 Compare and contrast their needs.

MINI CASE 12.2: A STRONG LOGO = AN IDENTIFIABLE BRAND

Source: Gaston Van de Laar and Lianne Van den Ber-Weitzel, Stagnito Communications – Brand Packaging

Research shows consumers associate easiest with an abstract shape. It's indefinable yet specific, such as the Nike 'swoosh'.

You've selected the colours, the shape and the materials. The package design is taking shape and perhaps you're even at the point of settling on the words. But is your packaging communications strategy complete? Some marketers might say 'yes', but those who operate the most successful brands know that one critical design component is missing.

The logo. And not just any shape or design will do. A great logo says it all about a brand. And new research from Claessens Product Consultants (CPC), the Netherlands, in collaboration with the University of Amsterdam, shows a strong correlation between an effective logo and consumers' ability to recognize and associate a brand with it.

An effective logo must be recognized when standing alone. It also needs to evoke the right associations in the consumer's mind. This makes the logo a cornerstone of a successful package design.

CPC's research finds that:

■ Consumers most easily recognize abstract logos. Specific, indefinable shapes – abstract logos – when used in an unfamiliar combination, generally display less complexity. This simplifies a logo's reconstruction in the consumer's mind and increases recognition.

- Consumers recognize abstract logos faster than other types of logos. The human mind constructs a distinctive, more specific shape relatively easy. Logo recognition comes faster. This is what makes logos more easily identifiable when walking past packaging on store shelves.

- Abstract logos require fewer consumer 'fixations' to achieve recognition. The research found that the average number of fixations on the logo was lower for abstract logos than for two other types of logos – descriptive and suggestive. The implication? Even with fewer viewings of a package, consumers recognize a brand easiest when the package contains an abstract logo.

- Suggestive logos tend to confuse consumers. They were the least effective in achieving recognition. They fail to provide enough reference points so consumers can immediately name and identify them.

Shape and colour

Creating a logo involves two key aspects: shape and colour. A 1997 study by Claessens Product Consultants demonstrated that shape is more important than colour in logo identification.

Although colour aids in logo recognition, correct identification does not depend on it. Logos appearing in different colours or in black-and-white are as easy to identify as logos in their actual colour combination.

This implies that a logo's impact hinges upon its principal shape. But what makes a shape strong or weak? How can we define this quality?

To determine the answers, Claessens Product Consultants conducted a study on the quality of logos. The study defines a logo as a brand's visually symbolic identifying mark.

Logos used in the study were taken from Rick Eiber's book *World Trademarks: 100 Years*, a collection of logos grouped thematically. To ensure that none of the logos in the study were familiar to the participants, the ones chosen were not currently in use in the Netherlands.

Testing for a strong image

A preliminary study and two experiments were conducted to determine how a logo can help build a strong brand image. In the preliminary study, about 100 University of Amsterdam students validated the logos by dividing them into the three categories – descriptive, suggestive and abstract.

Students selected a total of nine logos—three that they believe are the most representative of each of the three categories.

Perception research specialist Verify Nederland conducted the two experiments. One focused on eye-tracking and the other on tachistoscopic tests, both closely matching reality in how consumers look at logos. We also wanted to know which of the logos consumers would remember best a few days later. So we conducted a follow-up test after the first Verify experiment, which respondents completed at home.

First experiment

For the first experiment, we told 326 consumers we were conducting research on many recently designed logos for products that would be launched in the market soon. We showed them the nine logos, one at a time. Each had been selected in the preliminary study. The respondents decided for themselves how long they looked at each logo.

Thirty minutes after this pre-exposure, we showed each member of the group six logos on a touch screen. They had seen one of these logos earlier. The other five were unfamiliar to them but along the same theme as the 'target' logo.

Respondents were asked to select the logo they had seen earlier. Our experiment measured the accuracy of recognition and how long respondents took to select a logo. Next, 139 of the respondents participated in a follow-up test to measure logo recognition over time. Two days after our initial test, we sent a written test to their homes.

This test consisted of the same nine logos that Verify Nederland had shown them. The respondents were asked to indicate the nine logos they had seen earlier. The order in which the logos were presented within a field was changed. We wanted to ensure that recognition resulted from the logo itself rather than merely remembering its position in the field. We also sought to determine any differences in respondents' ability to recognize suggestive, descriptive and abstract logos, both shortly after pre-exposure and a few days later.

The results show that consumers recognize abstract and descriptive logos faster and more easily than suggestive logos. Suggestive logos had a significantly lower correct identification rate (60.7 per cent) than abstract logos (70.6 per cent) or descriptive logos (71.2 per cent).

In addition, consumers took longer to identify suggestive logos. In subsequent testing, abstract logos emerged clearly as the best option. They were correctly identified by 74.8 per cent of the respondents. This was significantly higher than the rates for suggestive logos (56.1) and descriptive logos (59).

Second experiment

In the second experiment, Verify Nederland conducted a so-called 'tacho test'. A respondent is shown a logo for about 24 milliseconds and is then asked to what he/she just saw. A group of 215 respondents participated. Once again, we explained that they were assisting with research into some new logos for various products nearing market launch.

We designed this experiment similarly to the first one. The main difference was that we let the respondents view the logos for only 24 milliseconds. We measured each logo's impact by presenting it tachistoscopically and then displaying it on a touch-screen in a field of six logos. Next, we asked respondents to touch the logo they had just been shown.

The experiment measured accuracy of identification and the time respondents took to make their choice. We wanted to measure any difference in how well consumers recognize abstract, suggestive and descriptive logos when they could view them only very briefly. This approach mirrors the short time frame consumers have to view messages on packaging.

The second experiment underscored results of the first experiment. Abstract logos were recognized significantly more easily and faster than suggestive or descriptive logos.

Our study found that suggestive logos lack enough reference points for consumers to recognize them easily. They are often less distinctive than abstract logos, making them harder to remember and identify. Abstract logos scored markedly higher on correct identification after a very brief exposure. Why? They exhibit little complexity, yet they are unique.

Minimal complexity makes an image easy to digest and remember. Abstract shapes are often unique, avoiding confusion with other shapes. This increases the likelihood that consumers will identify them correctly. BP

The authors, Gaston van de Laar and Lianne van den Berg-Weitzel, are Strategy Director and Brand Intelligence Manager, respectively, at Claessens Product Consultants in Hilversum, The Netherlands. Their research was conducted in collaboration with the Faculty of Communication Science at the University of Amsterdam. Bregje Jansen, a student at the university, carried out the study as part of her master's thesis.

Definitions of logo types

A logo can be designed in various ways. Claessens Product Consultants defines three types of logos:

Descriptive

Descriptive logos are shapes that are immediately recognizable; shapes that are familiar in our culture from their visual representation. Logo symbols in this group are easy to name and include common geometrical shapes (square, circle, etc.). The puma used by Puma is an example of this type.

Suggestive

The second category, suggestive logos, consists of shapes whose symbolism is more difficult to identify. A descriptive shape appears in a somewhat abstract way that makes it harder to associate a name with it. Suggestive logos include the Fjällräven fox.

Abstract

Abstract logos have no generally accepted, familiar meaning. Specific, indefinable shapes are used in an unfamiliar combination. This makes it impossible to identify the symbol instantly.

The Nike 'swoosh' – an abstract logo – is one of the most universally recognized brand symbols in the world.

Connecting a brand and product to a logo

Claessens Product Consultants' (CPC) research provides an initial idea about one important aspect in the performance of brand logos – recognition. But what about the link between brand or product and logo?

In practice, this link always exists. But CPC wanted to determine how far its experiments could translate to the 'real world' of brand communication.

Researchers conducted another test using the scenario of introducing a new line of skin-care products under the brand name Caress. They designed three packaging-dominant ads for the brand. The only differentiating element in each ad was the logo design.

CPC's first study had validated all three logos, each carrying a 'nature' theme. The advertisement was published as the back cover of *Libelle* – a popular women's magazine – in the eye-tracking test that Verify initially conducted during standard research.

In all cases, consumers easily associated the advertisement, logo and brand name (minimum of 95 per cent recognition, with an average of 111 respondents asked during each of the three test days). The advertisement clearly achieved its objective of publicizing the new brand and its associated logo.

Next, researchers presented the advertisements with the three different logos in 'pixelated' form. That is, the image was presented in a highly distorted view.

An image presented in this way can only be constructed in the consumer's mind if they recognize it from previous observation. The new study confirmed expectations – the abstract logo was the most easily recognized.

Questions:

1 Summarize the main points of the research findings.
2 What is the purpose of the tests?
3 What are the implications for package designers?

END OF CHAPTER CASE STUDY: HYUNDAI MISSES THE BIG IDEA

Source: Thirdway, brand trainers, advertising blog, 13 May 2007 © Hyundai

Last month at the Jacob Javitz center in New York, Hyundai introduced the Genesis sedan. This $35 000 sport sedan is an ambitious and impressive challenger to such auto industry heavyweights as BMW, Infiniti and Lexus.

More impressive than the styling of this new car (which looks far less like the odd panoply of competing design themes that defined the Hyundais of the 1980s) is the expected quality. In fact, in 2006, J.D. Power's rated Hyundai #3 in initial quality – above both Toyota (#4) and Honda (#6). In addition, Hyundai models in the past several years have been regularly recommended by Consumer Reports for reliability as well as value.

In spite of this good news, Hyundai is in a pickle. *BusinessWeek* reports that 'last year the Korean automaker's earnings fell 34% ... and its operating margin was halved ... Hyundai's sales bank [of unsold cars] has gone largely unnoticed.' The appreciation of the Korean won against the dollar has neutralized much of Hyundai's pricing advantage and the brand is under pressure to sustain premium pricing.

Hyundai's marketing chief, Steve Wilhite (COO of Hyundai Motors America), is struggling to find a recipe to make Hyundai a premium brand. The current plan of the company lies with an upcoming advertising campaign intended to position the brand as the choice for rational, clear-headed buyers unaffected by marketing hype.

This plan might or might not work in the long run, but it is an expensive and unlikely way to solve the brand's woes. Wilhite's thinking is one-dimensional, and his impressive resume (helping to lead turnarounds at Volkswagen, Apple and Nissan) points to the reason – he has primarily worked in single-brand environments.

Faced with the same challenge, a packaged-goods marketer might think differently. Instead of trying to reinvent a failing brand with a stable of good products, why not create a new brand for those good products?

Hyundai consumer research seems to bear this out. As *BusinessWeek* points out, consumers exposed to concepts for new Hyundai models were actually less likely to express purchase interest than when the concepts had no brand attached. Instead of being a sail for the brand, the Hyundai name is currently an anchor.

Of course, there are good examples of brands which have repositioned themselves in the automotive industry – and Mr Wilhite has worked on two of them. Volkswagen was in a brand netherworld before re-emerging with the 'Drivers Wanted' campaign and the New Beetle. Nissan was virtually a commodity when Wilhite helped reinvigorate the brand.

Unfortunately for Mr Wilhite, both of those brands had underlying heritage which made refreshing the brand more achievable. Nissan was beloved of a generation of drivers who remembered it bringing real sports cars to the masses with the 240Z – and these drivers were now of an age and family size to require a Maxima. Volkswagen captured the hearts of the masses with the original Beetle. Repositioning it as the brand that cared about drivers was more like reintroducing the original concept than arguing with consumers. (Nissan does of course have a second brand, Infiniti, but more on that later.)

Hyundai's problem is that it has no brand heritage to look back on. Hyundai came into the US market much as Yugo did – as a cheap car, cheaply made. The early Hyundai Accent was a dreadful tinny little car that did not engender much love.

To be fair, there are at least two examples of automakers with questionable initial offerings and poor brand reputations turning into automotive powerhouses – Toyota and Honda. The first Hondas were also tin pots known more for their propensity to rust than anything else. Toyotas had a similarly undistinguished brand as an inexpensive Japanese car.

These brands, however, were saved by a divine intervention that Hyundai and Mr Wilhite can hardly hope for – the OPEC oil crisis of the seventies which forced consumers to reconsider small cars.

These same two companies do offer a more useful model of dealing with entrenched consumer opinions about their automobiles, however, with their Lexus and Acura brands. Both Toyota and Honda (along with Nissan) faced the difficult question of how to move upscale as their consumers aged. They also saw a brand opportunity as no domestic or foreign carmaker was able to deliver 'reliable luxury' to the US consumer. They understood that their brand names did not connote luxury to US consumers and might never do so. So they chose to build new brands at huge expense. It was an investment well worth making.

For Hyundai, re-branding would be well worth the effort. Merely renaming the company and the dealerships would be difficult, and consumers might see through the effort. It might be smarter altogether to launch a new brand and begin to put updated versions of the smartly designed, reliable and clever new cars into this brand. Over time, the Hyundai name could be retired.

This begs the question of dealer networks. The US auto market is, unhelpfully for consumers, largely driven by distribution issues. Most dealerships still distribute only a single brand and consumers are reduced to driving all over town to shop for a new automobile. (Imagine doing the same thing to shop for a dishwasher and the absurdity becomes clearer.) This is justified by the service end of the business, but at the end of the day it does no favours to anyone.

Hyundai should look at partnering with another car manufacturer needing to penetrate the US market. This model is already common at the high end where brands like Aston Martin, Ferrari and Lotus lack the sales volume to support independent dealer networks. Renault might make a good partner as it is gearing up for a re-entry into this market.

There are reams of data to support the fact that consumers don't like to be argued with. The path Hyundai is pursuing with re-branding will be expensive and might fail which would be a shame, because the automaker is finally producing some vehicles worth considering.

Questions;

1 How would you characterize Hyundai's brand equity? What factors and decisions contributed to the building of this equity?

2 How would you suggest Hyundai be re-branded and re-positioned?

3 Can Hyundai successfully transfer the equity from the old name to the new one?

4 If Hyundai decides to re-brand and re-position, how should it follow up on its image and awareness programme campaign? What should be the next steps in the company's marketing programme?

5 What are the common problems that Hyundai has with other brands from less developed countries?

6 How would design enhance Hyundai's brand differentiation? Recommend a design that suits.

References

Anonymous author(s) 'A glimpse of food packaging in the future', at www.foodproductiondaily.com/news/news-NG.asp?id=51847.

Anonymous author(s) 'Green groceries: consumers, product labels and the environment', Policy Study No. 217, March 1996.

Barthel, M. (2005), 'Materials management for sustainability: WRAP's retail innovation programme', *Farapack Briefing*, 12–13 October, York.

Butler, P. (2005), 'Smart materials, smart packaging', *Farapack Briefing*, 12–13 October, York.

Costello, A., Hellier, E. and Edworthy, J. (2005), 'Voluntary GM free labeling, a big mistake?', *Farapack Briefing*, 12–13 October, York.

DEFRA (2005), *Securing the Future*, London: HMSO.

Gidda, S. (2005), 'Attracting consumers through package and product innovation', at www.brandchannel.com/print_page.asp?ar_id=111&section=brandspeak.

Kerwin, A. M. (1994), 'Seal, spiel: public opinion about the Good Housekeeping seal of approval', *Inside Media*, 2 February, pp. 1–5.

Kim, C. K. and Lavack, A. M. (1996), 'Vertical brand extensions: current research and managerial implications', *Journal of Product & Brand Management*, Vol. 5, No. 6, pp. 24–37.

Kronowitz, D. (1991), 'Packaging design: planning for today and the future', at www.foodproductdesign.com.

Laforet, S. and Saunders, J. A. (1994), 'Managing brand portfolios: how the leaders do it', *Journal of Advertising Research*, Vol. 34, No. 5, pp. 64–76.

Li, C. (1992), 'Effective design: brand identity + brand imagery = a potent marketing tool', at www.foodproductdesign.com/archive/1992/1292pk.html.

Mininni, T. (2005), 'Nothing says brand like the package', Brandchannel.com.

Mitchell, V. and Papavassiliou, V. (1999), 'Market causes and implications of consumer confusion', *Journal of Product and Brand Management*, Vol. 8, pp. 319–39.

Nelson, S. (2002), 'Corporate brand and packaging design', *Design Management Journal*, Fall.

Raghubir, P. and Krishna, A. (1999), 'Vital dimensions: biases in volume estimates', *Journal of Marketing Research*, Vol. xxxvi (August), pp. 313–26.

Raymond, J., Westoby, N. and Kaltreider, J. (2005), 'Consumers make mental links between healthy food and eco-responsibility: lessons for fmcg packaging?', *Farapack Briefing*, 12–13 October, York.

Rettie, R. and Brewer, C. (2000), 'The verbal and visual components of package design', *Journal of Product & Brand Management*, Vol. 9, No. 1, pp. 56–70.

Robertson, K. R. (1987), 'Recall and recognition effects of brand name imagery', *Psychology of Marketing*, Vol. 4, pp. 3–15.

Shimp, R. J. (1995), 'Eco labels: promise and reality – the illusion of environmental progress in the marketplace', Presentation to Institute of Economic Affairs, London, September.

Silayoi, P. and Speece, M. (2004), 'Packaging and purchase decisions', *British Food Journal*, Vol. 106, No. 8, pp. 607–28.

Swientek, B. (2001), 'Communicating trust, comfort to anxious consumers', *BrandPackaging Magazine*, November/December, Vol. 5, No. 6.

Underwood, L. R., Klein, M. N. and Burke, R. R. (2001), 'Packaging communication: attentional effects of product imagery', *Journal of Product & Brand Management*, Vol. 10, No. 7, pp. 403–22.

Van de laar, G. (2004), 'A strong logo = an identifiable brand', at www.brandpackaging.com/content.php?s=BP/2004/09&p=11.

Wilkinson, M. (2006), 'Nanotechnology', lecture notes in Laforet, S., Lectures on Consumer Behaviour, November.

Wynne, R. D. (1993), 'The emperor's new eco logos? A critical review of the scientific certification systems environmental report card and the green seal certification mark programs', *California Environmental Law Journal*, Vol. 14, pp. 51–149.

Further reading and online sites

Bitz, K. 'The power of packaging', at www.landor.com/portfolio.

Campbell, M. C. and Goodstein, R. C. (2001), 'The moderating effect of perceived risk on consumers' evaluations of product incongruity: preference for the norm', *Journal of Consumer Research*, Vol. 28, No. 3, pp. 439–449.

Chimboza, D. and Mutandwa, E. (2007), 'Measuring the determinants of brand preference in a dairy product market', *African Journal of Business Management*, Vol. 1, No. 9, pp. 230–7.

Herrmann, C. and Moller, G. (2004), 'Strategic design planning: the future of brand management', at www.brandchannel.com/print_page.asp?ar_id=84&section=brandspeak.

www.brandchannel.com

www.brandpackaging.com

www.cellpaksolutions.com/

www.happi.com/special/june001.html

Country-of-Origin Branding

Chapter overview

Competition among brands has become fiercer as the number of brands originating from foreign countries accrues in a number of markets, from durable to non-durable. There is also ample evidence to suggest that consumers pay significant attention to country-related information as well as brand reputation when evaluating and selecting brands. Country-of-origin branding (COOB) can be seen as a way for producers to brand a product, by taking advantage of the positively perceived image of the country where the product is made or comes from. The benefits of COOB can be seen to contribute to some companies' sales and market share.

In particular, COOB could contribute to the small company's brand equity and increase its international visibility and positioning. As part of the theme of competing in the new business environment, Chapter 10 examined new environmental pressures in branding, and the implications for companies around the world. Chapter 11 discussed competition from own-labels, and Chapter 12 examined innovative packaging design and branding to meet consumers' needs and purchase motivations. This chapter examines the concept of country-of-origin branding (COOB), the effects of country of origin (COO) on product evaluation, and multiple countries of origin (MCO) effects on brand equity and brand perception; it examines the benefits of COO in relation to increased market share, brand equity and positioning for small companies and services. It discusses the effects of country of manufacture (COM) on brand origin (BO), and the influence of BO and country image association on the perceptions and purchase intentions of Chinese brands. It discusses the overall managerial implications. Finally, it examines the concept of country or national branding. This is also the last chapter on the topic of 'The new business environment'.

❖ LEARNING OBJECTIVES

After completing this chapter, you should be able to

❖ Explain and distinguish the different meanings among the concepts of COOB, COM, BO and MCO

❖ Discuss the implications of the above from the company's and the consumer's perspectives

❖ Identify the potential problems of MCO and discuss its effect on brand equity

❖ Understand the nature of country umbrella branding and place branding

❖ Understand the role of country umbrella branding and the benefits it brings to the promotion of a country

❖ Discuss the challenges in national umbrella branding and success criteria of country associations

❖ Discuss the benefits of COO in relation to increased market share, and in relation to small companies and services

❖ Examine COO effects on BO

❖ Examine the issues in country image associations (CIA) for developing countries and their effects on foreign-investing companies

❖ Discuss BO and CIA in relation to the consumer's decision-making process

❖ Discuss how global companies could use the influence of COO and BO to benefit their brands

Introduction

With firms around the world pursuing a global expansion strategy, the impact of country-of-origin (COO) products on consumer product evaluations cannot be ignored. Furthermore, competition among brands has become fiercer as the number of brands originating from foreign countries accrues in a number of markets, from durable to non-durable. There is also ample evidence which suggests that consumers pay significant attention to country-related information as well as brand reputation, when evaluating and selecting brands.

Country of origin (COO) is often known by the term 'made in', which can mean manufactured in, but also assembled, designed or invented in (Papadopoulos and Heslop, 1993). Often the COO of a product is the country of manufacture (COM) of a product, but not always. For example, a Sony television can be manufactured in Mexico, in which case Mexico is the COM of Sony, but the COO of Sony is Japan, where it was originally designed and conceived.

Consumers' perception of brand origin (BO) will also impact on their buying behaviour. BO is where the product is manufactured or produced. For example, the brand origin of Sony is Japan. The BO is defined as the place, region or country to which the brand is perceived to belong by its target consumers (Tse and Gorn, 1993). The difference between COO and BO is that COO focuses more on the country as the origin cue of a product at the product level, while BO emphasizes brand perceptions and the influence of origin associations at the brand level. Consumers perceive the BO of a product to be associated with 'the country where the brand's corporate parent resides, rather than the country in which the product or its components are manufactured at any given time' (Thakor and Lavack, 2003).

BO and country-of-origin branding (COOB) have become the most common methods in brand marketing today. COOB can be seen as a way for producers to brand a product by taking advantage of the positive perceived image of the country where the product is made or comes from. The benefits of COOB can be seen to contribute to companies' sales and market share. For small companies, COOB could contribute to their brand equity and increase their international visibility and positioning.

The country of origin (COO) of a product has been found to influence consumers' perceptions of quality and purchase value (Ahmed and d'Astou, 1995). Consumers are also able to establish the connotations between certain products and their origins. For instance, since food products are naturally of land-based geographical origin, they appear to demonstrate strong associations with place. This favourable COO imagery can increase product satisfaction and further lead consumers' preferences for products from one country over another (Papadopoulos et al., 1991). BO can reflect the culture or heritage of brands – for example, 'French origins' indeed successfully strengthen the image of French wine brands as more sophisticated and having more status.

The globalization of businesses has nevertheless reached a point where it is sometimes difficult for consumers to determine with certainty the COO of a product. Furthermore, nowadays, a brand may have multiple countries of origin (MCO), thanks to mergers and acquisitions. For example, well-known brands are being taken over by different companies from different countries. The question then is to what extent the new nationality or brand ownership will have an impact on consumers' perceptions of brand equity (see Chapter 2). Another issue is that, given the importance of the service sector and the growth of international trade and services, the effects of COO in relation to consumers' evaluations of intangible services would also need to be examined along with the tangible goods (such as cars, electronics, wine or fashion).

Finally, a nation can behave just like a manufacturer brand, providing trust and a guarantee of quality. Like any brand, nations have individual fingerprints that are unique. This uniqueness gives power to a national brand. This is the focus of national branding or country branding, which is a new field of marketing. For example, in recent years, in order to build strong and beneficial provenance associations, many countries, including eastern and less-developed countries (LDCs), have initiated national cooperative marketing programmes to promote place as exporters of goods and services. In an attempt to build strong country associations, such national promotion is conducted to market nations on the basis of a wide variety of qualities. This is known as 'national umbrella branding'. These issues will be examined in this chapter.

COO effects on product evaluation

It has been established and empirically proven that the COO of a product affects consumers' product evaluations. Consumers tend to hold stereotyped images of products made in different countries. Thus, COO, like the price and brand name, constitutes an extrinsic cue in consumers' product evaluations. Consumers use COO cues to evaluate foreign products when they are not familiar with the product's intrinsic qualities.

Consumers also tend to evaluate domestic products more favourably than foreign products, and products from developed countries more favourably than products from developing countries. However, they do not perceive all products from a given foreign country in the same way. Research suggests that different countries have acquired distinctive images in consumers' minds in specific product categories. For instance, Nagashima (1977) found that Japanese respondents perceive Germany to be particularly good in the manufacture of luxury automobiles, France in cosmetics, and the United States in IT and aeroplanes. In a study currently under review, Laforet (2007) found that with regard to luxury brands, Japanese consumers desire different things from western and Japanese brands: history, tradition and status symbols from the former; quality, features and maintenance services from the latter.

Other researchers found greater consumer willingness to buy products made in countries with good reputations in those product categories, than the same products from countries that are not well known in those product categories (Okechuku, 1994). Thus, COO effects appear to be product specific. They also appear to vary from country to country.

Research shows COO effects on product evaluations vary with the following:

- The technical complexity of products – thus, COO effects would be less important with clothes than with TV sets and car radios and, possibly, luxury brands.
- The degree of availability, familiarity and perceived serviceability of foreign-made products, i.e. the degree of consumer ethnocentrism.
- The perceived level of economic development of the source country.
- The degree of similarity to the home country in terms of the economic, cultural and political systems of the foreign country.

Okechuku (1994), investigating the importance of COO of a product to consumers in four countries – the US, Canada, Germany and Holland – found that the COO of a product was one of the two or three most important attributes in preference evaluation. Consumers in each of the four countries studied preferred domestically made products most, followed by products made in other developed countries and, last, products made in LDCs. For Americans (and for TVs), COO was more important than the brand name, price, picture quality and warranty. For Canadians, it was more important than warranty and as important as the brand name, price and picture quality. For Germans, it was as important as the brand name, price, picture quality and warranty. For the Dutch it was more important than warranty, as important as price and picture quality, but less important than the brand name.

For car radio/cassette players, COO was more important than price in each country and as important as the brand name among respondents in all four countries. Americans also preferred American TVs to Japanese, Dutch and South Korean, regardless of the brand name, price or any other considerations. Canadians preferred American and Japanese TVs to Dutch and South Korean. Germans preferred Dutch and Japanese TVs to American and South Korean. Dutch consumers preferred Dutch and Japanese TVs to American and South Korean. For car radio/cassette players, Americans preferred American to German and Canadian as source countries. Canadians preferred Canadian to American or German. Germans preferred German to the other three sources countries. Dutch consumers preferred German to American and Canadian. All of them rated Mexico as a source country for car radio/cassette players as the poorest source.

Although the results of Okechuku's study suggest that COO effects are quite strong in some product categories, the actual effect on consumer purchasing behaviour is likely to be less in the real marketplace. This is because the study measured the importance of COO on consumers' product attitudes rather than their purchase intention. The actual effect on purchase behaviour may also depend on whether or not consumers notice COO or the 'made in' label at the time of purchase. In addition, the 'made in' label is not always prominently displayed on product packaging, and consumers might not notice or seek out this information at the time of purchase.

Nevertheless, the results of the study have implications for promotional strategy. When COO is an important decision attribute, the marketer manufacturing in, or importing from, a favoured foreign source should emphasize the product's COO (e.g. Mercedes emphasizing German engineering in its cars, or a wine importer emphasizing its Frenchness). Furthermore, when the preferred source is the home country itself, patriotic appeals used by both domestic and foreign companies may benefit both domestic companies and foreign companies manufacturing domestically (e.g. Honda Motor Company emphasizing 'Made in America' Honda Accords). Patriotic appeals are not likely to be effective when COO is unimportant in the product category, or when consumers prefer a foreign source.

Branding Brief 13.1: Country of origin as a branding statement

Source: Branding Strategy Insider by Martin Lindstrom, 19 March 2007

Imagine that I told you of a product that I knew nearly nothing about. I didn't know what its price was, what any of its unique features were, or even what type of product it was. But I did know the product's country of origin …

Let's say the product is from Switzerland. Now what would your impression of this product be? Even though this is a hypothetical scenario, I bet that you'd be able to tell me something about the mystery product's price, its quality, and the reputation it most likely enjoys. Such assumptions would be inspired by the preconceptions you, as a consumer, hold about the country in question.

Country branding means much more than adding a 'made in' label to a product. A product's country of origin constitutes an important piece of branding that, in many cases, can be so influential it overtakes the brand's other reputation builders.

If I were to tell you that the next super car was to come from Germany, you probably wouldn't be surprised. You would probably be immediately curious about it, expecting the fictional vehicle to be of superb engineering and design quality, expensive, and solid. Now imagine I surprised you by revealing that the forthcoming super car was actually a product of Greece. Your impression of the car would be totally different, your assumptions inspired by the apparent personality the country of origin communicates to your perceptions.

Have you ever wondered why some perfume bottles are accompanied by packaging that bears something along the lines of 'Paris – Milan – New York – Rome – London'? I'm sure you don't really think the perfume is produced in all of those places.

Now imagine if instead the packaging read as follows: 'Prague – Helsinki – Melbourne – Seattle – Auckland'. I guarantee your first impression of the perfume would be affected by the suppositions you made about the national affiliations. This is quite ironic considering none of us believe for a minute that any of the cited locales have anything to do with the product's manufacture.

I can't stop thinking about how valuable some countries are for their manufacturers. A high-tech brand coming from Japan seems logical for most of us. I'm convinced that promoting a high-tech brand in, say, the US would be substantially easier if the product hailed from Japan than it would be if the product hailed from Iceland. Why? Because the product's country of origin – in this case, Japan – has a reputation for producing superior high-tech products. Thus, the country establishes the brand's initial reputation.

Conversely, brands themselves can create countries' reputations. Consider Finland. If I asked you to respond to the notion of Finland ten years ago, you'd probably have said things like 'cold', 'midnight sun', and so on. Today, you're likely to think of high-tech, mobile-phone technology when you think of Finland. And this huge mind shift is purely thanks to Nokia (which, by the way, was a chainsaw manufacturer just 20 years ago).

So you can claim that brands create countries' reputations and that countries create brands' reputations. This is a very interesting theory to keep in mind the next time you have an opportunity to create a new brand from scratch. The theory should not only make you consider what values your brand should stand for, but also where it should be manufactured and where it should be perceived as being manufactured. Having the wrong country label on your package won't destroy your brand, but I'm convinced that having the right 'made in' label will save you a substantial amount of marketing money.

Rome wasn't built in a day. I'm sure we'll get there. The question is how long you can afford to wait? The rewards can be enormous.

MCO effects on brand perception and brand equity

China is a country where manufacturing has been growing steadily; it has, however, never owned a single brand that is recognized worldwide. Yet, despite this, China has recently become the owner of several well-known, worldwide brands, as the result of mergers and acquisitions (M&A) undertaken in the past couple of years. Examples include the Chinese computer maker Lenovo, which acquired IBM's global PC business for US$1.25 billion in cash and shares, and carmaker Nanjing Automotive, which acquired Rover's assets in 2005 (Wu and Ardley, 2006). These are only two examples of the many businesses that have been bought off, including some of the bigger and more established ones. A range of famous brands and iconic symbols like Thomson, RCA, Schneider, IBM, Rover, MG and Austin are now owned by companies from a different country. China, however, has a very different culture and no history of association with these brands before M&A took place.

The question is: how will consumers view brand equity following new ownership? What are the implications to their purchasing decisions following subsequent changes in brand ownership. To what extent will consumers' cultural views regarding product origin impact on their purchasing behaviour? Similarly, will the brand equity of these established products be sustained or improved, diluted or even damaged under the new ownership name? Clearly, this is a new phenomenon that cannot be explained by existing COO or BO concepts which focus only on issues of product quality and purchase value.

Wu and Ardley suggest that strong cultural and emotional connotations are two other factors influencing consumers' perception of products that come from multiple countries of origin (MCO), such as the cases mentioned above. These issues might also be more pronounced in the case of China, from the British or western consumer's viewpoint. They argue that it is unlikely that western consumers would hold neutral or equivocal views about China and the East.

Culturally conditioned factors are, therefore, likely to have an impact on consumers' perceptions of the brand and the company which takes it over or which has been taken over itself. Wu and Ardley also propose that consumers' perceptions of this factor are likely to be very significant in terms of the future success of the brands acquired by Chinese companies. These authors suggest that consumers are still very much ethnocentric, despite the acceptance of globalization and the fact that manufacturer origin is not a significant factor in buying behaviour. Their argument is that an increasing awareness of the global condition actually means that localization and identity become more important. Here 'localization' means not just a country, but also perhaps a trading bloc.

The second factor is brand equity. There is a clear link between COO perceptions held by consumers and brand equity. This link has, however, not been explored in relation to the change of ownership from western companies and brands to Chinese companies.

Wu and Ardley propose a new framework that will examine the extent to which the new brand ownership is likely to impact on consumers' perceptions and behaviour, and affect the management of brand equity, otherwise known as 'customer-based brand equity'. This framework can apply to other countries in similar situations to China – in particular, a change of ownership from a developed country to an LDC. The focus will also be on examining at a deep level consumer feelings towards COO and how this relates to perceptions of brand equity.

COO effects on market share

COO image and association have been shown to influence trust in, and judgements of, products. A country name of high equity can have a positive effect on a consumer's product evaluations at the individual level, and on the brand sales at the market level. For instance, there are some indications that Japanese names are perceived as being superior to American names within the car market. So, a country name with a favourable image can have a positive effect on the short-term market share of the brand.

It is also suggested that short-term marketing activities by a brand possessing high country image (CI) will be more effective than that of low country image. One can expect, generally, that products from high or favourable countries would charge premium prices for their favourable or unique image associations; and that consumers are more ready to accept premium prices for products from countries that have created a unique value or image for themselves. In other words, the higher the image of a country, the smaller is the price sensitivity.

These issues have been explored by Kim (1995), who found that, in the car market, the country name has a significant influence on price. Consumers were found to be less price-sensitive to the Japanese car make than their American counterparts. This means that Japanese car manufacturers can charge a premium price for their brands. Kim's study also supports the proposition that the higher the image of a country, the smaller the price sensitivity towards premium pricing. Furthermore, Kim found that there exist country-related equities. Japanese brands seem to have benefited from the positive assets associated with their country name, while the American and German names was found not to be significantly different from each other in the car market segment. Thus, the study found that Japanese cars benefited from the image of their country name in the sub-compact car market in the US. Japanese manufacturers were successful in creating intangible assets in the car market as well as in other markets, such as that of consumer electronics.

COO effects on brand equity

Research conducted by Yasin and Noor (2007) shows that COO image has effects on brand equity (Figure 13.1). The study focuses on electrical appliances and the Malaysian market. For electrical appliances, brand equity is determined by brand distinctiveness, brand loyalty and brand awareness/associations (see Chapter 2).

COO image is found to influence brand distinctiveness and plays an important role in consumer purchase decisions, particularly for electrical goods, including TVs, refrigerators and air-conditioners. Brand distinctiveness refers to the favourable and positive aspects that are associated with the brand, such as quality. This suggests that favourable country image leads to favourable brand image, which in turn influences brand distinctiveness.

COO image is found to influence brand loyalty and, thus, the good image of the COO leads to a high degree of customer loyalty. Although consumers are faced with many alternative brands in the market, which they perceive as equally good in terms of product attributes and functionality, information about the country is an added advantage. Consumers feel that brands from countries with a good image are more reliable than brands produced by countries with a less favourable one. As a result, these brands are preferred and often chosen during purchase decision-making. If repeat purchases occur, eventually consumers may develop loyalty towards these brands. Yasin and Noor found that Malaysian consumers perceive countries with good image as technologically advanced, and brands originating from these countries to be reliable and of high quality.

COO image is found to have an effect on brand awareness and associations. In the purchase of electrical goods, consumers often associate the quality of a brand with the image of the origin country. Countries with a good image are often familiar to consumers, and perceived as producers of quality brands. These authors argue that such a relationship exists between country image and brand awareness and associations.

Brand loyalty was also found to make the largest contribution to the formation of brand equity. It suggests that producers of household electrical appliances should place greater emphasis on creating brand loyalty for their products and through building long-term relationship with customers; and by providing good services, delivery and installation, as well as maintenance and repair after-sales services. This also implies that producers of household electrical appliances can use their COO image to enhance and promote the good image of their brand through advertising and personal selling.

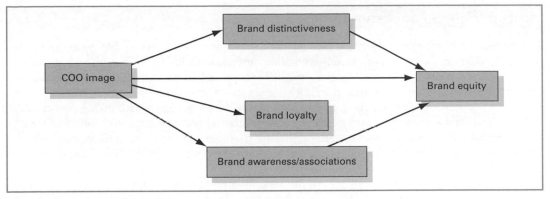

Source: Adapted from Yasin and Noor (2007)

FIGURE 13.1 COO image effects on brand equity

COO effects on SMEs' brand equity, visibility and positioning

COO can greatly enhance brand equity, especially for products that do not have famous names, such as Sony or Ford, Coca-Cola or Pepsi. Since COO is a factor linked to brand image, brands from countries with a more positive image have a better chance to establish a more positive image than those from countries with a less positive image. The existence of positive country images and stereotypes justifies the efforts of some companies to create strong associations with some countries for their brands (Thakor and Lavack, 2003).

Most well-known brands are strongly associated with a specific country, such as IBM and Ford with the US, Sony and Fuji with Japan, Virgin and Cadbury with Britain. Brands often use the image of a country to build their own image and convey information about the origin of their competencies, such as perfume brands and France, car brands and Germany. Depending on the country equity and how strong this equity is, it can generate added performance for companies' products. Similarly, some brands are strongly associated with their COO, while others are weakly associated with it, if at all (Spence and Hamzaoui, 2006).

Generally, any company of any size could seek to reinforce the associations between the brand and COO through its communication strategy, in order to benefit from its overall image and its perceived competencies. This is of particular importance when a brand is exported to countries in which it is not well known (Spence and Hamzaoui, 2006). In the case of small businesses it has been shown that communicating a brand is not a problem for a small business; the difficulty lies in establishing a clear position and personality for the organization. If properly used, COOB can provide good returns on brand equity for small companies with limited resources.

Spence and Hamzaoui's study confirms this. It focuses on four small firms operating in the consumer products market in Monaco, which use the COO effect to enhance their impact with foreign consumers and overcome the perceived liability of smallness which is attached both to themselves and to their COO. The COO is prominently displayed on the packaging twice for one company's products – the brand name is underlined in gold, with the line being interrupted in the middle by the mention of Monte-Carlo once, while on the back of the package the manufacturer's name is followed by the location, Monaco. For two companies' products, the Monaco image is advanced in order to sell the products, in the hope that it raises consumers' curiosity and differentiates them from other products. For the last of the four companies studied, the COO of the product was included in the brand name itself.

Spence and Hamzaoui's findings show all four companies benefiting from the appeal of the Monaco brand abroad, especially in Asia and the Middle East. In addition, the companies follow an integrated strategy, including a clear vision for the brands from the companies' executives, strong relationships with distributors, agents and retailers, and a presence at targeted trade shows.

COO effects on goods vs services

It is generally accepted that there are characteristic differences between tangible goods and intangible services in the heterogeneity, inseparability and perishability of services. These distinctive attributes, individually or in combination, might be expected to affect consumers' attitudes and behaviour towards services based on the COO of the service provider. For example, American and European companies enjoy a strong global presence in industries such as banking and finance, airlines, hospitality, consulting and business services (Hamin and Elliott, 2006). One can suggest therefore that consumers' attitudes towards HSBC, for example, may be different from their attitudes towards a locally owned bank, on the basis of the foreign ownership of the bank and the foreign origins of bank managers.

Furthermore, service characteristics are purportedly quite different from tangible goods. When limited information is available before a purchase decision, particularly concerning intangibility, inseparability and heterogeneity, consumers typically perceive buying services to be higher risk than buying tangible goods. Consumers may therefore display different behaviour between pre-purchase and purchase. This is due to the obvious differences between goods and services, and COO effects for goods and services must be different from one another.

This is an issue that has been examined by Hamin and Elliott (2006). Their study compares Indonesian consumers' purchase attitudes towards representative tangible goods such as TVs, and intangible services from airlines. Their investigation is also concerned with the broad issues of the effects of COO and consumer ethnocentrism (CE) on consumers' perception of quality, price and value, and, ultimately, on consumers' choice of both tangible goods and intangible services in Indonesia. They have designed a model to assess the effect of CE on purchase intention through perceived quality, perceived price and perceived value. Consumer ethnocentrism refers to consumers usually preferring to purchase products manufactured in their home country. Some consumers believe that buying products that are locally manufactured is morally appropriate in a normative sense (Shimp and Sharma, 1987). CE is an essential aspect of consumers' decision to purchase domestic or local products, and is central to the explanation of COO effects.

In their model, both tangible goods and intangible services are examined to see how closely the COO effect for services corresponds with the effect for tangible goods. Indonesian consumers who had previously purchased colour TVs and had travelled by international airlines were included in the survey sample. Respondents were asked their perceptions and purchasing intentions towards colour TVs and international airline travel.

Hamin and Elliott's findings show that there were no significant differences in consumers' perceptions relating to services and tangible goods. The study concludes that the mechanism for COO effects is broadly similar for both services and tangible goods. In other words, Indonesian consumers do not display any fundamental differences in COO effects between tangible goods and intangible services. Thus, CE is positively linked to perceptions of price, quality and value as well as to purchase intentions, and actual purchases for both tangible goods and intangible services. Thus Indonesian consumers see international airlines in much the same way as they see international brands of TVs. The study also shows that strongly ethnocentric consumers are positively disposed towards local companies and brands, whereas those low in ethnocentrism are predisposed towards international brands.

However, while the results of Hamin and Elliott's study support the proposition that the directionality in the relationships between CE and COO is broadly the same for goods and services, the authors also suggest that the magnitude of the COO effect for services may be more important than the COO effect for tangible goods. This is because for many services it is impossible to separate COO from brand. In their view, it is impossible for most consumers to separate Qantas from Australia, Citibank from the US and Marriott Hotels from the US. Thus the brand and the COO are inextricably linked. In contrast, Sony televisions can be made in Japan or anywhere else in the world. Thus, COO and the brand can act independently and often in opposite directions. Therefore, the influence of COO of a Sony television manufactured anywhere outside Japan is measurably less (Hamin and Elliott, 2005).

The authors argue that in this sense the impact of COO on intangible services may be greater, although it is possible that for international service companies the use of local staff may moderate the influence of the international brand. So, if Citibank or Qantas were to use predominantly Indonesian staff, it seems likely that the COO influence would be less. But this is, in their view, a hypothetical question.

Branding Brief 13.2: Stories from the food chain

Source: NFU online – Food Chain Roundup

Marks & Spencer has started marking food imported to the UK by air with a sticker displaying 'air freighted'. The label will initially appear on 20 products, including beans, mange tout and strawberries, rising to 150 products by the end of the year. The new labelling forms part of M&S Plan A commitment on climate change. Other initiatives include buying as much food from the UK and Ireland as possible and doubling regional food sourcing.

The Meat and Livestock Commission (MLC), through its campaign for menu transparency, is urging the farm industry to get behind initiatives that encourage restaurants and caterers to list the country of origin of the meat they use, rather than rely on government to introduce appropriate legislation which would take three years. The MLC has renewed its call for improved COO labelling on menus following the recent announcement by the Scottish Executive that Beef Labelling Regulations are to be extended to the catering sector.

COM effects on BO

Hui and Zhou (2003) found that country of manufacture (COM) information does not produce a significant effect on the evaluations of a branded product when the information is congruent with the BO, such as 'made in Japan' for a Sony or Sanyo. On the other hand, when COM information indicates that a branded product is manufactured in a country with a less reputable image than that of the BO, such as 'made in Mexico' for Sony or Sanyo, the information produces significant negative effects on product evaluations and the effects tend to be worst for low-equity than high-equity brands. Their study also confirms that, in the evaluation of a branded product, brand image tends to dominate country image for high-equity brands, while the opposite is true for low-equity brands.

It is not uncommon for well-known brands that originated in developed countries to have a substantial manufacturing presence in LDCs. Bearing an identical brand name may or may not be sufficient to convey equal values in the mind of the consumer, when the brand is associated with a negative manufacturing country. Hui and Zhou's study has demonstrated that the deterioration in consumer product evaluations as a result of moving production to countries with less positive images is significantly lower for high-equity than for low-equity brands.

For high-equity brands, foreign production affects global product attitude without changing any salient product beliefs. For low-equity brands, however, foreign production affects global product attitude directly and indirectly via a variety of salient product beliefs. Thus, moving production to low-cost countries is more feasible for high-equity brands than for low-equity ones. For high-equity brands, when manufacturers decide to move production to low-cost countries, they should strengthen and highlight the importance of all salient brand associations other than BO so as to minimize any negative effects from foreign production. For low-equity brands the primary marketing task is to convince prospective consumers that there is no decline in product performance on all salient attributes as a result of foreign production (Park et al., 1986).

Hui and Zhou further assert that it would be beneficial to strengthen product performance on all salient attributes and to communicate these values accordingly. The long-term goal is to improve brand image so that the negative effects of foreign production can be substantially reduced, as in the case of high-equity brands. This strategy has proved successful in the marketing history of most Japanese brands; they evolved from having a low-equity image in the 1950s to become extremely successful exemplars in relevant product categories today.

BO and CIA's influence on consumers' perceptions and purchase intentions of emerging Chinese brands

China has become one of the most globally influential economic powers since absorbing large amounts of inward foreign direct investment and engaging in exporting over the past two decades (Liu and Li, 2006). By 2004 Chinese MNCs are reported to have established 7470 companies in over 160 countries or regions. However, these companies have to overcome many strategic hurdles in international markets, which include a significantly lower level of brand recognition and poor BO and country image association (CIA) compared with their western European and Japanese counterparts. Other constraints include limited resources, inadequate R&D capabilities and lack of experience in international marketing (Liu and Li, 2002; Nolan, 2001).

With regard to CIA, consumers tend to resort to their knowledge of a country's image in considering products that they know little about. As discussed above, generally products from developing countries tend to be evaluated unfavourably, because of the negative associations of their country name, in particular during the pre-introduction stage. By contrast, products from developed countries such as those of western Europe, America and Japan tend to be positively perceived owing to their country's image of high technology and an advanced economy. For example, Germany is perceived as having a high level of crystallization for its engineering, with a favourable match between its country image and product category for luxury automobiles.

The concept of CIA is important for foreign-investing Chinese companies, in particular as the crystallization effect tends to happen during the introduction stage to which the Chinese brands are seen to belong (Liu and Li, 2006). Traditionally, products from China are often perceived by consumers in the western world as being cheap and of low quality. The country image of China possesses a low level of image crystallization and is seen by western consumers as 'copies of products from developed countries' (Doole and Lowe, 2004). This perception has thus created barriers against Chinese MNCs expanding globally.

However, in their study, Liu and Li examined the influence of BO and CIA on British consumers' perception of, and purchase intentions towards, emerging Chinese MNCs' brands. These authors show that, while the negative BO and CIA of China influence British consumers' perception of a Chinese household electrical appliance brand during the earlier stages of the decision-making process, brand familiarity seems to have the strongest influence on purchase intentions, followed by price during the later stages. Liu and Li found, indeed, that British consumers were influenced by their perception of BO in their evaluation of three household electrical appliances. They chose the Japanese Panasonic brand over the Turkish Beko brand and the Chinese Haier brand, which was also the least preferred brand. Panasonic was the most preferred brand in nearly all the attributes, except for good value. In contrast, Haier was rated the worst after both Panasonic and Beko in all attributes, but was thought to offer better value.

Similarly to previous research in the area, Liu and Li found that consumers are influenced by knowing the country owning the brand, which in turn influences their perception of the quality of the brand. British consumers were reported to prefer refrigerator brands with positive origin associations and that the country image crystallization effect is found to be present in their evaluation of the Japanese brand. Furthermore, their study shows a correlation between the perceived country image of China and the perceived brand image of Haier by British consumers, confirming that the stereotyped country image of China as a developing country has a strong impact on consumers' evaluation of the Chinese brand. The perceived low socio-economic character of China might have had an influence on British respondents' perception of the brand.

An interesting aspect of Liu and Li's findings is that their study shows that brand familiarity and price play a more important role in purchase intentions than BO and CIA. In respondents' evaluation of the Panasonic brand, brand familiarity was found to be more important than its origin and country image. Thus, respondents who identified the importance of the BO cue in evaluating Panasonic might have had the purchase of a familiar brand name in mind. Price is found to be of greater importance than BO in the respondents' purchase intentions towards Haier, followed by Beko.

In sum, Liu and Li's study shows that the level of BO and CIA influence varies during the different stages of the consumer's decision-making. BO and CIA are of greater importance than other extrinsic cues in brand evaluation during the early stages of the decision-making process; they are of lesser importance in consumers' purchase intentions during the later stages of the process. Brand familiarity is found to have the strongest influence on purchase intentions, followed by price and they both have a stronger impact on British consumers' purchase decision than BO and CIA. Indeed, their study also indicates that the positive effect of BO and CIA on brands should increase with brand familiarity.

The authors further suggest that it is of fundamental importance for Chinese companies to develop brand familiarity, popularity and recognition to allay consumers' negative BO and CIA. A familiar and popular brand would provide a better prospect for Chinese foreign-investing companies to succeed in international expansion.

Managerial implications of COO and BO

Although they are outside a company's control, country image, country equity and brand origin, influenced by country's economic status, technology, social desirability, the characteristics of its people, natural image, and so on are intangible assets for companies, especially when these are positively associated in the consumers' mind.

Figure 13.2 shows four situations in which global companies could use the influence of COO and BO to their benefit.

- *Situation 1 – High-equity or popular brand (or the market leader brand) and positive CIA.* Japanese electronics and German car models, such as Samsung and BMW, have high equity brands and the positive country images of Japan and Germany respectively. A top priority for these brands is to maintain their popularity by constantly updating their quality level, to maintain consistency with the images associated with their COO (Kim, 1995). They can also command a premium price because consumers are prepared to pay more for the favourable images. Hence, adopting a premium pricing strategy is appropriate here. They can also apply a defensive strategy by cutting price whenever needed. Price cuts can give effective results in this case. Kim (1995) has suggested that price reduction works very well for popular brands in taking sales away from other domestic brands of low quality, but not from high-quality brands. It also works well in the short term but not in the long term, because this would result in brand image dilution (see Chapters 9 and 10). Finally, companies in this situation should think of manufacturing or sourcing their products or major components in low-cost countries.

- *Situation 2 – High equity or popular brand but negative CIA.* Maintaining market share is a top priority. These brands should also focus on differentiating from competitive brands by providing distinctive bundles of products which are dissociated from their country images (Kim, 1995). Second, companies in this situation should emphasize functional quality, both in terms of product and support service-related quality. They need to use foreign manufacturing or sourcing from countries which are more favourably perceived. Finally, these brands must be competitive in price. As discussed above, price cuts are known to increase popular brands' shares in the short term.

- *Situation 3 – Low equity or less popular brand but positive CIA.* In the case of the Mazda 323, this situation applies to brands originating from a favourable country such as Japan, but which

	CIA	
	Positive	Negative
Brand equity		
High	Maintaining popularity Premium pricing Defensive strategy Sourcing from low-cost countries	Maintaining popularity Competitive pricing Quality differentiation FDI in favourable countries
Low	Building shares Creating images consistent with country associations Offensive strategy Identifying key success factors For small companies use integrated strategy including clear vision for the brands building strong relationships with distributors, agents and retailers and their presence at target trade show	Building shares Niche marketing strategy Creating functional images FDI in favourable countries or JV Develop brand familiarity, popularity and recognition Focus on product category Make use of brand names, e.g. Nokia a Finnish mobile brand that sounds like a Japanese name

Source: Based on Kim (1995), Spence and Hamzaoui (2006) and anonymous authors (2005)

FIGURE 13.2 High/low brand equity and positive/negative country image associations (CIA)

have yet to become popular in the market. The strategy for the company in this situation is either to try to strengthen and increase the brand's market share or let it phase out. To build up these brands, companies need to develop brand images which are consistent with their favourable country images. Pricing should not be used to build up market share, because the price effectiveness of these brands is low. Instead, companies must try to identify key factors contributing to an increase in the brand's market share, as well as advertising and improving product quality, which would significantly influence the brand's market share (Kim, 1995). This should also apply to the case of small companies' brands, which are often less well-known than their larger counterparts. As Spence and Hamzaoui's (2006) study shows, small companies can use positive CIA to overcome their smallness in international expansion. The examples referred to Monaco, the country and its brands. The Monaco CIA was positively perceived in Asia and the Middle East.

- *Situation 4 – Low equity or less popular brand and negative CIA.* Brands from China or LDCs are not as competitive as western or Japanese brands, and they do not have the back-up of positive CIA. These brands suffer from negative images of both country and brand equity. In order to compete in the global market, companies in this situation should try to develop a brand management strategy from a global and long-term perspective. They should first try to build brand share and base their reputation in a niche market that may be at the lower end of the market, then continually upgrade and improve product and service quality. Examples include many successful Korean companies in electronics, which started with negative images in both brand and country equity. Another option to deal with negative CIA is to establish a joint venture with a company that has a superior country image, or by manufacturing this company's products themselves (Kim, 1995). Alternatively, as suggested by Liu and Li (2006), in the case of Chinese MNCs to first develop brand familiarity, popularity and recognition to allay consumers' negative BO and CIA. Thus, a familiar and popular brand may provide a better prospect for companies that have a low-equity brand and negative country image to succeed in international expansion.

More and more, less industrialized countries are promoting their countries through major marketing communication programmes to overcome the negative perceived image of their countries. This is known as 'country branding' and is the subject of the next section. Examples include Colombia and Taiwan. The latter promotes itself using such slogans as 'Taiwan's symbol of excellence' and the brand slogan 'It's very well made in Taiwan'.

Country branding or national branding

A nation can behave just like a manufacturer brand, providing trust and a guarantee of quality. Like any brand, nations have individual fingerprints that are unique. This uniqueness gives power to a national brand. Country-of-origin brand can influence the positioning and differentiation of a nation's many products and brands (anonymous authors, 2005). A range of consumer brands may promote their 'made in' origin to benefit their own brand equity. However, unlike product branding, place or country branding is not under the control of a central authority. Place branding involves multiple stakeholders with competing interests (Frost, 2004). Many government officials are involved in country branding because their countries are in need of exports, tourism or foreign direct investment.

Major marketing programmes are often needed in country branding. For example, Colombia is today the major exporter of coffee to the US, largely because the National Federation of Coffee Growers of Colombia has built a successful marketing campaign for Café de Colombia. While some nations develop a national brand in a controlled or formalized way, with others it happens almost spontaneously (anonymous authors, 2005). For example, India has emerged in the last five years or so in a different way from how it was perceived a decade ago. Before, it signified spirituality and poverty, and now it stands for software and highly educated people (anonymous authors, 2005).

Promoting a country involves identifying spokespersons, product brands and events that can favourably influence public opinion in other countries. National cooperative marketing programmes are employed in some cases to promote place as exporters of goods and services. National promotion is sometimes conducted to market nations on a wide variety of qualities. National umbrella-branding programmes are also established in the country's effort to achieve unified promotion and build strong country associations, in the same way as a company serves as an umbrella brand for all its subsidiaries (see Chapter 6). Once a unitary and clear umbrella concept is established, individual constituents can go their separate ways within it, without the risk of inconsistent messaging (anonymous authors, 2005). The difficulty here is to devise approaches for coordinating within and across diverse brand partners to create synergies for all partners using the common umbrella brand logo. These synergies are derived from the branding of some shared qualities embedded in the brand partners' attribution. Another difficulty is that, to date, there are no guidelines for marketers on how to select country associations as core values of umbrella brands. Recent research outlines a set of criteria for marketers to evaluate country associations, which is discussed below. First, we look at the notion of national umbrella branding.

Umbrella branding is concerned with marketing a bundle of products and services under a shared brand identity that works as a bond for quality. An umbrella brand serves as a guarantee of consistent quality among the umbrella brand partners (Laforet and Saunders, 1994). Umbrella brands should serve as overall endorsers and provide additional brand equity to all brand partners (Aaker, 1991). The ultimate objectives of umbrella brands are to reduce perceived risk when introducing new products under the umbrella and to improve quality perceptions of new brand partners (Laforet and Saunders, 1994). The unique aspect of country umbrella brands (CUB) is their ability to identify and differentiate products on perceptions rooted in the brand partners' attribution.

An example of a CUB is the successful umbrella branding programme of New Zealand – 'The New Zealand Way' (NZW). This programme builds a strong brand concept that adds value to the marketing of NZ-origin products (Keller, 1998). By coordinating their marketing efforts, the NZ Tourism Board and Tradenz (a trade development board) have established a strong CUB that differentiates NZ-branded products in international markets. The brand is built on some selected core brand values that come from the country's natural, cultural and human resources (Keller, 1998). The core brand values of NZW umbrella brand are: quality excellence, environmental responsibility, innovation, contemporary values, honesty, integrity and openness of the people, and achievements of New Zealanders. These brand values are based on unique country associations that provide the brand partners carrying the NZW logo with some unique country qualities (anonymous authors, 2005).

Another successful national umbrella-branding example comes from a newly industrialized country, Taiwan. Taiwanese driver industries such as electronics, computers, auto parts and sporting goods have set up joint efforts to promote their products in international markets through the 'Innovalue marketing programmes' of Taiwan. Their umbrella-brand concept is based on the following motto: 'a country that provides excellent and innovative products of the best value-for-money'; and the most important brand components are Taiwanese brand logos – 'Taiwan's symbol of excellence' and, the brand slogan, 'It's very well made in Taiwan'. The rights are given to the most innovative and successful manufacturers of export products from Taiwan to use these brand components every year. Gradually, this symbol of excellence has increased in international recognition. Now Taiwan is seriously challenging the established reputation of Japan as the most advanced manufacturing country of technological goods from the Far East (anonymous authors, 2005).

The advantages of country umbrella branding are economies of scale and message consistency in terms of promoting a nation's exported goods, as well as promoting the country itself. The objectives of national umbrella branding are:

- To identify the actual place where a brand partner is manufactured and to make sure that the place of origin can be traced in cases of quality defects. To fulfil this objective, efforts are made to increase recall and recognition of the umbrella brand name.

- To differentiate brand partners by adding some unique local qualities associated with the product's attribution. To fulfil this objective, careful design of a CUB concept is undertaken. To build a strong CUB, increased brand recall and recognition, combined with consistent branding of country associations, are necessary.

A recent study shows how a framework of country umbrella branding is developed, by combining components of a country image with theories of umbrella branding. The challenge in national umbrella branding is to establish a brand concept that works across unrelated export products. The CUB should stimulate the spill-over effects of the marketing mix from one product category to another, and cause consumers to integrate existing brand beliefs with a portfolio with brand partners. This integration process should be triggered by some transcendent country associations, to make consumers identify new points of relatedness between the brand partners.

The major challenge in national umbrella branding is therefore to define core brand values, rooted in a place's attribution, which have a great potential to be extended across many product categories (anonymous authors, 2005). Another challenge is to identify links that match all the brand partners' attributes. It is equally difficult to identify logical links across disunited product categories.

Links can be found at two levels (Figure 13.3). The first is *vertical coordination,* where links are made on national characteristics that benefit products within one national industry, for example – Norway, where the second most important export industry is seafood from general fisheries and from farmed seafood. It is hard to identify links of tangible attributes that benefit all seafood products equally well. On the other hand, it should be easy to find common grounds for all categories of Norwegian seafood along some symbolic imagery based on clean nature, an environmentally concerned society and long cultural traditions in fisheries (anonymous authors, 2005). Second is *horizontal coordination*, where links are made using national or country characteristics that benefit products across industries. For example, Norway exports goods and services which range from tourism attractions to food and alcoholic beverages. It is hard to identify logical links of tangible attributes or functional utility that benefit all product categories in different industries. Yet, when one considers the symbolic images rooted in a cultural usage context, it is easier to see how

Norwegian smoked salmon could be eaten with with Norwegian Linie Aquavit in the surroundings of a Norwegian fjord (anonymous authors, 2005).

There is one question concerning country associations, which is whether these can be extended on an overall level, or whether they can be transferred on an attribute level (see Figure 13.4). Empirical evidence shows that American products, for instance, are associated with a youth lifestyle, e.g. Coca-Cola, Levi's and MTV, while French and Italian products are associated with style, elegance and good design. These examples show that country associations can be transferred across products on an overall level as well as on singular attributes (anonymous authors, 2005). On the other hand, the strength of country–brand similarity will determine the extendibility of country associations. Transference of country associations is expected when the associations match the brand partners.

Some country associations have a greater potential to reveal similarities between brand partners and, thus, have a greater potential to be extended. For example, for a BO to add some free equity, the product should resonate with its place of origin in the consumer's mind and some kind of logical link should be present between the two. This could be an abstract link, like the one between Caterpillar (a manufacturer of bulldozers) matching with rugged footwear (anonymous authors, 2005). It is also argued that a complex country image may contain a variety of associations of relevance for many products, while a simple country image is less flexible. The country equity of a complex image should therefore be easier to transfer.

Figure 13.4 shows that country associations that are strong, favourable, unique, relevant and abstract should have a higher propensity to reveal similarities or links across incongruent product categories. A higher level of perceived similarity will again lead to more transference of country associations. A strong country image is also built on a heterogeneous structure of associations, which might be both favourable and unfavourable. The relative positive versus negative aspects in a country image will determine its ability to influence product evaluations in a beneficial way. Research shows that developed countries are often more positively perceived than LDCs. Negative

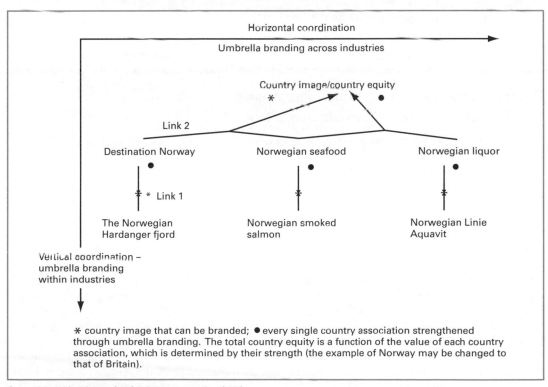

Source: Adapted from Iversen (1999) and anonymous authors (2005)
FIGURE 13.3 Country umbrella branding

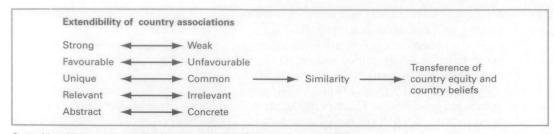

Source: Adapted from anonymous authors (Academy of Marketing Conference Proceedings, 2006)
FIGURE 13.4 Characteristics of country associations

effects of patriotism, consumer ethnocentrism and animosity are also found to be stronger for LDCs. Such negative aspects can influence product evaluations negatively and might be hard to overcome by marketing.

Country associations should be equally perceptions of a unique country feature that reveal shared product qualities, to be transferred as core values in national umbrella branding (anonymous authors, 2005), that is, when country associations are used as unique selling propositions (USPs) in national umbrella branding. Similarly, country associations should be relevant and must add an extra dimension that is meaningful to help consumers interpret new points of relatedness between umbrella brand partners.

For instance, Roth and Romeo (1992) found that evaluation of a product from a particular country is higher when the country association is perceived to be an important characteristic for the product category. According to these authors, the transferability of country associations depends on how relevant the country associations are in relation to the products under the umbrella brand. Finally, country associations should be at a high level of abstraction to be transferable as core values in national umbrella branding (anonymous authors, 2005). This is because meanings and abstract attributes in country associations tend to be more durable, accessible in memory and transcend easily across product classes (Keller, 1993).

Branding Brief 13.3: Brand India's image issue

Source: Adapted from the BBC News, December 2006

The concept of advertising a nation may seem bewildering, but the idea is the same as advertising a firm or its products.

The problem is, promoting a nation can be very expensive. The way to proceed is through a conglomerate of firms and the government.

India has done this with the Confederation of Indian Industry teaming up with the Government of India to invest heavily into promoting 'Brand India'.

But for such an initiative not to backfire it is important that the actual products live up to the promise.

For a variety of goods and services India is doing exceedingly well, but the one which is arguably the most visible, namely its national carrier, Air India (AI), leaves much to be desired. Right from the start, the appearance of passengers' seat covers which were peeling off, and the lack of cleanliness of the cabin and bathrooms did not make a favourable impression. This was coupled with the malfunctioning sound system and the narrow tray-like structures fitted to the handles, jutting out into the aisle some four inches.

Yet, undeterred, the November issue of *Namaskaar*, the in-flight magazine, proudly informs the traveller that Air India has been unanimously voted 'Best South Asian Airline' by readers across the continent.

'The airline was presented with the prestigious award at the glittering 17th annual travel awards ceremony by TTG Asia Media in Pattaya', the article proudly proclaims, without explaining what TTG stands for.

Clearly India is capable of better. India's domestic airlines are world class. The Jet Airways flights within India are of a quality as good as the best in the world. Why is AI languishing and what should be done?

Privatization is certainly worth considering. But that in itself may not be enough.

The domestic airline industry in the US is fully privatized, with minimal regulatory controls, but it is in dreadful shape – with abysmal punctuality and poor service quality.

Clearly, privatization is not sufficient – it has to be combined with intelligent regulation.

What matters above all is the love of excellence. That is what has made India's IT and pharmaceutical industries what they are, and that is what AI lacks.

Given that Air India has significance that goes beyond the airline industry to what people think of 'Brand India' itself, the plight of India's national carrier deserves attention at the highest level of government.

A proposed merger of AI with another airline has been much in the news, and it is a good time for such strategic thinking.

Conclusion

The COO of a product is sometimes the product's COM, but not always: Sony televisions can be manufactured in Mexico, Mexico is Sony's COM, but the COO of Sony is Japan, where it was originally designed and conceived. The difference between COO and BO is at the country and brand association level, on which the former and the latter focus respectively. COOB is a way for producers to brand a product by taking advantage of the positive perceived image of the country where the product was originally made.

The COO of a product influences consumers' product evaluation and perceptions of quality and purchase value. Consumers can establish the connotations between some products and their origin. Negative connotations are often associated with developing countries, while positive ones are associated with developed countries. The effects of COO on product evaluation vary with the technical complexity of products, the degree of availability/familiarity/degree of consumer ethnocentrism, the perceived level of economic development of the source country, the degree of similarity to the home country in terms of the economic, cultural and political systems of the foreign country, and product categories. Nevertheless, it has been argued that the actual effect on consumer purchasing behaviour is likely to be less in the real marketplace. This is because the actual effect on purchase behaviour depends whether or not consumers notice COO, or the 'made in' label, at the time of purchase.

A brand may have MCO, for example, in the case of mergers and acquisitions or where well-known brands are being taken over by a new COO. Cultural and strong emotional connotations are two factors influencing consumers' perception of products that come from MCO, which may affect their view of the brand equity as a result of the new ownership and, in turn, their purchasing behaviour. Another issue is whether the brand equity of these established products can be sustained or diluted, or even damaged under the new ownership. These issues are also more pronounced in the cases of China and the East.

There are benefits from COOB for companies in terms of increasing market share, brand equity, visibility and positioning for small companies, and the magnitude of the COO effect is greater for services than for tangible goods – because for many services, it is impossible to separate COO from brand.

COM information does not produce a significant effect on the evaluations of a branded product when the information is congruent with the BO, such as 'made in Japan' for a Sony or Sanyo. On the other hand, when COM information indicates that a branded product is manufactured in a country with a less reputable image than that of the BO, such as 'made in Mexico' for Sony or Sanyo, the information produces significant negative effects on product evaluations, and the effects tend to be worse for low-equity than high-equity brands. Moving production to low-cost countries is also more feasible for high-equity brands than for low-equity ones. In the evaluation of a branded product, brand image tends to dominate country image for high-equity brands, while the opposite is true for low-equity ones.

Generally, products from developing countries tend to be perceived unfavourably, but the reverse is true for products from developed countries. However, there are indications that the perceived negative BO and country image associations (CIA) of a country name take place during the earlier stages of the decision-making process. Brand familiarity has the strongest influence on purchase intentions, followed by price in the later stages of the decision-making process. Furthermore, brand familiarity and price seem to play a more important role in purchase intentions than BO and CIA; also, the positive effect of BO and CIA on brands should increase with brand familiarity. Depending on which of the four situations described in Figure 13.2 they are in, global companies can use the influence of COO and BO to their advantage.

CUB is developed by combining components of a country image with theories of umbrella branding. The challenge in country or national umbrella branding is to establish a brand concept that works across unrelated export products. The CUB should stimulate spill-over effects in the marketing mix from one product category to another, making consumers integrate existing brand beliefs in a portfolio of brand partners. This integration process should be triggered by some transcendent country associations, which make consumers identify new points of relatedness between the brand partners. Another challenge is to find links that match with all brand partners' attributes. It is also difficult to see logical links (vertical and horizontal) across disunited product categories.

🔑 Key terms

BO: (brand origin) is where the product is manufactured or produced. The brand origin of Sony is Japan. BO can reflect the cultural or history of brands, for example 'French origins'.

BO and CIA influence on decision-making: BO and CIA are of greater importance than other extrinsic cues in brand evaluation during the early stages of the decision-making process; they are of lesser importance in consumers' purchase intentions during the later stages of the process.

CA: (country associations) are perceptions of a given country that are structured as a cognitive schema in consumers' memory as an overall country image. CA include country stereotypes of the country, its citizens and their culture. Country associations are shown to influence trust in, and judgements of, products.

CI: (country image) is the 'total of all descriptive, inferential and informational beliefs one has about a particular country'. A country image is a structure of knowledge comprising country associations of varying complexity, strength, valence and uniqueness. The country image is shaped by external variables such as economic status, historical events, social and political climate of a country. Country image has two major functions: the **halo effect and the summary effect**.

COM: the country in which a product is manufactured. For example, many western products are manufactured in Asia, such as Mattel toys, which are manufactured in China.

COM effects on BO: it has been found that COM information does not produce a significant effect on the evaluations of a branded product when the information is congruent with the BO, such as 'made in Japan' for a Sony or Sanyo. On the other hand, when COM information indicates that a branded product is manufactured in a country with a less reputable image than that of the BO, such as 'made in Mexico' for Sony or Sanyo, the information produces significant negative effects on product evaluations, and the effects tend to be worse for low-equity than for high-equity brands.

Consumer decision-making process: in consumer behaviour, the buying decision-making process refers to the steps that consumers undertake before reaching a decision to buy the product. This involves recognizing a need to be fulfilled, or a problem to be solved, e.g. running out of a product, needing to buy a product to fulfil a need, gathering information on the product and evaluating alternatives (brand evaluation stage), making an informed decision to buy (intention to buy stage). Once sufficient information about the product and the alternatives is evaluated and sufficient funds are available, this will then lead to purchase.

COO: (country of origin) is known by the term 'made in' (manufactured in), while the term 'made in' can mean manufactured in, but also assembled, designed, invented in or made by a producer whose home country it is, and is often intended to look as if it was made in that country. The corporate headquarters is where the home country of company markets its product or where its brand is located. Often the COO of a product is the country of manufacture (COM) of a product, but not always. For example, a Sony television can be manufactured in Mexico; in this case, Mexico is the COM of Sony but the COO of Sony is Japan, where it was originally conceived and designed.

COO and product evaluation: the country of origin of a product influences product evaluation and perceptions of product quality and of purchase value. Domestic products are often evaluated more favourably than foreign ones, and products from developed countries are viewed more favourably than products from developing countries. However, different countries seem to have acquired distinctive images in consumers' minds in specific product categories. Germany is perceived as good in luxury automobiles and Japan in electronic goods.

COOB: a way for producers to brand a product by taking advantage of the positive perceived image of the country where the product is made or comes from.

COO effects on brand equity: country of origin image has been found to have effects on brand awareness/brand associations, brand loyalty and brand distinctiveness, which determine brand equity.

COO effects on market share: a country name of high equity can have a positive effect on consumers' product evaluations at the individual level, and on brand sales at the market level. A country name with a favourable image can have a positive effect on the short-term market share of the brand. For example, Japanese names are perceived as superior to American names within the car market.

▶

COO effects on product evaluation: vary with the technical complexity of products, degree of availability, familiarity, degree of consumer ethnocentrism, the perceived level of economic development of the source country, and the degree of similarity to the home country in terms of the economic, cultural and political systems of the foreign country.

COO effects on services: broadly similar for both services and tangible goods. However, the impact of COO on intangible services may be greater than on tangible goods, because for many services it is impossible to separate COO from brand. For example, it is impossible for most consumers to separate Qantas from Australia and Citibank from the US. In contrast, Sony televisions can be made in Japan or anywhere else in the world, although it is possible that for international service companies, the use of local staff may moderate the influence of the international brand. So, if Citibank or Qantas were to use predominantly Indonesian staff, then it seems likely that the COO influence would be less.

COO effects on SME: any company of any size could seek to reinforce the associations between the brand and COO through its communication strategy, in order to benefit from its overall image and/or its perceived competencies. This is of particular importance when a brand is exported to countries in which it is not well known. In the context of small businesses, it has been shown that communicating a brand is not a problem for a small business, but the difficulty lies in establishing a clear positioning and a personality for the organization. **COOB**, if properly used, can provide good returns on brand equity for small companies with limited resources. Spence and Hamzaoui's study (2006) confirms this.

Country equity: the commercial value that a country possesses. This is based on consumers' perception of the country's related associations, whether positive or negative. Such assets could be consumers' perception of technological advancement, workmanship, prestige, innovation, design and service.

Crystallization: means something very positive – for example, Germany is perceived as having a high level of crystallization for its engineering, with a favourable product match between its country image and product category for luxury automobiles.

CUB: (country umbrella branding) a range of consumer brands may promote their 'made in' origin to benefit their own brand equity. Country umbrella branding is about marketing a bundle of products and services under a shared country brand identity that works as a bond for quality. A country umbrella brand serves as a guarantee of consistent quality among the umbrella brand partners. The problem is to devise approaches for coordinating within and across diverse brand partners, to create synergies for all partners using the common umbrella brand logo. These synergies are derived from the branding of some shared qualities embedded in the brand partners' attribution. Another difficulty is how to select country associations as core values of umbrella brands. An example of successful CUB is 'The New Zealand Way' (NZW), whose core values are quality excellence, environmental responsibility, innovation, contemporary values, honesty, integrity and openness of the people, and achievements of New Zealanders. These brand values are based on unique country associations that provide the brand partners carrying the NZW logo with some unique country qualities.

Extendibility of country associations: the extent to which country associations have potential to have similarities with brand partners and, thereby, have potential to be extended.

Halo effect and summary effect: the halo effect occurs when consumers are unable to detect the true quality of a country's products before purchase, and the country image serves as a halo or signal (positive or negative) affecting product attitudes through deduction or assumption. The summary effect represents the accumulated experience of products from a given country, and this effect determines consumers' overall liking of a product.

MCO: used to describe a brand or a product that has been owned by a number of companies from different countries, due to mergers and acquisitions. For example, IBM is an American brand that has been bought by the Chinese computer maker Lenovo, and Rover, a British brand and car manufacturer, which was bought by Nanjing Automotive in 2005. Other examples are a range of famous brands and iconic symbols like Thomson, RCA, Schneider, IBM, Rover, MG and Austin, which are now owned by companies from a different countries.

MCO and consumer perception: cultural and strong emotional connotations are two other factors influencing consumers' perception of products that come from multiple countries of origin (**MCO**), apart from product quality and purchase value. These issues might also be more pronounced in the case of China, from a British or western consumer's perspective.

National umbrella branding: similar to **CUB**.

National umbrella branding programmes: established in an effort by the country in question to achieve unified promotion and build strong country associations, in the same way as a company serves as an umbrella brand for all its subsidiaries.

Place branding: unlike product branding, about developing and promoting positive associations, an image of a town or a city, through major marketing communication programmes, to market a city or town on the basis of a wide variety of qualities. It is not under the control of a central authority. Place branding involves multiple stakeholders with competing interests.

Place's attribution: the credit one gives to the place, such as a town or city.

Spill-over effects: the spilling over of the marketing mix from one product category to another, making consumers integrate existing brand beliefs into a portfolio of brand partners.

? Discussion questions

1 Explain and distinguish the different meanings among the concepts of COOB, COM, BO and MCO.

2 Discuss the implications of the above from a) the company's, b) the consumer's perspectives.

3 Identify the potential problems of MCO and discuss its effect on brand equity.

4 Discuss the challenges in country umbrella branding and success criteria for country associations.

5 Choose a product you would like to introduce in another country, and apply the lessons learned from the image and country of origin above to develop a strategy for that product.

6 Research branding and country-of-origin effects, and name changeover strategies. See the Campbell's case at: www.campbellsoupcompany.com/around_the_world.asp.

a) What are the reasons for Campbell's to change the names of its products sold in different countries of the world?

b) Explain how COO image affects consumer perception of food products.

7 Think of your own country. What image might it have for consumers in other countries? Are there some brands or products whose image is better for leveraging in global markets?

8 Develop a marketing communications programme using the country umbrella branding framework for your country.

9 What strategies would you recommend for your country using the framework of high/low brand equity and positive/negative country image associations (CIA) discussed above?

10 Discuss the benefits of COO in relation to small companies and services.

Projects

1 Find/buy a product which you cannot identify; write down your first impressions of what you think the product is made of and what it is used for. Bring it to class for discussion.

2 What cues are there on the product? If it is packaged, what information can you find? If it is not packaged, did the store signs give you any information? What information would you want as a consumer?

3 Describe what section of the store your product is placed in (i.e. describe what products were near it). (If you can not recognize these products, describe what they look like.)

4 Attempt to interview store management or one of the retail staff to find out what the product really is (you may not always be successful in this attempt!). If you fail to find out, please select another product whose identity can be explained to you.

5 After finding out what the product is, consider whether or not it would be marketable in the United States. Place yourself in the role of the product manager who is searching for products to import to the United States. Be prepared to describe why or why not you would want to proceed with this product:

a) Give the pros and cons.

b) Say if the product would be standardized, adapted or changed completely.

c) Discuss the types of data that you would want in order to make your presentation to management. Remember, your decision is simply a preliminary call as to whether to proceed with a market investigation!

6 Include all this information in your report. Be prepared to speak for about five to ten minutes on what you have found.

7 Please provide a photo of the product and its labelling, in an appendix.

MINI CASE 13.1: BEER BRANDS AND HOMELANDS

Simon Anholt, brand consultant and author of *Brand New Justice*, argues that the country of origin is an essential part of beer branding. 'Beer is the classic product parity market,' he says. 'Manufacturers are driven to intangible brand product features. Using the country of origin as part of the brand equity is essentially free, so you avoid having to build something up laboriously over decades. So long as you can credibly establish a connection between you and the place.'

In the automotive sector, if you were shown two identical cars and told that one was made in Turkey, the other in Switzerland, for example, you would immediately think that the Swiss car was better. 'But it is different with beer,' Anholt notes. 'The little, poor places can produce good beer. A Jamaican car is probably no good, but Jamaican beer, well that sounds good.'

Mainstream and niche products all free ride on their country of origin brand. For a long time Foster's used a kangaroo in its advertisements, while Lapin Kulta, from Lapland in Finland, relies heavily on its unusual provenance in its marketing. Images of Finland's stark landscapes adorn communications material and bottle labels.

South African Breweries Limited realizes that its national origins are important at a corporate level too. 'We have embarked on a corporate branding campaign to highlight the identity of SAB Limited,' says Michael Farr, the company's communications manager. 'The purpose is to strengthen the emotional attachment with our core market. Research conducted since the company's global expansion showed that the consumer was having confusion between SABMiller and SAB Limited. We felt it was important to encourage South African consumers to recognize SAB Limited is still the company they have always known.'

The corporate brand campaign from SAB Limited was fiercely patriotic. A two-minute TV commercial paid tribute to the South African nation and praised the country's achievements over the past ten years. The ad ends with some of the world's greatest landmarks, including the Statue of Liberty and the Sydney Opera House, sailing into Cape Town's Table Bay to symbolize international recognition for the country. SAB is unashamedly tapping into strong emotions and a proud heritage.

'Beer is sold on the story of its brewing heritage and you can't tell that story without tying it to the country of origin,' says Anholt. Companies deliberately emphasize the heritage and history of the beers they sell, to avoid being generic.

Given the success of country of origin branding in the beer sector, other industries should also consider the benefits. Consumers are too exposed to commercial messages. The only thing that marketers can leverage is emotions. In a world where people are well travelled, they are buying into emotion. If they've been to a country and had a good experience then, when they see a brand from that country, they are often buying into an emotion, not the product.

Country-of-origin branding is a cheaper bypass to build brand equity in a strong and reliable way. There are always dangers, especially when countries or famous citizens start behaving badly. The American brand, for instance, has suffered considerably abroad during the Iraq conflict, as did French products when President Chirac was vociferously anti-war. But the downside is usually short-lived.

Questions:

1 Explain in your own words what free branding means.

2 Discuss why COOB is more common for beer and wine than any other products. Give examples.

3 Discuss the strategy South African Breweries Ltd used to differentiate its product from the competition.

4 Explain what emotional branding means. Give examples of when this can be used.

MINI CASE 13.2: DEVELOPING AND MANAGING A BRAND – SCOTLAND

Source: Reprinted from *International Trade Forum* magazine, published by the International Trade Centre, based on presentations and a paper provided by Theresa Houston, Chief Executive, Scotland the Brand

Scotland's economic development agency, Scottish Enterprise, created a special project called 'Scotland the Brand' in 1994, to explore the benefits of integrating the marketing of Scottish trade, tourism and culture. They had noted that country of origin can be a key factor in a consumer's purchasing decision, and that countries such as New Zealand, Ireland and Spain had developed successful branding initiatives. The challenge for Scotland was to capitalize on an existing awareness, and become more cohesive in its marketing efforts.

Branding as an export development concept

The proposal was submitted to 150 business leaders at a conference, in order to determine whether it was a viable concept and would create commercial advantage. With support for the concept obtained, they tested the idea. They conducted a tourism drive, and simultaneously arranged a month-long pilot promotion in France with Marks & Spencer. Food, drink and cultural exports had a 200 per cent rise. Over 30 such integrated marketing events have been undertaken since then.

Developing and managing a generic mark

Authenticity, quality and tradition were put forth as traits. They developed a 'country of origin' mark to offer a guarantee of quality. Scotland the Brand took on membership status, to ensure a consistent message and accountability for companies using the generic mark. Today, 350 Scottish businesses from 23 sectors are members, and the mark is evident on a wide range of products, services and marketing and corporate materials.

Testing international perceptions of Scotland

Previous research work from both public and private bodies provided materials on values and perceptions of Scotland. Working with the organization responsible for re-branding New Zealand, Scotland the Brand tested four core values – integrity, tenacity, spirit and inventiveness – in seven countries.

Managing a brand image

Several key management concepts have been integrated in the Scottish approach. Quality assurance has been a management cornerstone. Early on it launched the Scotland Mark and developed a process to ensure quality. Members are proactively targeted and the assessment process uses an external panel, quality standards and benchmarking.

Assurance of quality standards was all the more challenging, given that operational targets for financing were numbers-based. Financial sustainability is another cornerstone. Originally funded by Scottish Enterprise, Scotland the Brand is member-owned and will be privatized in April 2003. There is a fee structure with membership benefits, and an annual licence. Awareness-raising through marketing has been another key element, with major promotional campaigns, marketing events and a web site. Public–private partnerships have been integrated in all the approaches to quality management, financial sustainability and marketing. Finally, the brand is based on solid research for core values that resonate with both exporters and consumers.

Measuring impact

Scotland the Brand set for itself several success indicators. These include: the number of companies applying for membership and using the generic mark; visibility of the Scotland mark in advertising materials, products and services (millions of opportunities); the number of integrated marketing events and their success in terms of press coverage, sales increase and new markets; increase in turnover, exports or market entry for member companies; increase in Scottish exports overall; increased awareness of Scotland and its products in the United Kingdom and international markets.

Some of these factors are easier to measure than others. The strongest, most reliable impact assessment figures available are from qualitative feedback and evaluations of marketing events.

Lessons learned

Management by a single organization and defined objectives and measurement helped create a unity of purpose and ownership in imaging, marketing and communicating brand values. A strong communications and marketing strategy to accompany the development was essential. Basing the core competencies and values on reality, and testing them through independent research was important. Finally, commitment, buy-in and funding from top-level decision-makers in the public and private sectors helped make the project a success.

Questions:

1 What are the core values of Scotland the Brand?

2 Conduct your own mini survey (thirty consumers, max.; ten questions, max.) on consumer perception of Scotland, and compare your results with the core values and image of Scotland the Brand created by the Scottish economic development agency.

3 Discuss the issue of extendibility of country associations, referring to Figure 13.3 in the text above, for Scotland.

END OF CHAPTER CASE STUDY: COUNTRY-OF-ORIGIN STEREOTYPING – THE CASE OF THE NEW ZEALAND MOTOR INDUSTRY

Before 1984 the New Zealand economy was heavily protected against imports, had high levels of subsidies for manufacturing exports, and sharply rising overseas debt. The Motor Industry Development Plan was formulated to open up the motor vehicle industry to competition from overseas. It aims were to encourage competition by altering the competitive environment; reduce the unit cost of NZ assembled automobiles; liberalize the marketplace; establish the appropriate levels of protection for domestically assembled vehicles.

As a result of these changes the European influence in the market is growing; no longer are imports from these countries destined only for the prestige market. Due to the easing of important barriers and the rise of the Yen, automobiles from European countries are competing with a greater degree of parity with Japanese offerings in NZ market.

Literature on COO effects on product evaluations suggests that NZ motor vehicle industry needs be made aware of the impact of COO stereotyping and its implications for automobile evaluation. With the advent of a considerably more deregulated motor vehicle market, NZ consumers are exposed to a wider range of automobiles than ever before.

Stereotyping has been shown to affect product evaluation for products in general and specific product categories. Currently, NZ research into COO bias phenomenon is extremely limited. The sample consisted of 275 contained purchasers, who had acquired their vehicle within the last six months at the time of formulation of the mailing list.

Made in Germany is seen as strong in performance, service and engineering. Made in Germany represented to consumers a more expensive, reliable, comfortable and spacious automobile than those manufactured by Japanese, Italians or French. Similarly, performance was perceived to be better than its competitors. German motor vehicles shared similar technical advancement levels with the Japanese, were superior to the French or Italians, but were seen as having poor availability of parts compared to the Japanese, something that they shared with other European COO. In all other service and engineering adjectives they were superior. Owning a German automobile was considered to be the most prestigious thing. Consumers felt there was little advertising of German brands compared to that undertaken for Japanese brands. German automobiles appeared as being more suited to consumers who were men, older and in the upper socio-economic classes. Japanese motor vehicles were perceived as providing a technically advanced product which offered good value for money.

Questions:

1 What can you conclude about the research?

2 What do New Zealanders value most in cars?

3 Explain the implications for producers of a repeat purchase cycle for automobiles.

4 Based on this research, what can you conclude on the consumers' perceptions of cars generally? What affects their purchase decisions?

5 How does COO image affect car producers?

6 Can you identify the external forces that impact on car producers?

7 What are the marketing implications for car producers – in terms of market segmentation, product positioning, branding and other strategic choices?

References

Aaker, D. A. (1991), *Managing Brand Equity*, New York, NY: The Free Press.

Ahmed, S. and d'Astou, A. (1995), 'Comparison of country of origin effects on household and organisational buyers product perceptions', *European Journal of Marketing*, Vol. 29, No. 3, pp. 35–51.

Anonymous author(s) (2005), 'Country associations as core values of country umbrella brands – a framework of characteristics', *Academy of Marketing, Critical Issues in Brand Management*, University of Birmingham Business School, November.

Del Rio, B. A., Vazquez, R. and Iglesias, V. (2001), 'The role of the brand name in obtaining differential advantages', *Journal of Product & Brand Management*, Vol. 10, No. 7, pp. 452–65.

Doole, I. and Lowe, R. (2004), *International Marketing Strategy: Analysis, Development and Implementation*, 4th edn, London: International Thomson.

Frost, R. (2004), 'Mapping a country's future', Brandchannel.com, Interbrand, UK.

Hamin, C. and Elliott, G. (2005), 'A less-developed country perspective of "country of origin" effects: Indonesian evidence', ANZMAC Conference: 'Marketing Issues in Asia'.

Hamin, C. and Elliott, G. (2006), 'A comparison of consumer ethnocentrism and country of origin effects for goods and services: Indonesian evidence', Academy of Marketing, Middlesex University, July.

Hui, M. K. and Zhou, L. (2003), 'Country-of-manufacture effects for known brands', *European Journal of Marketing*, Vol. 37, No. 1/2, pp. 133–53.

Iversen, N. M. (1999), 'Effekter av nasjonale image – pa vurdering av nasjonale merkeallianser', PhD proposal at Norwegian School of Economics and Business Administration, Norway.

Keller, K. L. (1993), 'Conceptualizing, measuring and managing customer-based brand equity', *Journal of Marketing*, Vol. 57, pp. 1–22.

Keller, K. L. (1998), *Strategic Brand Management: Building, Measuring, and Managing Brand Equity*, New Jersey: Prentice Hall.

Kim, C. K. (1995), 'Brand popularity and country image in global competition: managerial implications', *Journal of Product & Brand Management*, Vol. 4, No. 5, pp. 21–33.

Laforet, S. (2007), 'Japanese vs western luxury branding: a consumer's perspective', *International Journal of Retailing & Distribution* (under review).

Laforet, S. and Saunders, J. A. (1994), 'Managing brand portfolios: how the leaders do it', *Journal of Advertising Research*, Vol. 34, Sept/Oct, pp. 64–76.

Liu, H. and Li, K. (2002), 'Strategic implications of emerging Chinese multinationals: the Haier case study', *European Management Journal*, Vol. 20, pp. 669–706.

Liu, J. and Li, C. (2006), 'British consumers' evaluations of emerging Chinese MNC brands: the influence of brand origin and country image associations on Haier', Academy of Marketing, Middlesex University, July.

Nagashima, A. (1977), 'A comparative "made in" product image survey among Japanese businessmen', *Journal of Marketing*, Vol. 41, July, pp. 95–100.

Nolan, P. (2001), *China and the Global Economy*, Basingstoke, UK: Palgrave.

Okechuku, C. (1994), 'The importance of product country of origin: a conjoint analysis of the United States, Canada, Germany and the Netherlands', *European Journal of Marketing*, Vol. 28, No. 4, pp. 5–19.

Ozsomer, A. and Cavusgli, S. (1991), 'Country-of-origin effects on product evaluations: a sequel to Bilkey and Nes review', Gilly, AMA Educators Proceedings, Vol. 2, pp. 177–269, Chicago.

Papadopoulos, N. and Heslop, L. A. (1993), *Product-Country Images – Impact and Role in International Marketing*, New York: International Business Press.

Papadopoulos, N., Heslop, N. A. and Barmossy, G. (1991), 'A comparative image analysis of domestic versus imported products', *Research in Marketing*, Vol. 7, pp. 283–94.

Park, C. W., Jaworski, B. J. and MacInnis, D. J. (1986), 'Strategic brand concept-image management', *Journal of Marketing*, Vol. 50, October, pp. 135–45.

Roth, M. S. and Romeo, J. B. (1992), 'Matching product category and country image perceptions: a framework for managing country-of-origin effects', *Journal of International Business Studies*, pp. 477–97.

Shimp, T. A. and Sharma, S. (1987), 'Consumer ethnocentrism: construction and validation of the CETSCALE', *Journal of Marketing Research*, No. 24, pp. 280–90.

Spence, M. and Hamzaoui, L. (2006), 'Brand management and country of origin effects: liability of smallness for SMEs', Academy of Marketing, Middlesex University, July.

Thakor, M. V. and Lavack, A. M. (2003), 'Effect of perceived brand origin associations on consumer perceptions of quality', *Journal of Product & Brand Management*, Vol. 12, pp. 394–407.

Tse, D. K. and Gorn, G. J. (1993), 'An experiment on the salience of country-of-origin in the era of global brands', *Journal of International Marketing*, Vol. 1, No. 1, pp. 57–76.

Wu, Y. and Ardley, B. (2006), 'China and international ownership: exploring consumer perceptions of brand equity and a new country of origin', Academy of Marketing, Middlesex University, July.

Yasin, N. M. and Nasser Noor, M. (2007), 'Does image of country-of-origin matter to brand equity?', *Journal of Product & Brand Management*, Vol. 16, No. 1, pp. 38–48.

Further reading and online sites

Bilkey, W. J. and Nes, E. (1982), 'Country of origin effects on product evaluations', *Journal of International Business Studies*, No. 13, pp. 89–99.

BusinessWeek (2004), 'China's power brands', No. 8, pp. 44–50.

Iversen, N. M. and Hem, L. E. (2008), 'Provenance associations as core values of place umbrella brands: a framework of characteristics', *European Journal of Marketing*, Vol. 42, No. 5/6.

Leonidou, L. C., Palihawadana, D. and Talias, M. A. (2007), 'British consumers' evaluations of US versus Chinese goods: a multi-level and multi-cue comparison', *European Journal of Marketing*, Vol. 41, No. 7/8.

Wall, M., Heslop, L. A. and Hofstra, G. (1988), 'Male and female viewpoints of countries as producers of consumer goods', *Journal of International Consumer Marketing*, No. 1, pp. 1–25.

Wright, R. (2006), *Consumer Behaviour*, London: Thomson.

www.Brandchannel.com

www.nigeriavillagesquare1.com/articles/nworah/archives/2005_05_01_index

Index